Hu
RBT

DISC

MW01712198

CONTENTS

Members of the 90th Illinois General Assembly

(Following member name are party affiliation, district and page number.)

Senators

Representatives

* Appointed to fill the vacancy created by the death of Harry "Babe" Woodyard on January 31, 1997.

** Appointed to fill the vacancy created by Tom Dunn's resignation.

*** Appointed to fill the vacancy created by Ann Hughes' resignation.

**** Appointed July 16, 1997, to fill the vacancy created by the death of Terry Deering on June 26, 1997.

***** Appointed September 26, 1997, to fill the vacancy created by Mike Weaver's resignation.

List of Tables

Preface

The *Almanac of Illinois Politics—1998* is the latest in the biennial sequence of almanacs dating back to the original *Almanac* in 1990. Even though the names of people in politics and what they do change all the time, my purpose with this edition of the *Almanac* has not changed. My co-contributors and I want to make Illinois politics as understandable to the people of Illinois as we can. We believe that for democracy to work, the people have to know what government is doing and how to participate. People who grumble about politics but do not vote, write letters, or give a hand to good candidates deserve an unresponsive government. Those who take action often are delighted to find that their legislators respond to them. Our intent, then, is to make the General Assembly a less mysterious, more accessible body so that the people of our state are encouraged to get involved and take responsibility for their own good government.

Toward that end, we have continued the tradition of publishing the *Almanac* in its familiar, easy-to-use format. This edition, like its predecessors, is divided into three parts. Part one contains essays on the role of leadership in the House and Senate and an analysis of partisanship as reflected in the roll call votes of the 90th General Assembly.

Part two is a guide to the membership of the assembly. It also profiles the financial records of each legislator's most recent campaign as well as the campaign finances of his or her opponent. On top of that, we report how each Senate member voted on 134 key votes and how each House member voted on 172 key votes to come before the chamber in 1997.

Part three contains tables on political and demographic topics ranging from current salaries of Illinois' elected and appointed officials to the most recent gubernatorial election return results by county to Illinois popular vote returns for every presidential race since 1900 to a comparison of the General Assembly workloads over the sessions of the past decade.

While most of the tried-and-true features of our prior *Almanacs* remain, loyal readers will notice at least one informational casualty of the legislature's partisan battles: member pages in part two of this volume are without election data for University of Illinois board members. These election results were long recognized as an indicator of a legislative district's partisan leanings. But, because University of Illinois board members are now appointed, this indicator has been lost. As a partial remedy, we have gone to great effort to determine and report the results of voting for president, senator, and governor for each legislative district. We also still report the incidence of straight-party votes in legislative districts, but that voting information will disappear in 1998, because the General Assembly has determined to disallow onepunch, straight-party voting in Illinois.

Still, we have been encouraged by the response our *Almanacs* have received. Some of the most appreciative users of prior editions are legislators and the people in the lobbying business in Illinois. Even insiders who are active contributors and day-to-day practitioners welcome the detailed information provided here about which candidates received how much money from their top PAC contributors. Association executives and occasional lobbyists like the member pages and the information on how active legislators are in moving legislation and how they vote. The group ratings we report for each legislator relate how groups such as the Illinois Federation for the Right to Life or the American Civil Liberties Union rate the performance of members of the General Assembly based on their votes on high visibility questions. Citizens get help from the district office addresses and phone numbers we list for each member. From the tables in part three they also learn a good deal about the many offices and activities of Illinois state government. And, school teachers around the state have been introducing more and more students to the *Almanac* as a resource for term papers and as a means of becoming better acquainted with the legislators who represent them in Springfield. We want these pupils to become vigorous and knowledgeable citizens.

While this *Almanac* looks much the same as earlier ones, the team producing it has changed. The workhorse for this edition is David A. Joens, who joined the Illinois Legislative Studies Center after several years on the Illinois General Assembly Senate Democratic Staff. He succeeds Craig A. Roberts, now administrative assistant to Congressman John Shimkus, who did so much to make the earlier editions a success. Joens developed the data for the member pages in part two and directed research assistants Laura Cellini, Bridgette Heard, Danielle Madise, and Matthew Noffsinger in assembling and verifying data for the tables in part three. Paul Kleppner made available federal census data for Illinois legislative districts. The data are from 1990, of course, and while no longer completely accurate, they are the best information available. Kathleen Bottoms processed the words and numbers into the appropriate places. Lars Gaydos produced the detailed district maps.

The Publication Unit for the UIS Institute for Public Affairs produces the *Almanac*. For this edition, Rodd Whelpley, with help from graduate assistant Kimberly Allen, organized and edited information; Michelle Sutphin designed and typeset the project. Jacqueline Miles Wright handles the ongoing tasks of marketing and distribution.

It is my pleasure to work with all the people who make this *Almanac* accurate and timely. It is because of their excellence that I take pride in publishing the 1998 edition.

—Jack R. Van Der Slik
January 1998

Editor's Introduction: 1998—The Year of the Possible

It's a new year, and, as with any new year, 1998 comes with its share of uncertainties. One thing is sure, though, 1998 will pave the way for shifts in Illinois' political landscape. A relatively large shift would see the Democrats winning some (or all) of the state's constitutional offices, from which they have been absent since 1995. Or, a perhaps less dramatic shift would find Republicans remaining in control of the constitutional offices, with familiar politicians in new positions. Either way, by the end of the year, newcomers will be measuring for curtains in the governor's mansion, the lieutenant governor's office, the secretary of state's office, and the comptroller's office. To take a picture of the state of politics in January 1998, use a wide-angle lens. The possibilities are really that huge.

Political insiders waited impatiently until August 1997 to learn from Jim Edgar that he would retire from politics at the end of 1998. By saying he would not run for governor or the U.S. Senate, Edgar made space at the top of the Illinois political ladder, encouraging several to step up and some others to see if they can get on. It was his call. Personally popular with the voters, reelection as governor probably would have been easy, although many of his Republican running mates would have loved for him to lead the ticket by challenging Carol Moseley-Braun for her U.S. Senate seat.

Less conspicuous, but still surprising, Bob Kustra departs the lieutenant governorship without running for a statewide position. Kustra could have attempted to follow George Ryan's career path. Ryan went from the legislature to lieutenant governor to secretary of state in order to get his shot at the governorship. In fact, many observers expected Kustra to seek the secretary of state nomination. But, like the governor, Kustra opted out, and the scramble for nominations for the state's top offices became even more frenetic.

George Ryan's patience in waiting his turn and his diligence in helping legislative and county candidates around the state has earned him a lot of political capital. At the time of this writing, whether or not he can bring some discipline and order to the rest of the Republican ticket for statewide office remains to be seen.

For Democrats, 1998 has to be time for a change, and a time for "outsiders." None of their gubernatorial candidates currently holds a statewide elective office, which is not to say that the candidates for that office are unknowns. Quite the contrary. In fact, many would argue that the Democrat's most viable candidates have suffered the misfortune of announcing their candidacy for the same office. It seems the party's ability to produce a winning ticket has suffered since the ticket balancing art of slating died in the 1980s. Even so, fresh blood in the statewide office candidacies may yet invigorate the Democrats' electoral efforts in 1998.

Democrats do have an incumbent in the U.S. Senate with Carol Moseley-Braun. She has national friends and financial support. Like the nursery rhyme girl, "when she is good, she is very, very good; but when she is bad, she is horrid." In the last year or so she has shown that good side. Whether or not Republicans can shift her image in the other direction may depend on their nominee. As of January 1998, a divisive primary fight between Comptroller Lolita Didrickson and State Senator Peter Fitzgerald is taking shape. In this race there are echoes from the Kustra-Salvi primary of 1996, but the dynamics of an off-year primary differ from those in a presidential year.

While the U.S. Senate and statewide office primaries will get headlines, trench warfare for partisan control of the Illinois General Assembly goes into its fourth round since redistricting in 1991. After getting the Senate majority in 1992 and the Senate presidency, Republican James "Pate" Philip has hung on to a majority by a handful of seats. In 1996, Republicans kept a 31-28 edge with wins in the 24th and 58th districts with a combined electoral margin of only 212 votes. House Democrats, on the other hand, kept an edge in 1992, took a licking in 1994, but regained a narrow majority in 1996. Democratic leader Michael J. Madigan pursued a stoutly partisan agenda in the 88th General Assembly. As the new speaker, Republican Lee Daniels, with Philip's support in the Senate, ran a Republican fast track agenda into law in the 89th General Assembly. Chastened with small margins of party control in the 90th General Assembly, the four leaders have worked somewhat more bipartisanly on some significant issues in 1997, while arming for a renewal of the electoral battles in 1998.

The trend may be less apparent in the state legislature, but it—like the constitutional offices—is a robust, ever-changing group. There is now only one veteran of the Illinois Constitutional Convention who is still a member of the General Assembly, Speaker Michael J. Madigan. Members who served in the House from three-member districts in a 177-member body are still fairly numerous. But 15 currently are senators, with only 11 remaining in the House.

In the face of this nearly constant influx of new legislators, partisanship—as directed by House and Senate leaders—has become a chief means of political consistency. Our essays in part one of this edition of the *Almanac of Illinois Politics* look particularly at legislative partisanship. Kent Redfield, whose research on campaign finance has received wide attention from both the public and policymakers, looks at the way legislative leaders have increased the range of their influence in the legislative process. With Samuel J. Pernacciaro, I extend the analysis of partisan voting in the legislature for comparison to our findings in the 1996 edition of the *Almanac*.

The *Almanac* is intended to illuminate the processes of Illinois politics, especially the General Assembly. By the end of this year of almost infinite possibility, we will see new faces preparing to occupy new places. Even so, the process of Illinois politics moves steadily and constantly. Knowledge of the process, the political records of the policymakers, and specifics of policies they make, can only help us anticipate the type and style of government that will take this state into the next millennium.

In this spirit, I offer you the *Almanac of Illinois Politics—1998*. Some of the data reported here have been generated by research in the Illinois Legislative Studies Center, but most is gathered from other sources. The *Almanac* is as balanced, objective, and useful as we can make it. But your suggestions about information that should be included in future editions are always welcome.

—Jack R. Van Der Slik
January 1998

Part 1

The Politics of Illinois

Samuel J. Pernacciaro   Kent D. Redfield   Jack R. Van Der Slik

What Keeps the Four Tops on Top?

Leadership Power in the Illinois General Assembly

Kent D. Redfield

Where have all the slatemakers gone? In the old days (prior to 1980) party leaders in Illinois put together slates of candidates for statewide office. The Democrats publicly ratified private agreements as candidates presented their credentials first to a meeting of Cook County Democratic Party officials—presided over by the legendary Chicago Mayor Richard J. Daley—and then to state Democratic Party officials in Springfield. The Republicans worked more privately. But, however it was done, the result was slates of endorsed candidates who almost always won their respective primaries. In an era of party-based elections, it was the party organization that recruited the candidates, raised the funds, and ran the campaigns. The party organization got the message to the faithful and got the faithful to the polls. Once the election was over, the party became a vehicle for governing.

Those days are gone in Illinois. The trials and tribulations of Democratic and Republican leaders in Illinois in the fall of 1997 to reach some consensus over candidates for statewide office was merely another chapter in the continuing story of the decline of parties in Illinois (Merriner 1997). As of this writing (December 1997) a wide open, four- or five-way gubernatorial primary looms on the Democratic side. The Republican primary for the U.S. Senate seat will be a replay of the 1996 battle between a moderate candidate backed by most party leaders and a wealthy conservative candidate running as an outsider.

The story at local levels is largely the same. When Richard M. Daley, the son of the late Mayor Richard J. Daley, ran for mayor of Chicago in 1989 after the death of Mayor Harold Washington, the Cook County Democratic Party made no endorsement in the race. Compared to most county party organizations, the declining Cook County Democratic Party appears robust. In an era of elections which have become ever increasingly candidate centered, more than one observer has concluded that "the party is over."

Given what has happened to state and local parties in Illinois, it is surprising to find that political parties are alive and well in the Illinois General Assembly. But these are not the traditional Republican and Democratic parties. Rather, the parties that control the Illinois General Assembly are the Michael Madigan Party, the James "Pate" Philip Party, The Lee Daniels Party, and the Emil Jones Party. These legislative leaders perform all of the traditional functions of political parties. The legislative party leaders recruit the candidates, raise the funds, and run the campaigns. They also set the legislative agenda and consistently deliver the votes of their members on important roll calls. And they do all of this in a manner about which legislative leaders at the national level can only dream.

The Same Old Song

During the 1980s, decisions on key legislative matters in Springfield were almost always a product of a group that became know as Big Jim and the Four Tops (Parker 1984). Big Jim was Republican Governor James R. Thompson (1977-1991) and the Four Tops were Democratic House Speaker Michael Madigan, Democratic Senate President Phil Rock, Republican House Minority Leader Lee Daniels, and Republican Senate Minority Leader James "Pate" Philip. In 1991, Republican Jim Edgar replaced the retiring Jim Thompson as governor, and in 1993 Emil Jones, Jr. replaced the retiring Phil Rock as leader of the Senate Democrats. The Republicans gained control of the Illinois Senate in 1993, while control of the House shifted to the Republicans in 1995 and back to the Democrats in 1997. So, the current version of the Four Tops consists of Speaker Madigan, Senate President Philip, House Minority Leader Daniels, and Senate Minority Leader Jones. While one of the names has changed, the song remains the same. If anything, the Illinois legislature has become even more dominated by the legislative leaders during the 1990s, while the power of individual members has continued to decline.

Longevity and experience are certainly two sources of legislative leadership power in Springfield. All four of the legislative leaders came to Springfield before Jimmy Carter was elected president. Pate Philip was first elected to the state legislature in 1966, Michael Madigan in 1970, Emil Jones in 1972, and Lee Daniels in 1974. Madigan became the leader of the House Democrats in 1979. Philip became leader of the Senate Republicans in 1981, and Daniels became leader of the House Republicans in 1983. Before he retired and was replaced by Emil Jones in 1992, Phil Rock had been the leader of the Senate Democrats since 1979.

Having the same leaders for a decade is almost unprecedented in state legislatures in the modern era. Experience often produces wisdom. The legislative leaders in Springfield all benefit from having "been there and done that." It is also true that the leaders are all very talented, politically savvy men who have survived by making the right decision at the right time. Yet, the combination of long tenures and these leaders' political skills does not explain fully the reason why they are so powerful or why their power has increased steadily over the past decade.

At the heart of the legislative leaders' power in Illinois are the near monopolies on campaign fundraising and the mobilization of legislative staff efforts that each leader commands. Control of money and political expertise allows the leaders to control the course of legislative elections and to control the legislative process when the legislature comes into session. Individual legislators are simply not able, on their own, to raise the funds necessary to be competitive in a race targeted by the legislative leaders. Individual legislators also lack the personal and policy staff necessary to establish political and substantive autonomy apart from the leaders. Strong leaders and relatively weak members in Springfield mean that interest groups concentrate their campaign contributions on the leaders, which gives the leaders more control over the financing of elections, which makes them stronger in Springfield, which makes them more dominant in raising money, which means that interest groups continue to concentrate their campaign contributions on the leaders, and so on toward infinitude. Combine the effects of cornering the political money and staffing markets with the power of legislative leaders in Illinois to control legislative redistricting every ten years, and the result is a recipe for domination of the legislative process by the legislative leaders.

Show Me the Money

Illinois has the least restrictive campaign finance laws of any of the 50 states. There is no limit on who can contribute; no limit on how much an individual, corporation, or group can contribute; and, most important, no limit on how much an office-holder or party committee can raise and then contribute to another candidate or spend on another candidate's behalf. In Illinois, like many states with a partisan redistricting process, most legislative districts are drawn so that they are not usually competitive. Therefore, the outcome of elections in just a few races determines which party will be in the majority in each chamber for the next two year legislative session. For example, in 1996 control over the 118-seat Illinois House was determined by the outcome of 27 "targeted" races, and for the 59-seat Senate, partisan control hinged on just seven races.

The result of the ability to churn an unlimited amount of funds through the leaders' campaign committees and the fact that partisan control can be established by winning the few competitive seats in each chamber is that massive amounts money flow into a few targeted contests. In fact, the term "target" refers to a legislative race in which at least one of the legislative leaders accounts for a significant portion of the spending by one of the candidates. In one of 1996's featured Senate races, the two candidates in the 58th district spent $1.34 million in the general election, a new record for spending in a Senate race. Over $1 million of that total (77 percent) came from direct and in-kind contributions from the legislative leaders. The most expensive House race in 1996 was in the 107th legislative district. The two candidates spent over $841,000, also a new record for a House seat. Over $621,000 of the that total (74 percent) came from direct and in-kind contributions from the legislative leaders.

At the federal level and in most states, there are strict limitations or outright prohibitions on the transfer of funds from the political committee of one candidate to another and strict limits on the transfer of funds from party organizations directly to a candidate. Not in Illinois. Overall, in 1996 the legislative leaders accounted for 57 percent of the funding in targeted House races ($7.59 million) and 66% of the funding in targeted Senate races ($4.15 million).

One of the reasons that so much money can be concentrated on so few races is that the leadership—from a partisan perspective—has been able to draw the district boundaries very well. A three-tiered system of legislative elections exists in Illinois. Roughly 50 percent of the House and Senate races in any given election are perfectly safe for the incumbent party: the winner of the primary has no general election opponent, or one who does not spend any money. In the another 30 percent of the districts, the eventual winner, usually the incumbent, has an opponent, but the contest is not close and the spending by the losing candidate is very small. The average expenditures by losing candidates in nontargeted races has been flat over the past four election cycles, ranging from $10,000 to $23,000 for losing Senate candidates and from $11,00 to $15,000 for losing House candidates. In short, these lightly contested races are old-fashioned, amateur campaigns in which the incumbent wins almost without exception.

In sharp contrast to the relatively safe races stand the 20 percent of the House and Senate districts that are targeted by the legislative leaders in each election cycle. In 1996, the combined spending by both candidates in each of the 27 targeted House races averaged $497,000. This represents an increase of $309,000 per race over the 1990 spending figures for targeted House races. In the Senate, the average combined spending for the seven targeted Senate races topped $870,000, an increase of $482,000 per race over the comparable 1990 figures. Legislative leaders provided, on average, over $140,000 to each House candidate in a targeted race and $291,000 to each Senate candidate in a targeted race in 1996. Overall, the four legislative leaders raised $21 million for the 1996 elections, compared to $15.4 million in 1994, $11.5 million in 1992, and $7.1 million in 1990.

In the past four election cycles (between 1990 and 1996) only one incumbent, Representative Wayne Goforth (R-115), lost in a general election in a contest that could be considered a nontargeted race. In 1990 Goforth, spent $50,000 and lost to Terry Deering, who spent $15,000. While Speaker Madigan provided $5,000 of Deering's money, the outcome came as a great surprise to almost every one. Outside of that one contest, incumbents facing challengers not backed by a leader are pitching a no-hitter. In contrast, during that same time 36 incumbent legislators were defeated by challengers who were backed by legislative leaders. The number includes the 4 incumbent legislators who lost to another incumbent running for the same seat in 1992 after the 1991 redistricting. (There were also nine incumbent legislators who were defeated in primaries between 1990 and 1996.) Most incumbent legislators leave the legislature through retirement. These open seats, where the incumbent does not seek reelection, create opportunities for the opposing party to pick up seats. So, beating an incumbent with the help of a legislative leader is difficult, but clearly possible based on the experience of the past four elections. But, trying to beat an incumbent legislator in the general election without the help of a legislative leader is almost always a suicide mission.

A Little Help from my Friends

But money alone doesn't win elections. Anyone who has seen the documentary *The War Room* has an appreciation of how valuable expert advice is to the success of a campaign. Knowledgeable campaign staff get their candidate to the right place at the right time with the right message. And, contrary to popular opinion, political campaigns still have some basis in questions of public policy. A candidate going it alone, without an expert campaign staff well versed in the salient public policy issues of the day, runs at a disadvantage.

As I've noted previously, in Illinois the party leaders have monopolies not only on candidates' financial support but also on the partisan staff of the General Assembly. At election time, the leaders unleash this professional staff to run campaigns in targeted districts. To appreciate the power the leaders assert by their control over the mobilization of staff, it is helpful to compare the way partisan staffs operate on the federal level to how they operate in Illinois.

A number of Illinois congressmen are former state legislators. All of them surely found both getting to Washington and serving in Congress quite different from their state experiences. Representative Jerry Weller (R-11) was elected to the Illinois General Assembly in 1988 after losing a contested election in 1986. He served in the state legislature for six years before being elected to Congress in 1994 in a very hard-fought, close election. Operating under the more restrictive federal campaign finance laws, his run for Congress was not primarily financed by the Republican leader of the U.S. House of Representatives, then Minority Leader Newt Gingrich. Nor was his campaign directed by Gingrich's Washington-based leadership staff. This is a significant difference from what occurs in targeted legislative elections in Illinois, but it is not the only difference between being an individual member of the Illinois General Assembly and being an individual member of the U. S. Congress.

Once Congressman Weller took office, he was able to use the staffing allowance provided to every congressman or U.S. Senator to hire both a Washington-based legislative staff and a district office staff. A congressman's capital-based legislative staff provides support and analysis for the legislator. These staffers are on the congressman's payroll and have a vested interest in seeing that their congressman looks good. By providing the information and support, staffers enable their legislator to make the votes, take the positions, and achieve the recognition that maintains and builds the congressman's base of political support in the district back home. A congressman's own staff also performs Washington-based constituent work and provides a link to the constituent work and representation activities of the district office staff. If a congressman is a committee or subcommittee chairman or ranking minority member, he has authority to hire staff to provide policy analysis and expertise for himself and other members of the committee.

A congresswoman's district staff does constituent work, organizes home-district appearances, and puts out the press releases and newsletters that allow the legislator to present herself to constituents in the best possible light. When the congresswoman's formal reelection campaign activities begin, all of the capital and district staff resources she controls are used directly in the campaign effort. The staff organizes and runs the campaign in the district and provides policy expertise as needed. A U.S. congresswoman or senator's district and capitol staffs constitute a personal organization that continues to exist only as long as the legislator is reelected. All of these staff resources provide the incumbent with the means to control her own reelection fate and to develop policy expertise in areas of her choosing in ways that are largely independent of her legislative leader.

In contrast, the Illinois legislator does not control anywhere near the level of staff resources available to U.S. congressmen or senators. The Illinois legislator has a district office allowance of $47,000. (As of this writing, a pending bill on Governor Edgar's desk would increase it to $57,000.) This allowance is sufficient to open one or two offices in the district. These are usually staffed by one full-time person along with some part-time help and student volunteers. Rank-and-file House members have individual offices in the capitol, but usually they share a secretary with one or two other members. Each senator has a capital office and a secretary. When the General Assembly is in session, committee staff provide information on bills and amendments and support in drafting and shaping legislation. But those staff people are not hired by the legislative members or even the committee chairmen. All the partisan staff who do the substantive and appropriation committee work are part of four centralized staffs, each controlled by one of the legislative leaders. The committee chairmen and minority spokesmen are appointed by the leaders and work with staff people assigned from the leaders' staffs. Call up a democratic staff person who has responsibility for the House Transportation Committee or who analyzes the budget for mental health agencies for the one of the House appropriation committees and he will answer the phone, "Speaker Madigan's staff." The executive directors of the bipartisan legislative service agencies such as the Legislative Research Unit, the Legislative Reference Bureau, and the Economic and Fiscal Commission are hired by the four leaders and serve at their pleasure. In Illinois, ultimate control over staff rests not with individual members (or even committee chairmen) but with the legislative leaders.

Since 1993 when the Republicans took control of the Senate, the rules of the legislative process in both the Senate and the House have been significantly changed to increase the formal power of the legislative leaders over the movement, content, and passage of legislation. These powers have always been exercised by leaders informally, but the rule changes of 1993 created the formal steps that reduced the power of individual members and increased the control of the leaders. Longtime observers note that the process has come full circle. The 1970s was a period when a very closed, leader- and committee-chairman dominated process was opened up for individual members. Large increases in partisan committee staff and nonpartisan policy staff during that era also gave the individual members and the legislature as a whole more policy independence from the governor, interest groups, and the legislative leaders than had historically been the case. The 1990s have seen a wholesale retrenchment of the power and autonomy of individual members in the legislative process and a failure to extend the policy and bipartisan staffing resources of the legislature.

In addition to committee work, leadership staff provide the members with support that is more political in nature. They write press releases and write newsletters, organize district activities, and provide information on legislation directly to members. These are many of the same tasks performed by a U.S. congressmen's capital and district staff. The key difference is that these staff people work not for the individual member but for the legislative leader. These resources are directed at all members, but legislators who are potential targets need—and receive—the most support. This has been the real growth area in terms of the numbers of leadership staff. While the number of staff people analyzing legislation and creating agency budgets has remained stable or declined over the past decade, the number of staff whose responsibilities are to provide political support for members has increased dramatically.

The controversy of House passage of a bill sought by the cable TV industry during the 1997 fall veto session illustrates the problems for individual members that can arise from the current trends in the organization and focus of legislative staff. The bill, introduced during the fall veto session, would have had the effect of preempting cable customers' class-action lawsuits over the amount of late charges the industry applies to customers with past-due cable bills. New legislation is not considered and brought up for a vote in the veto session without the approval of the legislative leaders. The cable bill came up for a vote after passing out of committee earlier in the day. It was presented to the House as a consumer-oriented, noncontroversial bill. It passed with 78 votes, more than enough make the bill effective immediately. Press accounts of the impact of the bill combined with the public opposition of the State Attorney General Jim Ryan created a firestorm of criticism and fingerpointing that resulted in the Senate sponsor tabling the bill when the legislature came back a week later. Most of the media attention focused on the $198,448 in cable industry campaign contributions to the legislative leaders since January of 1995 and the $188,095 that went to individual members. However, the reported comments of individual legislators focused on the roles of the sponsor, the legislative leaders, and legislative staff (Pearson 1997). Members complained that they did not know what was in the bill, had not seen any staff analysis of the bill, and voted on the basis of the floor presentations made by the sponsor and other supporters of the bill. They also complained that while no one informed them of the implications of what they were voting on, members who were potential targets in the upcoming election received a "heads up" from somewhere and either voted against the bill or did not vote. The implication was that individual members have to depend on leadership staff and that the leadership did not take care of all members equally. Rank-and-file members of the U.S. Congress are much less likely to find themselves in this kind of embarrassing situation because they have large staffs whose primary job is keep them from looking bad. Nontargeted members of the General Assembly apparently have no such safety net.

As important as the general support provided by the political staff is to members, the real value of the partisan staffs lies in what they allow the legislative leaders to do during elections. Partisan staffers constitute an experienced, professional campaign organization that exists from election to election. Each election cycle, the leaders deploy their staffers to the work the races in the targeted districts. People from a legislative leader's political staff arrive in the targeted districts in the spring. They leave the state payroll in the summer and fall to work full-time organizing and running the campaigns. The centralization of staff and money gives the leaders incredible flexibility during the campaign season. If a targeted race becomes evidently lost halfway through the campaign, the leaders can shift resources and personnel, pulling the plug on a candidate whose campaign has failed to take off and pouring money and staff into a district where a contest is unexpectedly close.

Dancin' with the Guy that Brung Ya

When the legislature convenes in Springfield, the leaders have the political clout and the formal power necessary to control the legislative agenda and determine most of the outcomes. A number of members literally owe their seats to resources that leadership bestowed upon them during the election, and they realize that in order to retain their seats they may once again be dependent on the leadership's money and talent supply lines. The leadership uses its control over the staff and the campaign purse strings as its power base. It's an idealistic or naive legislator who habitually refuses to fall into step with his or her party's chamber leader.

The centralization of this power in the hands of the Four Tops means that almost every group that makes campaign contributions gives a significant portion of its contributions to the leaders, regardless of the nature of the issues or whether or not the group's concerns are partisan or regional. Because the leaders can never be sure how much is enough money for the next set of political campaigns, they exert great pressure on interest groups and corporations to contribute. Because these groups and corporations want to be important players in the process or, at a minimum, to have access to key legislators, they continue to contribute more each election cycle. Control in the capital enhances control in elections, and control in elections enhances control in the capital. No incentives exist for the leaders to share their power with individual members or to alter the campaign finance system they have created. The individual legislative members become less independent, less influential. The Four Tops stay on top. And the beat goes on.

Works Cited

Merriner, James L. 1997. Blank slate. *Illinois Issues,* June, 18-21.

Parker, Joan. 1984. *The Illinois tax increase of 1983.* Springfield, IL: Sangamon State University Press.

Pearson, Rick. 1997. Cable's capitol reception. *Chicago Tribune*, 9 November, Section 1: 1, 10.

Roll Call Voting in the 90th General Assembly

Samuel J. Pernacciaro and Jack R. Van Der Slik

Because voting on bills is what citizens expect their legislators to do, and because studying roll call votes is a difficult chore, we have devoted substantial space in this and previous *Almanacs* to identifying what we call key votes. As close legislative observers know, Illinois General Assembly members vote many hundreds of times in committee, on amendments, on third reading of bills, and on conference reports. There are too many votes to report them all here, so for this essay we have purposely gathered the more important ones that were cast in the first regular session of 1997. The detailed records of member voting on key votes" are recorded, one roll call at a time, on pages 285-341 of this *Almanac*. In this essay we provide some generalized results about the participation and partisanship of senators and representatives as they vote on roll calls.

Participation Scores

In the Illinois General Assembly bills pass only by obtaining a constitutional majority in each chamber. This means that in the House, constitutionally composed of 118 members, an actual majority of 60 "yes" votes is necessary to pass a bill. The members may vote "yes," "no," or "present"; they may be recorded as absent; they may be recorded as excused. But present, not voting, or any response other than yes is in opposition to the bill. The standard is the same in the Senate; with 59 members, 30 yes votes are necessary to pass a bill, regardless of the number of members absent or otherwise unsupportive of the bill in question. The Senate, unlike the House, does not record members as excused.

The actual rate of participation by legislators on roll call votes in 1997 is impressively high (see table 1). Senate members were present and voting 96 percent of the time on 149 roll calls, while House members voted 99 percent of the time on 189 roll calls in their chamber. Because the option of voting present is counted in this participation, we also determined the incidence of members voting actual yeas or nays on the key roll calls. In the Senate the percentage is 94, with 97 the number for the House. As the party breakdowns reveal, in the Senate, where Republicans hold a majority, Republican Senators vote more often than Democratic Senators. House Democrats, despite being in a majority, participated slightly less than House Republicans, but the difference is trivial. The high levels of participation reported here compare favorably to the results in 1995. In particular, the minority party members received higher scores in voting yea or nay in 1997 than they did in 1995.

Table 1: House and Senate roll call participation: key votes in 1997 and 1995

	1997 Roll Call Participation		1995 Roll Call Participation[1]	
	Percent Present & Voting	Percent Yeas/Nays	Percent Present & Voting	Percent Yeas/Nays
All Senators	96	94	94	89
Republican Senators	98	96	96	95
Democratic Senators	94	92	92	83
All Representatives	99	97	96	93
Republican Representatives	99	98	98	98
Democratic Representatives	98	96	94	87

[1]From *Almanac of Illinois Politics—1996* (Springfield, IL: The Institute for Public Affairs), 8.

Party Support Scores

The party support analysis for 1997 shows a substantial change from the partisanship in the legislature in 1995. There are several clear indicators. Perhaps the most striking one is the decline in "party votes," which are roll call votes in which a chamber's Democrats largely bloc-voted in opposition to a chamber's Republicans. We use a conventional measure of partisanship like that used on congressional voting by *Congressional Quarterly.* Of the 189 roll calls we have recorded as key votes in the Illinois House, only 33 produced a party vote (see table 2). This is in sharp contrast to 1995 when 93 of 159 key votes were classed as party votes. The picture is even more extreme in the Senate. In 1997, only 12 roll calls fit the definition of a party vote out of 149 key votes (see table 2). In the comparison year of 1995, there were 79 party votes out of 151. So the sharp differences between the parties on floor votes were muted a good deal of the time in 1997. We suspect that because the parties were so closely divided in both the Senate (with 31 Republicans and 28 Democrats) and the House (with 60 Democrats and 58 Republicans) that Senate President Philip and House Speaker Madigan avoided calling bills on which a few departures from party loyalty would result in a significant party loss.

Table 2 Party votes in the Illinois House and Senate in the first regular session of 1997

Party Votes in the House

Bill	Description
SB 21	Allows townships in Cook County to levy a special tax for improvements to streets.
SB 71	Provides that a first violation of carrying a firearm in a vehicle, concealed upon one's body, or upon a public street or lands within a municipality constitutes a Class A misdemeanor instead of a Class 4 felony.
SB 73	Provides that the provider of any tangible thing for which an employer is responsible for payment is bound by charges on payments ordered by the Industrial Commission.

SB 166	Increases the age for mandatory seat belt use from six to 16.
SB 645	A change in the education funding formula that would raise income tax by 1.5 billion, provide 900 million in property tax relief, and use the remaining 600 million for education funding.
SB 772	Increases penalties for hit and run drivers.
SB 899	Provides that contractually representative horsemen's organizations shall have the exclusive authority to represent horsemen.
HB 19	Amends the Bingo License and Tax Act to increase the aggregate prize limit from $2,250 to $3,250.
HB 38	Allows a municipality to demolish a vacant building that is considered hazardous.
HB 61	Regulates electricians and electrical engineers through licensing requirements.
HB 111	Requires health care plans to provide coverage for serious mental illness under the same terms as other illnesses.
HB 161	Provides that treatment for mental, emotional, or nervous disorders by a licensed clinical professional counselor shall be covered under the Illinois Insurance Code.
HB 229	Raises yearly personal service allowances for members of the General Assembly by $10,000.
HB 245	Provides that the standards of whether material is obscene is the standard in which the material is sold, delivered, advertised, or performed.
HB 314	Makes senior citizens aged 62 and older (now 65) eligible for the Circuit Breaker Program and increases the household income limit.
HB 319	Establishes the Freedom of Choice Act, establishing a state policy recognizing a woman's reproductive rights.
HB 383	Amends the Public Aid Code, replacing provisions concerning medical assistance and general assistance funding of abortions with identical language prohibiting payment of aid for abortions unless necessary for preserving the woman's life.
HB 391	Amends the State Employees Group Insurance Act to remove language prohibiting the coverage of abortions for state employees.
HB 523	Provides that any person who suffers damage (instead of actual damage) may bring an action under the Consumer Fraud and Deceptive Business Practices Act.
HB 585	Changes the method that multistate businesses use to apportion their income for Illinois tax purposes.
HB 644	Provides for the use of electronic ballot forms.
HB 851	Creates the offense of intentional interference with access to health care.
HB 1009	Requires that new outdoor swimming pools on private residential property be enclosed by a fence or wall at least 42 inches high.
HB 1090	Requires school administrators to report to local law enforcement agencies felony or misdemeanor violations that occur in the schools or at school-related activities.
HB 1211	Establishes fees for charities and professional fundraisers to be used

	by the Attorney General's office to disseminate information about charitable organizations.
HB 1271	Creates a Drycleaner Environmental Response Trust Fund to support remediation of dry cleaning solvent at dry cleaning facilities.
HB 1294	Establishes in Cook County a pilot program creating an Adolescent Family Life Program for high risk pregnant adolescents who are abusing drugs or alcohol.
HB 1525	Requires state universities to offer 50% tuition waivers for undergraduate education to the children of employees of other state universities.
HB 1627	Creates the Business Use Incentives for Large-Scale Development Act.
HB 1696	Creates an income tax credit for taxpayers who soundproof buildings located near O'Hare or Midway airports.
HB 1703	Creates the Illinois Family and Medical Leave Act, applicable to employers of 25 or more.
HB 1704	Creates the Flex-time Rights Act requiring certain employers to grant leave up to 24 hours.
HB 2061	Creates the Small Business Incubator Fund.

Party Votes in the Senate

Bill	Description
SB 55	Vehicle bill for electric deregulation.
SB 65	Creates a minority environmental scholarship program.
SB 71	Provides that a first violation of carrying a firearm in a vehicle, concealed upon one's body, or upon a public street or lands within a municipality constitutes a Class A misdemeanor instead of a Class 4 felony.
SB 81	Excludes park district recreational programs for the handicapped from the tax caps law.
SB 87	Increases authorization in General Obligation Bond Act.
SB 557	Creates the Alternative Route to Teacher Certification Program.
SB 895	Makes it a Class A misdemeanor for a business that makes deliveries to fail to deliver to a specific location because of the actual or perceived race, color, creed, religion, ancestry, sex, sexual orientation, physical or mental disability, or national origin of the location's residents.
SB 996	Allows the governing body of a municipality to impose an infrastructure maintenance fee on telecommunications retailers by ordinance or resolution.
SB 1103	Bans landscape waste burning in municipalities with a population over 75,000.
HB 449	A Senate GOP education funding plan that increases the telecommunications excise tax, imposes an additional tax on cigarettes. New revenues go into a common school fund.
HB 1087	Allows lotter prize winner to assign all or part of his or her winnings to another person.
HB 1696	Authorizes school districts to impose an income tax on corporations and individuals by referendum.

Although substantially fewer roll calls fell into the party vote category in 1997 than in 1995, the ones that did occur provide information for closer scrutiny. Of the two chambers, party loyalty is higher in the Senate than in the House (see table 3). As table 3 illustrates, on the dozen party votes in the Senate, party loyalty occurred on 87 percent of the member votes. Every subcategory of the breakdowns we use for party and region in tables 3 and 4 show loyalty in the Senate on 80 percent or more of the votes. The lowest score (80 percent) is by downstate Democrats, while the highest score (96 percent) is by Chicagoans in the Senate. Compared to 1995 results, the percentages in 1997 are similar but slightly lower except for the high score by Chicagoans.

Table 3 Senate and House party support: percent voting yea or nay with a majority of one's party

	1997	1995
All Senators	87	90
Republican Senators	86	92
Democratic Senators	88	87
All Representatives	78	92
Republican Representatives	75	94
Democratic Representatives	82	88

Table 4 Senate and House party support percentages: variation by region

Senate	**1997**	**1995**
Chicago Senators	96	91
Suburban Senators	82	91
Downstate Senators	85	88
Republicans	89	93
Democrats	80	82
House		
Chicago Representatives	89	92
Suburban Representatives	73	93
Downstate Representatives	77	90
Republicans	80	93
Democrats	74	85

In the House, not only did the number of party votes drop markedly, the loyalty of members went down on the party votes that are recorded. Overall party loyalty in the House in 1997 was shown to be 78 percent, noticeably less than in the Senate. The most loyal House subgroup was the Chicago representatives, Speaker Madigan's base. Overall, the House majority Democrats showed more party unity than minority

Republicans (82 percent to 75 percent). Note too that variation from party support is most conspicuous in the suburbs (see table 4). Traditionally downstate Democrats vary most from the party line, but that was not true in 1997. The suburbs have become the primary partisan battleground and the jockeying to keep or capture seats is shown in the way members from that region vote for their constituents. Party leaders evidently let legislators who may be targets in the next election stray from party positions on roll calls.

The decline in House party loyalty in 1997 compared to 1995 is substantial. Table 3 shows that the overall score of party loyalty as reflected in roll call voting declined from 92 percent in 1995 to 78 percent in 1997. The decline is especially notable among Republicans. No longer in the majority, their responsibility to be there for their leadership appears to have eroded substantially. Republican loyalty overall was 75 percent on party votes in 1997, compared to 94 percent in 1995. House Democrats, now the majority, recorded 82 percent party loyalty in 1997, down from 88 percent in 1995 when they were in the minority.

Table 5 provides detailed information on the participation of individual legislators on roll call votes and measures party support. The table captures a large amount of information. Take notice of the following explanations of the definitions and abbreviations used to describe the participation and party support scores for table 5.

Definitions for table 5:

P— Party affiliation

#— District number

R— Regional location

- **C**— Chicago: those districts in which all or most of the votes cast in primary and general elections are cast in Chicago.
- **S**— Suburban: those districts in which most or all of the votes cast in primary and general elections are cast in Cook County but outside Chicago, or the counties of DuPage, Kane, Lake, McHenry, and Will.
- **D**—Downstate: those districts in which most or all of the votes cast in primary and general elections are cast in the other 96 Illinois counties.

Participation scores for table 5 are determined as follows:

- **O**—The percentage of roll calls on which the member was on the record voting yes or no.
- **P**—The percentage of roll calls on which the member was recorded voting present.
- **N**—The percentage of roll calls on which the member was recorded as not voting.
- **E**—The percentage of roll calls on which the member was recorded as an excused absence. (Only recorded for members of the House.)

For each member, the sum of the scores (O, P, N, and E) is 100 percent. Variations are due to rounding.

Party support scores for table 5 are determined as follows:

S—The percentage of party vote roll calls on which the member voted yes, no, or present in support of a majority of the member's party. Present votes count as support if the majority of the member's party voted no.

O—The percentage of party vote roll calls on which the member voted yes, no, or present in opposition to the majority of the member's party. Present votes count as opposition if the majority of the member's party voted yes.

For each member the sum of the party support scores (S, O) is 100 percent. Variations are due to rounding.

Absence of members as recorded in table 5:

A—The percentage of party vote roll calls on which the member was recorded as not voting yes, no, or present. These entries do not lower party support or opposition scores.

Table 5 Participation and party support scores

Senators

				Participation				Party Support		
	P	**#**	**R**	**O**	**P**	**N**	**E**	**S**	**O**	**A**
Berman	D	9	C	95	1	3	0	92	8	0
Bomke	R	50	D	99	1	0	0	92	8	0
Bowles	D	56	D	93	1	5	0	83	17	0
Burzynski	R	35	D	97	2	1	0	100	0	0
Butler	R	28	S	97	1	3	0	75	25	0
Carroll	D	8	C	90	4	6	0	92	8	0
Clayborne	D	57	D	93	1	5	0	73	27	1
Collins	D	4	C	83	1	17	0	73	27	8
Cronin	R	39	S	91	3	6	0	91	9	8
Cullerton	D	6	C	90	4	6	0	100	0	17
del Valle	D	2	C	94	3	3	0	100	0	0
DeLeo	D	10	C	97	3	1	0	100	0	0
Demuzio	D	49	D	95	2	3	0	83	17	0
Dillard	R	41	S	97	3	0	0	75	25	0
Donahue	R	48	D	99	1	0	0	83	17	0
Dudycz	R	7	C	99	1	0	0	100	0	0
Farley	D	17	C	97	1	2	0	100	0	0
Fawell	R	20	S	97	3	0	0	83	17	0
Fitzgerald	R	27	S	91	5	3	0	73	27	8
Garcia	D	1	C	79	3	18	0	100	0	8
Geo-Karis	R	31	S	96	2	2	0	73	27	9
Halvorson	D	40	S	95	3	2	0	92	8	0

Senators *continued*

				Participation				Party Support		
	P	**#**	**R**	**O**	**P**	**N**	**E**	**S**	**O**	**A**
Hawkinson	R	47	D	96	1	3	0	82	18	1
Hendon	D	5	C	89	5	6	0	92	8	0
Jacobs	D	36	D	98	1	1	0	83	17	0
Jones	D	14	C	92	1	7	0	100	0	0
Karpiel	R	25	S	95	3	2	0	92	8	0
Klemm	R	32	S	95	3	2	0	92	8	0
Lauzen	R	21	S	92	4	4	0	92	8	0
Link	D	30	S	98	1	1	0	83	17	0
Luechtefeld	R	58	D	97	3	0	0	92	8	0
Madigan, R.	R	45	D	89	2	9	0	100	0	17
Mahar	R	19	S	94	1	5	0	64	36	8
Maitland	R	44	D	99	1	0	0	92	8	0
Molaro	D	12	C	84	3	13	0	100	0	8
Myers, J.	R	53	D	99	1	0	0	91	9	0
Obama	D	13	C	93	4	3	0	100	0	8
O'Daniel	D	54	D	97	0	3	0	75	25	0
O'Malley	R	18	S	93	5	3	0	83	17	0
Parker	R	29	S	99	0	1	0	67	33	0
Peterson	R	26	S	98	0	2	0	92	8	0
Petka	R	42	S	95	2	3	0	92	8	0
Philip	R	23	S	97	1	2	0	92	8	0
Radogno	R	24	S	98	1	1	0	75	25	0
Rauschenberger	R	33	S	93	2	5	0	83	17	0
Rea	D	59	D	95	1	5	0	90	10	17
Severns	D	51	D	99	0	1	0	75	25	0
Shadid	D	46	D	95	1	4	0	58	42	0
Shaw	D	15	S	54	3	43	0	80	20	58
Sieben	R	37	D	97	2	1	0	83	17	0
Smith	D	3	C	95	3	3	0	100	0	0
Syverson	R	34	D	89	1	9	0	100	0	8
Trotter	D	16	C	93	2	5	0	92	8	0
Viverito	D	11	C	95	3	2	0	75	25	0
Walsh, L.	D	43	S	100	0	0	0	50	50	0
Walsh, T.	R	22	S	95	5	0	0	92	8	0
Watson	R	55	D	99	1	0	0	83	17	0
Weaver, S.	R	52	D	96	3	1	0	83	17	0
Welch	D	38	D	99	1	1	0	82	18	8
Dunn	D	43	S	58	0	42	0	0	100	0
Woodyard	R	53	D	0	0	100	0	0	0	100

Representatives

				Participation				Party Support		
	P	**#**	**R**	**O**	**P**	**N**	**E**	**S**	**O**	**A**
Acevedo	D	2	C	98	1	1	0	91	9	0
Ackerman	R	89	D	96	3	2	0	91	9	3
Beaubien	R	52	S	98	0	2	0	66	34	3
Bergman	R	54	S	99	1	1	0	79	21	0
Biggert	R	81	S	100	0	0	0	67	33	0
Biggins	R	78	S	99	1	0	0	88	12	0
Black	R	105	D	98	2	0	1	73	27	0
Boland	D	71	D	84	1	0	15	77	23	0
Bost	R	115	D	98	1	1	1	76	24	0
Bradley	D	20	C	97	1	1	0	96	4	0
Brady	R	88	D	99	0	1	0	91	9	0
Brosnahan	D	36	S	100	0	0	0	67	33	0
Brown	R	63	S	0	0	0	0	0	0	0
Brunsvold	D	72	D	97	2	1	0	73	27	0
Bugielski	D	19	C	98	1	0	1	79	21	0
Burke	D	23	C	95	2	3	0	88	12	0
Capparelli	D	13	C	96	2	0	2	76	24	0
Churchill	R	62	S	99	1	0	0	88	12	0
Clayton	R	51	S	98	0	2	0	58	42	0
Coulson	R	57	S	98	2	1	0	50	50	3
Cowlishaw	R	41	S	99	0	1	0	85	15	0
Cross	R	84	D	97	1	2	0	64	36	0
Crotty	D	35	S	99	0	1	0	70	30	0
Currie	D	25	C	96	2	2	0	94	6	0
Curry	D	101	D	98	1	1	0	73	27	0
Daniels	R	46	S	99	0	0	1	85	15	0
Dart	D	28	C	92	2	3	3	93	7	18
Davis, M.	D	27	C	97	1	2	0	87	13	6
Davis, S.	D	111	D	99	0	1	0	82	18	0
Deuchler	R	42	S	97	1	2	1	61	39	0
Durkin	R	44	S	98	1	1	0	72	28	3
Erwin	D	11	C	98	1	1	0	91	9	0
Fantin	D	29	S	96	2	2	0	91	9	0
Feigenholtz	D	12	C	96	1	1	3	91	9	3
Flowers	D	21	C	97	0	2	1	97	3	3
Fritchey	D	33	C	95	3	2	0	84	16	3
Gash	D	60	S	92	0	0	8	74	26	6
Giglio	D	79	S	99	0	1	0	79	21	0
Giles	D	8	C	84	8	8	0	89	11	18
Granberg	D	109	D	95	1	4	0	69	31	3
Hannig	D	98	D	98	0	2	0	73	27	0

Representatives continued

				Participation				Party Support		
	P	#	R	O	P	N	E	S	O	A
Hartke	D	108	D	99	0	1	0	72	28	3
Hassert	R	83	S	98	0	2	0	63	38	3
Hoeft	R	66	S	98	1	1	0	67	33	0
Hoffman	D	112	D	0	0	0	0	0	0	0
Holbrook	D	113	D	99	0	0	1	70	30	0
Howard	D	32	C	91	4	5	0	90	10	6
Johnson, Thomas	R	50	S	97	2	1	0	82	18	0
Johnson, Timothy	R	104	D	96	3	1	0	82	18	0
Jones, J.	R	107	D	99	1	1	0	72	28	3
Jones, L.	D	5	C	87	5	7	0	87	13	6
Jones, S.	D	6	C	88	6	4	2	83	17	12
Kenner	D	24	C	93	6	1	0	91	9	0
Klingler	R	100	D	97	1	3	0	56	44	3
Kosel	R	38	S	98	0	2	0	69	31	3
Krause	R	56	S	98	1	1	0	33	67	0
Kubik	R	43	S	92	2	5	2	79	21	12
Lang	D	16	C	97	2	1	0	100	0	0
Lawfer	R	74	D	95	5	0	0	100	0	0
Leitch	R	93	D	97	0	3	0	86	14	12
Lindner	R	65	S	97	2	1	0	59	41	3
Lopez	D	4	C	95	2	1	3	97	3	9
Lyons, E.	R	47	S	94	1	4	2	70	30	9
Lyons, J.	D	15	C	99	0	1	0	88	12	0
Madigan, M.	D	22	C	97	2	1	0	91	9	3
Mautino	D	76	D	99	0	1	0	70	30	0
McAuliffe	R	14	C	100	0	0	0	58	42	0
McCarthy	D	37	S	99	0	1	0	64	36	0
McGuire	D	86	S	97	0	3	1	79	21	0
McKeon	D	34	C	98	1	1	0	100	0	0
Meyer	R	82	S	99	1	0	0	85	15	0
Mitchell	R	73	D	98	1	2	0	59	41	3
Moffitt	R	94	D	99	0	1	0	64	36	0
Moore, A.	R	61	D	99	0	1	0	61	39	0
Moore, E.	D	7	S	96	2	3	0	88	13	3
Morrow	D	26	C	90	6	3	1	88	13	3
Mulligan	R	55	S	96	2	3	0	60	40	9
Murphy	D	30	S	92	4	4	0	83	17	3
Myers, R.	R	95	D	99	1	0	0	82	18	0
Noland	R	102	D	99	0	1	0	85	15	0
Novak	D	85	D	99	1	1	0	70	30	0
O'Brien	D	75	D	99	0	1	0	55	45	0

Representatives continued

				Participation				Party Support		
	P	**#**	**R**	**O**	**P**	**N**	**E**	**S**	**O**	**A**
Pankau	R	49	S	99	1	1	0	79	21	0
Parke	R	53	S	97	0	2	1	83	17	9
Persico	R	39	S	100	0	0	0	58	42	0
Phelps	D	118	D	93	6	1	0	63	38	3
Poe	R	99	D	99	1	1	0	76	24	0
Pugh	D	10	C	90	8	2	0	88	13	3
Reitz	D	116	D	0	0	0	0	0	0	0
Ronen	D	17	C	98	2	0	0	97	3	0
Roskam	R	40	S	97	2	1	0	94	6	0
Rutherford	R	87	D	99	0	1	0	100	0	0
Ryder	R	97	D	89	0	0	11	89	11	18
Santiago	D	3	C	95	2	1	3	94	6	6
Saviano	R	77	S	97	1	2	0	61	39	0
Schakowsky	D	18	S	97	1	1	2	94	6	3
Schoenberg	D	58	S	88	0	6	6	77	23	6
Scott	D	67	D	99	0	1	0	94	6	0
Scully	D	80	S	99	1	0	1	73	27	0
Silva	D	1	C	95	2	3	0	90	10	0
Skinner	R	64	S	98	1	1	0	78	22	3
Slone	D	92	D	95	2	2	2	91	9	3
Smith, M.	D	91	D	98	0	2	0	81	19	3
Stephens	R	110	D	98	1	1	0	91	9	3
Stroger	D	31	C	94	6	0	0	88	12	0
Tenhouse	R	96	D	99	1	0	0	85	15	0
Turner, A.	D	9	C	94	4	3	0	87	13	9
Turner, J.	R	90	D	99	1	1	0	91	9	0
Wait	R	68	D	97	1	2	0	79	21	0
Winkel	R	103	D	99	1	1	0	73	27	0
Winters	R	69	D	99	1	1	0	82	18	0
Wirsing	R	70	D	99	0	1	0	97	3	0
Wojcik	R	45	S	97	1	3	0	88	13	3
Wood	R	59	S	98	0	2	0	66	34	3
Woolard	D	117	D	99	1	0	0	67	33	0
Younge	D	114	D	94	1	5	0	94	6	3
Zickus	R	48	S	97	2	1	0	79	21	0
Hughes	R	63	S	98	1	1	0	73	27	0
Deering	D	116	D	97	0	3	1	56	44	3
Kotlarz	D	20	C	17	0	17	67	0	0	100
Bradford	D	112	D	99	0	1	0	73	27	0
Weaver, M.	R	106	D	98	1	1	0	52	48	0

Part 2

General Assembly Members and Districts

David A. Joens Paul Kleppner

User's Guide to Members and Districts Pages

The Members and Districts section of the *Almanac of Illinois Politics* (pages 32-267) concentrates information on each Senate and House district in a series of four-page spreads. This user's guide explains the construction of the Members and Districts section and shows you how to get the most out of each page so that a wealth of information on each district and its legislator is, literally, at your finger tips.

The first page of each four-page spread features a map of one of the state's 59 Senate districts and the two House districts that comprise each Senate district. Below the map is a tabular representation of the demographic make up of the Senate and House districts in this geographical area. The next three pages introduce the senator and representatives from the two house districts of the geographic area. These pages reveal:

- the legislator's personal and professional background,
- his or her 1997 bill passage ratio,
- voting record on key votes,
- approval ratings from various political interest groups,
- election results, and
- campaign spending patterns.

Each member's page finishes with a look at how his or her district voted in the most recent presidential, U.S. Senate, and gubernatorial races.

The following paragraphs describe in more detail each of the elements that make up the pages of the Members and Districts section of the *Almanac.*

Demographics (1990)

The key to describing the state's legislative districts demographically is matching them with census data. Once the legislative map was accepted, Paul Kleppner, research professor at Northern Illinois University, obtained a computer file listing the assignment of tracts and blocks to legislative districts. He then matched the redistricting file with the appropriate census files, Summary Tape Files 1 and 3 (STF1 and STF3). STF1 is a block-level file, as is the redistricting file, so the two match directly. STF1 is the source for information on voting age and age structure of the population. STF3, the source for the other demographic information, reports the data at the level of block groups, therefore, it does not match directly with the redistricting file. When a block group contains blocks assigned to different legislative districts, values are determined by making the assignment based on proportionate shares of the total population. Specifically, if one block within a group belonged to a different legislative district than the other blocks and it contained 20 percent of the total population of the block group, then 20 percent of the value of the variable in question was assigned to the legislative district to which it belonged, and the remaining 80 percent was assigned to the other district.

Member Personal/Legislative Background

The member background information was obtained and updated by the members.

1997 Bill Passage Ratio

The 1997 Bill Passage Ratio was obtained from the Legislative Information System (LIS). The ratios reflect action on all legislation introduced during the first year of the 90th General Assembly as of June 1, 1997, the end of the spring session.

These ratios give the reader an indication of a member's rate of success in sponsoring legislation. It also gives an indication of a member's rate of success in passing legislation and having it sent to the governor for signature. The reader should not infer that passage ratios are the primary indicator of a given legislator's overall performance. Many legislators sponsor very few bills, yet the impact of that sponsorship may be more far-reaching than that of other legislators who sponsor numerous bills of minor consequence.

The 1997 Bill Passage Ratio are of two types: primary bills and primary/hyphenated bills.

Primary bills are those that the legislator has introduced and on which he or she is the first sponsor. Ideas for legislation could come from constituents, special interest groups, state agencies, departments, etc. However, these are the bills on which the legislator has taken the lead to seek enactment. The primary bills ratios reflect only those bills sponsored in the member's original chamber and not those bills on which the member was the primary sponsor after it passed from the other chamber.

Primary/hyphenated bills are a combination of those bills on which the member is the primary sponsor or one of the cosponsors as allowed by the House or Senate rules. Often the sponsor of a bill will have reason to seek out cosponsors. A downstate legislator may want a Chicago cosponsor, or a Democrat may seek a Republican for bipartisan support. Legislators who are hyphenated on a bill often lend a great deal of assistance to the sponsor in moving the bill through the legislative process. In addition, it is not uncommon for more than one member to introduce very similar bills, which they can combine. Such major contributors become cosponsors. Therefore, hyphenated sponsorship is a significant factor in determining legislative accomplishments. This ratio, too, reflects only those bills sponsored in the member's original chamber and not those bills on which the member was the primary or hyphenated sponsor after it passed from the other chamber.

Both sections then list the number of bills introduced by the legislator, the number that passed the chamber of origin, and the number of bills that passed the General Assembly. These figures reflect only the activity in the first year of the 90th General Assembly. Activity from the 1997 fall veto session is not reflected in this information. A complete picture of legislative sponsorship will be available only after the completion of the 90th General Assembly, in January 1999.

Key Votes

Fifteen key votes were selected for each chamber of the General Assembly based on the individual bill's impact on state government and the people of Illinois. Most of the bills are virtually identical for the Senate and the House. However, not all bills were voted on in both chambers. Where this occurred, we have attempted to select bills similar in content and/or controversy. During the spring 1997 session, several major pieces of legislation were voted on in one chamber but not the other. For example, Governor Edgar's proposed education funding plan was voted on in the House but not the Senate. The House vote on this proposal is listed among the 15 key votes for House members but the bill, which narrowly passed the House, was not called for a vote in the Senate. Instead, the vote on a Senate Republican education funding proposal is listed for Senate members. That bill, which passed the Senate, was never called for a vote in the House.

For legislation passed prior to midnight on May 31, a bill must have support from a constitutional majority (60 in the House and 30 in the Senate) if it is to be effective within a year. After May 31, bills require 71 votes in the House and 36 in the Senate (a three-fifths majority) if they are to go into effect within a year. While voting present or not voting at all differs from public opposition, these votes affect the roll call outcome the same as voting against a bill.

The following abbreviations have been used to designate the members' votes on these bills:

- Y - The member voted yes.
- N - The member voted no.
- P - The member voted present, which has the legal effect of a no vote.
- A - The member was absent when that roll call was taken; applies to House members only and has the legal effect of a no vote.
- E - The member received an excused absence for that roll call; applies to House members only and has the legal effect of a no vote.
- X - Was not a member of the General Assembly or of that chamber at the time of the roll call.
- O - The member was recorded as having not voted; applies only to Senate members and has the legal effect of a no vote.

Following are the key votes selected for 1997:

H1. Change education funding formula—SB645—3rd reading in the House. Raise income tax by $1.5 billion; provide $900 million in property tax relief; and use remaining $600 million for education funding. Adds several provisions on school reform. House vote on 3rd reading taken May 29, 1997: 62 yeas, 56 nays, 0 present. Passed the House.

S1. Senate GOP Education Funding Plan—HB449—3rd reading in the Senate. Increases telecommunications excise tax. Imposes additional tax on cigarettes. New revenues to go into common school fund. Revises state aid formula. Contains several provisions on school reform. Senate vote on 3rd reading taken May 30, 1997: 30 yeas, 28 nays, 0 present. Passed the Senate.

2. Budget—SB1129—Conference Committee Report #1 in the Senate and House. Makes appropriations and reappropriations to fund state operations for FY 98. Senate vote on CCR # 1 taken May 31, 1997: 49 yeas, 9 nays, 0 present. House vote on CCR # 1 taken on May 31, 1997: 116 yeas, 2 nays, 0 present. Passed the House and the Senate.

3. Tougher DUI level—SB 8—3rd reading in the House and the Senate. Lowers the blood alcohol concentration level at which a person is presumed to be under the influence of alcohol from 0.10 to 0.08. Senate 3rd reading taken March 6, 1997: 48 yeas, 8 nays, 0 present. House 3rd reading taken May 7, 1997: 106 yeas, 11 nays, 0 present. Passed the House and the Senate.

4. Ban partial birth abortions—HB 382—House 3rd reading, Senate 3rd reading. Prohibits partial birth abortions unless necessary to save the life of a mother. Makes performance of a partial birth abortion a Class 4 Felony. Prohibits prosecution of a woman on whom a partial birth abortion is performed. House third reading taken April 11, 1997: 74 yeas, 37 nays, 4 present. Senate third reading taken May 13, 1997: 49 yeas, 3 nays, 4 present. Passed the House and the Senate.

5. State Employees Pension—HB 110—3rd reading in the Senate, concurrence in the House. Provides a new retirement formula for state and university workers. Eliminates compensation for unused sick days. Senate third reading taken May 31, 1997: 58 yeas, 0 nays, 0 present. House concurrence with amendments 1, 3, and 4 taken May 31, 1997: 118 yeas, 0 nays, 0 present. Passed the House and the Senate.

6. Insurance/domestic violence—SB 490—3rd reading in the Senate, 3rd reading in the House. No company authorized to transact life, health, or disability insurance may deny coverage or charge a different rate because an individual has been the subject of abuse or has sought treatment or protection from abuse. Senate third reading taken March 20, 1997: 55 yeas, 0 nays and 0 present. House third reading taken May 8, 1997: 114 yeas, 0 nays, 2 present. Passed the House and the Senate.

7. Brownfields—SB939—Conference Committee Report in the House and the Senate. Establishes an environmental remediation tax credit for certain costs incurred by a person after Jan. 1, 1998 in performing site remediation activities. Creates the Brownfields Redevelopment Grant Program to provide municipalities with funding for Brownfields redevelopment efforts. House vote on CCR 1 taken May 31, 1997: 106 yeas, 8 nays, 0 present. Senate vote on CCR 1 taken June 1, 1997: 57 yeas, 0 nays, 0 present. Passed the House and the Senate.
8. Welfare reform—HB204—concurrence with Senate amendment # 3 in the House, 3rd reading in the Senate. Implements the provisions of the (federal) Personal Responsibility and Work Opportunity Reconciliation Act of 1996 regarding the Temporary Assistance to Needy Families Program. Senate 3rd reading taken May 31, 1997: 56 yeas, 1 nay, 0 present. House concurrence vote on Senate amendment 3 taken June 1, 1997: 112 yeas, 5 nays, 1 present. Passed the House and the Senate.
9. Concealed guns/misdemeanor—SB71—Senate concurrence with House amendments 1 and 2, House 3rd reading. Provides that a first violation of carrying a firearm in a vehicle, concealed upon one's body, or upon a public street or property lands within a municipality is a Class A misdemeanor instead of a Class 4 felony. House third reading taken May 15, 1997: 73 yeas, 40 nays, 3 present. Senate concurrence vote on House amendments 1 and 2 taken May 21, 1997: 36 yeas, 14 nays, 9 present. Passed the House and the Senate.
10. Banks sell insurance—HB586—3rd reading in the Senate, concurrence with Senate ammendment # 1 in the House. Authorizes financial institutions to act as agents for insurance companies. Senate 3rd reading taken May 16, 1997: 56 yeas, 0 nays, 2 present. House vote on concurrence taken May 22, 1997: 114 yeas, 1 nay, 3 present. Passed the House and the Senate.
11. Pre-paid college tuition—SB878 and HB 190—3rd reading on HB 190 in the Senate and 3rd reading on SB 878 in the House. Establishes the Illinois Pre-Paid Tuition Program, allowing a purchaser to enter into and make payments required on a pre-paid tuition contract in order to provide a higher education for a beneficiary. Senate vote on 3rd reading on HB 190 taken on May 16, 1997: 56 yeas, 1 nay, 2 present. House vote on 3rd reading on SB 878 taken May 16, 1997: 116 yeas, 0 nays, 0 present. Both bills passed the House and the Senate.
12. Increase pull tab prizes—HB 1840—3rd reading in the House and Senate. Fraternal organizations that conduct games under the Pull Tabs and Jar Games Act may now award prizes up to $500 (previously $250) and may sell as many as 6,000 tickets a game (previously 4,000) and may now charge up to $2 a game (previously $1). House 3rd reading taken April 11, 1997: 96 yeas, 18 nays, 1 present. Senate 3rd reading taken May 9, 1997: 35 yeas, 18 nays, 0 present. Passed the House and the Senate.

H13. Utility deregulation—SB 55—3rd reading in the House. Provides for the deregulation of the generation and sale of electricity and creates the electricity excise tax law. House vote on 3rd reading taken May 30, 1997: 85 yeas, 12 nays, 20 present. Passed the House.

S13. Telecommunications tax—SB996—3rd reading in the Senate. Allows the governing body of a municipality to impose an infrastructure maintenance fee on telecommunications retailers by ordinance or resolution. Senate vote on 3rd reading taken March 20, 1997: 23 yeas, 22 nays, 10 present. Failed in the Senate.

H14. County obscenity standards—HB245—3rd reading in the House. Provides that the standards of whether material is obscene is the standard of the county in which the material is sold, delivered, advertised, or performed. House vote on 3rd reading taken April 23, 1997: 58 yeas, 48 nays, 7 present. Failed in the House.

S14. Delivery discrimination—SB895—3rd reading in the Senate. Makes it a Class A misdemeanor for a business that makes deliveries to fail to deliver to a specific location because of actual or perceived race, color, creed, religion, ancestry, sex, sexual orientation, physical or mental disability, or national origin of the location's residents. Senate vote on 3rd reading taken March 19, 1997: 23 yeas, 6 nays, 26 present. Failed in the Senate.

H15. Managed care reform—HB626—3rd reading in the House. Creates the Managed Care Reform Act containing new controls and requirements on managed care plans. House vote on 3rd reading taken April 25, 1997: 73 yeas, 37 nays, 4 present. Passed the House.

S15. Sell drivers' data—SB 79—3rd reading in the Senate. Provides that the secretary of state shall, instead of may, furnish to an applicant vehicle and driver data at a specified fee. Senate vote on 3rd reading taken March 20, 1997: 19 yeas, 35 nays, 1 present. Failed in the Senate.

Group Ratings

Interest groups are close observers of legislative voting. Several groups rate members according to how the members voted on bills of interest to the group. We have assembled ratings from five significant interest groups. Five of the groups rate members on a percentage basis, while one group indicates how many of its key positions on bills each member supported. For example, the Illinois Federation for the Right to Life (PrLf) tracked six major bills in the state House of Representatives. The Right to Life group rating incidates how many times each member of the House supported the group's position on those six roll calls.

The special interest groups are:

- **Illinois Agriculture Association (FB).** Ratings provided based on 15 roll calls in the Senate and 16 roll calls in the House. For further information, contact the Illinois Agricultural Association (Illinois Farm Bureau), 1701 Towanda Ave., P.O. Box 2901, Bloomington, IL 61702-2901.

- **Illinois Chamber of Commerce (CoC).** Ratings provided based on five roll calls in the Senate and 13 roll calls in the House. For more information, contact the Illinois Chamber, 215 E. Adams St., Springfield, IL 62701-1199.
- **Illinois Federation for the Right to Life (PrLf).** Ratings provided based on two roll calls in the Senate and six roll calls in the House. For more information, contact the Illinois Federation for the Right to Life, 308 E. Monroe, Springfield, IL 62701.
- **Illinois Planned Parenthood Council (IPPC).** Ratings provided based on two votes in the Senate and six votes in the House. For more information, contact the Illinois Planned Parenthood Council, 313 W. Cook St., Springfield, IL 62704.
- **American Civil Liberties Union (ACLU).** Ratings provided based on four roll calls in the Senate and 10 roll calls in the House. For more information, contact the American Civil Liberties Union of Illinois at P.O. Box 5010, Springfield, IL 62705-5010.

Group ratings from the following interest groups have appeared in previous edition of the *Almanac*. These groups may issue ratings of General Assembly members at the end of the session. For the readers' convenience, we are providing names and addresses where information regarding such ratings might be obtained:

- AFL-CIO. For further information, contact the AFL-CIO, 828 S. 2nd, Springfield, IL 62704.
- National Taxpayers United of Illinois (NTU). For further information, contact the National Taxpayers United of Illinois, 59 E. Van Buren St., Suite 2517, Chicago, IL 60605.
- Illinois Environmental Council (IEC). For further information, contact the Illinois Environmental Council, 319 W. Cook St., Springfield, IL 62704.
- Manufacturers' Political Action Committee (MPAC). For further information, contact the Manufacturers' Political Action Committee, P.O. Box 2147, Springfield, IL 62705-2147.
- The National Federation of Independent Business (NFIB). The NIFB rates members of the General Assembly only at the end of the session. For further information, contact the National Federation of Independent Business, 600 S. 2nd St., Suite 101, Springfield, IL 62704.

The following rating abbreviation is used for some members of the General Assembly:

N/R—No rating; the legislator was not rated by that particular interest group. This rating is used for members who were not in the General Assembly during the session or who missed a certain number of the rated votes during the session.

Election Results

This portion of each member's page was compiled from the *Official Vote* books prepared by the Illinois State Board of Elections (SBE) for the general and primary elections of 1996, 1994, and 1992. Major candidates are listed first for the 1996 general election and then for the 1994 primary election by district. In some instances, primary elections attracted several candidates; in these instances the top-vote recipient was listed. As a result, not all total percentages equal 100.

The following abbreviations were used to identify partisan affiliation of the candidates:

R - Republican
D - Democrat
I - Independent
HWP - Harold Washington Party
LIB - Libertarian
REF - Reform
ERP - Economic Recovery Party
W-I - Write-In candidate

Campaign Resources and Expenditures

This information was compiled from the semiannual reports required of every political campaign committee registered in Illinois with the State Board of Elections. These reports cover the period from July 1, 1996, to December 31, 1996; therefore the information on contributions and expenditures primarily covers the November 1996 general election cycle. The information is not inclusive because candidates do receive contributions for the November election earlier than July 1 and often have expenditures outstanding beyond December 31 of the election year. However, the information does give an indication of the amounts of money raised and spent during a given election cycle.

The information for the beginning balance, receipts, expenditures, and on-hand funds was taken directly from the semiannual reports filed by the candidate's campaign committee. If that information was incomplete or inaccurate, attempts were made to provide the reader with the most accurate data available. All figures are rounded to the nearest dollar. The reader should also note that the receipts and expenditures include in-kind receipts and expenditures made on behalf of the committee. Often, party sources and others will spend money on behalf of a candidate and will also provide an in-kind contribution as opposed to a cash contribution. Those types of contributions are reported separately on the semiannual report but are combined here to give a more accurate reflection of the resources available to a given candidate. In many hotly contested races, contributions from party sources are so significant that you will see party sources among our listing of a candidate's top 10 PACs.

The breakdown of contributions by individuals, party sources, PACs (political action committees), the candidate, and the not-itemized section was compiled by doing a line-item check of the reports filed by the committee. The "candidate" line of this portion of the page includes money contributed to the campaign by the candidate, loans taken out by the candidate, and interest received by the campaign committee. In past editions of the *Almanac,* not-itemized contributions, which are contributions of under $150, were rolled into the individuals contribution line; interest income, which very few campaign committees had, was a separate line. In this edition, not-itemized contributions are a separate line and, as noted above, interest income is rolled into the candidate's contribution line.

The top 10 PAC contributors were identified by a line-item check of the reports filed by the committee. In listing the top 10 PACs, we included partisan committees, such as contributions from the candidate's state and local party funds and transfers from the campaign committees of other candidates. Of course, we also included nonpartisan special interest PACs as well. The abbreviations used for the PACs are identified in the last few pages of the book.

As with previous editions of the *Almanac,* we have provided the same information for incumbents' opponents starting on page 269. That information is provided for all opponents who, in accordance with state election law, after having raised or spent $1,000 in behalf of their campaign efforts, formed a campaign committee with the State Board of Elections.

General Election Data

For this portion of each member's page, general election data was compiled from precinct canvasses from each of the 111 election jurisdictions in the state of Illinois. To provide an overview of the electoral nature of the districts, the following information was compiled by hand for each district:

- 1996 registered voters and actual turnout, as well as percentage of those who voted;
- The number and percentage of those 1996 general election voters who cast straight-Republican or straight-Democratic ballots (Legislation passed by the 89th General Assembly in January 1997 ended straight party voting in Illinois);
- 1996 presidential vote returns and percentages;
- 1996 United States Senate vote returns and percentages;
- 1994 gubernatorial vote returns and percentages;
- 1992 presidential vote returns and percentages.

1st Senate District

House District 1
House District 2

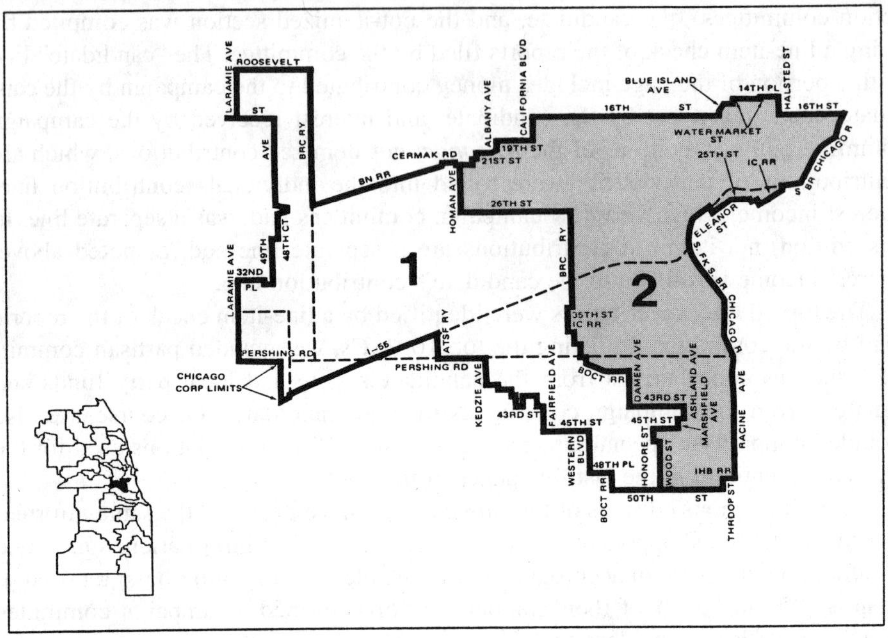

DEMOGRAPHICS (1990)

	S.D. #1	H.D. #1	H.D.#2
VOTING AGE POPULATION	126,178	64,327	61,851
White	23.5%	25.9%	20.9%
Black	4.5%	6.4%	2.6%
Hispanic	71.0%	66.6%	75.6%
Asian	0.7%	0.8%	0.6%
AGE (Total Population)	193,739	96,869	96,870
Under 6	12.9%	12.3%	13.5%
6 to 18	24.0%	23.4%	24.6%
65 and Over	6.8%	6.9%	6.7%
URBAN POPULATION	100.0%	100.0%	100.0%
HOUSING UNITS (Total)	56,366	26,523	29,843
Median Value	$50,182	$51,880	$46,834
Owner Occupied	33.7%	40.8%	27.4%
FAMILY INCOME (Total Families)	39,779	19,460	20,319
Median Income	$24,819	$26,656	$22,787
Below Poverty Level	21.0%	17.7%	24.1%
With Children Under 5	3.6%	3.1%	4.1%
With Children 5 to 17	7.1%	6.3%	7.9%
Headed by Females	8.3%	6.5%	10.0%
INDUSTRY (Total Employed)	73,643	36,596	37,048
Professional/Public Administration	11.7%	11.0%	12.4%
Manufacturing	38.0%	37.1%	39.0%
Retail	15.7%	16.3%	15.1%
Transportation/Communication	6.1%	6.3%	6.0%
Finance/Insurance/Real Estate	4.2%	4.8%	3.5%
Other Service	9.9%	10.1%	9.6%

Senator Jesus G. Garcia (D)

District Office: 2500 S. St. Louis St., Chicago 60623
Phone (773) 762-7089; (773) 762-1825 (fax)
Springfield Office: 119A Capitol Bldg., Springfield 62706
Phone (217) 782-9415

Legislative Assignments: Committees on Commerce & Industry (minority spokesperson); Public Health & Welfare.

Public Service: Senator (1993-present); committeeman, 22nd ward, Chicago; alderman, 22nd Ward, Chicago (1987-1993); board member of the Latino Elected Officials.

Personal: Full-time legislator; born April 12, 1956, Durango, Mexico; University of Illinois-Chicago, political science; married (Evelyn); two children.

1997 BILL PASSAGE RATIO	Introduced	Passed House of Origin	Passed GA
Primary	25	3	2
Primary/Hyphenated	48	15	8

KEY VOTES

1) Senate GOP Ed. $ Plan . . . . . . .N	6) Insurance/Domestic Violence . .Y	11) Pre-Paid College Tuition . . .Y
2) State Budget . . . . .Y	7) Brownfields . . . . .Y	12) Increase Pull Tab Prizes . . . .Y
3) Tougher DUI Level . . . . .O	8) Welfare Reform . . . . .Y	13) Telecommunications Tax . . .Y
4) Ban Partial Birth Abortions . . .O	9) Concealed guns/misdemeanor . .N	14) Delivery Discrimination . . . .Y
5) State Employees Pension . . . . .Y	10) Banks sell insurance . . . . .Y	15) Sell Drivers' Data . . . . .N

GROUP RATINGS

	FB	CoC	PrLf	IPPC	ACLU
1997	55	50	0/2	100	100

ELECTION RESULTS

1996 General	Jesus G. Garcia (D)	21,539	(100%)
1996 Primary	Jesus G. Garcia (D)	6,839	(59.3%)
1996 Primary	Juan M. Soliz (D)	4,686	(40.7%)

CAMPAIGN RESOURCES AND EXPENDITURES

1996 Campaign Funds				Top 10 PAC Contributors			
Beg. Balance . .	$8,951	Individuals . . .	$8,220	1) Teamsters . .	$3,250	6) ITLA	$1,000
Receipts	$52,823	Party	$650	2) PKMall . . .	$1,250	7) HOPE	$850
Expenditures .	$58,809	PACS	$34,900	3) TIP	$1,000	8) CHB	$800
On hand	$2,965	Candidate	$280	4) ElPasoAuto	$1,000	9) UAW	$750
		Not-itemized .	$8,773	5) CTU	$1,000	10) CoC	$750

NOTE: The General Election Opponent's Campaign Resources and Expenditures are reported in a separate section in the back of the book (pp. 269-284).

GENERAL ELECTION DATA

	Registered Voters	Voter Turnout		Straight Party Voting	
1996	 46,068	26,034	56.5%	(R) 1,096 . . . 4.2%	(D) 11,511 . . . 44.2%

PRESIDENT

1996	Bill Clinton (D)	20,271	82.1%
	Bob Dole (R)	3,171	12.8%
	Ross Perot (I)	1,248	5.1%
1992	Bill Clinton (D)	18,280	64.8%
	George Bush (R)	6,324	22.4%
	Ross Perot (I)	3,627	12.8%

UNITED STATES SENATE

1996	Richard J. Durbin (D)	19,555	79.6%
	Al Salvi (R)	4,322	17.6%

GOVERNOR

1994	Jim Edgar (R)	7,151	46.1%
	Dawn Clark Netsch (D)	8,345	53.9%

Representative Sonia Silva (D)

District Office: 2625 West 43rd St., Chicago 60632
Phone (773) 843-0096; (773) 843-1754 (fax)
Springfield Office: Rm. 2085-M, Stratton Bldg., Springfield 62706
Phone (217) 782-7752; (217) 782-0952 (fax)

Legislative Assignments: Committees on Appropriations-Education; Appropriations-General Services and Government Oversight; Aging; Insurance; Health Care Availability & Access.

Public Service: Representative (1997-present); member, National Association of Latino Elected Officials; Empowerment Zone.

Personal: Born December 28, 1950, Chicago; Northeastern Illinois University, B.A. in education; University of Chicago, A.M. in Public Policy/Urban Planning.

1997 BILL PASSAGE RATIO	Introduced	Passed House of Origin	Passed GA
Primary	19	1	1
Primary/Hyphenated	36	7	3

KEY VOTES

1) Change Ed. Funding Formula . . Y	6) Insurance/Domestic Violence . Y	11) Pre-Paid College Tuition . . . . Y
2) State Budget . . . . Y	7) Brownfields . . . . Y	12) Increase Pull Tab Prizes . . . . Y
3) Tougher DUI Level . . . . Y	8) Welfare Reform . . . . N	13) Utility Deregulation . . . . P
4) Ban Partial Birth Abortions . . . . P	9) Concealed Guns/Misdemeanor N	14) County Obscenity Standards . A
5) State Employees Pension . . . . . Y	10) Banks Sell Insurance . . . . Y	15) Managed Care Reform . . . . . Y

GROUP RATINGS

	FB	CoC	PrLf	IPPC	ACLU
1997	86	25	0/6	83	88

ELECTION RESULTS

1996 General	Sonia Silva (D)	9,832	(100%)
1996 Primary	Sonia Silva (D)	3,241	(59.2%)
1996 Primary	Fernando A. Frias (D)	2,236	(40.8%)
1994 General	Rafael "Ray" Frias (D)	5,642	(100%)

CAMPAIGN RESOURCES AND EXPENDITURES

1996 Campaign Funds			
Beg. Balance $965	Individuals $0
Receipts $7,385	Party $1,000
Expenditures . . $7,231	PACS $5,700
On hand $1,119	Candidate $0
	Not-itemized . . . $685

Top 10 PAC Contributors	
1) ITLA $2,000	6) CUPAC $350
2) CGarcia . . . $1,000	7) UAW $250
3) LAWPAC . . . $750	8) IUOE $250
4) HOPE $400	9) Ameritech . . . $250
5) AFLCIO $350	10) IFT $250

NOTE: The General Election Opponent's Campaign Resources and Expenditures are reported in a separate section in the back of the book (pp. 269-284).

GENERAL ELECTION DATA

	Registered Voters	Voter Turnout		Straight Party Voting	
1996	21,965	12,490	56.9%	(R) 691 . . . . . 5.5%	(D) 5,298 . . . 42.4%

PRESIDENT

1996	Bill Clinton (D)	9,482	79.4%
	Bob Dole (R)	1,761	14.7%
	Ross Perot (I)	616	5.2%
1992	Bill Clinton (D)	8,410	62.1%
	George Bush (R)	3,286	24.2%
	Ross Perot (I)	1,856	13.7%

UNITED STATES SENATE

1996	Richard J. Durbin (D)	9,067	77.1%
	Al Salvi (R)	2,352	20.0%

GOVERNOR

1994	Jim Edgar (R)	3,775	50.4%
	Dawn Clark Netsch (D)	3,717	49.6%

Representative Edward Acevedo (D)

District Office: 1939 S. Halsted, Chicago 60608
Phone (312) 829-2555; (312) 850-2886 (fax)
Springfield Office: 2032-J Stratton Bldg., Springfield 62706
Phone (217) 782-2855

Legislative Assignments: Committees on Local Government; Appropriations-Public Safety; Judiciary II-Criminal Law; Consumer Protection.

Public Service: Representative (1997-present)

Personal: Chicago police officer; born July 23, 1963, Chicago; married (Dianna); five children.

1997 BILL PASSAGE RATIO	Introduced	Passed House of Origin	Passed GA
Primary	8	3	3
Primary/Hyphenated	17	11	7

KEY VOTES

1) Change Ed. Funding Formula . . Y
2) State Budget . . . . Y
3) Tougher DUI Level . . . . Y
4) Ban Partial Birth Abortions . . . Y
5) State Employees Pension . . . . . Y
6) Insurance/Domestic Violence . . Y
7) Brownfields . . . . A
8) Welfare Reform . . . . Y
9) Concealed Guns/Misdemeanor . N
10) Banks Sell Insurance . . . . Y
11) Pre-Paid College Tuition . . . . Y
12) Increase Pull Tab Prizes . . . . Y
13) Utility Deregulation . . . . Y
14) County Obscenity Standards . N
15) Managed Care Reform . . . . . Y

GROUP RATINGS

	FB	CoC	PrLf	IPPC	ACLU
1997	82	23	3/6	33	60

ELECTION RESULTS

1996 General	Edward Acevedo (D)	10,274	(83.6%)
1996 General	Nancy Mercado (R)	2,017	(16.4%)
1996 Primary	Benjamin A. "Ben" Martinez (D)	2,238	(34.8%)
1996 Primary	Four others (D)	4,190	(65.2%)

CAMPAIGN RESOURCES AND EXPENDITURES

1996 Campaign Funds

Beg. Balance	$0	Individuals	$0
Receipts	$600	Party	$0
Expenditures	$109	PACS	$500
On hand	$491	Candidate	$0
		Not-itemized	$100

Top 10 PAC Contributors

1) ShyWays	$500	6) N/A	$N/A
2) N/A	$N/A	7) N/A	$N/A
3) N/A	$N/A	8) N/A	$N/A
4) N/A	$N/A	9) N/A	$N/A
5) N/A	$N/A	10) N/A	$N/A

NOTE: The General Election Opponent's Campaign Resources and Expenditures are reported in a separate section in the back of the book (pp. 269-284).

GENERAL ELECTION DATA

	Registered Voters	Voter Turnout		Straight Party Voting (R)		Straight Party Voting (D)	
1996	24,103	13,544	56.2%	405	3.0%	6,213	45.9%

PRESIDENT

1996	Bill Clinton (D)	10,789	83.2%
	Bob Dole (R)	1,410	10.9%
	Ross Perot (I)	632	4.9%
1992	Bill Clinton (D)	9,870	67.2%
	George Bush (R)	3,038	20.7%
	Ross Perot (I)	1,771	12.1%

UNITED STATES SENATE

1996	Richard J. Durbin (D)	10,488	82.0%
	Al Salvi (R)	1,970	15.4%

GOVERNOR

1994	Jim Edgar (R)	3,376	42.2%
	Dawn Clark Netsch (D)	4,628	57.8%

2nd Senate District

House District 3
House District 4

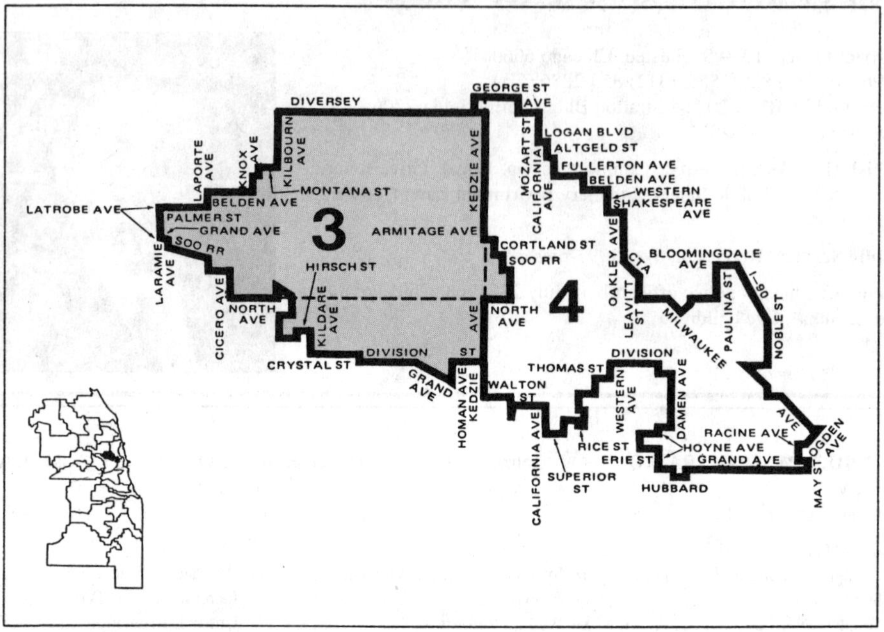

DEMOGRAPHICS (1990)

	S.D. #2	H.D. #3	H.D.#4
VOTING AGE POPULATION	126,813	62,947	63,866
White	25.0%	23.1%	27.0%
Black	7.4%	8.1%	6.7%
Hispanic	66.1%	67.3%	65.0%
Asian	1.0%	1.2%	0.8%
AGE (Total Population)	193,739	96,869	96,870
Under 6	12.6%	12.4%	12.7%
6 to 18	23.8%	24.4%	23.2%
65 and Over	6.7%	6.2%	7.1%
URBAN POPULATION	100.0%	100.0%	100.0%
HOUSING UNITS (Total)	65,281	30,252	35,029
Median Value	$67,741	$67,587	$68,194
Owner Occupied	25.7%	32.2%	20.0%
FAMILY INCOME (Total Families)	42,498	21,805	20,692
Median Income	$21,900	$23,420	$20,206
Below Poverty Level	28.5%	25.7%	31.5%
With Children Under 5	4.7%	4.2%	5.2%
With Children 5 to 17	10.7%	9.6%	11.9%
Headed by Females	16.5%	15.2%	17.8%
INDUSTRY (Total Employed)	73,875	37,394	36,481
Professional/Public Administration	17.9%	17.9%	17.9%
Manufacturing	34.5%	35.5%	33.4%
Retail	16.6%	15.7%	17.5%
Transportation/Communication	5.5%	6.2%	4.8%
Finance/Insurance/Real Estate	4.8%	4.7%	5.0%
Other Service	10.4%	9.3%	11.6%

Senator Miguel del Valle (D)

District Office: 3507 W. North Ave., Chicago 60647
Phone (773) 292-0202; (773) 292-1903 (fax)
Springfield Office: 311 Capitol Bldg., Springfield 62706
Phone (217) 782-5652

Legislative Assignments: Assistant Minority Leader; Committees on Executive; Licensed Activities.

Public Service: Senator (1987-present).

Personal: Full-time legislator; born July 24, 1951, Veja Baja, Puerto Rico; Northeastern Illinois University, B.A.in Spanish, M.A. in guidance; married (Lupe); four children.

1997 BILL PASSAGE RATIO	Introduced	Passed House of Origin	Passed GA
Primary	15	5	4
Primary/Hyphenated	27	8	5

KEY VOTES

1) Senate GOP Ed. $ Plan ......N	6) Insurance/Domestic Violence ..Y	11) Pre-Paid College Tuition ....Y
2) StateBudget ....Y	7) Brownfields ....Y	12) Increase Pull Tab Prizes ....Y
3) Tougher DUI Level ....Y	8) Welfare Reform ....N	13) Telecommunications Tax ...Y
4) Ban Partial Birth Abortions ....P	9) Concealed Guns/Misdemeanor .N	14) Delivery Discrimination ....Y
5) State Employees Pension .....Y	10) Banks Sell Insurance ....Y	15) Sell Drivers' Data ....N

GROUP RATINGS

	FB	CoC	PrLf	IPPC	ACLU
1997	73	50	0/2	100	100

ELECTION RESULTS

1994 General	Miguel del Valle (D)	15,741	(100%)
1994 Primary	Miguel del Valle (D)	11,753	(100%)
1992 General	Miguel del Valle (D)	34,463	(100%)

CAMPAIGN RESOURCES AND EXPENDITURES

1996 Campaign Funds			
Beg. Balance	$1,706	Individuals	$4,416
Receipts	$22,748	Party	$250
Expenditures	$23,360	PACS	$8,350
On hand	$1,094	Candidate	0
		Not-itemized	$9,732

Top 10 PAC Contributors			
1) AT&T	$1,000	6) Jimenez	$500
2) CTU	$1,000	7) UnityHMO	$500
3) IBA	$500	8) HOPE	$500
4) CB&T	$500	9) AlivioMC	$500
5) Humana	$500	10) UFCW	$500

NOTE: The General Election Opponent's Campaign Resources and Expenditures are reported in a separate section in the back of the book (pp. 269-284).

GENERAL ELECTION DATA

	Registered Voters	Voter Turnout		Straight Party Voting	
1996	72,364	37,058	51.2%	(R) 1,198 ....3.2%	(D) 17,423 ....47.0

PRESIDENT

1996	Bill Clinton (D)	29,436	84.2%
	Bob Dole (R)	3,722	10.7%
	Ross Perot (I)	1,372	3.9%
1992	Bill Clinton (D)	30,807	71.8%
	George Bush (R)	8,268	19.3%
	Ross Perot (I)	3,853	8.9%

UNITED STATES SENATE

1996	Richard J. Durbin (D)	28,575	83.2%
	Al Salvi (R)	4,701	13.7%

GOVERNOR

1994	Jim Edgar (R)	7,268	37.8%
	Dawn Clark Netsch (D)	11,973	62.2%

Representative Miguel A. Santiago (D)

District Office: 4502 West Fullerton Ave., Chicago 60639
Phone (773) 486-9779; (773) 276-2596 (fax)
Springfield Office: Room 618, Capitol Bldg., Springfield 62706
Phone (217) 782-0480; (217) 782-8917 (fax)

Legislative Assignments: Assistant Majority Leader; ex officio member of all committees; Committees on Executive; Financial Institutions; Registration & Regulation; Appropriations-Public Safety; Appropriations-Education.

Public Service: Representative (1989-present).

Personal: Full-time legislator, born May 24, 1953; Northeastern Illinois University and Governors State University; married (Leida); two children.

1997 BILL PASSAGE RATIO	Introduced	Passed House of Origin	Passed GA
Primary	31	10	5
Primary/Hyphenated	81	29	14

KEY VOTES

1) Change Ed. Funding Formula . . Y
2) State Budget . . . . Y
3) Tougher DUI Level . . . . Y
4) Ban Partial Birth Abortions . . . . P
5) State Employees Pension . . . . . Y
6) Insurance/Domestic Violence . . Y
7) Brownfields . . . . Y
8) Welfare Reform . . . . Y
9) Concealed Guns/Misdemeanor . N
10) Banks Sell Insurance . . . . Y
11) Pre-Paid College Tuition . . . . Y
12) Increase Pull Tab Prizes . . . . Y
13) Utility Deregulation . . . . Y
14) County Obscenity Standards . P
15) Managed Care Reform . . . . . Y

GROUP RATINGS

	FB	CoC	PrLf	IPPC	ACLU
1997	82	27	1/6	83	80

ELECTION RESULTS

1996 General	Miguel A. Santiago (D)	14,513	(90.1%)
1996 General	Augusto Montijo (R)	1,594	(9.9%)
1996 Primary	Miguel A. Santiago (D)	3,925	(54.3%)
1996 Primary	Two others (D)	3,305	(45.7%)

CAMPAIGN RESOURCES AND EXPENDITURES

1996 Campaign Funds

Beg. Balance	$24,672	Individuals	$1,600
Receipts	$36,100	Party	$1,000
Expenditures	$18,216	PACS	$28,800
On hand	$42,556	Candidate	$0
		Not-itemized	$4,700

Top 10 PAC Contributors

1) IPACE	$5,000	6) CAE	$1,000
2) IAC	$2,000	7) HI	$1,000
3) ITLA	$2,000	8) ISMS	$1,000
4) RPAC	$1,500	9) UPS	$500
5) IBA	$1,000	10) NJC	$500

NOTE: The General Election Opponent's Campaign Resources and Expenditures are reported in a separate section in the back of the book (pp. 269-284).

GENERAL ELECTION DATA

	Registered Voters	Voter Turnout		Straight Party Voting	
1996	35,464	17,534	49.4%	(R) 581 . . . . 3.4%	(D) 8,767 . . . . 50.5%

PRESIDENT

1996	Bill Clinton (D)	14,080	85.0%
	Bob Dole (R)	1,728	10.4%
	Ross Perot (I)	587	3.5%
1992	Bill Clinton (D)	14,213	70.1%
	George Bush (R)	4,335	21.4%
	Ross Perot (I)	1,737	8.5%

UNITED STATES SENATE

1996	Richard J. Durbin (D)	13,519	83.3%
	Al Salvi (R)	2,254	13.9%

GOVERNOR

1994	Jim Edgar (R)	3,624	40.1%
	Dawn Clark Netsch (D)	5,411	59.9%

Representative Edgar Lopez (D)

District Office: 1951 West Division, Chicago 60622
Phone (773) 252-9922; (773) 252-9926 (fax)
Springfield Office: Room 622, Capitol Bldg., Springfield 62706
Phone (217) 782-0150; (217) 782-8917 (fax)

Legislative Assignments: Committees on Consumer Protection (chairperson); Appropriations-Education (vice-chair); Executive; Financial Institutions; Insurance; Registration & Regulation.

Public Service: Representative (1993-present).

Personal: Accountant; born April 7, 1964, Chicago; Andrews University, business administration; married (Lillibeth); one daughter.

1997 BILL PASSAGE RATIO

	Introduced	Passed House of Origin	Passed GA
Primary	21	4	1
Primary/Hyphenated	67	28	12

KEY VOTES

1) Change Ed. Funding Formula . . Y	6) Insurance/Domestic Violence . . Y	11) Pre-Paid College Tuition . . . . Y
2) State Budget . . . . Y	7) Brownfields . . . . Y	12) Increase Pull Tab Prizes . . . . Y
3) Tougher DUI Level . . . . Y	8) Welfare Reform . . . . Y	13) Utility Deregulation . . . . Y
4) Ban Partial Birth Abortions . . . N	9) Concealed Guns/Misdemeanor . N	14) County Obscenity Standards . P
5) State Employees Pension . . . . . Y	10) Banks Sell Insurance . . . . Y	15) Managed Care Reform . . . . . Y

GROUP RATINGS

	FB	CoC	PrLf	IPPC	ACLU
1997	82	27	0/6	100	90

ELECTION RESULTS

1996 General	Edgar Lopez (D)	15,248	(86.2%)
1996 General	John W. Duda (R)	2,451	(13.9%)
1996 Primary	Edgar Lopez (D)	3,918	(100%)

CAMPAIGN RESOURCES AND EXPENDITURES

1996 Campaign Funds

Beg. Balance	$4,669	Individuals	$3,250
Receipts	$33,400	Party	$0
Expenditures	$23,925	PACS	$25,550
On hand	$14,144	Candidate	$500
		Not-itemized	$4,100

Top 10 PAC Contributors

1) MCMgt	$5,000	6) Ameritech	$750
2) ITLA	$2,000	7) FCNBD	$500
3) IBA	$1,500	8) FCB	$500
4) SJP	$1,000	9) IPACE	$500
5) ISMS	$1,000	10) PIIA	$500

NOTE: The General Election Opponent's Campaign Resources and Expenditures are reported in a separate section in the back of the book (pp. 269-284).

GENERAL ELECTION DATA

	Registered Voters	Voter Turnout		Straight Party Voting	
1996	36,900	19,524	52.9%	(R) 617 . . . . 3.2%	(D) 8,656 . . . 44.3%

PRESIDENT

1996	Bill Clinton (D)	15,356	83.5%
	Bob Dole (R)	1,994	10.9%
	Ross Perot (I)	785	4.3%
1992	Bill Clinton (D)	16,594	73.3%
	George Bush (R)	3,933	17.4%
	Ross Perot (I)	2,116	9.3%

UNITED STATES SENATE

1996	Richard J. Durbin (D)	15,056	83.0%
	Al Salvi (R)	2,447	13.5%

GOVERNOR

1994	Jim Edgar (R)	3,644	35.7%
	Dawn Clark Netsch (D)	6,562	64.3%

3rd Senate District

House District 5
House District 6

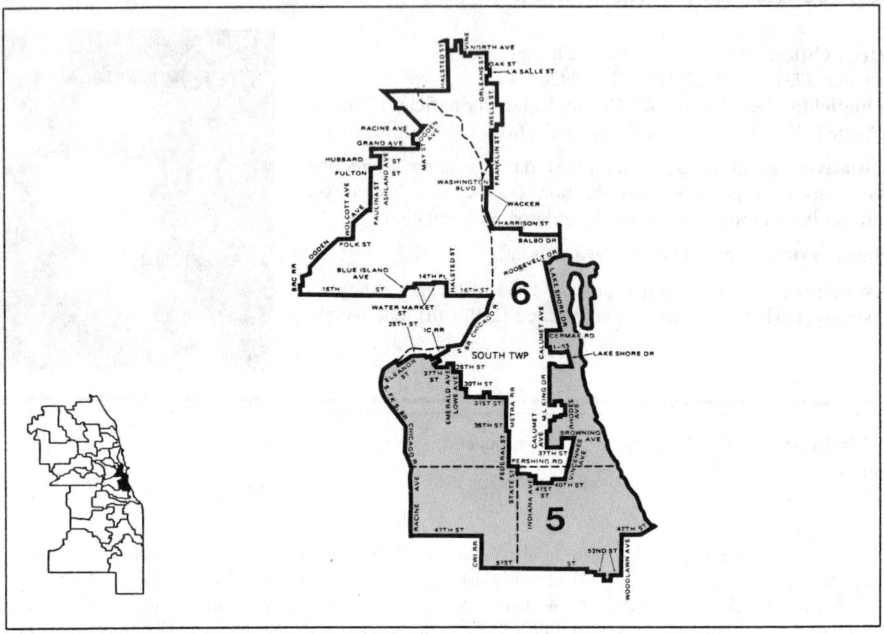

DEMOGRAPHICS (1990)

	S.D. #3	H.D. #5	H.D.#6
VOTING AGE POPULATION	135,518	66,782	68,736
White	25.6%	25.0%	26.2%
Black	59.9%	62.7%	57.2%
Hispanic	6.3%	7.9%	4.8%
Asian	7.9%	4.1%	11.6%
AGE (Total Population)	193,739	96,870	96,869
Under 6	11.2%	11.1%	11.3%
6 to 18	20.7%	21.5%	19.8%
65 and Over	12.2%	13.8%	10.7%
URBAN POPULATION	100.0%	100.0%	100.0%
HOUSING UNITS (Total)	91,033	45,083	45,950
Median Value	$73,131	$61,747	$134,124
Owner Occupied	13.5%	16.6%	10.5%
FAMILY INCOME (Total Families)	41,220	21,255	19,965
Median Income	$15,451	$16,547	$14,018
Below Poverty Level	42.5%	39.7%	45.4%
With Children Under 5	6.3%	5.1%	7.7%
With Children 5 to 17	16.5%	16.5%	16.6%
Headed by Females	34.3%	31.5%	37.4%
INDUSTRY (Total Employed)	60,619	28,159	32,460
Professional/Public Administration	35.1%	31.7%	38.0%
Manufacturing	13.0%	14.9%	11.3%
Retail	16.2%	17.1%	15.3%
Transportation/Communication	8.9%	9.9%	8.0%
Finance/Insurance/Real Estate	10.3%	8.6%	11.9%
Other Service	9.9%	9.8%	9.9%

Senator Margaret Smith (D)

District Office: 1233 S. Michigan Ave., Chicago 60605
Phone (312) 461-1908; (312) 461-1139 (fax)
Springfield Office: 103A Capitol Bldg., Springfield 62706
Phone (217) 782-5966; (217) 782-5252 (fax)

Legislative Assignments: Deputy Minority Caucus Chair; Committees on Public Health & Welfare (Minority Spokesperson); Appropriations; Commerce & Industry.

Public Service: Senator (1983-present); Representative (1981-1983).

Personal: Instructor of Religious Education; born Chicago; B.A. in Commerce, Tennessee State University.

1997 BILL PASSAGE RATIO	Introduced	Passed House of Origin	Passed GA
Primary	14	2	2
Primary/Hyphenated	39	19	18

KEY VOTES

1) Senate GOP Ed. $ Plan ...... N	6) Insurance/Domestic Violence .. O	11) Pre-Paid College Tuition .... Y
2) State Budget .... Y	7) Brownfields .... Y	12) Increase Pull Tab Prizes .... Y
3) Tougher DUI Level .... Y	8) Welfare Reform .... Y	13) Telecommunications Tax ... Y
4) Ban Partial Birth Abortions ... Y	9) Concealed Guns/Misdemeanor . N	14) Delivery Discrimination .... Y
5) State Employees Pension ..... Y	10) Banks Sell Insurance .... Y	15) Sell Drivers' Data .... N

GROUP RATINGS

	FB	CoC	PrLf	IPPC	ACLU
1997	73	60	1/2	50	75

ELECTION RESULTS

1996 General	Margaret Smith (D)	53,526	(96.4%)
1996 General	Maggie Kohls (LIB)	2,018	(3.6%)
1996 Primary	Margaret Smith (D)	20,257	(79.1%)
1996 Primary	Ken Dunkin (D)	5,362	(20.9%)

CAMPAIGN RESOURCES AND EXPENDITURES

1996 Campaign Funds				Top 10 PAC Contributors	
Beg. Balance	$7,309	Individuals	$6,110	1) CTU $1,000	6) Medco $400
Receipts	$22,702	Party	$120	2) ITLA $1,000	7) MaxManor .. $400
Expenditures	$18,284	PACS	$16,472	3) IBA $750	8) Ribs&Bibs .. $400
On hand	$11,727	Candidate	$0	4) IHCA $500	9) Haste $400
		Not-itemized	$0	5) UAW $500	10) Haymrkt ... $400

NOTE: The General Election Opponent's Campaign Resources and Expenditures are reported in a separate section in the back of the book (pp. 269-284).

GENERAL ELECTION DATA

	Registered Voters	Voter Turnout		Straight Party Voting	
1996	104,782	63,753	60.8%	(R) 1,648 .... 2.6%	(D) 27,241 .. 42.7%

PRESIDENT

1996	Bill Clinton (D)	53,387	87.9%
	Bob Dole (R)	5,088	8.4%
	Ross Perot (I)	1,698	2.8%
1992	Bill Clinton (D)	62,227	81.9%
	George Bush (R)	8,963	11.8%
	Ross Perot (I)	4,766	6.3%

UNITED STATES SENATE

1996	Richard J. Durbin (D)	52,211	87.4%
	Al Salvi (R)	6,129	10.3%

GOVERNOR

1994	Jim Edgar (R)	9,776	24.4%
	Dawn Clark Netsch (D)	30,333	75.6%

Representative Lovana "Lou" Jones (D)

District Office: 435 E. 35th, First Floor, Chicago, 60616
Phone (773) 373-9400; (773) 373-9787 (fax)
Springfield Office: 109 State Capitol Bldg., Springfield, 62706
Phone (217) 782-2023; (217) 782-8569 (fax)

Legislative Assignments: Assistant Majority Leader; ex officio member of all committees; committees on Appropriations-Public Safety; Public Utilities; Judiciary II-Criminal Law; Registration & Regulation; Prison Management Reform.

Public Service: Representative (1986-present).

Personal: Social worker; office administrator; born March 28, 1938, Mansfield, Ohio; Ohio State, B.A. in business administration; two children.

1997 BILL PASSAGE RATIO

	Introduced	Passed House of Origin	Passed GA
Primary	11	2	1
Primary/Hyphenated	36	15	12

KEY VOTES

1) Change Ed. Funding Formula. .Y
2) State Budget . . . . .Y
3) Tougher DUI Level . . . . .Y
4) Ban Partial Birth Abortions . . .N
5) State Employees Pension . . . . .Y
6) Insurance/Domestic Violence . .Y
7) Brownfields . . . . .Y
8) Welfare Reform . . . . .Y
9) Concealed Guns/Misdemeanor .N
10) Banks Sell Insurance . . . . .Y
11) Pre-Paid College Tuition . . .Y
12) Increase Pull Tab Prizes . . . .Y
13) Utility Deregulation . . . . . . .Y
14) County Obscenity Standards .N
15) Managed Care Reform . . . . .Y

GROUP RATINGS

	FB	CoC	PrLf	IPPC	ACLU
1997	75	36	0/6	100	100

ELECTION RESULTS

1996 General	Lovana S. "Lou" Jones (D)	27,772	(100%)
1996 Primary	Lovana S. "Lou" Jones (D)	9,264	(100%)
1994 General	Lovana S. "Lou" Jones (D)	19,339	(100%)

CAMPAIGN RESOURCES AND EXPENDITURES

1996 Campaign Funds

Beg. Balance	$4,467	Individuals	$1,000
Receipts	$18,600	Party	$500
Expenditures	$1,400	PACS	$17,100
On hand	$21,667	Candidate	$0
		Not-itemized	$0

Top 10 PAC Contributors

1) CPA's	$2,000	6) IPACE	$1,000
2) AB	$1,000	7) ITLA	$1,000
3) AQC	$1,000	8) LCRE	$1,000
4) Miller	$1,000	9) MPower	$800
5) ISMS	$1,000	10) IBA	$750

NOTE: The General Election Opponent's Campaign Resources and Expenditures are reported in a separate section in the back of the book (pp. 269-284).

GENERAL ELECTION DATA

	Registered Voters	Voter Turnout		Straight Party Voting			
1996	52,181	32,669	62.6%	(R) 619	1.9%	(D) 14,694	45.0%

PRESIDENT

1996	Bill Clinton (D)	27,776	89.0%
	Bob Dole (R)	2,159	6.9%
	Ross Perot (I)	939	3.0%
1992	Bill Clinton (D)	33,233	83.5%
	George Bush (R)	4,084	10.3%
	Ross Perot (I)	2,478	6.2%

UNITED STATES SENATE

1996	Richard J. Durbin (D)	27,116	88.6%
	Al Salvi (R)	2,777	9.0%

GOVERNOR

1994	Jim Edgar (R)	5,330	24.0%
	Dawn Clark Netsch (D)	16,900	76.0%

Representative Shirley M. Jones (D)

District Office: 47 West Polk St., Suite M-6, Chicago 60605
Phone (312) 786-1551; (312) 786-2177 (fax)
Springfield Office: Room 2078-K, Stratton Bldg., Springfield 62706
Phone (217) 782-5997

Legislative Assignments: Committees on Public Utilities (chair); Appropriations-Education; Electric Utility Deregulation; Environment and Energy; Financial Institutions; Labor and Commerce.

Public Service: Representative (1987-present).

Personal: Full-time legislator; born November 9, 1939, Chicago; George Williams College; one daughter.

1997 BILL PASSAGE RATIO	Introduced	Passed House of Origin	Passed GA
Primary	5	1	1
Primary/Hyphenated	9	3	1

KEY VOTES

1) Change Ed. Funding Formula . . Y
2) State Budget . . . . Y
3) Tougher DUI Level . . . . Y
4) Ban Partial Birth Abortions . . . N
5) State Employees Pension . . . . . Y
6) Insurance/Domestic Violence . . Y
7) Brownfields . . . . Y
8) Welfare Reform . . . . Y
9) Concealed Guns/Misdemeanor . N
10) Banks Sell Insurance . . . . Y
11) Pre-Paid College Tuition . . . . Y
12) Increase Pull Tab Prizes . . . . Y
13) Utility Deregulation . . . . Y
14) County Obscenity Standards . P
15) Managed Care Reform . . . . . A

GROUP RATINGS

	FB	CoC	PrLf	IPPC	ACLU
1997	86	38	0/6	83	100

ELECTION RESULTS

1996 General	Shirley M. Jones (D)	25,328	(90.1%)
1996 General	Bobby Belk (R)	2,790	(9.9%)
1996 Primary	Shirley M. Jones (D)	8,633	(78.5%)
1996 Primary	Derrick David Stinson (D)	2,375	(21.6%)

CAMPAIGN RESOURCES AND EXPENDITURES

1996 Campaign Funds

Beg. Balance	$43	Individuals	$600
Receipts	$17,685	Party	$500
Expenditures	$17,509	PACS	$13,650
On hand	$219	Candidate	$0
		Not-itemized	$2,935

Top 10 PAC Contributors

1) C&GL	$1,000	6) IBA	$500
2) Ameritech	$1,000	7) MBPlatt	$500
3) MPower	$1,000	8) NIGAS	$500
4) ITLA	$1,000	9) ABDI	$500
5) JJM	$500	10) Sprint	$500

NOTE: The General Election Opponent's Campaign Resources and Expenditures are reported in a separate section in the back of the book (pp. 269-284).

GENERAL ELECTION DATA

	Registered Voters	Voter Turnout		Straight Party Voting	
1996	52,601	31,084	59.1%	(R) 1,029 . . . 3.3%	(D) 12,547 . . 40.4%

PRESIDENT

1996	Bill Clinton (D)	25,611	86.6%
	Bob Dole (R)	2,929	9.9%
	Ross Perot (I)	759	2.6%
1992	Bill Clinton (D)	28,994	80.2%
	George Bush (R)	4,879	13.5%
	Ross Perot (I)	2,288	6.3%

UNITED STATES SENATE

1996	Richard J. Durbin (D)	25,095	86.1%
	Al Salvi (R)	3,352	11.5%

GOVERNOR

1994	Jim Edgar (R)	4,446	24.9%
	Dawn Clark Netsch (D)	13,433	75.1%

4th Senate District

House District 7
House District 8

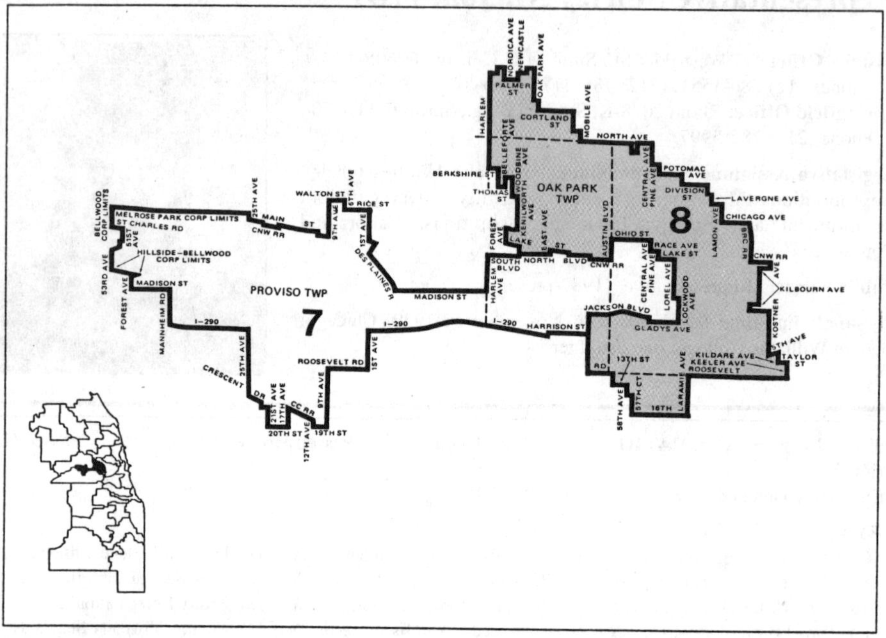

DEMOGRAPHICS (1990)

	S.D. #4	H.D. #7	H.D.#8
VOTING AGE POPULATION	137,738	69,982	67,756
White	31.6%	33.3%	29.8%
Black	63.4%	61.1%	65.7%
Hispanic	3.5%	3.9%	3.0%
Asian	1.4%	1.6%	1.3%
AGE (Total Population)	193,739	96,870	96,869
Under 6	9.9%	9.4%	10.3%
6 to 18	20.7%	20.0%	21.4%
65 and Over	8.7%	9.4%	8.0%
URBAN POPULATION	100.0%	100.0%	100.0%
HOUSING UNITS (Total)	70,090	36,841	33,249
Median Value	$83,077	$78,075	$97,399
Owner Occupied	47.1%	47.4%	46.8%
FAMILY INCOME (Total Families)	46,348	23,269	23,080
Median Income	$35,864	$37,644	$33,876
Below Poverty Level	14.5%	10.6%	18.4%
With Children Under 5	2.0%	1.5%	2.5%
With Children 5 to 17	6.0%	4.3%	7.8%
Headed by Females	10.8%	7.6%	13.9%
INDUSTRY (Total Employed)	85,031	45,978	39,053
Professional/Public Administration	32.6%	31.8%	33.6%
Manufacturing	17.7%	18.6%	16.5%
Retail	13.9%	13.6%	14.4%
Transportation/Communication	12.1%	12.7%	11.3%
Finance/Insurance/Real Estate	8.0%	7.7%	8.4%
Other Service	8.5%	8.3%	8.7%

Senator Earlean Collins (D)

District Office: 5943 W. Madison, Chicago 60644
Phone (773) 626-2184; (773) 626-2407 (fax).
Springfield Office: 309E Capitol Bldg., Springfield 62706
Phone (217) 782-8505; (217) 782-3242 (fax).

Legislative Assignments: Committees on Executive (minority spokesperson); Education.

Public Service: Senator (1977-present).

Personal: Full-time legislator; born Rolling Fork, Mississippi; B.A. sociology/education, University of Illinois-Chicago; one child.

1997 BILL PASSAGE RATIO	Introduced	Passed House of Origin	Passed GA
Primary	21	1	1
Primary/Hyphenated	24	4	4

KEY VOTES

1) Senate GOP Ed. $ Plan ......N	6) Insurance/Domestic Violence ..Y	11) Pre-Paid College Tuition ....Y
2) State Budget ....N	7) Brownfields ....Y	12) Increase Pull Tab Prizes ....N
3) Tougher DUI Level ....Y	8) Welfare Reform ....Y	13) Telecommunications Tax ...Y
4) Ban Partial Birth Abortions ...Y	9) Concealed Guns/Misdemeanor .N	14) Delivery Discrimination ....Y
5) State Employees Pension ....Y	10) Banks Sell Insurance ....O	15) Sell Drivers' Data ....N

GROUP RATINGS

	FB	CoC	PrLf	IPPC	ACLU
1997	73	60	2/2	0	67

ELECTION RESULTS

1996 General	Earlean Collins (D)	58,335	(100%)
1996 Primary	Earlean Collins (D)	20,532	(83.1%)
1996 Primary	Ronald Lawless (D)	4,164	(16.9%)
1992 General	Earlean Collins (D)	67,684	(100%)

CAMPAIGN RESOURCES AND EXPENDITURES

1996 Campaign Funds

Beg. Balance	$2,491	Individuals	$200
Receipts	$7,225	Party	$0
Expenditures	$8,271	PACS	$6,000
On hand	$1,445	Candidate	$0
		Not-itemized	$1,025

Top 10 PAC Contributors

1) ITLA	$1,000	6) ARC	$500
2) CTU	$1,000	7) ABDI	$300
3) Ameritech	$750	8) UNIPAC	$250
4) UAW	$500	9) Fremont	$250
5) HOPE	$500	10) CFFU	$250

NOTE: The General Election Opponent's Campaign Resources and Expenditures are reported in a separate section in the back of the book (pp. 269-284).

GENERAL ELECTION DATA

	Registered Voters	Voter Turnout		Straight Party Voting	
1996	116,095	69,726	60.1%	(R) 3,384 ....4.9%	(D) 26,847 ...38.5%

PRESIDENT

1996	Bill Clinton (D)	57,379	85.1%
	Bob Dole (R)	7,668	11.4%
	Ross Perot (I)	1,748	2.6%
1992	Bill Clinton (D)	69,425	80.8%
	George Bush (R)	10,997	12.8%
	Ross Perot (I)	5,499	6.4%

UNITED STATES SENATE

1996	Richard J. Durbin (D)	56,479	84.7%
	Al Salvi (R)	8,670	13.0%

GOVERNOR

1994	Jim Edgar (R)	13,212	30.6%
	Dawn Clark Netsch (D)	30,017	69.4%

Representative Eugene "Gene" Moore (D)

District Office: 1701 S. 1st Avenue, Maywood 60153
Phone (708) 345-0007; (708) 345-1647 (fax)
Springfield Office: 2041-J Stratton Bldg., Springfield 62706
Phone (217) 782-8120; (217) 782-1739 (fax)

Legislative Assignments: Committees on Revenue (chair); Registration & Regulation (vice-chair); Health Care Availability & Access; Personnel & Pensions; Insurance.

Public Service: Representative (1993-present).

Personal: Senior account executive, Metropolitan Life; born July 19, 1942, Baltzer, Mississippi; three children.

1997 BILL PASSAGE RATIO	Introduced	Passed House of Origin	Passed GA
Primary	16	1	0
Primary/Hyphenated	47	23	10

KEY VOTES

1) Change Ed. Funding Formula . . Y	6) Insurance/Domestic Violence . . Y	11) Pre-Paid College Tuition . . . . Y
2) State Budget . . . . Y	7) Brownfields . . . . Y	12) Increase Pull Tab Prizes . . . . Y
3) Tougher DUI Level . . . . Y	8) Welfare Reform . . . . Y	13) Utility Deregulation . . . . Y
4) Ban Partial Birth Abortions . . . N	9) Concealed Guns/Misdemeanor . N	14) County Obscenity Standards . N
5) State Employees Pension . . . . . Y	10) Banks Sell Insurance . . . . Y	15) Managed Care Reform . . . . . P

GROUP RATINGS

	FB	CoC	PrLf	IPPC	ACLU
1997	86	42	0/6	100	100

ELECTION RESULTS

1996 General	Eugene "Gene" Moore (D)	26,498	(84.5%)
1996 General	June Edvenson (R)	4,851	(15.5%)
1996 Primary	Eugene "Gene" Moore (D)	9,324	(100%)

CAMPAIGN RESOURCES AND EXPENDITURES

1996 Campaign Funds				Top 10 PAC Contributors	
Beg. Balance	$(5,272)	Individuals	$750	1) ITLA $2,000	6) AFSCME . . . $740
Receipts	$23,883	Party	$2,900	2) CDavis $1,000	7) CTaddeo $700
Expenditures	$28,218	PACS	$16,340	3) CTurner . . . $1,000	8) ABDI $600
On hand	$(9,607)	Candidate	$0	4) IPACE $1,000	9) UPS $600
		Not-itemized	$3,893	5) MPower . . . $1,000	10) Bankers L&C $600

NOTE: The General Election Opponent's Campaign Resources and Expenditures are reported in a separate section in the back of the book (pp. 269-284).

GENERAL ELECTION DATA

	Registered Voters	Voter Turnout		Straight Party Voting	
1996	57,570	33,783	58.7%	(R) 1,770 . . . . 5.2%	(D) 13,439 . . . 39.8%

PRESIDENT

1996	Bill Clinton (D)	27,913	85.0%
	Bob Dole (R)	3,745	11.4%
	Ross Perot (I)	919	2.8%
1992	Bill Clinton (D)	33,462	79.9%
	George Bush (R)	5,507	13.1%
	Ross Perot (I).	2,911	7.0%

UNITED STATES SENATE

1996	Richard J. Durbin (D)	27,345	84.2%
	Al Salvi (R)	4,367	13.4%

GOVERNOR

1994	Jim Edgar (R)	6,714	31.8%
	Dawn Clark Netsch (D)	14,401	68.2%

Representative Calvin L. Giles (D)

District Office: 5255 West North Ave., Chicago 60639
Phone (773) 745-6120; (773) 637-1496 (fax)
Springfield Office: Room 2090-M Stratton Bldg., Springfield 62706
Phone (217) 782-5962; (217) 782-2779 (fax)

Legislative Assignments: Committees on State Government Administration & Election Reform (chair); Aging; Elementary & Secondary Education; Financial Institutions; Higher Education; Insurance.

Public Service: Representative (1993-present).

Personal: Full-time legislator; born in Chicago; Northeastern Illinios University, B.S. in management.

1997 BILL PASSAGE RATIO	Introduced	Passed House of Origin	Passed GA
Primary	12	3	1
Primary/Hyphenated	23	9	2

KEY VOTES

1) Change Ed. Funding Formula . . Y	6) Insurance/Domestic Violence . . Y	11) Pre-Paid College Tuition . . . . Y
2) State Budget . . . . Y	7) Brownfields . . . . Y	12) Increase Pull Tab Prizes . . . . A
3) Tougher DUI Level . . . . Y	8) Welfare Reform . . . . P	13) Utility Deregulation . . . . Y
4) Ban Partial Birth Abortions . . . A	9) Concealed Guns/Misdemeanor . Y	14) County Obscenity Standards . N
5) State Employees Pension . . . . . Y	10) Banks Sell Insurance . . . . Y	15) Managed Care Reform . . . . . Y

GROUP RATINGS

	FB	CoC	PrLf	IPPC	ACLU
1997	79	33	0/6	50	80

ELECTION RESULTS

1996 General	Calvin L. Giles (D)	28,766	(87.4%)
1996 General	Les Golden (R)	4,140	(12.6%)
1996 Primary	Calvin L. Giles (D)	7,745	(60.8%)
1996 Primary	Grady C. Jordan (D)	4,986	(39.2%)

CAMPAIGN RESOURCES AND EXPENDITURES

1996 Campaign Funds

Beg. Balance	$2,577	Individuals	$600
Receipts	$17,320	Party	$1,250
Expenditures	$19,796	PACS	$10,230
On hand	$101	Candidate	$0
		Not-itemized	$5,240

Top 10 PAC Contributors

1) ITLA $1,500	6) Union Pacific $500
2) CTurner . . . $1,000	7) UAW $500
3) MPower . . . $1,000	8) CUPAC $500
4) UPS $800	9) IBA $500
5) IRMA $750	10) PIIA $500

NOTE: The General Election Opponent's Campaign Resources and Expenditures are reported in a separate section in the back of the book (pp. 269-284).

GENERAL ELECTION DATA

	Registered Voters	Voter Turnout		Straight Party Voting	
1996	58,525	35,943	61.4%	(R) 1,614 . . . 4.5%	(D) 13,408 . . 37.3%

PRESIDENT

1996	Bill Clinton (D)	29,466	85.1%
	Bob Dole (R)	3,923	11.3%
	Ross Perot (I)	829	2.4%
1992	Bill Clinton (D)	35,963	81.7%
	George Bush (R)	5,490	12.5%
	Ross Perot (I)	2,588	5.8%

UNITED STATES SENATE

1996	Richard J. Durbin (D)	29,134	85.2%
	Al Salvi (R)	4,303	12.6%

GOVERNOR

1994	Jim Edgar (R)	6,498	29.4%
	Dawn Clark Netsch (D)	15,616	70.6%

5th Senate District

House District 9
House District 10

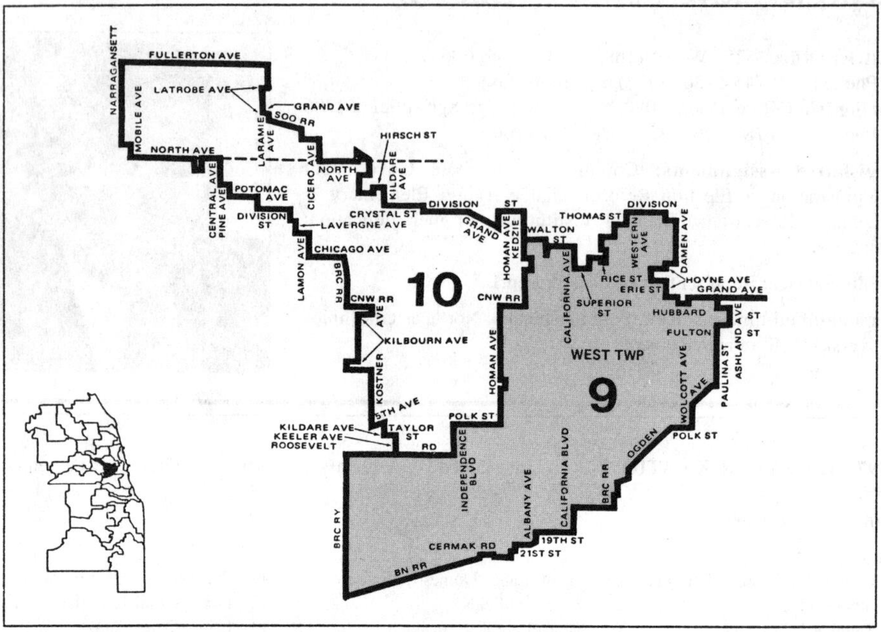

DEMOGRAPHICS (1990)

	S.D. #5	H.D. #9	H.D.#10
VOTING AGE POPULATION	126,638	63,136	63,502
White	11.4%	12.4%	10.5%
Black	77.0%	76.9%	77.1%
Hispanic	10.1%	9.3%	10.9%
Asian	1.3%	1.3%	1.4%
AGE (Total Population)	193,739	96,869	96,870
Under 6	11.9%	12.4%	11.4%
6 to 18	24.6%	24.2%	24.9%
65 and Over	8.1%	9.5%	6.8%
URBAN POPULATION	100.0%	100.0%	100.0%
HOUSING UNITS (Total)	67,748	36,228	31,520
Median Value	$59,578	$48,578	$62,708
Owner Occupied	26.4%	19.1%	34.7%
FAMILY INCOME (Total Families)	43,991	22,079	21,912
Median Income	$19,122	$14,690	$23,584
Below Poverty Level	35.3%	43.7%	26.9%
With Children Under 5	4.4%	5.9%	3.0%
With Children 5 to 17	14.0%	17.0%	11.0%
Headed by Females	27.0%	34.1%	19.8%
INDUSTRY (Total Employed)	58,494	25,941	32,553
Professional/Public Administration	27.7%	29.2%	26.6%
Manufacturing	22.3%	20.0%	24.2%
Retail	16.0%	16.3%	15.8%
Transportation/Communication	9.4%	8.7%	9.9%
Finance/Insurance/Real Estate	6.4%	6.7%	6.1%
Other Service	10.7%	11.4%	10.1%

Senator Rickey R. Hendon (D)

District Office: 538 N. Western Ave., Chicago 60612
Phone (312) 243-0009; (312) 243-2331 (fax)
Springfield Office: 105B Capitol Bldg., Springfield 62706
Phone (217) 782-6252; (217) 782-5340 (fax)

Legislative Assignments: Committees on Executive Appointments (minority spokesperson); Commerce & Industry; Financial Institutions.

Public Service: Senator (1993-present); Chicago alderman (27th Ward); Democratic committeeman (27th Ward); secretary/treasurer, Cook County Forest Preserve.

Personal: FCC licensed producer and writer; born December 8, 1953, Cleveland, Ohio; N.W. High School, Detroit, Michigan; married (Dawn); five children.

1997 BILL PASSAGE RATIO	Introduced	Passed House of Origin	Passed GA
Primary	6	1	1
Primary/Hyphenated	13	6	5

KEY VOTES

1) Senate GOP Ed. $ Plan ......N	6) Insurance/Domestic Violence ..Y	11) Pre-Paid College Tuition ....Y
2) State Budget ....Y	7) Brownfields ....Y	12) Increase Pull Tab Prizes ....Y
3) Tougher DUI Level ....Y	8) Welfare Reform ....Y	13) Telecommunications Tax ...Y
4) Ban Partial Birth Abortions ...Y	9) Concealed Guns/Misdemeanor .P	14) Delivery Discrimination ....Y
5) State Employees Pension ....Y	10) Banks Sell Insurance ....Y	15) Sell Drivers' Data ....N

GROUP RATINGS

	FB	CoC	PrLf	IPPC	ACLU
1997	73	60	2/2	0	75

ELECTION RESULTS

1994 General	Rickey R. Hendon (D)	26,576	(100%)
1994 Primary	Rickey R. Hendon (D)	12,399	(57.5%)
1994 Primary	Anthony B. Bass (D)	9,179	(42.5%)
1992 General	Rickey R. Hendon (D)	58,006	(100%)

CAMPAIGN RESOURCES AND EXPENDITURES

1996 Campaign Funds

Beg. Balance	$3,455	Individuals	$500
Receipts	$6,569	Party	$0
Expenditures	$8,740	PACS	$5,750
On hand	$1,284	Candidate	$0
		Not-itemized	$319

Top 10 PAC Contributors

1) Teamsters	$1,000	6) CFLabor	$300
2) CTU	$1,000	7) CFFU	$300
3) ISMS	$500	8) IBA	$250
4) UNIPAC	$500	9) ITLA	$250
5) CPA's	$400	10)HOPE	$250

NOTE: The General Election Opponent's Campaign Resources and Expenditures are reported in a separate section in the back of the book (pp. 269-284).

GENERAL ELECTION DATA

	Registered Voters	Voter Turnout		Straight Party Voting	
1996	99,284	53,345	53.7%	(R) 676 ....1.3%	(D) 22,559 ..42. 3%

PRESIDENT

1996	Bill Clinton (D)	47,222	93.0%
	Bob Dole (R)	1,982	3.9%
	Ross Perot (I)	724	1.4%
1992	Bill Clinton (D)	59,971	91.7%
	George Bush (R)	3,294	5.0%
	Ross Perot (I)	2,148	3.3%

UNITED STATES SENATE

1996	Richard J. Durbin (D)	45,499	91.6%
	Al Salvi (R)	2,984	6.0%

GOVERNOR

1994	Jim Edgar (R)	5,644	19.1%
	Dawn Clark Netsch (D)	23,945	80.9%

Representative Arthur L. Turner (D)

District Office: 3849 West Ogden Ave., Chicago 60623
Phone (773) 277-4700; (773) 277-5405 (fax)
Springfield Office: Room 300, Capitol Bldg., Springfield 62706
Phone (217) 782-8116; (217) 782-0888 (fax)

Legislative Assignments: Deputy Majority Leader; ex officio member of all committees. Committees on Revenue; Rules; Conflicts of Interest.

Public Service: Representative (1981-present).

Personal: Full-time legislator; born December 2, 1950, Chicago; Illinois State University, B.S. in business administration; Lewis University, M.S. in social justice; married (Rosalyn); two children.

1997 BILL PASSAGE RATIO	Introduced	Passed House of Origin	Passed GA
Primary	25	11	4
Primary/Hyphenated	41	18	10

KEY VOTES

1) Change Ed. Funding Formula . . Y	6) Insurance/Domestic Violence . . Y	11) Pre-Paid College Tuition . . . . A
2) State Budget . . . . Y	7) Brownfields . . . . Y	12) Increase Pull Tab Prizes . . . . Y
3) Tougher DUI Level . . . . Y	8) Welfare Reform . . . . Y	13) Utility Deregulation . . . . Y
4) Ban Partial Birth Abortions . . . N	9) Concealed Guns/Misdemeanor . P	14) County Obscenity Standards . P
5) State Employees Pension . . . . . Y	10) Banks Sell Insurance . . . . Y	15) Managed Care Reform . . . . . Y

GROUP RATINGS

	FB	CoC	PrLf	IPPC	ACLU
1997	86	38	0/6	83	100

ELECTION RESULTS

1996 General	Arthur L. Turner (D)	22,444	(94.3%)
1996 General	Marie Ciffone (R)	1,365	(5.7%)
1996 Primary	Arthur L. Turner (D)	7,301	(100%)

CAMPAIGN RESOURCES AND EXPENDITURES

1996 Campaign Funds

Beg. Balance	$4,630	Individuals	$1,825
Receipts	$46,525	Party	$0
Expenditure	$42,754	PACS	$44,700
On hand	$8,401	Candidate	$0
		Not-itemized	$0

Top 10 PAC Contributors

1) IPACE	$10,000	6) IBA	$1,000
2) MPower	$2,200	7) ABDI	$1,000
3) ITLA	$2,000	8) UPS	$1,000
4) HI	$1,000	9) IMHA	$700
5) PIIA	$1,000	10) AIA	$700

NOTE: The General Election Opponent's Campaign Resources and Expenditures are reported in a separate section in the back of the book (pp. 269-284).

GENERAL ELECTION DATA

	Registered Voters	Voter Turnout		Straight Party Voting	
1996	48,349	26,351	54.5%	(R) 404 . . . . 1.5%	(D) 10,451 . . 39.7%

PRESIDENT

1996	Bill Clinton (D)	22,984	92.6%
	Bob Dole (R)	1,134	4.6%
	Ross Perot (I)	412	1.6%
1992	Bill Clinton (D)	30,258	91.5%
	George Bush (R)	1,690	5.1%
	Ross Perot (I)	1,107	3.4%

UNITED STATES SENATE

1996	Richard J. Durbin (D)	22,207	90.9%
	Al Salvi (R)	1,624	6.7%

GOVERNOR

1994	Jim Edgar (R)	3,112	20.8%
	Dawn Clark Netsch (D)	11,861	79.2%

Representative Coy Pugh (D)

District Office: 1210 N. Pulaski Rd., Chicago 60651
Phone (773) 862-7844; (773) 862-0061 (fax)
Springfield Office: Room 2093M, Stratton Bldg., Springfield 62706
Phone (217) 782-8087; (217) 782-2779 (fax)

Legislative Assignments: Committees on Human Services (chair); Appropriations-Human Services (vice chair); Financial Institutions.

Public Service: Representative (1993-present).

Personal: Small business owner; born February 27, 1952; Northeastern University, B.A. in urban studies; married (Laura); two children.

1997 BILL PASSAGE RATIO	Introduced	Passed House of Origin	Passed GA
Primary	13	3	0
Primary/Hyphenated	17	5	2

KEY VOTES

1) Change Ed. Funding Formula . . Y	6) Insurance/Domestic Violence . . Y	11) Pre-Paid College Tuition . . . . Y
2) State Budget . . . . Y	7) Brownfields . . . . Y	12) Increase Pull Tab Prizes . . . . Y
3) Tougher DUI Level . . . . Y	8) Welfare Reform . . . . Y	13) Utility Deregulation . . . . Y
4) Ban Partial Birth Abortions . . . N	9) Concealed Guns/Misdemeanor . N	14) County Obscenity Standards . N
5) State Employees Pension . . . . . Y	10) Banks Sell Insurance . . . . Y	15) Managed Care Reform . . . . . Y

GROUP RATINGS

	FB	CoC	PrLf	IPPC	ACLU
1997	86	25	0/6	100	90

ELECTION RESULTS

1996 General	Coy Pugh (D)	23,699	(95.1%)
1996 General	Earnest L. Thomas (R)	1,222	(04.9%)
1996 Primary	Coy Pugh (D)	4,832	(50.9%)
1996 Primary	Two others (D)	4,656	(49.1%)

CAMPAIGN RESOURCES AND EXPENDITURES

1996 Campaign Funds		Top 10 PAC Contributors	
Beg. Balance . . $5,774	Individuals . . . $3,204	1) UDI $2,500	6) UAW $500
Receipts $15,629	Party $3,500	2) MPower $1,000	7) B&HCPA . . . $465
Expenditures . $20,806	PACS $8,925	3) ITLA $1,000	8) ABDI $300
On hand $597	Candidate $0	4) CTurner $1,000	9) USWA $300
	Not itemized $0	5) UPS $500	10) CFFU $250

NOTE: The General Election Opponent's Campaign Resources and Expenditures are reported in a separate section in the back of the book (pp. 269-284).

GENERAL ELECTION DATA

	Registered Voters	Voter Turnout	Straight Party Voting	
1996	50,935	26,994 . . . . 53.0%	(R) 272 . . . . . 1.0%	(D) 12,108 . . 44.9%

PRESIDENT

1996	Bill Clinton (D)	24,238	94.4%
	Bob Dole (R)	848	3.3%
	Ross Perot (I)	312	1.2%
1992	Bill Clinton (D)	29,713	91.8%
	George Bush (R)	1,604	5.0%
	Ross Perot (I)	1,041	3.2%

UNITED STATES SENATE

1996	Richard J. Durbin (D)	23,292	92.3%
	Al Salvi (R)	1,360	5.4%

GOVERNOR

1994	Jim Edgar (R)	2,532	17.3%
	Dawn Clark Netsch (D)	12,084	82.7%

6th Senate District

House District 11
House District 12

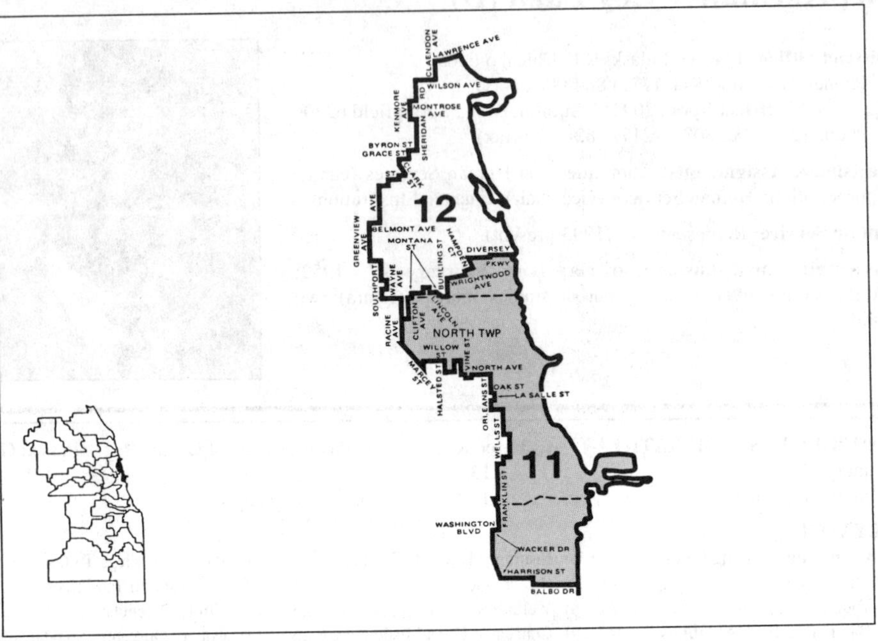

DEMOGRAPHICS (1990)

	S.D. #6	H.D. #11	H.D.#12
VOTING AGE POPULATION	178,178	90,860	87,318
White	82.5%	87.8%	77.1%
Black	7.5%	5.7%	9.3%
Hispanic	6.1%	3.5%	8.8%
Asian	3.6%	2.9%	4.4%
AGE (Total Population)	193,739	96,870	96,869
Under 6	3.7%	3.1%	4.4%
6 to 18	4.9%	3.7%	6.1%
65 and Over	11.2%	10.9%	11.4%
URBAN POPULATION	100.0%	100.0%	100.0%
HOUSING UNITS (Total)	132,605	69,719	62,886
Median Value	$311,772	$364,376	$242,812
Owner Occupied	26.5%	30.2%	22.3%
FAMILY INCOME (Total Families)	32,002	16,528	15,474
Median Income	$63,933	$81,901	$47,116
Below Poverty Level	6.1%	3.3%	9.1%
With Children Under 5	0.9%	0.5%	1.3%
With Children 5 to 17	1.9%	0.8%	3.0%
Headed by Females	3.1%	1.4%	4.8%
INDUSTRY (Total Employed)	136,384	69,223	67,161
Professional/Public Administration	34.6%	35.5%	33.7%
Manufacturing	9.5%	8.8%	10.1%
Retail	12.1%	10.4%	13.9%
Transportation/Communication	5.8%	5.8%	5.8%
Finance/Insurance/Real Estate	18.2%	20.7%	15.7%
Other Service	13.7%	13.1%	14.3%

Senator John J. Cullerton (D)

District Office: 1057 W. Belmont, Chicago 60657
Phone (773) 883-0770; (773) 525-5058 (fax)
Springfield Office: 417 Capitol Bldg., Springfield 62706
Phone (217) 782-7260

Legislative Assignments: Committees on Rules; Insurance & Pensions; and Judiciary (minority spokesperson).

Public Service: Senator (1991-present); representative (1979-1991).

Personal: Attorney; born October 28, 1948, Chicago; Loyola University, B.A. in political science and J.D.; married (Pamela); five children.

1997 BILL PASSAGE RATIO	Introduced	Passed House of Origin	Passed GA
Primary	47	12	6
Primary/Hyphenated	69	28	18

KEY VOTES

1) Senate GOP Ed. $ Plan . . . . . . .N	6) Insurance/Domestic Violence . .Y	11) Pre-Paid College Tuition . . . .Y
2) State Budget . . . . .N	7) Brownfields . . . . .Y	12) Increase Pull Tab Prizes . . . .Y
3) Tougher DUI Level . . . . .Y	8) Welfare Reform . . . . .Y	13) Telecommunications Tax . . .Y
4) Ban Partial Birth Abortions . . . .N	9) Concealed Guns/Misdemeanor .P	14) Delivery Discrimination . . . .O
5) State Employees Pension . . . . .Y	10) Banks Sell Insurance . . . . .Y	15) Sell Drivers' Data . . . . .Y

GROUP RATINGS

	FB	CoC	PrLf	IPPC	ACLU
1997	64	50	0/2	100	100

ELECTION RESULTS

1996 General	John J. Cullerton (D)	54,221	(70.6%)
1996 General	Robert N. Oberg (R)	22,538	(29.4%)
1996 Primary	John J. Cullerton (D)	15,582	(100%)
1996 Primary	Robert N. Oberg (R)	4,489	(100%)

CAMPAIGN RESOURCES AND EXPENDITURES

1996 Campaign Funds		Top 10 PAC Contributors	
Beg. Balance . .$32,813	Individuals . .$21,048	1) ISMS $3,000	6) CCEx $1,000
Receipts $83,474	Party $1,700	2) RepubTob $2,500	7) ILCable . . .$1,000
Expenditures . .$39,752	PACS $46,108	3) ITLA $2,000	8) CAE $1,000
On hand $76,535	Candidate $4,929	4) CFeigenholtz .$1,500	9)NCBank . . .$1,000
	Not-itemized .$9,689	5) LAWPAC $1,500	10)IBA $1,000

NOTE: The General Election Opponent's Campaign Resources and Expenditures are reported in a separate section in the back of the book (pp. 269-284).

GENERAL ELECTION DATA

	Registered Voters	Voter Turnout	Straight Party Voting	
1996	123,781	84,580 . . . . .68.3%	(R) 9,317 . . .11.0%	(D) 21,110 . . .25.0%

PRESIDENT

1996	Bill Clinton (D)	53,800	65.1%
	Bob Dole (R)	24,757	30.0%
	Ross Perot (I)	3,130	3.8%
1992	Bill Clinton (D)	66,258	60.3%
	George Bush (R)	31,164	28.4%
	Ross Perot (I)	12,392	11.3%

UNITED STATES SENATE

1996	Richard J. Durbin (D)	57,611	70.6%
	Al Salvi (R)	22,324	27.3%

GOVERNOR

1994	Jim Edgar (R)	23,971	45.4%
	Dawn Clark Netsch (D)	28,863	54.6%

Representative Judy Erwin (D)

District Office: 1545 N. Wells St., Chicago, 60610
Phone (312) 266-0340; (312) 266-0699 (fax)
Springfield Office: 2073-L Stratton Office Bldg, Springfield, 62706
Phone (217) 782-8404

Legislative Assignments: Committees on Higher Education (chair); Children & Youth; Judiciary II-Criminal Law; Prison Management Reform; Economic and Fiscal Commission.

Public Service: Representative (1993-present).

Personal: Manager, Grant Thornton LPP; born March 7, 1950; University of Wisconsin-Whitewater, B.S.; National College of Education, M.S. in state and local government; University of Illinois at Chicago, Ph.D. program.

1997 BILL PASSAGE RATIO	Introduced	Passed House of Origin	Passed GA
Primary	41	6	3
Primary/Hyphenated	105	36	12

KEY VOTES

1) Change Ed. Funding Formula . . Y
2) State Budget . . . . Y
3) Tougher DUI Level . . . . Y
4) Ban Partial Birth Abortions . . . . N
5) State Employees Pension . . . . . Y
6) Insurance/Domestic Violence . . Y
7) Brownfields . . . . Y
8) Welfare Reform . . . . Y
9) Concealed Guns/Misdemeanor . N
10) Banks Sell Insurance . . . . Y
11) Pre-Paid College Tuition . . . . Y
12) Increase Pull Tab Prizes . . . . Y
13) Utility Deregulation . . . . P
14) County Obscenity Standards . N
15) Managed Care Reform . . . . . Y

GROUP RATINGS

	FB	CoC	PrLf	IPPC	ACLU
1997	86	31	0/6	100	90

ELECTION RESULTS

1996 General	Judy Erwin (D)	29,816	(70.9%)
1996 General	Rudy Pamintuan (R)	12,267	(29.2%)
1996 Primary	Judy Erwin (D)	8,901	(100%)
1996 Primary	Rudy Pamintuan (R)	2,847	(100%)

CAMPAIGN RESOURCES AND EXPENDITURES

1996 Campaign Funds

Beg. Balance	$41,976	Individuals	$5,600
Receipts	$57,274	Party	$1,750
Expenditures	$61,692	PACS	$36,479
On hand	$37,558	Candidate	$0
		Not-itemized	$13,445

Top 10 PAC Contributors

1) ITLA	$3,000	6) FCNBD	$1,000
2) PersPAC	$1,779	7) UltraInk	$1,000
3) LAWPAC	$1,500	8) MPAC	$1,000
4) IBA	$1,500	9) CRock	$1,000
5) OBriens	$1,000	10) CUPAC	$550

NOTE: The General Election Opponent's Campaign Resources and Expenditures are reported in a separate section in the back of the book (pp. 269-284).

GENERAL ELECTION DATA

	Registered Voters	Voter Turnout		Straight Party Voting	
1996	64,490	44,941	69.7%	(R) 6,046 . . . 13.5%	(D) 9,920 . . . 22.1%

PRESIDENT

1996	Bill Clinton (D)	26,264	59.5%
	Bob Dole (R)	15,734	35.6%
	Ross Perot (I)	1,714	3.9%
1992	Bill Clinton (D)	31,550	54.5%
	George Bush (R)	19,404	33.5%
	Ross Perot (I)	6,977	12.0%

UNITED STATES SENATE

1996	Richard J. Durbin (D)	28,794	85.7%
	Al Salvi (R)	3,962	11.8%

GOVERNOR

1994	Jim Edgar (R)	14,799	50.7%
	Dawn Clark Netsch (D)	14,370	49.3%

Representative Sara Feigenholtz (D)

District Office: 1057 West Belmont, Chicago 60657
Phone (773) 296-4141; (773) 525-5058 (fax)
Springfield Office: Room 2035-J, Stratton Bldg., Springfield 62706
Phone (217) 782-8062; (217) 782-0927 (fax)

Legislative Assignments: Committees on Health Care Availability & Access (vice chair); Aging; Appropriations-General Services & Government Oversight; Children & Youth; Registration & Regulation.

Public Service: Representative (1995-present); executive director, Central Lakeview Business Association.

Personal: Full-time legislator; born December 11, 1956, Chicago; Northeastern University, B.A. in political science and speech and performing arts.

1997 BILL PASSAGE RATIO	Introduced	Passed House of Origin	Passed GA
Primary	17	5	4
Primary/Hyphenated	74	25	12

KEY VOTES

1) Change Ed. Funding Formula. .Y
2) State Budget ....Y
3) Tougher DUI Level ....Y
4) Ban Partial Birth Abortions ...N
5) State Employees Pension .....Y
6) Insurance/Domestic Violence ..Y
7) Brownfields ....Y
8) Welfare Reform ....Y
9) Concealed Guns/Misdemeanor .N
10) Banks Sell Insurance ....Y
11) Pre-Paid College Tuition ....Y
12) Increase Pull Tab Prizes ....Y
13) Utility Deregulation ....Y
14) County Obscenity Standards .E
15) Managed Care Reform .....Y

GROUP RATINGS

	FB	CoC	PrLf	IPPC	ACLU
1997	86	31	0/6	100	100

ELECTION RESULTS

1996 General	Sara Feigenholtz (D)	27,659	(77.0%)
1996 General	Beret A. Olson (R)	8,275	(23.0%)
1996 Primary	Sara Feigenholtz (D)	7,677	(100%)

CAMPAIGN RESOURCES AND EXPENDITURES

1996 Campaign Funds

Beg. Balance	$24,941	Individuals	$500
Receipts	$19,100	Party	$0
Expenditures	$20,266	PACS	$15,700
On hand	$23,775	Candidate	$440
		Not-itemized	$2,460

Top 10 PAC Contributors

1) ITLA	$2,000	6) LICID	$500
2) IPACE	$1,000	7) CTU	$500
3) LAWPAC	$1,000	8) Argosy	$500
4) ILCable	$500	9) UAW	$500
5) CoC	$500	10) ABDI	$500

NOTE: The General Election Opponent's Campaign Resources and Expenditures are reported in a separate section in the back of the book (pp. 269-284).

GENERAL ELECTION DATA

	Registered Voters	Voter Turnout		Straight Party Voting	
1996	59,291	39,639	66.9%	(R) 3,271 ....8.3%	(D) 11,190 ...28.2%

PRESIDENT

1996	Bill Clinton (D)	27,536	71.8%
	Bob Dole (R)	9,023	23.5%
	Ross Perot (I)	1,416	3.7%
1992	Bill Clinton (D)	34,708	66.9%
	George Bush (R)	11,760	22.7%
	Ross Perot (I)	5,415	10.4%

UNITED STATES SENATE

1996	Richard J. Durbin (D)	28,817	75.7%
	Al Salvi (R)	8,362	22.0%

GOVERNOR

1994	Jim Edgar (R)	9,172	38.8%
	Dawn Clark Netsch (D)	14,493	61.2%

7th Senate District

House District 13
House District 14

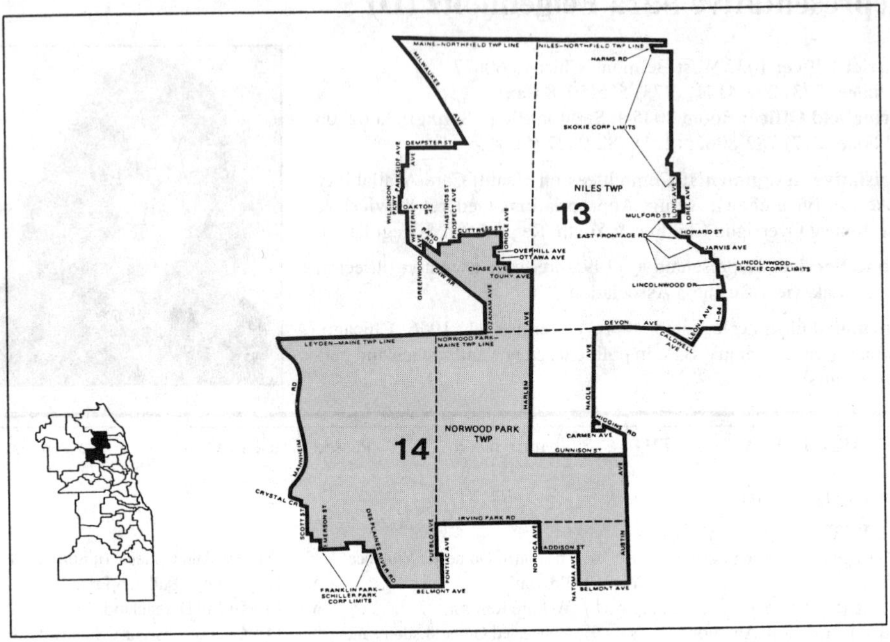

DEMOGRAPHICS (1990)

	S.D. #7	H.D. #13	H.D.#14
VOTING AGE POPULATION	159,588	79,589	79,999
White	92.6%	91.6%	93.7%
Black	0.3%	0.2%	0.5%
Hispanic	3.0%	2.3%	3.7%
Asian	3.9%	5.8%	2.1%
AGE (Total Population)	193,739	96,869	96,870
Under 6	6.0%	5.9%	6.1%
6 to 18	12.7%	13.0%	12.3%
65 and Over	20.9%	21.7%	20.1%
URBAN POPULATION	100.0%	100.0%	100.0%
HOUSING UNITS (Total)	76,972	36,733	40,239
Median Value	$140,732	$148,115	$131,684
Owner Occupied	75.8%	84.7%	67.7%
FAMILY INCOME (Total Families)	54,589	27,728	26,861
Median Income	$48,103	$51,292	$45,103
Below Poverty Level	1.8%	1.6%	1.9%
With Children Under 5	0.2%	0.2%	0.2%
With Children 5 to 17	0.4%	0.4%	0.4%
Headed by Females	0.5%	0.5%	0.5%
INDUSTRY (Total Employed)	100,882	49,937	50,945
Professional/Public Administration	25.7%	27.1%	24.3%
Manufacturing	19.5%	18.8%	20.2%
Retail	16.1%	17.0%	15.3%
Transportation/Communication	7.2%	6.3%	8.1%
Finance/Insurance/Real Estate	9.9%	9.7%	10.0%
Other Service	10.1%	9.7%	10.6%

Senator Walter W. Dudycz (R)

District Office: 6143 N. Northwest Highway, Chicago 60631
Phone (773) 774-7717; (773) 774-7877 (fax)
Springfield Office: M114 Capitol Bldg., Springfield 62706
Phone (217) 782-3650

Legislative Assignments: Assistant Majority Leader. Committees on Executive; Rules; Transportation; Local Government & Elections.

Public Service: Senator (1985-present).

Personal: Chicago police detective; born March 11, 1950, Chicago; graduated from the Chicago Police Academy; Northeastern Illinois University, B.A.; served in the U.S. Army (1968-71); married (Oksana); two daughters.

1997 BILL PASSAGE RATIO	Introduced	Passed House of Origin	Passed GA
Primary	30	15	11
Primary/Hyphenated	40	21	17

KEY VOTES

1) Senate GOP Ed. $ Plan . . . . . . .Y	6) Insurance/Domestic Violence . . .Y	11) Pre-Paid College Tuition . . . .Y
2) State Budget . . . . .Y	7) Brownfields . . . . .Y	12) Increase Pull Tab Prizes . . . .Y
3) Tougher DUI Level . . . . .Y	8) Welfare Reform . . . . .Y	13) Telecommunications Tax . . .P
4) Ban Partial Birth Abortions . . . .Y	9) Concealed Guns/Misdemeanor .P	14) Delivery Discrimination . . . .N
5) State Employees Pension . . . . .Y	10) Banks Sell Insurance . . . . .Y	15) Sell Drivers' Data . . . . .Y

GROUP RATINGS

	FB	CoC	PrLf	IPPC	ACLU
1997	68	100	2/2	0	50

ELECTION RESULTS

1996 General	Walter W. Dudycz (R)	41,218	(51.4%)
1996 General	Robert Martwick (D)	38,900	(48.6%)
1996 Primary	Walter W. Dudycz (R)	9,830	(100%)
1996 Primary	Robert Martwick (D)	13,807	(100%)

CAMPAIGN RESOURCES AND EXPENDITURES

1996 Campaign Funds				Top 10 PAC Contributors	
Beg. Balance	$166,615	Individuals	$9,448	1) RSSC . . .$420,221	6) CoC $3,500
Receipts	$560,414	Party	$433,871	2) ISMS $15,000	7) FOP $3,000
Expenditures	$625,576	PACS	$97,632	3) CRyan $5,500	8) MR&C $2,500
On hand	$101,453	Candidate	$1,713	4) ChgoCoC . .$5,000	9) ILCable . . .$2,500
		Not-itemized	$17,750	5) MPAC $4,000	10) HOPE $2,000

NOTE: The General Election Opponent's Campaign Resources and Expenditures are reported in a separate section in the back of the book (pp. 269-284).

GENERAL ELECTION DATA

	Registered Voters	Voter Turnout		Straight Party Voting	
1996	120,439	84,830	70.4%	(R) 13,248 . .15.6%	(D) 15,912 . . .18.8%

PRESIDENT

1996	Bill Clinton (D)	42,922	52.3%
	Bob Dole (R)	33,017	40.2%
	Ross Perot (I)	6,125	7.5%
1992	Bill Clinton (D)	39,903	40.3%
	George Bush (R)	41,770	42.2%
	Ross Perot (I)	17,306	17.5%

UNITED STATES SENATE

1996	Richard J. Durbin (D)	44,151	54.4%
	Al Salvi (R)	35,188	43.3%

GOVERNOR

1994	Jim Edgar (R)	44,671	71.2%
	Dawn Clark Netsch (D)	18,086	28.8%

Representative Ralph Capparelli (D)

District Office: 7452 North Harlem, Chicago 60631
Phone (773) 775-5775; (773) 775-5773 (fax)
Springfield Office: Room 300, Capitol Bldg., Springfield 62706
Phone (217) 782-8198

Legislative Assignments: Deputy Majority Leader; ex officio member of all committees. Committees on Executive; Financial Institutions; Registration & Regulation.

Public Service: Representative (1971-present); former school teacher.

Personal: Full-time legislator; born April 12, 1924, Chicago; Northern Illinois University, B.S. in education; married (Cora); two children; four grandchildren.

1997 BILL PASSAGE RATIO	Introduced	Passed House of Origin	Passed GA
Primary	55	15	12
Primary/Hyphenated	104	32	22

KEY VOTES

1)Change Ed. Funding Formula. . .N	6) Insurance/Domestic Violence. . .Y	11) Pre-Paid College Tuition . . . .Y
2)State Budget . . . . .Y	7) Brownfields . . . . .Y	12) Increase Pull Tab Prizes . . . .Y
3)Tougher DUI Level . . . . .Y	8) Welfare Reform . . . . .Y	13) Utility Deregulation . . . . . . .Y
4)Ban Partial Birth Abortions . . . .Y	9) Concealed Guns/Misdemeanor .Y	14) County Obscenity Standards .Y
5)State Employees Pension . . . . . .Y	10) Banks Sell Insurance . . . . .Y	15) Managed Care Reform . . . . .Y

GROUP RATINGS

	FB	CoC	PrLf	IPPC	ACLU
1997	64	38	5/6	16	30

ELECTION RESULTS

1996 General	Ralph C. Capparelli (D)	23,888	(58.5%)
1996 General	Peter Callaghan (R)	16,932	(41.5%)
1996 Primary	Ralph C. Capparelli (D)	7,833	(100%)
1996 Primary	Peter Callaghan (R)	2,639	(50.8%)

CAMPAIGN RESOURCES AND EXPENDITURES

1996 Campaign Funds				Top 10 PAC Contributors			
Beg. Balance	$574,227	Individuals	$23,726	1) IHDM	$30,719	6) ISMS	$6,000
Receipts	$232,066	Party	$51,567	2) CDStephens	$16,500	7) IBA	$5,000
Expenditures	$286,387	PACS	132,079	3) RosemontExpo	$15,000	8) IHIPAC	$5,000
On hand	$519,906	Candidate	$9,145	4) OGServices	$12,500	9) NDC	$4,000
		Not-itemized	$15,549	5) CSJBOP	$11,000	10) DPI	$2,660

NOTE: The General Election Opponent's Campaign Resources and Expenditures are reported in a separate section in the back of the book (pp. 269-284).

GENERAL ELECTION DATA

	Registered Voters	Voter Turnout		Straight Party Voting	
1996	61,483	43,890	71.4%	(R) 7,321 . . . 16.7%	(D) 8,427 . . . 19.2%

PRESIDENT

1996	Bill Clinton (D)	22,113	51.6%
	Bob Dole (R)	17,401	40.6%
	Ross Perot (I)	3,083	7.2%
1992	Bill Clinton (D)	21,300	40.9%
	George Bush (R)	22,058	42.3%
	Ross Perot (I)	8,772	16.8%

UNITED STATES SENATE

1996	Richard J. Durbin (D)	23,117	54.7%
	Al Salvi (R)	18,160	43.0%

GOVERNOR

1994	Jim Edgar (R)	23,252	70.2%
	Dawn Clark Netsch (D)	9,877	29.8%

Representative Michael P. McAuliffe (R)

District Office: 7818 West Higgins, Chicago 60631
Phone (773) 792-0749; (773) 792-1997 (fax)
Springfield Office: Room 2124-O, Stratton Bldg., Springfield 62706
Phone (217) 782-8182; (217) 782-4553 (fax)

Legislative Assignments: Committees on Transportation & Motor Vehicles; Financial Institutions; Appropriations-Public Safety; Personnel and Pensions; Legislative Printing Unit.

Public Service: Representative (1996-present); 41st Ward Republican Committeeman.

Personal: Born on December 7, 1963 in Chicago; Triton College.

1997 BILL PASSAGE RATIO	Introduced	Passed House of Origin	Passed GA
Primary	15	7	2
Primary/Hyphenated	58	30	14

KEY VOTES

1) Change Ed. Funding Formula . . N	6) Insurance/Domestic Violence . . Y	11) Pre-Paid College Tuition . . . . Y
2) State Budget . . . . Y	7) Brownfields . . . . N	12) Increase Pull Tab Prizes . . . . Y
3) Tougher DUI Level . . . . Y	8) Welfare Reform . . . . Y	13) Utility Deregulation . . . . N
4) Ban Partial Birth Abortions . . . . Y	9) Concealed Guns/Misdemeanor . Y	14) County Obscenity Standards . Y
5) State Employees Pension . . . . . Y	10) Banks Sell Insurance . . . . Y	15) Managed Care Reform . . . . . Y

GROUP RATINGS

	FB	CoC	PrLf	IPPC	ACLU
1997	54	31	6/6	0	20

ELECTION RESULTS

1996 General	Michael P. McAuliffe (R)	20,666	(52.4%)
1996 General	Thomas P. Needham (D)	18,771	(47.6%)
1996 Primary	Roger P. McAuliffe (R)	4,976	(100%)
1996 Primary	Thomas P. Needham (D)	7,490	(100%)

CAMPAIGN RESOURCES AND EXPENDITURES

1996 Campaign Funds				Top 10 PAC Contributors			
Beg. Balance	$0	Individuals	$38,122	1) HRCC	$130,442	6) CDStephens	$5,850
Receipts	$361,799	Party	$179, 213	2) FLAD	$20,741	7) RosemontExpo	$5,000
Expenditures	$346,917	PACS	$113,229	3) IPACE	$19,000	8) OGServices	$5,000
On hand	$14,882	Candidate	$0	4) ISMS	$10,000	9) FSaviano	$5,000
		Not-itemized	$31,235	5) CChurchill	$8,580	10) ChgoCoC	$3,000

NOTE: The General Election Opponent's Campaign Resources and Expenditures are reported in a separate section in the back of the book (pp. 269-284).

GENERAL ELECTION DATA

	Registered Voters	Voter Turnout		Straight Party Voting	
1996	58,956	40,940	69.4%	(R) 5,927 . . . 14.5%	(D) 7,485 . . . 18.3%

PRESIDENT

1996	Bill Clinton (D)	20,809	52.3%
	Bob Dole (R)	15,616	39.3%
	Ross Perot (I)	3,042	7.7%
1992	Bill Clinton (D)	18,603	39.7%
	George Bush (R)	19,712	42.1%
	Ross Perot (I)	8,534	18.2%

UNITED STATES SENATE

1996	Richard J. Durbin (D)	21,034	54.0%
	Al Salvi (R)	17,028	43.7%

GOVERNOR

1994	Jim Edgar (R)	21,419	72.3%
	Dawn Clark Netsch (D)	8,209	27.7%

8th Senate District

House District 15
House District 16

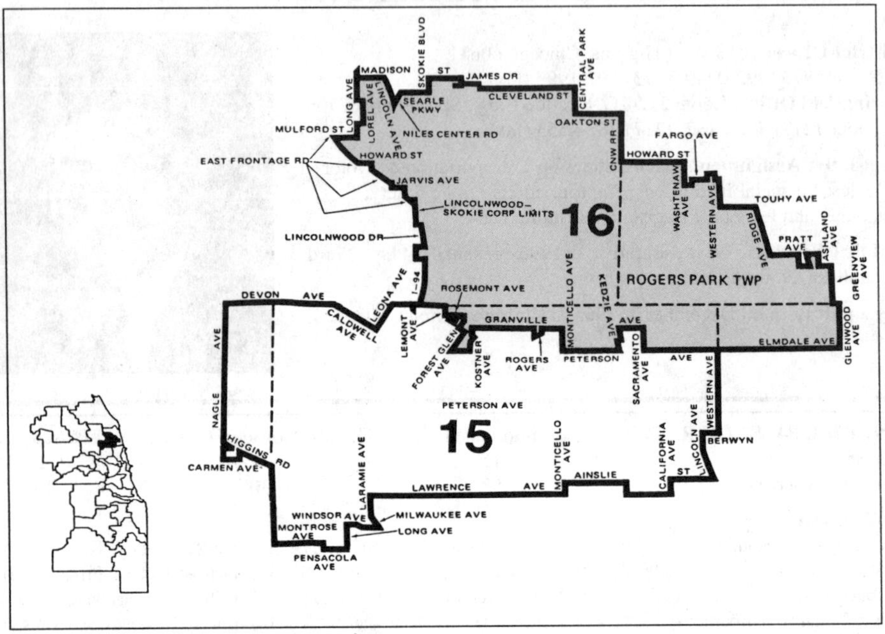

DEMOGRAPHICS (1990)

	S.D. #8	H.D. #15	H.D.#16
VOTING AGE POPULATION	152,691	76,996	75,695
White	75.8%	77.5%	74.1%
Black	1.8%	0.8%	2.8%
Hispanic	8.3%	8.8%	7.9%
Asian	13.8%	12.7%	14.9%
AGE (Total Population)	193,739	96,870	96,869
Under 6	7.9%	7.7%	8.0%
6 to 18	14.5%	14.0%	15.0%
65 and Over	18.5%	18.0%	19.0%
URBAN POPULATION	100.0%	100.0%	100.0%
HOUSING UNITS (Total)	77,076	39,053	38,023
Median Value	$133,850	$123,329	$144,380
Owner Occupied	53.2%	52.4%	54.2%
FAMILY INCOME (Total Families)	50,211	24,828	25,383
Median Income	$40,840	$40,859	$40,820
Below Poverty Level	7.3%	6.1%	8.6%
With Children Under 5	0.9%	0.8%	0.9%
With Children 5 to 17	3.1%	2.7%	3.4%
Headed by Females	2.0%	2.3%	1.8%
INDUSTRY (Total Employed)	95,302	48,518	46,784
Professional/Public Administration	29.2%	27.5%	31.0%
Manufacturing	17.8%	19.0%	16.5%
Retail	16.9%	16.0%	17.8%
Transportation/Communication	5.7%	6.2%	5.1%
Finance/Insurance/Real Estate	8.9%	8.8%	9.1%
Other Service	11.3%	11.8%	10.9%

Senator Howard W. Carroll (D)

District Office: 7344 N. Western Ave., Chicago 60645
Phone (773) 743-5015; (773) 743-8131 (fax)
Springfield Office: 309F Capitol Bldg., Springfield 62706
Phone (217) 782-5500; (217) 782-3242 (fax)

Legislative Assignments: Assistant Minority Leader; committees on Appropriations; Executive Appointments; Financial Institutions; Legislative Information System Commission.

Public Service: Senator (1973-present); representative (1971-1973).

Personal: Attorney; born July 28, 1942, Chicago; Roosevelt University, B.S./B.A.; DePaul University, J.D.; married (Eda); two children.

1997 BILL PASSAGE RATIO	Introduced	Passed House of Origin	Passed GA
Primary	20	4	4
Primary/Hyphenated	30	11	9

KEY VOTES

1) Senate GOP Ed. $ Plan ...... N	6) Insurance/Domestic Violence .. O	11) Pre-Paid College Tuition .... Y
2) State Budget .... N	7) Brownfields .... Y	12) Increase Pull Tab Prizes .... Y
3) Tougher DUI Level .... Y	8) Welfare Reform .... Y	13) Telecommunications Tax ... Y
4) Ban Partial Birth Abortions .... N	9) Concealed Guns/Misdemeanor . N	14) Delivery Discrimination .... Y
5) State Employees Pension ..... Y	10) Banks Sell Insurance .... Y	15) Sell Drivers' Data .... N

GROUP RATINGS

	FB	CoC	PrLf	IPPC	ACLU
1997	73	60	0/2	100	100

ELECTION RESULTS

1994 General	Howard W. Carroll (D)	32,416	(100%)
1994 Primary	Howard W. Carroll (D)	24,487	(100%)
1992 General	Howard W. Carroll (D)	48,581	(67.6%)
1992 General	Thomas H. Joseph (R)	23,337	(32.5%)

CAMPAIGN RESOURCES AND EXPENDITURES

1996 Campaign Funds				Top 10 PAC Contributors			
Beg. Balance	$175,059	Individuals	$12,000	1) IPACE	$4,000	6) TIP	$1,589
Receipts	$95,354	Party	$300	2) IAMB	$3,500	7) MPower	$1,500
Expenditures	$59,198	PACS	$57,834	3) UNIPAC	$2,300	8) Glencrest	$1,500
On hand	$211,215	Candidate	$4,180	4) PMorris	$1,850	9) HOPE	$1,500
		Not-itemized	$21,040	5) CFLabor	$1,614	10) IVendors	$1,000

NOTE: The General Election Opponent's Campaign Resources and Expenditures are reported in a separate section in the back of the book (pp. 269-284).

GENERAL ELECTION DATA

	Registered Voters	Voter Turnout		Straight Party Voting	
1996	95,266	63,494	66.7%	(R) 6,436 ... 10.1%	(D) 20,264 ... 31.9%

PRESIDENT

1996	Bill Clinton (D)	40,846	66.1%
	Bob Dole (R)	16,973	27.5%
	Ross Perot (I)	3,508	5.7%
1992	Bill Clinton (D)	43,575	55.9%
	George Bush (R)	24,174	31.0%
	Ross Perot (I)	10,199	13.1%

UNITED STATES SENATE

1996	Richard J. Durbin (D)	41,935	68.7%
	Al Salvi (R)	17,733	29.1%

GOVERNOR

1994	Jim Edgar (R)	24,667	52.8%
	Dawn Clark Netsch (D)	22,085	47.2%

Representative Joseph M. Lyons (D)

District Office: 4404 West Lawrence Ave., Chicago 60630
Phone (773) 286-1115; (773) 736-2333 (fax)
Springfield Office: Room 2103-N Stratton Bldg., Springfield 62706
Phone (217) 782-8400

Legislative Assignments: Committees on Aging (vice-chair); Executive; Appropriations-Public Safety; State Government Administration & Election Reform; Transportation & Motor Vehicles.

Public Service: Representative (1996-present); manager of Training and Education for Cook County Department of Human Resources.

Personal: Born June 24, 1951, Chicago; married (Kieran); two children.

1997 BILL PASSAGE RATIO	Introduced	Passed House of Origin	Passed GA
Primary	6	1	0
Primary/Hyphenated	45	14	5

KEY VOTES

1) Change Ed. Funding Formula . . Y	6) Insurance/Domestic Violence. . . Y	11) Pre-Paid College Tuition . . . . Y
2) State Budget . . . . Y	7) Brownfields . . . . Y	12) Increase Pull Tab Prizes . . . . Y
3) Tougher DUI Level . . . . Y	8) Welfare Reform . . . . Y	13) Utility Deregulation . . . . Y
4) Ban Partial Birth Abortions . . . Y	9) Concealed Guns/Misdemeanor . N	14) County Obscenity Standards . Y
5) State Employees Pension . . . . . Y	10) Banks Sell Insurance . . . . Y	15) Managed Care Reform . . . . . Y

GROUP RATINGS

	FB	CoC	PrLf	IPPC	ACLU
1997	86	31	5/6	16	40

ELECTION RESULTS

1996 General	Joseph M. Lyons (D)	21,307	(68.8%)
1996 General	Donald M. Hodgkinson (R)	9,684	(31.3%)
1996 Primary	Joseph M. Lyons (D)	7,335	(50.8%)
1996 Primary	Three others (D)	7,099	(49.2%)

CAMPAIGN RESOURCES AND EXPENDITURES

1996 Campaign Funds		Top 10 PAC Contributors	
Beg. Balance . . $13,904	Individuals . . . $2,450	1) ITLA $2,000	6) IBA $500
Receipts $23,065	Party $0	2) CUPAC $600	7) IHHSA $400
Expenditures . . $32,132	PACS $11,800	3) United $500	8) IFT $300
On hand $4,837	Candidate $0	4) ISMS $500	9) ABDI $300
	Not-itemized . $8,815	5) UAW $500	10) CNA $300

NOTE: The General Election Opponent's Campaign Resources and Expenditures are reported in a separate section in the back of the book (pp. 269-284).

GENERAL ELECTION DATA

	Registered Voters	Voter Turnout	Straight Party Voting	
1996	48,567	33,120 . . . . 68.2%	(R) 3,485 . . . 10.5%	(D) 9,083 . . . 27.4%

PRESIDENT

1996	Bill Clinton (D)	19,569	60.6%
	Bob Dole (R)	10,182	31.5%
	Ross Perot (I)	2,253	7.0%
1992	Bill Clinton (D)	19,319	47.4%
	George Bush (R)	14,948	36.7%
	Ross Perot (I)	6,489	15.9%

UNITED STATES SENATE

1996	Richard J. Durbin (D)	20,127	63.4%
	Al Salvi (R)	10,803	34.1%

GOVERNOR

1994	Jim Edgar (R)	14,437	58.9%
	Dawn Clark Netsch (D)	10,087	41.1%

Representative Louis I. Lang (D)

District Office: 4119 W. Main; Skokie 60076
Phone (847) 673-1131; (847) 673-2535 (fax)
Springfield Office: 109 Capitol Bldg., Springfield 62706
Phone (217) 782-1252; (217) 782-9903 (fax)

Legislative Assignments: Assistant Majority Leader; ex officio member of all committees. Committees on Conflicts of Interest (chair); Financial Institutions; Judiciary I - Civil Law; State Government Administration & Election Reform.

Public Service: Representative (1987-present); attorney, Niles Township.

Personal: Attorney; born November 26, 1949, Chicago; University of Illinois, B.A. in political science and DePaul College of Law, J.D.; married (Teri); five children.

1997 BILL PASSAGE RATIO	Introduced	Passed House of Origin	Passed GA
Primary	50	11	2
Primary/Hyphenated	109	39	14

KEY VOTES

1) Change Ed. Funding Formula. .Y	6) Insurance/Domestic Violence . .Y	11) Pre-Paid College Tuition . . . .Y
2) State Budget . . . . .Y	7) Brownfields . . . . .Y	12) Increase Pull Tab Prizes . . . .Y
3) Tougher DUI Level . . . . .Y	8) Welfare Reform . . . . .Y	13) Utility Deregulation . . . . . . .Y
4) Ban Partial Birth Abortions . . . .N	9) Concealed Guns/Misdemeanor .N	14) County Obscenity Standards .N
5) State Employees Pension . . . . .Y	10) Banks Sell Insurance . . . . .Y	15) Managed Care Reform . . . . .Y

GROUP RATINGS

	FB	CoC	PrLf	IPPC	ACLU
1997	86	23	0/6	100	90

ELECTION RESULTS

1996 General	Louis I. Lang (D)	22,972	(100%)
1996 Primary	Louis I. Lang (D)	7,115	(100%)
1994 General	Louis I. Lang (D)	15,517	(72.8%)
1994 General	Andrew J. Born (R)	5,792	(27.2%)

CAMPAIGN RESOURCES AND EXPENDITURES

1996 Campaign Funds

Beg. Balance	$29,530	Individuals	$2,900
Receipts	$97,661	Party	$20,000
Expenditures	$65,826	PACS	$66,350
On hand	$61,365	Candidate	$0
		Not-itemized	$8,411

Top 10 PAC Contributors

1) DSCC . . .$20,000	6) IPACE $2,000
2) Statesman .$12,500	7) SMW $1,500
3) ITLA $5,000	8) UNIPAC . . .$1,500
4) LAWPAC . .$2,000	9) IAMB $1,250
5) ABDI $2,000	10) JJM $1,000

NOTE: The General Election Opponent's Campaign Resources and Expenditures are reported in a separate section in the back of the book (pp. 269-284).

GENERAL ELECTION DATA

	Registered Voters	Voter Turnout		Straight Party Voting	
1996	46,699	30,374	65.0%	(R) 2,951 . . . 9.7%	(D) 11,181 . . .36.8%

PRESIDENT

1996	Bill Clinton (D)	21,277	72.0%
	Bob Dole (R)	6,791	23.0%
	Ross Perot (I)	1,255	4.3%
1992	Bill Clinton (D)	24,256	65.2%
	George Bush (R)	9,226	24.8%
	Ross Perot (I)	3,710	10.0%

UNITED STATES SENATE

1996	Richard J. Durbin (D)	21,808	37.1%
	Al Salvi (R)	6,930	11.8%

GOVERNOR

1994	Jim Edgar (R)	10,230	46.0%
	Dawn Clark Netsch (D)	11,998	54.0%

9th Senate District

House District 17
House District 18

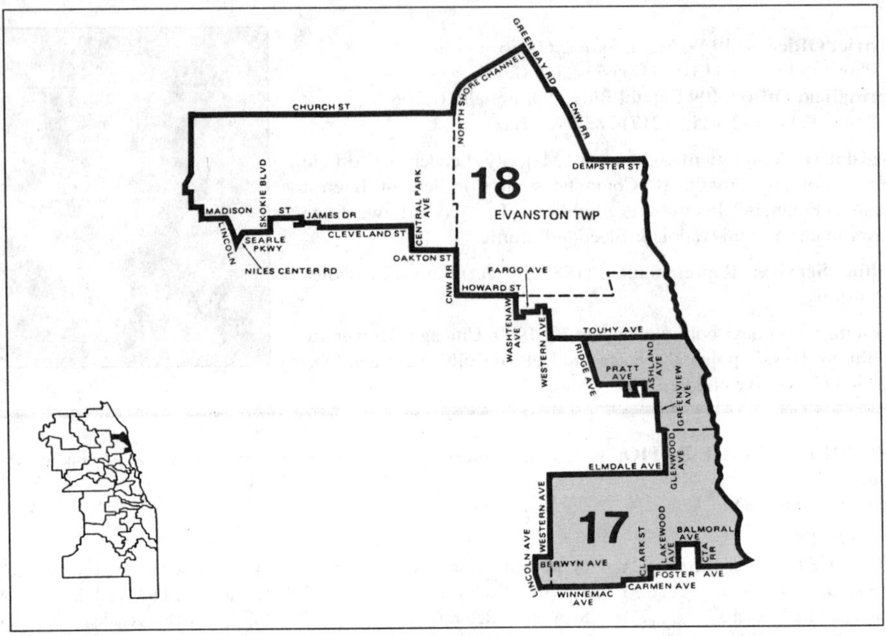

DEMOGRAPHICS (1990)

	S.D. #9	H.D. #17	H.D.#18
VOTING AGE POPULATION	155,727	79,814	75,913
White	59.6%	55.3%	64.0%
Black	19.7%	17.6%	21.8%
Hispanic	11.6%	15.9%	7.1%
Asian	8.7%	10.6%	6.8%
AGE (Total Population)	193,739	96,870	96,869
Under 6	7.7%	7.5%	7.8%
6 to 18	13.2%	11.5%	14.9%
65 and Over	13.1%	12.7%	13.6%
URBAN POPULATION	100.0%	100.0%	100.0%
HOUSING UNITS (Total)	91,521	50,406	41,115
Median Value	$135,406	$110,373	$139,184
Owner Occupied	31.1%	20.7%	43.9%
FAMILY INCOME (Total Families)	43,494	19,858	23,636
Median Income	$36,881	$30,398	$42,202
Below Poverty Level	10.3%	14.0%	7.2%
With Children Under 5	2.0%	2.9%	1.3%
With Children 5 to 17	3.8%	4.4%	3.2%
Headed by Females	5.2%	6.5%	4.1%
INDUSTRY (Total Employed)	107,102	54,018	53,084
Professional/Public Administration	34.6%	31.8%	37.5%
Manufacturing	13.5%	13.8%	13.2%
Retail	15.6%	16.8%	14.3%
Transportation/Communication	5.7%	6.4%	5.0%
Finance/Insurance/Real Estate	10.5%	10.1%	10.9%
Other Service	12.3%	13.1%	11.5%

Senator Arthur L. Berman (D)

District Office: 7344 N. Western Ave., Chicago 60657
Phone (773) 764-2200
Springfield Office: Rm. 413 Capitol Bldg., Springfield 62706
Phone (217) 782-8492

Legislative Assignments: Committees on Education (Minority Spokesman); Insurance & Pensions; Revenue.

Public Service: Senator (1977-present); representative (1969-1977).

Personal: Attorney; born May 4, 1935, Chicago; J.D., Northwestern University School of Law; University of Illinois-Champaign, B.S. in commerce; married (Barbara); two children.

1997 BILL PASSAGE RATIO	Introduced	Passed House of Origin	Passed GA
Primary	44	3	3
Primary/Hyphenated	60	10	8

KEY VOTES

1) Senate GOP Ed. $ Plan ......N	6) Insurance/Domestic Violence ..Y	11) Pre-Paid College Tuition ....Y
2) State Budget ....N	7) Brownfields ....Y	12) Increase Pull Tab Prizes ....Y
3) Tougher DUI Level ....Y	8) Welfare Reform ....Y	13) Telecommunications Tax ...Y
4) Ban Partial Birth Abortions ...N	9) Concealed Guns/Misdemeanor .N	14) Delivery Discrimination ....Y
5) State Employees Pension .....Y	10) Banks Sell Insurance ....Y	15) Sell Drivers' Data ....N

GROUP RATINGS

	FB	CoC	PrLf	IPPC	ACLU
1997	68	60	0/2	100	100

ELECTION RESULTS

1996 General	Arthur L. Berman (D)	48,178	(100%)
1996 Primary	Arthur L. Berman (D)	14,340	(100%)
1992 General	Arthur L. Berman (D)	53,556	(100%)
1992 Primary	Arthur L. Berman (D)	23,586	(100%)

CAMPAIGN RESOURCES AND EXPENDITURES

1996 Campaign Funds				Top 10 PAC Contributors	
Beg. Balance	$147,474	Individuals	$4,750	1) SMS $7,120	6) SachsErn ..$1,000
Receipts	$63,279	Party	$650	2) IPACE $5,000	7) CPA's $1,000
Expenditures	$37,162	PACS	$34,860	3) CCEx $1,000	8) HOPE $1,000
On hand	$173,591	Candidate	$7,120	4) ITLA $1,000	9) IVendors $900
		Not-itemized	$15,899	5) LAWPAC ..$1,000	10) LICID $500

NOTE: The General Election Opponent's Campaign Resources and Expenditures are reported in a separate section in the back of the book (pp. 269-284).

GENERAL ELECTION DATA

	Registered Voters	Voter Turnout		Straight Party Voting	
1996	93,304	61,823	66.3%	(R) 4,489 ....7.3%	(D) 22,743 ...36.8%

PRESIDENT

1996	Bill Clinton (D)	46,927	78.0%
	Bob Dole (R)	10,247	17.0%
	Ross Perot (I)	2,254	3.8%
1992	Bill Clinton (D)	54,605	72.1%
	George Bush (R)	14,138	18.7%
	Ross Perot (I)	7,032	9.2%

UNITED STATES SENATE

1996	Richard J. Durbin (D)	47,708	79.8%
	Al Salvi (R)	10,570	17.6%

GOVERNOR

1994	Jim Edgar (R)	14,756	36.6%
	Dawn Clark Netsch (D)	25,552	63.4%

Representative Carol Ronen (D)

District Office: 5600 North Sheridan Rd., Suite 2D, Chicago 60660
Phone (773) 769-1717; (773) 769-6901 (fax)
Springfield Office: Room 2075-K Stratton Bldg., Springfield 62706
Phone (217) 782-8088

Legislative Assignments: Committees on Children & Youth (chair); Appropriations-Human Services; Health Care Availability & Access.

Public Service: Representative (1993-present); executive director of the Chicago Commission on Women; Legislative & Community Affairs director for Chicago Human Services; director of Planning and Research for Chicago-Cook County.

Personal: Full-time legislator; born March 28, 1945, Chicago; Bradley University, B.A. in political science and Roosevelt University, M.A. in public administration.

1997 BILL PASSAGE RATIO	Introduced	Passed House of Origin	Passed GA
Primary	29	12	6
Primary/Hyphenated	63	25	11

KEY VOTES

1) Change Ed. Funding Formula . . Y	6) Insurance/Domestic Violence . . P	11) Pre-Paid College Tuition . . . . Y
2) State Budget . . . . Y	7) Brownfields . . . . Y	12) Increase Pull Tab Prizes . . . . Y
3) Tougher DUI Level . . . . Y	8) Welfare Reform . . . . Y	13) Utility Deregulation . . . . Y
4) Ban Partial Birth Abortions . . . N	9) Concealed Guns/Misdemeanor . N	14) County Obscenity Standards . N
5) State Employees Pension . . . . . Y	10) Banks Sell Insurance . . . . Y	15) Managed Care Reform . . . . . Y

GROUP RATINGS

	FB	CoC	PrLf	IPPC	ACLU
1997	86	23	0/6	100	100

ELECTION RESULTS

1996 General	Carol Ronen (D)	20,763	(83.8%)
1996 General	Kurt James Eckhardt (R)	4,009	(16.2%)
1996 Primary	Carol Ronen (D)	6,633	(100%)

CAMPAIGN RESOURCES AND EXPENDITURES

1996 Campaign Funds

Beg. Balance	$12,092	Individuals	$3,650
Receipts	$25,976	Party	$0
Expenditures	$18,916	PACS	$12,700
On hand	$19,152	Candidate	$0
		Not-itemized	$9,626

Top 10 PAC Contributors

1) ITLA $2,000	6) LAWPAC . . . $500
2) BCongress . $1,000	7) IBA $500
3) IPACE $1,000	8) Alt&Gray . . . $500
4) AFSCME . . . $800	9) UAW $500
5) SNAPI $600	10) CPA's $400

NOTE: The General Election Opponent's Campaign Resources and Expenditures are reported in a separate section in the back of the book (pp. 269-284).

GENERAL ELECTION DATA

	Registered Voters	Voter Turnout		Straight Party Voting	
1996	41,370	27,009	65.3%	(R) 1,771 . . . . 6.6%	(D) 9,802 . . . . 36.3%

PRESIDENT

1996	Bill Clinton (D)	20,388	77.9%
	Bob Dole (R)	4,348	16.6%
	Ross Perot (I)	1,066	4.1%
1992	Bill Clinton (D)	23,388	71.0%
	George Bush (R)	6,256	19.0%
	Ross Perot (I)	3,313	10.0%

UNITED STATES SENATE

1996	Richard J. Durbin (D)	20,610	79.3%
	Al Salvi (R)	4,647	17.9%

GOVERNOR

1994	Jim Edgar (R)	6,318	36.2%
	Dawn Clark Netsch (D)	11,132	63.8%

Representative Janice D. "Jan" Schakowsky (D)

District Office: 2100 Ridge Ave., Evanston 60201
Phone (847) 328-3399; (847) 328-3425 (fax)
Springfield Office: Room 2087-M Stratton Bldg., Springfield
Phone (217) 782-8052

Legislative Assignments: Committees on Labor & Commerce (chair); Appropriations-Human Services; Health Care Availability & Access; Electric Utility Deregulation.

Public Service: Representative (1991-present); board member of Citizen Action of Illinois.

Personal: Full-time legislator; born May 26, 1944, Chicago; University of Illinois, B.S. in elementary education; married (Robert Creamer); three children.

1997 BILL PASSAGE RATIO	Introduced	Passed House of Origin	Passed GA
Primary	46	7	0
Primary/Hyphenated	79	23	6

KEY VOTES

1) Change Ed. Funding Formula . . Y	6) Insurance/Domestic Violence . . Y	11) Pre-Paid College Tuition . . . . Y
2) State Budget . . . . Y	7) Brownfields . . . . Y	12) Increase Pull Tab Prizes . . . . Y
3) Tougher DUI Level . . . . Y	8) Welfare Reform . . . . Y	13) Utility Deregulation . . . . N
4) Ban Partial Birth Abortions . . . N	9) Concealed Guns/Misdemeanor . N	14) County Obscenity Standards . N
5) State Employees Pension . . . . . Y	10) Banks Sell Insurance . . . . N	15) Managed Care Reform . . . . . Y

GROUP RATINGS

	FB	CoC	PrLf	IPPC	ACLU
1997	75	23	0/6	100	100

ELECTION RESULTS

1996 General	Janice D. "Jan" Schakowsky (D)	26,910	(83.4%)
1996 General	Edward M. Potash (R)	5,353	(16.6%)
1996 Primary	Janice D. "Jan" Schakowsky (D)	7,533	(100%)
1996 Primary	Edward M. Potash (R)	1,337	(100%)

CAMPAIGN RESOURCES AND EXPENDITURES

1996 Campaign Funds				Top 10 PAC Contributors			
Beg. Balance	$10,825	Individuals	$2,850	1) ITLA	$2,000	6) LAWPAC	$500
Receipts	$25,865	Party	$0	2) Local1001	$500	7) AFSCME	$500
Expenditures	$24,952	PACS	$12,410	3) UAW	$500	8) SEIU/GSEU	$500
On hand	$11,738	Candidate	$0	4) AFLCIO	$500	9) Machinists	$500
		Not-itemized	$10,605	5) SEIU880	$500	10) HOPE	$400

NOTE: The General Election Opponent's Campaign Resources and Expenditures are reported in a separate section in the back of the book (pp. 269-284).

GENERAL ELECTION DATA

	Registered Voters	Voter Turnout		Straight Party Voting	
1996	51,934	34,814	67.0%	(R) 2,718 . . . 7.8%	(D) 12,941 . . . 37.2%

PRESIDENT

1996	Bill Clinton (D)	26,539	78.1%
	Bob Dole (R)	5,899	17.4%
	Ross Perot (I)	1,188	3.5%
1992	Bill Clinton (D)	31,217	73.0%
	George Bush (R)	7,882	18.4%
	Ross Perot (I)	3,719	8.6%

UNITED STATES SENATE

1996	Richard J. Durbin (D)	27,098	80.2%
	Al Salvi (R)	5,923	17.5%

GOVERNOR

1994	Jim Edgar (R)	8,438	36.9%
	Dawn Clark Netsch (D)	14,420	63.1%

10th Senate District

House District 19
House District 20

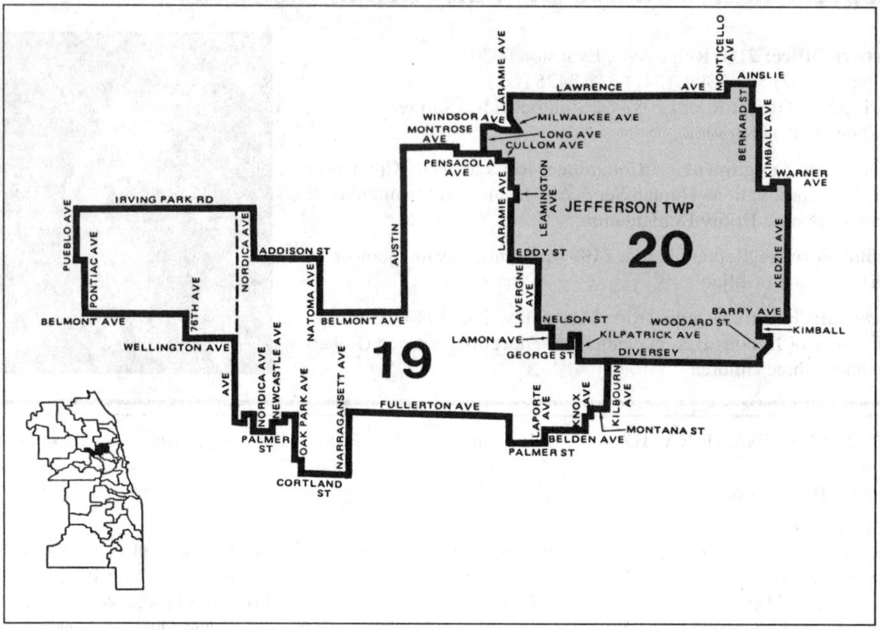

DEMOGRAPHICS (1990)

	S.D. #10	H.D. #19	H.D.#20
VOTING AGE POPULATION	153,631	77,859	75,772
White	79.7%	86.4%	72.9%
Black	0.4%	0.2%	0.6%
Hispanic	14.9%	10.9%	18.9%
Asian	4.7%	2.4%	7.2%
AGE (Total Population)	193,739	96,870	96,869
Under 6	7.7%	7.2%	8.2%
6 to 18	14.2%	13.6%	14.8%
65 and Over	16.2%	19.6%	12.7%
URBAN POPULATION	100.0%	100.0%	100.0%
HOUSING UNITS (Total)	77,707	38,357	39,350
Median Value	$101,325	$102,890	$97,493
Owner Occupied	51.2%	63.5%	39.3%
FAMILY INCOME (Total Families)	49,381	25,844	23,537
Median Income	$36,783	$38,862	$34,379
Below Poverty Level	5.8%	4.3%	7.4%
With Children Under 5	1.0%	0.4%	1.8%
With Children 5 to 17	2.0%	1.4%	2.6%
Headed by Females	2.3%	1.4%	3.3%
INDUSTRY (Total Employed)	97,573	47,337	50,237
Professional/Public Administration	20.3%	20.5%	20.2%
Manufacturing	23.8%	24.5%	23.2%
Retail	15.5%	16.2%	14.8%
Transportation/Communication	6.7%	6.9%	6.6%
Finance/Insurance/Real Estate	8.3%	9.0%	7.8%
Other Service	12.5%	10.7%	14.2%

Senator James A. DeLeo (D)

District Office: 6839 W. Belmont, Chicago 60634
Phone (773) 237-2525; (773) 237-7171 (fax)

Springfield Office: 218 Capitol Bldg., Springfield 62706
Phone (217) 782-1035

Legislative Assignments: Minority Conference Chair; Committees on Executive Appointments; Licensed Activities.

Public Service: Senator (1993-present); Representative (1985-1993).

Personal: Born August 10, 1951, Chicago; Chicago Loop Jr. College and DePaul University, political science; married (Ann), two children.

1997 BILL PASSAGE RATIO	Introduced	Passed House of Origin	Passed GA
Primary	7	0	0
Primary/Hyphenated	15	5	1

KEY VOTES

1) Senate GOP Ed. $ Plan ....N	6) Insurance/Domestic Violence ..Y	11) Pre-Paid College Tuition ....Y
2) State Budget ....Y	7) Brownfields ....Y	12) Increase Pull Tab Prizes ....Y
3) Tougher DUI Level ....Y	8) Welfare Reform ....Y	13) Telecommunications Tax ...Y
4) Ban Partial Birth Abortions ....Y	9) Concealed Guns/Misdemeanor .P	14) Delivery Discrimination ....Y
5) State Employees Pension .....Y	10) Banks Sell Insurance ....Y	15) Sell Drivers' Data ....N

GROUP RATINGS

	FB	CoC	PrLf	IPPC	ACLU
1997	73	60	2/2	0	50

ELECTION RESULTS

1996 General	James A. DeLeo (D)	40,814	(100%)
1996 Primary	James A. DeLeo (D)	19,512	(100%)
1996 Primary	Scott Tompkins (R)	2,567	(100%)
1992 General	James A. DeLeo (D)	43,873	(100%)

CAMPAIGN RESOURCES AND EXPENDITURES

1996 Campaign Funds				Top 10 PAC Contributors	
Beg. Balance	$165,191	Individuals	$2,050	1) INTIC ...$13,494	6) MCI $2,500
Receipts	$71,359	Party	$1,008	2) IPACE $5,000	7) ITLA $2,000
Expenditures	$88,274	PACS	$64,502	3) ISMS $3,500	8) Empress ...$2,000
On hand	$148,276	Candidate	$1,324	4) SASPAC ..$3,000	9) HI $2,000
		Not-itemized	$2,475	5) TIP $2,500	10) WMgt $1,900

NOTE: The General Election Opponent's Campaign Resources and Expenditures are reported in a separate section in the back of the book (pp. 269-284).

GENERAL ELECTION DATA

	Registered Voters	Voter Turnout		Straight Party Voting	
1996	86,074	56,916	66.1%	(R) 4,846 ....8.5%	(D) 18,153 ...31.9%

PRESIDENT

1996	Bill Clinton (D)	36,186	61.2%
	Bob Dole (R)	14,409	24.4%
	Ross Perot (I)	4,010	6.8%
1992	Bill Clinton (D)	33,932	49.1%
	George Bush (R)	23,271	33.7%
	Ross Perot (I)	11,893	17.2%

UNITED STATES SENATE

1996	Richard J. Durbin (D)	36,234	67.1%
	Al Salvi (R)	16,370	30.3%

GOVERNOR

1994	Jim Edgar (R)	25,138	60.9%
	Dawn Clark Netsch (D)	16,167	39.1%

Representative Robert J. Bugielski (D)

District Office: 6839 West Belmont Ave., Chicago 60634
Phone (773) 637-8770; (773) 622-6250 (fax)
Springfield Office: Room 2079-K Stratton Bldg., Springfield 62706
Phone (217) 782-0017

Legislative Assignments: Committees on Financial Institutions (chair); Executive; Insurance; Registration & Regulation; Banks Selling Insurance (co-chair).

Public Service: Representative (1987-present).

Personal: Applications analyst; born June 5, 1947 in Chicago; Chicago State University, B.S. in business education; married (Dona).

1997 BILL PASSAGE RATIO	Introduced	Passed House of Origin	Passed GA
Primary	20	4	4
Primary/Hyphenated	89	30	20

KEY VOTES

1) Change Ed. Funding Formula . . Y	6) Insurance/Domestic Violence . . Y	11) Pre-Paid College Tuition . . . . Y
2) State Budget . . . . Y	7) Brownfields . . . . Y	12) Increase Pull Tab Prizes . . . . Y
3) Tougher DUI Level . . . . Y	8) Welfare Reform . . . . Y	13) Utility Deregulation . . . . Y
4) Ban Partial Birth Abortions . . . . Y	9) Concealed Guns/Misdemeanor . Y	14) County Obscenity Standards . N
5) State Employees Pension . . . . . Y	10) Banks Sell Insurance . . . . Y	15) Managed Care Reform . . . . . Y

GROUP RATINGS

	FB	CoC	PrLf	IPPC	ACLU
1997	82	31	4/6	33	50

ELECTION RESULTS

1996 General	Robert J. Bugielski (D)	21,884	(73.3%)
1996 General	James J. Fiduccia (R)	7,973	(26.7%)
1996 Primary	Robert J. Bugielski (D)	11,325	(100%)

CAMPAIGN RESOURCES AND EXPENDITURES

1996 Campaign Funds				Top 10 PAC Contributors	
Beg. Balance	$76,655	Individuals	$0	1) ITLA $2,000	6) TIP $1,000
Receipts	$22,356	Party	$0	2) UPS $1,000	7) CAE $1,000
Expenditures	$40,866	PACS	$21,900	3) ABDI $1,000	8) MBPlatt . . . $500
On hand	$58,145	Candidate	$0	4) IPACE . . . $1,000	9) LAWPAC . . $500
		Not-itemized	$456	5) HI $1,000	10) IBA $500

NOTE: The General Election Opponent's Campaign Resources and Expenditures are reported in a separate section in the back of the book (pp. 269-284).

GENERAL ELECTION DATA

	Registered Voters	Voter Turnout		Straight Party Voting	
1996	47,699	32,232	67.6%	(R) 2,937 . . . 9.1%	(D) 10,174 . . . 31.6%

PRESIDENT

1996	Bill Clinton (D)	19,922	63.9%
	Bob Dole (R)	8,728	28.0%
	Ross Perot (I)	2,291	7.4%
1992	Bill Clinton (D)	18,060	46.4%
	George Bush (R)	13,996	36.0%
	Ross Perot (I)	6,846	17.6%

UNITED STATES SENATE

1996	Richard J. Durbin (D)	19,965	65.4%
	Al Salvi (R)	9,828	32.2%

GOVERNOR

1994	Jim Edgar (R)	15,651	64.1%
	Dawn Clark Netsch (D)	8,760	35.9%

Representative Richard T. Bradley (D)

District Office: 3616 N. Pulaski Rd., Chicago 60641
Phone (773) 794-9444; (773) 794-8576 (fax)
Springfield Office: 2089-M Stratton Building, Springfield, 62706
Phone (217) 782-8117

Legislative Assignments: Committees on Environment & Energy; Insurance; Judiciary II-Criminal Law; State Government Administration & Election Reform.

Public Service: Representative (1997-present); aldermanic secretary to Joseph Kotlarz.

Personal: Born May 18, 1955, Chicago; graduated from Concordia College; married (Cynthia); three children.

1997 BILL PASSAGE RATIO	Introduced	Passed House of Origin	Passed GA
Primary	0	0	0
Primary/Hyphenated	1	1	1

KEY VOTES

1) Change Ed. Funding Formula . .Y	6) Insurance/Domestic Violence . .Y	11) Pre-Paid College Tuition . . . .Y
2) State Budget . . . . .Y	7) Brownfields . . . . .Y	12) Increase Pull Tab Prizes X
3) Tougher DUI Level . . . . .Y	8) Welfare Reform . . . . .Y	13) Utility Deregulation . . . . . . .Y
4) Ban Partial Birth Abortions . . .X	9) Concealed Guns/Misdemeanor .N	14) County Obscenity Standards .Y
5) State Employees Pension . . . . .Y	10) Banks Sell Insurance . . . . .Y	15) Managed Care Reform . . . . .Y

GROUP RATINGS

	FB	CoC	PrLf	IPPC	ACLU
1997	91	30	N/R	N/R	N/R

ELECTION RESULTS

1996 General	Joseph S. Kotlarz, Jr. (D)	16,447	(73.3%)
1996 General	Joseph Anthony Hornowski (R)	5,987	(26.7%)
1996 Primary	Joseph S. Kotlarz, Jr. (D)	6,418	(63.4%)
1996 Primary	Elmer Haneberg (D)	3,705	(36.6%)

CAMPAIGN RESOURCES AND EXPENDITURES

1996 Campaign Funds				Top 10 PAC Contributors			
Beg. Balance	$N/A	Individuals	$N/A	1) N/A	$N/A	6) N/A	$N/A
Receipts	$N/A	Party	$N/A	2) N/A	$N/A	7) N/A	$N/A
Expenditures	$N/A	PACS	$N/A	3) N/A	$N/A	8) N/A	$N/A
On hand	$N/A	Candidate	$N/A	4) N/A	$N/A	9) N/A	$N/A
		Not-itemized	$N/A	5) N/A	$N/A	10) N/A	$N/A

NOTE: The General Election Opponent's Campaign Resources and Expenditures are reported in a separate section in the back of the book (pp. 269-284).

GENERAL ELECTION DATA

	Registered Voters	Voter Turnout		Straight Party Voting			
1996	38,375	24,684	64.3%	(R) 1,909	7.7%	(D) 7,979	32.3%

PRESIDENT

1996	Bill Clinton (D)	16,264	68.7%
	Bob Dole (R)	5,681	24.0%
	Ross Perot (I)	1,719	7.3%
1992	Bill Clinton (D)	15,872	52.6%
	George Bush (R)	9,275	30.7%
	Ross Perot (I)	5,047	16.7%

UNITED STATES SENATE

1996	Richard J. Durbin (D)	16,269	69.2%
	Al Salvi (R)	6,542	27.8%

GOVERNOR

1994	Jim Edgar (R)	9,487	56.2%
	Dawn Clark Netsch (D)	7,407	43.8%

11th Senate District

House District 21
House District 22

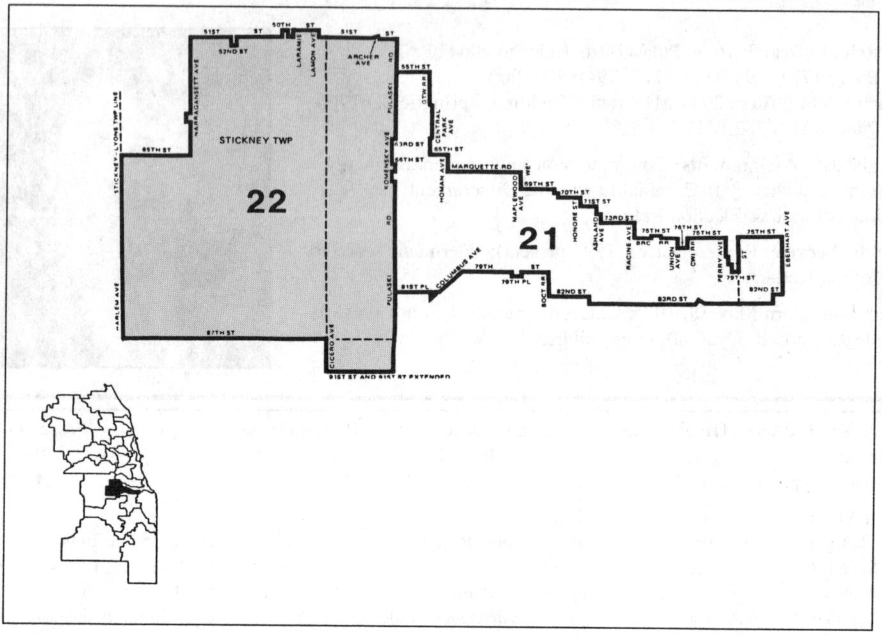

DEMOGRAPHICS (1990)

	S.D. #11	H.D. #21	H.D.#22
VOTING AGE POPULATION	147,669	71,592	76,077
White	62.9%	29.8%	94.0%
Black	31.3%	64.3%	0.1%
Hispanic	5.1%	5.1%	5.1%
Asian	0.7%	0.6%	0.7%
AGE (Total Population)	193,739	96,870	96.869
Under 6	7.8%	8.6%	7.3%
6 to 18	17.3%	19.2%	15.4%
65 and Over	16.1%	13.9%	18.5%
URBAN POPULATION	100.0%	100.0%	100.0%
HOUSING UNITS (Total)	71,520	34,995	36,525
Median Value	$77,054	$67,336	$83,982
Owner Occupied	70.7%	60.1%	80.3%
FAMILY INCOME (Total Families)	50,708	24,011	26,697
Median Income	$37,330	$33,199	$40,457
Below Poverty Level	7.4%	12.3%	2.9%
With Children Under 5	0.7%	1.2%	0.3%
With Children 5 to 17	3.1%	5.5%	1.0%
Headed by Females	4.8%	8.7%	1.2%
INDUSTRY (Total Employed)	86,577	40,011	46,566
Professional/Public Administration	26.3%	30.4%	22.8%
Manufacturing	18.0%	16.4%	19.3%
Retail	16.6%	14.9%	18.0%
Transportation/Communication	12.4%	13.3%	11.6%
Finance/Insurance/Real Estate	8.3%	8.2%	8.3%
Other Service	8.8%	9.4%	8.2%

Senator Louis S. "Lou" Viverito (D)

District Office: 6215 W. 79th Street., Suite 1A, Burbank 60459
Phone (708) 430-2510; (708) 430-2610 (fax)
Springfield Office: 105C Capitol Bldg., Springfield 62706
Phone (217) 782-0054

Legislative Assignments: Committees on State Government Operations (Minority Spokesperson); Licensed Activities.

Public Service: Senator (1995-present); Supervisor of Stickney Township (1973-present); Stickney Township Democratic Committeeman (1969-present); Commissioner, Metropolitan Sanitary District of Greater Chicago (1980-1986); member, Cook County Zoning Board of Appeals (1987-1995).

Personal: Born May 6, 1931, Chicago; three-time decorated Korean War veteran; married (Carolyn); three children.

1997 BILL PASSAGE RATIO	Introduced	Passed House of Origin	Passed GA
Primary	2	1	1
Primary/Hyphenated	15	9	8

KEY VOTES

1) Senate GOP Ed. $ Plan ...... N	6) Insurance/Domestic Violence .. Y	11) Pre-Paid College Tuition .... Y
2) State Budget .... Y	7) Brownfields .... Y	12) Increase Pull Tab Prizes .... Y
3) Tougher DUI Level .... Y	8) Welfare Reform .... Y	13) Telecommunications Tax ... Y
4) Ban Partial Birth Abortions ... Y	9) Concealed Guns/Misdemeanor . Y	14) Delivery Discrimination .... P
5) State Employees Pension ..... Y	10) Banks Sell Insurance .... Y	15) Sell Drivers' Data .... N

GROUP RATINGS

	FB	CoC	PrLf	IPPC	ACLU
1997	91	80	2/2	0	33

ELECTION RESULTS

1994 General	Louis S. "Lou" Viverito (D)	42,382	(76.8%)
1994 General	Thomas C. Petrick (R)	12,824	(23.2%)
1994 Primary	Louis S. "Lou" Viverito (D)	26,592	(100%)
1994 Primary	Thomas C. Petrick (R)	1,101	(69.9%)

CAMPAIGN RESOURCES AND EXPENDITURES

1996 Campaign Funds				Top 10 PAC Contributors	
Beg. Balance	$105,706	Individuals	$800	1) CWadas ... $2,500	6) Ameritech ... $500
Receipts	$18,317	Party	$2,500	2) FoxCollision $1,200	7) ILCable $500
Expenditures	$13,682	PACS	$14,150	3) UPS $1,000	8) CoC $500
On hand	$110,341	Candidate	$0	4) Sears $1,000	9) LCI $500
		Not-itemized	$867	5) CPA's $600	10) Walgreens .. $500

NOTE: The General Election Opponent's Campaign Resources and Expenditures are reported in a separate section in the back of the book (pp. 269-284).

GENERAL ELECTION DATA

	Registered Voters	Voter Turnout		Straight Party Voting	
1996	113,999	78,367	68.7%	(R) 4,198 ... 5.4%	(D) 29,086 ... 37.1%

PRESIDENT

1996	Bill Clinton (D)	56,189	74.0%
	Bob Dole (R)	14,292	18.8%
	Ross Perot (I)	4,843	6.4%
1992	Bill Clinton (D)	58,080	61.9%
	George Bush (R)	22,608	24.1%
	Ross Perot (I)	13,142	14.0%

UNITED STATES SENATE

1996	Richard J. Durbin (D)	56,024	74.9%
	Al Salvi (R)	16,919	22.6%

GOVERNOR

1994	Jim Edgar (R)	26,483	44.9%
	Dawn Clark Netsch (D)	32,525	55.1%

Representative Mary E. Flowers (D)

District Office: 7954 S. Western., Chicago 60620
Phone (773) 874-5200; (773) 471-1036 (fax)
Springfield Office: Room 2048-J Stratton Bldg., Springfield 62706
Phone (217) 782-4207; (217) 782-1130 (fax)

Legislative Assignments: Committees on Health Care Availability and Access (chair); Appropriations-Human Services; Human Services; Conference on Women Legislators (co-chair).

Public Service: Representative (1985-present).

Personal: Full-time legislator; born July 31, 1951, Inverness, Miss; Kennedy King Community College and University of Illinois-Chicago; married (Daniel L. Coutee); one daughter

1997 BILL PASSAGE RATIO	Introduced	Passed House of Origin	Passed GA
Primary	46	6	1
Primary/Hyphenated	80	24	5

KEY VOTES

1) Change Ed. Funding Formula . . Y	6) Insurance/Domestic Violence . . Y	11) Pre-Paid College Tuition . . . . Y
2) State Budget . . . . Y	7) Brownfields . . . . Y	12) Increase Pull Tab Prizes . . . . Y
3) Tougher DUI Level . . . . Y	8) Welfare Reform . . . . Y	13) Utility Deregulation . . . . Y
4) Ban Partial Birth Abortions . . . N	9) Concealed Guns/Misdemeanor . N	14) County Obscenity Standards . N
5) State Employees Pension . . . . . Y	10) Banks Sell Insurance . . . . Y	15) Managed Care Reform . . . . . Y

GROUP RATINGS

	FB	CoC	PrLf	IPPC	ACLU
1997	86	23	0/6	100	90

ELECTION RESULTS

1996 General	Mary E. Flowers (D)	32,623	(92.8%)
1996 General	Melvin R. Sexton (R)	2,524	(7.2%)
1996 Primary	Mary E. Flowers (D)	11,073	(100%)

CAMPAIGN RESOURCES AND EXPENDITURES

1996 Campaign Funds		Top 10 PAC Contributors	
Beg. Balance . . $1,993	Individuals $400	1) IBA $2,100	6) LICID $500
Receipts $25,115	Party $750	2) ITLA $2,000	7) CUPAC $500
Expenditures . $16,444	PACS $16,100	3) Ameritech . . . $750	8) CentTel $500
On hand $10,664	Candidate $2,000	4) UAW $750	9) CTurner $500
	Not-itemized . . $5,865	5) MPower $500	10) Sears $450

NOTE: The General Election Opponent's Campaign Resources and Expenditures are reported in a separate section in the back of the book (pp. 269-284).

GENERAL ELECTION DATA

	Registered Voters	Voter Turnout		Straight Party Voting	
1996	57,679	37,433	64.9%	(R) 827 . . . . . 2.2%	(D) 15,190 . . . 40.6%

PRESIDENT

1996	Bill Clinton (D)	31,746	88.1%
	Bob Dole (R)	2,875	8.0%
	Ross Perot (I)	1,086	3.0%
1992	Bill Clinton (D)	35,813	79.7%
	George Bush (R)	5,801	12.9%
	Ross Perot (I)	3,301	7.4%

UNITED STATES SENATE

1996	Richard J. Durbin (D)	30,888	87.1%
	Al Salvi (R)	3,729	10.5%

GOVERNOR

1994	Jim Edgar (R)	7,168	28.1%
	Dawn Clark Netsch (D)	18,380	71.9%

Representative Michael J. Madigan (D)

District Office: 6500 South Pulaski Rd., Chicago 60629
Phone (773) 581-8000; (773) 581-9414 (fax)
Springfield Office: Room 300 Capitol Bldg., Springfield 62706
Phone (217) 782-5350; (217) 524-1794 (fax)

Legislative Assignments: Speaker of the House; ex-officio member of all committees.

Public Service: Speaker of the House (1983-1995; 1997-present); Democratic leader of the House of Representatives (1995-1997); representative (1971-present); member of Illinois Constitutional Convention.

Personal: Attorney; born April 19, 1942, Chicago; University of Notre Dame, B.S. in economics; Loyola University Law School, J.D.; married (Shirley); four children.

1997 BILL PASSAGE RATIO	Introduced	Passed House of Origin	Passed GA
Primary	17	9	2
Primary/Hyphenated	27	17	4

KEY VOTES

1) Change Ed. Funding Formula . .Y	6) Insurance/Domestic Violence . .Y	11) Pre-Paid College Tuition . . . .Y
2) State Budget . . . . .Y	7) Brownfields . . . . .Y	12) Increase Pull Tab Prizes . . . .Y
3) Tougher DUI Level . . . . .Y	8) Welfare Reform . . . . .Y	13) Utility Deregulation . . . . . . .Y
4) Ban Partial Birth Abortions . . .Y	9) Concealed Guns/Misdemeanor .N	14) County Obscenity Standards .N
5) State Employees Pension . . . . .Y	10) Banks Sell Insurance . . . . .P	15) Managed Care Reform . . . . .Y

GROUP RATINGS

	FB	CoC	PrLf	IPPC	ACLU
1997	86	25	5/6	16	50

ELECTION RESULTS

1996 General	Michael J. Madigan (D)	31,049	(80.2%)
1996 General	Terrence F. Goggin (R)	7,651	(19.8%)
1996 Primary	Michael J. Madigan (D)	16,028	(100%)
1996 Primary	Terrence F. Goggin (R)	1,535	(100%)

CAMPAIGN RESOURCES AND EXPENDITURES

1996 Campaign Funds				Top 10 PAC Contributors	
Beg. Balance	$1,590,576	Individuals	$61,393	1) DSCC . .$605,000	6) Teamsters .$35,000
Receipts	$2,498,433	Party	$711,600	2) TIP $76,000	7) Machinists $33,000
Expenditures	$3,612,883	PACS	$1,665,077	3) IUOE399 .$51,550	8) CCapparelli $32,500
On hand	$476,126	Candidate	$28,091	4) AFSCME .$50,300	9) AO&R . . .$30,000
		Not-itemized	$32,272	5) UDI/DPI .$40,000	10) C&GL . .$28,000

NOTE: The General Election Opponent's Campaign Resources and Expenditures are reported in a separate section in the back of the book (pp. 269-284).

GENERAL ELECTION DATA

	Registered Voters	Voter Turnout		Straight Party Voting	
1996	56,320	40,934	72.7%	(R) 3,371 . . . .8.2%	(D) 13,896 . . .34.0%

PRESIDENT

1996	Bill Clinton (D)	24,443	61.3%
	Bob Dole (R)	11,417	28.6%
	Ross Perot (I)	3,757	9.4%
1992	Bill Clinton (D)	22,267	45.5%
	George Bush (R)	16,807	34.4%
	Ross Perot (I)	9,841	20.1%

UNITED STATES SENATE

1996	Richard J. Durbin (D)	25,136	63.9%
	Al Salvi (R)	13,190	33.5%

GOVERNOR

1994	Jim Edgar (R)	19,315	57.7%
	Dawn Clark Netsch (D)	14,145	42.3%

12th Senate District

House District 23
House District 24

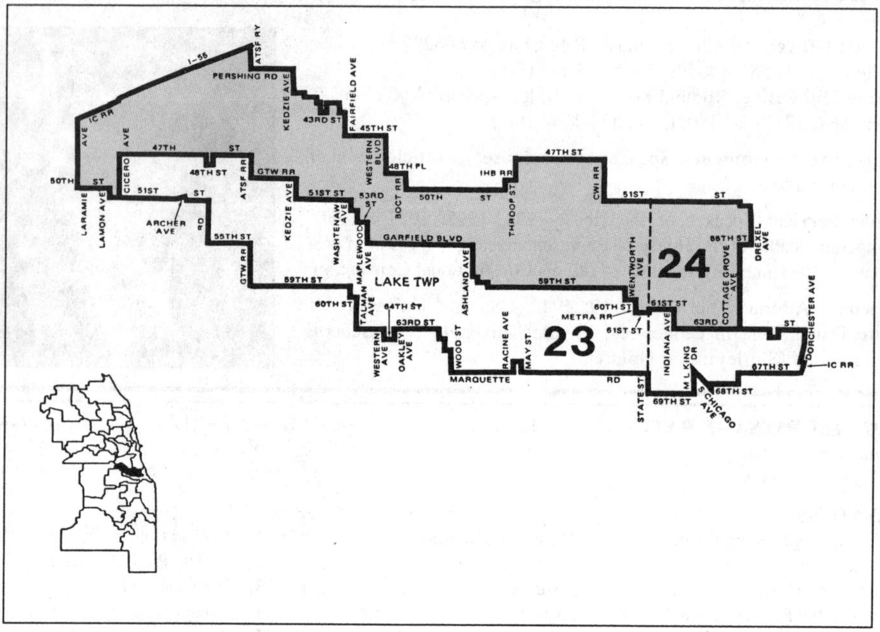

DEMOGRAPHICS (1990)

	S.D. #12	H.D. #23	H.D.#24
VOTING AGE POPULATION	131,570	67,507	64,063
White	25.3%	26.4%	24.1%
Black	63.7%	62.7%	64.8%
Hispanic	10.4%	10.4%	10.4%
Asian	0.5%	0.5%	0.5%
AGE (Total Population)	193,739	96,870	96,869
Under 6	11.3%	10.5%	12.1%
6 to 18	22.5%	21.5%	23.5%
65 and Over	11.9%	13.3%	10.4%
URBAN POPULATION	100.0%	100.0%	100.0%
HOUSING UNITS (Total)	71,843	35,547	36,296
Median Value	$57,556	$57,756	$57,151
Owner Occupied	35.0%	40.4%	29.7%
FAMILY INCOME (Total Families)	43,685	22,109	21,576
Median Income	$22,090	$24,406	$20,133
Below Poverty Level	28.6%	24.9%	32.3%
With Children Under 5	3.3%	2.6%	4.0%
With Children 5 to 17	10.9%	9.9%	11.8%
Headed by Females	21.6%	18.5%	24.8%
INDUSTRY (Total Employed)	61,295	31,820	29,475
Professional/Public Administration	25.7%	26.6%	24.8%
Manufacturing	20.3%	20.2%	20.3%
Retail	16.1%	15.8%	16.4%
Transportation/Communication	10.5%	10.3%	10.7%
Finance/Insurance/Real Estate	6.6%	6.4%	6.9%
Other Service	11.4%	11.4%	11.3%

Senator Robert S. Molaro (D)

District Office: 4204 S. Archer Ave., Suite 1212, Chicago 60632
Phone (773) 254-1212; (773) 254-8269 (fax)
Springfield Office: Room M-103-E, Capitol Bldg., Springfield 62706
Phone (217) 782-5280; (217) 782-1631 (fax)

Legislative Assignments: Committees on Licensed Activities (minority spokesman); Insurance & Pensions; Transportation.

Public Service: Senator (1993-present); former Democratic committeeman, 12th Ward, Chicago.

Personal: Attorney; born June 29, 1950, Chicago; Loyola University, B.S., John Marshall Law School, J.D.; married (Barbara); five children.

1997 BILL PASSAGE RATIO	Introduced	Passed House of Origin	Passed GA
Primary	20	1	0
Primary/Hyphenated	26	4	2

KEY VOTES

1) Senate GOP Ed. $ Plan ......N	6) Insurance/Domestic Violence ..Y	11) Pre-Paid College Tuition ....Y
2) State Budget ....O	7) Brownfields ....O	12) Increase Pull Tab Prizes ....Y
3) Tougher DUI Level ....Y	8) Welfare Reform ....O	13) Telecommunications Tax ...Y
4) Ban Partial Birth Abortions ...Y	9) Concealed Guns/Misdemeanor .P	14) Delivery Discrimination ....Y
5) State Employees Pension .....O	10) Banks Sell Insurance ....Y	15) Sell Drivers' Data ....N

GROUP RATINGS

	FB	CoC	PrLf	IPPC	ACLU
1997	68	60	1/2	50	75

ELECTION RESULTS

1996 General	Robert S. Molaro (D)	40,237	(86.4%)
1996 General	Glenn B. Wharton (HWP)	6,351	(13.6%)
1996 Primary	Robert S. Molaro (D)	11,136	(53.4%)
1996 Primary	Six candidates (D)	9,707	(46.6%)

CAMPAIGN RESOURCES AND EXPENDITURES

1996 Campaign Funds				Top 10 PAC Contributors	
Beg. Balance	$40,475	Individuals	$2,325	1) Statesman .$12,500	6) UPS $1,000
Receipts	$42,363	Party	$250	2) ISMS $3,000	7) G&S $1,000
Expenditures	$22,141	PACS	$37,325	3) IPACE $3,000	8) ABDI $1,000
On hand	$60,997	Candidate	$0	4) ITLA $2,000	9) IMAPAC $600
		Not-itemized	$2,463	5) C&GL $1,250	10) IHHA $500

NOTE: The General Election Opponent's Campaign Resources and Expenditures are reported in a separate section in the back of the book (pp. 269-284).

GENERAL ELECTION DATA

	Registered Voters	Voter Turnout		Straight Party Voting	
1996	91,824	53,645	58.4%	(R) 889 .....1.7%	(D) 23,222 ...43.3%

PRESIDENT

1996	Bill Clinton (D)	45,425	89.2%
	Bob Dole (R)	3,603	7.1%
	Ross Perot (I)	1,384	2.7%
1992	Bill Clinton (D)	58,016	83.1%
	George Bush (R)	7,373	10.6%
	Ross Perot (I)	4,436	6.3%

UNITED STATES SENATE

1996	Richard J. Durbin (D)	43,851	87.7%
	Al Salvi (R)	4,843	9.7%

GOVERNOR

1994	Jim Edgar (R)	9,887	28.8%
	Dawn Clark Netsch (D)	24,434	71.2%

Representative Daniel J. Burke (D)

District Office: 2650 West 51st St., Chicago 60632
Phone (773) 471-2299; (773) 471-1648 (fax)
Springfield Office: Room 2034-J Stratton Bldg., Springfield 62706
Phone (217) 782-1117

Legislative Assignments: Committees on Executive (chair); Financial Institutions; Registration & Regulation.

Public Service: Representative (1991-present).

Personal: Assistant city clerk, City of Chicago; born December 17, 1951, Chicago; Loyola University, communications 1971-73; DePaul University, business administration; single.

1997 BILL PASSAGE RATIO	Introduced	Passed House of Origin	Passed GA
Primary	22	7	4
Primary/Hyphenated	65	23	11

KEY VOTES

1) Change Ed. Funding Formula . . Y	6) Insurance/Domestic Violence . . Y	11) Pre-Paid College Tuition . . . . Y
2) State Budget . . . . Y	7) Brownfields . . . . A	12) Increase Pull Tab Prizes . . . . Y
3) Tougher DUI Level . . . . Y	8) Welfare Reform . . . . Y	13) Utility Deregulation . . . . A
4) Ban Partial Birth Abortions . . . N	9) Concealed Guns/Misdemeanor . N	14) County Obscenity Standards . N
5) State Employees Pension . . . . . Y	10) Banks Sell Insurance . . . . Y	15) Managed Care Reform . . . . . Y

GROUP RATINGS

	FB	CoC	PrLf	IPPC	ACLU
1997	86	38	0/6	100	90

ELECTION RESULTS

1996 General	Daniel J. Burke (D)	24,452	(100%)
1996 Primary	Daniel J. Burke (D)	7,589	(66.7%)
1996 Primary	Sabrina A. Barker (D)	1,876	(16.5%)
1996 Primary	Four others (D)	1,913	(16.8%)

CAMPAIGN RESOURCES AND EXPENDITURES

1996 Campaign Funds				Top 10 PAC Contributors			
Beg. Balance	$58,477	Individuals	$6,625	1) Egbert	$3,000	6) ITLA	$1,000
Receipts	$47,701	Party	$250	2) IBA	$2,000	7) IPACE	$1,000
Expenditures	$27,594	PACS	$35,150	3) AntiochMB	$1,500	8) BSIW	$700
On hand	$78,584	Candidate	$316	4) ANA	$1,500	9) FirstComm	$700
		Not-itemized	$5,360	5) TAC	$1,000	10) Sears	$650

NOTE: The General Election Opponent's Campaign Resources and Expenditures are reported in a separate section in the back of the book (pp. 269-284).

GENERAL ELECTION DATA

	Registered Voters	Voter Turnout		Straight Party Voting	
1996	47,569	28,369	59.6%	(R) 460 . . . . . 1.6%	(D) 12,188 . . . 43.0%

PRESIDENT

1996	Bill Clinton (D)	23,987	89.1%
	Bob Dole (R)	1,936	7.2%
	Ross Perot (I)	744	2.8%
1992	Bill Clinton (D)	30,962	83.0%
	George Bush (R)	3,967	10.6%
	Ross Perot (I)	2,387	6.4%

UNITED STATES SENATE

1996	Richard J. Durbin (D)	23,133	87.6%
	Al Salvi (R)	2,591	9.8%

GOVERNOR

1994	Jim Edgar (R)	5,431	29.6%
	Dawn Clark Netsch (D)	12,897	70.4%

Representative Howard Kenner (D)

District Office: 130 East Garfield Blvd., Chicago 60615
Phone (773) 624-2004; (773) 624-4450 (fax)
Springfield Office: Room 2101-N Stratton Bldg., Springfield 62706
Phone (217) 782-8197; (217) 782-3220 (fax)

Legislative Assignments: Committees on Labor and Commerce (vice chair); Appropriations-General Services & Government Oversight; Appropriations-Human Services; Health Care Availability & Access; Insurance.

Public Service: Representative (1995-present); chairman of the Illinois Legislative Black Caucus.

Personal: Certified public accountant; born December 26, 1957, Chicago; University of Illinois at Urbana, B.S. in accountancy; single.

1997 BILL PASSAGE RATIO	Introduced	Passed House of Origin	Passed GA
Primary	12	2	0
Primary/Hyphenated	30	10	0

KEY VOTES

1) Change Ed. Funding Formula . . Y	6) Insurance/Domestic Violence . . Y	11) Pre-Paid College Tuition . . . . Y
2) State Budget . . . . Y	7) Brownfields . . . . Y	12) Increase Pull Tab Prizes . . . . Y
3) Tougher DUI Level . . . . Y	8) Welfare Reform . . . . Y	13) Utility Deregulation . . . . Y
4) Ban Partial Birth Abortions . . . . P	9) Concealed Guns/Misdemeanor . P	14) County Obscenity Standards . N
5) State Employees Pension . . . . . Y	10) Banks Sell Insurance . . . . Y	15) Managed Care Reform . . . . . Y

GROUP RATINGS

	FB	CoC	PrLf	IPPC	ACLU
1997	86	33	0/6	100	100

ELECTION RESULTS

1996 General	Howard Kenner (D)	20,569	(89.9%)
1996 General	Patricia A. Krasowski (R)	2,300	(10.1%)
1996 Primary	Howard Kenner (D)	6,173	(100%)

CAMPAIGN RESOURCES AND EXPENDITURES

1996 Campaign Funds				Top 10 PAC Contributors			
Beg. Balance	$2,051	Individuals	$372	1) ITLA	$2,000	6) UAW	$500
Receipts	$13,372	Party	$500	2) MPower	$1,100	7) CPA's	$400
Expenditures	$9,754	PACS	$10,300	3) ABDI	$1,000	8) CUPAC	$350
On hand	$5,669	Candidate	$0	4) IPACE	$500	9) Sears	$300
		Not-itemized	$2,200	5) CTurner	$500	10) IBA	$300

NOTE: The General Election Opponent's Campaign Resources and Expenditures are reported in a separate section in the back of the book (pp. 269-284).

GENERAL ELECTION DATA

	Registered Voters	Voter Turnout		Straight Party Voting			
1996	44,255	25,276	57.1%	(R) 429	1.7%	(D) 11,034	43.7%

PRESIDENT

1996	Bill Clinton (D)	21,438	89.3%
	Bob Dole (R)	1,667	6.9%
	Ross Perot (I)	640	2.7%
1992	Bill Clinton (D)	27,054	83.2%
	George Bush (R)	3,406	10.5%
	Ross Perot (I)	2,049	6.3%

UNITED STATES SENATE

1996	Richard J. Durbin (D)	20,718	87.9%
	Al Salvi (R)	2,252	9.6%

GOVERNOR

1994	Jim Edgar (R)	4,456	27.9%
	Dawn Clark Netsch (D)	11,537	72.1%

13th Senate District

House District 25
House District 26

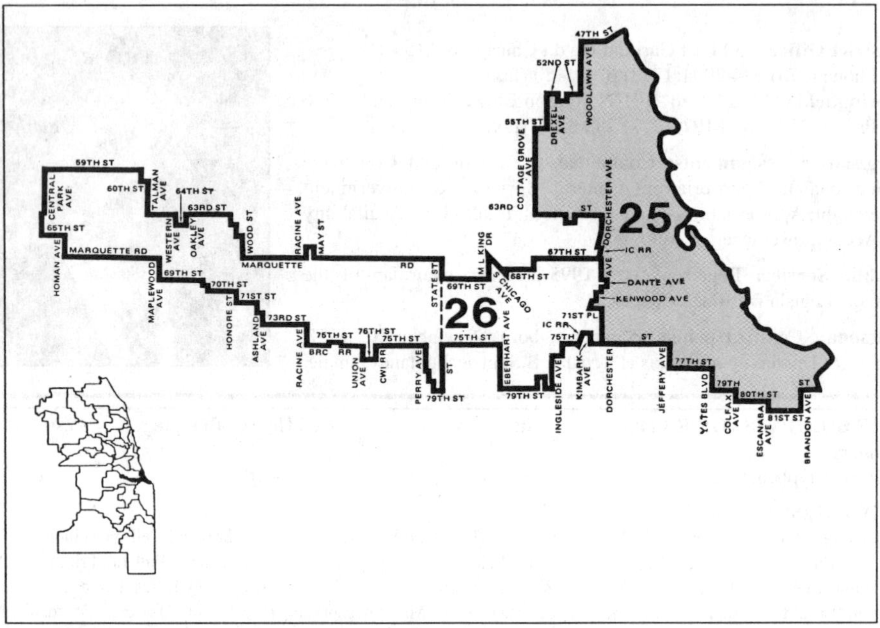

DEMOGRAPHICS (1990)

	S.D. #13	H.D. #25	H.D.#26
VOTING AGE POPULATION	142,164	75,154	67,010
White	20.3%	23.1%	17.1%
Black	71.7%	71.1%	72.4%
Hispanic	5.6%	2.0%	9.7%
Asian	2.2%	3.6%	0.6%
AGE (Total Population)	193,740	96,870	96,870
Under 6	9.3%	8.0%	10.7%
6 to 18	19.0%	16.1%	21.9%
65 and Over	11.3%	10.3%	12.2%
URBAN POPULATION	100.0%	100.0%	100.0%
HOUSING UNITS (Total)	83,671	49,168	34,503
Median Value	$57,964	$91,492	$53,024
Owner Occupied	28.3%	20.5%	39.5%
FAMILY INCOME (Total Families)	43,693	21,705	21,988
Median Income	$25,957	$28,090	$24,171
Below Poverty Level	22.6%	21.5%	23.7%
With Children Under 5	3.0%	2.9%	3.1%
With Children 5 to 17	9.0%	8.2%	9.8%
Headed by Females	16.2%	15.5%	16.9%
INDUSTRY (Total Employed)	77,482	43,882	33,599
Professional/Public Administration	40.3%	48.6%	29.5%
Manufacturing	12.0%	8.0%	17.2%
Retail	13.5%	10.3%	17.6%
Transportation/Communication	10.3%	9.8%	11.0%
Finance/Insurance/Real Estate	8.9%	10.2%	7.1%
Other Service	9.3%	8.8%	9.9%

Senator Barack Obama (D)

District Office: 2152 E. 71st St., Chicago 60649
Phone (773) 363-1996; (773) 363-5099 (fax)
Springfield Office: 105D Capitol Bldg., Springfield 62706
Phone (217) 782-5338; (217) 782-5340 (fax)

Legislative Assignments: Committees on Judiciary; Public Health & Welfare; State Government Operations.

Public Service: Senator (1997-present).

Personal: Attorney; law professor at the University of Chicago Law School; born August 4, 1961, Hawaii; Columbia University, B.A. in political science and Harvard Law School; married (Michelle).

1997 BILL PASSAGE RATIO	Introduced	Passed House of Origin	Passed GA
Primary	18	3	3
Primary/Hyphenated	39	8	8

KEY VOTES

1) Senate GOP Ed. $ Plan ......N	6) Insurance/Domestic Violence ..Y	11) Pre-Paid College Tuition ....Y
2) State Budget ....N	7) Brownfields ....Y	12) Increase Pull Tab Prizes ....N
3) Tougher DUI Level ....Y	8) Welfare Reform ....Y	13) Telecommunications Tax ...Y
4) Ban Partial Birth Abortions ....P	9) Concealed Guns/Misdemeanor .P	14) Delivery Discrimination ...Y
5) State Employees Pension .....Y	10) Banks Sell Insurance ....Y	15) Sell Drivers' Data ....N

GROUP RATINGS

	FB	CoC	PrLf	IPPC	ACLU
1997	91	75	0/2	100	100

ELECTION RESULTS

1996 General	Barack Obama (D)	48,592	(82.2%)
1996 General	David Whitehead (HWP)	7,461	(12.6%)
1996 General	Rosette Caldwell Peyton (R)	3,091	(5.2%)
1996 Primary	Barack Obama (D)	16,279	(100%)

CAMPAIGN RESOURCES AND EXPENDITURES

1996 Campaign Funds				Top 10 PAC Contributors	
Beg. Balance ..$4,177		Individuals ..$5,550		1) ITLA $1,000	6) PR&S $500
Receipts $19,457		Party $1,250		2) CDS $1,000	7) HOPE $300
Expenditures .$23,493		PACS $5,400		3) LAWPAC ..$1,000	8) FJacobs $250
On hand $141		Candidate ... $2,427		4) UAW $500	9) DystelInc ...$250
		Not-itemized .$4,830		5) AFSCME ...$500	10) Ameritech ..$250

NOTE: The General Election Opponent's Campaign Resources and Expenditures are reported in a separate section in the back of the book (pp. 269-284).

GENERAL ELECTION DATA

	Registered Voters	Voter Turnout		Straight Party Voting	
1996	105,428	65,745	62.4%	(R) 891 .....1.4%	(D) 24,644 ...37.5%

PRESIDENT

1996	Bill Clinton (D)	58,500	92.8%
	Bob Dole (R)	2,867	4.6%
	Ross Perot (I)	1,127	1.8%
1992	Bill Clinton (D)	72,413	90.5%
	George Bush (R)	4,554	5.7%
	Ross Perot (I)	3,077	3.8%

UNITED STATES SENATE

1996	Richard J. Durbin (D)	56,807	91.3%
	Al Salvi (R)	3,929	6.3%

GOVERNOR

1994	Jim Edgar (R)	7,426	18.1%
	Dawn Clark Netsch (D)	33,689	81.9%

Representative Barbara Flynn Currie (D)

District Office: 5225 South Harper Ave., Chicago 60615
Phone (773) 667-0550; (773) 667-3010 (fax)
Springfield Office: Room 300 Capitol Bldg., Springfield 62706
Phone (217) 782-8121

Legislative Assignments: House Majority Leader; ex officio member of all committees. Committees on Rules (chair); Revenue.

Public Service: Representative (1979-present).

Personal: Full-time legislator; born May 3, 1940, LaCrosse, WI; University of Chicago, A.B. (cum laude) in political science; University of Chicago, A.M. in political science; married (David P.); two children.

1997 BILL PASSAGE RATIO	Introduced	Passed House of Origin	Passed GA
Primary	29	7	3
Primary/Hyphenated	61	22	11

KEY VOTES

1) Change Ed. Funding Formula . . Y	6) Insurance/Domestic Violence . . P	11) Pre-Paid College Tuition . . . . Y
2) State Budget . . . . Y	7) Brownfields . . . . Y	12) Increase Pull Tab Prizes . . . . Y
3) Tougher DUI Level . . . . Y	8) Welfare Reform . . . . Y	13) Utility Deregulation . . . . Y
4) Ban Partial Birth Abortions . . . N	9) Concealed Guns/Misdemeanor . N	14) County Obscenity Standards . N
5) State Employees Pension . . . . . Y	10) Banks Sell Insurance . . . . Y	15) Managed Care Reform . . . . . Y

GROUP RATINGS

	FB	CoC	PrLf	IPPC	ACLU
1997	86	15	0/6	100	100

ELECTION RESULTS

1996 General	Barbara Flynn Currie (D)	32,036	(100%)
1996 Primary	Barbara Flynn Currie (D)	11,661	(100%)
1994 General	Barbara Flynn Currie (D)	21,531	(100%)

CAMPAIGN RESOURCES AND EXPENDITURES

1996 Campaign Funds				Top 10 PAC Contributors	
Beg. Balance	$87,331	Individuals	$784	1) ITLA $2,000	6) LICID $500
Receipts	$19,997	Party	$0	2) SNAPI $750	7) LAWPAC . . . $500
Expenditures	$8,128	PACS	$9,750	3) UAW $500	8) IVendors $500
On hand	$99,200	Candidate	$908	4) Sears $500	9) AFSCME . . . $500
		Not-itemized	$8,555	5) IBA $500	10) CPA's $400

NOTE: The General Election Opponent's Campaign Resources and Expenditures are reported in a separate section in the back of the book (pp. 269-284).

GENERAL ELECTION DATA

	Registered Voters	Voter Turnout		Straight Party Voting	
1996	55,207	36,343	65.8%	(R) 558 . . . . . 1.5%	(D) 12,433 . . . 34.2%

PRESIDENT

1996	Bill Clinton (D)	32,392	92.4%
	Bob Dole (R)	1,768	5.0%
	Ross Perot (I)	598	1.7%
1992	Bill Clinton (D)	42,019	91.6%
	George Bush (R)	2,312	5.0%
	Ross Perot (I)	1,546	3.4%

UNITED STATES SENATE

1996	Richard J. Durbin (D)	31,774	91.5%
	Al Salvi (R)	2,138	6.2%

GOVERNOR

1994	Jim Edgar (R)	3,657	15.8%
	Dawn Clark Netsch (D)	19,588	84.2%

Representative Charles G. Morrow, III (D)

District Office: 68 East 71st St., Chicago 60619
Phone (773) 224-1563; (773) 224-3074 (fax)
Springfield Office: Room 2097-M Stratton Bldg., Springfield 62706
Phone (217) 782-1702; (217) 782-9274 (fax)

Legislative Assignments: Committees on Appropriations-Public Safety (chairman); Public Utilities (vice-chair); Electric Utility Deregulation; Financial Institutions.

Public Service: Representative (1987-present).

Personal: Full-time legislator; born July 21, 1956, Chicago; Illinois Institute of Technology; married (Sherri); two children.

1997 BILL PASSAGE RATIO	Introduced	Passed House of Origin	Passed GA
Primary	12	3	2
Primary/Hyphenated	39	5	2

KEY VOTES

1) Change Ed. Funding Formula . . Y
2) State Budget . . . . Y
3) Tougher DUI Level . . . . Y
4) Ban Partial Birth Abortions . . . N
5) State Employees Pension . . . . . Y
6) Insurance/Domestic Violence . . Y
7) Brownfields . . . . Y
8) Welfare Reform . . . . Y
9) Concealed Guns/Misdemeanor . P
10) Banks Sell Insurance . . . . Y
11) Pre-Paid College Tuition . . . . Y
12) Increase Pull Tab Prizes . . . . Y
13) Utility Deregulation . . . . Y
14) County Obscenity Standards . N
15) Managed Care Reform . . . . . Y

GROUP RATINGS

	FB	CoC	PrLf	IPPC	ACLU
1997	86	23	0/6	100	100

ELECTION RESULTS

1996 General	Charles G. Morrow, III (D)	25,407	(95.5%)
1996 General	James V. Spring (R)	1,208	(4.5%)
1996 Primary	Charles G. Morrow, III (D)	7,825	(100%)

CAMPAIGN RESOURCES AND EXPENDITURES

1996 Campaign Funds

Beg. Balance	$7,864	Individuals	$0
Receipts	$9,450	Party	$500
Expenditures	$5,287	PACS	$8,400
On hand	$12,027	Candidate	$0
		Not-itemized	$550

Top 10 PAC Contributors

1) ITLA $2,000	6) LICID $500
2) IPACE . . . $1,000	7) ABDI $500
3) CTurner . . . $500	8) UAW $500
4) Ameritech . . $500	9) HBPAC $400
5) MPower . . . $500	10) CUPAC . . . $350

NOTE: The General Election Opponent's Campaign Resources and Expenditures are reported in a separate section in the back of the book (pp. 269-284).

GENERAL ELECTION DATA

	Registered Voters	Voter Turnout		Straight Party Voting	
1996	50,221	29,402	58.6%	(R) 333 . . . 1.1%	(D) 12,211 . . 41.5%

PRESIDENT

1996	Bill Clinton (D)	26,108	93.3%
	Bob Dole (R)	1,099	3.9%
	Ross Perot (I)	529	1.9%
1992	Bill Clinton (D)	30,394	89.0%
	George Bush (R)	2,242	6.6%
	Ross Perot (I)	1,531	4.4%

UNITED STATES SENATE

1996	Richard J. Durbin (D)	25,033	91.1%
	Al Salvi (R)	1,791	6.5%

GOVERNOR

1994	Jim Edgar (R)	3,751	21.0%
	Dawn Clark Netsch (D)	14,101	79.0%

14th Senate District

House District 27
House District 28

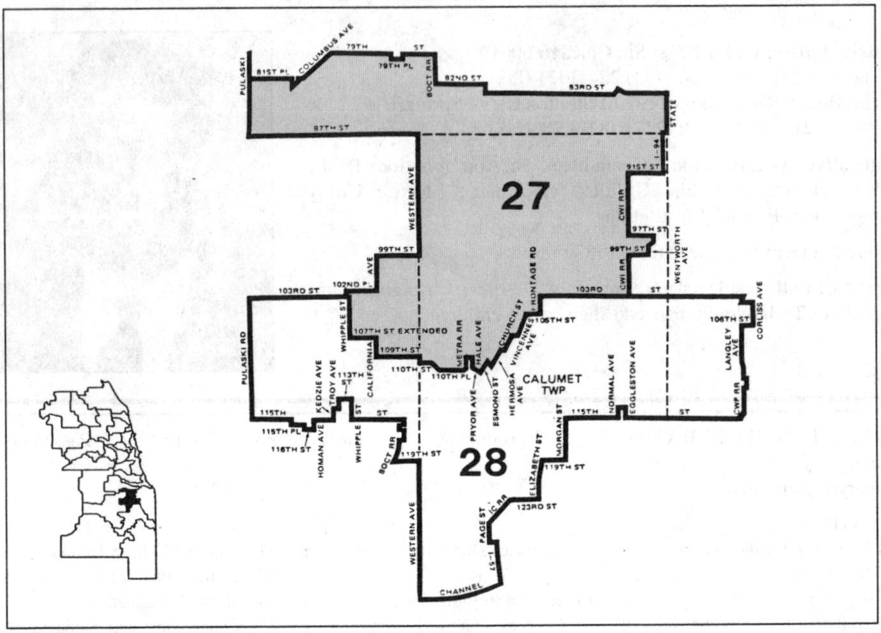

DEMOGRAPHICS (1990)

	S.D. #14	H.D. #27	H.D.#28
VOTING AGE POPULATION	143,167	72,453	70,714
White	32.8%	33.4%	32.3%
Black	64.4%	65.0%	63.9%
Hispanic	2.4%	1.2%	3.7%
Asian	0.3%	0.3%	0.2%
AGE (Total Population)	193,739	96,869	96,870
Under 6	8.5%	8.1%	8.9%
6 to 18	19.2%	18.7%	19.8%
65 and Over	11.8%	12.1%	11.4%
URBAN POPULATION	100.0%	100.0%	100.0%
HOUSING UNITS (Total)	64,993	32,204	32,789
Median Value	$71,768	$74,417	$68,567
Owner Occupied	71.6%	76.8%	66.4%
FAMILY INCOME (Total Families)	47,841	24,294	23,547
Median Income	$39,905	$42,449	$37,073
Below Poverty Level	9.1%	6.7%	11.6%
With Children Under 5	1.0%	1.1%	1.0%
With Children 5 to 17	3.6%	2.5%	4.7%
Headed by Females	6.1%	4.2%	8.0%
INDUSTRY (Total Employed)	85,852	44,834	41,017
Professional/Public Administration	36.2%	37.3%	35.0%
Manufacturing	12.5%	12.1%	12.9%
Retail	13.3%	12.8%	13.9%
Transportation/Communication	12.9%	13.0%	12.9%
Finance/Insurance/Real Estate	8.8%	9.7%	7.9%
Other Service	8.5%	8.1%	9.1%

Senator Emil Jones, Jr. (D)

District Office: 507 West 111th St., Chicago 60628
Phone (773) 995-7748; (773) 995-9061 (fax)
Springfield Office: 309A Capitol Bldg., Springfield 62706
Phone (217) 782-2728

Legislative Assignments: Minority Leader; Executive Committee; Joint Committee on Legislative Support (chair); General Assembly Retirement Systems Board of Trustees (vice-chair).

Public Service: Senator (1983-present); Senate minority leader (1993-present); representative (1973-83).

Personal: Full-time legislator; born October 18, 1935, Chicago; Chicago Loop College, A.A. in business administration; Roosevelt University, B.A. in business administration; married; four children.

1997 BILL PASSAGE RATIO	Introduced	Passed House of Origin	Passed GA
Primary	4	2	1
Primary/Hyphenated	11	5	2

KEY VOTES

1) Senate GOP Ed. $ Plan ......N	6) Insurance/Domestic Violence ..Y	11) Pre-Paid College Tuition ....Y
2) State Budget ....Y	7) Brownfields ....Y	12) Increase Pull Tab Prizes ....Y
3) Tougher DUI Level ....Y	8) Welfare Reform ....Y	13) Telecommunications Tax ...Y
4) Ban Partial Birth Abortions ...O	9) Concealed Guns/Misdemeanor .N	14) Delivery Discrimination ....Y
5) State Employees Pension .....Y	10) Banks Sell Insurance ....Y	15) Sell Drivers' Data ....N

GROUP RATINGS

	FB	CoC	PrLf	IPPC	ACLU
1997	91	40	1/2	50	N/R

ELECTION RESULTS

1994 General	Emil Jones, Jr. (D)	47,079	(77.7%)
1994 General	Richard D. Murphy (R)	13,521	(22.3%)
1994 Primary	Emil Jones, Jr. (D)	39,141	(100%)
1994 Primary	Richard D. Murphy (R)	1,217	(100%)

CAMPAIGN RESOURCES AND EXPENDITURES

1996 Campaign Funds				Top 10 PAC Contributors	
Beg. Balance	$929,687	Individuals	$15,854	1) UFCW ...$15,000	6) RAI $10,000
Receipts	$483,822	Party	$2,000	2) IPACE ...$15,000	7) PR&S $10,000
Expenditures	$1,257,231	PACS	$454,475	3) HOPE $12,500	8) USWA ...$10,000
On hand	$156,278	Candidate	$8,128	4) UNIPAC ..$12,000	9) AO&R ...$10,000
		Not-itemized.	$3,365	5) PSalvi $10,000	10) ITLA ...$10,000

NOTE: The General Election Opponent's Campaign Resources and Expenditures are reported in a separate section in the back of the book (pp. 269-284).

GENERAL ELECTION DATA

	Registered Voters	Voter Turnout		Straight Party Voting	
1996	130,638	88,291	67.6%	(R) 2,820 ...3.2%	(D) 29,712 ...33.7%

PRESIDENT

1996	Bill Clinton (D)	70,407	82.3%
	Bob Dole (R)	11,366	13.3%
	Ross Perot (I)	3,042	3.6%
1992	Bill Clinton (D)	79,480	76.8%
	George Bush (R)	15,764	15.2%
	Ross Perot (I)	8,212	8.0%

UNITED STATES SENATE

1996	Richard J. Durbin (D)	69,548	82.5%
	Al Salvi (R)	12,865	15.3%

GOVERNOR

1994	Jim Edgar (R)	18,894	30.3%
	Dawn Clark Netsch (D)	43,455	69.7%

Representative Monique D. Davis (D)

District Office: 1234 W. 95th St., Chicago 60643
Phone (773) 445-9700
Springfield Office: Room 2040-J Stratton Bldg., Springfield 62706
Phone (217) 782-0010; (217) 782-1795 (fax)

Legislative Assignments: Committees on Appropriations-Human Services (chair); Elementary & Secondary Education (vice-chair); Financial Institutions; Labor & Commerce; Public Utilities.

Public Service: Representative (1987-present).

Personal: Teacher/administrator; born August 19, 1936, Chicago; Chicago State University, B.S. in education and M.S. in guidance; two children.

1997 BILL PASSAGE RATIO	Introduced	Passed House of Origin	Passed GA
Primary	28	4	0
Primary/Hyphenated	70	17	5

KEY VOTES

1) Change Ed. Funding Formula . . Y	6) Insurance/Domestic Violence . . Y	11) Pre-Paid College Tuition . . . . Y
2) State Budget . . . . Y	7) Brownfields . . . . Y	12) Increase Pull Tab Prizes . . . . Y
3) Tougher DUI Level . . . . Y	8) Welfare Reform . . . . Y	13) Utility Deregulation . . . . Y
4) Ban Partial Birth Abortions . . . N	9) Concealed Guns/Misdemeanor . N	14) County Obscenity Standards . N
5) State Employees Pension . . . . . Y	10) Banks Sell Insurance . . . . Y	15) Managed Care Reform . . . . . Y

GROUP RATINGS

	FB	CoC	PrLf	IPPC	ACLU
1997	86	31	0/6	100	100

ELECTION RESULTS

1996 General	Monique D. Davis (D)	39,018	(100%)
1996 Primary	Monique D. Davis (D)	12,782	(62.9%)
1996 Primary	Ronald I. Gaines (D)	5,861	(28.9%)
1996 Primary	Audrey Jones Kenner (D)	1,671	(8.2%)

CAMPAIGN RESOURCES AND EXPENDITURES

1996 Campaign Funds				Top 10 PAC Contributors			
Beg. Balance	$1,743	Individuals	$0	1) ITLA	$1,000	6) AFSCME	$300
Receipts	$5,070	Party	$500	2) CTurner	$500	7) Ameritech	$250
Expenditures	$5,520	PACS	$3,650	3) MPower	$500	8) IBEW	$200
On hand	$1,293	Candidate	$0	4) ABDI	$500	9) IUOE	$200
		Not-itemized	$920	5) CFFU	$300	10) SNAPI	$200

NOTE: The General Election Opponent's Campaign Resources and Expenditures are reported in a separate section in the back of the book (pp. 269-284).

GENERAL ELECTION DATA

	Registered Voters	Voter Turnout		Straight Party Voting	
1996	67,691	46,781	69.1%	(R) 1,492 . . . . 3.2%	(D) 15,452 . . . 33.0%

PRESIDENT

1996	Bill Clinton (D)	37,723	83.2%
	Bob Dole (R)	5,823	12.8%
	Ross Perot (I)	1,465	3.2%
1992	Bill Clinton (D)	41,595	76.5%
	George Bush (R)	8,556	15.7%
	Ross Perot (I)	4,244	7.8%

UNITED STATES SENATE

1996	Richard J. Durbin (D)	37,236	83.3%
	Al Salvi (R)	6,400	14.3%

GOVERNOR

1994	Jim Edgar (R)	9,866	29.5%
	Dawn Clark Netsch (D)	23,607	70.5%

Representative Thomas J. Dart (D)

District Office: 10231 South Western Ave., Chicago 60643
Phone (773) 881-3720; (773) 881-9090 (fax)
507 West 111th St., Chicago 60643
Phone (312) 928-1747
Springfield Office: Room K-2 Stratton Bldg., Springfield 62706
Phone (217) 782-8200; (217) 525-1440 (fax)

Legislative Assignments: Committees on Judiciary I-Civil Law (chair); Prison Management Reform (chair); Revenue; State Government Administration & Election Reform; Health Care Availability & Access.

Public Service: Representative (1993-present); senator (1992-93).

Personal: Full-time legislator; Providence College, B.A. in history and general social studies; Loyola University School of Law, J.D.

1997 BILL PASSAGE RATIO	Introduced	Passed House of Origin	Passed GA
Primary	83	16	7
Primary/Hyphenated	119	31	13

KEY VOTES

1) Change Ed. Funding Formula . . Y
2) State Budget . . . . Y
3) Tougher DUI Level . . . . Y
4) Ban Partial Birth Abortions . . . . P
5) State Employees Pension . . . . . Y
6) Insurance/Domestic Violence . . Y
7) Brownfields . . . . Y
8) Welfare Reform . . . . Y
9) Concealed Guns/Misdemeanor . N
10) Banks Sell Insurance . . . . Y
11) Pre-Paid College Tuition . . . . Y
12) Increase Pull Tab Prizes . . . . Y
13) Utility Deregulation . . . . Y
14) County Obscenity Standards . P
15) Managed Care Reform . . . . . E

GROUP RATINGS

	FB	CoC	PrLf	IPPC	ACLU
1997	71	27	0/6	100	78

ELECTION RESULTS

1996 General	Thomas J. Dart (D)	31,173	(83.8%)
1996 General	Derek Banks (HWP)	6,028	(16.2%)
1996 Primary	Thomas J. Dart (D)	12,428	(67.4%)
1996 Primary	Five others (D)	6,000	(32.6%)

CAMPAIGN RESOURCES AND EXPENDITURES

1996 Campaign Funds

Beg. Balance	$4,110	Individuals	$17,072
Receipts	$85,253	Party	$10,000
Expenditures	$30,174	PACS	$41,336
On hand	$59,189	Candidate	$0
		Not-itemized	$16,845

Top 10 PAC Contributors

1) DSCC $6,500	6) IAMB $1,500
2) ITLA $3,000	7) CAR $1,000
3) TORVAC . . $1,625	8) CMEx $1,000
4) CBOT $1,500	9) LAWPAC . . $1,000
5) UrbRealEstate $1,500	10) CSheahan . $1,000

NOTE: The General Election Opponent's Campaign Resources and Expenditures are reported in a separate section in the back of the book (pp. 269-284).

GENERAL ELECTION DATA

	Registered Voters	Voter Turnout		Straight Party Voting	
1996	62,947	41,510	65.9%	(R) 1,328 . . . 3.2%	(D) 14,260 . . . 34.4%

PRESIDENT

1996	Bill Clinton (D)	32,684	81.4%
	Bob Dole (R)	5,543	13.8%
	Ross Perot (I)	1,577	3.9%
1992	Bill Clinton (D)	37,885	77.2%
	George Bush (R)	7,208	14.7%
	Ross Perot (I)	3,968	8.1%

UNITED STATES SENATE

1996	Richard J. Durbin (D)	32,312	81.5%
	Al Salvi (R)	6,465	16.3%

GOVERNOR

1994	Jim Edgar (R)	9,028	31.3%
	Dawn Clark Netsch (D)	19,848	68.7%

15th Senate District

House District 29
House District 30

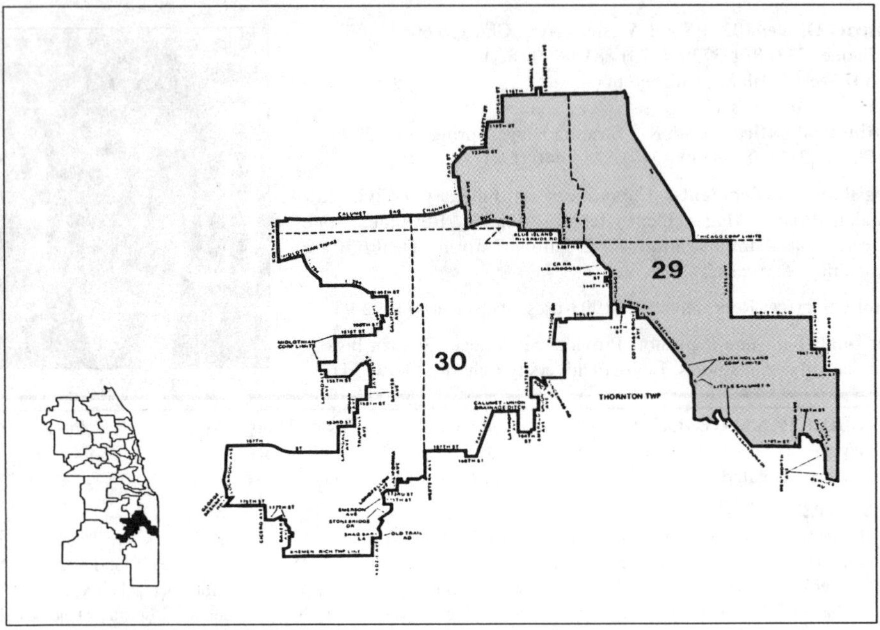

DEMOGRAPHICS (1990)

	S.D. #15	H.D. #29	H.D.#30
VOTING AGE POPULATION	134,046	67,597	66,449
White	34.1%	35.2%	33.0%
Black	60.8%	60.3%	61.3%
Hispanic	4.5%	4.0%	5.0%
Asian	0.5%	0.4%	0.6%
AGE (Total Population)	193,739	96,870	96,869
Under 6	10.0%	9.6%	10.3%
6 to 18	22.6%	22.4%	22.8%
65 and Over	9.9%	9.7%	10.2%
URBAN POPULATION	99.9%	100.0%	99.8%
HOUSING UNITS (Total)	68,123	34,679	33,444
Median Value	$59,721	$62,436	$57,155
Owner Occupied	61.2%	58.6%	64.0%
FAMILY INCOME (Total Families)	48,398	24,639	23,759
Median Income	$33,044	$33,055	$33,033
Below Poverty Level	15.2%	16.1%	14.3%
With Children Under 5	1.8%	1.7%	2.0%
With Children 5 to 17	6.6%	7.9%	5.3%
Headed by Females	10.7%	11.9%	9.4%
INDUSTRY (Total Employed)	79,978	40,151	39,826
Professional/Public Administration	28.6%	28.4%	28.7%
Manufacturing	16.4%	16.1%	16.8%
Retail	16.3%	16.0%	16.6%
Transportation/Communication	12.8%	13.5%	12.0%
Finance/Insurance/Real Estate	8.3%	8.3%	8.2%
Other Service	8.7%	9.1%	8.3%

Senator William "Bill" Shaw (D)

District Office: 3300 W. 159th St., Markham 60426
Phone (708) 333-4700; (708) 333-5392 (fax).
Springfield Office: 103D Capitol Bldg., Springfield 62706
Phone (217) 782-8066; (217) 782-5252 (fax).

Legislative Assignments: Assistant Minority Leader. Committees on Environment & Energy; Local Government & Elections; Judiciary.

Public Service: Senator (1993-present); representative (1983-1993); mayor of Dolton (1997-present).

Personal: Born July 31, 1937, Fulton, Arkansas; Fulton High School, Fulton, AR; married (Shirley); three children.

1997 BILL PASSAGE RATIO	Introduced	Passed House of Origin	Passed GA
Primary	8	2	1
Primary/Hyphenated	15	6	4

KEY VOTES

1) Senate GOP Ed. $ Plan ......N	6) Insurance/Domestic Violence ..O	11) Pre-Paid College Tuition ....Y
2) State Budget ....Y	7) Brownfields ....Y	12) Increase Pull Tab Prizes ....O
3) Tougher DUI Level ....N	8) Welfare Reform ....P	13) Telecommunications Tax ...O
4) Ban Partial Birth Abortions ....P	9) Concealed Guns/Misdemeanor .Y	14) Delivery Discrimination ....O
5) State Employees Pension .....Y	10) Banks Sell Insurance ....Y	15) Sell Drivers' Data ....O

GROUP RATINGS

	FB	CoC	PrLf	IPPC	ACLU
1997	45	N/R	0/2	100	N/R

ELECTION RESULTS

1996 General	William "Bill" Shaw (D)	52,208	(88.4%)
1996 General	Eugene James (R)	6,884	(11.6%)
1996 Primary	William "Bill" Shaw	15,978	(100%)

CAMPAIGN RESOURCES AND EXPENDITURES

1996 Campaign Funds

Beg. Balance	$1,890	Individuals	$8,425
Receipts	$60,991	Party	$6,281
Expenditures	$60,384	PACS	$41,780
On hand	$2,497	Candidate	$0
		Not-itemized	$4,505

Top 10 PAC Contributors

1) IPACE	$5,500	6) ABDI	$1,500
2) Elect	$4,431	7) ILCable	$1,250
3) ISMS	$3,000	8) CTU	$1,000
4) WMgt.	$2,000	9) ITLA	$1,000
5) FRobShaw	$1,850	10) UAW	$1,000

NOTE: The General Election Opponent's Campaign Resources and Expenditures are reported in a separate section in the back of the book (pp. 269-284).

GENERAL ELECTION DATA

	Registered Voters	Voter Turnout		Straight Party Voting	
1996	113,600	64,361	56.7%	(R) 2,835 ... 4.4%	(D) 27,800 ... 43.2%

PRESIDENT

1996	Bill Clinton (D)	53,571	86.2%
	Bob Dole (R)	6,159	9.9%
	Ross Perot (I)	2,432	3.9%
1992	Bill Clinton (D)	58,976	78.1%
	George Bush (R)	10,267	13.6%
	Ross Perot (I)	6,298	8.3%

UNITED STATES SENATE

1996	Richard J. Durbin (D)	51,832	84.1%
	Al Salvi (R)	8,453	13.7%

GOVERNOR

1994	Jim Edgar (R)	13,041	34.7%
	Dawn Clark Netsch (D)	24,504	65.3%

Representative Arline M. Fantin (D)

District Office: 523 Burnham, Calumet City, 60409
Phone (708) 730-0777; (708) 730-0799 (fax)
Springfield Office: 2031-J Stratton Bldg., Springfield 62706
Phone (217) 782-8077; (217) 782-7612 (fax)

Legislative Assignments: Committees on Revenue (vice-chair); Aging; Higher Education; Transportation & Motor Vehicles.

Public Service: Representative (1995-present); assessor, Thornton Township.

Personal: Full-time legislator; four children; two grandchildren.

1997 BILL PASSAGE RATIO	Introduced	Passed House of Origin	Passed GA
Primary	15	6	3
Primary/Hyphenated	72	38	15

KEY VOTES

1) Change Ed. Funding Formula . . Y	6) Insurance/Domestic Violence . . Y	11) Pre-Paid College Tuition . . . . Y
2) State Budget . . . . Y	7) Brownfields . . . . Y	12) Increase Pull Tab Prizes . . . . Y
3) Tougher DUI Level . . . . N	8) Welfare Reform . . . . Y	13) Utility Deregulation . . . . Y
4) Ban Partial Birth Abortions . . . N	9) Concealed Guns/Misdemeanor . N	14) County Obscenity Standards . N
5) State Employees Pension . . . . . Y	10) Banks Sell Insurance . . . . Y	15) Managed Care Reform . . . . . Y

GROUP RATINGS

	FB	CoC	PrLf	IPPC	ACLU
1997	86	23	0/6	83	80

ELECTION RESULTS

1996 General	Arline M. Fantin (D)	27,815	(91.0%)
1996 General	Rich Banske (R)	2,735	(9.0%)
1996 Primary	Arline M. Fantin (D)	4,412	(43.6%)
1996 Primary	Two others (D)	5,717	(56.4%)

CAMPAIGN RESOURCES AND EXPENDITURES

1996 Campaign Funds				Top 10 PAC Contributors			
Beg. Balance	$20,013	Individuals	$250	1) DSCC	$10,000	6) ITLA	$1,000
Receipts	$31,608	Party	$12,150	2) Signature	$1,500	7) UAW	$500
Expenditures	$30,631	PACS	$11,510	3) TDem	$1,000	8) Tombstone	$500
On hand	$20,990	Candidate	$0	4) ABDI	$1,000	9) CJHoffman	$500
		Not-itemized	$7,698	5) IPACE	$1,000	10) LICID	$500

NOTE: The General Election Opponent's Campaign Resources and Expenditures are reported in a separate section in the back of the book (pp. 269-284).

GENERAL ELECTION DATA

	Registered Voters	Voter Turnout		Straight Party Voting	
1996	55,329	33,118	59.9%	(R) 1,247 . . . 3.8%	(D) 13,738 . . . 41.5%

PRESIDENT

1996	Bill Clinton (D)	27,707	86.3%
	Bob Dole (R)	2,940	9.2%
	Ross Perot (I)	1,235	3.8%
1992	Bill Clinton (D)	31,083	79.3%
	George Bush (R)	4,936	12.6%
	Ross Perot (I)	3,168	8.1%

UNITED STATES SENATE

1996	Richard J. Durbin (D)	26,868	84.7%
	Al Salvi (R)	4,094	12.9%

GOVERNOR

1994	Jim Edgar (R)	6,606	32.8%
	Dawn Clark Netsch (D)	13,528	67.2%

Representative Harold Murphy (D)

District Office: 2959 W. 159th St., P.O. Box 25, Markham 60426
Phone (708) 339-8700; (708) 339-8738 (fax)
Springfield Office: Room 2046-J Stratton Bldg., Springfield 62706
Phone (217) 782-5961; (217) 782-1130 (fax)

Legislative Assignments: Committees on Personnel & Pensions (chair); Transportation & Motor Vehicles (vice-chair); Elementary & Secondary Education; Environment & Energy; Health Care Availability & Access; Labor & Commerce.

Public Service: Representative (1993-present); alderman, Markham; trustee, South Suburban College.

Personal: Full-time legislator; born April 1, 1938, Birmingham, AL; Northeastern Illinois University, B.A. in education; married (Loretta); three children.

1997 BILL PASSAGE RATIO	Introduced	Passed House of Origin	Passed GA
Primary	18	3	1
Primary/Hyphenated	25	6	4

KEY VOTES

1) Change Ed. Funding Formula . .Y	6) Insurance/Domestic Violence . .Y	11) Pre-Paid College Tuition . . . .Y
2) State Budget . . . . .Y	7) Brownfields . . . . .Y	12) Increase Pull Tab Prizes . . . .Y
3) Tougher DUI Level . . . . .Y	8) Welfare Reform . . . . .Y	13) Utility Deregulation . . . . . . .Y
4) Ban Partial Birth Abortions . . . .N	9) Concealed Guns/Misdemeanor .N	14) County Obscenity Standards .P
5) State Employees Pension . . . . .Y	10) Banks Sell Insurance . . . . .Y	15) Managed Care Reform . . . . .A

GROUP RATINGS

	FB	CoC	PrLf	IPPC	ACLU
1997	86	44	0/6	100	100

ELECTION RESULTS

1996 General	Harold Murphy (D)	25,649	(100%)
1996 Primary	Harold Murphy (D)	5,420	(78.5%)
1996 Primary	Ronald V. Cummings (D)	1,488	(21.5%)
1994 General	Harold Murphy (D)	13,441	(100%)

CAMPAIGN RESOURCES AND EXPENDITURES

1996 Campaign Funds		Top 10 PAC Contributors	
Beg. Balance . $17,922	Individuals . . .$2,500	1) MPower . . .$1,000	6) CTU $500
Receipts $32,392	Party $2,000	2) ITLA $1,000	7) ClarkR&M . .$500
Expenditures ..$22,796	PACS $19,095	3) CTurner $800	8) Do-All $500
On hand $27,518	Candidate $0	4) G&ESales . . .$525	9) TDem $500
	Not-itemized .$8,797	5) FZuccarelli . .$500	10) OGroup $500

NOTE: The General Election Opponent's Campaign Resources and Expenditures are reported in a separate section in the back of the book (pp. 269-284).

GENERAL ELECTION DATA

	Registered Voters	Voter Turnout	Straight Party Voting	
1996	58,271	31,243 . . . . .53.6%	(R) 1,588 . . . .5.1%	(D) 14,062 . . .45.0%

PRESIDENT

1996	Bill Clinton (D)	25,864	85.1%
	Bob Dole (R)	3,219	10.6%
	Ross Perot (I)	1,197	3.9%
1992	Bill Clinton (D)	27,893	76.7%
	George Bush (R)	5,331	14.7%
	Ross Perot (I)	3,130	8.6%

UNITED STATES SENATE

1996	Richard J. Durbin (D)	24,964	83.1%
	Al Salvi (R)	4,359	14.5%

GOVERNOR

1994	Jim Edgar (R)	6,435	37.0%
	Dawn Clark Netsch (D)	10,976	63.0%

16th Senate District

House District 31
House District 32

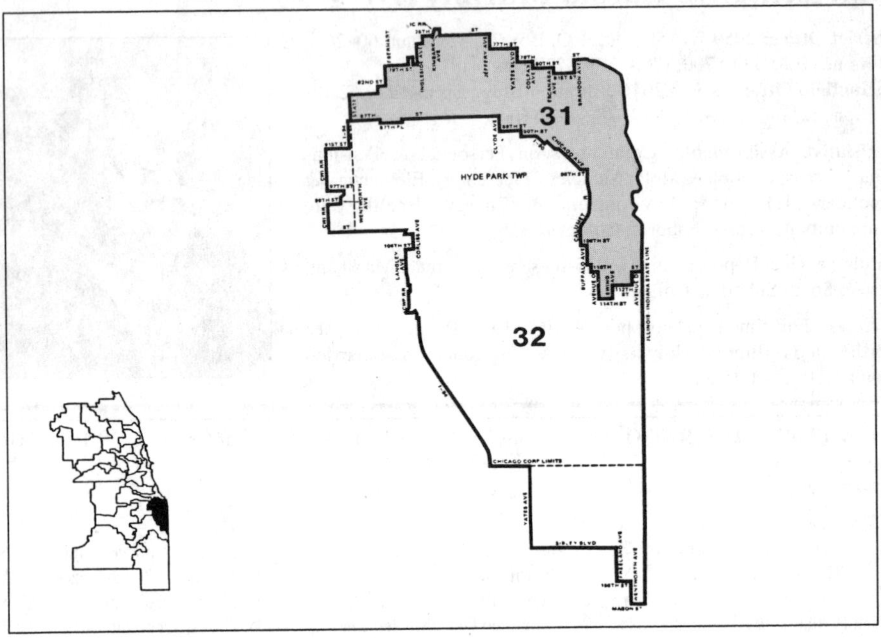

DEMOGRAPHICS (1990)

	S.D. #16	H.D. #31	H.D.#32
VOTING AGE POPULATION	143,779	70,969	72,810
White	20.6%	15.0%	26.1%
Black	65.7%	66.4%	64.9%
Hispanic	13.3%	18.2%	8.5%
Asian	0.2%	0.2%	0.3%
AGE (Total Population)	193,739	96,870	96,869
Under 6	8.4%	8.9%	7.8%
6 to 18	18.9%	19.3%	18.6%
65 and Over	12.8%	12.5%	13.1%
URBAN POPULATION	100.0%	100.0%	100.0%
HOUSING UNITS (Total)	73,474	38,284	35,190
Median Value	$63,131	$62,939	$63,253
Owner Occupied	54.8%	44.0%	66.5%
FAMILY INCOME (Total Families)	48,986	23,845	25,141
Median Income	$32,126	$29,913	$34,912
Below Poverty Level	13.1%	15.9%	10.5%
With Children Under 5	1.6%	2.0%	1.1%
With Children 5 to 17	5.4%	6.0%	4.8%
Headed by Females	8.9%	10.5%	7.4%
INDUSTRY (Total Employed)	82,206	40,194	42,012
Professional/Public Administration	33.3%	32.7%	33.9%
Manufacturing	15.1%	15.3%	14.9%
Retail	13.7%	13.8%	13.6%
Transportation/Communication	12.5%	12.5%	12.5%
Finance/Insurance/Real Estate	8.5%	8.8%	8.3%
Other Service	9.7%	10.5%	8.9%

Senator Donne E. Trotter (D)

District Office: 2954 E. 92nd St., Chicago 60617
Phone (773) 933-7715; (773) 933-5498 (fax)
Springfield Office: Rm. 417 Capitol Bldg., Springfield 62706
Phone (217) 782-320

Legislative Assignments: Committees on Appropriations (minority spokesperson); Local Government & Elections; Environment & Energy; Joint Committee on Rules.

Public Service: Senator (1993-present); representative (1989-1993).

Personal: Hospital administrator; born January 30, 1950, Cairo; Chicago State University, B.A. in history/political science; enrolled in Loyola School of Law; married (Rose); four children.

1997 BILL PASSAGE RATIO	Introduced	Passed House of Origin	Passed GA
Primary	22	0	0
Primary/Hyphenated	42	12	9

KEY VOTES

1) Senate GOP Ed. Plan ....N	6) Insurance/Domestic Violence ..Y	11) Pre-Paid College Tuition ....Y
2) State Budget ....Y	7) Brownfields ....Y	12) Increase Pull Tab Prizes ....Y
3) Tougher DUI Level ....Y	8) Welfare Reform ....Y	13) Telecommunications Tax ...Y
4) Ban Partial Birth Abortions ...O	9) Concealed Guns/Misdemeanor .P	14) Delivery Discrimination ....Y
5) State Employees Pension .....Y	10) Banks Sell Insurance ....Y	15) Sell Drivers' Data ....N

GROUP RATINGS

	FB	CoC	PrLf	IPPC	ACLU
1997	73	60	0/2	100	100

ELECTION RESULTS

1996 General	Donne E. Trotter (D)	65,933	(100%)
1996 Primary	Donne E. Trotter (D)	24,441	(100%)
1992 General	Donne E. Trotter (D)	75,031	(100%)

CAMPAIGN RESOURCES AND EXPENDITURES

1996 Campaign Funds

Beg. Balance	$6,025	Individuals	$1,925
Receipts	$19,200	Party	$0
Expenditures	$14,490	PACS	$14,975
On hand	$10,735	Candidate	$0
		Not-itemized.	$2,300

Top 10 PAC Contributors

1) Ameritech .$1,500	6) IPACE $500
2) ITLA $1,000	7) LICID $500
3) IHCA $1,000	8) IFT $500
4) IBA $750	9) HOPE $500
5) AFLCIO $500	10) RezCon $500

NOTE: The General Election Opponent's Campaign Resources and Expenditures are reported in a separate section in the back of the book (pp. 269-284).

GENERAL ELECTION DATA

	Registered Voters	Voter Turnout		Straight Party Voting	
1996	119,778	75,314	62.9%	(R) 1,444 ....1.9%	(D) 28,360 ...37.7%

PRESIDENT

1996	Bill Clinton (D)	66,036	90.8%
	Bob Dole (R)	4,195	5.8%
	Ross Perot (I)	2,000	2.8%
1992	Bill Clinton (D)	76,996	85.7%
	George Bush (R)	7,457	8.3%
	Ross Perot (I)	5,342	6.0%

UNITED STATES SENATE

1996	Richard J. Durbin (D)	63,670	88.9%
	Al Salvi (R)	6,247	8.7%

GOVERNOR

1994	Jim Edgar (R)	12,546	24.7%
	Dawn Clark Netsch (D)	38,297	75.3%

Representative Todd H. Stroger (D)

District Office: 8539 S. Cottage Grove Ave., Chicago 60619
Phone (773) 783-8492; (773) 783-8625 (fax)
Springfield Office: 2054-L Stratton Bldg., Springfield 62706
Phone (217) 782-8272; (217) 782-2404 (fax)

Legislative Assignments: Committees on Local Government (chair); Insurance; Health Care Availabilty & Access; Human Services; Personnel & Pensions.

Public Service: Representative (1993-present).

Personal: Born January 14, 1963; Xavier University, B.A. in history; married (Jeanine).

1997 BILL PASSAGE RATIO	Introduced	Passed House of Origin	Passed GA
Primary	14	3	1
Primary/Hyphenated	18	4	1

KEY VOTES

1) Change Ed. Funding Formula . . Y	6) Insurance/Domestic Violence . . Y	11) Pre-Paid College Tuition . . . . Y
2) State Budget . . . . Y	7) Brownfields . . . . Y	12) Increase Pull Tab Prizes . . . . Y
3) Tougher DUI Level . . . . Y	8) Welfare Reform . . . . Y	13) Utility Deregulation . . . . Y
4) Ban Partial Birth Abortions . . . N	9) Concealed Guns/Misdemeanor . N	14) County Obscenity Standards . N
5) State Employees Pension . . . . . Y	10) Banks Sell Insurance . . . . Y	15) Managed Care Reform . . . . . Y

GROUP RATINGS

	FB	CoC	PrLf	IPPC	ACLU
1997	86	15	0/6	100	90

ELECTION RESULTS

1996 General	Todd H. Stroger (D)	30,522	(93.0%)
1996 General	John E. Zart (R)	2,267	(6.9%)
1996 Primary	Todd H. Stroger (D)	13,148	(100%)
1996 Primary	John E. Zart (D)	467	(100%)

CAMPAIGN RESOURCES AND EXPENDITURES

1996 Campaign Funds

Beg. Balance	$13,634	Individuals	$11,026
Receipts	$43,650	Party	$950
Expenditures	$37,053	PACS	$31,674
On hand	$20,231	Candidate	$0
		Not-itemized	$0

Top 10 PAC Contributors

1) Excalibur . . $5,699	6) IBA $750
2) ITLA $2,000	7) PMC $500
3) MPower . . . $1,100	8) CTurner $500
4) KenwoodLiq$1,000	9) IPACE $500
5) ABDI $800	10) UAW $500

NOTE: The General Election Opponent's Campaign Resources and Expenditures are reported in a separate section in the back of the book (pp. 269-284).

GENERAL ELECTION DATA

	Registered Voters	Voter Turnout		Straight Party Voting	
1996	56,023	35,148	62.7%	(R) 598 . . . . . 1.7%	(D) 13,689 . . . 38.9%

PRESIDENT

1996	Bill Clinton (D)	31,095	91.8%
	Bob Dole (R)	1,768	5.2%
	Ross Perot (I)	787	2.3%
1992	Bill Clinton (D)	35,818	87.3%
	George Bush (R)	3,114	7.6%
	Ross Perot (I)	2,090	5.1%

UNITED STATES SENATE

1996	Richard J. Durbin (D)	29,921	89.7%
	Al Salvi (R)	2,670	8.0%

GOVERNOR

1994	Jim Edgar (R)	5,370	23.2%
	Dawn Clark Netsch (D)	17,804	76.8%

Representative Constance A. Howard (D)

District Office: 8800 South Cottage Grove, Chicago 60619
Phone (773) 783-8800; (773) 723-9688 (fax)
Springfield Office: Room 2094-M Stratton Bldg., Springfield
Phone (217) 782-6476

Legislative Assignments: Committees on Children & Youth (vice-chair); Appropriations-Education; Environment & Energy; Human Services; Labor & Commerce.

Public Service: Representative (1995-present); State Central Committeeperson, 1st Congressional District.

Personal: Full-time legislator; born December 14, 1942, Chicago; Chicago State University, B.S. and M.S. in corrections and criminal justice; married (Phillip, Jr.); one son; three granddaughters.

1997 BILL PASSAGE RATIO	Introduced	Passed House of Origin	Passed GA
Primary	10	3	2
Primary/Hyphenated	36	10	4

KEY VOTES

1) Change Ed. Funding Formula . . Y	6) Insurance/Domestic Violence . . Y	11) Pre-Paid College Tuition . . . . Y
2) State Budget . . . . Y	7) Brownfields . . . . A	12) Increase Pull Tab Prizes . . . . Y
3) Tougher DUI Level . . . . Y	8) Welfare Reform . . . . Y	13) Utility Deregulation . . . . Y
4) Ban Partial Birth Abortions . . . N	9) Concealed Guns/Misdemeanor . Y	14) County Obscenity Standards . N
5) State Employees Pension . . . . . Y	10) Banks Sell Insurance . . . . Y	15) Managed Care Reform . . . . . Y

GROUP RATINGS

	FB	CoC	PrLf	IPPC	ACLU
1997	86	23	0/6	100	100

ELECTION RESULTS

1996 General	Constance A. Howard (D)	34,798	(100%)
1996 Primary	Constance A. Howard (D)	12,031	(100%)
1994 General	Constance A. Howard (D)	22,423	(87.2%)
1994 General	Lee H. Anglin (R)	3,304	(12.8%)

CAMPAIGN RESOURCES AND EXPENDITURES

1996 Campaign Funds				Top 10 PAC Contributors			
Beg. Balance	$1,040	Individuals	$3,217	1) IPACE	$2,500	6) UAW	$500
Receipts	$19,119	Party	$1,351	2) ITLA	$2,000	7) CTurner	$500
Expenditures	$16,741	PACS	$12,300	3) Ameritech	$1,035	8) CPA's	$400
On hand	$3,418	Candidate	$0	4) MPower	$1,000	9) TriPClub	$400
		Not-itemized	$2,251	5) ILBC	$676	10) CUPAC	$350

NOTE: The General Election Opponent's Campaign Resources and Expenditures are reported in a separate section in the back of the book (pp. 269-284).

GENERAL ELECTION DATA

	Registered Voters	Voter Turnout		Straight Party Voting			
1996	63,755	40,166	63.0%	(R) 846	2.1%	(D) 14,671	36.5%

PRESIDENT

1996	Bill Clinton (D)	34,941	89.9%
	Bob Dole (R)	2,427	6.3%
	Ross Perot (I)	1,213	3.1%
1992	Bill Clinton (D)	41,178	84.4%
	George Bush (R)	4,343	8.9%
	Ross Perot (I)	3,252	6.7%

UNITED STATES SENATE

1996	Richard J. Durbin (D)	33,758	88.2%
	Al Salvi (R)	3,577	9.4%

GOVERNOR

1994	Jim Edgar (R)	7,176	25.9%
	Dawn Clark Netsch (D)	20,493	74.1%

17th Senate District

House District 33
House District 34

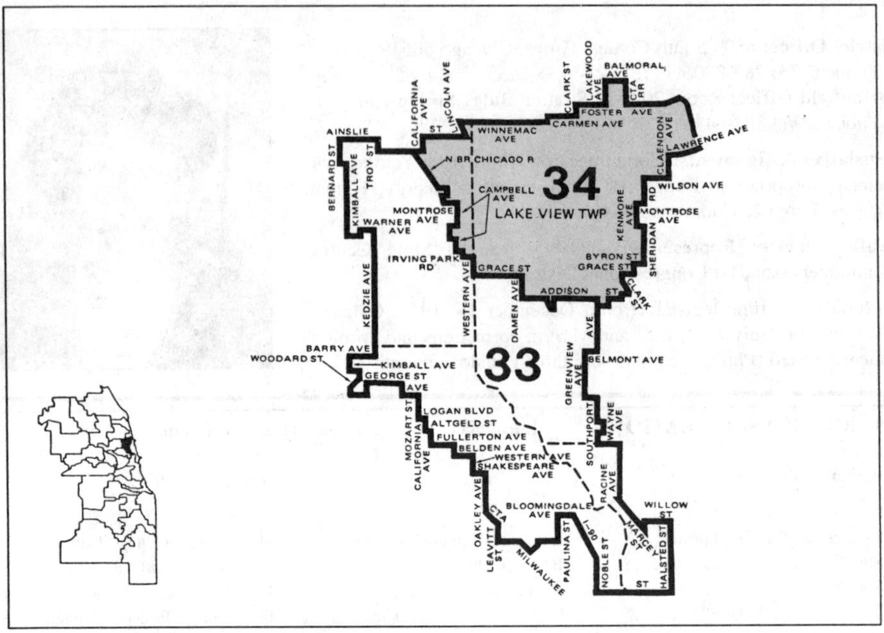

DEMOGRAPHICS (1990)

	S.D. #17	H.D. #33	H.D.#34
VOTING AGE POPULATION	149,195	72,623	76,572
White	56.1%	56.2%	56.1%
Black	6.6%	3.0%	9.9%
Hispanic	27.7%	33.9%	21.9%
Asian	8.9%	6.4%	11.2%
AGE (Total Population)	193,739	96,870	96,869
Under 6	8.8%	9.5%	8.1%
6 to 18	15.5%	16.9%	14.0%
65 and Over	10.8%	9.8%	11.7%
URBAN POPULATION	100.0%	100.0%	100.0%
HOUSING UNITS (Total)	86,458	40,728	45,730
Median Value	$111,321	$105,429	$121,050
Owner Occupied	24.9%	31.9%	18.7%
FAMILY INCOME (Total Families)	42,816	22,351	20,465
Median Income	$29,811	$30,664	$28,641
Below Poverty Level	16.3%	14.4%	18.5%
With Children Under 5	2.7%	2.0%	3.4%
With Children 5 to 17	6.0%	5.2%	6.8%
Headed by Females	8.6%	7.8%	9.5%
INDUSTRY (Total Employed)	95,974	47,590	48,384
Professional/Public Administration	26.3%	23.4%	29.1%
Manufacturing	21.0%	23.3%	18.7%
Retail	16.4%	15.8%	16.9%
Transportation/Communication	5.9%	6.0%	5.8%
Finance/Insurance/Real Estate	8.2%	8.0%	8.5%
Other Service	12.8%	12.7%	12.8%

Senator Bruce A. Farley (D)

District Office: 4740 North Lincoln Ave., Chicago 60625
Phone (773) 728-6300; (773) 728-9927 (fax)
Springfield Office: 105A Capitol Bldg., Springfield 62706
Phone (217) 782-8191; (217) 782-5340 (fax)

Legislative Assignments: Committees on Environment and Energy Committee (minority spokesperson); Commerce and Industry.

Public Service: Senator (1993-present); representative (1973-1993).

Personal: Full-time legislator; born April 12, 1943, Los Angeles, CA; Loyola University, B.S. in political science; married (Karen); two children.

1997 BILL PASSAGE RATIO	Introduced	Passed House of Origin	Passed GA
Primary	14	3	3
Primary/Hyphenated	44	26	18

KEY VOTES

1) Senate GOP Ed. $ Plan ......N
2) StateBudget ....Y
3) Tougher DUI Level ....Y
4) Ban Partial Birth Abortions ...Y
5) State Employees Pension .....Y
6) Insurance/Domestic Violence ..Y
7) Brownfields ....Y
8) Welfare Reform ....Y
9) Concealed Guns/Misdemeanor .N
10) Banks Sell Insurance ....Y
11) Pre-Paid College Tuition ....Y
12) Increase Pull Tab Prizes ....Y
13) Telecommunications Tax ...Y
14) Delivery Discrimination ....Y
15) Sell Drivers' Data ....O

GROUP RATINGS

	FB	CoC	PrLf	IPPC	ACLU
1997	68	60	1/2	50	75

ELECTION RESULTS

1994 General	Bruce A. Farley (D)	25,708	(99.9%)
1994 General	Mark J. Almberg (W-I)	21	(.1%)
1994 Primary	Bruce A. Farley (D)	17,809	(100%)
1992 General	Bruce A. Farley (D)	47,373	(100%)

CAMPAIGN RESOURCES AND EXPENDITURES

1996 Campaign Funds

Beg. Balance	$79,848	Individuals	$1,600
Receipts	$39,733	Party	$0
Expenditures	$20,477	PACS	$33,558
On hand	$99,104	Candidate	$0
		Not-itemized	$4,575

Top 10 PAC Contributors

1) ISMS	$2,498	6) ILCable	$1,000
2) HI.	$2,000	7) UNIPAC	$1,000
3) IBA	$1,500	8) Ameritech	$750
4) CTU	$1,000	9) Sears	$750
5) IPACE	$1,000	10) PetPec	$500

NOTE: The General Election Opponent's Campaign Resources and Expenditures are reported in a separate section in the back of the book (pp. 269-284).

GENERAL ELECTION DATA

	Registered Voters	Voter Turnout		Straight Party Voting	
1996	90,447	57,128	63.2%	(R) 3,611 ....6.3%	(D) 19,521 ...34.1%

PRESIDENT

1996	Bill Clinton (D)	41,149	74.5%
	Bob Dole (R)	10,459	18.9%
	Ross Perot (I)	2,972	5.4%
1992	Bill Clinton (D)	44,209	65.3%
	George Bush (R)	14,660	21.6%
	Ross Perot (I)	8,846	13.1%

UNITED STATES SENATE

1996	Richard J. Durbin (D)	42,048	76.9%
	Al Salvi (R)	11,045	20.2%

GOVERNOR

1994	Jim Edgar (R)	15,157	41.8%
	Dawn Clark Netsch (D)	21,109	58.2%

Representative John A. Fritchey (D)

District Office: 3649 North Kedzie Ave., Chicago 60618
Phone (773) 583-3338; (773) 478-8006 (fax)
Springfield Office: Room 2069-L Stratton Bldg., Springfield 62706
Phone (217) 782-2458

Legislative Assignments: Committees on Executive (vice chair); Local Government; Appropriations-General Services & Government Oversight; Consumer Protection.

Public Service: Representative (1997-present).

Personal: Attorney; born March 2, 1964, Bossier City, Louisiana; University of Michigan, B.A. in Economics; Northwestern University Law School, J.D.

1997 BILL PASSAGE RATIO	Introduced	Passed House of Origin	Passed GA
Primary	11	5	1
Primary/Hyphenated	18	8	2

KEY VOTES

1) Change Ed. Funding Formula . . Y	6) Insurance/Domestic Violence . . Y	11) Pre-Paid College Tuition . . . . Y
2) State Budget . . . . Y	7) Brownfields . . . . Y	12) Increase Pull Tab Prizes . . . . Y
3) Tougher DUI Level . . . . Y	8) Welfare Reform . . . . Y	13) Utility Deregulation . . . . Y
4) Ban Partial Birth Abortions . . . N	9) Concealed Guns/Misdemeanor . N	14) County Obscenity Standards . N
5) State Employees Pension . . . . . Y	10) Banks Sell Insurance . . . . Y	15) Managed Care Reform . . . . . Y

GROUP RATINGS

	FB	CoC	PrLf	IPPC	ACLU
1997	75	25	0/6	100	80

ELECTION RESULTS

1996 General	John A. Fritchey (D)	21,266	(100%)
1996 Primary	John A. Fritchey (D)	6,555	(64.6%)
1996 Primary	Kevin Lamm (D)	3,584	(35.3%)
1996 Primary	Jim R. Blasinski (R)	943	(100%)

CAMPAIGN RESOURCES AND EXPENDITURES

1996 Campaign Funds

Beg. Balance	$2,746	Individuals	$4,750
Receipts	$36,984	Party	$1,000
Expenditures	$39,072	PACS	$23,000
On hand	$658	Candidate	$2,284
		Not-itemized	$5,950

Top 10 PAC Contributors

1) TIP $5,000	6) WiltonInd . . $1,000
2) ITLA $3,000	7) NeidlesEnt . . $500
3) LAWPAC . . $1,000	8) IMPAC $500
4) Empress . . . $1,000	9) UAW $500
5) Carmichael . $1,000	10) C&GL $500

NOTE: The General Election Opponent's Campaign Resources and Expenditures are reported in a separate section in the back of the book (pp. 269-284).

GENERAL ELECTION DATA

	Registered Voters	Voter Turnout		Straight Party Voting	
1996	44,866	28,945	64.5%	(R) 1,808 . . . . 6.3%	(D) 9,989 . . . 34.5%

PRESIDENT

1996	Bill Clinton (D)	20,630	73.5%
	Bob Dole (R)	5,515	19.7%
	Ross Perot (I)	1,594	5.7%
1992	Bill Clinton (D)	21,996	63.7%
	George Bush (R)	7,720	22.4%
	Ross Perot (I)	4,796	13.9%

UNITED STATES SENATE

1996	Richard J. Durbin (D)	20,961	75.7%
	Al Salvi (R)	5,905	21.3%

GOVERNOR

1994	Jim Edgar (R)	8,135	43.5%
	Dawn Clark Netsch (D)	10,551	56.5%

Representative Larry McKeon (D)

District Office: 1967 West Montrose, Chicago 60613
Phone (773) 348-3434; (773) 348-3475 (fax)
Springfield Office: 2076 K Stratton Building, Springfield 62706
Phone (217) 782-3835

Legislative Assignments: Committees on Health Care Availability & Access; Human Services; Judiciary II-Criminal Law; Higher Education; Labor & Commerce; Aging.

Public Service: Representative (1997-present).

Personal: Born June 30, 1944; full-time legislator; California State University at Los Angeles, B.A. in Political Science and M.S. in Public Administration; School of Social Service Administration at the University of Chicago, Ph.D.; single.

1997 BILL PASSAGE RATIO	Introduced	Passed House of Origin	Passed GA
Primary	9	1	1
Primary/Hyphenated	61	27	9

KEY VOTES

1) Change Ed. Funding Formula . . Y	6) Insurance/Domestic Violence . . A	11) Pre-Paid College Tuition . . . . Y
2) State Budget . . . . Y	7) Brownfields . . . . Y	12) Increase Pull Tab Prizes . . . . Y
3) Tougher DUI Level . . . . Y	8) Welfare Reform . . . . Y	13) Utility Deregulation . . . . Y
4) Ban Partial Birth Abortions . . . N	9) Concealed Guns/Misdemeanor . N	14) County Obscenity Standards . N
5) State Employees Pension . . . . . Y	10) Banks Sell Insurance . . . . Y	15) Managed Care Reform . . . . . Y

GROUP RATINGS

	FB	CoC	PrLf	IPPC	ACLU
1997	86	23	0/6	100	90

ELECTION RESULTS

1996 General	Larry McKeon (D)	21,048	(80.5%)
1996 General	Robert F. Lytle (R)	5,086	(19.5%)
1996 Primary	Larry McKeon (D)	4,217	(39.2%)
1996 Primary	Three others (D)	6,533	(60.8%)

CAMPAIGN RESOURCES AND EXPENDITURES

1996 Campaign Funds

Beg. Balance . . $1,246	Individuals . . . $5,600		
Receipts $49,455	Party $2,350		
Expenditures . $40,537	PACS $28,100		
On hand $10,164	Candidate $0		
	Not-itemized $13,405		

Top 10 PAC Contributors

1) IMPACT . . $2,100	6) CSchulter . . $1,000
2) IFHR $2,000	7) IPACE $1,000
3) ITLA $2,000	8) CMSmith . . . $750
4) VictoryFund $1,000	9) NASW $600
5) SEIU $1,000	10) Ameritech . . $500

NOTE: The General Election Opponent's Campaign Resources and Expenditures are reported in a separate section in the back of the book (pp. 269-284).

GENERAL ELECTION DATA

	Registered Voters	Voter Turnout		Straight Party Voting	
1996	 45,581	28,183	. . . . 61.8%	(R) 1,803 . . . . 6.4%	(D) 9,532 . . . . 33.8%

PRESIDENT

1996	Bill Clinton (D)	20,519	75.4%
	Bob Dole (R)	4,944	18.2%
	Ross Perot (I)	1,378	5.1%
1992	Bill Clinton (D)	22,213	66.9%
	George Bush (R)	6,940	20.9%
	Ross Perot (I)	4,050	12.2%

UNITED STATES SENATE

1996	Richard J. Durbin (D)	21,087	78.1%
	Al Salvi (R)	5,140	19.1%

GOVERNOR

1994	Jim Edgar (R)	7,022	39.9%
	Dawn Clark Netsch (D)	10,558	60.1%

18th Senate District

House District 35
House District 36

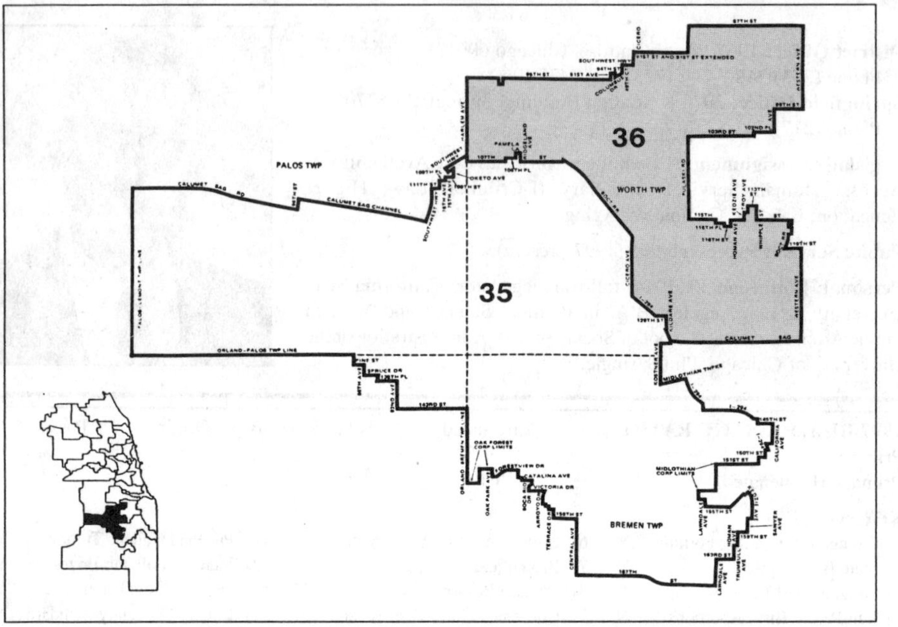

DEMOGRAPHICS (1990)

	S.D. #18	H.D. #35	H.D.#36
VOTING AGE POPULATION	147,911	72,360	75,551
White	94.4%	94.4%	94.3%
Black	1.7%	1.9%	1.4%
Hispanic	2.8%	2.3%	3.2%
Asian	1.1%	1.3%	0.9%
AGE (Total Population)	193,739	96,869	96,870
Under 6	8.5%	8.7%	8.3%
6 to 18	16.3%	17.9%	14.8%
65 and Over	15.0%	11.5%	18.5%
URBAN POPULATION	99.7%	99.3%	100.0%
HOUSING UNITS (Total)	72,994	34,079	38,915
Median Value	$98,658	$105,264	$94,450
Owner Occupied	73.3%	78.9%	68.4%
FAMILY INCOME (Total Families)	51,957	25,855	26,102
Median Income	$45,303	$47,151	$43,162
Below Poverty Level	3.3%	3.0%	3.7%
With Children Under 5	0.6%	0.4%	0.9%
With Children 5 to 17	1.1%	1.1%	1.2%
Headed by Females	1.7%	1.5%	1.9%
INDUSTRY (Total Employed)	97,093	49,815	47,278
Professional/Public Administration	25.8%	25.0%	26.5%
Manufacturing	14.5%	14.5%	14.5%
Retail	18.6%	18.8%	18.4%
Transportation/Communication	9.4%	9.6%	9.1%
Finance/Insurance/Real Estate	9.2%	9.2%	9.3%
Other Service	8.4%	8.1%	8.7%

Senator Patrick J. O'Malley (R)

District Office: 5100 W. 127th St., Alsip 60658
Phone (708) 396-1818; (708) 597-1580 (fax)
Springfield Office: 129 Capitol Bldg., Springfield 62706
Phone (217) 782-5145; (217) 782-4079 (fax)

Legislative Assignments: Committees on Financial Institutions (chair); Education (vice-chair); Judiciary; Insurance & Pensions.

Public Service: Senator (1993-present); Trustee, Moraine Valley Community College (1989-92); Trustee, Palos Fire Protection District (1986-95).

Personal: Attorney; born October 22, 1950, Evergreen Park; Purdue University, B.S. in economics, M.S.in finance; John Marshall Law School, J.D.; married (Mary Judith); two children.

1997 BILL PASSAGE RATIO	Introduced	Passed House of Origin	Passed GA
Primary	39	22	15
Primary/Hyphenated	51	29	21

KEY VOTES

1) Senate GOP Ed. $ Plan . . . . . .Y	6) Insurance/Domestic Violence . .Y	11) Pre-Paid College Tuition . . . .Y
2) State Budget . . . . .Y	7) Brownfields . . . . .Y	12) Increase Pull Tab Prizes . . . .N
3) Tougher DUI Level . . . . .Y	8) Welfare Reform . . . . .Y	13) Telecommunications Tax . . . .P
4) Ban Partial Birth Abortions . . .Y	9) Concealed Guns/Misdemeanor .Y	14) Delivery Discrimination . . . .P
5) State Employees Pension . . . . .Y	10) Banks Sell Insurance . . . . .Y	15) Sell Drivers' Data . . . . .N

GROUP RATINGS

	FB	CoC	PrLf	IPPC	ACLU
1997	86	80	2/2	0	50

ELECTION RESULTS

1996 General	Patrick J. O'Malley (R)	42,933	(59.3%)
1996 General	Dennis Kibby (D)	29,498	(40.7%)
1996 Primary	Patrick J. O'Malley (R)	10,161	(100%)
1996 Primary	Dennis Kibby (D)	7,573	(100%)

CAMPAIGN RESOURCES AND EXPENDITURES

1996 Campaign Funds		Top 10 PAC Contributors	
Beg. Balance .$66,503	Individuals . .$17,199	1) RSSC $9,154	6) ABDI $2,500
Receipts $153,512	Party $15,179	2) ISMS $3,700	7) Ameritech . .$2,370
Expenditures .$209,595	PACS $94,987	3) CRausch . .$3,000	8) PIIA $2,250
On hand $10,420	Candidate $9,000	4) LIPAC $3,000	9) ClarkR&M .$1,850
	Not-itemized $17,147	5) BankersL&C$2,779	10) LICID . . .$1,750

NOTE: The General Election Opponent's Campaign Resources and Expenditures are reported in a separate section in the back of the book (pp. 269-284).

GENERAL ELECTION DATA

Registered Voters	Voter Turnout	Straight Party Voting	
1996 114,449	74,159 . . . . .64.8%	(R) 13,717 . .18.5%	(D) 12,016 . . .16.2%

PRESIDENT

1996	Bill Clinton (D)	33,477	46.0%
	Bob Dole (R)	32,062	44.0%
	Ross Perot (I)	6,831	9.4%
1992	Bill Clinton (D)	30,863	34.8%
	George Bush (R)	39,502	44.6%
	Ross Perot (I)	18,272	20.6%

UNITED STATES SENATE

1996	Richard J. Durbin (D)	34,998	48.9%
	Al Salvi (R)	34,508	48.2%

GOVERNOR

1994	Jim Edgar (R)	39,970	73.0%
	Dawn Clark Netsch (D)	14,802	27.0%

Representative M. Maggie Crotty (D)

District Office: 16150 South Cicero, Suite 11, Oak Forest 60452
Phone (708) 687-9696; (708) 687-0308 (fax)
Springfield Office: Room 2086-M Stratton Bldg., Springfield 62706
Phone (217) 782-9747

Legislative Assignments: Committees on Aging; Appropriations-Education; Elementary & Secondary Education; Registration & Regulation; Children & Youth.

Public Service: Representative (1997-present); District 145 school board president (1986-1993); school board member (1978-1993).

Personal: Born October 16, 1948; Mercy High School; married (Larry); three children.

1997 BILL PASSAGE RATIO	Introduced	Passed House of Origin	Passed GA
Primary	7	1	0
Primary/Hyphenated	24	8	2

KEY VOTES

1) Change Ed. Funding Formula . .N	6) Insurance/Domestic Violence . .Y	11) Pre-Paid College Tuition . . . .Y
2) State Budget . . . . .Y	7) Brownfields . . . . .N	12) Increase Pull Tab Prizes . . . .Y
3) Tougher DUI Level . . . . .Y	8) Welfare Reform . . . . .N	13) Utility Deregulation . . . . . . .N
4) Ban Partial Birth Abortions . . .N	9) Concealed Guns/Misdemeanor .N	14) County Obscenity Standards .Y
5) State Employees Pension . . . . .Y	10) Banks Sell Insurance . . . . .Y	15) Managed Care Reform . . . . .Y

GROUP RATINGS

	FB	CoC	PrLf	IPPC	ACLU
1997	50	31	2/6	66	50

ELECTION RESULTS

1996 General	M. Maggie Crotty (D)	19,711	(53.7%)
1996 General	Jack O'Connor (R)	16,981	(46.3%)
1996 Primary	M. Maggie Crotty (D)	2,321	(100%)
1996 Primary	Jack O'Connor (R)	5,532	(100%)

CAMPAIGN RESOURCES AND EXPENDITURES

1996 Campaign Funds

Beg. Balance	$7,312	Individuals	$10,803
Receipts	$295,021	Party	$188,097
Expenditures	$259,457	PACS	$87,002
On hand	$42,876	Candidate	$0
		Not-itemized	$9,119

Top 10 PAC Contributors

1)IHDM	$139,750	6) WVWV	$8,000
2) IPACE	$29,135	7) IFT	$5,891
3) DSCC	$28,813	8) PersPAC	$5,309
4) DPI	$8,670	9) SEIU	$5,000
5) ITLA	$8,000	10) CLang	$3,000

NOTE: The General Election Opponent's Campaign Resources and Expenditures are reported in a separate section in the back of the book (pp. 269-284).

GENERAL ELECTION DATA

	Registered Voters	Voter Turnout		Straight Party Voting	
1996	58,223	37,466	64.4%	(R) 7,589 . . 20.3%	(D) 5,539 . . . 14.8%

PRESIDENT

1996	Bill Clinton (D)	15,886	43.1%
	Bob Dole (R)	17,097	46.4%
	Ross Perot (I)	3,686	10.0%
1992	Bill Clinton (D)	14,407	32.4%
	George Bush (R)	19,959	44.9%
	Ross Perot (I)	9,641	22.7%

UNITED STATES SENATE

1996	Richard J. Durbin (D)	16,562	45.7%
	Al Salvi (R)	18,548	51.2%

GOVERNOR

1994	Jim Edgar (R)	20,175	74.8%
	Dawn Clark Netsch (D)	6,802	25.2%

Representative James D. "Jim" Brosnahan (D)

District Office: 5309 West 95th St., Oak Lawn 60453
Phone (708) 499-2810
Springfield Office: Room K-1 Stratton Bldg., Springfield 62706
Phone (217) 782-0515

Legislative Assignments: Committees on Health Care Availability & Access; Judiciary I-Civil Law; Labor & Commerce; Appropriations-General Services; Aging.

Public Service: Representative (1997-present); assistant state's attorney.

Personal: Born July 5, 1963; Loyola University of Chicago, B.A., and J.D.; married (Janet); two children.

1997 BILL PASSAGE RATIO	Introduced	Passed House of Origin	Passed GA
Primary	12	2	1
Primary/Hyphenated	31	10	5

KEY VOTES

1) Change Ed. Funding Formula . . Y	6) Insurance/Domestic Violence . . Y	11) Pre-Paid College Tuition . . . . Y
2) State Budget . . . . Y	7) Brownfields . . . . N	12) Increase Pull Tab Prizes . . . N
3) Tougher DUI Level . . . . Y	8) Welfare Reform . . . . N	13) Utility Deregulation . . . . N
4) Ban Partial Birth Abortions . . . Y	9) Concealed Guns/Misdemeanor . N	14) County Obscenity Standards . Y
5) State Employees Pension . . . . . Y	10) Banks Sell Insurance . . . . Y	15) Managed Care Reform . . . . . Y

GROUP RATINGS

	FB	CoC	PrLf	IPPC	ACLU
1997	71	23	6/6	0	10

ELECTION RESULTS

1996 General	James D. "Jim" Brosnahan (D)	20,201	(56.1%)
1996 General	Maureen Murphy (R)	15,798	(43.9%)
1996 Primary	James D. "Jim" Brosnahan (D)	4,528	(100%)
1996 Primary	Maureen Murphy (R)	4,625	(100%)

CAMPAIGN RESOURCES AND EXPENDITURES

1996 Campaign Funds		Top 10 PAC Contributors	
Beg. Balance . . $8,922	Individuals $390	1) IHDM . . $119,083	6) UDI $3,000
Receipts $184,443	Party $142,668	2) DSCC . . . $10,000	7) CDart $2,000
Expenditures . $184,950	PACS $22,990	3) DPI $7,939	8) CFLabor . . . $1,500
On hand $8,415	Candidate $0	4) ITLA $5,000	9) LAWPAC . . $1,500
	Not-itemized $18,395	5) C&GL $3,000	10) USWA . . . $1,500

NOTE: The General Election Opponent's Campaign Resources and Expenditures are reported in a separate section in the back of the book (pp. 269-284).

GENERAL ELECTION DATA

Registered Voters	Voter Turnout	Straight Party Voting	
1996 56,226	36,693 . . . . 65.3%	(R) 6,128 . . . 16.7%	(D) 6,477 . . . . 17.7%

PRESIDENT

1996	Bill Clinton (D)	17,591	48.9%
	Bob Dole (R)	14,965	41.6%
	Ross Perot (I)	3,145	8.8%
1992	Bill Clinton (D)	16,456	36.9%
	George Bush (R)	19,543	43.8%
	Ross Perot (I)	8,631	19.3%

UNITED STATES SENATE

1996	Richard J. Durbin (D)	18,436	52.1%
	Al Salvi (R)	15,960	45.1%

GOVERNOR

1994	Jim Edgar (R)	19,795	71.2%
	Dawn Clark Netsch (D)	8,000	28.8%

19th Senate District

House District 37
House District 38

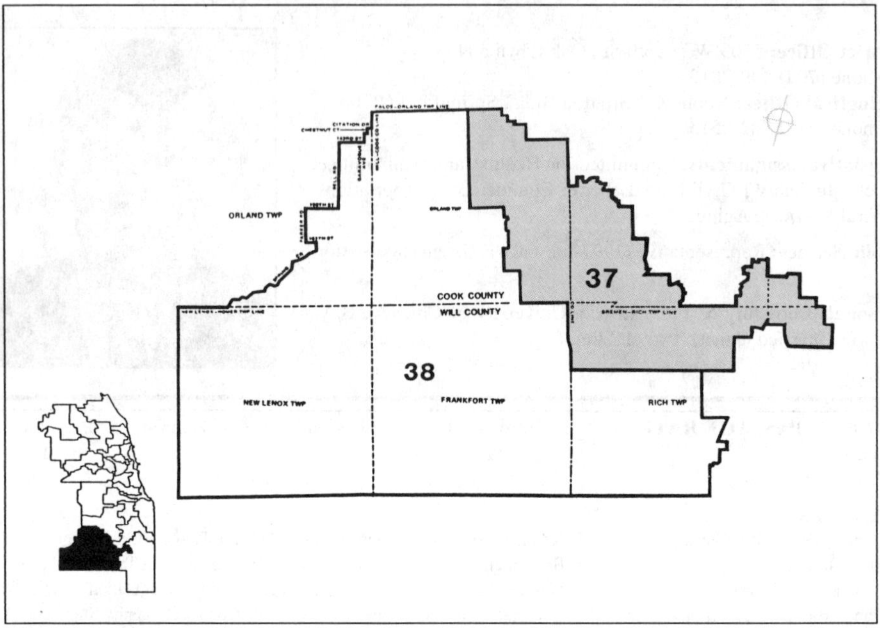

DEMOGRAPHICS (1990)

	S.D. #19	H.D. #37	H.D.#38
VOTING AGE POPULATION	137,660	70,567	67,093
White	89.3%	89.7%	89.0%
Black	7.0%	6.5%	7.6%
Hispanic	2.0%	1.8%	2.2%
Asian	1.5%	1.9%	1.1%
AGE (Total Population)	193,739	96,869	96,870
Under 6	9.5%	9.0%	10.0%
6 to 18	20.8%	19.5%	22.2%
65 and Over	8.9%	10.6%	7.2%
URBAN POPULATION	92.8%	99.2%	86.4%
HOUSING UNITS (Total)	66,890	34,551	32,339
Median Value	$114,816	$117,040	$112,447
Owner Occupied	81.3%	82.5%	80.1%
FAMILY INCOME (Total Families)	52,636	26,430	26,206
Median Income	$51,301	$52,479	$50,139
Below Poverty Level	2.0%	1.5%	2.5%
With Children Under 5	0.2%	0.1%	0.3%
With Children 5 to 17	0.7%	0.5%	0.9%
Headed by Females	0.8%	0.5%	1.2%
INDUSTRY (Total Employed)	98,873	49,362	49,512
Professional/Public Administration	27.0%	28.2%	25.8%
Manufacturing	15.5%	14.4%	16.6%
Retail	17.8%	17.8%	17.7%
Transportation/Communication	9.6%	9.5%	9.7%
Finance/Insurance/Real Estate	9.8%	10.7%	9.0%
Other Service	7.5%	7.5%	7.4%

Senator William F. Mahar (R)

District Office: 14700 Ravinia, Orland Park 60462
Phone (708) 349-1400; (708) 403-9212 (fax)
Springfield Office: 121C State Capitol Bldg., Springfield 62706
Phone (217) 782-9595

Legislative Assignments: Committees on Environment and Energy (chair); Public Health & Welfare; Transportation.

Public Service: Senator (1985-present); village trustee, Homewood (1979-1985).

Personal: Full-time legislator; born Feb. 13, 1947, Chicago Heights; Southern Illinois University-Carbondale, Bachelor's degree in psychology; Purdue University, master's degree in personnel services; U.S. Army (1970-1972); married (Beth); two children.

1997 BILL PASSAGE RATIO	Introduced	Passed House of Origin	Passed GA
Primary	25	13	10
Primary/Hyphenated	35	19	15

KEY VOTES

1) Senate GOP Ed. $ Plan ......Y	6) Insurance/Domestic Violence ..Y	11) Pre-Paid College Tuition ....Y
2) State Budget ....Y	7) Brownfields ....Y	12) Increase Pull Tab Prizes ....N
3) Tougher DUI Level ....Y	8) Welfare Reform ....Y	13) Telecommunications Tax ...Y
4) Ban Partial Birth Abortions ...Y	9) Concealed Guns/Misdemeanor .N	14) Delivery Discrimination ....P
5) State Employees Pension .....Y	10) Banks Sell Insurance ....Y	15) Sell Drivers' Data ....N

GROUP RATINGS

	FB	CoC	PrLf	IPPC	ACLU
1997	86	100	2/2	0	50

ELECTION RESULTS

1996 General	William F. Mahar (R)	48,563	(57.0%)
1996 General	Richard R. Della Croce (D)	34,524	(40.6%)
1996 General	Lance Del Goebel (REF)	2,047	(2.4%)

CAMPAIGN RESOURCES AND EXPENDITURES

1996 Campaign Funds		Top 10 PAC Contributors	
Beg. Balance . $95,923	Individuals ...$5,819	1) IPACE ...$17,500	6) Ameritech ..$2,310
Receipts $137,661	Party $15,704	2) ISMS $15,110	7) IBA $2,000
Expenditures .$121,206	PACS $88,811	3) RSSC $12,530	8) ChgoCoC ..$2,000
On hand $112,378	Candidate $1,482	4) MPAC $3,000	9) HeritBank ..$1,682
	Not-itemized $25,845	5) ILCable ...$2,500	10) IP $1,500

NOTE: The General Election Opponent's Campaign Resources and Expenditures are reported in a separate section in the back of the book (pp. 269-284).

GENERAL ELECTION DATA

	Registered Voters	Voter Turnout		Straight Party Voting	
1996	130,991	89,992	68.7%	(R) 18,115 . .20.1%	(D) 14,911 . . .16.6%

PRESIDENT

1996	Bill Clinton (D)	42,138	47.7%
	Bob Dole (R)	38,084	43.1%
	Ross Perot (I)	7,602	8.6%
1992	Bill Clinton (D)	34,125	36.7%
	George Bush (R)	39,527	42.5%
	Ross Perot (I)	19,256	20.8%

UNITED STATES SENATE

1996	Richard J. Durbin (D)	43,206	49.7%
	Al Salvi (R)	41,148	47.3%

GOVERNOR

1994	Jim Edgar (R)	41,453	71.7%
	Dawn Clark Netsch (D)	16,353	28.3%

Representative Kevin A. McCarthy (D)

District Office: 7711 West 159th St., Tinley Park 60477
Phone (708) 633-9696; (708) 633-0226 (fax)
Springfield Office: Room 2080-M Stratton Bldg., Springfield 62706
Phone (217) 782-3316

Legislative Assignments: Committees on Health Care Availability & Access; Consumer Protection; Higher Education; Public Utilities; State Government Administration & Election Reform.

Public Service: Representative (1997-present).

Personal: Teacher; born Dec. 5, 1950 in Chicago; Chicago State University, B.A.; De Paul University, M.A. in Educational Administration & Supervision; married (Judy); two children.

1997 BILL PASSAGE RATIO	Introduced	Passed House of Origin	Passed GA
Primary	15	2	0
Primary/Hyphenated	34	10	2

KEY VOTES

1) Change Ed. Funding Formula . .N	6) Insurance/Domestic Violence . .Y	11) Pre-Paid College Tuition . . . .Y
2) State Budget . . . . .Y	7) Brownfields . . . . .N	12) Increase Pull Tab Prizes . . . .N
3) Tougher DUI Level . . . . .Y	8) Welfare Reform . . . . .N	13) Utility Deregulation . . . . . . .N
4) Ban Partial Birth Abortions . . .Y	9) Concealed Guns/Misdemeanor .N	14) County Obscenity Standards .Y
5) State Employees Pension . . . . .Y	10) Banks Sell Insurance . . . . .Y	15) Managed Care Reform . . . . .Y

GROUP RATINGS

	FB	CoC	PrLf	IPPC	ACLU
1997	50	38	6/6	0	10

ELECTION RESULTS

1996 General	Kevin A. McCarthy (D)	20,498	(51.1%)
1996 General	John T. Doody, Jr. (R)	19,615	(48.9%)
1996 Primary	Kevin A. McCarthy (D)	3,584	(100%)
1996 Primary	John T. Doody, Jr. (R)	5,291	(100%)

CAMPAIGN RESOURCES AND EXPENDITURES

1996 Campaign Funds		Top 10 PAC Contributors	
Beg. Balance . . $5,742	Individuals . . .$2,775	1) IHDM . .$129,162	6) C&GL $3,000
Receipts $234,560	Party $163,985	2) DSCC . . .$22,892	7) CCCTU . . .$2,750
Expenditures .$223,951	PACS $42,900	3) SEIU $13,000	8) DPI $2,682
On hand $16,351	Candidate $0	4) ITLA $4,000	9) UDI $2,500
	Not-itemized $24,900	5) CLang $3,000	10) IUOE $2,500

NOTE: The General Election Opponent's Campaign Resources and Expenditures are reported in a separate section in the back of the book (pp. 269-284).

GENERAL ELECTION DATA

	Registered Voters	Voter Turnout		Straight Party Voting	
1996	61,349	41,875	68.3%	(R) 7,986 . . .19.1%	(D) 7,395 . . . .17.7%

PRESIDENT

1996	Bill Clinton (D)	20,576	49.9%
	Bob Dole (R)	17,213	41.7%
	Ross Perot (I)	3,241	7.9%
1992	Bill Clinton (D)	17,871	37.7%
	George Bush (R)	20,324	42.8%
	Ross Perot (I)	9,237	19.5%

UNITED STATES SENATE

1996	Richard J. Durbin (D)	21,248	52.4%
	Al Salvi (R)	18,277	45.1%

GOVERNOR

1994	Jim Edgar (R)	20,025	69.7%
	Dawn Clark Netsch (D)	8,718	30.3%

Representative Renee Kosel (R)

District Office: 205 West Maple, New Lenox 60451
Phone (815) 462-3838; (815) 462-3818 (fax)

Springfield Office: Room 2008-H Stratton Bldg., Springfield 62706
Phone (217) 782-0424; (217) 782-5257 (fax)

Legislative Assignments: Committees on Transportation & Motor Vehicles; Elementary & Secondary Education; Local Government; Aging; Task Force on Education.

Public Service: Representative (1997-present); Lincoln-Way Community High School Board of Education.

Personal: Born April 3, 1943; Western Illinois University, B.S. in education; married (Alfred); three children.

1997 BILL PASSAGE RATIO	Introduced	Passed House of Origin	Passed GA
Primary	5	3	2
Primary/Hyphenated	16	10	5

KEY VOTES

1) Change Ed. Funding Formula . .N	6) Insurance/Domestic Violence . .Y	11) Pre-Paid College Tuition . . . .Y
2) State Budget . . . . .Y	7) Brownfields . . . . .N	12) Increase Pull Tab Prizes . . . .Y
3) Tougher DUI Level . . . . .Y	8) Welfare Reform . . . . .Y	13) Utility Deregulation . . . . . . .Y
4) Ban Partial Birth Abortions . . .Y	9) Concealed Guns/Misdemeanor .Y	14) County Obscenity Standards .Y
5) State Employees Pension . . . . .Y	10) Banks Sell Insurance . . . . .Y	15) Managed Care Reform . . . . .N

GROUP RATINGS

	FB	CoC	PrLf	IPPC	ACLU
1997	54	69	4/6	33	30

ELECTION RESULTS

1996 General	Renee Kosel (R)	23,503	(51.0%)
1996 General	Lois R. Mayer (D)	22,600	(49.0%)
1996 Primary	Larry Wennlund (R)	8,399	(100%)
1996 Primary	Lois R. Mayer (D)	4,485	(100%)

CAMPAIGN RESOURCES AND EXPENDITURES

1996 Campaign Funds

Beg. Balance	$0	Individuals	$13,811
Receipts	$371,567	Party	$283,927
Expenditures	$364,149	PACS	$61,910
On hand	$7,418	Candidate	$0
		Not-itemized	$11,919

Top 10 PAC Contributors

1) HRCC . .$218,513	6) CWennlund . .$6,785
2) FLAD . . .$24,357	7) Alliance $6,125
3) CRyan . . .$10,300	8) ChgoCoC . . .$5,000
4) CChurchill $10,000	9) MPAC $2,500
5) ISMS $10,000	10) GOPWom . .$2,000

NOTE: The General Election Opponent's Campaign Resources and Expenditures are reported in a separate section in the back of the book (pp. 269-284).

GENERAL ELECTION DATA

	Registered Voters	Voter Turnout		Straight Party Voting	
1996	69,642	48,117	69.1%	(R) 10,129 . .21.1%	(D) 7,516 . . . .15.6%

PRESIDENT

1996	Bill Clinton (D)	21,562	45.8%
	Bob Dole (R)	20,871	44.4%
	Ross Perot (I)	4,361	9.3%
1992	Bill Clinton (D)	16,254	35.7%
	George Bush (R)	19,203	42.2%
	Ross Perot (I)	10,019	22.1%

UNITED STATES SENATE

1996	Richard J. Durbin (D)	21,958	47.3%
	Al Salvi (R)	22,871	49.3%

GOVERNOR

1994	Jim Edgar (R)	21,428	73.7%
	Dawn Clark Netsch (D)	7,635	26.3%

20th Senate District

House District 39
House District 40

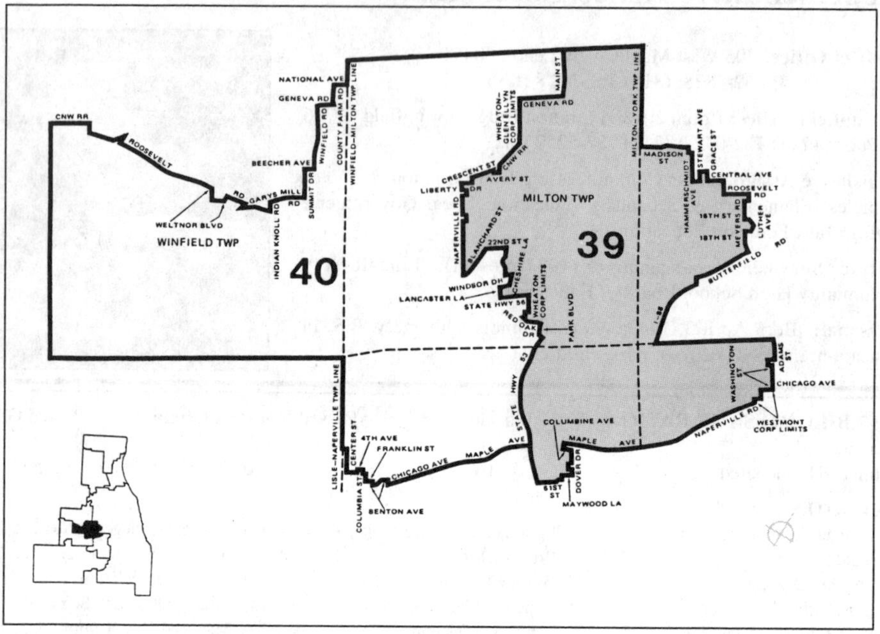

DEMOGRAPHICS (1990)

	S.D. #20	H.D. #39	H.D.#40
VOTING AGE POPULATION	143,433	73,240	70,193
White	91.5%	92.3%	90.6%
Black	2.1%	1.9%	2.2%
Hispanic	2.8%	2.2%	3.4%
Asian	3.6%	3.4%	3.7%
AGE (Total Population)	193,739	96,869	96,870
Under 6	9.8%	9.2%	10.5%
6 to 18	17.4%	16.4%	18.5%
65 and Over	9.5%	11.5%	7.5%
URBAN POPULATION	99.2%	100.0%	98.4%
HOUSING UNITS (Total)	74,385	38,705	35,680
Median Value	$142,105	$136,641	$149,763
Owner Occupied	68.7%	70.4%	66.9%
FAMILY INCOME (Total Families)	51,557	26,406	25,151
Median Income	$56,758	$54,868	$59,027
Below Poverty Level	1.8%	1.6%	2.0%
With Children Under 5	0.3%	0.2%	0.5%
With Children 5 to 17	0.6%	0.6%	0.7%
Headed by Females	0.9%	0.6%	1.2%
INDUSTRY (Total Employed)	106,657	53,878	52,779
Professional/Public Administration	28.3%	27.8%	28.8%
Manufacturing	15.6%	15.1%	16.1%
Retail	15.7%	16.6%	14.8%
Transportation/Communication	8.2%	8.1%	8.2%
Finance/Insurance/Real Estate	9.8%	10.0%	9.5%
Other Service	10.1%	9.9%	10.4%

Senator Beverly Fawell (R)

District Office: 213 W. Wesley, Suite 105, Wheaton 60187
Phone (630) 752-1100; (630) 752-1103 (fax)
Springfield Office: 121A Capitol Bldg., Springfield 62706
Phone (217) 782-8022; (217) 782-9586 (fax)

Legislative Assignments: Committees on Transportation (chair); Revenue; Appropriations.

Public Service: Senator (1983-present); representative (1981-1983).

Personal: Full-time legislator; born September 17, 1930, Oak Park; Elmhurst College, B.A. in elementary education/business administration and Northern Illinois University, political science; four children.

1997 BILL PASSAGE RATIO	Introducted	Passed House of Origin	Passed GA
Primary	23	13	11
Primary/Hyphenated	29	16	13

KEY VOTES

1) Senate GOP Ed. $ Plan ......Y	6) Insurance/Domestic Violence ..Y	11) Pre-Paid College Tuition ....Y
2) State Budget ....Y	7) Brownfields ....Y	12) Increase Pull Tab Prizes ....N
3) Tougher DUI Level ....Y	8) Welfare Reform ....Y	13) Telecommunications Tax ....P
4) Ban Partial Birth Abortions ...Y	9) Concealed Guns/Misdemeanor .N	14) Delivery Discrimination ....P
5) State Employees Pension .....Y	10) Banks Sell Insurance ....Y	15) Sell Drivers' Data ....N

GROUP RATINGS

	FB	CoC	PrLf	IPPC	ACLU
1997	73	100	2/2	0	50

ELECTION RESULTS

1994 General	Beverly Fawell (R)	45,063	(75.5%)
1994 General	Larry Nelson (D)	14,662	(24.5%)
1994 Primary	Beverly Fawell (R)	13,378	(47.7%)
1994 Primary	Two others (R)	14,676	(52.3%)

CAMPAIGN RESOURCES AND EXPENDITURES

1996 Campaign Funds

Beg. Balance	$13,938	Individuals	$0
Receipts	$6,262	Party	$0
Expenditures	$3,913	PACS	$5,650
On hand	$16,287	Candidate	$0
		Not-itemized	$612

Top 10 PAC Contributors

1) UnionPacific .$500	6) HOPE $500
2) Norfolk $500	7) ChgoCoC ...$500
3) Monsanto ...$500	8) Auto $500
4) CPA's $500	9) NIGAS $300
5) ICAPAC $500	10) ILCentral ...$250

NOTE: The General Election Opponent's Campaign Resources and Expenditures are reported in a separate section in the back of the book (pp. 269-284).

GENERAL ELECTION DATA

	Registered Voters	Voter Turnout		Straight Party Voting	
1996	109,650	86,465	78.9%	(R) 28,553 ..33.0%	(D) 9,731 ....11.3%

PRESIDENT

1996	Bill Clinton (D)	32,267	38.0%
	Bob Dole (R)	45,508	53.5%
	Ross Perot (I)	6,448	7.6%
1992	Bill Clinton (D)	29,675	30.6%
	George Bush (R)	48,353	49.9%
	Ross Perot (I)	18,881	19.5%

UNITED STATES SENATE

1996	Richard J. Durbin (D)	35,091	41.8%
	Al Salvi (R)	45,717	54.5%

GOVERNOR

1994	Jim Edgar (R)	48,010	79.6%
	Dawn Clark Netsch (D)	12,316	21.4%

Representative Vincent A. Persico (R)

District Office: 478 Pennsylvania, Suite 101, Glen Ellyn 60137
Phone (630)858-0860; (630) 858-0868 (fax)
Springfield Office: Room 2127-O, Stratton Bldg., Springfield 62706
Phone (217) 782-8037; (217) 782-0709 (fax)

Legislative Assignments: Committees on Electric Utility Deregulation (minority spokesperson); Elementary & Secondary Education; Environment & Energy; Financial Institutions; Insurance.

Public Service: Representative (1991-present); trustee, Milton Township.

Personal: Educator; born December 9, 1948, Oak Park; University of Illinois, B.A. in history; Northern Illinios University, M.A. in education; married (Donna); three children.

1997 BILL PASSAGE RATIO	Introduced	Passed House of Origin	Passed GA
Primary	8	6	4
Primary/Hyphenated	29	16	9

KEY VOTES

1) Change Ed. Funding Formula . . N
2) State Budget . . . . Y
3) Tougher DUI Level . . . . Y
4) Ban Partial Birth Abortions . . . Y
5) State Employees Pension . . . . . Y
6) Insurance/Domestic Violence . . Y
7) Brownfields . . . . Y
8) Welfare Reform . . . . Y
9) Concealed Guns/Misdemeanor . Y
10) Banks Sell Insurance . . . . Y
11) Pre-Paid College Tuition . . . . Y
12) Increase Pull Tab Prizes . . . . Y
13) Utility Deregulation . . . . Y
14) County Obscenity Standards . Y
15) Managed Care Reform . . . . . Y

GROUP RATINGS

	FB	CoC	PrLf	IPPC	ACLU
1997	68	69	3/6	50	50

ELECTION RESULTS

1996 General	Vincent A. Persico (R)	26,178	(65.2%)
1996 General	Keith Murphy (D)	13,946	(34.8%)
1996 Primary	Vincent A. Persico (R)	11,859	(76.5%)
1996 Primary	Lee Sila (R)	3,644	(23.5%)

CAMPAIGN RESOURCES AND EXPENDITURES

1996 Campaign Funds

Beg. Balance	$98,607	Individuals	$600
Receipts	$39,915	Party	$0
Expenditures	$37,976	PACS	$36,815
On hand	$100,546	Candidate	$0
		Not-itemized	$2,500

Top 10 PAC Contributors

1) IPACE	$3,000	6) IMPAC	$750
2) HI	$2,000	7) PetPec	$600
3) WMgt	$1,600	8) Empress	$600
4) ISMS	$1,000	9) CUPAC	$600
5) ABDI	$800	10)BFerris	$600

NOTE: The General Election Opponent's Campaign Resources and Expenditures are reported in a separate section in the back of the book (pp. 269-284).

GENERAL ELECTION DATA

	Registered Voters	Voter Turnout		Straight Party Voting	
1996	54,289	43,058	79.3%	(R) 13,224 . . 30.7%	(D) 5,274 . . . . 12.3%

PRESIDENT

1996	Bill Clinton (D)	17,101	40.4%
	Bob Dole (R)	21,450	50.7%
	Ross Perot (I)	3,314	7.8%
1992	Bill Clinton (D)	16,193	32.8%
	George Bush (R)	23,286	47.2%
	Ross Perot (I)	9,866	20.0%

UNITED STATES SENATE

1996	Richard J. Durbin (D)	18,452	44.2%
	Al Salvi (R)	21,618	51.8%

GOVERNOR

1994	Jim Edgar (R)	23,699	77.7%
	Dawn Clark Netsch (D)	6,819	22.3%

Representative Peter Roskam (R)

District Office: 202 West Willow, Suite 102, Wheaton 60187
Phone (630) 221-0040; (603) 221-9466 (fax)
Springfield Office: Room 2139-O Stratton Bldg., Springfield 62706
Phone (217) 782-1653

Legislative Assignments: Committees on Judiciary II-Criminal Law (minority spokesperson); Appropriations-General Services; Labor & Commerce; Prison Management Reform; Children & Youth.

Public Service: Representative (1993-present).

Personal: Partner, Salvi & Roskam, attorneys at law; born September 13, 1961, Hinsdale; University of Illinois, B.A. in political science/history; married (Elizabeth); four children.

1997 BILL PASSAGE RATIO	Introduced	Passed House of Origin	Passed GA
Primary	22	7	6
Primary/Hyphenated	30	15	8

KEY VOTES

1) Change Ed. Funding Formula . . N	6) Insurance/Domestic Violence . . Y	11) Pre-Paid College Tuition . . . . Y
2) State Budget . . . . Y	7) Brownfields . . . . Y	12) Increase Pull Tab Prizes . . . N
3) Tougher DUI Level . . . . Y	8) Welfare Reform . . . . Y	13) Utility Deregulation . . . . P
4) Ban Partial Birth Abortions . . . Y	9) Concealed Guns/Misdemeanor . Y	14) County Obscenity Standards . Y
5) State Employees Pension . . . . . Y	10) Banks Sell Insurance . . . . Y	15) Managed Care Reform . . . . . N

GROUP RATINGS

	FB	CoC	PrLf	IPPC	ACLU
1997	75	92	6/6	0	20

ELECTION RESULTS

1996 General	Peter Roskam (R)	28,858	(70.8%)
1996 General	Kevin D. Schuele (D)	11,907	(29.2%)
1996 Primary	Peter Roskam (R)	13,657	(100%)
1996 Primary	Kevin D. Schuele (D)	2,108	(100%)

CAMPAIGN RESOURCES AND EXPENDITURES

1996 Campaign Funds

Beg. Balance	$18,311	Individuals	$4,115
Receipts	$27,620	Party	$0
Expenditures	$18,828	PACS	$13,228
On hand	$27,103	Candidate	$0
		Not-itemized	$10,277

Top 10 PAC Contributors

1) LAWPAC	$1,500	6) CoC	$500
2) FCCSPAC	$925	7) LICID	$500
3) IBA	$750	8) MPAC	$500
4) Quidlibet	$525	9) ACPA	$500
5) WCLA	$500	10) HOPE	$500

NOTE: The General Election Opponent's Campaign Resources and Expenditures are reported in a separate section in the back of the book (pp. 269-284).

GENERAL ELECTION DATA

	Registered Voters	Voter Turnout		Straight Party Voting	
1996	55,361	43,407	78.4%	(R) 15,329 . . 35.3%	(D) 4,457 . . . . 10.3%

PRESIDENT

1996	Bill Clinton (D)	15,166	35.5%
	Bob Dole (R)	24,058	56.3%
	Ross Perot (I)	3,134	7.3%
1992	Bill Clinton (D)	13,482	28.3%
	George Bush (R)	25,067	52.7%
	Ross Perot (I)	9,015	19.0%

UNITED STATES SENATE

1996	Richard J. Durbin (D)	16,639	39.5%
	Al Salvi (R)	24,099	57.2%

GOVERNOR

1994	Jim Edgar (R)	24,311	81.6%
	Dawn Clark Netsch (D)	5,497	18.4%

21st Senate District

House District 41
House District 42

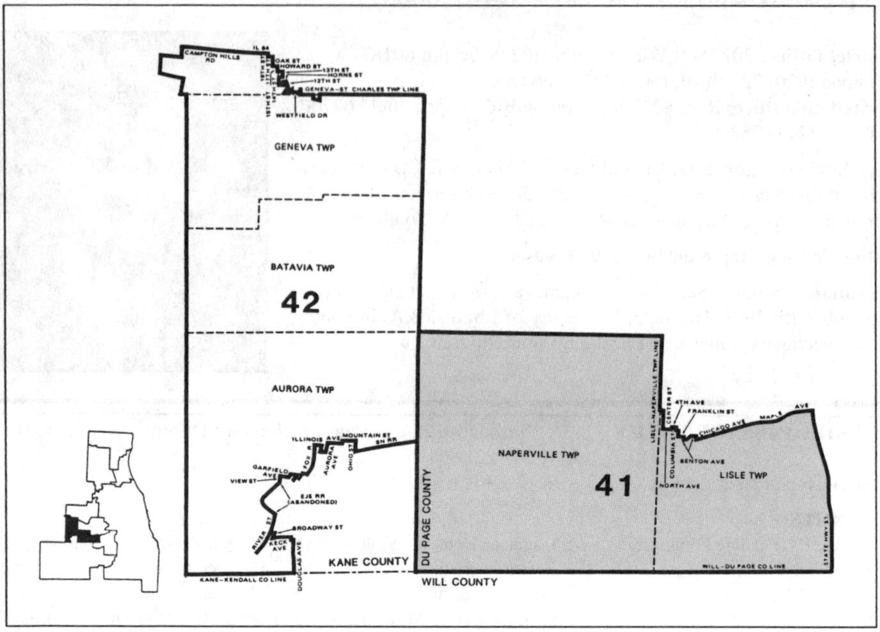

DEMOGRAPHICS (1990)

	S.D. #21	H.D. #41	H.D.#42
VOTING AGE POPULATION	139,344	69,725	69,619
White	88.8%	91.6%	86.0%
Black	4.3%	2.4%	6.1%
Hispanic	4.3%	2.0%	6.6%
Asian	2.5%	3.9%	1.1%
AGE (Total Population)	193,739	96,869	96,870
Under 6	10.2%	10.2%	10.2%
6 to 18	19.2%	19.1%	19.3%
65 and Over	8.1%	5.3%	11.0%
URBAN POPULATION	98.0%	98.9%	97.0%
HOUSING UNITS (Total)	73,983	37,584	36,399
Median Value	$135,706	$165,157	$104,874
Owner Occupied	64.7%	65.3%	64.1%
FAMILY INCOME (Total Families)	50,908	25,624	25,284
Median Income	$54,818	$64,840	$46,464
Below Poverty Level	2.4%	1.1%	3.8%
With Children Under 5	0.3%	0.1%	0.6%
With Children 5 to 17	0.8%	0.6%	1.0%
Headed by Females	1.3%	0.6%	1.9%
INDUSTRY (Total Employed)	104,582	54,754	49,828
Professional/Public Administration	26.4%	25.8%	27.2%
Manufacturing	19.3%	16.3%	22.5%
Retail	15.8%	15.8%	15.7%
Transportation/Communication	7.7%	8.5%	6.7%
Finance/Insurance/Real Estate	9.7%	11.6%	7.6%
Other Service	8.8%	9.4%	8.1%

Senator Chris Lauzen (R)

District Office: 28 S. Fifth St., P.O. Box 111, Geneva, 60134
Phone (630) 232-1576; (630) 232-1194 (fax)
Springfield Office: 613 B, Capitol Bldg., Springfield 62706
Phone (217) 782-0052

Legislative Assignments: Committees on Commerce and Industry (chair); Revenue (vice-chair); Appropriations; Legislative Audit Commission.

Public Service: Senator (1993-present); public building commissioner, Kane County; elected delegate, 1995 White House Conference on Small Business.

Personal: CPA; born Dec. 30, 1952; Duke University, B.S. in management science and English and Harvard Business School, M.B.A.; married (Sarah Longley); four children.

1997 BILL PASSAGE RATIO	Introduced	Passed House of Origin	Passed GA
Primary	43	12	4
Primary/Hyphenated	52	14	6

KEY VOTES

1) Senate GOP Ed. $ Plan . . . . . .Y	6) Insurance/Domestic Violence . .Y	11) Pre-Paid College Tuition . . . .P
2) State Budget . . . . .N	7) Brownfields . . . . .Y	12) Increase Pull Tab Prizes . . . .N
3) Tougher DUI Level . . . . .Y	8) Welfare Reform . . . . .Y	13) Telecommunications Tax . . . .P
4) Ban Partial Birth Abortions . . .Y	9) Concealed Guns/Misdemeanor .Y	14) Delivery Discrimination . . . .N
5) State Employees Pension . . . . .Y	10) Banks Sell Insurance . . . . .Y	15) Sell Drivers' Data . . . . .O

GROUP RATINGS

	FB	CoC	PrLf	IPPC	ACLU
1997	45	100	2/2	0	33

ELECTION RESULTS

1996 General	Chris Lauzen (R)	53,084	(65.1%)
1996 General	Jennifer Lawson Finlay (D)	28,402	(34.9%)
1996 Primary	Chris Lauzen (R)	19,493	(100%)

CAMPAIGN RESOURCES AND EXPENDITURES

1996 Campaign Funds

Beg. Balance	$7,774	Individuals	$41,362
Receipts	$103,259	Party	$430
Expenditures	$110,000	PACS	$31,535
On hand	$1,033	Candidate	$14,377
		Not-itemized	$15,555

Top 10 PAC Contributors

1) ASBA	$14,378	6) Hollywood	$570
2) CPA's	$1,000	7) Macom	$550
3) ChgoCoC	$1,000	8) GOA	$550
4) AlarmDet	$785	9) IPMA	$500
5) Starrett	$750	10) Sec-Master	$500

NOTE: The General Election Opponent's Campaign Resources and Expenditures are reported in a separate section in the back of the book (pp. 269-284).

GENERAL ELECTION DATA

	Registered Voters	Voter Turnout		Straight Party Voting	
1996	121,617	86,964	71.5%	(R) 25,131 . . 28.8%	(D) 10,799 . . . 12.4%

PRESIDENT

1996	Bill Clinton (D)	34,597	40.4%
	Bob Dole (R)	43,502	50.1%
	Ross Perot (I)	6,736	7.9%
1992	Bill Clinton (D)	31,589	32.6%
	George Bush (R)	46,071	47.6%
	Ross Perot (I)	19,179	19.8%

UNITED STATES SENATE

1996	Richard J. Durbin (D)	36,579	43.3%
	Al Salvi (R)	44,399	52.6%

GOVERNOR

1994	Jim Edgar (R)	45,112	79.4%
	Dawn Clark Netsch (D)	11,715	20.6%

Representative Mary Lou Cowlishaw (R)

District Office: 552 South Washington St., Ste. 119, Naperville 60540
Phone (630) 355-4113; (630) 355-2847 (fax)
Springfield Office: Room 2016-H Stratton Bldg., Springfield 62706
Phone (217) 782-6507; (217) 782-5257 (fax)

Legislative Assignments: Committees on Elementary & Secondary Education (minority spokesperson); Appropriations-Education; Public Utilities; Aging; Electric Utility Deregulation.

Public Service: Representative (1983-present); school board, Naperville District # 203 (1972-1983).

Personal: Full-time legislator; born February 20, 1932, Rockford; University of Illinois, B.S. in journalism; married (Wayne); three children.

1997 BILL PASSAGE RATIO	Introduced	Passed House of Origin	Passed GA
Primary	16	3	1
Primary/Hyphenated	32	14	8

KEY VOTES

1) Change Ed. Funding Formula . . N	6) Insurance/Domestic Violence . . Y	11) Pre-Paid College Tuition . . . . Y
2) State Budget . . . . Y	7) Brownfields . . . . Y	12) Increase Pull Tab Prizes . . . . N
3) Tougher DUI Level . . . . Y	8) Welfare Reform . . . . Y	13) Utility Deregulation . . . . N
4) Ban Partial Birth Abortions . . . Y	9) Concealed Guns/Misdemeanor . Y	14) County Obscenity Standards . N
5) State Employees Pension . . . . . Y	10) Banks Sell Insurance . . . . Y	15) Managed Care Reform . . . . . Y

GROUP RATINGS

	FB	CoC	PrLf	IPPC	ACLU
1997	68	62	6/6	0	30

ELECTION RESULTS

1996 General	Mary Lou Cowlishaw (R)	31,489	(71.3%)
1996 General	Suzanne Tobin Frankel (D)	12,657	(28.7%)
1996 Primary	Mary Lou Cowlishaw (R)	10,376	(100%)
1996 Primary	Suzanne Tobin Frankel (D)	2,138	(100%)

CAMPAIGN RESOURCES AND EXPENDITURES

1996 Campaign Funds				Top 10 PAC Contributors			
Beg. Balance	$35,350	Individuals	$1,400	1) ALEX	$1,000	6) UNIPAC	$600
Receipts	$24,385	Party	$0	2) ABDI	$1,000	7) ISPP	$500
Expenditures	$18,881	PACS	$18,550	3) AT&T	$1,000	8) LICID	$500
On hand	$40,854	Candidate	$0	4) MPAC	$1,000	9) CoC	$500
		Not-itemized	$4,435	5) IBA	$750	10) ChgoCoC	$500

NOTE: The General Election Opponent's Campaign Resources and Expenditures are reported in a separate section in the back of the book (pp. 269-284).

GENERAL ELECTION DATA

	Registered Voters	Voter Turnout		Straight Party Voting	
1996	61,351	47,237	77.0%	(R) 15,734 . . 33.3%	(D) 5,045 . . . 10.6%

PRESIDENT

1996	Bill Clinton (D)	17,745	38.1%
	Bob Dole (R)	25,251	54.2%
	Ross Perot (I)	3,254	7.0%
1992	Bill Clinton (D)	14,610	29.1%
	George Bush (R)	25,841	51.4%
	Ross Perot (I)	9,777	19.5%

UNITED STATES SENATE

1996	Richard J. Durbin (D)	19,415	42.3%
	Al Salvi (R)	24,946	54.3%

GOVERNOR

1994	Jim Edgar (R)	25,669	81.5%
	Dawn Clark Netsch (D)	5,839	18.5%

Representative Suzanne L. Deuchler (R)

District Office: 1128-A Prairie St., Aurora 60506
Phone (630) 896-4021; (630) 896-4596 (fax)
Springfield Office: Room 2131-O, Stratton Bldg., Springfield 62706
Phone (217) 782-5457

Legislative Assignments: Committees on Financial Institutions (minority spokesperson); Appropriations-General Services; Human Services; Personnel & Pensions; Banks Selling Insurance.

Public Service: Representative (1981-present); Kane County Board.

Personal: Full-time legislator; born July 21, 1929, Chicago; University of Illinois, B.A. in Spanish and speech; married (Walter); two children.

1997 BILL PASSAGE RATIO	Introduced	Passed House of Origin	Passed GA
Primary	9	2	1
Primary/Hyphenated	19	9	5

KEY VOTES

1) Change Ed. Funding Formula . . Y
2) State Budget . . . . Y
3) Tougher DUI Level . . . . Y
4) Ban Partial Birth Abortions . . . N
5) State Employees Pension . . . . . Y
6 Insurance/Domestic Violence . . Y
7) Brownfields . . . . Y
8) Welfare Reform . . . . Y
9) Concealed Guns/Misdemeanor . Y
10) Banks Sell Insurance . . . . Y
11) Pre-Paid College Tuition . . . . Y
12) Increase Pull Tab Prizes . . . . Y
13) Utility Deregulation . . . . Y
14) County Obscenity Standards . N
15) Managed Care Reform . . . . . Y

GROUP RATINGS

	FB	CoC	PrLf	IPPC	ACLU
1997	82	46	0/6	100	100

ELECTION RESULTS

1996 General	Suzanne L. Deuchler (R)	23,810	(64.7%)
1996 General	Barbara Connell Vondrak (D)	13,015	(35.3%)
1996 Primary	Suzanne L. Deuchler (R)	9,266	(100%)
1994 General	Suzanne L. Deuchler (R)	21,177	(100%)

CAMPAIGN RESOURCES AND EXPENDITURES

1996 Campaign Funds

Beg. Balance	$15,358	Individuals	$960
Receipts	$28,217	Party	$0
Expenditures	$23,587	PACS	$19,850
On hand	$19,988	Candidate	$191
		Not-itemized	$7,216

Top 10 PAC Contributors

1) IPACE	$5,000	6) ILFI	$500
2) IBA	$2,500	7) CatCEG	$500
3) CUPAC	$1,000	8) COBANK	$500
4) HI	$1,000	9) ILCon	$500
5) ABDI	$800	10) ISMS	$500

NOTE: The General Election Opponent's Campaign Resources and Expenditures are reported in a separate section in the back of the book (pp. 269-284).

GENERAL ELECTION DATA

	Registered Voters	Voter Turnout		Straight Party Voting	
1996	60,266	39,727	65.9%	(R) 9,397 . . 23.7%	(D) 5,754 . . . 14.5%

PRESIDENT

1996	Bill Clinton (D)	16,852	43.2%
	Bob Dole (R)	18,251	46.8%
	Ross Perot (I)	3,482	8.9%
1992	Bill Clinton (D)	16,979	36.4%
	George Bush (R)	20,230	43.4%
	Ross Perot (I)	9,402	20.2%

UNITED STATES SENATE

1996	Richard J. Durbin (D)	17,164	44.6%
	Al Salvi (R)	19,453	50.6%

GOVERNOR

1994	Jim Edgar (R)	19,443	76.8%
	Dawn Clark Netsch (D)	5,876	23.2%

22nd Senate District

House District 43
House District 44

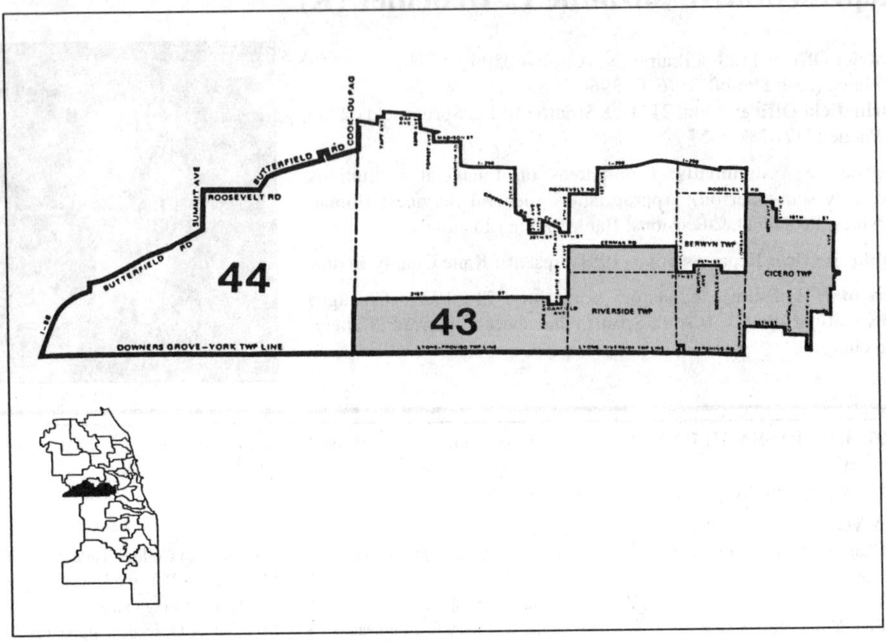

DEMOGRAPHICS (1990)

	S.D. #22	H.D. #43	H.D.#44
VOTING AGE POPULATION	152,179	74,366	77,813
White	87.2%	84.8%	89.4%
Black	1.2%	0.1%	2.3%
Hispanic	8.7%	13.6%	4.0%
Asian	2.8%	1.2%	4.3%
AGE (Total Population)	193,739	96,870	96,869
Under 6	7.9%	8.7%	7.1%
6 to 18	14.6%	15.7%	13.5%
65 and Over	18.9%	18.3%	19.4%
URBAN POPULATION	100.0%	100.0%	100.0%
HOUSING UNITS (Total)	79,339	38,858	40,481
Median Value	$109,012	$97,384	$118,601
Owner Occupied	65.2%	62.2%	68.0%
FAMILY INCOME (Total Families)	51,952	25,396	26,555
Median Income	$43,931	$39,614	$48,456
Below Poverty Level	4.1%	5.7%	2.6%
With Children Under 5	0.5%	0.9%	0.2%
With Children 5 to 17	1.6%	2.4%	0.7%
Headed by Females	1.7%	2.7%	0.7%
INDUSTRY (Total Employed)	94,770	45,264	49,506
Professional/Public Administration	26.0%	23.8%	28.0%
Manufacturing	19.6%	22.4%	17.1%
Retail	16.2%	15.5%	16.9%
Transportation/Communication	7.6%	8.0%	7.2%
Finance/Insurance/Real Estate	9.2%	8.6%	9.7%
Other Service	9.4%	9.7%	9.1%

Senator Thomas J. Walsh (R)

District Office: 10544 W. Cermak Rd., Westchester 60154
Phone (708) 531-0390; (708) 531-0467 (fax)
Springfield Office: 118 Capitol Bldg., Springfield 62704
Phone (217) 782-2015

Legislative Assignments: Committees on Insurance and Pensions (vice-chair); Financial Institutions (vice-chair); Appropriations; Executive Appointments.

Public Service: Senator (1994-present); representative (1993-1995); commissioner, Metropolitan Water Reclamation District of Greater Chicago (1988-1990).

Personal: Public relations; born July 4, 1960, Chicago; Loras College, B.A. in business administration.

1997 BILL PASSAGE RATIO	Introduced	Passed House of Origin	Passed GA
Primary	37	16	11
Primary/Hyphenated	61	33	23

KEY VOTES

1) Senate GOP Ed. $ Plan ......Y
2) State Budget ....Y
3) Tougher DUI Level ....Y
4) Ban Partial Birth Abortions ...Y
5) State Employees Pension .....Y
6) Insurance/Domestic Violence ..Y
7) Brownfields ....Y
8) Welfare Reform ....Y
9) Concealed Guns/Misdemeanor .P
10) Banks Sell Insurance ....Y
11) Pre-Paid College Tuition ....Y
12) Increase Pull Tab Prizes ....Y
13) Telecommunications Tax ....P
14) Delivery Discrimination ....P
15) Sell Drivers' Data ....Y

GROUP RATINGS

	FB	CoC	PrLf	IPPC	ACLU
1997	68	100	2/2	0	50

ELECTION RESULTS

1996 General	Thomas J. Walsh (R)	46,947	(100%)
1996 Primary	Thomas J. Walsh (R)	15,130	(100%)
1992 General	Judy Baar Topinka (R)	59,187	(71.0%)
1992 General	Thomas N. Geovanis (D)	24,148	(29.0%)

CAMPAIGN RESOURCES AND EXPENDITURES

1996 Campaign Funds

Beg. Balance	$51,033	Individuals	$7,650
Receipts	$51,367	Party	$4,160
Expenditures	$40,926	PACS	$29,740
On hand	$61,474	Candidate	$0
		Not-itemized	$9,817

Top 10 PAC Contributors

1) ILCable ...$2,500	6) VIPNR $1,000
2) ABDI $1,000	7) Oak $800
3) ConElectric $1,000	8) ARC $800
4) HI $1,000	9) IFDA $800
5) IndFinance .$1,000	10) ILCon $800

NOTE: The General Election Opponent's Campaign Resources and Expenditures are reported in a separate section in the back of the book (pp. 269-284).

GENERAL ELECTION DATA

	Registered Voters	Voter Turnout		Straight Party Voting	
1996	107,632	71,568	66.5%	(R) 16,293 .. 22.8%	(D) 13,169 ... 18.4%

PRESIDENT

1996	Bill Clinton (D)	33,596	47.9%
	Bob Dole (R)	30,337	43.3%
	Ross Perot (I)	5,624	8.0%
1992	Bill Clinton (D)	32,818	37.7%
	George Bush (R)	38,171	43.8%
	Ross Perot (I)	16,069	18.5%

UNITED STATES SENATE

1996	Richard J. Durbin (D)	34,071	49.3%
	Al Salvi (R)	32,883	47.5%

GOVERNOR

1994	Jim Edgar (R)	40,920	75.2%
	Dawn Clark Netsch (D)	13,487	24.8%

Representative Jack L. Kubik (R)

District Office: 2601 S. Harlem Ave. Suite A, Berwyn 60402
Phone (708) 442-0149; (708) 442-0172 (fax)
Springfield Office: Room 630 Capitol Bldg., Springfield 62706
Phone (217) 782-5821

Legislative Assignments: Committees on Executive; Revenue; Conflicts of Interest.

Public Service: Representative (1985-present).

Personal: Businessman; born May 20, 1955, Riverside; DePaul University, B.A. in Business Administration; University of Illinois, Business Administration; married (Aggie).

1997 BILL PASSAGE RATIO	Introduced	Passed House of Origin	Passed GA
Primary	32	12	5
Primary/Hyphenated	47	21	11

KEY VOTES

1) Change Ed. Funding Formula . . N	6) Insurance/Domestic Violence . . Y	11) Pre-Paid College Tuition . . . . Y
2) State Budget . . . . Y	7) Brownfields . . . . A	12) Increase Pull Tab Prizes . . . . N
3) Tougher DUI Level . . . . Y	8) Welfare Reform . . . . Y	13) Utility Deregulation . . . . Y
4) Ban Partial Birth Abortions . . . Y	9) Concealed Guns/Misdemeanor . N	14) County Obscenity Standards . N
5) State Employees Pension . . . . . Y	10) Banks Sell Insurance . . . . Y	15) Managed Care Reform . . . . . Y

GROUP RATINGS

	FB	CoC	PrLf	IPPC	ACLU
1997	68	54	5/6	0	44

ELECTION RESULTS

1996 General	Jack L. Kubik (R)	21,849	(100%)
1996 Primary	Jack L. Kubik (R)	8,319	(100%)
1994 General	Jack L. Kubik (R)	19,455	(77.0%)
1994 General	William P. Karmia (D)	5,807	(23.0%)

CAMPAIGN RESOURCES AND EXPENDITURES

1996 Campaign Funds		Top 10 PAC Contributors					
Beg. Balance	$49,663	Individuals	$2,780	1) SMCorp	$3,000	6) PMorris	$750
Receipts	$40,382	Party	$1,890	2) Corey	$1,500	7) MidAmFed	$600
Expenditures	$46,230	PACS	$25,090	3) MPAC	$1,000	8) CLM	$600
On hand	$43,815	Candidate	$0	4) HuntInc	$1,000	9) MAMP	$600
		Not-itemized	$10,622	5) IMPACT	$1,000	10) VIPNR	$600

NOTE: The General Election Opponent's Campaign Resources and Expenditures are reported in a separate section in the back of the book (pp. 269-284).

GENERAL ELECTION DATA

	Registered Voters	Voter Turnout		Straight Party Voting	
1996	50,462	33,125	65.6%	(R) 6,116 . . . 18.5%	(D) 6,399 . . . 19.3%

PRESIDENT

1996	Bill Clinton (D)	16,230	50.1%
	Bob Dole (R)	13,206	40.8%
	Ross Perot (I)	2,719	8.4%
1992	Bill Clinton (D)	15,631	38.6%
	George Bush (R)	17,179	42.5%
	Ross Perot (I)	7,653	18.9%

UNITED STATES SENATE

1996	Richard J. Durbin (D)	16,133	50.6%
	Al Salvi (R)	14,724	46.1%

GOVERNOR

1994	Jim Edgar (R)	19,440	75.8%
	Dawn Clark Netsch (D)	6,221	24.2%

Representative James B. Durkin (R)

District Office: 10544 West Cermak, Westchester 60154
Phone (708) 531-1444; (708) 531-0467 (fax)
Springfield Office: Room G-1 Stratton Bldg., Springfield 62706
Phone (217) 782-1061; (217) 782-1023 (fax)

Legislative Assignments: Committees on House Appropriations-Education (minority spokesperson); Judiciary II-Criminal Law; Financial Institutions; Environment & Energy; Personnel & Pensions; Prison Management Reform.

Public Service: Representative (1995-present); Triton Community College Board of Trustees.

Personal: Attorney; born January 28, 1961, Chicago; Illinois State University, B.S.; John Marshall Law School, J.D.

1997 BILL PASSAGE RATIO	Introduced	Passed House of Origin	Passed GA
Primary	16	8	5
Primary/Hyphenated	48	28	17

KEY VOTES

1) Change Ed. Funding Formula . . N	6) Insurance/Domestic Violence . . Y	11) Pre-Paid College Tuition . . . . Y
2) State Budget . . . . Y	7) Brownfields . . . . Y	12) Increase Pull Tab Prizes . . . . Y
3) Tougher DUI Level . . . . Y	8) Welfare Reform . . . . Y	13) Utility Deregulation . . . . Y
4) Ban Partial Birth Abortions . . . Y	9) Concealed Guns/Misdemeanor . N	14) County Obscenity Standards . N
5) State Employees Pension . . . . . Y	10) Banks Sell Insurance . . . . Y	15) Managed Care Reform . . . . . Y

GROUP RATINGS

	FB	CoC	PrLf	IPPC	ACLU
1997	57	77	5/6	16	50

ELECTION RESULTS

1996 General	James B. Durkin (R)	25,212	(100%)
1996 Primary	James B. Durkin (R)	6,868	(100%)
1996 Primary	Thomas F. Lorenz (D)	4,191	(100%)

CAMPAIGN RESOURCES AND EXPENDITURES

1996 Campaign Funds			
Beg. Balance	$57,594	Individuals	$2,690
Receipts	$41,331	Party	$1,135
Expenditures	$43,681	PACS	$27,496
On hand	$55,244	Candidate	$545
		Not-itemized	$9,465

Top 10 PAC Contributors			
1) UNISTAT	$5,040	6) GOInc	$806
2) LAWPAC	$1,500	7) ITLA	$750
3) IndFinance	$1,000	8) PMorris	$500
4) MPAC	$1,000	9) ISMS	$500
5) SMCorp	$1,000	10) HI	$500

NOTE: The General Election Opponent's Campaign Resources and Expenditures are reported in a separate section in the back of the book (pp. 269-284).

GENERAL ELECTION DATA

	Registered Voters	Voter Turnout		Straight Party Voting	
1996	57,170	38,443	67.2%	(R) 10,177 . . 26.5%	(D) 6,770 . . . . 17.6%

PRESIDENT

1996	Bill Clinton (D)	17,366	46.1%
	Bob Dole (R)	17,131	45.4%
	Ross Perot (I)	2,905	7.7%
1992	Bill Clinton (D)	17,187	36.9%
	George Bush (R)	20,992	45.1%
	Ross Perot (I)	8,416	18.0%

UNITED STATES SENATE

1996	Richard J. Durbin (D)	17,938	48.2%
	Al Salvi (R)	18,159	48.7%

GOVERNOR

1994	Jim Edgar (R)	21,480	74.7%
	Dawn Clark Netsch (D)	7,266	25.3%

23rd Senate District

House District 45
House District 46

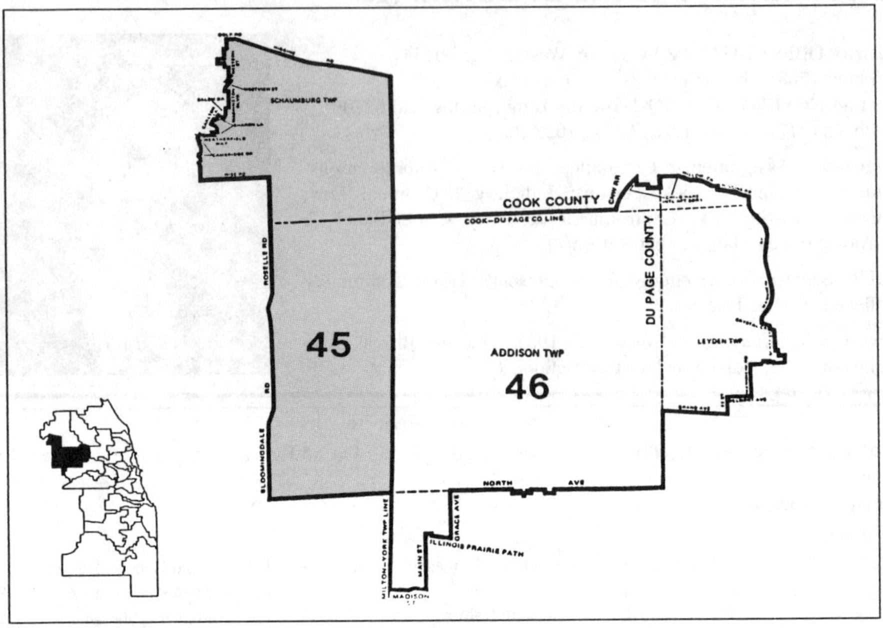

DEMOGRAPHICS (1990)

	S.D. #23	H.D. #45	H.D.#46
VOTING AGE POPULATION	145,035	71,653	73,382
White	87.3%	88.0%	86.6%
Black	1.1%	1.7%	0.6%
Hispanic	6.4%	3.9%	8.8%
Asian	5.1%	6.4%	3.8%
AGE (Total Population)	193,739	96,870	96,869
Under 6	8.7%	9.0%	8.5%
6 to 18	17.8%	18.4%	17.1%
65 and Over	8.8%	7.6%	10.1%
URBAN POPULATION	100.0%	100.0%	100.0%
HOUSING UNITS (Total)	70,980	36,344	34,636
Median Value	$123,414	$129,846	$118,806
Owner Occupied	72.5%	73.2%	71.7%
FAMILY INCOME (Total Families)	51,763	25,798	25,965
Median Income	$50,543	$52,684	$48,190
Below Poverty Level	2.2%	2.3%	2.1%
With Children Under 5	0.3%	0.4%	0.2%
With Children 5 to 17	0.9%	0.9%	0.8%
Headed by Females	1.1%	1.3%	0.9%
INDUSTRY (Total Employed)	109,803	55,949	53,854
Professional/Public Administration	16.6%	17.4%	15.7%
Manufacturing	23.0%	21.4%	24.7%
Retail	16.6%	16.4%	16.9%
Transportation/Communication	10.4%	10.8%	9.9%
Finance/Insurance/Real Estate	8.3%	8.9%	7.6%
Other Service	9.5%	9.5%	9.5%

Senator James "Pate" Philip (R)

District Office: 50 East Oak St., Suite 250, Addison 60101
Phone (630) 941-0094; (630) 832-2356 (fax)
Springfield Office: 327 Capitol Bldg., Springfield 62706
Phone (217) 782-3840

Legislative Assignments: Senate President; Executive Committee.

Public Service: Senator (1975-present); senate president (1993-present); senate minority leader (1981-93); representative (1967-74).

Personal: Full-time legislator; born May 26, 1930, Elmhurst; Kansas City Junior College and Kansas City State College; married (Nancy); four children.

1997 BILL PASSAGE RATIO	Introduced	Passed House of Origin	Passed GA
Primary	15	5	1
Primary/Hyphenated	26	12	5

KEY VOTES

1) Senate GOP Ed. $ Plan ......Y	6) Insurance/Domestic Violence ..Y	11) Pre-Paid College Tuition ....Y
2) State Budget ....Y	7) Brownfields ....Y	12) Increase Pull Tab Prizes ....Y
3) Tougher DUI Level ....Y	8) Welfare Reform ....Y	13) Telecommunications Tax ...N
4) Ban Partial Birth Abortions ...Y	9) Concealed Guns/Misdemeanor .Y	14) Delivery Discrimination ....P
5) State Employees Pension .....Y	10) Banks Sell Insurance ....Y	15) Sell Drivers' Data ....Y

GROUP RATINGS

	FB	CoC	PrLf	IPPC	ACLU
1997	86	100	1/2	0	50

ELECTION RESULTS

1994 General	James "Pate" Philip (R)	29,452	(69.2%)
1994 General	Keith Petropoulos (D)	13,100	(30.8%)
1994 Primary	James "Pate" Philip (R)	12,753	(100%)

CAMPAIGN RESOURCES AND EXPENDITURES

1996 Campaign Funds		Top 10 PAC Contributors	
Beg. Balance $1,077,317	Individuals ...$32,975	1) NRCC ...$180,000	6) MPAC $15,000
Receipts $614,386	Party $183,280	2) ISMS $25,000	7) WMgt $10,660
Expenditures .$560,412	PACS $344,555	3) Empress ..$25,000	8) IRLA $10,000
On hand ...$1,131,291	Candidate ...$18,006	4) UPS $15,000	9) BAGChgo $10,000
	Not-itemized $35,570	5) HOPE ...$15,000	10) ILCable .$10,000

NOTE: The General Election Opponent's Campaign Resources and Expenditures are reported in a separate section in the back of the book (pp. 269-284).

GENERAL ELECTION DATA

	Registered Voters	Voter Turnout		Straight Party Voting	
1996	90,910	65,689	72.3%	(R) 17,566 ..26.7%	(D) 9,566 ....14.6%

PRESIDENT

1996	Bill Clinton (D)	28,714	44.5%
	Bob Dole (R)	28,771	44.6%
	Ross Perot (I)	6,528	10.1%
1992	Bill Clinton (D)	25,574	32.8%
	George Bush (R)	34,802	44.7%
	Ross Perot (I)	17,534	22.5%

UNITED STATES SENATE

1996	Richard J. Durbin (D)	28,953	45.5%
	Al Salvi (R)	31,805	50.0%

GOVERNOR

1994	Jim Edgar (R)	34,555	79.7%
	Dawn Clark Netsch (D)	8,777	20.3%

Representative Kathleen L. "Kay" Wojcik (R)

District Office: 514 West Wise Rd., Schaumburg 60193
Phone (847) 524-0461; (847) 524-6938 (fax)
Springfield Office: Room 632 Capitol Bldg., Springfield 62706
Phone (217) 782-8192; (217) 782-1873 (fax)

Legislative Assignments: Assistant Republican Leader; ex officio member of all committees. Committees on Consumer Protection; Registration & Regulation; Financial Institutions.

Public Service: Representative (1983-present); former clerk, Schaumburg Township.

Personal: Full-time legislator; born July 15, 1936, Chicago; William Harper College, Palatine; married (Norbert); two children; five grandchildren.

1997 BILL PASSAGE RATIO	Introduced	Passed House of Origin	Passed GA
Primary	5	3	1
Primary/Hyphenated	13	10	3

KEY VOTES

1) Change Ed. Funding Formula . . N	6) Insurance/Domestic Violence . . Y	11) Pre-Paid College Tuition . . . . Y
2) State Budget . . . . Y	7) Brownfields . . . . Y	12) Increase Pull Tab Prizes . . . . Y
3) Tougher DUI Level . . . . Y	8) Welfare Reform . . . . Y	13) Utility Deregulation . . . . Y
4) Ban Partial Birth Abortions . . . Y	9) Concealed Guns/Misdemeanor . Y	14) County Obscenity Standards . Y
5) State Employees Pension . . . . . Y	10) Banks Sell Insurance . . . . Y	15) Managed Care Reform . . . . . Y

GROUP RATINGS

	FB	CoC	PrLf	IPPC	ACLU
1997	64	69	5/6	0	20

ELECTION RESULTS

1996 General	Kathleen L. "Kay" Wojcik (R)	23,025	(100%)
1996 Primary	Kathleen L. "Kay" Wojcik (R)	6,718	(100%)
1994 General	Kathleen L. "Kay" Wojcik (R)	16,977	(100%)
1994 Primary	Kathleen L. "Kay" Wojcik (R)	5,406	(100%)

CAMPAIGN RESOURCES AND EXPENDITURES

1996 Campaign Funds				Top 10 PAC Contributors			
Beg. Balance	$70,743	Individuals	$9,817	1) ILCable	$2,500	6) ABDI	$1,300
Receipts	$65,581	Party	$0	2) Laidlaw	$1,700	7) ILCon	$1,200
Expenditures	$55,082	PACS	$48,684	3) SR&D	$1,600	8) FBSchaum	$1,200
On hand	$81,242	Candidate	$0	4) RJR	$1,500	9) HI	$1,000
		Not-itemized	$7,080	5) IBA	$1,500	10) ARC	$1,000

NOTE: The General Election Opponent's Campaign Resources and Expenditures are reported in a separate section in the back of the book (pp. 269-284).

GENERAL ELECTION DATA

	Registered Voters	Voter Turnout		Straight Party Voting	
1996	46,444	32,133	69.2%	(R) 8,632 . . . 26.9%	(D) 4,812 . . . 15.0%

PRESIDENT

1996	Bill Clinton (D)	13,973	44.2%
	Bob Dole (R)	14,439	45.6%
	Ross Perot (I)	2,992	9.5%
1992	Bill Clinton (D)	12,948	32.4%
	George Bush (R)	18,250	45.7%
	Ross Perot (I)	8,769	21.9%

UNITED STATES SENATE

1996	Richard J. Durbin (D)	14,223	45.6%
	Al Salvi (R)	15,662	50.2%

GOVERNOR

1994	Jim Edgar (R)	16,440	79.6%
	Dawn Clark Netsch (D)	4,216	20.4%

Representative Lee A. Daniels (R)

District Office: 611 N. York Rd., Elmhurst 60126
Phone (630) 530-2700; (630) 279-8660 (fax)
Springfield Office: Room 316 Capitol Bldg., Springfield 62706
Phone (217) 782-4014; (217) 782-7012 (fax)

Legislative Assignments: Minority Leader, ex officio member of all committees.

Public Service: Representative (1975-present); minority leader (1997-present, 1983-1995); speaker (1995-97); board of trustees, York Township.

Personal: Attorney, Bell, Boyd and Lloyd; born April 15, 1942, Lansing, MI; University of Iowa, B.A. in political science; John Marshall Law School, J.D.; married (Pam); five children.

1997 BILL PASSAGE RATIO	Introduced	Passed House of Origin	Passed GA
Primary	27	6	0
Primary/Hyphenated	31	9	1

KEY VOTES

1) Change Ed. Funding Formula . . N	6) Insurance/Domestic Violence . . Y	11) Pre-Paid College Tuition . . . . Y
2) State Budget . . . . Y	7) Brownfields . . . . Y	12) Increase Pull Tab Prizes . . . Y
3) Tougher DUI Level . . . . Y	8) Welfare Reform . . . . Y	13) Utility Deregulation . . . . Y
4) Ban Partial Birth Abortions . . . Y	9) Concealed Guns/Misdemeanor . Y	14) County Obscenity Standards . Y
5) State Employees Pension . . . . . Y	10) Banks Sell Insurance . . . . Y	15) Managed Care Reform . . . . . N

GROUP RATINGS

	FB	CoC	PrLf	IPPC	ACLU
1997	68	69	6/6	0	20

ELECTION RESULTS

1996 General	Lee A. Daniels (R)	21,655	(68.5%)
1996 General	Dennis Hamm (D)	9,958	(31.5%)
1996 Primary	Lee A. Daniels (R)	9,187	(100%)
1996 Primary	Dennis Hamm (D)	2,527	(100%)

CAMPAIGN RESOURCES AND EXPENDITURES

1996 Campaign Funds

Beg. Balance	$2,240,097	Individuals	$103,864
Receipts	$1,395,461	Party	$165,300
Expenditures	$2,848,998	PACS	$763,014
On hand	$786,560	Candidate	$337,412
		Not-itemized	$25,871

Top 10 PAC Contributors

1) NRCC . . $160,000	6) MPAC . . . $20,000
2) ISMS $30,000	7) ILCable . . $20,000
3) Cent21 . . . $25,000	8) IPACE . . . $19,000
4) PMorris . . $25,000	9) Portillo's . . $10,000
5) CMC $20,000	10) Kraft $10,000

NOTE: The General Election Opponent's Campaign Resources and Expenditures are reported in a separate section in the back of the book (pp. 269-284).

GENERAL ELECTION DATA

	Registered Voters	Voter Turnout		Straight Party Voting			
1996	44,466	33,556	75.5%	(R) 8,934	26.6%	(D) 4,754	14.2%

PRESIDENT

1996	Bill Clinton (D)	14,741	44.9%
	Bob Dole (R)	14,332	43.6%
	Ross Perot (I)	3,536	10.8%
1992	Bill Clinton (D)	12,626	33.3%
	George Bush (R)	16,552	43.6%
	Ross Perot (I)	8,765	23.1%

UNITED STATES SENATE

1996	Richard J. Durbin (D)	14,370	45.4%
	Al Salvi (R)	16,143	49.8%

GOVERNOR

1994	Jim Edgar (R)	18,115	79.9%
	Dawn Clark Netsch (D)	4,561	20.1%

24th Senate District

House District 47
House District 48

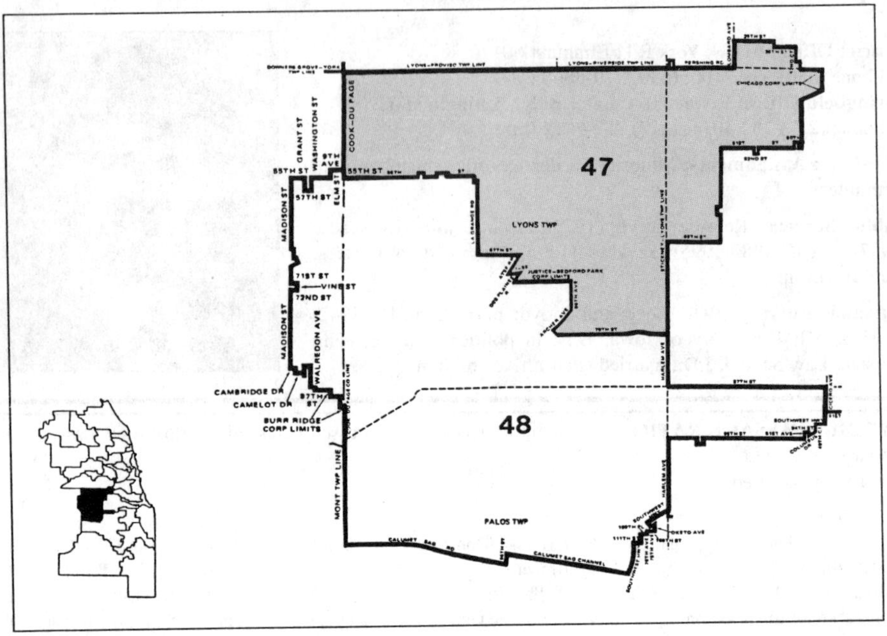

DEMOGRAPHICS (1990)

	S.D. #24	H.D. #47	H.D.#48
VOTING AGE POPULATION	149,537	74,882	74,655
White	91.8%	90.5%	93.1%
Black	2.2%	2.3%	2.1%
Hispanic	4.4%	6.0%	2.7%
Asian	1.5%	1.0%	2.0%
AGE (Total Population)	193,739	96,869	96,870
Under 6	8.0%	8.2%	7.8%
6 to 18	16.1%	15.7%	16.5%
65 and Over	14.4%	15.8%	12.9%
URBAN POPULATION	99.9%	100.0%	99.8%
HOUSING UNITS (Total)	74,140	37,349	36,791
Median Value	$111,319	$101,164	$120,065
Owner Occupied	74.3%	73.9%	74.8%
FAMILY INCOME (Total Families)	53,007	26,503	26,504
Median Income	$46,405	$45,773	$46,967
Below Poverty Level	3.3%	3.8%	2.7%
With Children Under 5	0.5%	0.6%	0.4%
With Children 5 to 17	1.0%	1.0%	0.9%
Headed by Females	1.4%	1.4%	1.4%
INDUSTRY (Total Employed)	98,778	48,337	50,441
Professional/Public Administration	22.7%	24.4%	21.1%
Manufacturing	19.5%	20.8%	18.3%
Retail	17.7%	16.8%	18.5%
Transportation/Communication	9.8%	8.6%	11.0%
Finance/Insurance/Real Estate	8.7%	9.0%	8.4%
Other Service	8.7%	8.8%	8.5%

Senator Christine Radogno (R)

District Office: 521 S. LaGrange Rd., Suite 104, LaGrange 60525
Phone (708) 354-6700; (708) 354-6730 (fax)
Springfield Office: M108 Capitol Bldg., Springfield 62706
Phone (217) 782-9407

Legislative Assignments: Committees on Commerce and Industry (vice-chair); Revenue, Public Health and Welfare.

Public Service: Senator (1997-present); former LaGrange village trustee; founder, Citizens Active in Reclaiming the Environment (CARE).

Personal: Bachelor's Degree and Master's Degree in Social Work from Loyola University; married (Nunzio); three daughters.

1997 BILL PASSAGE RATIO	Introduced	Passed House of Origin	Passed GA
Primary	15	9	9
Primary/Hyphenated	26	14	13

KEY VOTES

1) Senate GOP Ed. $ Plan ...... Y
2) StateBudget .... Y
3) Tougher DUI Level .... Y
4) Ban Partial Birth Abortions ... Y
5) State Employees Pension ..... Y
6) Insurance/Domestic Violence .. Y
7) Brownfields .... Y
8) Welfare Reform .... Y
9) Concealed Guns/Misdemeanor . N
10) Banks Sell Insurance .... Y
11) Pre-Paid College Tuition .... Y
12) Increase Pull Tab Prizes .... N
13) Telecommunications Tax .. N
14) Delivery Discrimination .... N
15) Sell Drivers' Data .... Y

GROUP RATINGS

	FB	CoC	PrLf	IPPC	ACLU
1997	82	100	2/2	0	75

ELECTION RESULTS

1996 General	Christine Radogno (R)	36,680	(50.1%)
1996 General	Nancy C. Kenney (D)	36,598	(49.9%)
1996 Primary	Christine Radogno (R)	7,611	(50.3%)
1996 Primary	Robert M. Raica (R)	7,529	(49.7%)

CAMPAIGN RESOURCES AND EXPENDITURES

1996 Campaign Funds

Beg. Balance	$9,969	Individuals	$5,045
Receipts	$691,419	Party	$591,242
Expenditures	$692,785	PACS	$90,879
On hand	$8,603	Candidate	$0
		Not-itemized	$4,253

Top 10 PAC Contributors

1) RSSC ...$561,512	6) MPAC $4,750
2) ISMS $15,158	7) Mentzer ...$4,095
3) CRausch ..$7,000	8) ChgoCoC ..$4,000
4) CoC $5,000	9) CWalsh ...$4,000
5) CRyan $5,000	10) GOPWom .$3,000

NOTE: The General Election Opponent's Campaign Resources and Expenditures are reported in a separate section in the back of the book (pp. 269-284).

GENERAL ELECTION DATA

	Registered Voters	Voter Turnout		Straight Party Voting	
1996	113,847	76,701	67.4%	(R) 13,931 .. 18.2%	(D) 13,719 ... 17.9%

PRESIDENT

1996	Bill Clinton (D)	36,088	47.9%
	Bob Dole (R)	31,617	42.0%
	Ross Perot (I)	6,937	9.2%
1992	Bill Clinton (D)	34,538	38.3%
	George Bush (R)	36,980	41.0%
	Ross Perot (I)	18,773	20.7%

UNITED STATES SENATE

1996	Richard J. Durbin (D)	37,619	52.6%
	Al Salvi (R)	33,916	47.4%

GOVERNOR

1994	Jim Edgar (R)	41,669	72.3%
	Dawn Clark Netsch (D)	15,938	26.7%

Representative Eileen Lyons (R)

District Office: 1030 South LaGrange Rd., Suite 5, LaGrange 60525
Phone (708) 352-7700; (708) 352-7702 (fax)
Springfield Office: Room 2123-O Stratton Bldg., Springfield 62706
Phone (217) 782-0494; (217) 782-1336 (fax)

Legislative Assignments: Committees on Health Care Availability & Access; Labor & Commerce; Judiciary II-Criminal Law; Aging.

Public Service: Representative (1995-present).

Personal: Full-time legislator; born July 4, 1941, New York, NY; Elmhurst College; married (Arthur); four children.

1997 BILL PASSAGE RATIO	Introduced	Passed House of Origin	Passed GA
Primary	3	2	2
Primary/Hyphenated	26	20	10

KEY VOTES

1) Change Ed. Funding Formula . .N	6) Insurance/Domestic Violence . .Y	11) Pre-Paid College Tuition . . . .Y
2) State Budget . . . . .Y	7) Brownfields . . . . .Y	12) Increase Pull Tab Prizes . . . .Y
3) Tougher DUI Level . . . . .Y	8) Welfare Reform . . . . .Y	13) Utility Deregulation . . . . .P
4) Ban Partial Birth Abortions . . .Y	9) Concealed Guns/Misdemeanor .Y	14) County Obscenity Standards .Y
5) State Employees Pension . . . . .Y	10) Banks Sell Insurance . . . . .Y	15) Managed Care Reform . . . . .N

GROUP RATINGS

	FB	CoC	PrLf	IPPC	ACLU
1997	57	54	6/6	0	20

ELECTION RESULTS

1996 General	Eileen Lyons (R)	20,393	(51.7%)
1996 General	Mark Pera (D)	19,031	(48.3%)
1996 Primary	Eileen Lyons (R)	8,013	(100%)
1996 Primary	Mark Pera (D)	7,078	(100%)

CAMPAIGN RESOURCES AND EXPENDITURES

1996 Campaign Funds		Top 10 PAC Contributors	
Beg. Balance .$31,468	Individuals . . .$8,368	1) HRCC . .$182,076	6) FKubik . . .$10,000
Receipts $352,006	Party $262,526	2) FLAD . . .$45,150	7) MPAC $3,500
Expenditures .$347,606	PACS $65,064	3) CChurchill $10,000	8) ChgoCoC . .$2,500
On hand $35,868	Candidate $263	4) ISMS $10,000	9) GOPWom . .$2,000
	Not-itemized $15,785	5) CBiggert .$10,000	10) SMCorp . .$2,000

NOTE: The General Election Opponent's Campaign Resources and Expenditures are reported in a separate section in the back of the book (pp. 269-284).

GENERAL ELECTION DATA

	Registered Voters	Voter Turnout	Straight Party Voting	
1996	57,813	40,929 . . . . .70.8%	(R) 6,225 . . .15.2%	(D) 7,861 . . . .19.2%

PRESIDENT

1996	Bill Clinton (D)	20,148	50.3%
	Bob Dole (R)	15,914	39.7%
	Ross Perot (I)	3,646	9.1%
1992	Bill Clinton (D)	19,500	40.6%
	George Bush (R)	19,140	39.8%
	Ross Perot (I)	9,407	19.6%

UNITED STATES SENATE

1996	Richard J. Durbin (D)	20,793	52.8%
	Al Salvi (R)	17,252	43.8%

GOVERNOR

1994	Jim Edgar (R)	23,393	71.6%
	Dawn Clark Netsch (D)	9,277	28.4%

Representative Anne Zickus (R)

District Office: 10600 South Roberts Rd., Palos Hills 60465
Phone (708) 974-8080; (708) 974-8083 (fax)
Springfield Office: Room G-4 Stratton Bldg., Springfield 62706
Phone (217) 782-8017

Legislative Assignments: Committees on Human Services (minority spokesperson); Consumer Protection; Transportation & Motor Vehicles; Health Care Availability & Access; Registration & Regulation; Legislative Audit Commission.

Public Service: Representative 47th district (1989-91); representative 48th district (1993-present).

Personal: Realtor; born April 6, 1939, Chicago; married (Charles); two children.

1997 BILL PASSAGE RATIO	Introduced	Passed House of Origin	Passed GA
Primary	20	7	4
Primary/Hyphenated	28	15	9

KEY VOTES

1) Change Ed. Funding Formula . .N
2) State Budget . . . . .Y
3) Tougher DUI Level . . . . .Y
4) Ban Partial Birth Abortions . . .Y
5) State Employees Pension . . . . .Y
6) Insurance/Domestic Violence . .Y
7) Brownfields . . . . .Y
8) Welfare Reform . . . . .Y
9) Concealed Guns/Misdemeanor .Y
10) Banks Sell Insurance . . . . .Y
11) Pre-Paid College Tuition . . . .A
12) Increase Pull Tab Prizes . . . .Y
13) Utility Deregulation . . . . .P
14) County Obscenity Standards .Y
15) Managed Care Reform . . . . .Y

GROUP RATINGS

	FB	CoC	PrLf	IPPC	ACLU
1997	64	54	6/6	0	20

ELECTION RESULTS

1996 General	Anne Zickus (R)	22,503	(65.1%)
1996 General	Michael W. Schadt (D)	11,834	(34.9%)
1996 Primary	Anne Zickus (R)	6,051	(100%)
1996 Primary	Michael W. Schadt (D)	3,502	(100%)

CAMPAIGN RESOURCES AND EXPENDITURES

1996 Campaign Funds

Beg. Balance	$11,404	Individuals	$2,335
Receipts	$70,849	Party	$32,597
Expenditures	$75,525	PACS	$32,900
On hand	$6,728	Candidate	$0
		Not-itemized	$3,017

Top 10 PAC Contributors

1) HRCC	$26,597	6) ABDI	$1,000
2) ISMS	$5,500	7) MPAC	$1,000
3) RPAC	$5,000	8) IAMB	$750
4) CChurchill	$2,500	9) Zeman	$500
5) FLAD	$2,000	10) LICID	$500

NOTE: The General Election Opponent's Campaign Resources and Expenditures are reported in a separate section in the back of the book (pp. 269-284).

GENERAL ELECTION DATA

	Registered Voters	Voter Turnout		Straight Party Voting	
1996	56,034	35,772	63.8%	(R) 7,706 . . .21.5%	(D) 5,858 . . . .16.4%

PRESIDENT

1996	Bill Clinton (D)	15,940	45.4%
	Bob Dole (R)	15,703	44.7%
	Ross Perot (I)	3,291	9.4%
1992	Bill Clinton (D)	15,038	35.6%
	George Bush (R)	17,840	42.2%
	Ross Perot (I)	9,366	22.2%

UNITED STATES SENATE

1996	Richard J. Durbin (D)	16,826	48.6%
	Al Salvi (R)	16,664	48.1%

GOVERNOR

1994	Jim Edgar (R)	18,276	73.3%
	Dawn Clark Netsch (D)	6,661	26.7%

25th Senate District

House District 49
House District 50

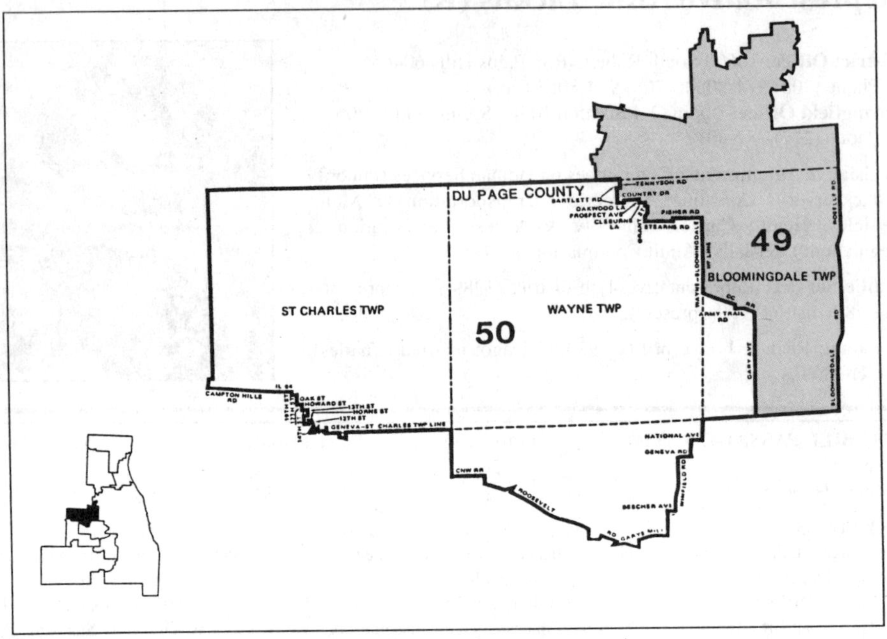

DEMOGRAPHICS (1990)

	S.D. #25	H.D. #49	H.D.#50
VOTING AGE POPULATION	134,689	67,864	66,825
White	86.9%	84.5%	89.3%
Black	1.6%	2.1%	1.2%
Hispanic	6.3%	6.2%	6.5%
Asian	5.0%	7.1%	2.9%
AGE (Total Population)	193,739	96,870	96,869
Under 6	11.2%	10.7%	11.7%
6 to 18	20.7%	20.7%	20.6%
65 and Over	5.5%	4.8%	6.2%
URBAN POPULATION	94.9%	100.0%	89.9%
HOUSING UNITS (Total)	66,227	33,172	33,055
Median Value	$121,340	$116,338	$128,225
Owner Occupied	77.0%	75.5%	78.5%
FAMILY INCOME (Total Families)	51,661	25,543	26,119
Median Income	$52,119	$50,344	$53,687
Below Poverty Level	1.8%	1.9%	1.8%
With Children Under 5	0.3%	0.3%	0.3%
With Children 5 to 17	0.7%	0.8%	0.6%
Headed by Females	0.7%	0.7%	0.7%
INDUSTRY (Total Employed)	107,105	54,755	52,350
Professional/Public Administration	19.8%	18.1%	21.5%
Manufacturing	21.8%	21.4%	22.3%
Retail	16.2%	16.9%	15.5%
Transportation/Communication	9.0%	9.4%	8.5%
Finance/Insurance/Real Estate	8.3%	8.9%	7.7%
Other Service	9.4%	9.8%	8.9%

Senator Doris C. Karpiel (R)

District Office: 400 W. Lake St., Suite 220, Roselle 60172
Phone (630) 894-2008; (630) 894-2871 (fax)
Springfield Office: 123 Capitol Bldg., Springfield 62706
Phone (217) 782-5572;

Legislative Assignments: Majority Caucus Chair. Committees on Licensed Activities (vice-chair); Education; Executive; Environment & Energy.

Public Service: Senator (1984-present); representative (1979-1984); supervisor, Bloomingdale Township; trustee, Bloomingdale Township.

Personal: Full-time legislator; born September 21, 1935, Chicago; Morton Jr. College, A.A. and Northern Illinois University, B.A. in political science; four children; five grandchildren.

1997 BILL PASSAGE RATIO	Introduced	Passed House of Origin	Passed GA
Primary	13	8	6
Primary/Hyphenated	31	17	12

KEY VOTES

1) Senate GOP Ed. $ Plan . . . . . . .Y	6) Insurance/Domestic Violence . .Y	11) Pre-Paid College Tuition . . . .Y
2) State Budget . . . . .Y	7) Brownfields . . . . .Y	12) Increase Pull Tab Prizes . . . .N
3) Tougher DUI Level . . . . .Y	8) Welfare Reform . . . . .Y	13) Telecommunications Tax . . .N
4) Ban Partial Birth Abortions . . .Y	9) Concealed Guns/Misdemeanor .Y	14) Delivery Discrimination . . . .N
5) State Employees Pension . . . . .Y	10) Banks Sell Insurance . . . . .Y	15) Sell Drivers' Data . . . . .N

GROUP RATINGS

	FB	CoC	PrLf	IPPC	ACLU
1997	73	100	2/2	0	50

ELECTION RESULTS

1996 General	Doris C. Karpiel (R)	43,282	(64.5%)
1996 General	Geraldine Vance Carter (D)	23,812	(35.5%)
1996 Primary	Doris C. Karpiel (R)	15,669	(100%)

CAMPAIGN RESOURCES AND EXPENDITURES

1996 Campaign Funds				Top 10 PAC Contributors			
Beg. Balance	$19,649	Individuals	$1,383	1) ISMS	$1,000	6) NIGAS	$750
Receipts	$38,052	Party	$830	2) FloodBros	$1,000	7) WMgt	$750
Expenditures	$27,060	PACS	$26,725	3) MPAC	$1,000	8) Benchmark	$750
On hand	$30,641	Candidate	$0	4) IBA	$1,000	9) GOA	$695
		Not-itemized	$9,114	5) ABDI	$1,000	10) CRausch	$630

NOTE: The General Election Opponent's Campaign Resources and Expenditures are reported in a separate section in the back of the book (pp. 269-284).

GENERAL ELECTION DATA

	Registered Voters	Voter Turnout		Straight Party Voting			
1996	101,811	72,442	71.2%	(R) 20,007	27.6%	(D) 9,668	13.4%

PRESIDENT

1996	Bill Clinton (D)	29,991	42.1%
	Bob Dole (R)	33,821	47.4%
	Ross Perot (I)	6,965	9.8%
1992	Bill Clinton (D)	26,199	31.7%
	George Bush (R)	37,807	45.8%
	Ross Perot (I)	18,628	22.5%

UNITED STATES SENATE

1996	Richard J. Durbin (D)	30,747	43.9%
	Al Salvi (R)	36,336	51.8%

GOVERNOR

1994	Jim Edgar (R)	37,006	79.5%
	Dawn Clark Netsch (D)	9,548	20.5%

Representative Carole Pankau (R)

District Office: 1278-B West Lake St., Roselle 60172
Phone (630) 582-0390; (630) 582-0391 (fax)
Springfield Office: Room 2122-0 Stratton Bldg., Springfield 62706
Phone (217) 782-8158; (217) 782-1336 (fax)

Legislative Assignments: Committees on Registration & Regulation (minority spokesperson); Health Care Availability & Access; Appropriations-Public Safety; Revenue.

Public Service: Representative (1993-present); board member, DuPage County; board member, Kenneyville School District 20.

Personal: Born August 13, 1947, Valparaiso, IN; University of Illinois, B.S. in accounting; married (John); four children.

1997 BILL PASSAGE RATIO	Introduced	Passed House of Origin	Passed GA
Primary	8	3	3
Primary/Hyphenated	12	5	4

KEY VOTES

1) Change Ed. Funding Formula . .N	6) Insurance/Domestic Violence . .Y	11) Pre-Paid College Tuition . . . .Y
2) State Budget . . . . .Y	7) Brownfields . . . . .Y	12) Increase Pull Tab Prizes . . . .Y
3) Tougher DUI Level . . . . .Y	8) Welfare Reform . . . . .Y	13) Utility Deregulation . . . . . . .Y
4) Ban Partial Birth Abortions . . .Y	9) Concealed Guns/Misdemeanor .Y	14) County Obscenity Standards .Y
5) State Employees Pension . . . . .Y	10) Banks Sell Insurance . . . . .Y	15) Managed Care Reform . . . . .N

GROUP RATINGS

	FB	CoC	PrLf	IPPC	ACLU
1997	64	62	6/6	0	20

ELECTION RESULTS

1996 General	Carole Pankau (R)	17,590	(62.0%)
1996 General	Robert "Bob" Banks (D)	10,769	(38.0%)
1996 Primary	Carole Pankau (R)	5,335	(100%)
1996 Primary	Robert "Bob" Banks (D)	1,736	(100%)

CAMPAIGN RESOURCES AND EXPENDITURES

1996 Campaign Funds

Beg. Balance	$9,933	Individuals	$2,384
Receipts	$33,265	Party	$842
Expenditures	$22,269	PACS	$18,298
On hand	$20,929	Candidate	$167
		Not-itemized	$11,574

Top 10 PAC Contributors

1) Benchmark . $1,500	6) MPAC $500
2) Pacini $1,000	7) IBA $500
3) CPA's $600	8) Empress $500
4) PetPec $500	9) ICAPAC $500
5) LICID $500	10) HOPE $500

NOTE: The General Election Opponent's Campaign Resources and Expenditures are reported in a separate section in the back of the book (pp. 269-284).

GENERAL ELECTION DATA

	Registered Voters	Voter Turnout		Straight Party Voting	
1996	45,259	30,758	68.0%	(R) 7,793 . . .25.3%	(D) 4,811 . . . .15.6%

PRESIDENT

1996	Bill Clinton (D)	13,996	46.2%
	Bob Dole (R)	13,154	43.4%
	Ross Perot (I)	2,943	9.7%
1992	Bill Clinton (D)	12,637	34.6%
	George Bush (R)	15,778	43.2%
	Ross Perot (I)	8,126	22.2%

UNITED STATES SENATE

1996	Richard J. Durbin (D)	14,034	47.1%
	Al Salvi (R)	14,516	48.7%

GOVERNOR

1994	Jim Edgar (R)	15,368	77.9%
	Dawn Clark Netsch (D)	4,355	22.1%

Representative Thomas L. Johnson (R)

District Office: 27W031 North Ave., West Chicago 60185-5122
Phone (630) 231-0340; (630) 231-0464 (fax)
Springfield Office: Room G-3 Stratton Bldg., Springfield 62706
Phone (217) 782-1565

Legislative Assignments: Committees on Prison Management Reform (minority spokesperson); Elementary & Secondary Education; Judiciary II-Criminal Law; Labor & Commerce; Veterans' Affairs.

Public Service: Representative (1993-present).

Personal: Attorney; born April 30, 1945, Oakland, CA.; University of Michigan; DePaul Law School, J.D.; married (Virginia); three children.

1997 BILL PASSAGE RATI0	Introduced	Passed House of Origin	Passed GA
Primary	11	3	2
Primary/Hyphenated	23	11	5

KEY VOTES

1) Change Ed. Funding Formula . .N	6) Insurance/Domestic Violence . .Y	11) Pre-Paid College Tuition . . . .Y
2) State Budget . . . . .Y	7) Brownfields . . . . .Y	12) Increase Pull Tab Prizes . . . .N
3) Tougher DUI Level . . . . .Y	8) Welfare Reform . . . . .Y	13) Utility Deregulation . . . . .P
4) Ban Partial Birth Abortions . . .Y	9) Concealed Guns/Misdemeanor .Y	14) County Obscenity Standards .Y
5) State Employees Pension . . . . .Y	10) Banks Sell Insurance . . . . .Y	15) Managed Care Reform . . . . .N

GROUP RATINGS

	FB	CoC	PrLf	IPPC	ACLU
1997	57	92	6/6	0	20

ELECTION RESULTS

1996 General	Thomas L. Johnson (R)	23,462	(61.4%)
1996 General	Mary Frances Potts (D)	14,725	(38.6%)
1996 Primary	Thomas L. Johnson (R)	9,828	(100%)

CAMPAIGN RESOURCES AND EXPENDITURES

1996 Campaign Funds		Top 10 PAC Contributors	
Beg. Balance $495	Individuals . .$32,440	1) Dominick's . .$250	6) N/A . . . .$N/A
Receipts $37,066	Party $0	2) M&B $250	7) N/A . . . .$N/A
Expenditures .$26,421	PACS $650	3) CSX $150	8) N/A . . . .$N/A
On hand $11,140	Candidate $500	4) N/A . . . .$N/A	9) N/A . . . .$N/A
	Not-itemized .$3,476	5) N/A . . . .$N/A	10) N/A . . . . . .$N/A

NOTE: The General Election Opponent's Campaign Resources and Expenditures are reported in a separate section in the back of the book (pp. 269-284).

GENERAL ELECTION DATA

	Registered Voters	Voter Turnout		Straight Party Voting	
1996	56,552	41,684	73.7%	(R) 12,214 . .29.3%	(D) 4,857 . . . .11.6%

PRESIDENT

1996	Bill Clinton (D)	15,995	40.0%
	Bob Dole (R)	20,667	50.4%
	Ross Perot (I)	4,022	9.8%
1992	Bill Clinton (D)	13,562	29.4%
	George Bush (R)	22,029	47.8%
	Ross Perot (I)	10,502	22.8%

UNITED STATES SENATE

1996	Richard J. Durbin (D)	16,713	42.5%
	Al Salvi (R)	21,820	55.5%

GOVERNOR

1994	Jim Edgar (R)	21,638	80.6%
	Dawn Clark Netsch (D)	5,193	19.4%

26th Senate District

House District 51
House District 52

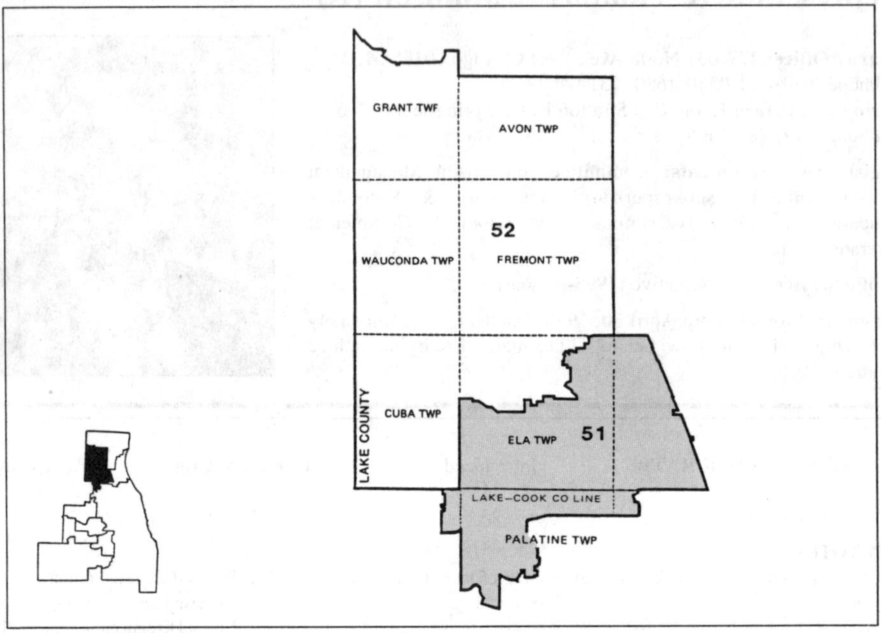

DEMOGRAPHICS (1990)

	S.D. #26	H.D. #51	H.D.#52
VOTING AGE POPULATION	137,654	68,351	69,303
White	91.4%	89.3%	93.4%
Black	0.8%	1.3%	0.4%
Hispanic	5.2%	5.3%	5.1%
Asian	2.5%	4.1%	1.0%
AGE (Total Population)	193,739	96,870	96,869
Under 6	11.1%	11.8%	10.4%
6 to 18	19.1%	18.7%	19.4%
65 and Over	6.2%	4.4%	8.0%
URBAN POPULATION	92.9%	99.7%	86.1%
HOUSING UNITS (Total)	69,932	35,067	34,865
Median Value	$149,538	$178,730	$113,220
Owner Occupied	76.2%	74.7%	77.7%
FAMILY INCOME (Total Families)	52,818	26,498	26,320
Median Income	$56,652	$64,937	$49,346
Below Poverty Level	2.6%	2.1%	3.1%
With Children Under 5	0.5%	0.5%	0.4%
With Children 5 to 17	0.8%	0.7%	1.0%
Headed by Females	1.4%	1.0%	1.7%
INDUSTRY (Total Employed)	105,984	54,413	51,571
Professional/Public Administration	20.3%	21.0%	19.7%
Manufacturing	22.3%	21.3%	23.3%
Retail	16.2%	15.8%	16.7%
Transportation/Communication	6.0%	6.1%	6.0%
Finance/Insurance/Real Estate	10.6%	12.2%	8.9%
Other Service	9.2%	9.5%	8.9%

Senator William E. Peterson (R)

District Office: 3050 North Main St., Prairie View 60069
Phone (847) 634-6060; (847) 634-1569 (fax)
Springfield Office: 307 Capitol Bldg., Springfield 62706
Phone (217) 782-8010

Legislative Assignments: Committees on Revenue (chair); Insurance & Pensions; Licensed Activities; Intergovernmental Cooperation Commission.

Public Service: Senator (1993-present); representative (1983-93), school board member; township trustee and supervisor.

Personal: Full-time legislator; born February 2, 1936, Chicago; military veteran; North Park College, B.A.; Northern Illinois University, M.S. in education; Loyola University, post-graduate studies; married (Patricia); three children; three grandchildren.

1997 BILL PASSAGE RATIO	Introduced	Passed House of Origin	Passed GA
Primary	18	12	8
Primary/Hyphenated	28	20	15

KEY VOTES

1) Senate GOP Ed. $ Plan ......Y	6) Insurance/Domestic Violence ..Y	11) Pre-Paid College Tuition ....Y
2) State Budget ....Y	7) Brownfields ....Y	12) Increase Pull Tab Prizes ....Y
3) Tougher DUI Level ....Y	8) Welfare Reform ....Y	13) Telecommunications Tax ...N
4) Ban Partial Birth Abortions ...Y	9) Concealed Guns/Misdemeanor .Y	14) Delivery Discrimination ....P
5) State Employees Pension .....Y	10) Banks Sell Insurance ....Y	15) Sell Drivers' Data ....N

GROUP RATINGS

	FB	CoC	PrLf	IPPC	ACLU
1997	91	100	2/2	0	50

ELECTION RESULTS

1994 General	William E. Peterson (R)	34,592	(72.8%)
1994 General	Nancy Sass Scotillo (D)	12,917	(27.2%)
1994 Primary	William E. Peterson (R)	15,940	(100%)

CAMPAIGN RESOURCES AND EXPENDITURES

1996 Campaign Funds				Top 10 PAC Contributors			
Beg. Balance	$165,343	Individuals	$1,920	1) IPACE	$5,500	6) CPA's	$600
Receipts	$46,086	Party	$560	2) PIIA	$1,500	7) CNA	$500
Expenditures	$51,681	PACS	$28,340	3) AFFI	$1,000	8) LCR	$500
On hand	$159,748	Candidate	$2,426	4) HI	$1,000	9) IBA	$500
		Not-itemized	$12,840	5) MPAC	$1,000	10) IHHA	$500

NOTE: The General Election Opponent's Campaign Resources and Expenditures are reported in a separate section in the back of the book (pp. 269-284).

GENERAL ELECTION DATA

	Registered Voters	Voter Turnout		Straight Party Voting	
1996	116,708	81,291	69.7%	(R) 24,195 ..29.8%	(D) 8,560 ....10.5%

PRESIDENT

1996	Bill Clinton (D)	33,395	40.9%
	Bob Dole (R)	40,457	49.6%
	Ross Perot (I)	7,034	8.6%
1992	Bill Clinton (D)	27,761	30.9%
	George Bush (R)	42,807	47.7%
	Ross Perot (I)	19,195	21.4%

UNITED STATES SENATE

1996	Richard J. Durbin (D)	34,566	43.1%
	Al Salvi (R)	42,615	53.1%

GOVERNOR

1994	Jim Edgar (R)	39,256	79.9%
	Dawn Clark Netsch (D)	9,881	20.1%

Representative Verna L. Clayton (R)

District Office: 314 McHenry Rd., Suite D-1, Buffalo Grove 60089
Phone (847) 520-3555; (847) 520-4091 (fax)

Springfield Office: Room 2119-N Stratton Bldg., Springfield 62706
Phone (217) 782-1664; (217) 782-1139 (fax)

Legislative Assignments: Committees on State Government Administration & Election Reform (minority spokesperson); Executive; Health Care Availability & Access; Transportation & Motor Vehicles; Legislative Printing Unit.

Public Service: Representative (1993-present); former mayor and village clerk, Buffalo Grove.

Personal: Full-time legislator; born February 28, 1937, Hamden, OH; Oklahoma State University; married (Frank); two children.

1997 BILL PASSAGE RATIO	Introduced	Passed House of Origin	Passed GA
Primary	15	7	5
Primary/Hyphenated	29	18	7

KEY VOTES

1) Change Ed. Funding Formula . . N	6) Insurance/Domestic Violence . . Y	11) Pre-Paid College Tuition . . . . Y
2) State Budget . . . . Y	7) Brownfields . . . . Y	12) Increase Pull Tab Prizes . . . . N
3) Tougher DUI Level . . . . Y	8) Welfare Reform . . . . Y	13) Utility Deregulation . . . . Y
4) Ban Partial Birth Abortions . . . N	9) Concealed Guns/Misdemeanor . Y	14) County Obscenity Standards . N
5) State Employees Pension . . . . . Y	10) Banks Sell Insurance . . . . Y	15) Managed Care Reform . . . . . N

GROUP RATINGS

	FB	CoC	PrLf	IPPC	ACLU
1997	68	92	0/6	100	89

ELECTION RESULTS

1996 General	Verna L. Clayton (R)	26,107	(70.5%)
1996 General	Hyman Riebman (D)	10,922	(29.5%)
1996 Primary	Verna L. Clayton (R)	6,480	(58.5%)
1996 Primary	Mike Salvi (R)	4,596	(41.5%)

CAMPAIGN RESOURCES AND EXPENDITURES

1996 Campaign Funds				Top 10 PAC Contributors	
Beg. Balance	$60,644	Individuals	$0	1) IPACE $3,700	6) ILCon $300
Receipts	$15,499	Party	$0	2) CUPAC $500	7) IRoad $300
Expenditures	$24,683	PACS	$9,043	3) ISMS $500	8) Fidelity $250
On hand	$51,460	Candidate	$0	4) CPA's $500	9) IBA $250
		Not-itemized	$6,456	5) IMAPAC $300	10) IHCA $250

NOTE: The General Election Opponent's Campaign Resources and Expenditures are reported in a separate section in the back of the book (pp. 269-284).

GENERAL ELECTION DATA

Registered Voters		Voter Turnout		Straight Party Voting	
1996	53,267	38,976	73.2%	(R) 10,852 . . 27.8%	(D) 4,374 . . . . 11.2%

PRESIDENT

1996	Bill Clinton (D)	17,123	44.6%
	Bob Dole (R)	18,468	48.1%
	Ross Perot (I)	2,568	6.7%
1992	Bill Clinton (D)	15,281	33.3%
	George Bush (R)	21,881	47.8%
	Ross Perot (I)	8,604	18.9%

UNITED STATES SENATE

1996	Richard J. Durbin (D)	18,023	47.7%
	Al Salvi (R)	18,668	49.4%

GOVERNOR

1994	Jim Edgar (R)	18,113	79.5%
	Dawn Clark Netsch (D)	4,660	20.5%

Representative Mark H. Beaubien, Jr. (R)

District Office: 124-A East Liberty St., Wauconda 60084
Phone (847) 487-5252; (847) 487-0956 (fax)
Springfield Office: Room 2108-N Stratton Bldg., Springfield 62706
Phone (217) 782-1517; (217) 782-0595 (fax)

Legislative Assignments: Committees on Registration & Regulation; Environment & Energy; Appropriations-Human Services; Personnel & Pensions.

Public Service: Representative (1996-present); board member, district 17, Lake County; township supervisor, Cuba.

Personal: Born October 30, 1942 in Waukegan; Northwestern University, J.D.; married (Dee); two sons.

1997 BILL PASSAGE RATIO	Introduced	Passed House of Origin	Passed GA
Primary	8	6	2
Primary/Hyphenated	18	12	6

KEY VOTES

1) Change Ed. Funding Formula . .N
2) State Budget . . . . .Y
3) Tougher DUI Level . . . . .Y
4) Ban Partial Birth Abortions . . .N
5) State Employees Pension . . . . .Y
6) Insurance/Domestic Violence . .Y
7) Brownfields . . . . .Y
8) Welfare Reform . . . . .Y
9) Concealed Guns/Misdemeanor .Y
10) Banks Sell Insurance . . . . .Y
11) Pre-Paid College Tuition . . . .Y
12) Increase Pull Tab Prizes . . . .Y
13) Utility Deregulation . . . . . . .Y
14) County Obscenity Standards .A
15) Managed Care Reform . . . . .N

GROUP RATINGS

	FB	CoC	PrLf	IPPC	ACLU
1997	57	85	0/6	100	100

ELECTION RESULTS

1996 General	Mark H. Beaubien, Jr. (R)	25,875	(65.2%)
1996 General	Robert Boness (D)	13,789	(34.8%)
1996 Primary	Mark H. Beaubien, Jr. (R)	7,114	(53.1%)
1996 Primary	Philip A. Mullenix (R)	6,288	(46.9%)

CAMPAIGN RESOURCES AND EXPENDITURES

1996 Campaign Funds

Beg. Balance	$5,200	Individuals	$5,050
Receipts	$32,215	Party	$5,250
Expenditures	$32,530	PACS	$13,087
On hand	$4,885	Candidate	$5,000
		Not-itemized	$3,828

Top 10 PAC Contributors

1) CubaGOP . .$4,000	6) IMPAC $500
2) IPACE $2,500	7) CatCEG $500
3) CChurchill .$1,000	8) EPAC $500
4) LAWPAC . .$1,000	9) ILLumber . . .$500
5) TrustmarkIns .$687	10) ISMS $500

NOTE: The General Election Opponent's Campaign Resources and Expenditures are reported in a separate section in the back of the book (pp. 269-284).

GENERAL ELECTION DATA

	Registered Voters	Voter Turnout		Straight Party Voting	
1996	63,441	42,315	66.7%	(R) 13,343 . . 31.5%	(D) 4,186 . . . . 9.9%

PRESIDENT

1996	Bill Clinton (D)	16,272	37.7%
	Bob Dole (R)	21,989	51.0%
	Ross Perot (I)	4,466	10.4%
1992	Bill Clinton (D)	12,480	28.4%
	George Bush (R)	20,926	47.5%
	Ross Perot (I)	10,591	24.1%

UNITED STATES SENATE

1996	Richard J. Durbin (D)	16,543	39.0%
	Al Salvi (R)	23,947	56.4%

GOVERNOR

1994	Jim Edgar (R)	21,143	80.2%
	Dawn Clark Netsch (D)	5,221	19.8%

27th Senate District

House District 53
House District 54

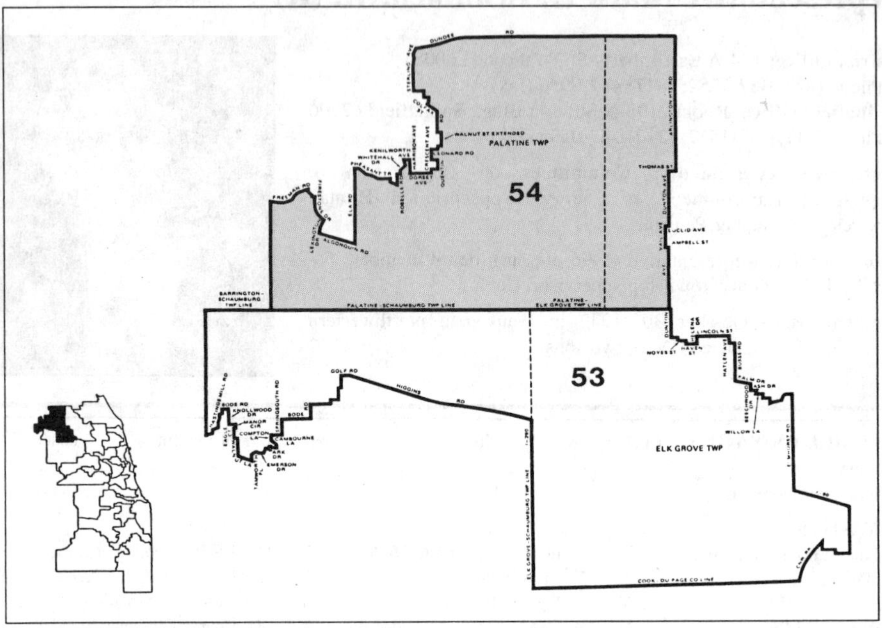

DEMOGRAPHICS (1990)

	S.D. #27	H.D. #53	H.D.#54
VOTING AGE POPULATION	149,843	75,233	74,610
White	88.8%	84.8%	92.8%
Black	1.6%	2.3%	1.0%
Hispanic	5.0%	6.8%	3.2%
Asian	4.4%	5.9%	3.0%
AGE (Total Population)	193,739	96,869	96,870
Under 6	8.2%	8.2%	8.3%
6 to 18	15.6%	15.4%	15.8%
65 and Over	8.7%	7.2%	10.2%
URBAN POPULATION	100.0%	100.0%	100.0%
HOUSING UNITS (Total)	80,340	41,756	38,584
Median Value	$142,944	$135,253	$148,785
Owner Occupied	57.7%	49.8%	66.2%
FAMILY INCOME (Total Families)	50,027	24,447	25,580
Median Income	$53,210	$49,019	$57,794
Below Poverty Level	2.0%	2.5%	1.6%
With Children Under 5	0.3%	0.3%	0.3%
With Children 5 to 17	0.6%	0.8%	0.5%
Headed by Females	1.0%	1.2%	0.8%
INDUSTRY (Total Employed)	115,729	59,585	56,144
Professional/Public Administration	19.5%	17.0%	22.1%
Manufacturing	21.4%	22.4%	20.3%
Retail	16.3%	17.1%	15.3%
Transportation/Communication	8.8%	10.3%	7.2%
Finance/Insurance/Real Estate	9.9%	8.4%	11.5%
Other Service	9.6%	9.7%	9.4%

Senator Peter G. Fitzgerald (R)

District Office: 117 W. Slade Street, Palatine 60067
Phone (847) 934-1992; (847) 934-2064 (fax)
Springfield Office: 611C Capitol Bldg., Springfield 62706
Phone (217) 782-4471; (217) 782-0116 (fax)

Legislative Assignments: Committees on State Government Operations (chair); Insurance & Pensions; Revenue.

Public Service: Senator (1993-present).

Personal: Attorney; born October 20, 1960; University of Michigan Law School, J.D. and Dartmouth College A.B.; married (Nina); one child.

1997 BILL PASSAGE RATIO	Introduced	Passed House of Origin	Passed GA
Primary	22	12	10
Primary/Hyphenated	47	31	24

KEY VOTES

1) Senate GOP Ed. $ Plan ......Y	6) Insurance/Domestic Violence ..Y	11) Pre-Paid College Tuition ....Y
2) State Budget ....Y	7) Brownfields ....Y	12) Increase Pull Tab Prizes ....N
3) Tougher DUI Level ....Y	8) Welfare Reform ....Y	13) Telecommunications Tax ...N
4) Ban Partial Birth Abortions ...Y	9) Concealed Guns/Misdemeanor .N	14) Delivery Discrimination ....P
5) State Employees Pension .....Y	10) Banks Sell Insurance ....P	15) Sell Drivers' Data ....N

GROUP RATINGS

	FB	CoC	PrLf	IPPC	ACLU
1997	86	100	2/2	0	50

ELECTION RESULTS

1996 General	Peter G. Fitzgerald (R)	44,850	(100%)
1996 Primary	Peter G. Fitzgerald (R)	10,166	(100%)
1992 General	Peter G. Fitzgerald (R)	50,999	(67.6%)
1992 General	Gene Diemer (D)	24,477	(32.4%)

CAMPAIGN RESOURCES AND EXPENDITURES

1996 Campaign Funds				Top 10 PAC Contributors			
Beg. Balance	$2,535	Individuals	$23,250	1) ABDI	$5,000	6) LIPAC	$1,000
Receipt	$82,107	Party	$1,250	2) ARC	$1,500	7) GOA	$1,000
Expenditures	$51,221	PACS	$51,600	3) MPAC	$1,000	8) LAWPAC	$1,000
On hand	$33,421	Candidate	$240	4) OxfordFin	$1,000	9) PIIA	$1,000
		Not-itemized	$5,767	5) NSBSI	$1,000	10) ISMS	$1,000

NOTE: The General Election Opponent's Campaign Resources and Expenditures are reported in a separate section in the back of the book (pp. 269-284).

GENERAL ELECTION DATA

	Registered Voters	Voter Turnout		Straight Party Voting	
1996	96,831	65,308	67.4%	(R) 16,046 ..24.6%	(D) 9,754 ....14.9%

PRESIDENT

1996	Bill Clinton (D)	27,759	43.1%
	Bob Dole (R)	30,852	47.9%
	Ross Perot (I)	5,294	8.2%
1992	Bill Clinton (D)	27,203	32.8%
	George Bush (R)	38,775	46.8%
	Ross Perot (I)	16,834	20.4%

UNITED STATES SENATE

1996	Richard J. Durbin (D)	29,309	46.2%
	Al Salvi (R)	32,076	50.5%

GOVERNOR

1994	Jim Edgar (R)	33,584	79.0%
	Dawn Clark Netsch (D)	8,931	21.0%

Representative Terry Parke (R)

District Office: 837 West Higgins Rd., Schaumburg 60195
Phone (847) 882-0270; (847) 884-6885 (fax)
Springfield Office: Room 2002-G Stratton Bldg., Springfield 62706
Phone (217) 782-0347; (217) 782-3189 (fax)

Legislative Assignments: Committees on Labor & Commerce (minority spokesperson); Insurance; Environment & Energy; Consumer Protection; Economic & Fiscal Commission.

Public Service: Representative (1985-present); school trustee Schaumberg Township.

Personal: Life insurance agent; born February 21, 1944, Pittsfield; Southern Illinois University, B.S. in education; U.S. Army veteran; married (Joanne); two children.

1997 BILL PASSAGE RATIO	Introduced	Passed House of Origin	Passed GA
Primary	9	3	2
Primary/Hyphenated	19	12	6

KEY VOTES

1) Change Ed. Funding Formula . . N
2) State Budget . . . . Y
3) Tougher DUI Level . . . . Y
4) Ban Partial Birth Abortions . . . Y
5) State Employees Pension . . . . . Y
6) Insurance/Domestic Violence . . Y
7) Brownfields . . . . Y
8) Welfare Reform . . . . Y
9) Concealed Guns/Misdemeanor . Y
10) Banks Sell Insurance . . . . Y
11) Pre-Paid College Tuition . . . . Y
12) Increase Pull Tab Prizes . . . . N
13) Utility Deregulation . . . . P
14) County Obscenity Standards . Y
15) Managed Care Reform . . . . . N

GROUP RATINGS

	FB	CoC	PrLf	IPPC	ACLU
1997	68	92	6/6	0	20

ELECTION RESULTS

1996 General	Terry Parke (R)	18,382	(100%)
1996 Primary	Terry Parke (R)	3,516	(100%)
1994 General	Terry Parke (R)	11,727	(67.2%)
1994 General	Mary E. Ecker (D)	5,718	(32.8%)

CAMPAIGN RESOURCES AND EXPENDITURES

1996 Campaign Funds

Beg. Balance	$98,685	Individuals	$450
Receipts	$41,446	Party	$250
Expenditures	$29,747	PACS	$31,157
On hand	$110,384	Candidate	$2,290
		Not-itemized	$7,299

Top 10 PAC Contributors

1) Fremont	$2,000	6) UST	$1,000
2) GOA	$1,500	7) ARC	$1,000
3) TCI	$1,000	8) NAII	$1,000
4) WCLA	$1,000	9) ABDI	$800
5) Zurich-Amer	$1,000	10) IMHA	$750

NOTE: The General Election Opponent's Campaign Resources and Expenditures are reported in a separate section in the back of the book (pp. 269-284).

GENERAL ELECTION DATA

	Registered Voters	Voter Turnout		Straight Party Voting	
1996	42,566	27,582	64.8%	(R) 6,412 . . . 23.2%	(D) 4,741 . . . 17.2%

PRESIDENT

1996	Bill Clinton (D)	12,752	46.8%
	Bob Dole (R)	11,885	43.7%
	Ross Perot (I)	2,385	8.8%
1992	Bill Clinton (D)	13,053	35.8%
	George Bush (R)	15,774	43.3%
	Ross Perot (I)	7,589	20.9%

UNITED STATES SENATE

1996	Richard J. Durbin (D)	13,023	48.7%
	Al Salvi (R)	12,790	47.8%

GOVERNOR

1994	Jim Edgar (R)	13,668	77.8%
	Dawn Clark Netsch (D)	3,909	22.2%

Representative Robert L. Bergman (R)

District Office: 865 East Wilmette Rd., Suite F-1(b), Palatine 60067
Phone (847) 358-1829; (847) 358-4296 (fax)
Springfield Office: Room 2129-0 Stratton Bldg., Springfield 62706
Phone (217) 782-8026; (217) 782-4553 (fax)

Legislative Assignments: Committees on Local Government; Human Services; Consumer Protection; Appropriations-General Services & Government Oversight.

Public Service: Representative (Appointed November 14, 1996-present); former Palatine Township Highway Commissioner.

Personal: Born November 10, 1948, Elgin; William Rainey Harper College; four children.

1997 BILL PASSAGE RATIO	Introduced	Passed House of Origin	Passed GA
Primary	5	3	1
Primary/Hyphenated	13	8	3

KEY VOTES

1) Change Ed. Funding Formula . . N
2) State Budget . . . . Y
3) Tougher DUI Level . . . . Y
4) Ban Partial Birth Abortions . . . Y
5) State Employees Pension . . . . Y
6) Insurance/Domestic Violence . . Y
7) Brownfields . . . . Y
8) Welfare Reform . . . . Y
9) Concealed Guns/Misdemeanor . Y
10) Banks Sell Insurance . . . . Y
11) Pre-Paid College Tuition . . . Y
12) Increase Pull Tab Prizes . . . . Y
13) Utility Deregulation . . . . P
14) County Obscenity Standards . Y
15) Managed Care Reform . . . . . N

GROUP RATINGS

	FB	CoC	PrLf	IPPC	ACLU
1997	54	85	6/6	0	20

ELECTION RESULTS

1996 General	Bernard E. Pedersen (R)	20,016	(55.9%)
1996 General	Sue A. Walton (D)	15,760	(44.1%)
1996 Primary	Bernard E. Pedersen (R)	5,202	(63.3%)
1996 Primary	Suzanne (Suzie) Bassi (R)	3,017	(36.7%)

CAMPAIGN RESOURCES AND EXPENDITURES

1996 Campaign Funds

Beg. Balance	$N/A	Individuals	$N/A
Receipts	$N/A	Party	$N/A
Expenditures	$N/A	PACS	$N/A
On hand	$N/A	Candidate	$N/A
		Not-itemized	$N/A

Top 10 PAC Contributors

1) N/A	$N/A	6) N/A	$N/A
2) N/A	$N/A	7) N/A	$N/A
3) N/A	$N/A	8) N/A	$N/A
4) N/A	$N/A	9) N/A	$N/A
5) N/A	$N/A	10) N/A	$N/A

NOTE: The General Election Opponent's Campaign Resources and Expenditures are reported in a separate section in the back of the book (pp. 269-284).

GENERAL ELECTION DATA

	Registered Voters	Voter Turnout		Straight Party Voting	
1996	54,265	37,726	69.5%	(R) 9,634 . . . 25.5%	(D) 5,013 . . . 13.3%

PRESIDENT

1996	Bill Clinton (D)	15,007	40.3%
	Bob Dole (R)	18,967	51.0%
	Ross Perot (I)	2,909	7.8%
1992	Bill Clinton (D)	14,150	30.5%
	George Bush (R)	23,001	49.6%
	Ross Perot (I)	9,245	19.9%

UNITED STATES SENATE

1996	Richard J. Durbin (D)	16,286	44.4%
	Al Salvi (R)	19,286	52.5%

GOVERNOR

1994	Jim Edgar (R)	19,916	79.9%
	Dawn Clark Netsch (D)	5,022	20.1%

28th Senate District

House District 55
House District 56

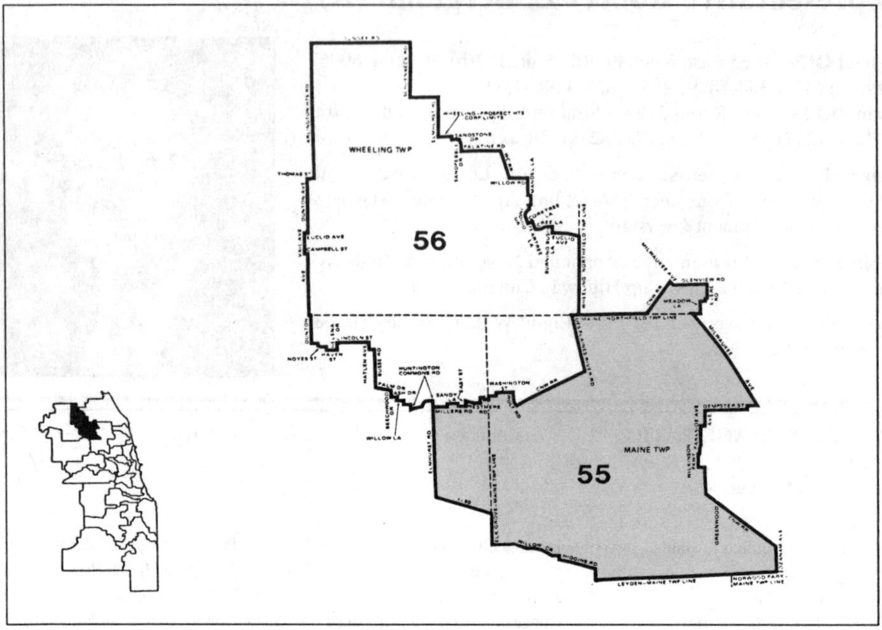

DEMOGRAPHICS (1990)

	S.D. #28	H.D. #55	H.D.#56
VOTING AGE POPULATION	152,507	77,569	74,938
White	90.0%	87.0%	93.1%
Black	0.8%	1.0%	0.5%
Hispanic	4.4%	5.8%	2.9%
Asian	4.8%	6.1%	3.4%
AGE (Total Population)	193,739	96,870	96,869
Under 6	7.6%	7.1%	8.1%
6 to 18	14.8%	13.9%	15.7%
65 and Over	13.9%	15.3%	12.5%
URBAN POPULATION	100.0%	100.0%	100.0%
HOUSING UNITS (Total)	77,463	40,077	37,386
Median Value	$149,343	$138,203	$158,416
Owner Occupied	74.0%	68.2%	80.1%
FAMILY INCOME (Total Families)	53,703	25,916	27,787
Median Income	$53,177	$47,648	$58,166
Below Poverty Level	2.0%	2.6%	1.4%
With Children Under 5	0.3%	0.3%	0.2%
With Children 5 to 17	0.8%	1.0%	0.6%
Headed by Females	0.6%	0.8%	0.4%
INDUSTRY (Total Employed)	108,089	54,362	53,727
Professional/Public Administration	23.1%	22.7%	23.4%
Manufacturing	19.6%	19.9%	19.3%
Retail	16.5%	16.7%	16.4%
Transportation/Communication	7.1%	7.1%	7.1%
Finance/Insurance/Real Estate	10.3%	9.4%	11.2%
Other Service	9.9%	10.6%	9.1%

Senator Martin J. Butler (R)

District Office: 800 E. Northwest Highway, Suite 102,
Mount Prospect 60056
Phone (847) 670-0280; (847) 670-0291 (fax)
Springfield Office: M113 Capitol Bldg., Springfield 62706
Phone (217) 782-3875

Legislative Assignments: Committees on Local Government & Elections (chairperson); Education; Financial Institutions; Senate Committee on Education Reform.

Public Service: Senator (1991-present); mayor and alderman, Park Ridge.

Personal: Born April 18, 1924; President, Distributors Institute; served in U.S. Army Air Force (1942-45); married (Gerry); two daughters.

1997 BILL PASSAGE RATIO	Introduced	Passed House of Origin	Passed GA
Primary	24	12	10
Primary/Hyphenated	31	18	16

KEY VOTES

1) Senate GOP Ed. $ Plan ....Y	6) Insurance/Domestic Violence ..Y	11) Pre-Paid College Tuition ....Y
2) State Budget ....Y	7) Brownfields ....Y	12) Increase Pull Tab Prizes ....Y
3) Tougher DUI Level ....Y	8) Welfare Reform ....Y	13) Telecommunications Tax ...N
4) Ban Partial Birth Abortions ...Y	9) Concealed guns/misdemeanor ..Y	14) Delivery Discrimination ....P
5) State Employees Pension .....Y	10) Banks sell insurance ....Y	15) Sell Drivers' Data ....Y

GROUP RATINGS

	FB	CoC	PrLf	IPPC	ACLU
1997	82	100	2/2	0	50

ELECTION RESULTS

1996 General	Martin J. Butler (R)	42,633	(58.8%)
1996 General	William M. "Bill" Blaine, Jr. (D)	29,858	(41.2%)
1996 Primary	Martin J. Butler (R)	10,154	(63.2%)
1996 Primary	George A. Clowes (R)	5,910	(36.8%)

CAMPAIGN RESOURCES AND EXPENDITURES

1996 Campaign Funds

Beg. Balance	$37,252	Individuals	$5,915
Receipts	$63,605	Party	$1,450
Expenditures	$75,638	PACS	$33,990
On hand	$25,219	Candidate	$0
		Not-itemized	$22,250

Top 10 PAC Contributors

1) IBA	$2,000	6) GOA	$1,000
2) Fremont	$1,100	7) ARC	$1,000
3) AbbeyBlders	$1,000	8) UPS	$1,000
4) HOPE	$1,000	9) ISMS	$1,000
5) NTGOP	$1,000	10) AT&T	$1,000

NOTE: The General Election Opponent's Campaign Resources and Expenditures are reported in a separate section in the back of the book (pp. 269-284).

GENERAL ELECTION DATA

	Registered Voters	Voter Turnout		Straight Party Voting	
1996	111,103	77,122	69.4%	(R) 16,599 ..21.5%	(D) 11,598 ...15.0%

PRESIDENT

1996	Bill Clinton (D)	34,756	45.7%
	Bob Dole (R)	35,024	46.1%
	Ross Perot (I)	5,661	7.5%
1992	Bill Clinton (D)	33,374	35.9%
	George Bush (R)	42,248	45.5%
	Ross Perot (I)	17,215	18.6%

UNITED STATES SENATE

1996	Richard J. Durbin (D)	36,925	49.3%
	Al Salvi (R)	35,899	47.9%

GOVERNOR

1994	Jim Edgar (R)	42,405	76.9%
	Dawn Clark Netsch (D)	12,722	23.1%

Representative Rosemary Mulligan (R)

District Office: 932 Lee St., Suite 204, Des Plaines 60016
Phone (847) 297-6533; (847) 297-2978 (fax)
Springfield Office: Room 2133-0 Stratton Bldg., Springfield 62706
Phone (217) 782-8007

Legislative Assignments: Committees on Appropriations-Human Services (minority spokesperson); Children & Youth; Health Care Availability & Access; Human Services; Registration & Regulation.

Public Service: Representative (1993-present).

Personal: Born July 8, 1941, Chicago; Harper College, A.A.S.; Illinois State University, education; two children.

1997 BILL PASSAGE RATIO	Introduced	Passed House of Origin	Passed GA
Primary	11	6	2
Primary/Hyphenated	37	21	9

KEY VOTES

1) Change Ed. Funding Formula . . N	6) Insurance/Domestic Violence . . Y	11) Pre-Paid College Tuition . . . . Y
2) State Budget . . . . Y	7) Brownfields . . . . Y	12) Increase Pull Tab Prizes . . . . Y
3) Tougher DUI Level . . . . Y	8) Welfare Reform . . . . Y	13) Utility Deregulation . . . . Y
4) Ban Partial Birth Abortions . . . N	9) Concealed Guns/Misdemeanor . Y	14) County Obscenity Standards . N
5) State Employees Pension . . . . . Y	10) Banks Sell Insurance . . . . Y	15) Managed Care Reform . . . . . Y

GROUP RATING

	FB	CoC	PrLf	IPPC	ACLU
1997	68	38	0/6	100	80

ELECTION RESULTS

1996 General	Rosemary Mulligan (R)	18,982	(56.6%)
1996 General	Thomas P. Cahill (D)	14,539	(43.4%)
1996 Primary	Rosemary Mulligan (R)	5,151	(63.6%)
1996 Primary	Robert J. Cassidy (R)	2,943	(36.4%)

CAMPAIGN RESOURCES AND EXPENDITURES

1996 Campaign Funds

Beg. Balance	$36,018	Individuals	$5,350
Receipts	$41,287	Party	$550
Expenditures	$58,189	PACS	$24,187
On hand	$19,116	Candidate	$944
		Not-itemized	$10,256

Top 10 PAC Contributors

1) PersPAC . . . $5,387	6) TMRS $550
2) WomensCamp $1,000	7) ChaufCars . . . $550
3) Sprint $1,000	8) CKrause $550
4) LynnMarketing $944	9) DelCar $550
5) CPA's $600	10) IPACE $500

NOTE: The General Election Opponent's Campaign Resources and Expenditures are reported in a separate section in the back of the book (pp. 269-284).

GENERAL ELECTION DATA

	Registered Voters	Voter Turnout		Straight Party Voting			
1996	52,236	35,088	67.2%	(R) 6,408	18.3	(D) 5,973	17.0%

PRESIDENT

1996	Bill Clinton (D)	17,024	49.3%
	Bob Dole (R)	14,597	42.3%
	Ross Perot (I)	2,603	7.5%
1992	Bill Clinton (D)	16,877	39.6%
	George Bush (R)	17,994	42.2%
	Ross Perot (I)	7,778	18.2%

UNITED STATES SENATE

1996	Richard J. Durbin (D)	17,886	52.6%
	Al Salvi (R)	15,080	44.3%

GOVERNOR

1994	Jim Edgar (R)	18,584	73.9%
	Dawn Clark Netsch (D)	6,575	26.1%

Representative Carolyn H. Krause (R)

District Office: 111 East Busse Ave., Suite 605, Mt. Prospect 60056
Phone (847) 255-3100; (847) 255-3184 (fax)
Springfield Office: Room 2004-G Stratton Bldg., Springfield 62706
Phone (217) 782-3739; (217) 782-3189 (fax)

Legislative Assignments: Committees on Health Care Availability & Access (minority spokesperson); Revenue; Aging; Registration & Regulation.

Public Service: Representative (1993-present); mayor, Village of Mt. Prospect (1977-1989).

Personal: Attorney; born October 20, 1938, Milwaukee, WI; University of Wisconsin at Madison, B.A., IIT-Chicago Kent College of Law, J.D.; married (David).

1997 BILL PASSAGE RATIO	Introduced	Passed House of Origin	Passed GA
Primary	15	6	4
Primary/Hyphenated	37	22	8

KEY VOTES

1) Change Ed. Funding Formula . . N	6) Insurance/Domestic Violence . . Y	11) Pre-Paid College Tuition . . . . Y
2) State Budget . . . . Y	7) Brownfields . . . . Y	12) Increase Pull Tab Prizes . . . N
3) Tougher DUI Level . . . . Y	8) Welfare Reform . . . . Y	13) Utility Deregulation . . . . Y
4) Ban Partial Birth Abortions . . . Y	9) Concealed Guns/Misdemeanor . N	14) County Obscenity Standards . N
5) State Employees Pension . . . . . Y	10) Banks Sell Insurance . . . . Y	15) Managed Care Reform . . . . . Y

GROUP RATINGS

	FB	CoC	PrLf	IPPC	ACLU
1997	68	45	1/6	83	70

ELECTION RESULTS

1996 General	Carolyn H. Krause (R)	31,182	(100%)
1996 Primary	Carolyn H. Krause (R)	7,640	(100%)
1994 General	Carolyn H. Krause (R)	22,616	(76.8%)
1994 General	Richard A. Valentino (D)	6,819	(23.2%)

CAMPAIGN RESOURCES AND EXPENDITURES

1996 Campaign Funds		Top 10 PAC Contributors	
Beg. Balance . $43,111	Individuals $500	1) IBA $1,500	6) GOA $600
Receipts $20,515	Party $0	2) ISMS $1,000	7) Merck $500
Expenditures . . $5,825	PACS $15,575	3) IHCA $1,000	8) EmergMed . . $500
On hand $57,801	Candidate $855	4) IPACE $1,000	9) United $500
	Not-itemized . . $3,585	5) HOPE $600	10) MPAC $500

NOTE: The General Election Opponent's Campaign Resources and Expenditures are reported in a separate section in the back of the book (pp. 269-284).

GENERAL ELECTION DATA

	Registered Voters	Voter Turnout		Straight Party Voting	
1996	58,867	42,034	71.4%	(R) 10,191 . . 24.2%	(D) 5,625 . . . 13.4%

PRESIDENT

1996	Bill Clinton (D)	17,732	42.7%
	Bob Dole (R)	20,427	49.2%
	Ross Perot (I)	3,058	7.4%
1992	Bill Clinton (D)	16,497	32.9%
	George Bush (R)	24,254	48.3%
	Ross Perot (I)	9,437	18.8%

UNITED STATES SENATE

1996	Richard J. Durbin (D)	19,039	46.5%
	Al Salvi (R)	20,819	50.9%

GOVERNOR

1994	Jim Edgar (R)	23,821	79.5%
	Dawn Clark Netsch (D)	6,147	20.5%

29th Senate District

House District 57
House District 58

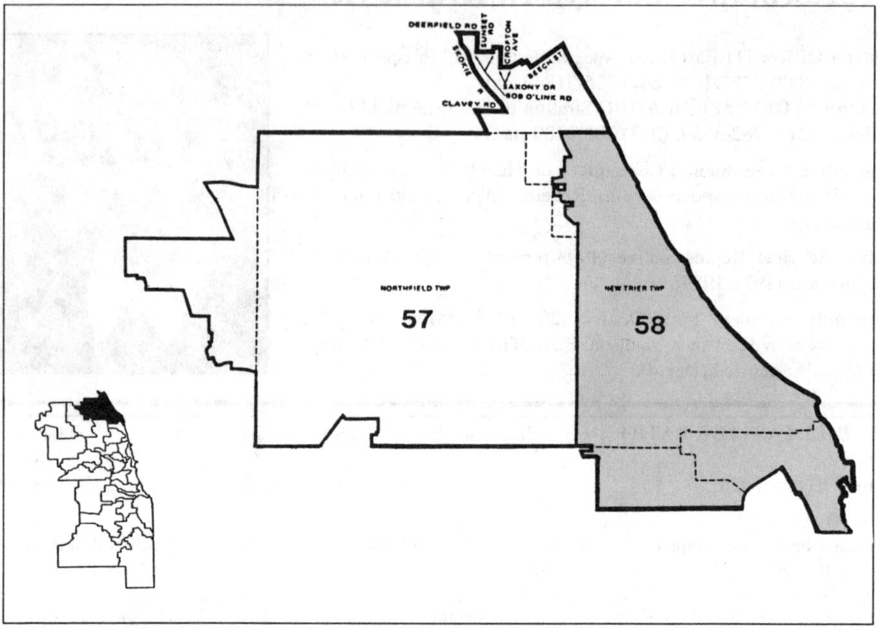

DEMOGRAPHICS (1990)

	S.D. #29	H.D. #57	H.D.#58
VOTING AGE POPULATION	150,156	73,861	76,295
White	89.8%	90.0%	89.7%
Black	1.6%	0.8%	2.4%
Hispanic	2.8%	4.1%	1.6%
Asian	5.7%	5.1%	6.3%
AGE (Total Population)	193,739	96,870	96,869
Under 6	7.9%	8.3%	7.6%
6 to 18	16.0%	16.5%	15.6%
65 and Over	14.4%	12.9%	15.8%
URBAN POPULATION	100.0%	100.0%	100.0%
HOUSING UNITS (Total)	72,252	36,581	35,671
Median Value	$266,418	$249,317	$285,962
Owner Occupied	77.4%	78.9%	75.9%
FAMILY INCOME (Total Families)	52,822	27,667	25,155
Median Income	$76,331	$71,373	$81,154
Below Poverty Level	1.6%	1.5%	1.6%
With Children Under 5	0.2%	0.1%	0.3%
With Children 5 to 17	0.5%	0.6%	0.3%
Headed by Females	0.4%	0.4%	0.4%
INDUSTRY (Total Employed)	99,604	51,367	48,236
Professional/Public Administration	35.2%	29.2%	41.5%
Manufacturing	13.3%	15.7%	10.8%
Retail	14.7%	16.2%	13.1%
Transportation/Communication	3.7%	4.2%	3.1%
Finance/Insurance/Real Estate	13.4%	12.4%	14.5%
Other Service	9.8%	9.9%	9.8%

Senator Kathleen K. Parker (R)

District Office: 191 Waukegan Rd., Suite 210, Northfield 60093
Phone (847) 441-0077; (847) 441-0322 (fax)
Springfield Office: 118M State Capitol Bldg., Springfield 62706
Phone (217) 782-2119

Legislative Assignments: Committees on Transportation (vice-chair); Public Health & Welfare (vice-chair); Financial Institutions.

Public Service: Senator (1995-present); member, Regional Transportation Authority Board (1983-1995).

Personal: Born September 21, 1943; University of Miami, B.A. in mass communications; married (Keith); two children.

1997 BILL PASSAGE RATIO	Introduced	Passed House of Origin	Passed GA
Primary	49	16	12
Primary/Hyphenated	76	37	26

KEY VOTES

1) Senate GOP Ed. $ Plan ...... Y	6) Insurance/Domestic Violence .. Y	11) Pre-Paid College Tuition .... Y
2) State Budget .... Y	7) Brownfields .... Y	12) Increase Pull Tab Prizes .... N
3) Tougher DUI Level .... Y	8) Welfare Reform .... Y	13) Telecommunications Tax .. N
4) Ban Partial Birth Abortions ... Y	9) Concealed Guns/Misdemeanor . N	14) Delivery Discrimination .... N
5) State Employees Pension ..... Y	10) Banks Sell Insurance .... Y	15) Sell Drivers' Data .... N

GROUP RATINGS

	FB	CoC	PrLf	IPPC	ACLU
1997	73	100	1/2	50	50

ELECTION RESULTS

1994 General	Kathleen K. Parker (R)	35,531	(53.8%)
1994 General	Grace Mary Stern (D)	30,516	(46.2%)
1994 Primary	Kathleen K. Parker (R)	7,203	(57.8%)
1994 Primary	Two others (R)	5,267	(42.2%)

CAMPAIGN RESOURCES AND EXPENDITURES

1996 Campaign Funds				Top 10 PAC Contributors	
Beg. Balance	$22,066	Individuals	$1,350	1) KP&A $1,378	6) Sears $750
Receipts	$31,882	Party	$0	2) IBA $1,000	7) HOPE $750
Expenditures	$30,844	PACS	$26,128	3) MPAC $1,000	8) ILCon $600
On hand	$23,104	Candidate	$159	4) ILCable ...$1,000	9) FCNBD $600
		Not-itemized	$4,245	5) VSGrinding ..$900	10) ISMS $600

NOTE: The General Election Opponent's Campaign Resources and Expenditures are reported in a separate section in the back of the book (pp. 269-284).

GENERAL ELECTION DATA

	Registered Voters	Voter Turnout		Straight Party Voting	
1996	124,783	91,777	73.5%	(R) 18,933 . . 20.6%	(D) 16,379 . . . 17.8%

PRESIDENT

1996	Bill Clinton (D)	48,288	53.4%
	Bob Dole (R)	37,751	41.8%
	Ross Perot (I)	3,657	4.1%
1992	Bill Clinton (D)	50,136	47.4%
	George Bush (R)	42,629	40.3%
	Ross Perot (I)	13,001	12.3%

UNITED STATES SENATE

1996	Richard J. Durbin (D)	54,141	60.6%
	Al Salvi (R)	33,491	37.5%

GOVERNOR

1994	Jim Edgar (R)	43,751	64.3%
	Dawn Clark Netsch (D)	24,363	35.7%

Representative Elizabeth Coulson (R)

District Office: 3801 West Lake Ave., Glenview 60025
Phone (847) 724-3233; (847) 724-8682 (fax)
Springfield Office: Room 2140-O Stratton Bldg., Springfield 62706
Phone (217) 782-4194

Legislative Assignments: Committees on Aging; Appropriations-General Services & Government Oversight; Health Care Availability & Access; Registration & Regulation.
Public Service: Representative (1997-present); trustee, Northfield Township.
Personal: Born September 8, 1954, Hastings, NE; Wellesley College and the University of Kansas, B.S. in education; Northwestern University Medical School, A.C. in physical therapy; Keller Graduate School of Management, M.A. in business admin.; University of Illinois at Chicago, Ph.D. candidate in health policy & admin.; married (Bill).

1997 BILL PASSAGE RATIO	Introduced	Passed House of Origin	Passed GA
Primary	4	2	0
Primary/Hyphenated	22	14	7

KEY VOTES

1) Change Ed. Funding Formula . . N
2) State Budget . . . . Y
3) Tougher DUI Level . . . . Y
4) Ban Partial Birth Abortions . . . N
5) State Employees Pension . . . . . Y
6) Insurance/Domestic Violence . . Y
7) Brownfields . . . . Y
8) Welfare Reform . . . . Y
9) Concealed Guns/Misdemeanor . A
10) Banks Sell Insurance . . . . Y
11) Pre-Paid College Tuition . . . . Y
12) Increase Pull Tab Prizes . . . . Y
13) Utility Deregulation . . . . Y
14) County Obscenity Standards . N
15) Managed Care Reform . . . . . Y

GROUP RATINGS

	FB	CoC	PrLf	IPPC	ACLU
1997	54	54	0/6	100	89

ELECTION RESULTS

1996 General	Elizabeth Coulson (R)	21,903	(53.2%)
1996 General	Elaine Nekritz (D)	19.247	(46.8%)
1996 Primary	Elizabeth Coulson (R)	4,354	(60.9%)
1996 Primary	Two others (R)	2,799	(39.1%)

CAMPAIGN RESOURCES AND EXPENDITURES

1996 Campaign Funds

Beg. Balance	$13,289	Individuals	$1,550
Receipts	$37,198	Party	$3,000
Expenditures	$48,370	PACS	$14,338
On hand	$2,117	Candidate	$10,000
		Not-itemized	$8,310

Top 10 PAC Contributors

1) ISMS	$1,633	6) Kraft	$500
2) IPTPAC	$1,025	7) HI	$500
3) GOPAC	$1,000	8) IBA	$500
4) CChurchill	$1,000	9) CParker	$500
5) Ameritech	$750	10) Fremont	$500

NOTE: The General Election Opponent's Campaign Resources and Expenditures are reported in a separate section in the back of the book (pp. 269-284).

GENERAL ELECTION DATA

	Registered Voters	Voter Turnout		Straight Party Voting			
1996	59,189	43,518	73.5%	(R) 9,702	22.3%	(D) 7,111	16.3%

PRESIDENT

1996	Bill Clinton (D)	21,632	50.5%
	Bob Dole (R)	18,940	44.2%
	Ross Perot (I)	2,013	4.7%
1992	Bill Clinton (D)	21,252	42.0%
	George Bush (R)	22,155	43.7%
	Ross Perot (I)	7,235	14.3%

UNITED STATES SENATE

1996	Richard J. Durbin (D)	24,083	56.9%
	Al Salvi (R)	17,317	40.9%

GOVERNOR

1994	Jim Edgar (R)	22,197	70.4%
	Dawn Clark Netsch (D)	9,344	29.6%

Representative Jeffrey M. Schoenberg (D)

District Office: 1000 Skokie Blvd., Suite LL33, Wilmette 60091
Phone (847) 853-0130; (847) 853-0135 (fax)
Springfield Office: M-2 Stratton Bldg., Springfield 62706
Phone (217) 782-0499

Legislative Assignments: Appropriations-General Services & Government Oversight (chair); Human Services (vice-chair); Financial Institutions; Economic and Fiscal Commission.

Public Service: Representative (1991-present).

Personal: Full-time legislator; born July 28, 1959, Chicago; Rutgers University, B.S. in philosophy and Jewish Theological Seminary; married (Lynne Sered).

1997 BILL PASSAGE RATIO	Introduced	Passed House of Origin	Passed GA
Primary	36	8	4
Primary/Hyphenated	103	24	11

KEY VOTES

1) Change Ed. Funding Formula . . Y
2) State Budget . . . . Y
3) Tougher DUI Level . . . . Y
4) Ban Partial Birth Abortions . . . N
5) State Employees Pension . . . . . Y
6) Insurance/Domestic Violence . . Y
7) Brownfields . . . . Y
8) Welfare Reform . . . . Y
9) Concealed Guns/Misdemeanor . N
10) Banks Sell Insurance . . . . Y
11) Pre-Paid College Tuition . . . . Y
12) Increase Pull Tab Prizes . . . . Y
13) Utility Deregulation . . . . Y
14) County Obscenity Standards . E
15) Managed Care Reform . . . . . Y

GROUP RATINGS

	FB	CoC	PrLf	IPPC	ACLU
1997	79	25	0/6	100	100

ELECTION RESULTS

1996 General	Jeffrey M. Schoenberg (D)	27,964	(59.4%)
1996 General	Kristina "Tina" Escamilla (R)	19,123	(40.6%)
1996 Primary	Jeffrey M. Schoenberg (D)	6,747	(100%)
1996 Primary	Kristina "Tina" Escamilla (R)	5,037	(100%)

CAMPAIGN RESOURCES AND EXPENDITURES

1996 Campaign Funds

Beg. Balance	$27,129	Individuals	$40,106
Receipts	$231,399	Party	$69,486
Expenditures	$241,636	PACS	$103,245
On hand	$16,892	Candidate	$0
		Not-itemized	$18,562

Top 10 PAC Contributors

1) IHDM	$68,786	6) RPLMgt	$2,000
2) IPACE	$17,652	7) Statesman	$2,000
3) PersPAC	$4,663	8) CTU	$2,000
4) ITLA	$4,500	9) UAW	$1,500
5) C&GL	$2,000	10) LAWPAC	$1,500

NOTE: The General Election Opponent's Campaign Resources and Expenditures are reported in a separate section in the back of the book (pp. 269-284).

GENERAL ELECTION DATA

	Registered Voters	Voter Turnout		Straight Party Voting	
1996	65,594	48,259	73.6%	(R) 9,231 . . . 19.1%	(D) 9,268 . . . 19.2%

PRESIDENT

1996	Bill Clinton (D)	26,656	56.1%
	Bob Dole (R)	18,811	39.6%
	Ross Perot (I)	1,644	3.4%
1992	Bill Clinton (D)	28,884	52.4%
	George Bush (R)	20,474	37.1%
	Ross Perot (I)	5,766	10.5%

UNITED STATES SENATE

1996	Richard J. Durbin (D)	30,058	63.9%
	Al Salvi (R)	16,174	34.4%

GOVERNOR

1994	Jim Edgar (R)	21,554	58.9%
	Dawn Clark Netsch (D)	15,019	41.1%

30th Senate District

House District 59
House District 60

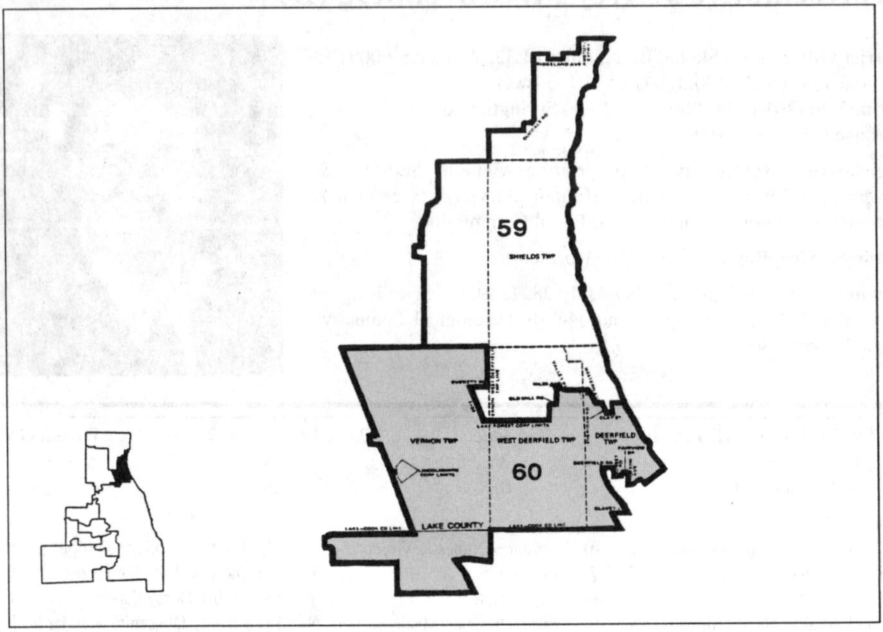

DEMOGRAPHICS (1990)

	S.D. #30	H.D. #59	H.D.#60
VOTING AGE POPULATION	144,568	71,814	72,754
White	76.7%	63.3%	89.9%
Black	10.8%	20.2%	1.5%
Hispanic	9.6%	13.8	5.5%
Asian	2.7%	2.3%	3.0%
AGE (Total Population)	193,739	96,869	96,870
Under 6	9.4%	9.5%	9.3%
6 to 18	18.4%	20.3%	16.6%
65 and Over	9.0%	8.5%	9.5%
URBAN POPULATION	99.2%	99.0%	99.3%
HOUSING UNITS (Total)	65,870	29,035	36,835
Median Value	$180,471	$174,852	$181,467
Owner Occupied	64.2%	52.5%	73.4%
FAMILY INCOME (Total Families)	47,277	20,356	26,921
Median Income	$53,402	$41,364	$61,450
Below Poverty Level	4.4%	7.6%	2.0%
With Children Under 5	0.7%	1.4%	0.3%
With Children 5 to 17	1.2%	2.1%	0.5%
Headed by Females	2.2%	4.1%	0.9%
INDUSTRY (Total Employed)	89,869	36,032	53,837
Professional/Public Administration	29.1%	31.6%	27.5%
Manufacturing	18.6%	21.7%	16.5%
Retail	15.5%	13.9%	16.6%
Transportation/Communication	5.0%	4.8%	5.1%
Finance/Insurance/Real Estate	10.1%	8.7%	11.0%
Other Service	9.9%	9.6%	10.1%

Senator Terry Link (D)

District Office: 425 Sheridan Road, Suite B, Highwood 60040
Phone (847) 266-1997; (847) 266-1920 (fax)
Springfield Office: 119B Capitol Bldg., Springfield 62706
Phone (217) 782-8181; (217) 785-0552 (fax)

Legislative Assignments: Committees on Local Government & Elections; State Government Operations; Agriculture & Conservation.

Public Service: Senator (1997-present).

Personal: Partner in Lake County Industrial Equipment business; born March 20, 1947, Waukegan; attended Stout State University; married (Susan); four daughters.

1997 BILL PASSAGE RATIO	Introduced	Passed House of Origin	Passed GA
Primary	11	1	0
Primary/Hyphenated	25	11	8

KEY VOTES

1) Senate GOP Ed. $ Plan . . . . . . .N	6) Insurance/Domestic Violence . .Y	11) Pre-Paid College Tuition . . . .Y
2) State Budget . . . . .Y	7) Brownfields . . . . .Y	12) Increase Pull Tab Prizes . . . .Y
3) Tougher DUI Level . . . . .Y	8) Welfare Reform . . . . .Y	13) Telecommunications Tax . . .N
4) Ban Partial Birth Abortions . . . .P	9) Concealed Guns/Misdemeanor .N	14) Delivery Discrimination . . . .Y
5) State Employees Pension . . . . .Y	10) Banks Sell Insurance . . . . .Y	15) Sell Drivers' Data . . . . .N

GROUP RATINGS

	FB	CoC	PrLf	IPPC	ACLU
1997	73	60	0/2	100	100

ELECTION RESULTS

1996 General	Terry Link (D)	31,133	(50.7%)
1996 General	Thomas F. Lachner (R)	30,301	(49.3%)
1996 Primary	Terry Link (D)	3,349	(65.2%)
1996 Primary	Lawrence T. Krulewich (D)	1,785	(34.8%)
1996 Primary	Thomas F. Lachner (R)	6,627	(52.8%)

CAMPAIGN RESOURCES AND EXPENDITURES

1996 Campaign Funds				Top 10 PAC Contributors			
Beg. Balance	$6,128	Individuals	$1,277	1) CDS	$99,313	6) IFT	$2,000
Receipts	$151,348	Party	$107,513	2) LCTU	$10,000	7) AFLCIO	$2,000
Expenditures	$157,256	PACS	$35,025	3) FCarroll	$4,850	8) ITLA	$2,000
On hand	$220	Candidate	$0	4) PSalvi	$2,125	9) Plumb93	$2,000
		Not-itemized	$7,533	5) IBEW	$2,000	10) WauDems	$1,600

NOTE: The General Election Opponent's Campaign Resources and Expenditures are reported in a separate section in the back of the book (pp. 269-284).

GENERAL ELECTION DATA

	Registered Voters	Voter Turnout		Straight Party Voting	
1996	95,458	67,096	70.3%	(R) 14,519 . .21.6%	(D) 11,639 . . .17.3%

PRESIDENT

1996	Bill Clinton (D)	35,100	53.5%
	Bob Dole (R)	26,451	40.3%
	Ross Perot (I)	3,647	5.6%
1992	Bill Clinton (D)	34,304	45.5%
	George Bush (R)	30,033	39.8%
	Ross Perot (I)	11,068	14.7%

UNITED STATES SENATE

1996	Richard J. Durbin (D)	37,363	58.0%
	Al Salvi (R)	25,164	39.1%

GOVERNOR

1994	Jim Edgar (R)	29,788	68.5%
	Dawn Clark Netsch (D)	13,712	31.5%

Representative Corinne G. Wood (R)

District Office: 191 East Deerpath, Suite 103, Lake Forest 60045
Phone (847) 295-7511; (847) 295-7512 (fax)
Springfield Office: Room 2110-N Stratton Bldg., Springfield 62706
Phone (217) 782-6400

Legislative Assignments: Committees on Aging; Appropriations-Education; Financial Institutions; Labor & Commerce; Legislative Research Unit.

Public Service: Representative (1997-present); Plan Commissioner and Senior Housing Commissioner, Lake Forest (1993-1996).

Personal: Attorney; born May 28, 1954, Barrington; University of Illinois, B.S. in Psychology; Loyola University, J.D.; married (Paul); three children.

1997 BILL PASSAGE RATIO	Introduced	Passed House of Origin	Passed GA
Primary	12	8	4
Primary/Hyphenated	38	27	14

KEY VOTES

1) Change Ed. Funding Formula . . N	6) Insurance/Domestic Violence . . Y	11) Pre-Paid College Tuition . . . . Y
2) State Budget . . . . Y	7) Brownfields . . . . Y	12) Increase Pull Tab Prizes . . . . Y
3) Tougher DUI Level . . . . Y	8) Welfare Reform . . . . Y	13) Utility Deregulation . . . . Y
4) Ban Partial Birth Abortions . . . N	9) Concealed Guns/Misdemeanor . A	14) County Obscenity Standards . Y
5) State Employees Pension . . . . . Y	10) Banks Sell Insurance . . . . Y	15) Managed Care Reform . . . . . N

GROUP RATINGS

	FB	CoC	PrLf	IPPC	ACLU
1997	57	62	0/6	100	78

ELECTION RESULTS

1996 General	Corinne G. Wood (R)	15,717	(100%)
1996 Primary	Corinne G. Wood (R)	5,304	(100%)
1994 General	Thomas F. Lachner (R)	10,209	(65.7%)
1994 General	Christopher J. Wakefield (D)	5,332	(34.3%)

CAMPAIGN RESOURCES AND EXPENDITURES

1996 Campaign Funds

Beg. Balance	$16,103	Individuals	$30,605
Receipts	$58,284	Party	$2,450
Expenditures	$50,912	PACS	$18,908
On hand	$23,475	Candidate	$0
		Not-itemized	$6,321

Top 10 PAC Contributors

1) ISMS	$1,000	6) IBA	$500
2) K&Ellis	$1,000	7) CatCEG	$500
3) LCR	$650	8) NFBC	$500
4) WilsonCon	$600	9) Ameritech	$500
5) IFT504	$500	10) ABDI	$500

NOTE: The General Election Opponent's Campaign Resources and Expenditures are reported in a separate section in the back of the book (pp. 269-284).

GENERAL ELECTION DATA

	Registered Voters	Voter Turnout		Straight Party Voting	
1996	38,751	25,178	65.0%	(R) 6,986 . . . 27.7%	(D) 4,818 . . . 19.1%

PRESIDENT

1996	Bill Clinton (D)	11,606	47.3%
	Bob Dole (R)	11,445	46.6%
	Ross Perot (I)	1,302	5.3%
1992	Bill Clinton (D)	12,290	42.7%
	George Bush (R)	12,484	43.4%
	Ross Perot (I)	3,989	13.9%

UNITED STATES SENATE

1996	Richard J. Durbin (D)	12,298	51.2%
	Al Salvi (R)	10,883	45.3%

GOVERNOR

1994	Jim Edgar (R)	11,257	71.9%
	Dawn Clark Netsch (D)	4,403	28.1%

Representative Lauren Beth Gash (D)

District Office: 108 Wilmot Rd., Suite 210, Deerfield 60015
Phone (847) 948-1080; (847) 948-1082 (fax)
Springfield Office: Room 2052-L Stratton, Springfield 62706
Phone (217) 782-0902

Legislative Assignments: Committees on Judiciary II-Criminal Law (chair); Appropriations-General Services & Government Oversight (vice-chair); State Government Administration & Election Reform; Elementary & Secondary Education; Children & Youth; Prison Management Reform.

Public Service: Representative (1993-present).

Personal: Attorney; born June 11, 1960, Summit, NJ; Clark University, B.A. in Psychology and Government; Northwestern University Law School and Georgetown University Law Center; J.D.; married (Gregg A. Garmisa); two children.

1997 BILL PASSAGE RATIO	Introduced	Passed House of Origin	Passed GA
Primary	33	8	2
Primary/Hyphenated	66	25	12

KEY VOTES

1) Change Ed. Funding Formula . . Y	6) Insurance/Domestic Violence . . Y	11) Pre-Paid College Tuition . . . . Y
2) State Budget . . . . Y	7) Brownfields . . . . Y	12) Increase Pull Tab Prizes . . . . Y
3) Tougher DUI Level . . . . Y	8) Welfare Reform . . . . Y	13) Utility Deregulation . . . . Y
4) Ban Partial Birth Abortions . . . N	9) Concealed Guns/Misdemeanor . N	14) County Obscenity Standards . N
5) State Employees Pension . . . . . Y	10) Banks Sell Insurance . . . . Y	15) Managed Care Reform . . . . . Y

GROUP RATINGS

	FB	CoC	PrLf	IPPC	ACLU
1997	86	31	0/6	100	100

ELECTION RESULTS

1996 General	Lauren Beth Gash (D)	24,007	(60.0%)
1996 General	Joel D. Gingiss (R)	15,990	(40.0%)
1996 Primary	Lauren Beth Gash (D)	3,529	(100%)
1996 Primary	Joel D. Gingiss (R)	4,929	(100%)

CAMPAIGN RESOURCES AND EXPENDITURES

1996 Campaign Funds				Top 10 PAC Contributors			
Beg. Balance	$30,609	Individuals	$17,445	1) IHDM	$107,877	6) IFT	$4,285
Receipts	$233,784	Party	$137,248	2) DSCC	$10,000	7) PersPAC	$4,092
Expenditures	$244,560	PACS	$55,386	3) FMJM	$7,495	8) CLang	$3,500
On hand	$19,833	Candidate	$201	4) DPI	$6,126	9) IFT504	$3,000
		Not-itemized	$23,504	5) IPACE	$5,000	10) ITLA	$3,000

NOTE: The General Election Opponent's Campaign Resources and Expenditures are reported in a separate section in the back of the book (pp. 269-284).

GENERAL ELECTION DATA

	Registered Voters	Voter Turnout		Straight Party Voting	
1996	56,707	41,918	73.9%	(R) 7,533 . . .18.0%	(D) 6,821 . . . .16.3%

PRESIDENT

1996	Bill Clinton (D)	23,494	57.1%
	Bob Dole (R)	15,006	36.5%
	Ross Perot (I)	2,345	5.7%
1992	Bill Clinton (D)	22,014	47.2%
	George Bush (R)	17,549	37.6%
	Ross Perot (I)	7,079	15.2%

UNITED STATES SENATE

1996	Richard J. Durbin (D)	25,065	62.0%
	Al Salvi (R)	14,281	35.3%

GOVERNOR

1994	Jim Edgar (R)	18,531	66.6%
	Dawn Clark Netsch (D)	9,309	33.4%

31st Senate District

House District 61
House District 62

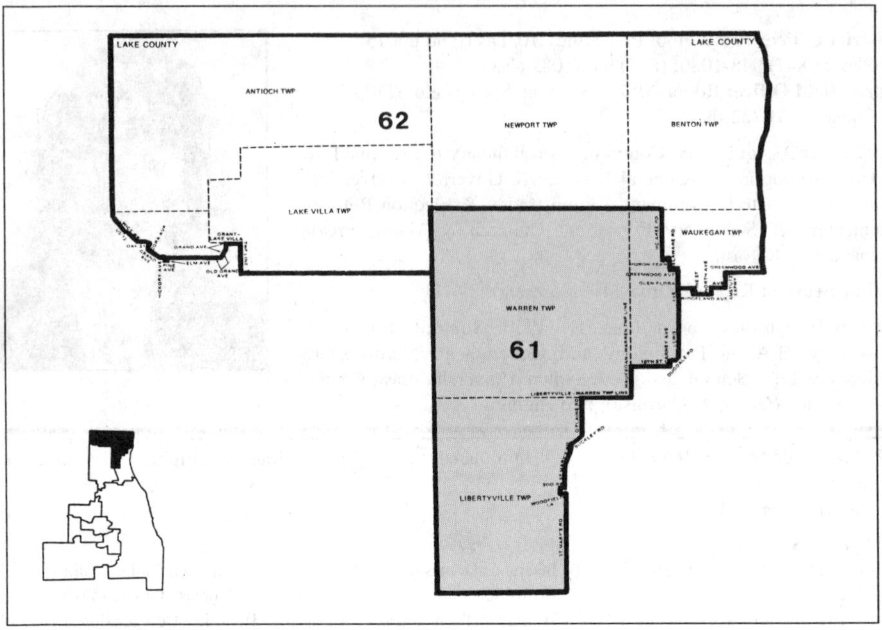

DEMOGRAPHICS (1990)

	S.D. #31	H.D. #61	H.D.#62
VOTING AGE POPULATION	140,389	71,312	69,077
White	87.5%	86.3%	88.8%
Black	4.8%	3.9%	5.7%
Hispanic	5.2%	6.3%	4.0%
Asian	2.3%	3.2%	1.2%
AGE (Total Population)	193,739	96,870	96,869
Under 6	9.9%	9.8%	10.0%
6 to 18	18.9%	17.8%	20.1%
65 and Over	9.2%	9.1%	9.4%
URBAN POPULATION	90.7%	93.3%	88.1%
HOUSING UNITS (Total)	73,754	37,299	36,455
Median Value	$101,299	$118,626	$91,186
Owner Occupied	68.0%	67.7%	68.3%
FAMILY INCOME (Total Families)	52,237	26,077	26,159
Median Income	$47,112	$50,463	$44,586
Below Poverty Level	3.8%	2.5%	5.0%
With Children Under 5	0.8%	0.6%	1.0%
With Children 5 to 17	1.3%	0.8%	1.8%
Headed by Females	2.0%	1.2%	2.8%
INDUSTRY (Total Employed)	101,389	52,791	48,598
Professional/Public Administration	25.1%	26.0%	24.1%
Manufacturing	24.1%	24.0%	24.3%
Retail	16.5%	16.2%	16.8%
Transportation/Communication	6.0%	5.4%	6.8%
Finance/Insurance/Real Estate	7.4%	8.2%	6.6%
Other Service	8.1%	8.2%	8.0%

Senator Adeline Jay Geo-Karis (R)

District Office: 2610 Sheridan Road, P.O. Box 248, Zion 60099
Phone (847) 872-7500, (847) 623-8811; (847) 872-3131 (fax)
Springfield Office: 323 Capitol Bldg., Springfield 62706
Phone (217) 782-7353; (217) 782-7818 (fax)

Legislative Assignments: Assistant Majority Leader. Committees on Commerce and Industry; Financial Institutions; Judiciary.

Public Service: Senator (1979-present); representative (1973-79); attorney; former mayor of Zion; former justice of the peace; assistant state's attorney.

Personal: Born in Tegeas, Greece; Northwestern University; DePaul University College of Law, LL.B.; Lt. Commander, U.S.N.R.

1997 BILL PASSAGE RATIO	Introduced	Passed House of Origin	Passed GA
Primary	15	8	8
Primary/Hyphenated	27	20	16

KEY VOTES

1) Senate GOP Ed. $ Plan ......Y	6) Insurance/Domestic Violence ..Y	11) Pre-Paid College Tuition ....Y
2) State Budget ....Y	7) Brownfields ....Y	12) Increase Pull Tab Prizes ....Y
3) Tougher DUI Level ....Y	8) Welfare Reform ....Y	13) Telecommunications Tax ...N
4) Ban Partial Birth Abortions ...Y	9) Concealed Guns/Misdemeanor .Y	14) Delivery Discrimination ....P
5) State Employees Pension .....Y	10) Banks Sell Insurance ....P	15) Sell Drivers' Data ....N

GROUP RATINGS

	FB	CoC	PrLf	IPPC	ACLU
1997	91	100	2/2	0	50

ELECTION RESULTS

1996 General	Adeline Jay Geo-Karis (R)	57,067	(100%)
1996 Primary	Adeline Jay Geo-Karis (R)	20,593	(100%)
1992 General	Adeline Jay Geo-Karis (R)	53,238	(67.0%)
1992 General	John H. Gordon (D)	21,989	(27.7%)
1992 General	Barbara Goudeaux (ERP)	4,266	(5.4%)

CAMPAIGN RESOURCES AND EXPENDITURES

1996 Campaign Funds				Top 10 PAC Contributors	
Beg. Balance	$38,878	Individuals	$0	1) CPhilip $1,000	6) CUPAC $500
Receipts	$7,623	Party	$1,000	2) Monsanto ...$750	7) ABDI $500
Expenditures	$20,426	PACS	$6,623	3) IRoad $500	8) HOPE $500
On hand	$26,075	Candidate	$0	4) AB $500	9) IFT504 .....$500
		Not-itemized	$0	5) ChgoCoC ...$500	10) LICID $500

NOTE: The General Election Opponent's Campaign Resources and Expenditures are reported in a separate section in the back of the book (pp. 269-284).

GENERAL ELECTION DATA

	Registered Voters	Voter Turnout		Straight Party Voting			
1996	115,695	78,556	67.9%	(R) 20,414	26.0%	(D) 9,383	11.9%

PRESIDENT

1996	Bill Clinton (D)	32,728	42.5%
	Bob Dole (R)	35,920	46.7%
	Ross Perot (I)	7,696	10.0%
1992	Bill Clinton (D)	27,183	32.7%
	George Bush (R)	38,380	46.2%
	Ross Perot (I)	17,488	21.1%

UNITED STATES SENATE

1996	Richard J. Durbin (D)	33,210	44.0%
	Al Salvi (R)	38,959	51.6%

GOVERNOR

1994	Jim Edgar (R)	37,210	77.0%
	Dawn Clark Netsch (D)	10,975	23.0%

Representative Andrea S. Moore (R)

District Office: 733 N. Milwaukee, Libertyville 60048
Phone (847) 549-1133; (847) 549-0051 (fax)
Springfield Office: Room 2014-H Stratton Bldg., Springfield 62706
Phone (217) 782-3696; (217) 782-5257 (fax)

Legislative Assignments: Committees on Revenue (minority spokesperson); Environment & Energy; Health Care Availability & Access; Labor & Commerce; Public Utilities.

Public Service: Representative (1993-present); commissioner, Lake County Board; trustee, village of Libertyville.

Personal: Full-time legislator; born September 2, 1944; married (Bill); three children.

1997 BILL PASSAGE RATIO	Introduced	Passed House of Origin	Passed GA
Primary	18	9	4
Primary/Hyphenated	39	22	11

KEY VOTES

1) Change Ed. Funding Formula . . N	6) Insurance/Domestic Violence . . Y	11) Pre-Paid College Tuition . . . . Y
2) State Budget . . . . Y	7) Brownfields . . . . Y	12) Increase Pull Tab Prizes . . . . Y
3) Tougher DUI Level . . . . Y	8) Welfare Reform . . . . Y	13) Utility Deregulation . . . . Y
4) Ban Partial Birth Abortions . . . Y	9) Concealed Guns/Misdemeanor . Y	14) County Obscenity Standards . Y
5) State Employees Pension . . . . . Y	10) Banks Sell Insurance . . . . Y	15) Managed Care Reform . . . . . Y

GROUP RATINGS

	FB	CoC	PrLf	IPPC	ACLU
1997	68	58	1/6	83	66

ELECTION RESULTS

1996 General	Andrea S. Moore (R)	29,203	(100%)
1996 Primary	Andrea S. Moore (R)	9,713	(100%)
1994 General	Andrea S. Moore (R)	18,127	(75.8%)
1994 General	James W. Yonker (D)	5,778	(24.2%)

CAMPAIGN RESOURCES AND EXPENDITURES

1996 Campaign Funds				Top 10 PAC Contributors			
Beg. Balance	$21,252	Individuals	$650	1) LibertyLM	$1,000	6) LICID	$500
Receipts	$25,795	Party	$0	2) S&Austin	$1,000	7) HOPE	$500
Expenditures	$16,410	PACS	$14,800	3) Classic Chev	$1,000	8) CentTel	$500
On hand	$30,637	Candidate	$0	4) WMgt	$550	9) MPAC	$500
		Not-itemized	$10,345	5) IFT504	$500	10) Ameritech	$500

NOTE: The General Election Opponent's Campaign Resources and Expenditures are reported in a separate section in the back of the book (pp. 269-284).

GENERAL ELECTION DATA

	Registered Voters	Voter Turnout		Straight Party Voting			
1996	59,810	41,270	69.0%	(R) 10,976	26.6%	(D) 5,062	12.3%

PRESIDENT

1996	Bill Clinton (D)	17,658	43.7%
	Bob Dole (R)	19,120	47.3%
	Ross Perot (I)	3,341	8.3%
1992	Bill Clinton (D)	15,067	33.6%
	George Bush (R)	20,897	46.6%
	Ross Perot (I)	8,917	19.8%

UNITED STATES SENATE

1996	Richard J. Durbin (D)	18,313	46.1%
	Al Salvi (R)	19,886	50.1%

GOVERNOR

1994	Jim Edgar (R)	18,386	77.0%
	Dawn Clark Netsch (D)	5,480	23.0%

Representative Robert W. Churchill (R)

District Office: 976 Hillside Ave., Antioch 60002
Phone (847) 395-7000; (847) 395-9277 (fax)
Springfield Office: Room 314 Capitol Bldg., Springfield 62706
Phone (217) 782-8151; (217) 782-7012 (fax)

Legislative Assignments: Deputy Republican Leader; ex officio member of all committees. Committees on Rules (minority spokesperson); Conflicts of Interest; Legislative Space Needs Commission.

Public Service: Representative (1983-present); trustee, Lake Villa Township (1981-1983).

Personal: Attorney; born April 10, 1947, Waukegan; Northwestern University, B.A. in History/Political Science; University of Iowa, J.D.; married (Sandra); three children.

1997 BILL PASSAGE RATIO	Introduced	Passed House of Origin	Passed GA
Primary	7	2	2
Primary/Hyphenated	14	9	9

KEY VOTES

1) Change Ed. Funding Formula . . N
2) State Budget . . . . Y
3) Tougher DUI Level . . . . Y
4) Ban Partial Birth Abortions . . . Y
5) State Employees Pension . . . . . Y
6) Insurance/Domestic Violence . . Y
7) Brownfields . . . . Y
8) Welfare Reform . . . . Y
9) Concealed Guns/Misdemeanor . Y
10) Banks Sell Insurance . . . . Y
11) Pre-Paid College Tuition . . . . Y
12) Increase Pull Tab Prizes . . . . Y
13) Utility Deregulation . . . . Y
14) County Obscenity Standards . Y
15) Managed Care Reform . . . . . N

GROUP RATINGS

	FB	CoC	PrLf	IPPC	ACLU
1997	68	85	6/6	0	20

ELECTION RESULTS

1996 General	Robert W. Churchill (R)	21,864	(63.8%)
1996 General	Ronald Lee Molinaro III (D)	12,427	(36.2%)
1996 Primary	Robert W. Churchill (R)	10,242	(100%)
1996 Primary	Ronald Lee Molinaro III (D)	2,437	(100%)

CAMPAIGN RESOURCES AND EXPENDITURES

1996 Campaign Funds				Top 10 PAC Contributors			
Beg. Balance	$117,606	Individuals	$4,200	1) IPACE	$10,500	6) ABDI	$5,000
Receipts	$216,449	Party	$6,000	2) MPAC	$8,500	7) ILCon	$5,000
Expenditures	$245,231	PACS	$185,725	3) PetPec	$6,000	8) Midas	$5,000
On hand	$88,824	Candidate	$2,338	4) RPAC	$5,250	9) ISMS	$5,000
		Not-itemized	$18,186	5) UNIPAC	$5,100	10) IRoad	$5,000

NOTE: The General Election Opponent's Campaign Resources and Expenditures are reported in a separate section in the back of the book (pp. 269-284).

GENERAL ELECTION DATA

	Registered Voters	Voter Turnout		Straight Party Voting			
1996	55,885	37,286	66.7%	(R) 9,438	25.3%	(D) 4,321	11.6%

PRESIDENT

1996	Bill Clinton (D)	15,070	41.3%
	Bob Dole (R)	16,800	46.0%
	Ross Perot (I)	4,355	11.9%
1992	Bill Clinton (D)	12,116	31.7%
	George Bush (R)	17,483	45.8%
	Ross Perot (I)	8,571	22.5%

UNITED STATES SENATE

1996	Richard J. Durbin (D)	14,897	41.6%
	Al Salvi (R)	19,073	53.2%

GOVERNOR

1994	Jim Edgar (R)	18,824	77.4%
	Dawn Clark Netsch (D)	5,495	22.6%

32nd Senate District

House District 63
House District 64

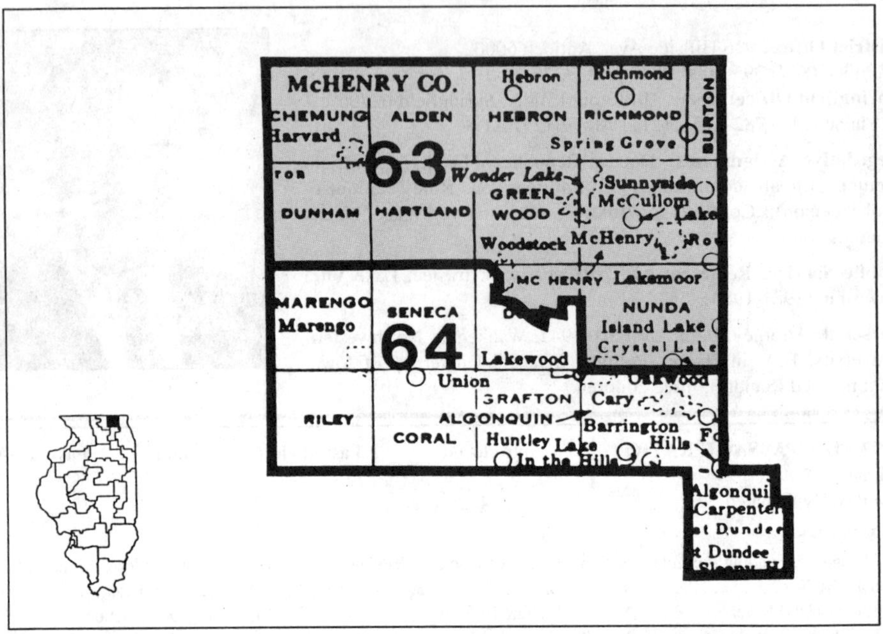

DEMOGRAPHICS (1990)

	S.D. #32	H.D. #63	H.D.#64
VOTING AGE POPULATION	137,365	68,774	68,591
White	95.9%	95.9%	95.8%
Black	0.2%	0.1%	0.2%
Hispanic	2.9%	3.2%	2.6%
Asian	0.9%	0.6%	1.3%
AGE (Total Population)	193,739	96,870	96,869
Under 6	10.3%	10.2%	10.4%
6 to 18	20.1%	20.1%	20.1%
65 and Over	9.4%	10.8%	8.0%
URBAN POPULATION	76.5%	70.0%	83.0%
HOUSING UNITS (Total)	69,415	35,176	34,239
Median Value	$114,249	$99,807	$126,471
Owner Occupied	76.7%	74.0%	79.4%
FAMILY INCOME (Total Families)	53,141	26,209	26,931
Median Income	$49,066	$44,994	$53,186
Below Poverty Level	2.5%	3.1%	1.8%
With Children Under 5	0.4%	0.5%	0.3%
With Children 5 to 17	0.9%	1.2%	0.7%
Headed by Females	1.1%	1.5%	0.7%
INDUSTRY (Total Employed)	101,042	49,323	51,719
Professional/Public Administration	20.5%	19.1%	21.8%
Manufacturing	24.1%	25.1%	23.1%
Retail	15.3%	15.3%	15.3%
Transportation/Communication	7.1%	7.2%	7.0%
Finance/Insurance/Real Estate	7.8%	6.8%	8.7%
Other Service	7.7%	7.9%	7.5%

Senator Dick Klemm (R)

District Office: 3 West Crystal Lake Ave., Crystal Lake 60014
Phone (815) 455-6330; (815) 455-8284 (fax)
Springfield Office: 124 Capitol Bldg., Springfield 62706
Phone (217) 782-8000

Legislative Assignments: Committees on Executive (chair); Commerce & Industry ; Local Government & Elections.

Public Service: Senator (1993-present); representative (1981-93); chairman, McHenry County Board; president, Board of Education District 46; township trustee.

Personal: President and Chairman of Board, Food Warming Equipment Co., Inc.; born May 5, 1932 in Chicago; Purdue University, B.S. in engineering/industrial economics; married (Nancy).

1997 BILL PASSAGE RATIO	Introduced	Passed House of Origin	Passed GA
Primary	9	7	6
Primary/Hyphenated	14	12	8

KEY VOTES

1) Senate GOP Ed. $ Plan . . . . . . .Y	6) Insurance/Domestic Violence . .Y	11) Pre-Paid College Tuition . . . .P
2) State Budget . . . . .Y	7) Brownfields . . . . .Y	12) Increase Pull Tab Prizes . . . .Y
3) Tougher DUI Level . . . . .Y	8) Welfare Reform . . . . .Y	13) Telecommunications Tax . . .N
4) Ban Partial Birth Abortions . . .Y	9) Concealed Guns/Misdemeanor .Y	14) Delivery Discrimination . . . .P
5) State Employees Pension . . . . .Y	10) Banks Sell Insurance . . . . .Y	15) Sell Drivers' Data . . . . .N

GROUP RATINGS

	FB	CoC	PrLf	IPPC	ACLU
1997	86	100	2/2	0	50

ELECTION RESULTS

1994 General	Dick Klemm (R)	43,685	(73.0%)
1994 General	Michael J. Walkup (D)	16,164	(27.0%)
1994 Primary	Dick Klemm (R)	25,730	(100%)
1994 Primary	Michael J. Walkup (D)	6,675	(100%)

CAMPAIGN RESOURCES AND EXPENDITURES

1996 Campaign Funds				Top 10 PAC Contributors	
Beg. Balance	$11,920	Individuals	$700	1) IPACE . . .$2,500	6) Ameritech . . .$500
Receipts	$18,870	Party	$160	2) CAR $500	7) ISMS $500
Expenditures	$16,359	PACS	$10,930	3) Dominick's . .$500	8) Uno-Ven $500
On hand	$14,431	Candidate	$0	4) IBA $500	9) PetPec $500
		Not-itemized	$7,080	5) IMPAC $500	10) HBPAC $400

NOTE: The General Election Opponent's Campaign Resources and Expenditures are reported in a separate section in the back of the book (pp. 269-284).

GENERAL ELECTION DATA

	Registered Voters	Voter Turnout		Straight Party Voting	
1996	136,029	89,044	65.5%	(R) 25,514 . . 28.7%	(D) 7,885 . . . . 8.9%

PRESIDENT

1996	Bill Clinton (D)	32,449	37.0%
	Bob Dole (R)	44,142	50.3%
	Ross Perot (I)	10,345	11.8%
1992	Bill Clinton (D)	25,857	27.7%
	George Bush (R)	44,571	47.8%
	Ross Perot (I)	22,769	24.5%

UNITED STATES SENATE

1996	Richard J. Durbin (D)	32,881	38.2%
	Al Salvi (R)	48,717	56.5%

GOVERNOR

1994	Jim Edgar (R)	46,956	78.4%
	Dawn Clark Netsch (D)	12,972	21.6%

Representative Michael J. Brown (R)

District Office: 5400 W. Elm, McHenry, 60050
Phone (815) 344-2019

Springfield Office: Room 2001-G Stratton Bldg., Springfield 62706
Phone (217) 782-1717; (217) 782-3189 (Fax)

Legislative Assignments: Committees on Environment & Energy; Health Care Availabilty & Access; Insurance.

Public Service: Representative (appointed July 1997); McHenry County Board member; Nunda Township Assessor; Illinois State Property Tax Appeal Board member.

Personal: Independent fee appraiser; born March 11, 1941, McHenry; Illinois Institute of Technology, Bachelor of Science; married (Carolyn); five children; five grandchildren.

1997 BILL PASSAGE RATIO	Introduced	Passed House of Origin	Passed GA
Primary	N/A	N/A	N/A
Primary/Hyphenated	N/A	N/A	N/A

KEY VOTES

1) Change Ed. Funding Formula . . X
2) State Budget X
3) Tougher DUI Level X
4) Ban Partial Birth Abortions . . X
5) State Employees Pension X
6) Insurance/Domestic Violence . . X
7) Brownfields X
8) Welfare Reform X
9) Concealed Guns/Misdemeanor . X
10) Banks Sell Insurance X
11) Pre-Paid College Tuition X
12) Increase Pull Tab Prizes X
13) Utility Deregulation X
14) County Obscenity Standards . X
15) Managed Care Reform X

GROUP RATINGS

	FB	CoC	PrLf	IPPC	ACLU
1997	N/R	N/R	N/R	N/R	N/R

ELECTION RESULTS

1996 General	Ann Hughes (R)	27,672	(72.6%)
1996 General	James S. Kappel (D)	10,435	(27.4%)
1996 Primary	Ann Hughes (R)	7,478	(56.9%)
1996 Primary	Steven Robert Verr (R)	5,653	(43.0%)

CAMPAIGN RESOURCES AND EXPENDITURES

1996 Campaign Funds

Beg. Balance	$N/A	Individuals	$N/A
Receipts	$N/A	Party	$N/A
Expenditures	$N/A	PACS	$N/A
On hand	$N/A	Candidate	$N/A
		Not-itemized	$N/A

Top 10 PAC Contributors

1) N/A	$N/A	6) N/A	$N/A
2) N/A	$N/A	7) N/A	$N/A
3) N/A	$N/A	8) N/A	$N/A
4) N/A	$N/A	9) N/A	$N/A
5) N/A	$N/A	10) N/A	$N/A

NOTE: The General Election Opponent's Campaign Resources and Expenditures are reported in a separate section in the back of the book (pp. 269-284).

GENERAL ELECTION DATA

	Registered Voters	Voter Turnout		Straight Party Voting			
1996	63,429	40,848	64.4%	(R) 11,145	27.3%	(D) 3,530	8.6%

PRESIDENT

1996	Bill Clinton (D)	14,899	37.1%
	Bob Dole (R)	19,446	48.4%
	Ross Perot (I)	5,390	13.4%
1992	Bill Clinton (D)	12,484	28.4%
	George Bush (R)	20,261	46.1%
	Ross Perot (I)	11,233	25.5%

UNITED STATES SENATE

1996	Richard J. Durbin (D)	14,886	37.5%
	Al Salvi (R)	22,249	56.1%

GOVERNOR

1994	Jim Edgar (R)	21,730	77.7%
	Dawn Clark Netsch (D)	6,241	22.3%

Representative Cal Skinner, Jr. (R)

District Office: 7103 Manor Rd., Suite 1, Crystal Lake 60014
Phone (815) 477-0066; (815) 477-0098 (fax)
Springfield Office: Room G-2 Stratton Bldg., Springfield 62706
Phone (217) 782-0432; (217) 782-2289 (fax)

Legislative Assignments: Committees on Appropriations-Public Safety (minority spokesperson); Health Care Availability & Access; Labor & Commerce; Appropriations-Education; Prison Management Reform.

Public Service: Representative (1973-81; 1993-present); treasurer, McHenry County (1966-1970); U.S. Bureau of the Budget (1965-1966).

Personal: Full-time legislator; born June 11, 1942, Easton, MD; Oberlin College, A.B. in economics; University of Michigan, master's degree in public administration; married (Michele); one child.

1997 BILL PASSAGE RATIO	Introduced	Passed House of Origin	Passed GA
Primary	11	3	1
Primary/Hyphenated	25	8	3

KEY VOTES

1) Change Ed. Funding Formula . . N	6) Insurance/Domestic Violence . . Y	11) Pre-Paid College Tuition . . . . Y
2) State Budget . . . . Y	7) Brownfields . . . . Y	12) Increase Pull Tab Prizes . . . . N
3) Tougher DUI Level . . . . Y	8) Welfare Reform . . . . Y	13) Utility Deregulation . . . . N
4) Ban Partial Birth Abortions . . . Y	9) Concealed Guns/Misdemeanor . Y	14) County Obscenity Standards . Y
5) State Employees Pension . . . . . Y	10) Banks Sell Insurance . . . . Y	15) Managed Care Reform . . . . . Y

GROUP RATINGS

	FB	CoC	PrLf	IPPC	ACLU
1997	68	85	6/6	0	20

ELECTION RESULTS

1996 General	Cal Skinner, Jr. (R)	30,246	(67.8%)
1996 General	Joseph H. "Big Joe" Powalowski (D)	14,394	(32.2%)
1996 Primary	Cal Skinner, Jr. (R)	7,478	(52.0%)
1996 Primary	John H. Brehmer (R)	6,916	(48.0%)

CAMPAIGN RESOURCES AND EXPENDITURES

1996 Campaign Funds				Top 10 PAC Contributors			
Beg. Balance	$38,519	Individuals	$2,100	1) IMPAC	$500	6) Ameritech	$250
Receipts	$19,411	Party	$0	2) Sears	$400	7) Fremont	$250
Expenditures	$9,512	PACS	$6,500	3) CPA's	$400	8) Geske	$250
On hand	$48,418	Candidate	$6,722	4) RPAC	$350	9) ILRest	$250
		Not-itemized	$4,089	5) IMAPAC	$300	10) RJR	$250

NOTE: The General Election Opponent's Campaign Resources and Expenditures are reported in a separate section in the back of the book (pp. 269-284).

GENERAL ELECTION DATA

	Registered Voters	Voter Turnout		Straight Party Voting			
1996	72,600	48,196	66.4%	(R) 14,369	29.8%	(D) 4,355	9.0%

PRESIDENT

1996	Bill Clinton (D)	17,550	36.9%
	Bob Dole (R)	24,696	51.9%
	Ross Perot (I)	4,955	10.4%
1992	Bill Clinton (D)	13,373	27.2%
	George Bush (R)	24,310	49.4%
	Ross Perot (I)	11,536	23.4%

UNITED STATES SENATE

1996	Richard J. Durbin (D)	17,995	38.7%
	Al Salvi (R)	26,468	56.9%

GOVERNOR

1994	Jim Edgar (R)	25,226	78.9%
	Dawn Clark Netsch (D)	6,731	21.1%

33rd Senate District

House District 65
House District 66

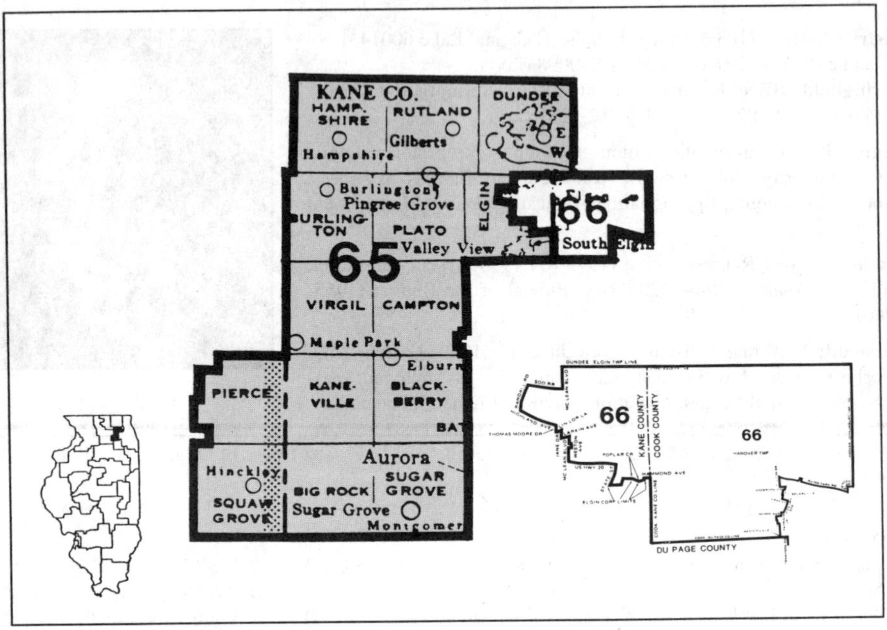

DEMOGRAPHICS (1990)

	S.D. #33	H.D. #65	H.D.#66
VOTING AGE POPULATION	136,863	67,592	69,271
White	85.0%	91.4%	78.6%
Black	3.2%	1.9%	4.4%
Hispanic	9.6%	5.4%	13.8%
Asian	2.1%	1.1%	3.0%
AGE (Total Population)	193,739	96,869	96,870
Under 6	10.7%	10.1%	11.4%
6 to 18	20.1%	21.5%	18.6%
65 and Over	8.0%	7.2%	8.8%
URBAN POPULATION	78.0%	57.2%	98.9%
HOUSING UNITS (Total)	66,878	31,972	34,906
Median Value	$108,274	$118,782	$101,022
Owner Occupied	71.5%	76.4%	67.0%
FAMILY INCOME (Total Families)	50,938	26,177	24,762
Median Income	$46,945	$50,174	$44,166
Below Poverty Level	4.0%	3.9%	4.2%
With Children Under 5	0.9%	0.8%	1.1%
With Children 5 to 17	1.6%	1.7%	1.4%
Headed by Females	2.2%	2.1%	2.3%
INDUSTRY (Total Employed)	102,553	50,454	52,099
Professional/Public Administration	19.9%	19.7%	20.0%
Manufacturing	25.3%	24.2%	26.3%
Retail	16.1%	16.0%	16.2%
Transportation/Communication	7.9%	7.9%	7.8%
Finance/Insurance/Real Estate	7.1%	7.0%	7.2%
Other Service	8.3%	8.5%	8.1%

Senator Steven J. Rauschenberger (R)

District Office: 1112 South St., Elgin 60123
Phone (847) 622-1049; (847) 622-0948 (fax)
Springfield Office: 615A State Capitol Bldg., Springfield 62706
Phone (217) 782-7746

Legislative Assignments: Committees on Appropriations (Chair); Environment and Energy; Local Government and Elections; Economic and Fiscal Commission; Joint Committee on Administrative Rules.

Public Service: Senator (1993-present)

Personal: Furniture retailer; born August 29, 1956, Elgin; College of William and Mary, B.B.A.in accounting; married (Betty); two children.

1997 BILL PASSAGE RATIO	Introduced	Passed House of Origin	Passed GA
Primary	72	24	12
Primary/Hyphenated	91	32	18

KEY VOTES

1) Senate GOP Ed. $ Plan . . . . . . .Y	6) Insurance/Domestic Violence . .Y	11) Pre-Paid College Tuition . . . .N
2) State Budget . . . . .Y	7) Brownfields . . . . .O	12) Increase Pull Tab Prizes . . . .O
3) Tougher DUI Level . . . . .Y	8) Welfare Reform . . . . .Y	13) Telecommunications Tax . . .N
4) Ban Partial Birth Abortions . . .Y	9) Concealed Guns/Misdemeanor .Y	14) Delivery Discrimination . . . .P
5) State Employees Pension . . . . .Y	10) Banks Sell Insurance . . . . .Y	15) Sell Drivers' Data . . . . .Y

GROUP RATINGS

	FB	CoC	PrLf	IPPC	ACLU
1997	82	100	2/2	0	50

ELECTION RESULTS

1996 General	Steven J. Rauschenberger (R)	43,966	(67.0%)
1996 General	Charles A. Marwig (D)	21,679	(33.0%)
1996 Primary	Steven J. Rauschenberger (R)	16,453	(100%)

CAMPAIGN RESOURCES AND EXPENDITURES

1996 Campaign Funds		Top 10 PAC Contributors	
Beg. Balance .$70,379	Individuals . .$27,375	1) Prohealth . .$5,000	6) ValleyAm . .$3,500
Receipts $172,309	Party $2,475	2) UPS $5,000	7) BSDCorp . .$3,000
Expenditures .$128,459	PACS $123,190	3) MPower . . .$4,000	8) ILCable . . .$2,500
On hand $114,229	Candidate $0	4) J&BElectric $3,500	9) ILCon $2,500
	Not-itemized $19,269	5) HOPE $3,500	10) GGCouncil $2,500

NOTE: The General Election Opponent's Campaign Resources and Expenditures are reported in a separate section in the back of the book (pp. 269-284).

GENERAL ELECTION DATA

Registered Voters	Voter Turnout	Straight Party Voting	
1996 108,129	70,210 . . . . .64.9%	(R) 18,483 . .26.3%	(D) 8,764 . . . .12.5%

PRESIDENT

1996	Bill Clinton (D) 28,094	40.7%
	Bob Dole (R) 32,997	47.8%
	Ross Perot (I) 7,304	10.6%
1992	Bill Clinton (D) 25,000	32.4%
	George Bush (R) 34,246	44.4%
	Ross Perot (I) 17,899	23.2%

UNITED STATES SENATE

1996	Richard J. Durbin (D) 28,404	42.0%
	Al Salvi (R) 35,701	52.7%

GOVERNOR

1994	Jim Edgar (R) 33,755	76.5%
	Dawn Clark Netsch (D) 10,350	23.5%

Representative Patricia Reid Lindner (R)

District Office: 32 Main St., Suite A, Sugar Grove 60554
Phone (630) 466-9791; (630) 466-7124 (fax)
Springfield Office: Room 2116-N Stratton Bldg., Springfield 62706
Phone (217) 782-1486; (217) 782-1275 (fax)

Legislative Assignments: Committees on Children & Youth (minority spokesperson); Financial Institutions; Appropriations-General Services & Government Oversight; Registration & Regulation; Judiciary II-Criminal Law.

Public Service: Representative (1993-present).

Personal: Attorney; born November 29, 1939; Northwestern University, B.S. in speech; University of Colorado, M.A. in political science; Northern Illinois University, J.D.; married (George); four children.

1997 BILL PASSAGE RATIO	Introduced	Passed House of Origin	Passed GA
Primary	20	5	3
Primary/Hyphenated	41	16	8

KEY VOTES

1) Change Ed. Funding Formula . . N	6) Insurance/Domestic Violence . . Y	11) Pre-Paid College Tuition . . . . Y
2) State Budget . . . . Y	7) Brownfields . . . . Y	12) Increase Pull Tab Prizes . . . . Y
3) Tougher DUI Level . . . . Y	8) Welfare Reform . . . . Y	13) Utility Deregulation . . . . P
4) Ban Partial Birth Abortions . . . Y	9) Concealed Guns/Misdemeanor . Y	14) County Obscenity Standards . N
5) State Employees Pension . . . . . Y	10) Banks Sell Insurance . . . . Y	15) Managed Care Reform . . . . . Y

GROUP RATINGS

	FB	CoC	PrLf	IPPC	ACLU
1997	68	54	1/6	83	70

ELECTION RESULTS

1996 General	Patricia Reid Lindner (R)	31,043	(100%)
1996 Primary	Patricia Reid Lindner (R)	10,772	(100%)
1994 General	Patricia Reid Lindner (R)	22,312	(100%)

CAMPAIGN RESOURCES AND EXPENDITURES

1996 Campaign Funds				Top 10 PAC Contributors	
Beg. Balance	$15,071	Individuals	$250	1) LAWPAC . . $1,500	6) WCLA $500
Receipts	$16,678	Party	$0	2) MPAC $1,500	7) HOPE $400
Expenditures	$20,183	PACS	$12,249	3) CatCEG $750	8) CPA's $400
On hand	$11,566	Candidate	$0	4) RPAC $500	9) N&STruck . . $399
		Not-itemized	$4,179	5) Ameritech . . . $500	10) Sears $350

NOTE: The General Election Opponent's Campaign Resources and Expenditures are reported in a separate section in the back of the book (pp. 269-284).

GENERAL ELECTION DATA

	Registered Voters	Voter Turnout		Straight Party Voting	
1996	60,779	41,472	68.2%	(R) 11,674 . . 28.1%	(D) 4,055 . . . . 9.8%

PRESIDENT

1996	Bill Clinton (D)	14,789	36.3%
	Bob Dole (R)	21,010	51.5%
	Ross Perot (I)	4,603	11.3%
1992	Bill Clinton (D)	12,281	28.7%
	George Bush (R)	19,994	46.7%
	Ross Perot (I)	10,502	24.6%

UNITED STATES SENATE

1996	Richard J. Durbin (D)	15,118	37.8%
	Al Salvi (R)	22,606	56.5%

GOVERNOR

1994	Jim Edgar (R)	20,431	79.2%
	Dawn Clark Netsch (D)	5,362	20.8%

Representative Douglas L. Hoeft (R)

District Office: 1112 South St., Elgin 60123
Phone (847) 622-1048; (847) 622-0948 (fax)
Springfield Office: Room 2136-O Stratton Bldg., Springfield 62706
Phone (217) 782-8020

Legislative Assignments: Committees on Personnel & Pensions (minority spokesperson); Insurance; Elementary & Secondary Education; Environment & Energy.

Public Service: Representative (1993-present); regional superintendent of schools, Kane County.

Personal: Born May 26, 1942, Rochester, MN; Denison University, B.A. in liberal arts; Northwestern University, M.A. in education; Northern Illinois University, Ed.D. in administration; married (Libby); two children.

1997 BILL PASSAGE RATIO	Introduced	Passed House of Origin	Passed GA
Primary	6	2	2
Primary/Hyphenated	14	7	4

KEY VOTES

1) Change Ed. Funding Formula . . N
2) State Budget . . . . N
3) Tougher DUI Level . . . . Y
4) Ban Partial Birth Abortions . . . Y
5) State Employees Pension . . . . . Y
6) Insurance/Domestic Violence . . Y
7) Brownfields . . . . Y
8) Welfare Reform . . . . Y
9) Concealed Guns/Misdemeanor . Y
10) Banks Sell Insurance . . . . Y
11) Pre-Paid College Tuition . . . . Y
12) Increase Pull Tab Prizes . . . . Y
13) Utility Deregulation . . . . Y
14) County Obscenity Standards . Y
15) Managed Care Reform . . . . . N

GROUP RATINGS

	FB	CoC	PrLf	IPPC	ACLU
1997	64	77	4/6	33	40

ELECTION RESULTS

1996 General	Douglas L. Hoeft (R)	19,468	(100%)
1996 Primary	Douglas L. Hoeft (R)	5,318	(100%)
1994 General	Douglas L. Hoeft (R)	14,722	(100%)

CAMPAIGN RESOURCES AND EXPENDITURES

1996 Campaign Funds

Beg. Balance	$23,110	Individuals	$500
Receipts	$17,974	Party	$450
Expenditures	$14,940	PACS	$10,200
On hand	$26,144	Candidate	$0
		Not-itemized	$6,824

Top 10 PAC Contributors

1) MPAC	$2,000	6) PIIA	$500
2) Ameritech	$1,000	7) CPA's	$400
3) ChgoCoC	$500	8) HOPE	$400
4) IBA	$500	9) CAR	$400
5) ISMS	$500	10) LUPAC	$300

NOTE: The General Election Opponent's Campaign Resources and Expenditures are reported in a separate section in the back of the book (pp. 269-284).

GENERAL ELECTION DATA

	Registered Voters	Voter Turnout		Straight Party Voting (R)		Straight Party Voting (D)	
1996	47,350	28,738	60.7%	6,809	23.7%	4,709	16.4%

PRESIDENT

1996	Bill Clinton (D)	13,305	47.1%
	Bob Dole (R)	11,987	42.4%
	Ross Perot (I)	2,701	9.6%
1992	Bill Clinton (D)	12,719	37.0%
	George Bush (R)	14,252	41.5%
	Ross Perot (I)	7,397	21.5%

UNITED STATES SENATE

1996	Richard J. Durbin (D)	13,286	47.9%
	Al Salvi (R)	13,095	47.3%

GOVERNOR

1994	Jim Edgar (R)	13,324	72.8%
	Dawn Clark Netsch (D)	4,988	27.2%

34th Senate District

House District 67
House District 68

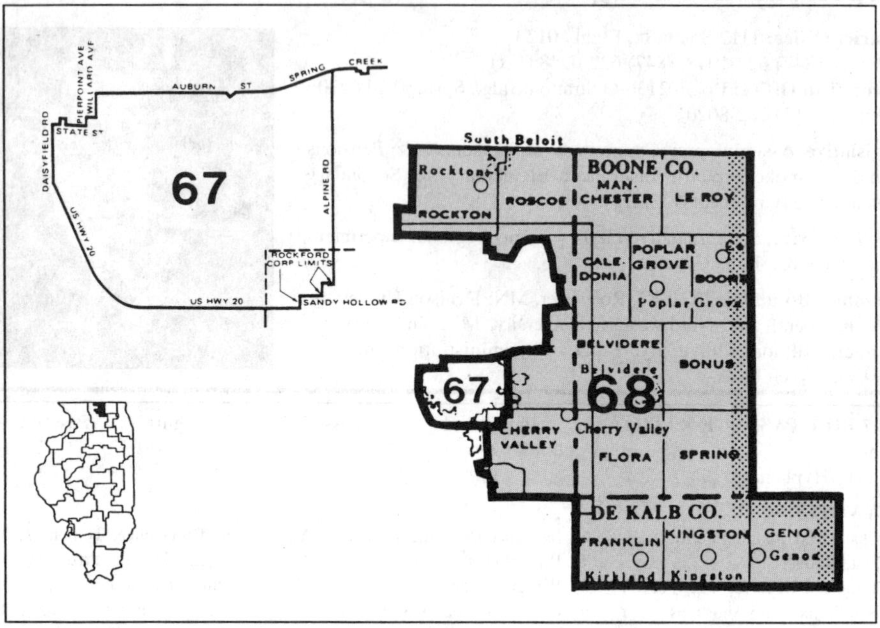

DEMOGRAPHICS (1990)

	S.D. #34	H.D. #67	H.D.#68
VOTING AGE POPULATION	141,727	70,756	70,971
White	86.2%	77.4%	94.9%
Black	9.1%	16.9%	1.2%
Hispanic	3.5%	4.3%	2.8%
Asian	1.0%	1.2%	0.9%
AGE (Total Population)	193,739	96,869	96,870
Under 6	9.4%	10.2%	8.6%
6 to 18	18.9%	18.1%	19.6%
65 and Over	12.3%	14.2%	10.5%
URBAN POPULATION	82.8%	99.1%	66.4%
HOUSING UNITS (Total)	78,140	41,665	36,475
Median Value	$63,302	$50,095	$75,892
Owner Occupied	61.5%	52.6%	71.7%
FAMILY INCOME (Total Families)	52,416	25,341	27,075
Median Income	$36,872	$30,224	$42,774
Below Poverty Level	8.8%	14.3%	3.6%
With Children Under 5	2.1%	3.4%	0.9%
With Children 5 to 17	2.8%	4.5%	1.2%
Headed by Females	5.9%	10.2%	1.9%
INDUSTRY (Total Employed)	94,340	43,569	50,771
Professional/Public Administration	21.4%	21.6%	21.3%
Manufacturing	34.3%	34.1%	34.6%
Retail	16.3%	17.3%	15.5%
Transportation/Communication	5.6%	5.9%	5.4%
Finance/Insurance/Real Estate	4.9%	4.6%	5.1%
Other Service	7.6%	8.3%	7.1%

Senator Dave Syverson (R)

District Office: 200 S. Wyman, Suite 302, Rockford 61101
Phone (815) 987-7555; (815) 987-7563 (fax)
Springfield Office: M115 Capitol Bldg., Springfield 62706
Phone (217) 782-5413; (217) 782-0650 (fax)

Legislative Assignments: Committees on Public Health & Welfare (chair); Appropriations; Transportation; Illinois Tollway Advisory Committee.

Public Service: Senator (1993 - present)

Personal: Born June 29, 1957, Chicago; attended Rock Valley College, communications; Partner in Market Insurance Service, Inc.; married (Shirley); two children.

1997 BILL PASSAGE RATIO	Introduced	Passed House of Origin	Passed GA
Primary	15	10	10
Primary/Hyphenated	23	13	11

KEY VOTES

1) Senate GOP Ed. $ Plan ......Y	6) Insurance/Domestic Violence ..Y	11) Pre-Paid College Tuition ....Y
2) State Budget ....Y	7) Brownfields ....Y	12) Increase Pull Tab Prizes ....N
3) Tougher DUI Level ....Y	8) Welfare Reform ....Y	13) Telecommunications Tax ...N
4) Ban Partial Birth Abortions ...Y	9) Concealed Guns/Misdemeanor .Y	14) Delivery Discrimination ....O
5) State Employees Pension .....Y	10) Banks Sell Insurance ....Y	15) Sell Drivers' Data ....Y

GROUP RATINGS

	FB	CoC	PrLf	IPPC	ACLU
1997	82	100	2/2	0	50

ELECTION RESULTS

1996 General	Dave Syverson (R)	45,351	(62.1%)
1996 General	Carol Jambor-Smith (D)	27,686	(37.9%)
1996 Primary	Dave Syverson (R)	19,254	(100%)
1996 Primary	Carol Jambor-Smith (D)	5,759	(100%)

CAMPAIGN RESOURCES AND EXPENDITURES

1996 Campaign Funds				Top 10 PAC Contributors	
Beg. Balance	$112,247	Individuals	$7,325	1) RSSC ...$172,297	6) Sundstrand .$2,160
Receipts	$261,686	Party	$174,497	2) ISMS $12,500	7) PIIA $2,000
Expenditures	$371,713	PACS	$66,555	3) MPAC $6,500	8) ILCon $2,000
On hand	$2,220	Candidate	$0	4) CoC $3,547	9) NICA $2,000
		Not-itemized	$13,309	5) RubloffDevlp$3,000	10) Pioneer ...$1,585

NOTE: The General Election Opponent's Campaign Resources and Expenditures are reported in a separate section in the back of the book (pp. 269-284).

GENERAL ELECTION DATA

	Registered Voters	Voter Turnout		Straight Party Voting	
1996	111,866	75,895	67.8%	(R) 17,513 . .23.1%	(D) 10,782 . . .14.2%

PRESIDENT

1996	Bill Clinton (D)	34,247	46.1%
	Bob Dole (R)	33,266	44.7%
	Ross Perot (I)	6,133	8.3%
1992	Bill Clinton (D)	36,097	43.3%
	George Bush (R)	31,405	37.7%
	Ross Perot (I)	15,767	19.0%

UNITED STATES SENATE

1996	Richard J. Durbin (D)	32,374	44.1%
	Al Salvi (R)	38,319	52.2%

GOVERNOR

1994	Jim Edgar (R)	36,220	73.8%
	Dawn Clark Netsch (D)	2,869	26.2%

Representative Douglas P. Scott (D)

District Office: 200 S. Wyman, Suite 304, Rockford 61101
Phone (815) 987-7433; (815) 987-7225 (fax)
Springfield Office: Room 2071-L Stratton Bldg., Springfield 62706
Phone (217) 782-3167; (217) 782-1290 (fax)

Legislative Assignments: Committees on Judiciary I - Civil Law (vice-chair); Aging; Local Government; Environment & Energy; Conflicts of Interest; Electric Utility Deregulation; Intergovernmental Cooperation Commission.

Public Service: Representative (1995-present); city attorney, Rockford (1987-95); assistant city attorney, Rockford (1985-87).

Personal: Full-time legislator; born January 17, 1960, Rockford; University of Tulsa, B.A. in political science & history; Marquette University, J.D.; married (Tammy).

1997 BILL PASSAGE RATIO	Introduced	Passed House of Origin	Passed GA
Primary	48	10	4
Primary/Hyphenated	151	40	13

KEY VOTES

1) Change Ed. Funding Formula . . Y	6) Insurance/Domestic Violence . . Y	11) Pre-Paid College Tuition . . . . Y
2) State Budget . . . . Y	7) Brownfields . . . . Y	12) Increase Pull Tab Prizes . . . . Y
3) Tougher DUI Level . . . . Y	8) Welfare Reform . . . . Y	13) Utility Deregulation . . . . Y
4) Ban Partial Birth Abortions . . . N	9) Concealed Guns/Misdemeanor . N	14) County Obscenity Standards . N
5) State Employees Pension . . . . . Y	10) Banks Sell Insurance . . . . Y	15) Managed Care Reform . . . . . Y

GROUP RATINGS

	FB	CoC	PrLf	IPPC	ACLU
1997	86	23	0/6	100	100

ELECTION RESULTS

1996 General	Douglas P. Scott (D)	18,527	(63.6%)
1996 General	Thomas J. Seymour (R)	10,622	(36.4%)
1996 Primary	Douglas P. Scott (D)	3,551	(100%)

CAMPAIGN RESOURCES AND EXPENDITURES

1996 Campaign Funds

Beg. Balance	$24,200	Individuals	$8,427
Receipts	$80,569	Party	$6,700
Expenditures	$101,819	PACS	$53,655
On hand	$2,950	Candidate	$0
		Not-itemized	$11,787

Top 10 PAC Contributors

1) IPACE . . . $14,000	6) Laidlaw . . . $2,600
2) DSCC $5,000	7) AFSCME . . $2,400
3) PersPAC . . . $3,930	8) UAW $2,000
4) ITLA $3,000	9) LAWPAC . . $1,500
5) NWICA . . . $3,000	10) AFLCIO . . $1,150

NOTE: The General Election Opponent's Campaign Resources and Expenditures are reported in a separate section in the back of the book (pp. 269-284).

GENERAL ELECTION DATA

	Registered Voters	Voter Turnout		Straight Party Voting	
1996	46,640	30,601	65.6%	(R) 5,184 . . . 16.9%	(D) 6,238 . . . 20.4%

PRESIDENT

1996	Bill Clinton (D)	16,704	55.6%
	Bob Dole (R)	10,872	36.2%
	Ross Perot (I)	2,126	7.1%
1992	Bill Clinton (D)	19,542	53.2%
	George Bush (R)	11,383	31.0%
	Ross Perot (I)	5,815	15.8%

UNITED STATES SENATE

1996	Richard J. Durbin (D)	15,974	53.8%
	Al Salvi (R)	12,587	42.4%

GOVERNOR

1994	Jim Edgar (R)	12,752	65.8%
	Dawn Clark Netsch (D)	6,625	34.2%

Representative Ronald A. Wait (R)

District Office: 411 South State St., Belvidere 61008; 200 South Wyman, Suite 303, Rockford 61101
Phone (815) 987-7478; (815) 987-7767 (fax)
Springfield Office: Room 2022-H Stratton Bldg., Springfield 62706
Phone (217) 782-0548; (217) 782-1275 (fax)

Legislative Assignments: Committees on Transportation & Motor Vehicles (minority spokesperson); Appropriations - Public Safety; Judiciary I - Civil Law; Local Government.

Public Service: Representative (1983-93; 1995-present).

Personal: Full-time legislator; born April 15, 1944; Drake University, B.S. in accounting; Northern Illinois University, M.A. in education/business administration; Drake University Law School, J.D.; one child.

1997 BILL PASSAGE RATIO	Introduced	Passed House of Origin	Passed GA
Primary	13	3	2
Primary/Hyphenated	17	6	3

KEY VOTES

1) Change Ed. Funding Formula . .N
2) State Budget . . . . .Y
3) Tougher DUI Level . . . . .Y
4) Ban Partial Birth Abortions . . .Y
5) State Employees Pension . . . . .Y
6) Insurance/Domestic Violence . .Y
7) Brownfields . . . . .Y
8) Welfare Reform . . . . .Y
9) Concealed Guns/Misdemeanor .Y
10) Banks Sell Insurance . . . . .Y
11) Pre-Paid College Tuition . . . .Y
12) Increase Pull Tab Prizes . . . .Y
13) Utility Deregulation . . . . .P
14) County Obscenity Standards .Y
15) Managed Care Reform . . . . .Y

GROUP RATINGS

	FB	CoC	PrLf	IPPC	ACLU
1997	54	69	6/6	0	20

ELECTION RESULTS

1996 General	Ronald A. Wait (R)	27,364	(63.7%)
1996 General	William A. Vedra (D)	15,574	(36.3%)
1996 Primary	Ronald A. Wait (R)	11,678	(100%)
1996 Primary	William A. Vedra (D)	2,404	(100%)

CAMPAIGN RESOURCES AND EXPENDITURES

1996 Campaign Funds

Beg. Balance	$10,837	Individuals	$6,775
Receipts	$182,737	Party	$110,324
Expenditures	$185,144	PACS	$58,038
On hand	$8,430	Candidate	$0
		Not-itemized	$7,600

Top 10 PAC Contributors

1) FLAD	$56,688	6) IRoad	$2,500
2) HRCC	$49,541	7) NICA	$2,000
3) ISMS	$10,000	8) Activator	$1,455
4) Truck	$2,500	9) Landmark	$1,000
5) CChurchill	$2,500	10) LAWPAC	$1,000

NOTE: The General Election Opponent's Campaign Resources and Expenditures are reported in a separate section in the back of the book (pp. 269-284).

GENERAL ELECTION DATA

	Registered Voters	Voter Turnout		Straight Party Voting	
1996	65,226	45,294	69.4%	(R) 12,329 . .27.3%	(D) 4,544 . . . .10.0%

PRESIDENT

1996	Bill Clinton (D)	17,543	39.6%
	Bob Dole (R)	22,394	50.5%
	Ross Perot (I)	4,007	9.0%
1992	Bill Clinton (D)	16,555	35.6%
	George Bush (R)	20,022	43.0%
	Ross Perot (I)	9,952	21.4%

UNITED STATES SENATE

1996	Richard J. Durbin (D)	16,400	37.5%
	Al Salvi (R)	25,732	58.8%

GOVERNOR

1994	Jim Edgar (R)	23,468	79.0%
	Dawn Clark Netsch (D)	6,244	21.0%

35th Senate District

House District 69
House District 70

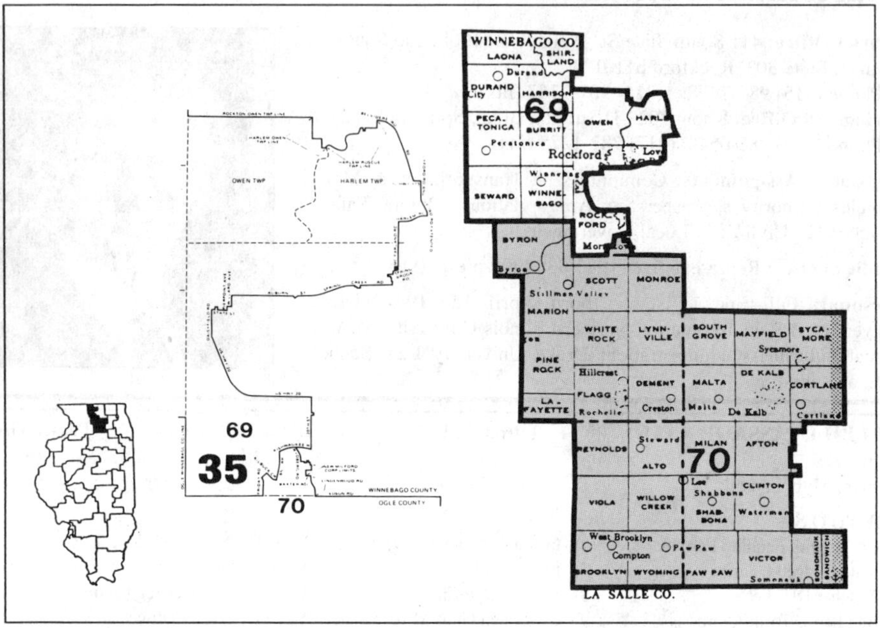

DEMOGRAPHICS (1990)

	S.D. #35	H.D. #69	H.D.#70
VOTING AGE POPULATION	146,598	71,999	74,599
White	94.2%	95.7%	92.8%
Black	2.0%	1.9%	2.2%
Hispanic	2.2%	1.4%	2.9%
Asian	1.4%	0.7%	2.0%
AGE (Total Population)	193,740	96,870	96,870
Under 6	8.3%	8.6%	8.0%
6 to 18	18.2%	18.5%	17.8%
65 and Over	11.8%	12.9%	10.7%
URBAN POPULATION	71.7%	81.5%	61.8%
HOUSING UNITS (Total)	72,170	37,511	34,659
Median Value	$65,279	$59,179	$73,610
Owner Occupied	65.9%	73.1%	58.2%
FAMILY INCOME (Total Families)	49,814	27,145	22,669
Median Income	$38,147	$38,700	$37,408
Below Poverty Level	5.2%	4.7%	5.9%
With Children Under 5	1.0%	0.8%	1.4%
With Children 5 to 17	1.6%	1.6%	1.6%
Headed by Females	2.3%	1.8%	2.8%
INDUSTRY (Total Employed)	98,493	49,426	49,067
Professional/Public Administration	26.2%	22.0%	30.4%
Manufacturing	27.0%	32.9%	21.1%
Retail	16.8%	16.0%	17.5%
Transportation/Communication	5.6%	4.8%	6.4%
Finance/Insurance/Real Estate	5.0%	5.3%	4.7%
Other Service	6.9%	7.6%	6.2%

Senator J. Bradley Burzynski (R)

District Office: 505 DeKalb Ave., Sycamore 60178
Phone (815) 895-6318; (815) 895-2905 (fax)
Springfield Office: Room M-121 Capitol Bldg., Springfield 62706
Phone (217) 782-1977

Legislative Assignments: Committees on Licensed Activities (chair); State Government Operations; Executive Appointments.

Public Service: Senator (1993-present); representative (1990-1993).

Personal: Full-time legislator; born July 13, 1955, Christopher; Rend Lake Community College, A.A.; Illinois Wesleyan, B.A. in education; married (Judy); two children.

1997 BILL PASSAGE RATIO	Introduced	Passed House of Origin	Passed GA
Primary	32	12	10
Primary/Hyphenated	40	19	17

KEY VOTES

1) Senate GOP Ed. $ Plan ......Y	6) Insurance/Domestic Violence ..Y	11) Pre-Paid College Tuition ....Y
2) State Budget ....Y	7) Brownfields ....Y	12) Increase Pull Tab Prizes ....N
3) Tougher DUI Level ....Y	8) Welfare Reform ....Y	13) Telecommunications Tax ...N
4) Ban Partial Birth Abortions ...Y	9) Concealed Guns/Misdemeanor .Y	14) Delivery Discrimination ....P
5) State Employees Pension .....Y	10) Banks Sell Insurance ....Y	15) Sell Drivers' Data ....N

GROUP RATINGS

	FB	CoC	PrLf	IPPC	ACLU
1997	86	100	2/2	0	50

ELECTION RESULTS

1994 General	J. Bradley Burzynski (R)	33,966	(66.0%)
1994 General	Lorraine Chaussee (D)	17,528	(34.0%)
1994 Primary	J. Bradley Burzynski (R)	11,959	(100%)
1994 Primary	Lorraine Chaussee (D)	5,912	(100%)

CAMPAIGN RESOURCES AND EXPENDITURES

1996 Campaign Funds				Top 10 PAC Contributors			
Beg. Balance	$31,892	Individuals	$2,050	1) LamonicaBev	$1,414	6) ABDI	$600
Receipts	$21,679	Party	$0	2) IMHA	$1,000	7) NIBC	$600
Expenditures	$21,373	PACS	$17,889	3) ILCon	$1,000	8) IMPAC	$600
On hand	$32,198	Candidate	$340	4) RPAC	$750	9) LUPAC	$600
		Not-itemized	$1,400	5) CPA's	$600	10) MedMan	$575

NOTE: The General Election Opponent's Campaign Resources and Expenditures are reported in a separate section in the back of the book (pp. 269-284).

GENERAL ELECTION DATA

	Registered Voters	Voter Turnout		Straight Party Voting			
1996	119,868	78,687	65.6%	(R) 18,203	23.1%	D) 9,486	12.1%

PRESIDENT

1996	Bill Clinton (D)	33,976	44.1%
	Bob Dole (R)	34,726	45.1%
	Ross Perot (I)	7,466	9.7%
1992	Bill Clinton (D)	34,823	40.1%
	George Bush (R)	33,684	38.8%
	Ross Perot (I)	18,383	21.1%

UNITED STATES SENATE

1996	Richard J. Durbin (D)	32,796	43.2%
	Al Salvi (R)	39,675	52.3%

GOVERNOR

1994	Jim Edgar (R)	38,498	75.5%
	Dawn Clark Netsch (D)	12,509	24.5%

Representative Dave Winters (R)

District Office: 3600 North Main St., North Towne Mall, Suite 80, Rockford 61103
Phone (815) 282-0083; (815) 282-0085 (fax)
Springfield Office: Room 2118-N Stratton Bldg., Springfield 62706
Phone (217) 782-0455; (217) 782-1139 (fax)

Legislative Assignments: Committees on Appropriations-General Services & Government Oversight; Human Services; Insurance; Labor & Commerce.

Public Service: Representative (1995-present); chair, Winnebago County Zoning Board of Appeals (1993-1995); Winnebago County Board (1986-1992).

Personal: Farmer; born June 30, 1952, Springfield; Dartmouth College, B.A. in History; University of Illinois, M.S. in Agricultural Economics; married (Kathleen); two children.

1997 BILL PASSAGE RATIO	Introduced	Passed House of Origin	Passed GA
Primary	15	3	1
Primary/Hyphenated	25	10	3

KEY VOTES

1) Change Ed. Funding Formula . . N
2) State Budget . . . . Y
3) Tougher DUI Level . . . . Y
4) Ban Partial Birth Abortions . . . Y
5) State Employees Pension . . . . . Y
6) Insurance/Domestic Violence . . Y
7) Brownfields . . . . Y
8) Welfare Reform . . . . Y
9) Concealed Guns/Misdemeanor . Y
10) Banks Sell Insurance . . . . Y
11) Pre-Paid College Tuition . . . . Y
12) Increase Pull Tab Prizes . . . . N
13) Utility Deregulation . . . . Y
14) County Obscenity Standards . Y
15) Managed Care Reform . . . . . N

GROUP RATINGS

	FB	CoC	PrLf	IPPC	ACLU
1997	68	92	5/6	16	30

ELECTION RESULTS

1996 General	Dave Winters (R)	23,320	(61.6%)
1996 General	Victor W. Verni (D)	14,532	(38.4%)
1996 Primary	Dave Winters (R)	9,966	(100%)
1996 Primary	Victor W. Verni (D)	3,416	(100%)

CAMPAIGN RESOURCES AND EXPENDITURES

1996 Campaign Funds

Beg. Balance	$8,776	Individuals	$14,060
Receipts	$309,252	Party	$223,777
Expenditures	$313,916	PACS	$58,983
On hand	$4,112	Candidate	$0
		Not-itemized	$12,432

Top 10 PAC Contributors

1) FLAD . . $114,708	6) MPAC $4,500
2) HRCC . . . $87,069	7) CoC $2,250
3) ISMS $10,077	8) NWICA . . . $2,000
4) CChurchill $10,000	9) SyversonFS $2,000
5) CRyan . . . $10,000	10) Fremont . . $1,500

NOTE: The General Election Opponent's Campaign Resources and Expenditures are reported in a separate section in the back of the book (pp. 269-284).

GENERAL ELECTION DATA

	Registered Voters	Voter Turnout		Straight Party Voting	
1996	62,936	42,179	67.0%	(R) 8,827 . . . 20.9%	(D) 5,004 . . . 11.9%

PRESIDENT

1996	Bill Clinton (D)	18,316	44.5%
	Bob Dole (R)	18,711	45.4%
	Ross Perot (I)	3,763	9.1%
1992	Bill Clinton (D)	18,210	40.6%
	George Bush (R)	17,579	39.2%
	Ross Perot (I)	9,107	20.2%

UNITED STATES SENATE

1996	Richard J. Durbin (D)	17,383	42.7%
	Al Salvi (R)	21,605	53.1%

GOVERNOR

1994	Jim Edgar (R)	21,396	76.1%
	Dawn Clark Netsch (D)	6,730	23.9%

Representative David Wirsing (R)

District Office: 115 N. Third St., Suite 400, DeKalb 60115-3365
Phone (815) 748-3494; (815) 748-4630 (fax)
Springfield Office: 2028-H Stratton Bldg., Springfield 62706
Phone (217) 782-0425

Legislative Assignments: Committees on Higher Education (minority spokesman); Appropriations-Education; Public Utilities; State Government Administration & Election Reform.

Public Service: Representative (1993-present); member, Sycamore school board.

Personal: Farmer; born August 5, 1937, Sycamore; married (Nancy) four children; four grandchildren.

1997 BILL PASSAGE RATIO	Introduced	Passed House of Origin	Passed GA
Primary	11	4	2
Primary/Hyphenated	24	11	5

KEY VOTES

1) Change Ed. Funding Formula . .N	6) Insurance/Domestic Violence . .Y	11) Pre-Paid College Tuition . . . .Y
2) State Budget . . . . .Y	7) Brownfields . . . . .Y	12) Increase Pull Tab Prizes . . . .Y
3) Tougher DUI Level . . . . .Y	8) Welfare Reform . . . . .Y	13) Utility Deregulation . . . . . . .Y
4) Ban Partial Birth Abortions . . .Y	9) Concealed Guns/Misdemeanor .Y	14) County Obscenity Standards .Y
5) State Employees Pension . . . . .Y	10) Banks Sell Insurance . . . . .Y	15) Managed Care Reform . . . . .N

GROUP RATINGS

	FB	CoC	PrLf	IPPC	ACLU
1997	71	77	6/6	0	30

ELECTION RESULTS

1996 General	David Wirsing (R)	25,160	(100%)
1996 Primary	David Wirsing (R)	9,464	(100%)
1994 General	David Wirsing (R)	16,539	(71.7%)
1994 General	Su Bute (D)	6,533	(28.3%)

CAMPAIGN RESOURCES AND EXPENDITURES

1996 Campaign Funds				Top 10 PAC Contributors			
Beg. Balance	$8,147	Individuals	$690	1) CatCEG	$1,000	6) ISMS	$500
Receipts	$20,461	Party	$0	2) IBA	$750	7) IPACE	$500
Expenditures	$24,359	PACS	$11,700	3) LICID	$500	8) GTE	$500
On hand	$4,249	Candidate	$0	4) ABCI	$500	9) MPAC	$500
		Not-itemized	$8,071	5) Ameritech	$500	10) CPA's	$400

NOTE: The General Election Opponent's Campaign Resources and Expenditures are reported in a separate section in the back of the book (pp. 269-284).

GENERAL ELECTION DATA

	Registered Voters	Voter Turnout		Straight Party Voting	
1996	56,932	36,508	64.1%	(R) 9,376 . . .25.7%	(D) 4,482 . . . .12.3%

PRESIDENT

1996	Bill Clinton (D)	15,660	43.7%
	Bob Dole (R)	16,015	44.7%
	Ross Perot (I)	3,703	10.3%
1992	Bill Clinton (D)	16,613	39.6%
	George Bush (R)	16,105	38.4%
	Ross Perot (I)	9,276	22.0%

UNITED STATES SENATE

1996	Richard J. Durbin (D)	15,413	43.7%
	Al Salvi (R)	18,070	51.3%

GOVERNOR

1994	Jim Edgar (R)	17,102	74.7%
	Dawn Clark Netsch (D)	5,779	25.3%

36th Senate District

House District 71
House District 72

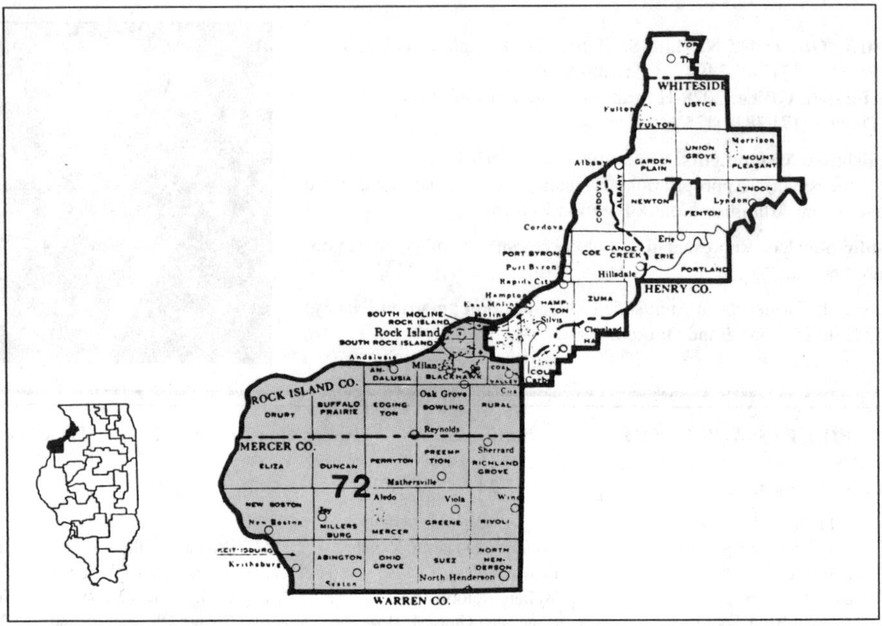

DEMOGRAPHICS (1990)

	S.D. #36	H.D. #71	H.D.#72
VOTING AGE POPULATION	143,457	71,648	71,809
White	91.2%	92.5%	89.9%
Black	4.5%	2.8%	6.3%
Hispanic	3.6%	4.0%	3.2%
Asian	0.5%	0.5%	0.4%
AGE (Total Population)	193,739	96,870	96,869
Under 6	8.3%	8.3%	8.3%
6 to 18	19.1%	19.0%	19.1%
65 and Over	14.8%	14.1%	15.4%
URBAN POPULATION	75.8%	76.0%	75.5%
HOUSING UNITS (Total)	81,355	40,238	41,117
Median Value	$46,756	$48,838	$44,364
Owner Occupied	64.6%	66.6%	62.5%
FAMILY INCOME (Total Families)	52,692	26,905	25,786
Median Income	$33,043	$34,449	$31,818
Below Poverty Level	9.6%	8.9%	10.4%
With Children Under 5	2.5%	2.5%	2.5%
With Children 5 to 17	3.3%	3.1%	3.4%
Headed by Females	5.3%	4.8%	5.8%
INDUSTRY (Total Employed)	86,833	43,658	43,174
Professional/Public Administration	27.0%	25.4%	28.7%
Manufacturing	19.4%	22.0%	16.8%
Retail	17.9%	17.4%	18.4%
Transportation/Communication	7.0%	6.8%	7.2%
Finance/Insurance/Real Estate	5.1%	4.7%	5.5%
Other Service	7.8%	8.1%	7.6%

Senator Denny Jacobs (D)

District Office: 606 19th St., Moline 61265
Phone (309) 797-0001; (309) 797-0003 (fax)
Springfield Office: M103C, Capitol Bldg., Springfield 62706
Phone (217) 782-5957

Legislative Assignments: Minority Caucus Whip. Committees on Insurance and Pensions (minority spokesman); Environment & Energy.

Public Service: Senator (1986-present); mayor of East Moline (1973 – 1987).

Personal: Full-time legislator; born November 8, 1937, East Moline; Augustana College, B.A. in business administration; married (Mary Ellen); six children.

1997 BILL PASSAGE RATIO	Introduced	Passed House of Origin	Passed GA
Primary	20	6	5
Primary/Hyphenated	43	16	12

KEY VOTES

1) Senate GOP Ed. $ Plan ......N	6) Insurance/Domestic Violence ..Y	11) Pre-Paid College Tuition ....Y
2) State Budget ....N	7) Brownfields ....Y	12) Increase Pull Tab Prizes ....Y
3) Tougher DUI Level ....N	8) Welfare Reform ....Y	13) Telecommunications Tax ...Y
4) Ban Partial Birth Abortions ...Y	9) Concealed Guns/Misdemeanor .Y	14) Delivery Discrimination ....Y
5) State Employees Pension .....Y	10) Banks Sell Insurance ....Y	15) Sell Drivers' Data ....Y

GROUP RATINGS

	FB	CoC	PrLf	IPPC	ACLU
1997	86	80	2/2	0	50

ELECTION RESULTS

1996 General	Denny Jacobs (D)	57,793	(100%)
1996 Primary	Denny Jacobs (D)	11,406	(75.2%)
1996 Primary	Marlys Vermeire (D)	3,754	(24.8%)

CAMPAIGN RESOURCES AND EXPENDITURES

1996 Campaign Funds				Top 10 PAC Contributors			
Beg. Balance	$71,893	Individuals	$2,918	1) DSCC	$5,000	6) FLEvans	$1,130
Receipts	$78,227	Party	$6,943	2) Ameritech	$3,500	7) ILCable	$1,000
Expenditures	$69,677	PACS	$54,983	3) AFFI	$2,600	8) MPAC	$1,000
On hand	$80,443	Candidate	$0	4) IPACE	$2,500	9) IVendors	$1,000
		Not-itemized	$13,383	5) IBEW	$1,500	10) ISMS	$1,000

NOTE: The General Election Opponent's Campaign Resources and Expenditures are reported in a separate section in the back of the book (pp. 269-284).

GENERAL ELECTION DATA

	Registered Voters	Voter Turnout		Straight Party Voting	
1996	125,467	81,875	65.3%	(R) 12,272 ..15.0%	(D) 25,597 ...31.3%

PRESIDENT

1996	Bill Clinton (D)	44,353	55.7%
	Bob Dole (R)	28,105	35.3%
	Ross Perot (I)	7,168	9.0%
1992	Bill Clinton (D)	46,517	50.8%
	George Bush (R)	31,201	34.1%
	Ross Perot (I)	13,827	15.1%

UNITED STATES SENATE

1996	Richard J. Durbin (D)	43,768	55.6%
	Al Salvi (R)	32,446	41.2%

GOVERNOR

1994	Jim Edgar (R)	37,916	67.8%
	Dawn Clark Netsch (D)	17,997	32.2%

Representative Michael J. Boland (D)

District Office: 605 17th Ave., Suite 2, East Moline 61244
Phone (309) 752-7171; (309) 752-7186 (fax)
Springfield Office: Room 2098-M Stratton Bldg., Springfield 62706
Phone (217) 782-3992

Legislative Assignments: Committees on Veterans' Affairs (vice-chair); Elementary & Secondary Education; Insurance; Registration & Regulation.

Public Service: Representative (1995-present); former member, UTHS school board.

Personal: Full-time legislator; educator; born August 20, 1942, Davenport, IA; Upper Iowa University, B.A. Henderson State University, M.S. in Education; post-masters degree work at Western Illinois University and the University of Iowa; married (Mary); two children.

1997 BILL PASSAGE RATIO	Introduced	Passed House of Origin	Passed GA
Primary	16	7	4
Primary/Hyphenated	69	36	13

KEY VOTES

1) Change Ed. Funding Formula . . Y	6) Insurance/Domestic Violence . . E	11) Pre-Paid College Tuition . . . . Y
2) State Budget . . . . Y	7) Brownfields . . . . Y	12) Increase Pull Tab Prizes . . . . Y
3) Tougher DUI Level . . . . E	8) Welfare Reform . . . . Y	13) Utility Deregulation . . . . Y
4) Ban Partial Birth Abortions . . . Y	9) Concealed Guns/Misdemeanor . Y	14) County Obscenity Standards . N
5) State Employees Pension . . . . . Y	10) Banks Sell Insurance . . . . Y	15) Managed Care Reform . . . . . Y

GROUP RATINGS

	FB	CoC	PrLf	IPPC	ACLU
1997	75	31	2/6	66	70

ELECTION RESULTS

1996 General	Michael J. Boland (D)	23,881	(60.5%)
1996 General	Phil Banaszek (R)	15,588	(39.5%)
1996 Primary	Michael J. Boland (D)	4,069	(50.2%)
1996 Primary	Two others (D)	4,036	(49.8%)

CAMPAIGN RESOURCES AND EXPENDITURES

1996 Campaign Funds

Beg. Balance	$9,478	Individuals	$500
Receipts	$92,232	Party	$62,683
Expenditures	$76,859	PACS	$24,500
On hand	$24,851	Candidate	$0
		Not-itemized	$4,549

Top 10 PAC Contributors

1) IHDM	$53,818	6) USWA	$1,500
2) DSCC	$6,615	7) IPACE	$1,000
3) ITLA	$6,000	8) LICID	$1,000
4) CLang	$2,000	9) IBEW	$1,000
5) QCFL	$1,500	10) ABDI	$1,000

NOTE: The General Election Opponent's Campaign Resources and Expenditures are reported in a separate section in the back of the book (pp. 269-284).

GENERAL ELECTION DATA

	Registered Voters	Voter Turnout		Straight Party Voting	
1996	62,917	41,625	66.2%	(R) 6,701 . . .16.1%	(D) 12,364 . . .29.7%

PRESIDENT

1996	Bill Clinton (D)	22,049	54.1%
	Bob Dole (R)	14,853	36.4%
	Ross Perot (I)	3,641	9.0%
1992	Bill Clinton (D)	23,316	50.1%
	George Bush (R)	16,409	35.3%
	Ross Perot (I)	6,808	14.6%

UNITED STATES SENATE

1996	Richard J. Durbin (D)	21,884	54.6%
	Al Salvi (R)	16,914	42.2%

GOVERNOR

1994	Jim Edgar (R)	19,934	68.2%
	Dawn Clark Netsch (D)	9,312	31.8%

Representative Joel Brunsvold (D)

District Office: 303 18th St., Rock Island 61201
Phone (309) 793-4716; (309) 793-4764 (fax)
Springfield Office: Room 109 Capitol Bldg., Springfield 62706
Phone (217) 782-5970

Legislative Assignments: Assistant Majority Leader; ex officio member of all committees. Committees on Agriculture & Conservation; Revenue.

Public Service: Representative (1983-present); trustee and president, Milan Village.

Personal: Full-time legislator; born February 26, 1942, Mason City, IA; Augustana College, B.A. in Education; married (Barbara); two children.

1997 BILL PASSAGE RATIO	Introduced	Passed House of Origin	Passed GA
Primary	24	7	6
Primary/Hyphenated	44	19	14

KEY VOTES

1) Change Ed. Funding Formula . . Y	6) Insurance/Domestic Violence . . Y	11) Pre-Paid College Tuition . . . . Y
2) State Budget . . . . Y	7) Brownfields . . . . Y	12) Increase Pull Tab Prizes . . . . Y
3) Tougher DUI Level . . . . Y	8) Welfare Reform . . . . Y	13) Utility Deregulation . . . . Y
4) Ban Partial Birth Abortions . . . Y	9) Concealed Guns/Misdemeanor . Y	14) County Obscenity Standards . N
5) State Employees Pension . . . . . Y	10) Banks Sell Insurance . . . . Y	15) Managed Care Reform . . . . . N

GROUP RATINGS

	FB	CoC	PrLf	IPPC	ACLU
1997	86	54	4/6	33	50

ELECTION RESULTS

1996 General	Joel Brunsvold (D)	29,342	(100%)
1996 Primary	Joel Brunsvold (D)	6,636	(100%)
1994 General	Joel Brunsvold (D)	20,727	(100%)
1994 Primary	Joel Brunsvold (D)	7,705	(100%)

CAMPAIGN RESOURCES AND EXPENDITURES

1996 Campaign Funds

Beg. Balance	$81,058	Individuals	$1,180
Receipts	$67,959	Party	$11,450
Expenditures	$36,824	PACS	$48,850
On hand	$112,193	Candidate	$0
		Not-itemized	$6,479

Top 10 PAC Contributors

1) Statesman $12,500	6) ABDI $1,000
2) DSCC $11,000	7) PIIA $1,000
3) IPACE $5,000	8) ILCable $1,000
4) ITLA $2,000	9) ILCasualty $1,000
5) IBEW $1,000	10) Argosy $1,000

NOTE: The General Election Opponent's Campaign Resources and Expenditures are reported in a separate section in the back of the book (pp. 269-284).

GENERAL ELECTION DATA

	Registered Voters	Voter Turnout		Straight Party Voting (R)		Straight Party Voting (D)	
1996	62,550	40,250	64.3%	5,571	13.8%	13,233	32.9%

PRESIDENT

1996	Bill Clinton (D)	22,304	56.7%
	Bob Dole (R)	13,252	33.7%
	Ross Perot (I)	3,527	9.0%
1992	Bill Clinton (D)	23,201	51.5%
	George Bush (R)	14,792	32.9%
	Ross Perot (I)	7,019	15.6%

UNITED STATES SENATE

1996	Richard J. Durbin (D)	21,884	56.6%
	Al Salvi (R)	15,532	40.2%

GOVERNOR

1994	Jim Edgar (R)	17,982	67.4%
	Dawn Clark Netsch (D)	8,685	32.6%

37th Senate District

House District 73
House District 74

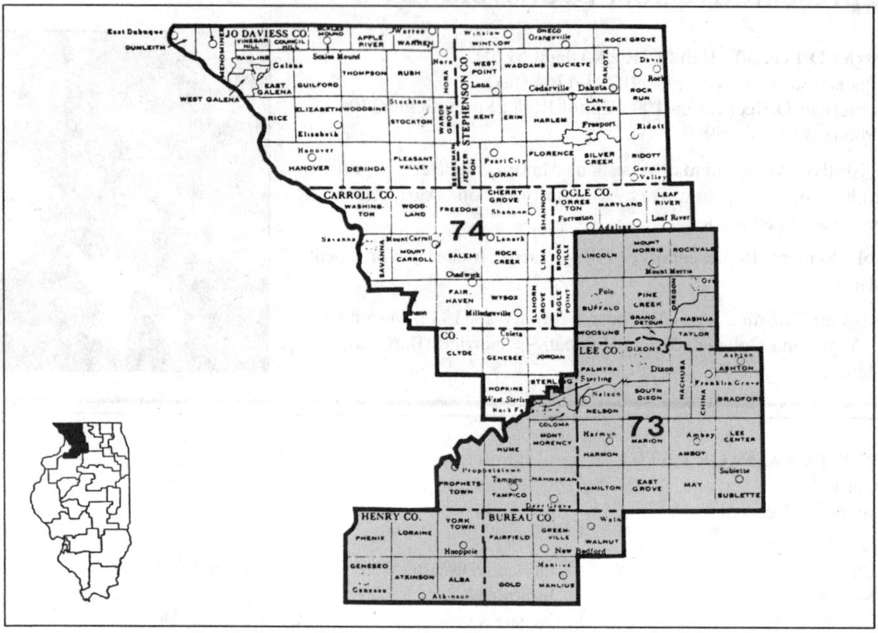

DEMOGRAPHICS (1990)

	S.D. #37	H.D. #73	H.D.#74
VOTING AGE POPULATION	143,359	71,531	71,828
White	94.8%	93.7%	95.9%
Black	2.3%	1.8%	2.8%
Hispanic	2.4%	4.0%	0.9%
Asian	0.3%	0.3%	0.4%
AGE (Total Population)	193,739	96,870	96,869
Under 6	8.3%	8.3%	8.2%
6 to 18	19.1%	19.3%	19.0%
65 and Over	16.0%	15.6%	16.4%
URBAN POPULATION	48.4%	56.0%	40.8%
HOUSING UNITS (Total)	81,213	38,815	42,398
Median Value	$47,058	$46,189	$48,063
Owner Occupied	65.1%	65.9%	64.4%
FAMILY INCOME (Total Families)	53,877	26,514	27,363
Median Income	$32,483	$31,992	$33,069
Below Poverty Level	7.5%	7.8%	7.2%
With Children Under 5	1.3%	1.6%	1.0%
With Children 5 to 17	2.7%	3.0%	2.4%
Headed by Females	3.4%	3.7%	3.1%
INDUSTRY (Total Employed)	91,013	44,272	46,741
Professional/Public Administration	22.1%	23.9%	20.5%
Manufacturing	28.5%	28.8%	28.3%
Retail	14.7%	15.9%	13.6%
Transportation/Communication	5.7%	5.9%	5.4%
Finance/Insurance/Real Estate	5.5%	4.2%	6.8%
Other Service	6.8%	6.4%	7.1%

Senator Todd Sieben (R)

District Office: 137 S. State Street, Geneseo 61254
Phone (309) 944-5681; (309) 944-3392 (fax)
Springfield Office: Room 307 Capitol Bldg., Springfield 62706
Phone (217) 782-0180

Legislative Assignments: Committees on Agriculture & Conservation (chair); Education; State Government Operations; Governor's Council on Health & Fitness; Human Services Consolidation Task Force.

Public Service: Senator (1993-present); representative (1987-93).

Personal: Vice-President and co-owner, Sieben Hybrids; born July 11, 1945, Geneseo; Western Illinois University, B.S. in business administration; married (Kay); three children.

1997 BILL PASSAGE RATIO	Introduced	Passed House of Origin	Passed GA
Primary	21	10	9
Primary/Hyphenated	35	19	15

KEY VOTES

1) Senate GOP Ed. $ Plan ...... Y	6) Insurance/Domestic Violence .. Y	11) Pre-Paid College Tuition .... Y
2) State Budget .... Y	7) Brownfields .... Y	12) Increase Pull Tab Prizes .... N
3) Tougher DUI Level .... Y	8) Welfare Reform .... Y	13) Telecommunications Tax .... P
4) Ban Partial Birth Abortions ... Y	9) Concealed Guns/Misdemeanor . Y	14) Delivery Discrimination .... P
5) State Employees Pension ..... Y	10) Banks Sell Insurance .... Y	15) Sell Drivers' Data .... Y

GROUP RATINGS

	FB	CoC	PrLf	IPPC	ACLU
1997	82	100	2/2	0	50

ELECTION RESULTS

1996 General	Todd Sieben (R)	55,740	(100%)
1996 Primary	Todd Sieben (R)	18,567	(100%)
1992 General	Todd Sieben (R)	47,031	(54.5%)
1992 General	Eric Gubelman (D)	39,204	(45.5%)

CAMPAIGN RESOURCES AND EXPENDITURES

1996 Campaign Funds

Beg. Balance	$52,304	Individuals	$1,305
Receipts	$30,926	Party	$165
Expenditures	$27,304	PACS	$14,800
On hand	$55,926	Candidate	$3,752
		Not-itemized	$10,904

Top 10 PAC Contributors

1) IPACE $4,000	6) Monsanto ... $500
2) ISMS $1,000	7) Ameritech ... $500
3) HI $1,000	8) LICID $500
4) RPAC $700	9) LIPAC $500
5) CoC $600	10) PetPec $500

NOTE: The General Election Opponent's Campaign Resources and Expenditures are reported in a separate section in the back of the book (pp. 269-284).

GENERAL ELECTION DATA

	Registered Voters	Voter Turnout		Straight Party Voting	
1996	119,244	80,269	67.3%	(R) 19,834 . 24.7%	(D) 11,019 ... 13.7%

PRESIDENT

1996	Bill Clinton (D)	34,206	43.8%
	Bob Dole (R)	34,891	44.7%
	Ross Perot (I)	8,389	10.7%
1992	Bill Clinton (D)	34,861	39.1%
	George Bush (R)	36,583	41.0%
	Ross Perot (I)	17,821	19.9%

UNITED STATES SENATE

1996	Richard J. Durbin (D)	33,322	43.5%
	Al Salvi (R)	40,094	52.3%

GOVERNOR

1994	Jim Edgar (R)	44,424	75.4%
	Dawn Clark Netsch (D)	4,529	24.6%

Representative Gerald L. "Jerry" Mitchell (R)

District Office: 100 East 5th St., Rock Falls 61071
Phone (815) 625-0820; (815) 625-0839 (fax)
Springfield Office: Room 2117-N Stratton Bldg., Springfield 62706
Phone (217) 782-0535; (217) 782-1275 (fax)

Legislative Assignments: Committees on Elementary & Secondary Education; Local Government; Appropriations-Education; Aging.

Public Service: Representative (1995-present); former superintendent of schools and high school principal.

Personal: Full-time legislator; born June 18, 1942, Jacksonville; Eureka College, B.A. in teaching; Illinois State University, M.S. in educational administration; Western Illinois University, Ed.S. in educational administration; married (Jan); three children.

1997 BILL PASSAGE RATIO	Introduced	Passed House of Origin	Passed GA
Primary	7	5	3
Primary/Hyphenated	15	11	6

KEY VOTES

1) Change Ed. Funding Formula . . Y	6) Insurance/Domestic Violence . . Y	11) Pre-Paid College Tuition . . . . Y
2) State Budget . . . . Y	7) Brownfields . . . . Y	12) Increase Pull Tab Prizes . . . . N
3) Tougher DUI Level . . . . Y	8) Welfare Reform . . . . Y	13) Utility Deregulation . . . . P
4) Ban Partial Birth Abortions . . . Y	9) Concealed Guns/Misdemeanor . Y	14) County Obscenity Standards . N
5) State Employees Pension . . . . . Y	10) Banks Sell Insurance . . . . Y	15) Managed Care Reform . . . . . N

GROUP RATINGS

	FB	CoC	PrLf	IPPC	ACLU
1997	82	77	3/6	50	70

ELECTION RESULTS

1996 General	Gerald L. "Jerry" Mitchell (R)	19,813	(51.3%)
1996 General	Pennie L. von Bergen Wessels (D)	18,816	(48.7%)
1996 Primary	Gerald L. "Jerry" Mitchell (R)	9,870	(100%)
1996 Primary	Pennie L. von Bergen Wessels (D)	3,174	(100%)

CAMPAIGN RESOURCES AND EXPENDITURES

1996 Campaign Funds				Top 10 PAC Contributors			
Beg. Balance	$37,545	Individuals	$16,196	1) HRCC	$196,190	6) ISMS	$10,000
Receipts	$466,091	Party	$339,473	2) FLAD	$106,658	7) MPAC	$7,000
Expenditures	$485,227	PACS	$91,487	3) IPACE	$30,868	8) CRyder	$5,000
On hand	$18,409	Candidate	$0	4) CRyan	$11,000	9) CoC	$2,180
		Not-itemized	$18,935	5) CChurchill	$10,500	10) CatCEG	$2,000

NOTE: The General Election Opponent's Campaign Resources and Expenditures are reported in a separate section in the back of the book (pp. 269-284).

GENERAL ELECTION DATA

	Registered Voters	Voter Turnout		Straight Party Voting	
1996	59,628	40,661	68.2%	(R) 7,967 . . . 19.6%	(D) 6,120 . . . 15.1%

PRESIDENT

1996	Bill Clinton (D)	18,223	46.1%
	Bob Dole (R)	16,997	43.0%
	Ross Perot (I)	4,071	10.3%
1992	Bill Clinton (D)	18,177	40.8%
	George Bush (R)	17,922	40.2%
	Ross Perot (I)	8,470	19.0%

UNITED STATES SENATE

1996	Richard J. Durbin (D)	17,743	45.7%
	Al Salvi (R)	19,540	50.4%

GOVERNOR

1994	Jim Edgar (R)	21,898	73.7%
	Dawn Clark Netsch (D)	7,781	26.3%

Representative I. Ronald Lawfer (R)

District Office: 19 South Chicago Ave., Freeport 61032
Phone (815) 232-0774; (815) 232-0777 (fax)
Springfield Office: Room 2029-H Stratton Bldg., Springfield 62706
Phone (217) 782-8186

Legislative Assignments: Committees on Aging (minority spokesperson); Agriculture & Conservation; Local Government; Environment & Energy.

Public Service: Representative (1993-present); Wards Grove Township supervisor (1974-1982); JoDaviess County Board (1982-1992); public commissioner, Illinois Rural Bond Bank; U.S. Army veteran.

Personal: Farmer; born May 15, 1934, Stockton; University of Illinois, B.S. in agriculture; married (Patricia); five children.

1997 BILL PASSAGE RATIO	Introduced	Passed House of Origin	Passed GA
Primary	6	1	1
Primary/Hyphenated	14	5	5

KEY VOTES

1) Change Ed. Funding Formula . . N
2) State Budget . . . . Y
3) Tougher DUI Level . . . . Y
4) Ban Partial Birth Abortions . . . Y
5) State Employees Pension . . . . . Y
6) Insurance/Domestic Violence . . Y
7) Brownfields . . . . Y
8) Welfare Reform . . . . Y
9) Concealed Guns/Misdemeanor . Y
10) Banks Sell Insurance . . . . P
11) Pre-Paid College Tuition . . . . Y
12) Increase Pull Tab Prizes . . . . N
13) Utility Deregulation . . . . P
14) County Obscenity Standards . Y
15) Managed Care Reform . . . . . N

GROUP RATINGS

	FB	CoC	PrLf	IPPC	ACLU
1997	75	85	6/6	0	30

ELECTION RESULTS

1996 General	I. Ronald Lawfer (R)	23,671	(63.3%)
1996 General	Mickey R. Martin (D)	13,747	(36.7%)
1996 Primary	I. Ronald Lawfer (R)	8,809	(100%)

CAMPAIGN RESOURCES AND EXPENDITURES

1996 Campaign Funds				Top 10 PAC Contributors			
Beg. Balance	$20,946	Individuals	$3,087	1) FLAD	$72,500	6) CatCEG	$1,000
Receipts	$160,459	Party	$129,250	2) HRCC	$54,174	7) CChurchill	$1,000
Expenditures	$177,452	PACS	$18,671	3) Activator	$2,521	8) ISMS	$1,000
On hand	$3,953	Candidate	$0	4) IPACE	$1,500	9) MPAC	$1,000
		Not-itemized	$9,451	5) CSieben	$1,466	10) CoC	$1,000

NOTE: The General Election Opponent's Campaign Resources and Expenditures are reported in a separate section in the back of the book (pp. 269-284).

GENERAL ELECTION DATA

	Registered Voters	Voter Turnout		Straight Party Voting	
1996	59,616	39,608	66.4%	(R) 11,867 . . 30.0%	(D) 4,899 . . . . 12.4%

PRESIDENT

1996	Bill Clinton (D)	15,983	41.5%
	Bob Dole (R)	17,894	46.4%
	Ross Perot (I)	4,318	11.2%
1992	Bill Clinton (D)	16,684	37.3%
	George Bush (R)	18,661	41.8%
	Ross Perot (I)	9,351	20.9%

UNITED STATES SENATE

1996	Richard J. Durbin (D)	15,579	41.1%
	Al Salvi (R)	20,554	54.2%

GOVERNOR

1994	Jim Edgar (R)	22,526	76.9%
	Dawn Clark Netsch (D)	6,748	23.1%

38th Senate District

House District 75
House District 76

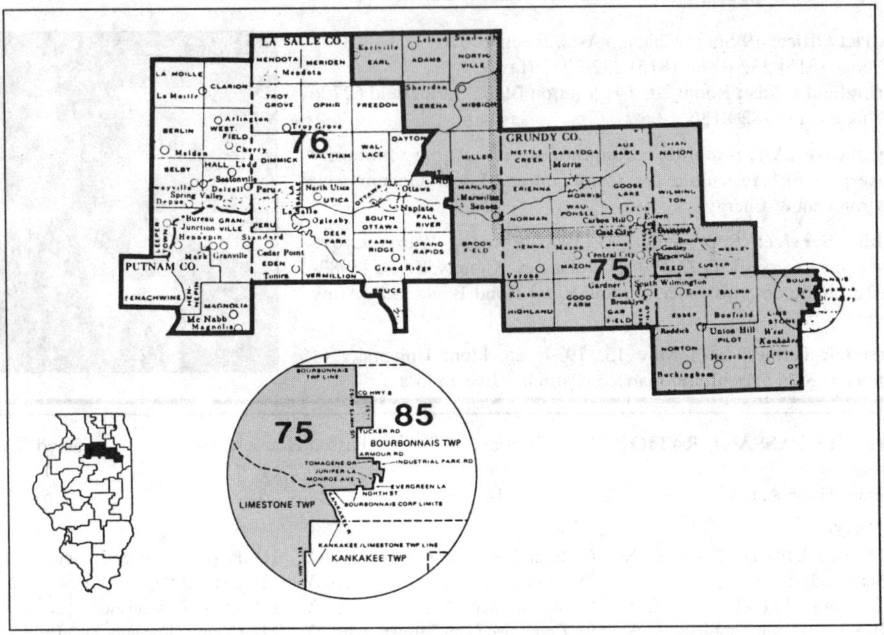

DEMOGRAPHICS (1990)

	S.D. #38	H.D. #75	H.D.#76
VOTING AGE POPULATION	141,863	69,320	72,543
White	96.3%	96.7%	95.9%
Black	0.8%	1.2%	0.4%
Hispanic	2.3%	1.4%	3.1%
Asian	0.5%	0.5%	0.4%
AGE (Total Population)	193,739	96,870	96,869
Under 6	8.5%	8.8%	8.1%
6 to 18	19.8%	21.3%	18.3%
65 and Over	14.7%	11.0%	18.4%
URBAN POPULATION	57.4%	48.7%	66.0%
HOUSING UNITS (Total)	76,525	35,721	40,804
Median Value	$56,893	$68,439	$47,361
Owner Occupied	68.8%	69.5%	68.2%
FAMILY INCOME (Total Families)	52,943	26,304	26,639
Median Income	$36,231	$40,603	$32,606
Below Poverty Level	7.1%	5.2%	8.9%
With Children Under 5	1.1%	1.0%	1.3%
With Children 5 to 17	2.6%	1.8%	3.3%
Headed by Females	3.2%	2.1%	4.2%
INDUSTRY (Total Employed)	87,068	45,009	42,058
Professional/Public Administration	23.3%	23.3%	23.2%
Manufacturing	23.2%	23.2%	23.2%
Retail	17.7%	16.0%	19.5%
Transportation/Communication	9.0%	9.9%	8.0%
Finance/Insurance/Real Estate	4.5%	4.8%	4.2%
Other Service	7.1%	7.1%	7.1%

Senator Patrick D. Welch (D)

District Office: 1025 Peoria St., Peru 61354
Phone (815) 223-3747; (815) 223-8446 (fax)
Springfield Office: 218 Capitol Bldg., Springfield 62706
Phone (217) 782-8287; (217) 782-0715 (fax)

Legislative Assignments: Assistant Minority Leader. Committees on Revenue; Appropriations; Tax Increment Financing and Tax Increases Expenditures; Economic & Fiscal Commission (co-chair).

Public Service: Senator (1983-present).

Personal: Attorney; born December 12, 1948, Chicago; Southern Illinois University, B.A. in government; Kent College of Law, J.D.; one child.

1997 BILL PASSAGE RATIO	Introduced	Passed House of Origin	Passed GA
Primary	9	0	0
Primary/Hyphenated	17	7	5

KEY VOTES

1) Senate GOP Ed. $ Plan ....N	6) Insurance/Domestic Violence ..Y	11) Pre-Paid College Tuition ....Y
2) State Budget ....Y	7) Brownfields ....Y	12) Increase Pull Tab Prizes ....Y
3) Tougher DUI Level ....Y	8) Welfare Reform ....Y	13) Telecommunications Tax ...Y
4) Ban Partial Birth Abortions ...Y	9) Concealed Guns/Misdemeanor .Y	14) Delivery Discrimination ....Y
5) State Employees Pension .....Y	10) Banks Sell Insurance ....Y	15) Sell Drivers' Data ....Y

GROUP RATINGS

	FB	CoC	PrLf	IPPC	ACLU
1997	86	50	2/2	0	50

ELECTION RESULTS

1994 General	Patrick D. Welch (D)	31,917	(50.3%)
1994 General	Robert W. Studzinski (R)	31,524	(49.7%)
1994 Primary	Patrick D. Welch (D)	12,849	(100%)
1994 Primary	Robert W. Studzinski (R)	12,053	(100%)

CAMPAIGN RESOURCES AND EXPENDITURES

1996 Campaign Funds				Top 10 PAC Contributors			
Beg. Balance	$49,149	Individuals	$0	1) IPACE	$5,000	6) Sears	$200
Receipts	$8,150	Party	$0	2) MCI	$750	7) NIGAS	$200
Expenditures	$16,384	PACS	$7,550	3) CPA's	$400	8) HOPE	$200
On hand	$40,915	Candidate	$525	4) Emerson	$300	9) Harrah's	$150
		Not-itemized	$75	5) Walgreens	$200	10) AB	$150

NOTE: The General Election Opponent's Campaign Resources and Expenditures are reported in a separate section in the back of the book (pp. 269-284).

GENERAL ELECTION DATA

	Registered Voters	Voter Turnout		Straight Party Voting	
1996	119,038	83,523	70.2%	(R) 11,866 ..14.2%	(D) 15,135 ...18.1%

PRESIDENT

1996	Bill Clinton (D)	39,767	48.6%
	Bob Dole (R)	31,281	38.3%
	Ross Perot (I)	10,127	12.4%
1992	Bill Clinton (D)	39,957	44.0%
	George Bush (R)	31,369	34.6%
	Ross Perot (I)	19,390	21.4%

UNITED STATES SENATE

1996	Richard J. Durbin (D)	39,674	49.2%
	Al Salvi (R)	38,041	47.1%

GOVERNOR

1994	Jim Edgar (R)	45,106	72.1%
	Dawn Clark Netsch (D)	17,412	27.9%

Representative Mary K. O'Brien (D)

District Office: 760 East Division, Coal City 60416
Phone (815) 634-3096; (815) 634-3137 (fax)
Springfield Office: Room 2045-J Stratton Bldg., Springfield 62706
Phone (217) 782-4535

Legislative Assignments: Committees on Agriculture & Conservation; Transportation & Motor Vehicles; Environment & Energy; Judiciary II-Criminal Law.

Public Service: Representative (1997-present).

Personal: Attorney; born June 4, 1965, Kankakee; Western Illinois University, Bachelor of Arts Cum Laude; University of Illinois College of Law, J.D.; married (John Thompson).

1997 BILL PASSAGE RATIO	Introduced	Passed House of Origin	Passed GA
Primary	11	5	1
Primary/Hyphenated	31	19	8

KEY VOTES

1) Change Ed. Funding Formula . . N	6) Insurance/Domestic Violence . . Y	11) Pre-Paid College Tuition . . . . Y
2) State Budget . . . . Y	7) Brownfields . . . . Y	12) Increase Pull Tab Prizes . . . . Y
3) Tougher DUI Level . . . . Y	8) Welfare Reform . . . . Y	13) Utility Deregulation . . . . . . Y
4) Ban Partial Birth Abortions . . . Y	9) Concealed Guns/Misdemeanor . Y	14) County Obscenity Standards . Y
5) State Employees Pension . . . . . Y	10) Banks Sell Insurance . . . . Y	15) Managed Care Reform . . . . Y

GROUP RATINGS

	FB	CoC	PrLf	IPPC	ACLU
1997	61	38	3/6	50	50

ELECTION RESULTS

1996 General	Mary K. O'Brien (D)	21,006	(52.8%)
1996 General	Stephen Alan Spangler (R)	18,763	(47.2%)
1996 Primary	Mary K. O'Brien (D)	3,352	(100%)
1996 Primary	Stephen Alan Spangler (R)	8,822	(100%)

CAMPAIGN RESOURCES AND EXPENDITURES

1996 Campaign Funds				Top 10 PAC Contributors			
Beg. Balance	$10,577	Individuals	$3,894	1) IHDM	$86,415	6) WVWV	$4,000
Receipts	$190,331	Party	$137,217	2) DSCC	$13,036	7) CGranberg	$4,000
Expenditures	$189,824	PACS	$41,721	3) PNovak	$8,141	8) ITLA	$3,000
On hand	$11,084	Candidate	$0	4) PersPAC	$5,531	9) CLang	$2,500
		Not-itemized	$7,499	5) SEIU	$5,000	10) UDI	$2,500

NOTE: The General Election Opponent's Campaign Resources and Expenditures are reported in a separate section in the back of the book (pp. 269-284).

GENERAL ELECTION DATA

	Registered Voters	Voter Turnout		Straight Party Voting	
1996	59,844	42,532	71.1%	(R) 7,283 . . . 17.1%	(D) 5,830 . . . 13.7%

PRESIDENT

1996	Bill Clinton (D)	18,139	43.4%
	Bob Dole (R)	17,880	42.8%
	Ross Perot (I)	5,458	13.1%
1992	Bill Clinton (D)	16,754	37.9%
	George Bush (R)	17,215	38.9%
	Ross Perot (I)	10,258	23.2%

UNITED STATES SENATE

1996	Richard J. Durbin (D)	17,990	43.7%
	Al Salvi (R)	21,532	52.3%

GOVERNOR

1994	Jim Edgar (R)	23,950	77.9%
	Dawn Clark Netsch (D)	6,777	22.1%

Representative Frank J. Mautino (D)

District Office: 108 West St. Paul, Spring Valley 61362
Phone (815) 664-2717; (815) 663-1629 (fax)
Springfield Office: Room 2082-M Stratton Bldg., Springfield 62706
Phone (217) 782-0140

Legislative Assignments: Committees on Insurance (chair); Appropriations-Public Safety (vice-chair); Elementary & Secondary Education; Financial Institutions; Local Government; Personnel & Pensions; Banks Selling Insurance (co-chair); Comprehensive Health Insurance Program Board; Economic & Fiscal Commission.

Public Service: Representative (1991-present).

Personal: Full-time legislator; born August 7, 1962, Spring Valley; Illinois State University, B.S. in marketing/administration; Illinois Valley Community College, A.A.; married (Lena); one child.

1997 BILL PASSAGE RATIO	Introduced	Passed House of Origin	Passed GA
Primary	24	11	5
Primary/Hyphenated	42	22	14

KEY VOTES

1) Change Ed. Funding Formula . . Y	6) Insurance/Domestic Violence . . Y	11) Pre-Paid College Tuition . . . . Y
2) State Budget . . . . Y	7) Brownfields . . . . Y	12) Increase Pull Tab Prizes . . . . Y
3) Tougher DUI Level . . . . N	8) Welfare Reform . . . . Y	13) Utility Deregulation . . . . . . Y
4) Ban Partial Birth Abortions . . . Y	9) Concealed Guns/Misdemeanor . Y	14) County Obscenity Standards . N
5) State Employees Pension . . . . . Y	10) Banks Sell Insurance . . . . Y	15) Managed Care Reform . . . . . N

GROUP RATINGS

	FB	CoC	PrLf	IPPC	ACLU
1997	82	69	3/6	50	60

ELECTION RESULTS

1996 General	Frank J. Mautino (D)	27,379	(70.6%)
1996 General	Donald Schwanke (R)	11,392	(29.4%)
1996 Primary	Frank J. Mautino (D)	6,829	(100%)
1996 Primary	Donald Schwanke (R)	5,040	(100%)

CAMPAIGN RESOURCES AND EXPENDITURES

1996 Campaign Funds

Beg. Balance	$4,274	Individuals	$4,000
Receipts	$66,237	Party	$5,350
Expenditures	$70,506	PACS	$41,588
On hand	$5	Candidate	$0
		Not-itemized	$15,299

Top 10 PAC Contributors

1) DSCC $5,000	6) Amoco $1,000
2) ITLA $2,000	7) PIIA $1,000
3) Activator . . $1,533	8) IRLA $925
4) ABDI $1,200	9) Ameritech . . . $900
5) Chamelin . . $1,000	10) RPAC $850

NOTE: The General Election Opponent's Campaign Resources and Expenditures are reported in a separate section in the back of the book (pp. 269-284).

GENERAL ELECTION DATA

	Registered Voters	Voter Turnout		Straight Party Voting	
1996	59,194	40,991	69.3%	(R) 4,583 . . . 11.2%	(D) 9,305 . . . 22.7%

PRESIDENT

1996	Bill Clinton (D)	21,628	54.1%
	Bob Dole (R)	13,401	33.5%
	Ross Perot (I)	4,669	11.7%
1992	Bill Clinton (D)	23,203	49.9%
	George Bush (R)	14,154	30.4%
	Ross Perot (I)	9,132	19.7%

UNITED STATES SENATE

1996	Richard J. Durbin (D)	21,684	54.8%
	Al Salvi (R)	16,509	41.7%

GOVERNOR

1994	Jim Edgar (R)	21,156	66.5%
	Dawn Clark Netsch (D)	10,635	33.5%

39th Senate District

House District 77
House District 78

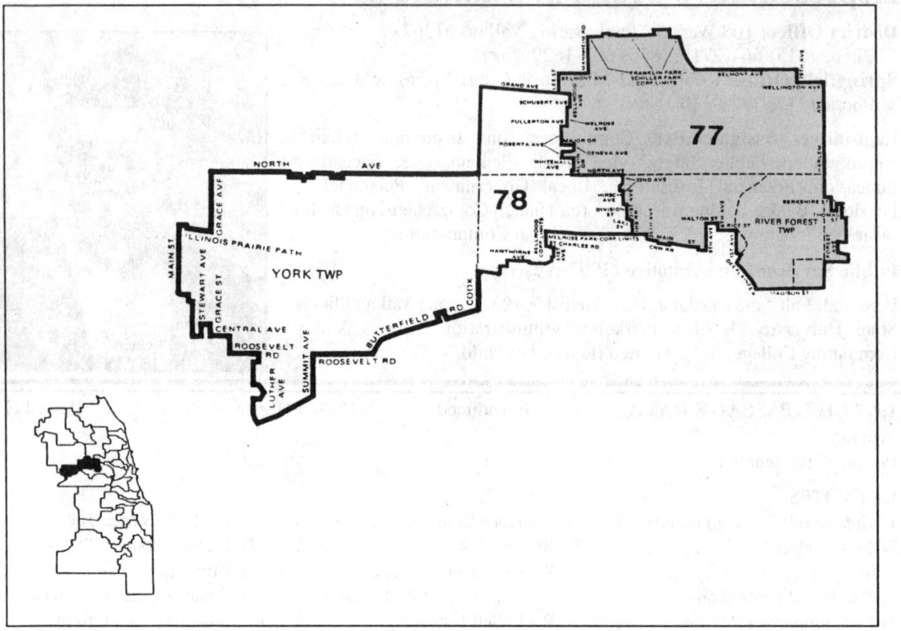

DEMOGRAPHICS (1990)

	S.D. #39	H.D. #77	H.D.#78
VOTING AGE POPULATION	150,016	76,572	73,444
White	87.1%	84.8%	89.6%
Black	1.8%	2.6%	0.9%
Hispanic	8.8%	10.7%	6.8%
Asian	2.2%	1.9%	2.5%
AGE (Total Population)	193,739	96,870	96,869
Under 6	8.4%	7.8%	9.0%
6 to 18	15.4%	14.3%	16.4%
65 and Over	15.3%	17.2%	13.3%
URBAN POPULATION	100.0%	100.0%	100.0%
HOUSING UNITS (Total)	74,971	39,032	35,939
Median Value	$112,623	$110,493	$114,027
Owner Occupied	68.5%	61.2%	76.3%
FAMILY INCOME (Total Families)	51,463	25,338	26,125
Median Income	$45,936	$42,513	$48,785
Below Poverty Level	2.8%	3.6%	2.0%
With Children Under 5	0.4%	0.6%	0.3%
With Children 5 to 17	0.9%	1.2%	0.6%
Headed by Females	1.1%	1.5%	0.7%
INDUSTRY (Total Employed)	101,651	50,228	51,423
Professional/Public Administration	23.2%	24.1%	22.2%
Manufacturing	21.9%	23.2%	20.7%
Retail	16.6%	16.1%	17.0%
Transportation/Communication	8.3%	7.5%	9.1%
Finance/Insurance/Real Estate	7.9%	8.2%	7.7%
Other Service	9.4%	8.9%	9.9%

Senator Dan Cronin (R)

District Office: 105 East First St., Elmhurst 60126
Phone (630) 941-0040; (630) 941-1205 (fax)
Springfield Office: Room 127 Capitol Bldg., Springfield 62706
Phone (217) 782-8107

Legislative Assignments: Committees on Education (chair); Public Health & Welfare; Judiciary.

Public Service: Senator (1993-present); representative (1991-93).

Personal: Attorney; born November 7, 1959, Elmhurst; Northwestern University, B.A. in economics; Loyola University, J.D.; married (Juliann Ashley); two daughters.

1997 BILL PASSAGE RATIO	Introduced	Passed House of Origin	Passed GA
Primary	30	12	4
Primary/Hyphenated	41	16	7

KEY VOTES

1) Senate GOP Ed. $ Plan . . . . . . .Y	6) Insurance/Domestic Violence . .Y	11) Pre-Paid College Tuition . . . .Y
2) State Budget . . . . .Y	7) Brownfields . . . . .Y	12) Increase Pull Tab Prizes . . . .Y
3) Tougher DUI Level . . . . .Y	8) Welfare Reform . . . . .Y	13) Telecommunications Tax . . . P
4) Ban Partial Birth Abortions . . .Y	9) Concealed Guns/Misdemeanor .Y	14) Delivery Discrimination . . . .P
5) State Employees Pension . . . . .Y	10) Banks Sell Insurance . . . . .Y	15) Sell Drivers' Data . . . . .Y

GROUP RATINGS

	FB	CoC	PrLf	IPPC	ACLU
1997	59	100	2/2	0	75

ELECTION RESULTS

1996 General	Dan Cronin (R)	42,016	(61.8%)
1996 General	Larry Craig (D)	25,925	(38.2%)
1996 Primary	Dan Cronin (R)	16,024	(100%)

CAMPAIGN RESOURCES AND EXPENDITURES

1996 Campaign Funds				Top 10 PAC Contributors			
Beg. Balance	$41,988	Individuals	$12,224	1) EMS	$5,321	6) ProSelect	$1,200
Receipts	$71,761	Party	$1,000	2) UPS	$3,900	7) PIIA	$1,000
Expenditures	$87,178	PACS	$54,494	3) ABDI	$2,000	8) Guerine	$1,000
On hand	$26,571	Candidate	$184	4) ILCable	$1,500	9) CAR	$1,000
		Not-itemized	$3,859	5) LAWPAC	$1,500	10) Gottlieb	$1,000

NOTE: The General Election Opponent's Campaign Resources and Expenditures are reported in a separate section in the back of the book (pp. 269-284).

GENERAL ELECTION DATA

	Registered Voters	Voter Turnout		Straight Party Voting			
1996	104,309	71,510	68.6%	(R) 16,616	23.2%	(D) 12,366	17.3%

PRESIDENT

1996	Bill Clinton (D)	34,128	48.7%
	Bob Dole (R)	29,266	41.8%
	Ross Perot (I)	6,065	8.7%
1992	Bill Clinton (D)	33,181	37.8%
	George Bush (R)	37,327	42.6%
	Ross Perot (I)	17,208	19.6%

UNITED STATES SENATE

1996	Richard J. Durbin (D)	34,323	49.8%
	Al Salvi (R)	32,289	46.8%

GOVERNOR

1994	Jim Edgar (R)	40,261	74.8%
	Dawn Clark Netsch (D)	13,580	25.2%

Representative Angelo "Skip" Saviano (R)

District Office: 8153 West Grand Ave., River Grove 60171
Phone (708) 453-7547; (708) 453-7594 (fax)
Springfield Office: Room 2107-N Stratton Bldg., Springfield 62706
Phone (217) 782-3374; (217) 782-1275 (fax)

Legislative Assignments: Committees on Registration & Regulation (chair); Aging; Financial Institutions; Appropriations-Human Services.

Public Service: Representative (1993-present); former supervisor, Leyden Township.

Personal: Full-time legislator; born May 20, 1958, Chicago; DePaul University, B.A. in history/political science; married (Julie); two children.

1997 BILL PASSAGE RATIO	Introduced	Passed House of Origin	Passed GA
Primary	59	19	11
Primary/Hyphenated	150	60	32

KEY VOTES

1) Change Ed. Funding Formula . . N	6) Insurance/Domestic Violence . . Y	11) Pre-Paid College Tuition . . . . Y
2) State Budget . . . . Y	7) Brownfields . . . . Y	12) Increase Pull Tab Prizes . . . . Y
3) Tougher DUI Level . . . . Y	8) Welfare Reform . . . . Y	13) Utility Deregulation . . . . Y
4) Ban Partial Birth Abortions . . . Y	9) Concealed Guns/Misdemeanor . Y	14) County Obscenity Standards . P
5) State Employees Pension . . . . . Y	10) Banks Sell Insurance . . . . Y	15) Managed Care Reform . . . . . Y

GROUP RATINGS

	FB	CoC	PrLf	IPPC	ACLU
1997	68	38	4/6	33	40

ELECTION RESULTS

1996 General	Angelo "Skip" Saviano (R)	22,707	(100%)
1996 Primary	Angelo "Skip" Saviano (R)	6,680	(100%)
1994 General	Angelo "Skip" Saviano (R)	18,329	(68.7%)
1994 General	Ted E. Leverenz (D)	8,334	(31.3%)

CAMPAIGN RESOURCES AND EXPENDITURES

1996 Campaign Funds				Top 10 PAC Contributors			
Beg. Balance	$111,995	Individuals	$6,300	1) Statesman	$12,500	6) ITLA	$1,000
Receipts	$86,457	Party	$1,050	2) ISMS	$2,000	7) ISPP	$1,000
Expenditures	$86,499	PACS	$56,700	3) CPA's	$1,500	8) IRLA	$1,000
On hand	$111,953	Candidate	$0	4) HI	$1,500	9) ABDI	$1,000
		Not-itemized	$22,407	5) CFFU	$1,000	10) AB	$1,000

NOTE: The General Election Opponent's Campaign Resources and Expenditures are reported in a separate section in the back of the book (pp. 269-284).

GENERAL ELECTION DATA

	Registered Voters	Voter Turnout		Straight Party Voting	
1996	51,728	33,589	64.9%	(R) 6,524 . . . 19.4%	(D) 6,807 . . . 20.3%

PRESIDENT

1996	Bill Clinton (D)	17,475	53.2%
	Bob Dole (R)	12,419	37.8%
	Ross Perot (I)	2,685	8.2%
1992	Bill Clinton (D)	17,551	41.2%
	George Bush (R)	17,231	40.5%
	Ross Perot (I)	7,800	18.3%

UNITED STATES SENATE

1996	Richard J. Durbin (D)	17,028	52.8%
	Al Salvi (R)	14,318	44.4%

GOVERNOR

1994	Jim Edgar (R)	19,255	72.7%
	Dawn Clark Netsch (D)	7,218	27.3%

Representative Robert A. "Bob" Biggins (R)

District Office: 114 West Park Ave., Elmhurst 60126
Phone (630) 941-1278; (630) 941-1285 (fax)
Springfield Office: Room 2010-H Stratton Bldg., Springfield 62706
Phone (217) 782-6578; (217) 782-5257 (fax)

Legislative Assignments: Committees on Appropriations-General Services & Government Oversight (minority spokesperson); Financial Institutions; Executive; Revenue; Legislative Audit Commission.

Public Service: Representative (1993-present); Addison Township assessor (1973-1977).

Personal: Board member, Suburban Bank of Elmhurst; born October 20, 1946, Oak Park; Northeastern Illinois University, B.A. in education; married (Judy); two children.

1997 BILL PASSAGE RATIO	Introduced	Passed House of Origin	Passed GA
Primary	4	2	1
Primary/Hyphenated	21	7	2

KEY VOTES

1) Change Ed. Funding Formula . .N	6) Insurance/Domestic Violence . .Y	11) Pre-Paid College Tuition . . . .Y
2) State Budget . . . . .Y	7) Brownfields . . . . .Y	12) Increase Pull Tab Prizes . . . .Y
3) Tougher DUI Level . . . . .Y	8) Welfare Reform . . . . .Y	13) Utility Deregulation . . . . . . .Y
4) Ban Partial Birth Abortions . . .Y	9) Concealed Guns/Misdemeanor .Y	14) County Obscenity Standards .Y
5) State Employees Pension . . . . .Y	10) Banks Sell Insurance . . . . .Y	15) Managed Care Reform . . . . .N

GROUP RATINGS

	FB	CoC	PrLf	IPPC	ACLU
1997	68	77	6/6	0	20

ELECTION RESULTS

1996 General	Bob Biggins (R)	21,677	(60.1%)
1996 General	Tom Berry (D)	14,407	(39.9%)
1996 Primary	Bob Biggins (R)	9,491	(100%)

CAMPAIGN RESOURCES AND EXPENDITURES

1996 Campaign Funds				Top 10 PAC Contributors			
Beg. Balance	$21,059	Individuals	$2,792	1) Inland	$1,000	6) HOPE	$500
Receipts	$32,321	Party	$750	2) PetPec	$500	7) LICID	$500
Expenditures	$22,607	PACS	$18,212	3) IMPAC	$500	8) MPAC	$500
On hand	$30,773	Candidate	$0	4) RPAC	$500	9) PMorris	$500
		Not-itemized	$10,567	5) ISMS	$500	10) IHCA	$500

NOTE: The General Election Opponent's Campaign Resources and Expenditures are reported in a separate section in the back of the book (pp. 269-284).

GENERAL ELECTION DATA

	Registered Voters	Voter Turnout		Straight Party Voting			
1996	52,581	37,921	72.1%	(R) 10,092	26.6%	(D) 5,559	14.7%

PRESIDENT

1996	Bill Clinton (D)	16,653	44.8%
	Bob Dole (R)	16,847	45.3%
	Ross Perot (I)	3,380	9.1%
1992	Bill Clinton (D)	15,630	34.6%
	George Bush (R)	20,096	44.5%
	Ross Perot (I)	9,408	20.9%

UNITED STATES SENATE

1996	Richard J. Durbin (D)	17,295	47.1%
	Al Salvi (R)	17,971	50.0%

GOVERNOR

1994	Jim Edgar (R)	21,006	76.8%
	Dawn Clark Netsch (D)	6,362	23.2%

40th Senate District

House District 79
House District 80

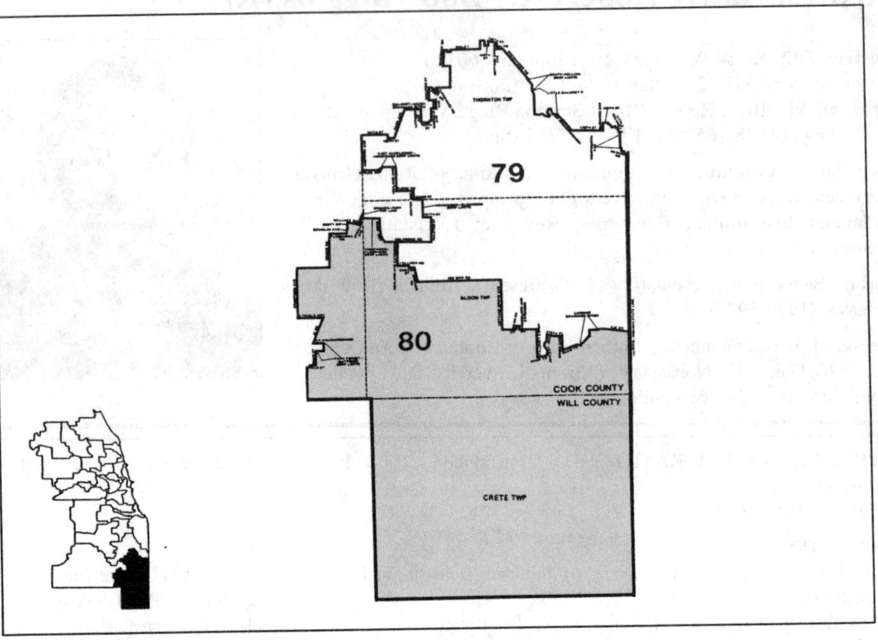

DEMOGRAPHICS (1990)

	S.D. #40	H.D. #79	H.D.#80
VOTING AGE POPULATION	142,713	72,742	69,971
White	79.0%	83.0%	74.8%
Black	15.2%	13.3%	17.2%
Hispanic	4.8%	2.9%	6.8%
Asian	0.9%	0.8%	1.1%
AGE (Total Population)	193,739	96,869	96,870
Under 6	8.7%	8.1%	9.3%
6 to 18	19.0%	18.1%	20.0%
65 and Over	12.5%	13.9%	11.2%
URBAN POPULATION	95.9%	98.8%	93.1%
HOUSING UNITS (Total)	70,609	35,486	35,123
Median Value	$73,225	$78,194	$67,012
Owner Occupied	74.5%	79.6%	69.3%
FAMILY INCOME (Total Families)	52,652	26,902	25,751
Median Income	$41,747	$42,687	$40,868
Below Poverty Level	6.1%	4.6%	7.8%
With Children Under 5	0.8%	0.4%	1.2%
With Children 5 to 17	2.2%	1.7%	2.8%
Headed by Females	3.7%	2.7%	4.8%
INDUSTRY (Total Employed)	93,190	47,330	45,860
Professional/Public Administration	26.9%	26.0%	27.9%
Manufacturing	17.4%	16.8%	18.0%
Retail	17.5%	16.9%	18.1%
Transportation/Communication	9.2%	10.5%	7.9%
Finance/Insurance/Real Estate	8.2%	8.3%	8.1%
Other Service	7.9%	8.3%	7.6%

Senator Debbie DeFrancesco Halvorson (D)

District Office: 241 W. Joe Orr Rd., Chicago Heights 60411
Phone (708) 756-0882; (708) 756-0885 (fax)
Springfield Office: Rm 105-E, Capitol Bldg., Springfield 62706
Phone (217) 782-7419

Legislative Assignments: Committees on Education; Financial Institutions.

Public Service: Senator (1997-present); Crete Township Clerk (1993-1996).

Personal: Born March 1, 1958; independent salesperson; Robert Morris and Prairie State Colleges; married (Gordy); two children.

1997 BILL PASSAGE RATIO	Introduced	Passed House of Origin	Passed GA
Primary	20	4	3
Primary/Hyphenated	29	6	5

KEY VOTES

1) Senate GOP Ed. $ Plan . . . . . . .N	6) Insurance/Domestic Violence . .Y	11) Pre-Paid College Tuition . . . .Y
2) State Budget . . . . .Y	7) Brownfields . . . . .Y	12) Increase Pull Tab Prizes . . . .N
3) Tougher DUI Level . . . . .Y	8) Welfare Reform . . . . .Y	13) Telecommunications Tax . . .Y
4) Ban Partial Birth Abortions . . .Y	9) Concealed Guns/Misdemeanor .Y	14) Delivery Discrimination . . . .Y
5) State Employees Pension . . . . .Y	10) Banks Sell Insurance . . . . . . .Y	15) Sell Drivers' Data . . . . .N

GROUP RATINGS

	FB	CoC	PrLf	IPPC	ACLU
1997	77	60	2/2	0	50

ELECTION RESULTS

1996 General	Debbie DeFrancesco Halvorson (D)	40,813	(55.62%)
1996 General	Aldo A. DeAngelis (R)	32,554	(44.37%)
1996 Primary	Debbie DeFrancesco Halvorson (D)	8,490	(100%)
1996 Primary	Aldo A. DeAngelis (R)	12,003	(100%)

CAMPAIGN RESOURCES AND EXPENDITURES

1996 Campaign Funds		Top 10 PAC Contributors	
Beg. Balance .$16,748	Individuals . .$16,167	1) CDS $270,460	6) CCCTU . . .$7,397
Receipts $390,527	Party $294,537	2) CEJones . .$12,200	7) IFT $7,000
Expenditures .$407,184	PACS $84,823	3) ITLA $10,000	8) IPACE $6,320
On hand $91	Candidate $0	4) AFSCME . .$8,621	9) FCarroll . . .$4,500
	Not-itemized $0	5) WVWV . . .$8,000	10) IUOE $4,000

NOTE: The General Election Opponent's Campaign Resources and Expenditures are reported in a separate section in the back of the book (pp. 269-284).

GENERAL ELECTION DATA

Registered Voters	Voter Turnout		Straight Party Voting	
1996 118,213	75,439	63.8%	(R) 14,888 . .19.7%	(D) 18,292 . . .24.3%

PRESIDENT

1996	Bill Clinton (D)	40,614	54.9%
	Bob Dole (R)	27,088	36.6%
	Ross Perot (I)	5,793	7.8%
1992	Bill Clinton (D)	37,217	44.4%
	George Bush (R)	32,274	38.5%
	Ross Perot (I)	14,349	17.1%

UNITED STATES SENATE

1996	Richard J. Durbin (D)	40,260	55.3%
	Al Salvi (R)	30,534	41.0%

GOVERNOR

1994	Jim Edgar (R)	35,779	67.9%
	Dawn Clark Netsch (D)	16,891	32.1%

Representative Michael Giglio (D)

District Office: 18511 Torrence, Lansing 60438
Phone (708) 895-1996; (708) 895-4250 (fax)
Springfield Office: Room 2051-L Stratton Bldg., Springfield 62706
Phone (217) 782-5971

Legislative Assignments: Committees on Labor & Commerce; Veterans' Affairs; Transportation & Motor Vehicles.

Public Service: Representative (1997-present).

Personal: Licensed plumbing contractor; Roosevelt University, B.A.; married (Lisa); two children.

1997 BILL PASSAGE RATIO	Introduced	Passed House of Origin	Passed GA
Primary	10	2	0
Primary/Hyphenated	25	10	4

KEY VOTES

1) Change Ed. Funding Formula . . Y	6) Insurance/Domestic Violence . . Y	11) Pre-Paid College Tuition . . . . Y
2) State Budget . . . . Y	7) Brownfields . . . . N	12) Increase Pull Tab Prizes . . . . Y
3) Tougher DUI Level . . . . Y	8) Welfare Reform . . . . N	13) Utility Deregulation . . . . N
4) Ban Partial Birth Abortions . . . N	9) Concealed Guns/Misdemeanor . N	14) County Obscenity Standards . Y
5) State Employees Pension . . . . . Y	10) Banks Sell Insurance . . . . Y	15) Managed Care Reform . . . . . Y

GROUP RATINGS

	FB	CoC	PrLf	IPPC	ACLU
1997	71	23	0/6	100	70

ELECTION RESULTS

1996 General	Michael Giglio (D)	21,292	(56.9%)
1996 General	Marvin Lyzenga (R)	16,133	(43.1%)
1996 Primary	Michael Giglio (D)	4,822	(66.6%)
1996 Primary	Robert L. Ryan (D)	2,413	(33.4%)

CAMPAIGN RESOURCES AND EXPENDITURES

1996 Campaign Funds		Top 10 PAC Contributors	
Beg. Balance . . $7,487	Individuals . . . $4,925	1) IHDM . . $122,332	6) PersPAC . . . $4,500
Receipts $243,124	Party $145,627	2) DSCC . . . $10,000	7) AFSCME . . $3,216
Expenditures . $237,314	PACS $82,876	3) SEIU $10,000	8) IFT $3,000
On hand $13,297	Candidate $0	4) FHalvorson $6,150	9) CLang $3,000
	Not-itemized . $9,696	5) ITLA $6,000	10) UAW $3,000

NOTE: The General Election Opponent's Campaign Resources and Expenditures are reported in a separate section in the back of the book (pp. 269-284).

GENERAL ELECTION DATA

	Registered Voters	Voter Turnout		Straight Party Voting	
1996	 58,844	37,724 . . . . 64.1%		(R) 8,380 . . . 22.2%	(D) 8,577 . . . . 22.7%

PRESIDENT

1996	Bill Clinton (D)	19,766	53.3%
	Bob Dole (R)	14,425	38.9%
	Ross Perot (I)	2,682	7.2%
1992	Bill Clinton (D)	17,645	41.3%
	George Bush (R)	17,847	41.8%
	Ross Perot (I)	7,212	16.9%

UNITED STATES SENATE

1996	Richard J. Durbin (D)	19,354	53.1%
	Al Salvi (R)	16,223	44.5%

GOVERNOR

1994	Jim Edgar (R)	18,839	70.7%
	Dawn Clark Netsch (D)	7,811	29.3%

Representative George F. Scully, Jr. (D)

District Office: 414 West Lincoln Highway, Chicago Heights 60411
Phone (708) 503-9350; (708) 503-9611 (fax)
Springfield Office: Room 2036-J Stratton Bldg., Springfield 62706
Phone (217) 782-1719

Legislative Assignments: Committees on Aging; Appropriations-Education; Appropriations-General Services & Government Oversight; Judiciary I-Civil Law; Local Government.

Public Service: Representative (1997-present).

Personal: Attorney; born February 28, 1952, Evergreen Park; Northern Illinois University, B.S. in finance; John Marshall Law School, J.D.; married (Barbara); three children.

1997 BILL PASSAGE RATIO	Introduced	Passed House of Origin	Passed GA
Primary	10	4	1
Primary/Hyphenated	41	12	2

KEY VOTES

1) Change Ed. Funding Formula . . Y	6) Insurance/Domestic Violence . . Y	11) Pre-Paid College Tuition . . . . Y
2) State Budget . . . . Y	7) Brownfields . . . . N	12) Increase Pull Tab Prizes . . . . Y
3) Tougher DUI Level . . . . Y	8) Welfare Reform . . . . N	13) Utility Deregulation . . . . N
4) Ban Partial Birth Abortions . . . Y	9) Concealed Guns/Misdemeanor . N	14) County Obscenity Standards . Y
5) State Employees Pension . . . . . Y	10) Banks Sell Insurance . . . . Y	15) Managed Care Reform . . . . . Y

GROUP RATINGS

	FB	CoC	PrLf	IPPC	ACLU
1997	71	23	3/6	50	50

ELECTION RESULTS

1996 General	George F. Scully, Jr. (D)	19.506	(54.1%)
1996 General	Flora L. Ciarlo (R)	16,579	(45.9%)
1996 Primary	George F. Scully, Jr. (D)	4,108	(100%)
1996 Primary	Flora L. Ciarlo (R)	5,227	(67.4%)

CAMPAIGN RESOURCES AND EXPENDITURES

1996 Campaign Funds				Top 10 PAC Contributors			
Beg. Balance	$7,150	Individuals	$9,864	1) IHDM	$124,850	6) ITLA	$4,000
Receipts	$254,956	Party	$141,460	2) IPACE	$30,000	7) LavinPC	$3,000
Expenditures	$260,330	PACS	$86,787	3) DSCC	$13,262	8) UAW	$3,000
On hand	$1,776	Candidate	$0	4) SEIU	$10,000	9) C&GL	$3,000
		Not-itemized	$16,845	5) AFSCME	$6,577	10) Statesman	$2,500

NOTE: The General Election Opponent's Campaign Resources and Expenditures are reported in a separate section in the back of the book (pp. 269-284).

GENERAL ELECTION DATA

	Registered Voters	Voter Turnout		Straight Party Voting			
1996	59,369	37,715	63.5%	(R) 6,508	17.3%	(D) 9,715	25.8%

PRESIDENT

1996	Bill Clinton (D)	20,848	56.9%
	Bob Dole (R)	12,663	34.6%
	Ross Perot (I)	3,111	8.5%
1992	Bill Clinton (D)	19,572	47.6%
	George Bush (R)	14.427	35.1%
	Ross Perot (I)	7,137	17.3%

UNITED STATES SENATE

1996	Richard J. Durbin (D)	20,906	57.6%
	Al Salvi (R)	14,311	39.4%

GOVERNOR

1994	Jim Edgar (R)	16,940	65.1%
	Dawn Clark Netsch (D)	9,080	34.9%

41st Senate District

House District 81
House District 82

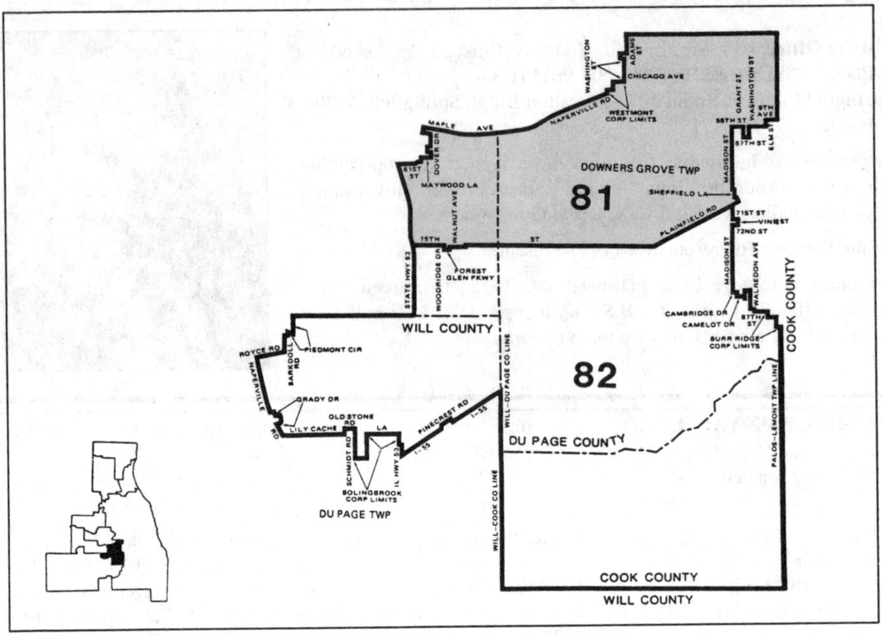

DEMOGRAPHICS (1990)

	S.D. #41	H.D. #81	H.D.#82
VOTING AGE POPULATION	140,587	72,702	67,885
White	87.6%	90.3%	84.6%
Black	4.2%	1.7%	6.9%
Hispanic	3.0%	2.7%	3.4%
Asian	5.0%	5.2%	4.8%
AGE (Total Population)	193,738	96,869	96,869
Under 6	9.7%	9.2%	10.3%
6 to 18	18.9%	16.9%	21.0%
65 and Over	8.0%	9.9%	6.1%
URBAN POPULATION	97.5%	99.9%	95.1%
HOUSING UNITS (Total)	71,673	37,628	34,045
Median Value	$136,772	$147,833	$119,891
Owner Occupied	72.2%	72.1%	72.2%
FAMILY INCOME (Total Families)	52,251	26,688	25,563
Median Income	$54,100	$56,440	$52,048
Below Poverty Level	2.0%	1.9%	2.0%
With Children Under 5	0.3%	0.3%	0.3%
With Children 5 to 17	0.7%	0.6%	0.8%
Headed by Females	1.0%	0.9%	1.1%
INDUSTRY (Total Employed)	107,052	53,845	53,207
Professional/Public Administration	26.2%	28.6%	23.8%
Manufacturing	16.2%	15.2%	17.3%
Retail	16.9%	15.8%	18.0%
Transportation/Communication	8.9%	7.8%	10.0%
Finance/Insurance/Real Estate	10.4%	11.4%	9.5%
Other Service	9.3%	9.6%	9.1%

Senator Kirk W. Dillard (R)

District Office: 942 Maple Ave., Downers Grove 60515
Phone (630) 969-0990; (630) 969-1007 (fax)
Springfield Office: 120M Capitol Bldg., Springfield 62706
Phone (217) 782-8148

Legislative Assignments: Committees on Rules (vice-chair); Judiciary (vice-chair); Energy and Environment; Commerce and Industry.

Public Service: Senator (1993-present); chief of staff for Governor Jim Edgar (1991-94); judge for the Illinois Court of Claims (1987-90); director of Legislative Affairs for Governor James R. Thompson (1982-87).

Personal: Partner, Lord, Bissoll & Brook (Chicago); born June 1, 1955, Chicago; Western Illinois University, B.A. in political science and economics; DePaul University College of Law, J.D.; married (Carol).

1997 BILL PASSAGE RATIO	Introduced	Passed House of Origin	Passed GA
Primary	46	11	8
Primary/Hyphenated	59	21	17

KEY VOTES

1) Senate GOP Ed. $ Plan . . . . . . .Y	6) Insurance/Domestic Violence . .Y	11) Pre-Paid College Tuition . . . .Y
2) State Budget . . . . .Y	7) Brownfields . . . . .Y	12) Increase Pull Tab Prizes . . . .Y
3) Tougher DUI Level . . . . .Y	8) Welfare Reform . . . . .Y	13) Telecommunications Tax . . . .P
4) Ban Partial Birth Abortions . . .Y	9) Concealed Guns/Misdemeanor .Y	14) Delivery Discrimination . . . .P
5) State Employees Pension . . . . .Y	10) Banks Sell Insurance . . . . .Y	15) Sell Drivers' Data . . . . .Y

GROUP RATINGS

	FB	CoC	PrLf	IPPC	ACLU
1997	82	100	2/2	0	50

ELECTION RESULTS

1994 General	Kirk W. Dillard (R)	39,112	(73.4%)
1994 General	R. Christine Hotchkin (D)	14,202	(26.6%)
1994 Primary	Kirk W. Dillard (R)	10,541	(53.0%)
1994 Primary	S. Patricia "Pat" Trowbridge (R)	9,364	(47.0%)

CAMPAIGN RESOURCES AND EXPENDITURES

1996 Campaign Funds				Top 10 PAC Contributors	
Beg. Balance	$14,831	Individuals	$7,100	1) IPACE $7,800	6) HOPE $1,450
Receipts	$94,724	Party	$900	2) ILCable . . .$4,583	7) PIIA $1,200
Expenditures	$59,295	PACS	$80,233	3) UPS $2,500	8) Duchossois .$1,200
On hand	$50,260	Candidate	$0	4) MPAC $2,500	9) IUOE $1,200
		Not-itemized	$6,491	5) CyborFire . .$1,500	10) BFerris . . .$1,200

NOTE: The General Election Opponent's Campaign Resources and Expenditures are reported in a separate section in the back of the book (pp. 269-284).

GENERAL ELECTION DATA

	Registered Voters	Voter Turnout		Straight Party Voting	
1996	110,481	81,146	73.4%	(R) 22,316 . . 27.5%	(D) 11,778 . . . 14.5%

PRESIDENT

1996	Bill Clinton (D)	34,054	42.7%
	Bob Dole (R)	38,188	47.9%
	Ross Perot (I)	6,782	8.5%
1992	Bill Clinton (D)	30,371	33.9%
	George Bush (R)	40,086	44.7%
	Ross Perot (I)	19,177	21.4%

UNITED STATES SENATE

1996	Richard J. Durbin (D)	35,746	45.4%
	Al Salvi (R)	39,846	50.6%

GOVERNOR

1994	Jim Edgar (R)	42,861	77.9%
	Dawn Clark Netsch (D)	12,161	22.1%

Representative Judy Biggert (R)

District Office: 6301 South Cass Ave., Suite 303, Westmont 60559
Phone (630) 852-8633; (630) 852-6530 (fax)
Springfield Office: Room 220 Capitol Bldg., Springfield 62706
Phone (217) 782-1448

Legislative Assignments: Assistant Republican Leader; ex officio member of all committees. Committees on Judiciary I - Civil Law; Appropriations-Human Services; Labor & Commerce; Conflicts of Interest.

Public Service: Representative (1993-present); Hinsdale planning commission; board of education, district 86.

Personal: Attorney; born August 15, 1937, Chicago; Stanford University, B.A. in international relations; Northwestern University, J.D.; married (Rody); four children.

1997 BILL PASSAGE RATIO	Introduced	Passed House of Origin	Passed GA
Primary	14	7	3
Primary/Hyphenated	38	25	10

KEY VOTES

1) Change Ed. Funding Formula . . N	6) Insurance/Domestic Violence . . Y	11) Pre-Paid College Tuition . . . . Y
2) State Budget . . . . Y	7) Brownfields . . . . Y	12) Increase Pull Tab Prizes . . . . Y
3) Tougher DUI Level . . . . Y	8) Welfare Reform . . . . Y	13) Utility Deregulation . . . . Y
4) Ban Partial Birth Abortions . . . N	9) Concealed Guns/Misdemeanor . Y	14) County Obscenity Standards . N
5) State Employees Pension . . . . . Y	10) Banks Sell Insurance . . . . Y	15) Managed Care Reform . . . . . N

GROUP RATINGS

	FB	CoC	PrLf	IPPC	ACLU
1997	68	62	0/6	100	100

ELECTION RESULTS

1996 General	Judy Biggert (R)	28,597	(71.2%)
1996 General	Dave Brockway (D)	11,573	(28.8%)
1996 Primary	Judy Biggert (R)	14,142	(100%)
1996 Primary	Dave Brockway (D)	3,564	(100%)

CAMPAIGN RESOURCES AND EXPENDITURES

1996 Campaign Funds

Beg. Balance	$46,836	Individuals	$6,170
Receipts	$48,120	Party	$200
Expenditures	$51,174	PACS	$30,550
On hand	$43,782	Candidate	$0
		Not-itemized	$11,200

Top 10 PAC Contributors

1) TuthillCorp $3,000	6) LAWPAC . $1,000
2) IPACE $2,000	7) AT&T $1,000
3) MPAC $2,000	8) MBPlatt . . . $750
4) WCLA $1,000	9) WMgt $750
5) MASILA . . $1,000	10) Ameritech . . $750

NOTE: The General Election Opponent's Campaign Resources and Expenditures are reported in a separate section in the back of the book (pp. 269-284).

GENERAL ELECTION DATA

	Registered Voters	Voter Turnout		Straight Party Voting	
1996	54,003	42,548	78.8%	(R) 12,800 . . 30.1%	(D) 5,062 . . . . 11.9%

PRESIDENT

1996	Bill Clinton (D)	16,824	40.3%
	Bob Dole (R)	21,245	50.8%
	Ross Perot (I)	3,336	8.0%
1992	Bill Clinton (D)	15,592	32.5%
	George Bush (R)	22,639	47.2%
	Ross Perot (I)	9,768	20.3%

UNITED STATES SENATE

1996	Richard J. Durbin (D)	18,149	43.9%
	Al Salvi (R)	21,560	52.2%

GOVERNOR

1994	Jim Edgar (R)	22,616	78.3%
	Dawn Clark Netsch (D)	6,251	21.7%

Representative James H. "Jim" Meyer (R)

District Office: 277 S. Schmidt Rd., Suite 100, Bolingbrook 60440
Phone (630) 759-3465; (630) 759-3554 (fax)
Springfield Office: Room 2005-G Stratton Bldg., Springfield 62706
Phone (217) 782-8028; (217) 782-3189 (fax)

Legislative Assignments: Committees on Veterans' Affairs (minority spokesperson); Insurance; Financial Institutions; Registration & Regulation; Environment & Energy.

Public Service: Representative (1993-present); former village trustee and plan commissioner, Village of Bolingbrook.

Personal: Born October 28, 1943, Sibley, IA; Upper Iowa University, B.A. in political science; married (Bonnie); one child.

1997 BILL PASSAGE RATIO	Introduced	Passed House of Origin	Passed GA
Primary	16	9	5
Primary/Hyphenated	21	11	6

KEY VOTES

1) Change Ed. Funding Formula . . N	6) Insurance/Domestic Violence . . Y	11) Pre-Paid College Tuition . . . . Y
2) State Budget . . . . Y	7) Brownfields . . . . Y	12) Increase Pull Tab Prizes . . . . N
3) Tougher DUI Level . . . . Y	8) Welfare Reform . . . . Y	13) Utility Deregulation . . . . Y
4) Ban Partial Birth Abortions . . . Y	9) Concealed Guns/Misdemeanor . Y	14) County Obscenity Standards . Y
5) State Employees Pension . . . . . Y	10) Banks Sell Insurance . . . . Y	15) Managed Care Reform . . . . . N

GROUP RATINGS

	FB	CoC	PrLf	IPPC	ACLU
1997	64	69	5/6	16	30

ELECTION RESULTS

1996 General	James H. "Jim" Meyer (R)	20,590	(60.3%)
1996 General	Tom Wolfe (D)	13,556	(39.7%)
1996 Primary	James H. "Jim" Meyer (R)	8,681	(100%)
1996 Primary	Tom Wolfe (D)	3,008	(100%)

CAMPAIGN RESOURCES AND EXPENDITURES

1996 Campaign Funds				Top 10 PAC Contributors			
Beg. Balance	$21,473	Individuals	$300	1) IPACE	$1,500	6) Monroe	$700
Receipts	$27,349	Party	$200	2) UPS	$1,200	7) QMS	$600
Expenditures	$36,146	PACS	$24,281	3) Quantum	$750	8) IVendors	$600
On hand	$12,676	Candidate	$0	4) SASPAC	$750	9) Uno-Ven	$600
		Not-itemized	$2,568	5) BFerris	$700	10) HOPE	$600

NOTE: The General Election Opponent's Campaign Resources and Expenditures are reported in a separate section in the back of the book (pp. 269-284).

GENERAL ELECTION DATA

	Registered Voters	Voter Turnout		Straight Party Voting	
1996	56,478	38,598	68.3%	(R) 9,516 . . .24.7%	(D) 6,716 . . . .17.4%

PRESIDENT

1996	Bill Clinton (D)	17,230	45.5%
	Bob Dole (R)	16,943	44.7%
	Ross Perot (I)	3,446	9.1%
1992	Bill Clinton (D)	14,779	35.5%
	George Bush (R)	17,447	41.9%
	Ross Perot (I)	9,409	22.6%

UNITED STATES SENATE

1996	Richard J. Durbin (D)	17,597	47.0%
	Al Salvi (R)	18,286	48.8%

GOVERNOR

1994	Jim Edgar (R)	20,245	77.4%
	Dawn Clark Netsch (D)	5,910	22.6%

42nd Senate District

House District 83
House District 84

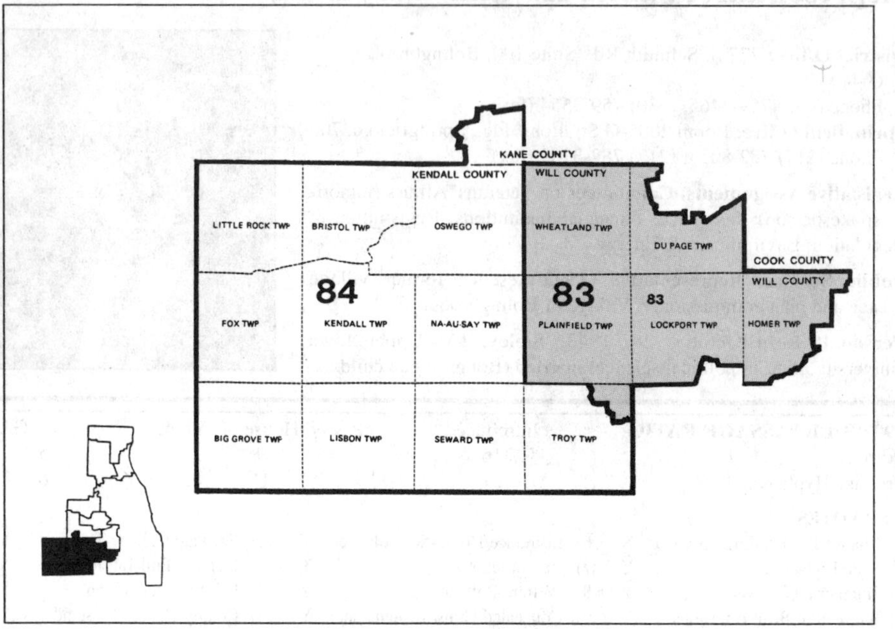

DEMOGRAPHICS (1990)

	S.D. #42	H.D. #83	H.D.#84
VOTING AGE POPULATION	134,123	68,187	65,936
White	83.4%	90.4%	76.2%
Black	4.9%	4.3%	5.4%
Hispanic	10.6%	3.9%	17.6%
Asian	1.0%	1.3%	0.6%
AGE (Total Population)	193,739	96,870	96,869
Under 6	10.5%	10.0%	11.0%
6 to 18	21.9%	21.1%	22.6%
65 and Over	7.3%	6.4%	8.2%
URBAN POPULATION	84.2%	85.5%	82.9%
HOUSING UNITS (Total)	64,288	31,914	32,374
Median Value	$93,928	$103,195	$85,168
Owner Occupied	73.7%	79.5%	68.0%
FAMILY INCOME (Total Families)	49,937	25,640	24,297
Median Income	$45,690	$49,442	$41,452
Below Poverty Level	4.5%	2.4%	6.7%
With Children Under 5	0.9%	0.2%	1.6%
With Children 5 to 17	1.4%	0.9%	1.9%
Headed by Females	2.1%	0.9%	3.4%
INDUSTRY (Total Employed)	95,989	48,671	47,319
Professional/Public Administration	21.9%	23.5%	20.2%
Manufacturing	24.6%	19.6%	29.7%
Retail	16.7%	17.9%	15.5%
Transportation/Communication	8.3%	9.7%	7.0%
Finance/Insurance/Real Estate	6.8%	7.5%	6.2%
Other Service	8.0%	7.8%	8.2%

Senator Edward Petka (R)

District Office: 501 N. Division, P.O. Box 188, Plainfield 60544
Phone (815) 436-5577; (815) 436-8065 (fax)
Springfield Office: 122 Capitol Bldg., Springfield 62706
Phone (217) 782-0422

Legislative Assignments: Majority Caucus Secretary; Committees on Executive Appointments (chair); Judiciary, Insurance & Pensions; Executive.

Public Service: Senator (1993-present); representative (1987-93); state's attorney, Will County (1976-1986).

Personal: Attorney; born March 10, 1943, Chicago; B.A., Southern Illinois University; J.D., John Marshall Law School; married (Phyllis); four children.

1997 BILL PASSAGE RATIO	Introduced	Passed House of Origin	Passed GA
Primary	13	4	4
Primary/Hyphenated	15	6	5

KEY VOTES

1) Senate GOP Ed. $ Plan . . . . . . .Y	6) Insurance/Domestic Violence . .Y	11) Pre-Paid College Tuition . . . .Y
2) State Budget . . . . .Y	7) Brownfields . . . . .Y	12) Increase Pull Tab Prizes . . . .Y
3) Tougher DUI Level . . . . .N	8) Welfare Reform . . . . .Y	13) Telecommunications Tax . . .N
4) Ban Partial Birth Abortions . . .Y	9) Concealed Guns/Misdemeanor .Y	14) Delivery Discrimination . . . .N
5) State Employees Pension . . . . .Y	10) Banks Sell Insurance . . . . .Y	15) Sell Drivers' Data . . . . .P

GROUP RATINGS

	FB	CoC	PrLf	IPPC	ACLU
1997	77	100	2/2	0	50

ELECTION RESULTS

1996 General	Edward Petka (R)	44,843	(59.2%)
1996 General	Ed Kelly (D)	30,913	(40.8%)
1996 Primary	Edward Petka (R)	16,418	(100%)
1996 Primary	Ed Kelly (D)	2,841	(55.6%)
1996 Primary	Jennifer J. Flowers (D)	2,267	(44.4%)

CAMPAIGN RESOURCES AND EXPENDITURES

1996 Campaign Funds

Beg. Balance	$48,191	Individuals	$7,090
Receipts	$93,465	Party	$42,571
Expenditures	$121,681	PACS	$42,506
On hand	$19,975	Candidate	$436
		Not-itemized	$862

Top 10 PAC Contributors

1) RSSC	$42,071	6) PIIA	$2,000
2) ISMS	$5,000	7) LIPAC	$1,500
3) BankersL&C	$3,506	8) LAWPAC	$1,500
4) MPAC	$3,000	9) NRA	$1,000
5) ABDI	$2,000	10) Fremont	$1,000

NOTE: The General Election Opponent's Campaign Resources and Expenditures are reported in a separate section in the back of the book (pp. 269-284).

GENERAL ELECTION DATA

	Registered Voters	Voter Turnout		Straight Party Voting	
1996	126,261	80,327	63.6%	(R) 18,169 . .22.6%	(D) 11,591 . . .14.4%

PRESIDENT

1996	Bill Clinton (D)	34,055	43.4%
	Bob Dole (R)	35,460	45.2%
	Ross Perot (I)	8,394	10.7%
1992	Bill Clinton (D)	28,966	36.2%
	George Bush (R)	33,246	41.5%
	Ross Perot (I)	17,812	22.3%

UNITED STATES SENATE

1996	Richard J. Durbin (D)	33,779	43.7%
	Al Salvi (R)	40,068	51.8%

GOVERNOR

1994	Jim Edgar (R)	40,052	78.2%
	Dawn Clark Netsch (D)	11,183	21.8%

Representative Brent Hassert (R)

District Office: 1413 Sherman Rd., Ste. 60, Romeoville 60446
Phone (630) 739-7063; (630) 739-4055 (fax)
Springfield Office: Room 2135-O Stratton Bldg., Springfield 62706
Phone (217) 782-4179

Legislative Assignments: Committees on Environment & Energy (minority spokesperson); Insurance; Financial Institutions; Executive; Electric Utility Deregulation.

Public Service: Representative (1993-present); board commissioner, Will County.

Personal: Owner, Hassert Landscaping; born October 29, 1952, Joliet; Joliet Junior College, ornamental horticulture; married (Patty); two children.

1997 BILL PASSAGE RATIO	Introduced	Passed House of Origin	Passed GA
Primary	12	8	4
Primary/Hyphenated	24	18	11

KEY VOTES

1) Change Ed. Funding Formula . . N
2) State Budget . . . . Y
3) Tougher DUI Level . . . . Y
4) Ban Partial Birth Abortions . . . Y
5) State Employees Pension . . . . . Y
6) Insurance/Domestic Violence . . Y
7) Brownfields . . . . Y
8) Welfare Reform . . . . Y
9) Concealed Guns/Misdemeanor . Y
10) Banks Sell Insurance . . . . Y
11) Pre-Paid College Tuition . . . . Y
12) Increase Pull Tab Prizes . . . . Y
13) Utility Deregulation . . . . Y
14) County Obscenity Standards . N
15) Managed Care Reform . . . . . N

GROUP RATINGS

	FB	CoC	PrLf	IPPC	ACLU
1997	68	75	3/6	50	50

ELECTION RESULTS

1996 General	Brent Hassert (R)	34,252	(100%)
1996 Primary	Brent Hassert (R)	7,329	(100%)
1994 General	Brent Hassert (R)	19,670	(70.4%)
1994 General	Terry M. Hogan (D)	8,272	(29.6%)

CAMPAIGN RESOURCES AND EXPENDITURES

1996 Campaign Funds

Beg. Balance	$56,931	Individuals	$600
Receipts	$16,861	Party	$405
Expenditures	$27,996	PACS	$12,951
On hand	$45,796	Candidate	$0
		Not-itemized	$2,905

Top 10 PAC Contributors

1) RJR	$1,200	6) Empress	$500
2) ABDI	$800	7) HI	$500
3) BFerris	$750	8) ISMS	$500
4) Uno-Ven	$600	9) Players	$500
5) CatCEG	$500	10) ARC	$500

NOTE: The General Election Opponent's Campaign Resources and Expenditures are reported in a separate section in the back of the book (pp. 269-284).

GENERAL ELECTION DATA

	Registered Voters	Voter Turnout		Straight Party Voting	
1996	72,624	47,956	66.0%	(R) 10,294 . . 21.5%	(D) 6,410 . . . 13.4%

PRESIDENT

1996	Bill Clinton (D)	20,002	42.7%
	Bob Dole (R)	21,495	45.9%
	Ross Perot (I)	5,009	10.7%
1992	Bill Clinton (D)	15,003	34.4%
	George Bush (R)	18,486	42.3%
	Ross Perot (I)	10,165	23.3%

UNITED STATES SENATE

1996	Richard J. Durbin (D)	20,130	43.6%
	Al Salvi (R)	23,958	51.9%

GOVERNOR

1994	Jim Edgar (R)	23,432	78.6%
	Dawn Clark Netsch (D)	6,386	21.4%

Representative Tom Cross (R)

District Office: 541 Countryside Shopping Center, Yorkville 60560
Phone (630) 553-0000; (630) 553-9999 (fax)
Springfield Office: Room 2023-H Stratton Bldg., Springfield 62706
Phone (217) 782-1331

Legislative Assignments: Committees on Judiciary I-Civil Law (minority spokesperson); Judiciary II-Criminal Law; Health Care Availability & Access; Children & Youth; State Government Administration & Election Reform.

Public Service: Representative (1993-present).

Personal: Attorney; born July 31, 1958, Nashville, TN; Illinois Wesleyan University, B.A. in political science; Samford University, Cumberland School of Law; married (Genie); two children.

1997 BILL PASSAGE RATIO	Introduced	Passed House of Origin	Passed GA
Primary	45	14	9
Primary/Hyphenated	59	21	14

KEY VOTES

1) Change Ed. Funding Formula . .N	6) Insurance/Domestic Violence . .Y	11) Pre-Paid College Tuition . . . .Y
2) State Budget . . . . .Y	7) Brownfields . . . . .Y	12) Increase Pull Tab Prizes . . . .Y
3) Tougher DUI Level . . . . .Y	8) Welfare Reform . . . . .Y	13) Utility Deregulation . . . . . . .Y
4) Ban Partial Birth Abortions . . .Y	9) Concealed Guns/Misdemeanor .Y	14) County Obscenity Standards .N
5) State Employees Pension . . . . .Y	10) Banks Sell Insurance . . . . .Y	15) Managed Care Reform . . . . .Y

GROUP RATINGS

	FB	CoC	PrLf	IPPC	ACLU
1997	57	46	1/6	83	80

ELECTION RESULTS

1996 General	Tom Cross (R)	19,794	(65.3%)
1996 General	Alex Arroyo (D)	10,502	(34.7%)
1996 Primary	Tom Cross (R)	8,258	(78.4%)
1996 Primary	Dale Stahl (R)	2,271	(21.6%)

CAMPAIGN RESOURCES AND EXPENDITURES

1996 Campaign Funds				Top 10 PAC Contributors			
Beg. Balance	$62,085	Individuals	$6,150	1) IPACE	$5,000	6) PIIA	$1,000
Receipts	$57,710	Party	$300	2) LAWPAC	$2,500	7) Argosy	$1,000
Expenditures	$42,245	PACS	$42,220	3) ABDI	$2,000	8) IBA	$1,000
On hand	$77,550	Candidate	$0	4) ISMS	$1,600	9) HI	$1,000
		Not-itemized	$9,040	5) Activator	$1,437	10) MPAC	$1,000

NOTE: The General Election Opponent's Campaign Resources and Expenditures are reported in a separate section in the back of the book (pp. 269-284).

GENERAL ELECTION DATA

	Registered Voters	Voter Turnout		Straight Party Voting	
1996	53,637	32,371	60.3%	(R) 7,875 . . 24.3%	(D) 5,181 . . . .16.0%

PRESIDENT

1996	Bill Clinton (D)	14,053	44.3%
	Bob Dole (R)	13,965	44.0%
	Ross Perot (I)	3,385	10.7%
1992	Bill Clinton (D)	13,963	38.4%
	George Bush (R)	14,760	40.6%
	Ross Perot (I)	7,647	21.0%

UNITED STATES SENATE

1996	Richard J. Durbin (D)	13,649	43.8%
	Al Salvi (R)	16,110	51.7%

GOVERNOR

1994	Jim Edgar (R)	16,620	77.6%
	Dawn Clark Netsch (D)	4,797	22.4%

43rd Senate District

House District 85
House District 86

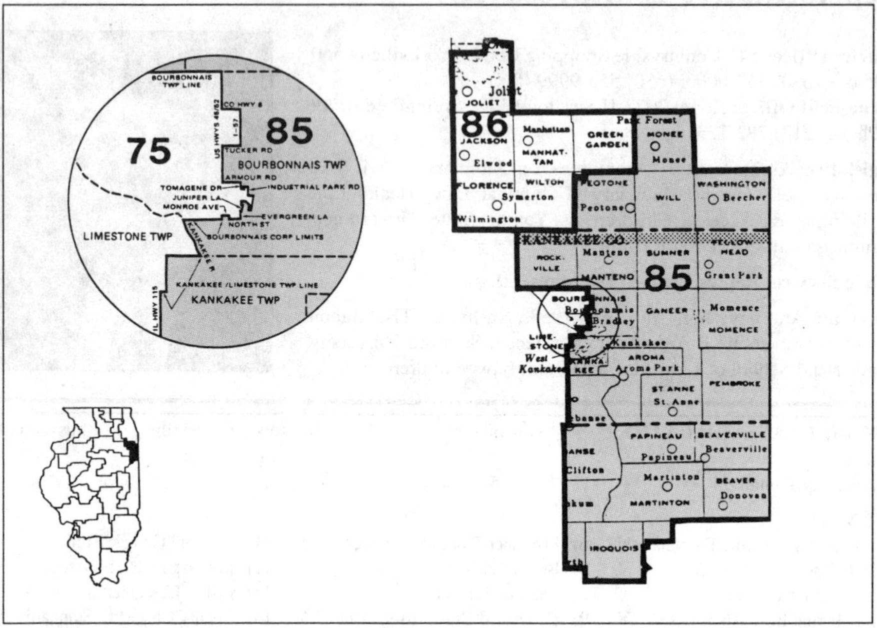

DEMOGRAPHICS (1990)

	S.D. #43	H.D. #85	H.D.#86
VOTING AGE POPULATION	139,645	69,637	70,008
White	75.8%	81.0%	70.6%
Black	17.8%	16.7%	19.0%
Hispanic	5.7%	1.8%	9.6%
Asian	0.4%	0.4%	0.5%
AGE (Total Population)	193,739	96,870	96,869
Under 6	9.5%	9.3%	9.8%
6 to 18	19.9%	20.3%	19.5%
65 and Over	14.1%	14.2%	13.9%
URBAN POPULATION	77.2%	65.2%	89.2%
HOUSING UNITS (Total)	74,064	37,910	36,154
Median Value	$57,862	$55,210	$60,135
Owner Occupied	61.5%	62.2%	60.9%
FAMILY INCOME (Total Families)	49,320	25,217	24,104
Median Income	$35,002	$33,311	$36,516
Below Poverty Level	9.8%	10.5%	9.2%
With Children Under 5	1.5%	1.8%	1.2%
With Children 5 to 17	3.6%	3.8%	3.3%
Headed by Females	6.0%	6.4%	5.5%
INDUSTRY (Total Employed)	83,782	42,492	41,289
Professional/Public Administration	27.3%	27.6%	27.1%
Manufacturing	21.4%	21.1%	21.7%
Retail	16.9%	17.1%	16.6%
Transportation/Communication	8.5%	7.4%	9.6%
Finance/Insurance/Real Estate	5.0%	5.1%	4.9%
Other Service	7.6%	8.2%	7.0%

Senator Lawrence M. Walsh (D)

District Office: 1100 Plainfield Rd., Joliet 60435
Phone (815) 722-4200; (815) 722-4657 (fax)
Springfield Office: 309G Capitol Bldg., Springfield 62706
Phone (217) 782-8800; (217) 782-3242 (fax)

Legislative Assignments: Committees on Agriculture and Conservation; State Government Operations.

Public Service: Senator (apptd. 1997-present); Jackson Township supervisor (1973-present); former Will County board member.

Personal: Farmer; born March 3, 1948, Joliet; Joliet Junior College, A.A. in agriculture/business; married (Irene); six children; 1 grandchild.

1997 BILL PASSAGE RATIO	Introduced	Passed House of Origin	Passed GA
Primary	0	0	0
Primary/Hyphenated	1	1	1

KEY VOTES

1) Senate GOP Ed. $ Plan . . . . . . .N	6) Insurance/Domestic Violence . .X	11) Pre-Paid College Tuition . . . .Y
2) State Budget . . . . .Y	7) Brownfields . . . . .Y	12) Increase Pull Tab Prizes . . . .Y
3) Tougher DUI Level X	8) Welfare Reform . . . . .Y	13) Telecommunications Tax . . .X
4) Ban Partial Birth Abortions . . .Y	9) Concealed Guns/Misdemeanor .Y	14) Delivery Discrimination X
5) State Employees Pension . . . . .Y	10) Banks Sell Insurance . . . . .Y	15) Sell Drivers' Data X

GROUP RATINGS

	FB	CoC	PrLf	IPPC	ACLU
1997	82	N/R	N/R	0	67

ELECTION RESULTS

1996 General	Tom Dunn (D)	48,059	(100%)
1996 Primary	Tom Dunn (D)	7, 062	(100%)
1996 Primary	Richard E. Carroll (R) (W-I)	161	(100%)

CAMPAIGN RESOURCES AND EXPENDITURES

1996 Campaign Funds				Top 10 PAC Contributors			
Beg. Balance	$N/A	Individuals	$N/A	1) N/A	$N/A	6) N/A	$N/A
Receipts	$N/A	Party	$N/A	2) N/A	$N/A	7) N/A	$N/A
Expenditures	$N/A	PACS	$N/A	3) N/A	$N/A	8) N/A	$N/A
On hand	$N/A	Candidate	$N/A	4) N/A	$N/A	9) N/A	$N/A
		Not-itemized	$N/A	5) N/A	$N/A	10) N/A	$N/A

NOTE: The General Election Opponent's Campaign Resources and Expenditures are reported in a separate section in the back of the book (pp. 269-284).

GENERAL ELECTION DATA

	Registered Voters	Voter Turnout		Straight Party Voting	
1996	107,619	67,318	62.6%	(R) 9,155 . . .13.6%	(D) 16,526 . . .24.5%

PRESIDENT

1996	Bill Clinton (D)	35,756	54.5%
	Bob Dole (R)	23,190	35.3%
	Ross Perot (I)	6,280	9.6%
1992	Bill Clinton (D)	37,323	49.0%
	George Bush (R)	25,296	33.2%
	Ross Perot (I)	13,545	17.8%

UNITED STATES SENATE

1996	Richard J. Durbin (D)	34,910	53.9%
	Al Salvi (R)	27,441	42.4%

GOVERNOR

1994	Jim Edgar (R)	32,416	67.5%
	Dawn Clark Netsch (D)	15,588	32.5%

Representative John "Phil" Novak (D)

District Office: 135 South Schuyler Ave., Kankakee 60901
Phone (815) 939-1983; (815) 939-0081 (fax)
Springfield Office: Room 2064-L Stratton Bldg., Springfield 62706
Phone (217) 782-5981; (217) 782-0945 (fax)

Legislative Assignments: Committees on Environment & Energy (chair); Electric Utility Deregulation (chair); Financial Institutions; Transportation & Motor Vehicles; Veterans' Affairs.

Public Service: Representative (1987-present); former treasurer, Kankakee County; village trustee, Bradley; U.S. Army veteran.

Personal: Full-time legislator; born February 15, 1946, Berwyn; Eastern Illinois University, B.S. in education and M.A. in political science; married (Rebecca); one child.

1997 BILL PASSAGE RATIO	Introduced	Passed House of Origin	Passed GA
Primary	36	12	7
Primary/Hyphenated	69	34	18

KEY VOTES

1) Change Ed. Funding Formula . . Y	6) Insurance/Domestic Violence . . Y	11) Pre-Paid College Tuition . . . . Y
2) State Budget . . . . Y	7) Brownfields . . . . Y	12) Increase Pull Tab Prizes . . . . Y
3) Tougher DUI Level . . . . Y	8) Welfare Reform . . . . Y	13) Utility Deregulation . . . . Y
4) Ban Partial Birth Abortions . . . Y	9) Concealed Guns/Misdemeanor . Y	14) County Obscenity Standards . Y
5) State Employees Pension . . . . . Y	10) Banks Sell Insurance . . . . Y	15) Managed Care Reform . . . . . Y

GROUP RATINGS

	FB	CoC	PrLf	IPPC	ACLU
1997	86	31	5/6	16	30

ELECTION RESULTS

1996 General	John "Phil" Novak (D)	25,633	(100%)
1996 Primary	John "Phil" Novak (D)	2,237	(100%)
1996 Primary	Judith E. Shepherd (R) (W-I)	127	(100%)

CAMPAIGN RESOURCES AND EXPENDITURES

1996 Campaign Funds				Top 10 PAC Contributors			
Beg. Balance	$53,948	Individuals	$2,149	1) DSCC	$15,000	6) IAMB	$1,400
Receipts	$76,687	Party	$15,850	2) ITLA	$2,000	7) ABDI	$1,150
Expenditures	$59,637	PACS	$46,495	3) RPAC	$1,800	8) Teamsters	$1,150
On hand	$70,998	Candidate	$0	4) PIIA	$1,500	9) Argosy	$1,000
		Not-itemized	$12,193	5) ILCable	$1,500	10) ChgoCoC	$1,000

NOTE: The General Election Opponent's Campaign Resources and Expenditures are reported in a separate section in the back of the book (pp. 269-284).

GENERAL ELECTION DATA

	Registered Voters	Voter Turnout		Straight Party Voting	
1996	54,047	35,672	66.0%	(R) 5,970 . . .16.7%	(D) 7,277 . . . .20.4%

PRESIDENT

1996	Bill Clinton (D)	17,525	50.1%
	Bob Dole (R)	13,692	39.2%
	Ross Perot (I)	3,530	10.1%
1992	Bill Clinton (D)	17,953	45.1%
	George Bush (R)	14,621	36.7%
	Ross Perot (I)	7,220	18.2%

UNITED STATES SENATE

1996	Richard J. Durbin (D)	17,193	49.9%
	Al Salvi (R)	15,957	46.4%

GOVERNOR

1994	Jim Edgar (R)	17,867	70.0%
	Dawn Clark Netsch (D)	7,648	30.0%

Representative Jack McGuire (D)

District Office: 560 Ruby St., Joliet 60435
Phone (815) 722-0083; (815) 722-7197 (fax)
Springfield Office: Room 2037-J Stratton Bldg., Springfield 62706
Phone (217) 782-8090

Legislative Assignments: Committees on Aging (chair); Appropriations-Public Safety; Executive; Labor & Commerce; Transportation & Motor Vehicles.

Public Service: Representative (1991-present); supervisor and trustee, Joliet Township.

Personal: Full-time legislator; born May 12, 1933, Joliet; Colorado State College, B.A. in education; married (Marilyn); four children; eight grandchildren.

1997 BILL PASSAGE RATIO	Introduced	Passed House Of Origin	Passed GA
Primary	24	9	3
Primary/Hyphenated	35	12	3

KEY VOTES

1) Change Ed. Funding Formula . . Y	6) Insurance/Domestic Violence . . Y	11) Pre-Paid College Tuition . . . . Y
2) State Budget . . . . Y	7) Brownfields . . . . Y	12) Increase Pull Tab Prizes . . . . Y
3) Tougher DUI Level . . . . Y	8) Welfare Reform . . . . Y	13) Utility Deregulation . . . . Y
4) Ban Partial Birth Abortions . . . Y	9) Concealed Guns/Misdemeanor . N	14) County Obscenity Standards . N
5) State Employees Pension . . . . . Y	10) Banks Sell Insurance . . . . Y	15) Managed Care Reform . . . . . Y

GROUP RATINGS

	FB	CoC	PrLf	IPPC	ACLU
1997	82	23	5/6	16	55

ELECTION RESULTS

1996 General	Jack McGuire (D)	24,073	(100%)
1996 Primary	Jack McGuire (D)	4,876	(100%)
1996 Primary	Louise A. Thompson (R) (W-I)	25	(100%)

CAMPAIGN RESOURCES AND EXPENDITURES

1996 Campaign Funds

Beg. Balance	$6,062	Individuals	$0
Receipts	$8,068	Party	$0
Expenditures	$8,113	PACS	$7,850
On hand	$6,017	Candidate	$0
		Not-itemized	$218

Top 10 PAC Contributors

1) ITLA $1,000	6) RPAC $350
2) ABDI $800	7) AGC $300
3) LICID $500	8) Sears $300
4) HOPE $400	9) IMAPAC $300
5) CPA's $400	10) Ameritech . .$250

NOTE: The General Election Opponent's Campaign Resources and Expenditures are reported in a separate section in the back of the book (pp. 269-284).

GENERAL ELECTION DATA

	Registered Voters	Voter Turnout		Straight Party Voting	
1996	53,572	31,646	59.1%	(R) 3,185 . . .10.1%	(D) 9,249 . . . .29.2%

PRESIDENT

1996	Bill Clinton (D)	18,231	59.4%
	Bob Dole (R)	9,498	31.0%
	Ross Perot (I)	2,750	9.0%
1992	Bill Clinton (D)	19,370	53.3%
	George Bush (R)	10,675	29.4%
	Ross Perot (I)	6,325	17.3%

UNITED STATES SENATE

1996	Richard J. Durbin (D)	17,717	58.3%
	Al Salvi (R)	11,484	37.8%

GOVERNOR

1994	Jim Edgar (R)	14,549	64.7%
	Dawn Clark Netsch (D)	7,940	35.3%

44th Senate District

House District 87
House District 88

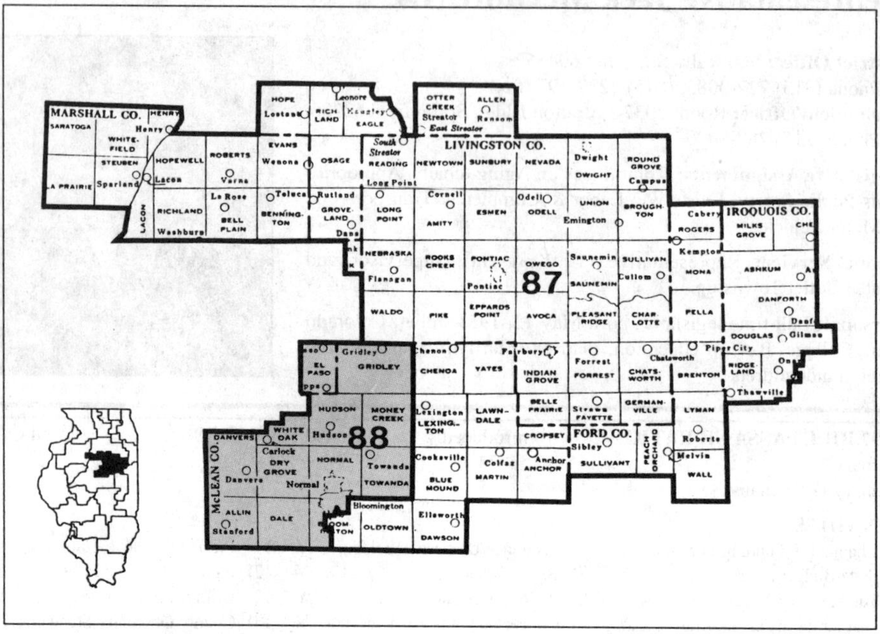

DEMOGRAPHICS (1990)

	S.D. #44	H.D. #87	H.D.#88
VOTING AGE POPULATION	147,717	71,951	75,766
White	93.6%	94.3%	92.9%
Black	3.9%	3.5%	4.4%
Hispanic	1.4%	1.5%	1.3%
Asian	0.9%	0.5%	1.3%
AGE (Total Population)	193,739	96,869	96,870
Under 6	8.0%	8.1%	7.8%
6 to 18	18.0%	18.8%	17.3%
65 and Over	12.9%	16.0%	9.7%
URBAN POPULATION	61.2%	38.6%	83.8%
HOUSING UNITS (Total)	74,066	37,836	36,230
Median Value	$57,609	$49,245	$65,818
Owner Occupied	62.9%	68.6%	57.0%
FAMILY INCOME (Total Families)	47,818	26,148	21,669
Median Income	$36,920	$35,012	$39,559
Below Poverty Level	6.6%	6.7%	6.4%
With Children Under 5	1.1%	1.2%	1.1%
With Children 5 to 17	2.4%	2.2%	2.6%
Headed by Females	3.3%	2.9%	3.8%
INDUSTRY (Total Employed)	95,493	44,250	51,243
Professional/Public Administration	27.8%	24.1%	31.0%
Manufacturing	14.9%	20.1%	10.4%
Retail	18.3%	15.9%	20.3%
Transportation/Communication	6.0%	6.5%	5.6%
Finance/Insurance/Real Estate	12.1%	9.2%	14.7%
Other Service	7.2%	6.1%	8.2%

Senator John W. Maitland, Jr. (R)

District Office: 525 North East St., Bloomington 61701
Phone (309) 828-7733; (309) 828-4907 (fax)
Springfield Office: 627A Capitol Bldg., Springfield 62706
Phone (217) 782-6216; (217) 782-0116 (fax)

Legislative Assignments: Assistant Majority Leader; Committees on Appropriations; Executive; Environment and Energy (vice chair).

Public Service: Senator (1979-present).

Personal: Grain farmer in McLean County; born July 29, 1936, Normal; U.S. Marine Corps veteran; attended Illinois State University; married (Joanne); three children; five grandchildren.

1997 BILL PASSAGE RATIO	Introduced	Passed House of Origin	Passed GA
Primary	16	1	1
Primary/Hyphenated	26	6	3

KEY VOTES

1) Senate GOP Ed. $ Plan . . . . . . .Y	6) Insurance/Domestic Violence . .Y	11) Pre-Paid College Tuition . . . .Y
2) State Budget . . . . .Y	7) Brownfields . . . . .Y	12) Increase Pull Tab Prizes . . . .Y
3) Tougher DUI Level . . . . .N	8) Welfare Reform . . . . .Y	13) Telecommunications Tax . . .N
4) Ban Partial Birth Abortions . . .Y	9) Concealed Guns/Misdemeanor .Y	14) Delivery Discrimination . . . .P
5) State Employees Pension . . . . .Y	10) Banks Sell Insurance . . . . .Y	15) Sell Drivers' Data . . . . .Y

GROUP RATINGS

	FB	CoC	PrLf	IPPC	ACLU
1997	86	100	2/2	0	50

ELECTION RESULTS

1994 General	John W. Maitland, Jr. (R)	46,562	(100%)
1994 Primary	John W. Maitland, Jr. (R)	18,317	(100%)
1992 General	John W. Maitland, Jr. (R)	65,109	(100%)
1992 Primary	John W. Maitland, Jr. (R)	27,316	(100%)

CAMPAIGN RESOURCES AND EXPENDITURES

1996 Campaign Funds				Top 10 PAC Contributors	
Beg. Balance	$40,614	Individuals	$150	1) UPS $5,000	6) MBPlatt . . .$1,000
Receipts	$23,835	Party	$0	2) IHCA $1,500	7) MetroPrim .$1,000
Expenditures	$37,003	PACS	$22,650	3) MPAC $1,100	8) Monsanto . . .$750
On hand	$27,446	Candidate	$240	4) Heritage . . .$1,000	9) NIGAS $750
		Not-itemized	$795	5) GTENorth .$1,000	10) CoC $750

NOTE: The General Election Opponent's Campaign Resources and Expenditures are reported in a separate section in the back of the book (pp. 269-284).

GENERAL ELECTION DATA

	Registered Voters	Voter Turnout		Straight Party Voting	
1996	121,099	80,543	66.5%	(R) 25,031 . . 31.1%	(D) 10,772 . . . 13.4%

PRESIDENT

1996	Bill Clinton (D)	33,050	41.9%
	Bob Dole (R)	38,695	49.1%
	Ross Perot (I)	6,449	8.2%
1992	Bill Clinton (D)	34,110	38.4%
	George Bush (R)	38,975	43.8%
	Ross Perot (I)	15,808	17.8%

UNITED STATES SENATE

1996	Richard J. Durbin (D)	33,010	42.5%
	Al Salvi (R)	42,327	54.5%

GOVERNOR

1994	Jim Edgar (R)	43,930	79.3%
	Dawn Clark Netsch (D)	11,501	20.7%

Representative Dan Rutherford (R)

District Office: 732 West Madison St., Pontiac 61764
Phone (815) 842-3632; (815) 842-2875 (fax)
Springfield Office: Room H-2 Stratton Bldg., Springfield 62706
Phone (217) 782-7776

Legislative Assignments: Committees on Executive (minority spokesperson); Insurance; Financial Institutions; State Government Administration & Election Reform.

Public Service: Representative (1993-present).

Personal: Vice president, Service Master, International Division; born May 26, 1955, Pontiac; Illinois State University, B.A. in business.

1997 BILL PASSAGE RATIO	Introduced	Passed House of Origin	Passed GA
Primary	16	7	6
Primary/Hyphenated	23	11	9

KEY VOTES

1) Change Ed. Funding Formula . .N	6) Insurance/Domestic Violence . .Y	11) Pre-Paid College Tuition . . . .Y
2) State Budget . . . . .Y	7) Brownfields . . . . .Y	12) Increase Pull Tab Prizes . . . .Y
3) Tougher DUI Level . . . . .N	8) Welfare Reform . . . . .Y	13) Utility Deregulation . . . . . . .N
4) Ban Partial Birth Abortions . . .Y	9) Concealed Guns/Misdemeanor .Y	14) County Obscenity Standards .Y
5) State Employees Pension . . . . .Y	10) Banks Sell Insurance . . . . .Y	15) Managed Care Reform . . . . .N

GROUP RATINGS

	FB	CoC	PrLf	IPPC	ACLU
1997	68	92	6/6	0	40

ELECTION RESULTS

1996 General	Dan Rutherford (R)	27,519	(100%)
1996 Primary	Dan Rutherford (R)	13,927	(100%)
1994 General	Dan Rutherford (R)	22,267	(72.0%)
1994 General	Karen Schmidt (D)	8,662	(28.0%)

CAMPAIGN RESOURCES AND EXPENDITURES

1996 Campaign Funds

Beg. Balance	$123,221	Individuals	$6,245
Receipts	$93,043	Party	$0
Expenditures	$118,832	PACS	$44,894
On hand	$97,432	Candidate	$2,150
		Not-itemized	$39,754

Top 10 PAC Contributors

1) MPAC	$1,650	6) CBA	$1,000
2) Empress	$1,000	7) ABDI	$1,000
3) ILCable	$1,000	8) ADS	$1,000
4) RRDonnelly	$1,000	9) Fremont	$1,000
5) CatCEG	$1,000	10) ISMS	$1,000

NOTE: The General Election Opponent's Campaign Resources and Expenditures are reported in a separate section in the back of the book (pp. 269-284).

GENERAL ELECTION DATA

	Registered Voters	Voter Turnout		Straight Party Voting			
1996	57,148	40,236	70.4%	(R) 12,538	31.2%	(D) 5,002	12.4%

PRESIDENT

1996	Bill Clinton (D)	15,647	39.8%
	Bob Dole (R)	19,630	50.0%
	Ross Perot (I)	3,736	9.5%
1992	Bill Clinton (D)	16,629	36.4%
	George Bush (R)	20,501	44.9%
	Ross Perot (I)	8,580	18.7%

UNITED STATES SENATE

1996	Richard J. Durbin (D)	15,218	39.4%
	Al Salvi (R)	22,194	57.4%

GOVERNOR

1994	Jim Edgar (R)	24,837	79.9%
	Dawn Clark Netsch (D)	6,233	20.1%

Representative William E. Brady (R)

District Office: 2203 Eastland Dr., Suite 3, Bloomington 61704
Phone (309) 663-2455; (309) 663-7055 (fax)
Springfield Office: Room 2126-O Stratton Bldg., Springfield 62706
Phone (217) 782-1118

Legislative Assignments: Committees on Insurance (minority spokesperson); Financial Institutions; Environment & Energy; State Government Administration & Election Reform; Banks Selling Insurance.

Public Service: Representative (1993-present).

Personal: Real estate broker; born May 15, 1961, Bloomington; Illinois Wesleyan University, B.S. in political science/economics/business; married (Nancy); three children.

1997 BILL PASSAGE RATIO	Introduced	Passed House of Origin	Passed GA
Primary	13	7	4
Primary/Hyphenated	32	17	12

KEY VOTES

1) Change Ed. Funding Formula . . N	6) Insurance/Domestic Violence . . Y	11) Pre-Paid College Tuition . . . . Y
2) State Budget . . . . Y	7) Brownfields . . . . Y	12) Increase Pull Tab Prizes . . . . Y
3) Tougher DUI Level . . . . Y	8) Welfare Reform . . . . Y	13) Utility Deregulation . . . . Y
4) Ban Partial Birth Abortions . . . Y	9) Concealed Guns/Misdemeanor . Y	14) County Obscenity Standards . Y
5) State Employees Pension . . . . . Y	10) Banks Sell Insurance . . . . Y	15) Managed Care Reform . . . . . N

GROUP RATINGS

	FB	CoC	PrLf	IPPC	ACLU
1997	68	100	6/6	0	30

ELECTION RESULTS

1996 General	Bill Brady (R)	25,499	(100%)
1996 Primary	Bill Brady (R)	14,222	(100%)
1994 General	Bill Brady (R)	20,587	(100%)
1994 Primary	Bill Brady (R)	5,719	(100%)

CAMPAIGN RESOURCES AND EXPENDITURES

1996 Campaign Funds				Top 10 PAC Contributors			
Beg. Balance	$49,627	Individuals	$1,200	1) IPACE	$3,000	6) AULife	$1,000
Receipts	$50,844	Party	$0	2) PIIA	$2,000	7) C&L	$1,000
Expenditures	$35,546	PACS	$37,310	3) RPAC	$1,250	8) ILCable	$1,000
On hand	$64,925	Candidate	$1,269	4) ABDI	$1,000	9) CIEquip	$750
		Not-itemized	$11,065	5) MPAC	$1,000	10) PoliceBPAC	$750

NOTE: The General Election Opponent's Campaign Resources and Expenditures are reported in a separate section in the back of the book (pp. 269-284).

GENERAL ELECTION DATA

	Registered Voters	Voter Turnout		Straight Party Voting	
1996	63,951	40,307	63.0%	(R) 12,493 . . 31.0%	(D) 5,770 . . . . 14.3%

PRESIDENT

1996	Bill Clinton (D)	17,403	43.9%
	Bob Dole (R)	19,065	48.1%
	Ross Perot (I)	2,713	6.8%
1992	Bill Clinton (D)	17,481	40.5%
	George Bush (R)	18,474	45.7%
	Ross Perot (I)	7,228	13.8%

UNITED STATES SENATE

1996	Richard J. Durbin (D)	17,792	45.6%
	Al Salvi (R)	20,133	51.6%

GOVERNOR

1994	Jim Edgar (R)	19,093	78.4%
	Dawn Clark Netsch (D)	5,268	21.6%

45th Senate District

House District 89
House District 90

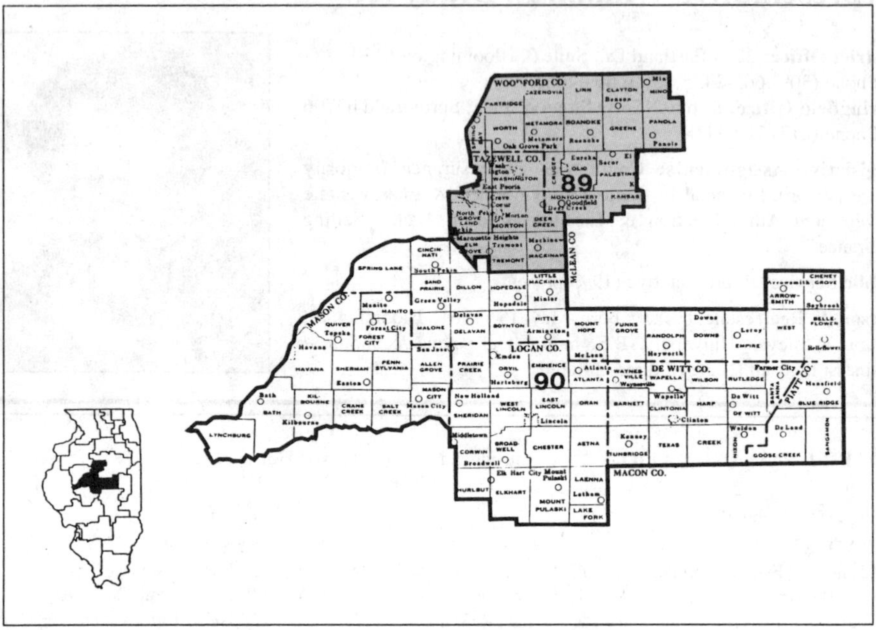

DEMOGRAPHICS (1990)

	S.D. #45	H.D. #89	H.D.#90
VOTING AGE POPULATION	142,303	70,436	71,867
White	98.1%	98.9%	97.3%
Black	0.9%	0.2%	1.7%
Hispanic	0.6%	0.6%	0.6%
Asian	0.3%	0.3%	0.3%
AGE (Total Population)	193,739	96,869	96,870
Under 6	8.3%	8.4%	8.2%
6 to 18	19.7%	20.3%	19.1%
65 and Over	14.0%	12.6%	15.3%
URBAN POPULATION	48.3%	61.9%	34.6%
HOUSING UNITS (Total)	75,952	36,754	39,198
Median Value	$50,741	$56,347	$45,274
Owner Occupied	69.9%	73.3%	66.7%
FAMILY INCOME (Total Families)	54,341	27,419	26,922
Median Income	$36,286	$39,299	$33,106
Below Poverty Level	6.4%	5.1%	7.8%
With Children Under 5	1.0%	0.9%	1.1%
With Children 5 to 17	2.3%	1.7%	2.8%
Headed by Females	2.7%	2.4%	2.9%
INDUSTRY (Total Employed)	90,930	46,872	44,058
Professional/Public Administration	25.9%	24.6%	27.3%
Manufacturing	21.0%	23.6%	18.1%
Retail	16.5%	17.6%	15.3%
Transportation/Communication	7.0%	6.2%	7.7%
Finance/Insurance/Real Estate	6.5%	5.6%	7.5%
Other Service	7.0%	7.7%	6.2%

Senator Robert A. Madigan (R)

District Office: 618 N. Chicago St., Lincoln 62656; 106 S. Main St., P.O. Box 152, Eureka 61530
Phone (217) 732-1323; (217) 735-4319 (fax) (Lincoln); (309) 467-5464 (Eureka)
Springfield Office: 121-B Capitol Bldg., Springfield 62706
Phone (217) 782-6597; (217) 782-9586 (fax).

Legislative Assignments: Committees on Insurance and Pensions (chair); Agriculture & Conservation; Licensed Activities.

Public Service: Senator (1987-present); city clerk, Lincoln.

Personal: Born November 28, 1942, Lincoln; Millikin University, B.S. in education; married (Connie); two children.

1997 BILL PASSAGE RATIO	Introduced	Passed House of Origin	Passed GA
Primary	36	12	7
Primary/Hyphenated	46	14	9

KEY VOTES

1) Senate GOP Ed. $ Plan . . . . Y	6) Insurance/Domestic Violence . . Y	11) Pre-Paid College Tuition . . . . Y
2) State Budget . . . . Y	7) Brownfields . . . . Y	12) Increase Pull Tab Prizes . . . . O
3) Tougher DUI Level . . . . O	8) Welfare Reform . . . . Y	13) Telecommunications Tax . . . O
4) Ban Partial Birth Abortions . . . Y	9) Concealed Guns/Misdemeanor . Y	14) Delivery Discrimination . . . . P
5) State Employees Pension . . . . . Y	10) Banks Sell Insurance . . . . Y	15) Sell Drivers' Data . . . . Y

GROUP RATINGS

	FB	CoC	PrLf	IPPC	ACLU
1997	86	80	2/2	0	50

ELECTION RESULTS

1996 General	Robert A. Madigan (R)	61,993	(100%)
1996 Primary	Robert A. Madigan (R)	24,795	(100%)
1992 General	Robert A. Madigan (R)	68,377	(100%)
1992 Primary	Robert A. Madigan (R)	22,243	(100%)

CAMPAIGN RESOURCES AND EXPENDITURES

1996 Campaign Funds				Top 10 PAC Contributors			
Beg. Balance	$159,132	Individuals	$4,525	1) IPACE	$10,815	6) LIPAC	$2,000
Receipts	$109,410	Party	$1,888	2) ISMS	$3,000	7) ABDI	$2,000
Expenditures	$51,817	PACS	$91,078	3) LUPAC	$3,000	8) IAHMO	$1,500
On hand	$216,725	Candidate	$3,618	4) PIIA	$3,000	9) ILCable	$1,500
		Not-itemized	$8,301	5) RPAC	$2,000	10) LICID	$1,500

NOTE: The General Election Opponent's Campaign Resources and Expenditures are reported in a separate section in the back of the book (pp. 269-284).

GENERAL ELECTION DATA

	Registered Voters	Voter Turnout		Straight Party Voting			
1996	132,298	86,269	65.2%	(R) 20,774	24.1%	(D) 12,123	14.1%

PRESIDENT

1996	Bill Clinton (D)	34,441	40.7%
	Bob Dole (R)	42,260	49.9%
	Ross Perot (I)	7,476	8.8%
1992	Bill Clinton (D)	37,368	39.2%
	George Bush (R)	41,530	43.5%
	Ross Perot (I)	16,529	17.3%

UNITED STATES SENATE

1996	Richard J. Durbin (D)	34,559	41.3%
	Al Salvi (R)	46,497	55.6%

GOVERNOR

1994	Jim Edgar (R)	50,814	77.0%
	Dawn Clark Netsch (D)	15,184	23.0%

Representative Jay Ackerman (R)

District Office: 205 West Jefferson, Morton 61550
Phone (309) 266-9533
Springfield Office: Room 2018-H Stratton Bldg., Springfield 62706
Phone (217) 782-0221

Legislative Assignments: Committees on Public Utilities (minority spokesman); Agriculture & Conservation; Executive; Labor & Commerce.

Public Service: Representative (1979-83; 1987-present); former president, Morton Park Board; Tazewell County Board.

Personal: Born November 23, 1933, Morton; University of Illinois, agricultural program; married (Joann); four children; five grandchildren.

1997 BILL PASSAGE RATIO	Introduced	Passed House of Origin	Passed GA
Primary	4	0	0
Primary/Hyphenated	7	0	0

KEY VOTES

1) Change Ed. Funding Formula . . N	6) Insurance/Domestic Violence . . Y	11) Pre-Paid College Tuition . . . . Y
2) State Budget . . . . Y	7) Brownfields . . . . Y	12) Increase Pull Tab Prizes . . . . Y
3) Tougher DUI Level . . . . Y	8) Welfare Reform . . . . Y	13) Utility Deregulation . . . . P
4) Ban Partial Birth Abortions . . . Y	9) Concealed Guns/Misdemeanor . Y	14) County Obscenity Standards . Y
5) State Employees Pension . . . . . Y	10) Banks Sell Insurance . . . . Y	15) Managed Care Reform . . . . . P

GROUP RATINGS

	FB	CoC	PrLf	IPPC	ACLU
1997	68	75	5/6	0	40

ELECTION RESULTS

1996 General	Jay Ackerman (R)	22,957	(53.4%)
1996 General	Mike Goodman (D)	19,998	(46.6%)
1996 Primary	Jay Ackerman (R)	6,404	(49.5%)
1996 Primary	Two others (R)	6,531	(50.5%)

CAMPAIGN RESOURCES AND EXPENDITURES

1996 Campaign Funds

Beg. Balance	$28,853	Individuals	$1,150
Receipts	$29,852	Party	$750
Expenditures	$47,344	PACS	$18,411
On hand	$11,361	Candidate	$0
		Not-itemized	$9,541

Top 10 PAC Contributors

1) ISMS	$5,023	6) MPAC	$500
2) Activator	$1,638	7) GTE	$500
3) ABDI	$800	8) Ameritech	$500
4) RMadigan	$750	9) RPAC	$500
5) ILCon	$500	10) CILCO	$400

NOTE: The General Election Opponent's Campaign Resources and Expenditures are reported in a separate section in the back of the book (pp. 269-284).

GENERAL ELECTION DATA

	Registered Voters	Voter Turnout		Straight Party Voting	
1996	65,996	45,067	68.3%	(R) 11,730 . . 26.0%	(D) 6,359 . . . . 14.1%

PRESIDENT

1996	Bill Clinton (D)	17,287	39.0%
	Bob Dole (R)	23,139	52.2%
	Ross Perot (I)	3,603	8.1%
1992	Bill Clinton (D)	18,921	38.2%
	George Bush (R)	22,177	44.8%
	Ross Perot (I)	8,273	16.7%

UNITED STATES SENATE

1996	Richard J. Durbin (D)	17,136	39.2%
	Al Salvi (R)	25,154	57.5%

GOVERNOR

1994	Jim Edgar (R)	26,755	77.9%
	Dawn Clark Netsch (D)	7,606	22.1%

Representative John Turner (R)

District Office: 1201 Woodlawn, Lincoln 62656
Phone (217) 732-4011; (217) 732-8791 (fax)
Springfield Office: Room 2011-H Stratton Bldg., Springfield 62706
Phone (217) 782-0428; (217) 782-5257 (fax)

Legislative Assignments: Committees on Local Government (minority spokesperson); Agriculture & Conservation; Judiciary I - Civil Law; Judiciary II - Criminal Law; Registration & Regulation.

Public Service: Representative (1994-present); state's attorney and public defender, Logan County.

Personal: Attorney; born March 23, 1956, Lincoln; University of Illinois, B.A.; DePaul University College of Law, J.D.; married (Kimberly); one child.

1997 BILL PASSAGE RATIO	Introduced	Passed House of Origin	Passed GA
Primary	14	6	1
Primary/Hyphenated	32	21	11

KEY VOTES

1) Change Ed. Funding Formula . . N	6) Insurance/Domestic Violence . . Y	11) Pre-Paid College Tuition . . . . Y
2) State Budget . . . . Y	7) Brownfields . . . . Y	12) Increase Pull Tab Prizes . . . . Y
3) Tougher DUI Level . . . . Y	8) Welfare Reform . . . . Y	13) Utility Deregulation . . . . Y
4) Ban Partial Birth Abortions . . . Y	9) Concealed Guns/Misdemeanor . Y	14) County Obscenity Standards . Y
5) State Employees Pension . . . . . Y	10) Banks Sell Insurance . . . . Y	15) Managed Care Reform . . . . . N

GROUP RATINGS

	FB	CoC	PrLf	IPPC	ACLU
1997	68	92	6/6	0	20

ELECTION RESULTS

1996 General	John Turner (R)	28,787	(100%)
1996 Primary	John Turner (R)	13,094	(100%)
1994 General	John Turner (R)	25,378	(100%)

CAMPAIGN RESOURCES AND EXPENDITURES

1996 Campaign Funds			
Beg. Balance	$43,891	Individuals	$1,200
Receipts	$12,464	Party	$0
Expenditures	$15,188	PACS	$9,750
On hand	$41,167	Candidate	$445
		Not-itemized	$1,069

Top 10 PAC Contributors			
1) CatCEG	$1,000	6) LIPAC	$500
2) IPACE	$500	7) WCLA	$500
3) ITLA	$500	8) Railroad	$500
4) HMLTD	$500	9) LICID	$500
5) Allstate	$500	10) McLFB	$500

NOTE: The General Election Opponent's Campaign Resources and Expenditures are reported in a separate section in the back of the book (pp. 269-284).

GENERAL ELECTION DATA

	Registered Voters	Voter Turnout		Straight Party Voting	
1996	66,302	41,202	62.1%	(R) 9,044 . . . 22.0%	(D) 5,764 . . . . 14.0%

PRESIDENT

1996	Bill Clinton (D)	17,154	42.5%
	Bob Dole (R)	19,121	47.4%
	Ross Perot (I)	3,873	9.6%
1992	Bill Clinton (D)	18,447	40.1%
	George Bush (R)	19,353	42.0%
	Ross Perot (I)	8,256	17.9%

UNITED STATES SENATE

1996	Richard J. Durbin (D)	17,423	43.6%
	Al Salvi (R)	21,343	53.4%

GOVERNOR

1994	Jim Edgar (R)	24,059	76.0%
	Dawn Clark Netsch (D)	7,578	24.0%

46th Senate District

House District 91
House District 92

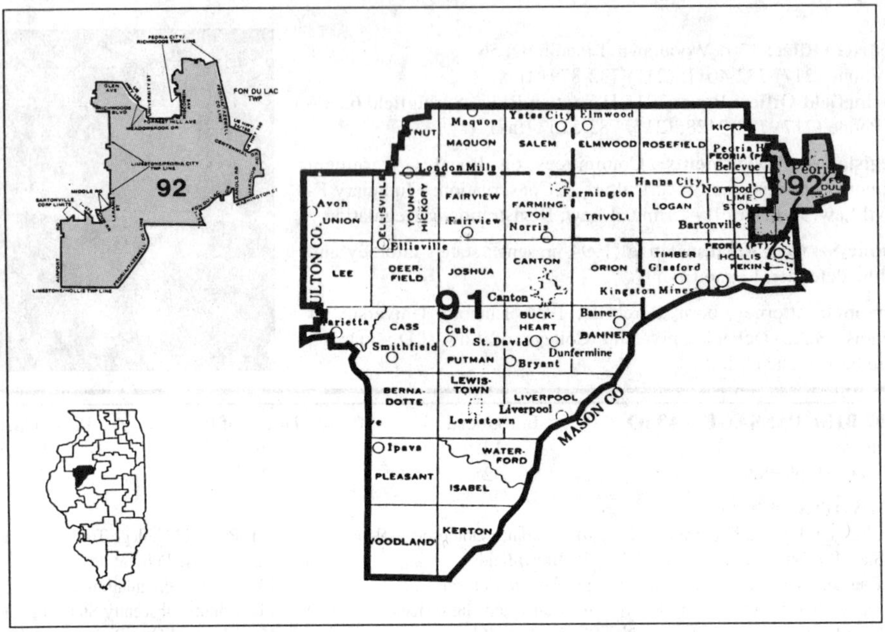

DEMOGRAPHICS (1990)

	S.D. #46	H.D. #91	H.D.#92
VOTING AGE POPULATION	143,234	72,031	71,203
White	88.7%	97.2%	80.0%
Black	9.5%	1.7%	17.3%
Hispanic	1.0%	0.6%	1.4%
Asian	0.7%	0.3%	1.0%
AGE (Total Population)	193,739	96,869	96,870
Under 6	8.5%	7.8%	9.2%
6 to 18	19.2%	19.2%	19.1%
65 and Over	15.5%	15.7%	15.2%
URBAN POPULATION	82.3%	64.7%	100.0%
HOUSING UNITS (Total)	80,935	39,958	40,977
Median Value	$38.848	$39,133	$38,552
Owner Occupied	58.8%	66.1%	51.6%
FAMILY INCOME (Total Families)	50,835	27,059	23,776
Median Income	$29,302	$30,885	$27,307
Below Poverty Level	14.1%	10.7%	17.9%
With Children Under 5	2.7%	2.5%	3.0%
With Children 5 to 17	5.9%	4.0%	8.2%
Headed by Females	8.8%	5.5%	12.4%
INDUSTRY (Total Employed)	79,914	40,804	39,110
Professional/Public Administration	27.7%	25.3%	30.2%
Manufacturing	20.9%	22.1%	19.6%
Retail	19.8%	19.1%	20.5%
Transportation/Communication	6.5%	7.0%	5.9%
Finance/Insurance/Real Estate	5.7%	5.8%	5.7%
Other Service	8.4%	7.2%	9.6%

Senator George P. Shadid (D)

District Office: 410 Court St., Pekin 61554
Phone (309) 353-6276; (309) 353-1819 (fax)
Springfield Office: 309-H Capitol Bldg., Springfield 62706
Phone (217) 782-8250

Legislative Assignments: Committees on Transportation (minority spokesman); Judiciary; Executive Appointments

Public Service: Senator (1993-present); sheriff, Peoria County.

Personal: Full-time legislator; born May 15, 1929, Clinton, IA; married (Lorraine); two children; four grandchildren.

1997 BILL PASSAGE RATIO	Introduced	Passed House of Origin	Passed GA
Primary	10	2	2
Primary/Hyphenated	18	17	5

KEY VOTES

1) Senate GOP Ed. $ Plan . . . . . . .N	6) Insurance/Domestic Violence . .Y	11) Pre-Paid College Tuition . . . .Y
2) State Budget . . . . .N	7) Brownfields . . . . .Y	12) Increase Pull Tab Prizes . . . .Y
3) Tougher DUI Level . . . . .N	8) Welfare Reform . . . . .Y	13) Telecommunications Tax . . .N
4) Ban Partial Birth Abortions . . .Y	9) Concealed Guns/Misdemeanor .P	14) Delivery Discrimination . . . .P
5) State Employees Pension . . . . .Y	10) Banks Sell Insurance . . . . .Y	15) Sell Drivers' Data . . . . .N

GROUP RATINGS

	FB	CoC	PrLf	IPPC	ACLU
1997	73	80	2/2	0	67

ELECTION RESULTS

1996 General	George P. Shadid (D)	56,334	(100%)
1996 Primary	George P. Shadid (D)	14,953	(100%)
1994 General	George P. Shadid (D)	41,279	(100%)
1994 Primary	George P. Shadid (D)	14,936	(100%)

CAMPAIGN RESOURCES AND EXPENDITURES

1996 Campaign Funds				Top 10 PAC Contributors			
Beg. Balance	$57,256	Individuals	$3,380	1) WilliamsBros	$2,500	6) MCIDC	$800
Receipts	$37,778	Party	$0	2) Steam353	$1,450	7) ABDI	$800
Expenditures	$18,140	PACS	$26,350	3) IBA	$1,000	8) CIPS	$700
On hand	$76,894	Candidate	$0	4) IPACE	$1,000	9) AFLCIO	$500
		Not-itemized	$8,048	5) ITLA	$1,000	10) LICID	$500

NOTE: The General Election Opponent's Campaign Resources and Expenditures are reported in a separate section in the back of the book (pp. 269-284).

GENERAL ELECTION DATA

	Registered Voters	Voter Turnout		Straight Party Voting	
1996	116,263	76,830	66.1%	(R) 7,710 . . .10.0%	(D) 20,317 . .26.4%.

PRESIDENT

1996	Bill Clinton (D)	42,737	56.8%
	Bob Dole (R)	25,705	34.1%
	Ross Perot (I)	6,347	8.4%
1992	Bill Clinton (D)	43,785	54.4%
	George Bush (R)	24,436	30.3%
	Ross Perot (I)	12,332	15.3%

UNITED STATES SENATE

1996	Richard J. Durbin (D)	42,428	57.0%
	Al Salvi (R)	29,427	39.5%

GOVERNOR

1994	Jim Edgar (R)	33,179	66.4%
	Dawn Clark Netsch (D)	16,784	33.6%

Representative Michael K. Smith (D)

District Office: 2 N. Main Street, Canton 61520
Phone (309) 647-7479; (309) 647-7482 (fax)
Springfield Office: 2068-L Stratton Bldg., Springfield 62706
Phone (217) 782-8152; (217) 782-1333 (fax)

Legislative Assignments: Committees on Judiciary II - Criminal Law (vice-chair); Agriculture & Conservation; Elementary & Secondary Education; Local Government; Environment & Energy; Pension Laws Commission.

Public Service: Representative (1995-present).

Personal: Full-time legislator; born May 23, 1966, Canton; Bradley University, B.A. in political science; married (Donna).

1997 BILL PASSAGE RATIO	Introduced	Passed House of Origin	Passed GA
Primary	16	7	3
Primary/Hyphenated	39	22	8

KEY VOTES

1) Change Ed. Funding Formula . . Y
2) State Budget . . . . Y
3) Tougher DUI Level . . . . Y
4) Ban Partial Birth Abortions . . . Y
5) State Employees Pension . . . . . Y
6) Insurance/Domestic Violence . . Y
7) Brownfields . . . . Y
8) Welfare Reform . . . . Y
9) Concealed Guns/Misdemeanor . Y
10) Banks Sell Insurance . . . . Y
11) Pre-Paid College Tuition . . . . Y
12) Increase Pull Tab Prizes . . . . Y
13) Utility Deregulation . . . . Y
14) County Obscenity Standards . N
15) Managed Care Reform . . . . . Y

GROUP RATINGS

	FB	CoC	PrLf	IPPC	ACLU
1997	93	15	3/6	50	70

ELECTION RESULTS

1996 General	Michael K. Smith (D)	24,236	(65.2%)
1996 General	Phil Philipps (R)	12,950	(34.8%)
1996 Primary	Michael K. Smith (D)	8,639	(100%)
1996 Primary	Phil Philipps (R)	5,475	(100%)

CAMPAIGN RESOURCES AND EXPENDITURES

1996 Campaign Funds

Beg. Balance	$13,591	Individuals	$600
Receipts	$53,963	Party	$5,500
Expenditures	$45,133	PACS	$37,829
On hand	$22,421	Candidate	$0
		Not-itemized	$10,034

Top 10 PAC Contributors

1) IPACE	$16,000	6) Activator	$1,679
2) DSCC	$5,000	7) IBEW	$1,000
3) Steam	$2,000	8) IMPAC	$750
4) MCIDC	$2,000	9) Laborers	$750
5) ITLA	$2,000	10) IBEWEd	$700

NOTE: The General Election Opponent's Campaign Resources and Expenditures are reported in a separate section in the back of the book (pp. 269-284).

GENERAL ELECTION DATA

	Registered Voters	Voter Turnout		Straight Party Voting	
1996	64,260	42,163	65.6%	(R) 4,273 . . . 10.1%	(D) 9,961 . . . 23.6%

PRESIDENT

1996	Bill Clinton (D)	22,488	54.4%
	Bob Dole (R)	14,483	35.0%
	Ross Perot (I)	4,153	10.0%
1992	Bill Clinton (D)	23,105	53.0%
	George Bush (R)	13,234	30.4%
	Ross Perot (I)	7,245	16.6%

UNITED STATES SENATE

1996	Richard J. Durbin (D)	22,346	54.8%
	Al Salvi (R)	16,932	41.5%

GOVERNOR

1994	Jim Edgar (R)	19,436	68.4%
	Dawn Clark Netsch (D)	8,972	31.6%

Representative Ricca C. Slone (D)

District Office: 456 Fulton St., Suite 150, Peoria 61602
Phone (309) 673-0921; (309) 673-0923 (fax)
Springfield Office: Room 2072-L Stratton Bldg., Springfield 62706
Phone (217) 782-3186

Legislative Assignments: Committees on Health Care Availabilty & Access; Environment & Energy; Appropriations-Education; Labor & Commerce.

Public Service: Representative (1997-present); Peoria City-County Landfill Committee.

Personal: Attorney; born February 19, 1947; Washington University, B.A.; University of California-Los Angeles, M.A. in anthropology; Ohio State University, M.A. in public administration; University of Illinois, J.D.; married (Dr. William Berkman); three sons.

1997 BILL PASSAGE RATIO	Introduced	Passed House of Origin	Passed GA
Primary	11	2	1
Primary/Hyphenated	27	10	6

KEY VOTES

1) Change Ed. Funding Formula . . Y	6) Insurance/Domestic Violence . . Y	11) Pre-Paid College Tuition . . . . Y
2) State Budget . . . . Y	7) Brownfields . . . . Y	12) Increase Pull Tab Prizes . . . . N
3) Tougher DUI Level . . . . Y	8) Welfare Reform . . . . Y	13) Utility Deregulation . . . . P
4) Ban Partial Birth Abortions . . . N	9) Concealed Guns/Misdemeanor . N	14) County Obscenity Standards . N
5) State Employees Pension . . . . . Y	10) Banks Sell Insurance . . . . Y	15) Managed Care Reform . . . . . Y

GROUP RATINGS

	FB	CoC	PrLf	IPPC	ACLU
1997	86	23	0/6	100	100

ELECTION RESULTS

1996 General	Ricca C. Slone (D)	22,395	(70.2%)
1996 General	Walter "Wally" Hellstrom, Jr. (R)	9,493	(29.8%)
1996 Primary	Ricca C. Slone (D)	3,790	(53.5%)
1996 Primary	Donald L. Saltsman (D)	3,296	(46.5%)

CAMPAIGN RESOURCES AND EXPENDITURES

1996 Campaign Funds				Top 10 PAC Contributors			
Beg. Balance	$18,797	Individuals	$2,055	1) IHDM	$17,618	6) WVWV	$2,000
Receipts	$58,894	Party	$23,893	2) DSCC	$5,000	7) AFSCME	$1,777
Expenditures	$71,556	PACS	$27,477	3) MCIDC	$5,000	8) UAW	$1,500
On hand	$6,135	Candidate	$1,000	4) ISMS	$3,000	9) LAWPAC	$1,500
		Not-itemized	$4,469	5) ITLA	$3,000	10) AFLCIO	$1,500

NOTE: The General Election Opponent's Campaign Resources and Expenditures are reported in a separate section in the back of the book (pp. 269-284).

GENERAL ELECTION DATA

	Registered Voters	Voter Turnout		Straight Party Voting	
1996	52,003	34,667	66.7%	(R) 3,437 . . . 9.9%	(D) 10,356 . . . 29.9%

PRESIDENT

1996	Bill Clinton (D)	20,249	59.6%
	Bob Dole (R)	11,222	33.1%
	Ross Perot (I)	2,194	6.5%
1992	Bill Clinton (D)	20,680	55.9%
	George Bush (R)	11,202	30.3%
	Ross Perot (I)	5,087	13.8%

UNITED STATES SENATE

1996	Richard J. Durbin (D)	20,082	59.7%
	Al Salvi (R)	12,495	37.1%

GOVERNOR

1994	Jim Edgar (R)	13,743	63.8%
	Dawn Clark Netsch (D)	7,812	36.2%

47th Senate District

House District 93
House District 94

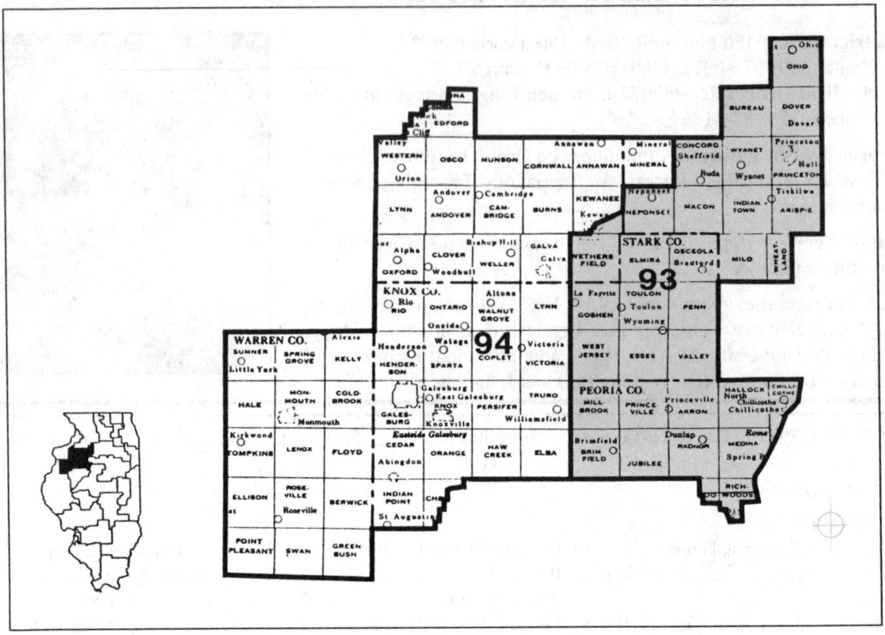

DEMOGRAPHICS (1990)

	S.D. #47	H.D. #93	H.D.#94
VOTING AGE POPULATION	145,364	72,680	72,684
White	94.9%	95.5%	94.3%
Black	3.0%	2.4%	3.5%
Hispanic	1.3%	0.9%	1.7%
Asian	0.8%	1.1%	0.4%
AGE (Total Population)	193,739	96,870	96,869
Under 6	7.7%	7.7%	7.7%
6 to 18	18.6%	18.5%	18.7%
65 and Over	16.5%	15.8%	17.1%
URBAN POPULATION	63.6%	68.3%	58.9%
HOUSING UNITS (Total)	81,115	40,414	40,701
Median Value	$45,301	$58,395	$35,982
Owner Occupied	66.1%	67.4%	64.9%
FAMILY INCOME (Total Families)	53,855	27,395	26,460
Median Income	$34,211	$39,506	$29,672
Below Poverty Level	7.7%	5.8%	9.7%
With Children Under 5	1.2%	0.9%	1.6%
With Children 5 to 17	2.9%	1.9%	3.8%
Headed by Females	3.4%	2.5%	4.4%
INDUSTRY (Total Employed)	90,426	46,966	43,460
Professional/Public Administration	28.0%	28.8%	27.2%
Manufacturing	21.1%	23.1%	18.9%
Retail	17.0%	16.4%	17.7%
Transportation/Communication	7.0%	5.4%	8.7%
Finance/Insurance/Real Estate	5.5%	6.9%	4.0%
Other Service	7.1%	7.1%	7.0%

Senator Carl E. Hawkinson (R)

District Office: 4 Weinberg Arcade, Galesburg 61401
Phone (309) 343-8176; (309) 343-2683 (fax)
Springfield Office: 623 Capitol Bldg., Springfield 62706
Phone (217) 782-1942; (217) 782-0116 (fax)

Legislative Assignments: Committees on Judiciary (chair); Agriculture and Conservation; Transportation.

Public Service: Senator (1987-present); representative (1983-87); state's attorney, Knox County.

Personal: Attorney; born October 7, 1947, Galesburg; North Park College, B.A. and Harvard Law School, J.D.; married (Karen), three children.

1997 BILL PASSAGE RATIO	Introduced	Passed House of Origin	Passed GA
Primary	19	16	11
Primary/Hyphenated	33	25	20

KEY VOTES

1) Senate GOP Ed. $ Plan ....O	6) Insurance/Domestic Violence ..Y	11) Pre-Paid College Tuition ....Y
2) State Budget ....N	7) Brownfields ....Y	12) Increase Pull Tab Prizes ....N
3) Tougher DUI Level ....N	8) Welfare Reform ....Y	13) Telecommunications Tax ...N
4) Ban Partial Birth Abortions ...Y	9) Concealed Guns/Misdemeanor .Y	14) Delivery Discrimination ....P
5) State Employees Pension .....Y	10) Banks Sell Insurance ....Y	15) Sell Drivers' Data ....N

GROUP RATINGS

	FB	CoC	PrLf	IPPC	ACLU
1997	91	100	2/2	0	67

ELECTION RESULTS

1994 General	Carl E. Hawkinson (R)	53,632	(100%)
1994 Primary	Carl E. Hawkinson (R)	22,271	(100%)
1992 General	Carl E. Hawkinson (R)	57,223	(63.8%)
1992 General	Fred Kirkpatrick (D)	32,423	(36.2%)

CAMPAIGN RESOURCES AND EXPENDITURES

1996 Campaign Funds

Beg. Balance	$127,422	Individuals	$1,017
Receipts	$39,515	Party	$0
Expenditures	$13,933	PACS	$16,900
On hand	$153,004	Candidate	$2,655
		Not-itemized	$18,943

Top 10 PAC Contributors

1) IPACE $5,000	6) BNRR $500
2) IBA $1,000	7) CentTel $500
3) ISMS $1,000	8) HOPE $500
4) LAWPAC ...$500	9) PetPec $500
5) Ameritech ...$500	10) MPAC $500

NOTE: The General Election Opponent's Campaign Resources and Expenditures are reported in a separate section in the back of the book (pp. 269-284).

GENERAL ELECTION DATA

	Registered Voters	Voter Turnout		Straight Party Voting			
1996	122,668	86,490	70.5%	(R) 14,270	16.5%	(D) 12,314	14.2%

PRESIDENT

1996	Bill Clinton (D)	39,694	46.8%
	Bob Dole (R)	37,152	43.8%
	Ross Perot (I)	7,367	8.7%
1992	Bill Clinton (D)	39,443	42.0%
	George Bush (R)	38,416	40.9%
	Ross Perot (I)	15,987	17.1%

UNITED STATES SENATE

1996	Richard J. Durbin (D)	39,467	47.3%
	Al Salvi (R)	41,368	49.6%

GOVERNOR

1994	Jim Edgar (R)	49,036	77.1%
	Dawn Clark Netsch (D)	14,584	22.9%

Representative David R. Leitch (R)

District Office: 3114 North University, Peoria 61604
Phone (309) 685-3900; (309) 685-3936 (fax)
Springfield Office: Room 220 Capitol Bldg., Springfield 62706
Phone (217) 782-8108; (217) 782-5309 (fax)

Legislative Assignments: Assistant Republican Leader; ex officio member of all committees. Committees on Appropriations-Human Services; Public Utilities; Electric Utility Deregulation; Pension Laws Commission.

Public Service: Representative (1989-present); senator (1986-87).

Personal: Bank vice president; born August 22, 1948, Three Rivers, Michigan; Kalamazoo College, B.A. in history; married (Marlene); three children.

1997 BILL PASSAGE RATIO	Introduced	Passed House of Origin	Passed GA
Primary	24	12	8
Primary/Hyphenated	40	20	14

KEY VOTES

1) Change Ed. Funding Formula . . N	6) Insurance/Domestic Violence . . Y	11) Pre-Paid College Tuition . . . . Y
2) State Budget . . . . Y	7) Brownfields . . . . Y	12) Increase Pull Tab Prizes . . . . N
3) Tougher DUI Level . . . . Y	8) Welfare Reform . . . . Y	13) Utility Deregulation . . . . N
4) Ban Partial Birth Abortions . . . Y	9) Concealed Guns/Misdemeanor . Y	14) County Obscenity Standards . N
5) State Employees Pension . . . . . Y	10) Banks Sell Insurance . . . . Y	15) Managed Care Reform . . . . . N

GROUP RATINGS

	FB	CoC	PrLf	IPPC	ACLU
1997	68	85	5/6	0	33

ELECTION RESULTS

1996 General	David R. Leitch (R)	34,652	(100%)
1996 Primary	David R. Leitch (R)	11,607	(100%)
1994 General	David R. Leitch (R)	29,558	(100%)
1994 Primary	David R. Leitch (R)	12,088	(100%)

CAMPAIGN RESOURCES AND EXPENDITURES

1996 Campaign Funds

Beg. Balance	$100,509	Individuals	$7,250
Receipts	$53,383	Party	$6,208
Expenditures	$65,534	PACS	$29,700
On hand	$88,358	Candidate	$0
		Not-itemized	$10,225

Top 10 PAC Contributors

1) FLAD	$5,000	6) PCPLTD	$1,000
2) IPACE	$3,000	7) ABDI	$1,000
3) AVentures	$2,500	8) SEIU	$800
4) IBA	$1,500	9) IHCA	$750
5) HRCC	$1,208	10) HOPE	$750

NOTE: The General Election Opponent's Campaign Resources and Expenditures are reported in a separate section in the back of the book (pp. 269-284).

GENERAL ELECTION DATA

	Registered Voters	Voter Turnout		Straight Party Voting	
1996	63,712	46,950	73.7%	(R) 7,843 . . . 16.7%	(D) 5,928 . . . . 12.6%

PRESIDENT

1996	Bill Clinton (D)	19,208	41.6%
	Bob Dole (R)	23,103	50.0%
	Ross Perot (I)	3,590	7.7%
1992	Bill Clinton (D)	18,828	37.4%
	George Bush (R)	23,114	46.0%
	Ross Perot (I)	8,353	16.6%

UNITED STATES SENATE

1996	Richard J. Durbin (D)	19,595	42.9%
	Al Salvi (R)	24,733	54.2%

GOVERNOR

1994	Jim Edgar (R)	27,082	77.9%
	Dawn Clark Netsch (D)	7,678	22.1%

Representative Donald L. Moffitt (R)

District Office: 5 Weinberg Arcade, Galesburg 61401
Phone (309) 343-8000; (309) 343-2683 (fax)
Springfield Office: Room 2025-H Stratton Bldg., Springfield 62706
Phone (217) 782-8032; (217) 782-0179 (fax)

Legislative Assignments: Committees on Consumer Protection (minority spokesperson); Appropriations-Public Safety; Local Government; Transportation & Motor Vehicles.

Public Service: Representative (1993-present); former treasurer and board member, Knox County; city council, Knoxville; mayor, Oneida.

Personal: Full-time legislator; born February 18, 1947, Galesburg; University of Illinois, B.S. in agricultural education and economics; married (Carolyn); three children.

1997 BILL PASSAGE RATIO	Introduced	Passed House of Origin	Passed GA
Primary	10	7	5
Primary/Hyphenated	23	17	11

KEY VOTES

1) Change Ed. Funding Formula . . Y	6) Insurance/Domestic Violence . . Y	11) Pre-Paid College Tuition . . . . Y
2) State Budget . . . . Y	7) Brownfields . . . . Y	12) Increase Pull Tab Prizes . . . . Y
3) Tougher DUI Level . . . . Y	8) Welfare Reform . . . . Y	13) Utility Deregulation . . . . Y
4) Ban Partial Birth Abortions . . . Y	9) Concealed Guns/Misdemeanor . Y	14) County Obscenity Standards . Y
5) State Employees Pension . . . . . Y	10) Banks Sell Insurance . . . . Y	15) Managed Care Reform . . . . . N

GROUP RATINGS

	FB	CoC	PrLf	IPPC	ACLU
1997	86	69	6/6	0	22

ELECTION RESULTS

1996 General	Donald L. Moffitt (R)	22,255	(60.7%)
1996 General	Caroline Porter (D)	14,413	(39.3%)
1996 Primary	Donald L. Moffitt (R)	8,165	(100%)

CAMPAIGN RESOURCES AND EXPENDITURES

1996 Campaign Funds				Top 10 PAC Contributors			
Beg. Balance	$30,109	Individuals	$1,573	1) IPACE	$7,750	6) WCLA	$500
Receipts	$29,540	Party	$200	2) CatCEG	$1,000	7) RPAC	$500
Expenditures	$43,287	PACS	$16,925	3) ADM	$600	8) AFFI	$500
On hand	$16,362	Candidate	$0	4) ILCon	$500	9) AFSCME	$500
		Not-itemized	$10,842	5) LICID	$500	10) CPA's	$400

NOTE: The General Election Opponent's Campaign Resources and Expenditures are reported in a separate section in the back of the book (pp. 269-284).

GENERAL ELECTION DATA

	Registered Voters	Voter Turnout		Straight Party Voting	
1996	58,956	39,540	67.1%	(R) 6,427 . . . 16.3%	(D) 6,386 . . . 16.2%

PRESIDENT

1996	Bill Clinton (D)	20,486	53.2%
	Bob Dole (R)	14,049	36.5%
	Ross Perot (I)	3,777	9.8%
1992	Bill Clinton (D)	20,615	47.3%
	George Bush (R)	15,302	35.1%
	Ross Perot (I)	7,634	17.6%

UNITED STATES SENATE

1996	Richard J. Durbin (D)	19,872	52.5%
	Al Salvi (R)	16,635	44.0%

GOVERNOR

1994	Jim Edgar (R)	21,954	76.1%
	Dawn Clark Netsch (D)	6,906	23.9%

48th Senate District

House District 95
House District 96

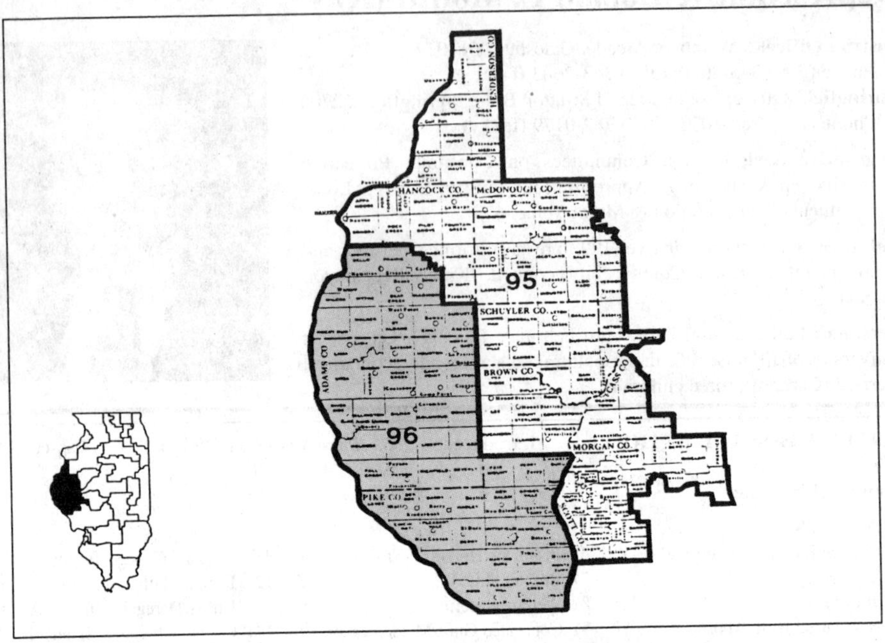

DEMOGRAPHICS (1990)

	S.D. #48	H.D. #95	H.D.#96
VOTING AGE POPULATION	146,926	74,868	72,058
White	96.3%	94.8%	97.8%
Black	2.4%	3.3%	1.5%
Hispanic	0.6%	0.8%	0.3%
Asian	0.6%	1.0%	0.3%
AGE (Total Population)	193,739	96,870	96,869
Under 6	7.7%	7.0%	8.3%
6 to 18	18.4%	18.2%	18.7%
65 and Over	17.0%	15.7%	18.3%
URBAN POPULATION	45.6%	39.8%	51.5%
HOUSING UNITS (Total)	82,062	40,058	42,004
Median Value	$37.088	$33,497	$40,224
Owner Occupied	63.4%	61.9%	64.9%
FAMILY INCOME (Total Families)	50,840	24,225	26,615
Median Income	$27,871	$27,468	$28,215
Below Poverty Level	10.8%	11.0%	10.7%
With Children Under 5	1.6%	1.5%	1.7%
With Children 5 to 17	3.8%	3.7%	4.0%
Headed by Females	4.1%	4.0%	4.2%
INDUSTRY (Total Employed)	86,430	42,643	43,787
Professional/Public Administration	29.8%	31.6%	28.1%
Manufacturing	17.9%	16.7%	18.9%
Retail	17.1%	16.3%	17.9%
Transportation/Communication	6.0%	5.8%	6.2%
Finance/Insurance/Real Estate	4.1%	3.9%	4.3%
Other Service	6.8%	6.4%	7.1%

Senator Laura Kent Donahue (R)

District Office: 640 Maine St., Quincy 62301
Phone (217) 224-0644; (217) 223-1565 (fax)
Springfield Office: 323 Capitol Bldg., Springfield 62706
Phone (217) 782-2479

Legislative Assignments: Assistant Majority Leader. Committees on Appropriations (vice-chair); Environment & Energy; Public Health and Welfare; State Government Operations.

Public Service: Senator (1981-present).

Personal: Full-time legislator; born April 22, 1949, Quincy; Stephens College, B.A.

1997 BILL PASSAGE RATIO	Introduced	Passed House of Origin	Passed GA
Primary	16	5	4
Primary/Hyphenated	26	10	9

KEY VOTES

1) Senate GOP Ed. $ Plan . . . . . . .Y
2) State Budget . . . . .Y
3) Tougher DUI Level . . . . .N
4) Ban Partial Birth Abortions . . .Y
5) State Employees Pension . . . . .Y
6) Insurance/Domestic Violence . .Y
7) Brownfields . . . . .Y
8) Welfare Reform . . . . .Y
9) Concealed Guns/Misdemeanor .Y
10) Banks Sell Insurance . . . . .Y
11) Pre-Paid College Tuition . . . .Y
12) Increase Pull Tab Prizes . . . .N
13) Telecommunications Tax . . .N
14) Delivery Discrimination . . . .P
15) Sell Drivers' Data . . . . .N

GROUP RATINGS

	FB	CoC	PrLf	IPPC	ACLU
1997	91	100	2/2	0	50

ELECTION RESULTS

1996 General	Laura Kent Donahue (R)	60,015	(100%)
1996 Primary	Laura Kent Donahue (R)	17,912	(100%)
1992 General	Laura Kent Donahue (R)	56,878	(65.1%)
1992 General	Verne Hagstrom (D)	30,469	(34.9%)

CAMPAIGN RESOURCES AND EXPENDITURES

1996 Campaign Funds				Top 10 PAC Contributors			
Beg. Balance	$86,569	Individuals	$7,078	1) UPS	$2,500	6) ISMS	$1,000
Receipts	$60,603	Party	$1,475	2) Ameritech	$1,200	7) PIIA	$1,000
Expenditures	$86,470	PACS	$37,486	3) HOPE	$1,100	8) MPAC	$1,000
On hand	$60,702	Candidate	$1,328	4) Knapheide	$1,000	9) CIPS	$700
		Not-itemized	$13,236	5) ILCable	$1,000	10) GDC	$700

NOTE: The General Election Opponent's Campaign Resources and Expenditures are reported in a separate section in the back of the book (pp. 269-284).

GENERAL ELECTION DATA

	Registered Voters	Voter Turnout		Straight Party Voting	
1996	124,772	81,580	65.4%	(R) 11,700 . .14.3%	(D) 9,092 . . . .11.1%

PRESIDENT

1996	Bill Clinton (D)	34,849	43.9%
	Bob Dole (R)	34,771	43.8%
	Ross Perot (I)	9,084	11.5%
1992	Bill Clinton (D)	36,659	41.4%
	George Bush (R)	34,577	39.1%
	Ross Perot (I)	17,302	19.5%

UNITED STATES SENATE

1996	Richard J. Durbin (D)	39,681	50.7%
	Al Salvi (R)	36,599	46.8%

GOVERNOR

1994	Jim Edgar (R)	46,057	76.1%
	Dawn Clark Netsch (D)	14,498	23.9%

Representative Richard P. Myers (R)

District Office: 331 North Lafayette, Macomb 61455
Phone (309) 836-2707; (309) 836-2231 (fax)
Springfield Office: Room 2109-N Stratton Bldg., Springfield 62706
Phone (217) 782-0416

Legislative Assignments: Committees on Agriculture & Conservation; Higher Education; Appropriations-Education; Transportation & Motor Vehicles.

Public Service: Representative (1995-present); former board member, Illinois Farm Bureau.

Personal: Farmer; born December 27, 1947, Colchester; Western Illinois University, B.S. in agriculture; married (Christine); one child.

1997 BILL PASSAGE RATIO	Introduced	Passed House of Origin	Passed GA
Primary	9	3	1
Primary/Hyphenated	15	9	6

KEY VOTES

1) Change Ed. Funding Formula . .N	6) Insurance/Domestic Violence . .Y	11) Pre-Paid College Tuition . . . .Y
2) State Budget . . . . .Y	7) Brownfields . . . . .Y	12) Increase Pull Tab Prizes . . . .Y
3) Tougher DUI Level . . . . .Y	8) Welfare Reform . . . . .Y	13) Utility Deregulation . . . . . . .Y
4) Ban Partial Birth Abortions . . .Y	9) Concealed Guns/Misdemeanor .Y	14) County Obscenity Standards .Y
5) State Employees Pension . . . . .Y	10) Banks Sell Insurance . . . . .Y	15) Managed Care Reform . . . . .N

GROUP RATINGS

	FB	CoC	PrLf	IPPC	ACLU
1997	68	69	6/6	0	30

ELECTION RESULTS

1996 General	Richard P. Myers (R)	18,539	(51.0%)
1996 General	Tab Turke (D)	17,820	(49.0%)
1996 Primary	Richard P. Myers (R)	8,724	(100%)
1996 Primary	Tab Turke (D)	3,355	(100%)

CAMPAIGN RESOURCES AND EXPENDITURES

1996 Campaign Funds

Beg. Balance	$15,668	Individuals	$7,087
Receipts	$391,840	Party	$301, 796
Expenditures	$405,938	PACS	$58,672
On hand	$1,570	Candidate	$0
		Not-itemized	$24,285

Top 10 PAC Contributors

1) HRCC . .$206,922	6) JACPAC . . .$5,000
2) FLAD . . .$59,439	7) CChurchill .$5,000
3) CRyan . . .$10,000	8) MPAC $3,000
4) ISMS $10,000	9) Activator . .$2,429
5) CRyder $9,500	10) CDonahue $2,250

NOTE: The General Election Opponent's Campaign Resources and Expenditures are reported in a separate section in the back of the book (pp. 269-284).

GENERAL ELECTION DATA

	Registered Voters	Voter Turnout	Straight Party Voting (R)	Straight Party Voting (D)
1996	59,209	38,364 . . . .64.8%	6,056 . . .15.8%	4,876 . . . .12.7%

PRESIDENT

1996	Bill Clinton (D)	17,456	46.8%
	Bob Dole (R)	15,198	40.8%
	Ross Perot (I)	4,311	11.6%
1992	Bill Clinton (D)	18,288	43.7%
	George Bush (R)	15,349	36.7%
	Ross Perot (I)	8,205	19.6%

UNITED STATES SENATE

1996	Richard J. Durbin (D)	18,438	50.4%
	Al Salvi (R)	17,084	46.7%

GOVERNOR

1994	Jim Edgar (R)	22,261	72.7%
	Dawn Clark Netsch (D)	8,375	27.3%

Representative Arthur "Art" Tenhouse (R)

District Office: 640 Maine, P.O. Box 1161, Quincy 62301
Phone (217) 223-0833; (217) 223-1565 (fax)
Springfield Office: Room O-2 Stratton Bldg., Springfield 62706
Phone (217) 782-8096; (217) 782-1275 (fax)

Legislative Assignments: Republican Conference Chairperson; committees on Health Care Availability & Access; Veterans' Affairs.

Public Service: Representative (1989-present).

Personal: Full-time legislator; born December 27, 1950, Quincy; University of Illinois, B.S. in agriculture science/economics; M.B.A. in finance accounting; married (Sharon); three children.

1997 BILL PASSAGE RATIO	Introduced	Passed House of Origin	Passed GA
Primary	9	5	5
Primary/Hyphenated	20	13	9

KEY VOTES

1) Change Ed. Funding Formula . . N	6) Insurance/Domestic Violence . . Y	11) Pre-Paid College Tuition . . . . Y
2) State Budget . . . . Y	7) Brownfields . . . . Y	12) Increase Pull Tab Prizes . . . . Y
3) Tougher DUI Level . . . . N	8) Welfare Reform . . . . Y	13) Utility Deregulation . . . . P
4) Ban Partial Birth Abortions . . . Y	9) Concealed Guns/Misdemeanor . Y	14) County Obscenity Standards . Y
5) State Employees Pension . . . . . Y	10) Banks Sell Insurance . . . . Y	15) Managed Care Reform . . . . . N

GROUP RATINGS

	FB	CoC	PrLf	IPPC	ACLU
1997	57	85	6/6	0	30

ELECTION RESULTS

1996 General	Art Tenhouse (R)	30,935	(75.8%)
1996 General	Paul Lange (D)	9,874	(24.2%)
1996 Primary	Art Tenhouse (R)	8,896	(100%)
1996 Primary	Paul Lange (D)	3,824	(100%)

CAMPAIGN RESOURCES AND EXPENDITURES

1996 Campaign Funds			
Beg. Balance	$39,539	Individuals	$1,000
Receipts	$42,006	Party	$500
Expenditures	$72,622	PACS	$31,650
On hand	$8,923	Candidate	$0
		Not-itemized	$8,856

Top 10 PAC Contributors			
1) IPACE	$10,000	6) CPA's	$1,000
2) MPAC	$2,000	7) PIIA	$1,000
3) ABDI	$1,000	8) Fremont	$500
4) IHCA	$1,000	9) IMPAC	$500
5) CatCEG	$1,000	10) Ameritech	$500

NOTE: The General Election Opponent's Campaign Resources and Expenditures are reported in a separate section in the back of the book (pp. 269-284).

GENERAL ELECTION DATA

	Registered Voters	Voter Turnout		Straight Party Voting			
1996	65,563	43,216	65.9%	(R) 5,644	13.1%	(D) 4,216	9.8%

PRESIDENT

1996	Bill Clinton (D)	17,393	41.4%
	Bob Dole (R)	19,573	46.6%
	Ross Perot (I)	4,773	11.3%
1992	Bill Clinton (D)	18,371	39.3%
	George Bush (R)	19,228	41.2%
	Ross Perot (I)	9,097	19.5%

UNITED STATES SENATE

1996	Richard J. Durbin (D)	21,243	51.0%
	Al Salvi (R)	19,515	46.8%

GOVERNOR

1994	Jim Edgar (R)	23,796	79.5%
	Dawn Clark Netsch (D)	6,123	20.5%

49th Senate District

House District 97
House District 98

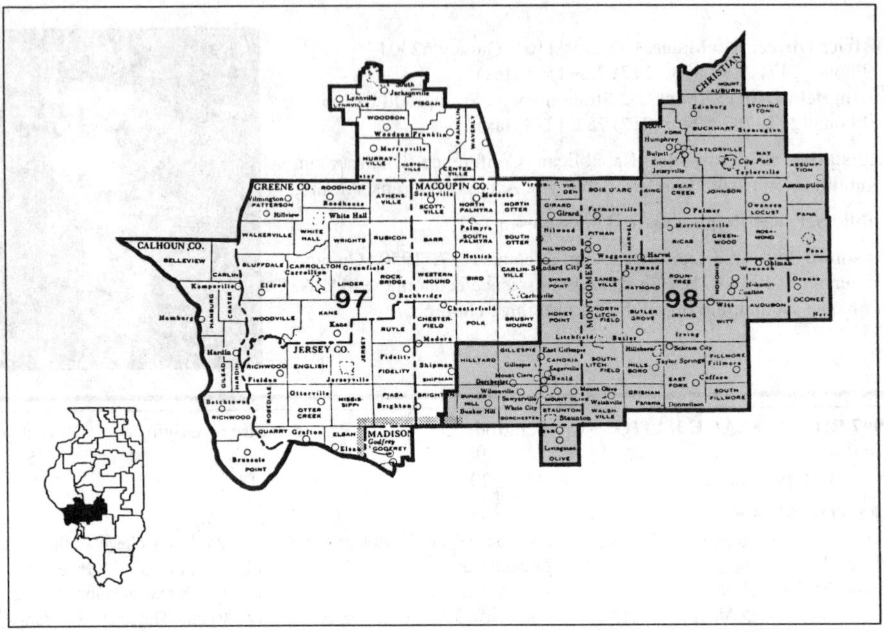

DEMOGRAPHICS (1990)

	S.D. #49	H.D. #97	H.D.#98
VOTING AGE POPULATION	144,545	72,424	72,121
White	98.2%	98.2%	98.2%
Black	1.0%	0.9%	1.1%
Hispanic	0.4%	0.5%	0.4%
Asian	0.2%	0.3%	0.2%
AGE (Total Population)	193,739	96,870	96,869
Under 6	8.0%	8.0%	8.1%
6 to 18	18.7%	18.7%	18.8%
65 and Over	17.3%	16.2%	18.4%
URBAN POPULATION	45.3%	46.4%	44.2%
HOUSING UNITS (Total)	80,681	39,978	40,703
Median Value	$41,731	$47,237	$37,000
Owner Occupied	69.5%	68.8%	70.2%
FAMILY INCOME (Total Families)	53,686	26,709	26,976
Median Income	$31,019	$32,434	$29,483
Below Poverty Level	8.9%	7.8%	10.0%
With Children Under 5	1.4%	1.3%	1.5%
With Children 5 to 17	3.2%	2.7%	3.7%
Headed by Females	3.2%	2.6%	3.8%
INDUSTRY (Total Employed)	83,719	43,248	40,471
Professional/Public Administration	28.7%	30.2%	27.1%
Manufacturing	17.6%	18.1%	17.1%
Retail	16.7%	17.1%	16.3%
Transportation/Communication	7.1%	6.7%	7.6%
Finance/Insurance/Real Estate	5.5%	5.2%	5.8%
Other Service	6.7%	6.6%	6.8%

Senator Vince Demuzio (D)

District Office: 140 Carlinville Plaza, Carlinville 62626
Phone (217) 854-4441; (217) 854-5311 (fax)
Springfield Office: 309-D Capitol Bldg., Springfield 62706
Phone (217) 782-8206

Legislative Assignments: Assistant Minority Leader; Committees on Education; Executive; Rules (minority spokesperson); Legislative Audit Commission.

Public Service: Senator (1975-present); executive director of Illinois Valley Economic Development Corporation; former chairman, Illinois Democratic Party.

Personal: Born May 7, 1941, Gillespie; University of Illinois at Springfield, M.A. in education & public policy; Sangamon State University, B.A. in education & human services; married (Deanna Clemonds); two children and two grandchildren.

1997 BILL PASSAGE RATIO	Introduced	Passed House of Origin	Passed GA
Primary	11	3	1
Primary/Hyphenated	23	8	3

KEY VOTES

1) Senate GOP Ed. $ Plan . . . . . . .N
2) State Budget . . . . .Y
3) Tougher DUI Level . . . . .Y
4) Ban Partial Birth Abortions . . .Y
5) State Employees Pension . . . . .Y
6) Insurance/Domestic Violence . .Y
7) Brownfields . . . . .Y
8) Welfare Reform . . . . .Y
9) Concealed Guns/Misdemeanor .Y
10) Banks Sell Insurance . . . . .Y
11) Pre-Paid College Tuition . . .Y
12) Increase Pull Tab Prizes . . . .Y
13) Telecommunications Tax . . . .P
14) Delivery Discrimination . . . .Y
15) Sell Drivers' Data . . . . .N

GROUP RATINGS

	FB	CoC	PrLf	IPPC	ACLU
1997	77	60	2/2	0	67

ELECTION RESULTS

1996 General	Vince Demuzio (D)	60,446	(100%)
1996 Primary	Vince Demuzio (D)	16,285	(100%)
1992 General	Vince Demuzio (D)	72,409	(100%)
1992 Primary	Vince Demuzio (D)	24,502	(100%)

CAMPAIGN RESOURCES AND EXPENDITURES

1996 Campaign Funds

Beg. Balance	$231,301	Individuals	$1,000
Receipts	$69,595	Party	$250
Expenditures	$47,630	PACS	$46,430
On hand	$253,266	Candidate	$5,381
		Not-itemized	$16,534

Top 10 PAC Contributors

1) IPACE	$20,000	6) ITLA	$1,000
2) AFFI	$2,000	7) ABDI	$800
3) ILCable	$1,000	8) IHCA	$750
4) PIIA	$1,000	9) JACPAC	$750
5) WMgt	$1,000	10) Sears	$750

NOTE: The General Election Opponent's Campaign Resources and Expenditures are reported in a separate section in the back of the book (pp. 269-284).

GENERAL ELECTION DATA

	Registered Voters	Voter Turnout		Straight Party Voting	
1996	129,386	86,247	66.7%	(R) 11,108 . .12.9%	(D) 16,030 . . .18.6%

PRESIDENT

1996	Bill Clinton (D)	41,207	48.9%
	Bob Dole (R)	32,058	38.1%
	Ross Perot (I)	10,182	12.1%
1992	Bill Clinton (D)	46,116	48.0%
	George Bush (R)	29,963	31.2%
	Ross Perot (I)	20,036	20.8%

UNITED STATES SENATE

1996	Richard J. Durbin (D)	44,028	52.8%
	Al Salvi (R)	36,671	44.0%

GOVERNOR

1994	Jim Edgar (R)	43,514	65.8%
	Dawn Clark Netsch (D)	22,587	34.2%

Representative Tom Ryder (R)

District Office: 100 South State St., Jerseyville 62052
Phone (618) 498-6456; (618) 498-3384 (fax)
Springfield Office: Room 314 Capitol Bldg., Springfield 62706
Phone (217) 782-1840; (217) 782-7012 (fax)

Legislative Assignments: Deputy Republican Leader; ex officio member of all committees. Joint Committee on Administrative Rules (co-chair); committees on Rules; Insurance; Health Care Availability & Access.

Public Service: Representative (1983-present).

Personal: Attorney; born May 17, 1949, Alton; Northern Illinois University, B.A. in political science; Washington and Lee University, J.D.; married (Peggy); two children.

1997 BILL PASSAGE RATIO	Introduced	Passed House of Origin	Passed GA
Primary	21	8	5
Primary/Hyphenated	61	21	12

KEY VOTES

1) Change Ed. Funding Formula . . Y
2) State Budget . . . . Y
3) Tougher DUI Level . . . . Y
4) Ban Partial Birth Abortions . . . . E
5) State Employees Pension . . . . . Y
6) Insurance/Domestic Violence . . Y
7) Brownfields . . . . Y
8) Welfare Reform . . . . Y
9) Concealed Guns/Misdemeanor . Y
10) Banks Sell Insurance . . . . Y
11) Pre-Paid College Tuition . . . . Y
12) Increase Pull Tab Prizes . . . . E
13) Utility Deregulation . . . . Y
14) County Obscenity Standards . Y
15) Managed Care Reform . . . . . N

GROUP RATINGS

	FB	CoC	PrLf	IPPC	ACLU
1997	79	77	N/R	0	N/R

ELECTION RESULTS

1996 General	Tom Ryder (R)	30,924	(100%)
1996 Primary	Tom Ryder (R)	7,155	(100%)
1994 General	Tom Ryder (R)	22,077	(62.9%)
1994 General	Jerry Montague (D)	13,010	(37.1%)

CAMPAIGN RESOURCES AND EXPENDITURES

1996 Campaign Funds

Beg. Balance	$106,439	Individuals	$1,600
Receipts	$ 80,088	Party	$0
Expenditures	$102,684	PACS	$58,170
On hand	$83,843	Candidate	$1,152
		Not-itemized	$19,166

Top 10 PAC Contributors

1) IPACE	$12,000	6) CPA's	$1,500
2) ISMS	$5,000	7) MetroPrim	$1,000
3) ARC	$3,000	8) AB	$1,000
4) Ameritech	$1,750	9) AFFI	$1,000
5) LAWPAC	$1,500	10) CatCEG	$1,000

NOTE: The General Election Opponent's Campaign Resources and Expenditures are reported in a separate section in the back of the book (pp. 269-284).

GENERAL ELECTION DATA

	Registered Voters	Voter Turnout		Straight Party Voting	
1996	63,357	43,814	69.2%	(R) 6,189 . . . 14.1%	(D) 6,656 . . . 15.2%

PRESIDENT

1996	Bill Clinton (D)	19,490	45.6%
	Bob Dole (R)	17,565	41.1%
	Ross Perot (I)	5,296	12.4%
1992	Bill Clinton (D)	20,865	43.5%
	George Bush (R)	16,722	34.8%
	Ross Perot (I)	10,431	21.7%

UNITED STATES SENATE

1996	Richard J. Durbin (D)	20,979	49.6%
	Al Salvi (R)	19,931	47.2%

GOVERNOR

1994	Jim Edgar (R)	24,290	70.8%
	Dawn Clark Netsch (D)	10,032	29.2%

Representative Gary Hannig (D)

District Office: 225 South Macoupin, Gillespie 62033
Phone (217) 839-2859; (217) 839-2577 (fax)
Springfield Office: Room 300 Capitol Bldg., Springfield 62706
Phone (217) 782-8071

Legislative Assignments: Assistant Majority Leader; ex officio member of all committees. Committees on Rules; Agriculture & Conservation.

Public Service: Representative (1979-present).

Personal: Full-time legislator; born July 22, 1952, Litchfield; University of Illinois-Chicago, B.S. in accounting; married (Elizabeth).

1997 BILL PASSAGE RATIO	Introduced	Passed House of Origin	Passed GA
Primary	137	8	3
Primary/Hyphenated	160	20	10

KEY VOTES

1) Change Ed. Funding Formula . . Y	6) Insurance/Domestic Violence . . Y	11) Pre-Paid College Tuition . . . . Y
2) State Budget . . . . Y	7) Brownfields . . . . Y	12) Increase Pull Tab Prizes . . . . Y
3) Tougher DUI Level . . . . Y	8) Welfare Reform . . . . Y	13) Utility Deregulation . . . . Y
4) Ban Partial Birth Abortions . . . Y	9) Concealed Guns/Misdemeanor . Y	14) County Obscenity Standards . Y
5) State Employees Pension . . . . . Y	10) Banks Sell Insurance . . . . Y	15) Managed Care Reform . . . . . Y

GROUP RATINGS

	FB	CoC	PrLf	IPPC	ACLU
1997	86	46	5/6	33	30

ELECTION RESULTS

1996 General	Gary Hannig (D)	23,224	(57.4%)
1996 General	Rodney Davis (R)	17,230	(42.6%)
1996 Primary	Gary Hannig (D)	10,261	(100%)
1996 Primary	Rodney Davis (R)	4,888	(100%)

CAMPAIGN RESOURCES AND EXPENDITURES

1996 Campaign Funds				Top 10 PAC Contributors			
Beg. Balance	$60,815	Individuals	$0	1) IPACE	$20,158	6) AFFI	$2,000
Receipts	$79,962	Party	$33,131	2) DSCC	$16,480	7) WMgt	$2,000
Expenditures	$94,557	PACS	$45,434	3) IHDM	$9,452	8) ILCable	$1,300
On hand	$46,220	Candidate	$0	4) DPI	$7,200	9) ISMS	$1,000
		Not-itemized	$1,397	5) ITLA	$2,000	10) IHCA	$1,000

NOTE: The General Election Opponent's Campaign Resources and Expenditures are reported in a separate section in the back of the book (pp. 269-284).

GENERAL ELECTION DATA

	Registered Voters	Voter Turnout		Straight Party Voting	
1996	66,029	42,433	64.3%	(R) 4,919 . . . 11.6%	(D) 9,374 . . . 22.1%

PRESIDENT

1996	Bill Clinton (D)	21,717	52.4%
	Bob Dole (R)	14,493	35.0%
	Ross Perot (I)	4,886	11.8%
1992	Bill Clinton (D)	25,251	52.5%
	George Bush (R)	13,241	27.5%
	Ross Perot (I)	9,605	20.0%

UNITED STATES SENATE

1996	Richard J. Durbin (D)	23,049	56.1%
	Al Salvi (R)	16,740	40.7%

GOVERNOR

1994	Jim Edgar (R)	19,224	60.5%
	Dawn Clark Netsch (D)	12,555	39.5%

50th Senate District

House District 99
House District 100

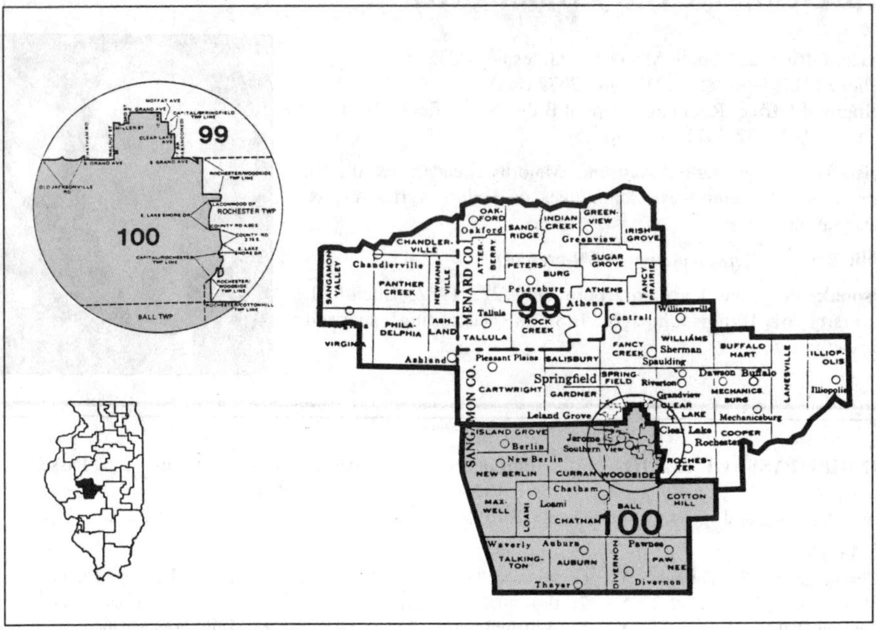

DEMOGRAPHICS (1990)

	S.D. #50	H.D. #99	H.D.#100
VOTING AGE POPULATION	144,019	72,306	71,713
White	92.4%	96.9%	87.8%
Black	6.2%	1.8%	10.6%
Hispanic	0.6%	0.5%	0.7%
Asian	0.7%	0.5%	0.8%
AGE (Total Population)	193,739	96,870	96,869
Under 6	8.7%	8.3%	9.0%
6 to 18	18.2%	18.3%	18.2%
65 and Over	13.8%	13.9%	13.8%
URBAN POPULATION	72.1%	59.8%	84.4%
HOUSING UNITS (Total)	83,366	40,629	42,737
Median Value	$59,697	$59,094	$60,428
Owner Occupied	62.8%	68.1%	57.8%
FAMILY INCOME (Total Families)	52,170	26,427	25,743
Median Income	$37,158	$37,792	$36,465
Below Poverty Level	7.3%	5.4%	9.2%
With Children Under 5	1.6%	1.0%	2.1%
With Children 5 to 17	2.6%	1.8%	3.4%
Headed by Females	3.9%	1.9%	6.0%
INDUSTRY (Total Employed)	99,212	50,560	48,652
Professional/Public Administration	44.5%	43.0%	46.1%
Manufacturing	5.4%	5.6%	5.2%
Retail	15.0%	14.2%	15.8%
Transportation/Communication	7.4%	7.9%	6.8%
Finance/Insurance/Real Estate	8.5%	8.7%	8.3%
Other Service	7.8%	8.0%	7.5%

Senator Larry K. Bomke (R)

District Office: 111 Capitol Bldg., Springfield 62706
Phone (217) 782-0228; (217) 782-4079 (fax)
Springfield Office: 111 Capitol Bldg., Springfield 62706
Phone (217) 782-0228; (217) 782-4079 (fax)

Legislative Assignments: Committees on Executive Appointments (vice chair); Local Government & Elections (vice chair); Appropriations.

Public Service: Senator (1995-present); former chairman and member, Sangamon County Board.

Personal: Small business owner; born June 6, 1950; Lincoln Land Community College; married (Sally Jo); two children.

1997 BILL PASSAGE RATIO	Introduced	Passed House of Origin	Passed GA
Primary	8	3	2
Primary/Hyphenated	18	8	6

KEY VOTES

1) Senate GOP Ed. $ Plan . . . . . . .Y	6) Insurance/Domestic Violence . .Y	11) Pre-Paid College Tuition . . . .Y
2) State Budget . . . . .Y	7) Brownfields . . . . .Y	12) Increase Pull Tab Prizes . . . .N
3) Tougher DUI Level . . . . .Y	8) Welfare Reform . . . . .Y	13) Telecommunications Tax . . .N
4) Ban Partial Birth Abortions . . .Y	9) Concealed Guns/Misdemeanor .Y	14) Delivery Discrimination . . . .P
5) State Employees Pension . . . . .Y	10) Banks Sell Insurance . . . . .Y	15) Sell Drivers' Data . . . . .Y

GROUP RATINGS

	FB	CoC	PrLf	IPPC	ACLU
1997	86	100	2/2	0	50

ELECTION RESULTS

1996 General	Larry K. Bomke (R)	49,241	(52.3%)
1996 General	Tom Londrigan (D)	44,921	(47.7%)
1996 Primary	Larry K. Bomke (R)	25,309	(100%)
1996 Primary	Tom Londrigan (D)	9,287	(100%)

CAMPAIGN RESOURCES AND EXPENDITURES

1996 Campaign Funds

Beg. Balance	$44,088	Individuals	$35,509
Receipts	$522,595	Party	$358,837
Expenditures	$514,748	PACS	$128,249
On hand	$51,935	Candidate	$0
		Not-itemized	$0

Top 10 PAC Contributors

1) RSSC . . .$346,724	6) CRausch . . .$3,000
2) IPACE . . .$33,223	7) Alliance . . .$2,556
3) ISMS $15,193	8) PIIA $2,500
4) MPAC $9,500	9) ILCon $2,000
5) CoC $5,059	10) HOPE $2,000

NOTE: The General Election Opponent's Campaign Resources and Expenditures are reported in a separate section in the back of the book (pp. 269-284).

GENERAL ELECTION DATA

	Registered Voters	Voter Turnout		Straight Party Voting	
1996	133,189	103,504	77.7%	(R) 22,173 . .21.4%	(D) 13,568 . . .13.1%

PRESIDENT

1996	Bill Clinton (D)	44,689	43.9%
	Bob Dole (R)	48,823	47.8%
	Ross Perot (I)	7,577	7.4%
1992	Bill Clinton (D)	43,270	41.2%
	George Bush (R)	43,229	41.2%
	Ross Perot (I)	18,457	17.6%

UNITED STATES SENATE

1996	Richard J. Durbin (D)	48,972	48.3%
	Al Salvi (R)	50,720	50.0%

GOVERNOR

1994	Jim Edgar (R)	57,640	69.4%
	Dawn Clark Netsch (D)	25,360	30.6%

Representative Raymond Poe (R)

District Office: Room E-1 Stratton Bldg., Springfield 62706
Phone (217) 782-0044; (217) 782-0897 (fax)
Springfield Office: Room E-1 Stratton Bldg., Springfield 62706
Phone (217) 782-0044; (217) 782-0897 (fax)

Legislative Assignments: Committees on Elementary & Secondary Education; Higher Education; Appropriations-Education; Agriculture & Conservation; Personnel & Pensions.

Public Service: Representative (1995-present); former board member, Williamsville School District.

Personal: Farmer; born March 26, 1944, Lincoln; DeVry Institute of Technology; married (Carol); three children.

1997 BILL PASSAGE RATIO	Introduced	Passed House of Origin	Passed Ga
Primary	6	4	3
Primary/Hyphenated	23	16	8

KEY VOTES

1) Change Ed. Funding Formula . . N	6) Insurance/Domestic Violence . . Y	11) Pre-Paid College Tuition . . . . Y
2) State Budget . . . . Y	7) Brownfields . . . . N	12) Increase Pull Tab Prizes . . . . N
3) Tougher DUI Level . . . . Y	8) Welfare Reform . . . . Y	13) Utility Deregulation . . . . P
4) Ban Partial Birth Abortions . . . Y	9) Concealed Guns/Misdemeanor . Y	14) County Obscenity Standards . Y
5) State Employees Pension . . . . . Y	10) Banks Sell Insurance . . . . Y	15) Managed Care Reform . . . . . N

GROUP RATINGS

	FB	CoC	PrLf	IPPC	ACLU
1997	64	69	6/6	0	20

ELECTION RESULTS

1996 General	Raymond Poe (R)	27,158	(56.6%)
1996 General	Leslie J. Graves (D)	20,830	(43.4%)
1996 Primary	Raymond Poe (R)	13,704	(100%)
1996 Primary	Leslie J. Graves (D)	4,231	(100%)

CAMPAIGN RESOURCES AND EXPENDITURES

1996 Campaign Funds

Beg. Balance	$24,878	Individuals	$6,034
Receipts	$204,334	Party	$110,173
Expenditures	$226,978	PAC	$58,281
On hand	$2,234	Candidate	$218
		Not-itemized	$29,628

Top 10 PAC Contributors

1) FLAD	$56,310	6) MPAC	$3,500
2) HRCC	$45,701	7) Alliance	$2,750
3) CChurchill	$5,000	8) LLDC	$2,400
4) ISMS	$5,000	9) Fremont	$1,500
5) IPACE	$4,500	10) IHCA	$1,500

NOTE: The General Election Opponent's Campaign Resources and Expenditures are reported in a separate section in the back of the book (pp. 269-284).

GENERAL ELECTION DATA

	Registered Voters	Voter Turnout		Straight Party Voting	
1996	68,691	53,037	77.2%	(R) 11,562 . . 21.8%	(D) 6,476 . . . . 12.2%

PRESIDENT

1996	Bill Clinton (D)	22,347	42.8%
	Bob Dole (R).	25,246	48.4%
	Ross Perot (I)	4,263	8.2%
1992	Bill Clinton (D)	22,057	39.2%
	George Bush (R)	23,847	42.3%
	Ross Perot (I)	10,425	18.5%

UNITED STATES SENATE

1996	Richard J. Durbin (D)	24,388	46.9%
	Al Salvi (R)	26,669	51.3%

GOVERNOR

1994	Jim Edgar (R)	30,279	70.2%
	Dawn Clark Netsch (D)	12,829	29.8%

Representative Gwenn Klingler (R)

District Office: Room 1128-E Stratton Bldg., Springfield 62706
Phone (217) 782-0053; (217) 782-0897 (fax)
Springfield Office: Room 1128-E Stratton Bldg., Springfield 62706
Phone (217) 782-0053; (217) 782-0897 (fax)

Legislative Assignments: Committees on Children & Youth; Health Care Availability & Access; Higher Education; Aging.

Public Service: Representative (1995-present); Springfield city council alderwoman (1991-1995); board member, Springfield School District 186 (1987-1991); president, School Board (1988).

Personal: Attorney; born May 28, 1944, Toledo, OH; Ohio Wesleyan University, B.A. in biology; University of Michigan, M.A. in zoology; George Washington University, J.D. with honors; married (Gerald); two children.

1997 BILL PASSAGE RATIO	Introduced	Passed Houseof Origin	Passed GA
Primary	11	5	1
Primary/Hyphenated	33	20	9

KEY VOTES

1) Change Ed. Funding Formula . . N
2) State Budget . . . . Y
3) Tougher DUI Level . . . . Y
4) Ban Partial Birth Abortions . . . N
5) State Employees Pension . . . . . Y
6) Insurance/Domestic Violence . . Y
7) Brownfields . . . . Y
8) Welfare Reform . . . . Y
9) Concealed Guns/Misdemeanor . Y
10) Banks Sell Insurance . . . . Y
11) Pre-Paid College Tuition . . . . Y
12) Increase Pull Tab Prizes . . . . Y
13) Utility Deregulation . . . . P
14) County Obscenity Standards . Y
15) Managed Care Reform . . . . . Y

GROUP RATINGS

	FB	CoC	PrLf	IPPC	ACLU
1997	64	46	0/6	100	80

ELECTION RESULTS

1996 General	Gwenn Klingler (R)	24,536	(53.9%)
1996 General	Marylou Lowder Kent (D)	21,023	(46.1%)
1996 Primary	Gwenn Klingler (R)	11,873	(100%)
1996 Primary	Marylou Lowder Kent (D)	4,885	(100%)

CAMPAIGN RESOURCES AND EXPENDITURES

1996 Campaign Funds

Beg. Balance	$12,104	Individuals	$11,520
Receipts	$350,965	Party	$220,733
Expenditures	$356,944	PACS	$98,960
On hand	$6,125	Candidate	$0
		Not-itemized	$19,752

Top 10 PAC Contributors

1) HRCC	$119,254	6) CChurchill	$10,000
2) FLAD	$70,301	7) MPAC	$7,000
3) IPACE	$29,197	8) CRyder	$5,000
4) ISMS	$15,123	9) CoC	$3,600
5) CRyan	$10,000	10) Alliance	$2,500

NOTE: The General Election Opponent's Campaign Resources and Expenditures are reported in a separate section in the back of the book (pp. 269-284).

GENERAL ELECTION DATA

	Registered Voters	Voter Turnout		Straight Party Voting	
1996	64,498	50,467	78.2%	(R) 10,611 . . 21.0%	(D) 7,092 . . . . 14.1%

PRESIDENT

1996	Bill Clinton (D)	22,342	45.0%
	Bob Dole (R)	23,577	47.5%
	Ross Perot (I)	3,314	6.7%
1992	Bill Clinton (D)	21,213	43.6%
	George Bush (R)	19,382	39.9%
	Ross Perot (I)	8,032	16.5%

UNITED STATES SENATE

1996	Richard J. Durbin (D)	24,584	49.8%
	Al Salvi (R)	24,051	48.7%

GOVERNOR

1994	Jim Edgar (R)	27,361	68.6%
	Dawn Clark Netsch (D)	12,531	31.4%

51st Senate District

House District 101
House District 102

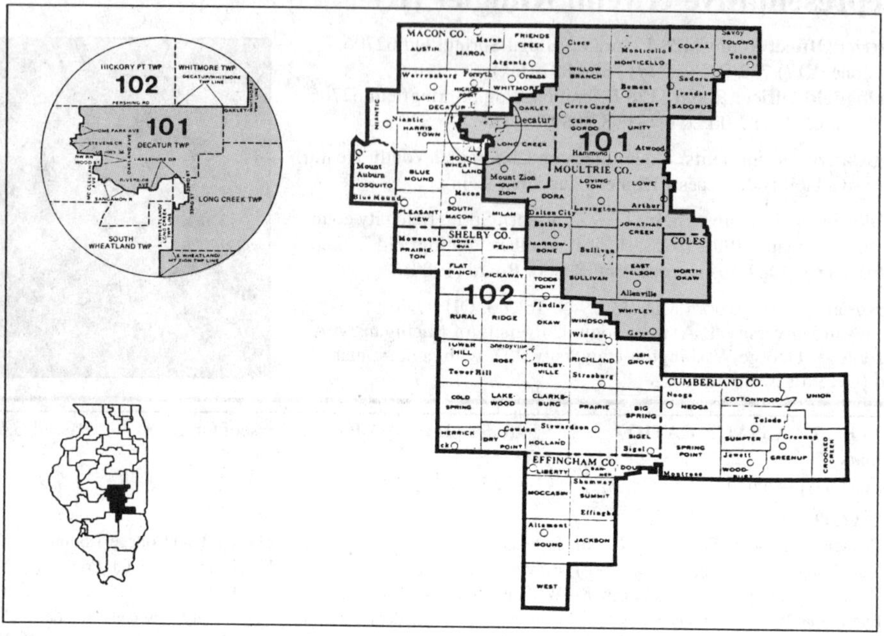

DEMOGRAPHICS (1990)

	S.D. #51	H.D. #101	H.D.#102
VOTING AGE POPULATION	142,707	71,217	71,490
White	93.3%	89.0%	97.6%
Black	6.0%	10.4%	1.7%
Hispanic	0.3%	0.3%	0.3%
Asian	0.3%	0.2%	0.3%
AGE (Total Population)	193,739	96,869	96,870
Under 6	8.4%	8.7%	8.1%
6 to 18	19.4%	19.2%	19.6%
65 and Over	15.3%	16.1%	14.5%
URBAN POPULATION	58.3%	72.7%	43.8%
HOUSING UNITS (Total)	80,864	41,706	39,158
Median Value	$44,819	$40,138	$49,607
Owner Occupied	67.7%	62.1%	73.6%
FAMILY INCOME (Total Families)	54,164	26,308	27,856
Median Income	$33,550	$31,156	$36,200
Below Poverty Level	8.8%	11.8%	6.0%
With Children Under 5	1.6%	2.1%	1.1%
With Children 5 to 17	3.3%	4.7%	1.9%
Headed by Females	4.9%	7.3%	2.6%
INDUSTRY (Total Employed)	87,656	42,330	45,326
Professional/Public Administration	24.9%	24.8%	24.9%
Manufacturing	23.5%	23.2%	23.8%
Retail	16.6%	17.2%	15.9%
Transportation/Communication	8.3%	8.3%	8.3%
Finance/Insurance/Real Estate	5.1%	5.0%	5.1%
Other Service	7.4%	8.3%	6.6%

Senator Penny Severns (D)

District Office: 101B Ashland Ave., Mt. Zion 62549
Phone (217) 864-6026; (217) 864-3696 (fax)
Springfield Office: 311 Capitol Bldg., Springfield 62706
Phone (217) 782-5284; (217) 782-3242 (fax)

Legislative Assignments: Minority Caucus Whip. Committees on Revenue (minority spokesperson) and Executive; Legislative Audit Commission.

Public Service: Senator (1987-present); Decatur City Council.

Personal: Full-time legislator; born January 21, 1952, Decatur; Southern Illinois University, B.A. in political science; John F. Kennedy School of Government; Harvard University.

1997 BILL PASSAGE RATIO	Introduced	Passed House of Origin	Passed GA
Primary	23	6	5
Primary/Hyphenated	48	22	13

KEY VOTES

1) Senate GOP Ed. $ Plan . . . . . . .N	6) Insurance/Domestic Violence . .Y	11) Pre-Paid College Tuition . . . .Y
2) State Budget . . . . .Y	7) Brownfields . . . . .Y	12) Increase Pull Tab Prizes . . . .Y
3) Tougher DUI Level . . . . .Y	8) Welfare Reform . . . . .Y	13) Telecommunications Tax . . .Y
4) Ban Partial Birth Abortions . . .Y	9) Concealed Guns/Misdemeanor .Y	14) Delivery Discrimination . . . .Y
5) State Employees Pension . . . . .Y	10) Banks Sell Insurance . . . . .Y	15) Sell Drivers' Data . . . . .N

GROUP RATINGS

	FB	CoC	PrLf	IPPC	ACLU
1997	91	80	2/2	0	50

ELECTION RESULTS

1996 General	Penny Severns(D)	53,248	(67.7%)
1996 General	P. Duane Potter (R)	25,362	(32.3%)
1996 Primary	Penny Severns (D)	11,290	(100%)
1996 Primary	P. Duane Potter (R)	10,957	(100%)

CAMPAIGN RESOURCES AND EXPENDITURES

1996 Campaign Funds				Top 10 PAC Contributors	
Beg. Balance	$12,199	Individuals	$4,855	1) IPACE . . .$80,000	6) PersPAC . . .$4,179
Receipts	$204,719	Party	$35,122	2) CDS $16,572	7) ITLA $3,000
Expenditures	$150,162	PACS	$147,622	3) MCIDC . .$10,000	8) ISMS $3,000
On hand	$66,756	Candidate	$0	4) CEJones . .$10,000	9) WVWV . . .$2,000
		Not-itemized	$17,120	5) CClayborne $5,000	10) UAW $2,000

NOTE: The General Election Opponent's Campaign Resources and Expenditures are reported in a separate section in the back of the book (pp. 269-284).

GENERAL ELECTION DATA

	Registered Voters	Voter Turnout		Straight Party Voting	
1996	121,262	81,852	67.5%	(R) 11,167 . .13.6%	(D) 14,158 . . .17.3%

PRESIDENT

1996	Bill Clinton (D)	38,174	47.8%
	Bob Dole (R)	32,838	41.1%
	Ross Perot (I)	8,424	10.5%
1992	Bill Clinton (D)	43,394	46.8%
	George Bush (R)	31,921	34.4%
	Ross Perot (I)	17,368	18.8%

UNITED STATES SENATE

1996	Richard J. Durbin (D)	41,510	52.3%
	Al Salvi (R)	36,005	45.3%

GOVERNOR

1994	Jim Edgar (R)	42,717	67.1%
	Dawn Clark Netsch (D)	20,955	32.9%

Representative Julie A. Curry (D)

District Office: 101-A Ashland Ave., Mt. Zion 62549
Phone (217) 864-3746; (217) 864-4576 (fax)
Springfield Office: Room 2080-M Stratton Bldg., Springfield 62706
Phone (217) 782-8398

Legislative Assignments: Committees on State Government Administration & Election Reform (vice chair); Appropriations-General Services & Government Oversight; Consumer Protection; Elementary & Secondary Education; Legislative Audit Commission.

Public Service: Representative (1995-present); treasurer, Macon County (1990-1994).

Personal: Full-time legislator; born June 7, 1962, Granite City; Eastern Illinois University, B.A. and M.A. in political science; one child.

1997 BILL PASSAGE RATIO	Introduced	Passed House of Origin	Passed GA
Primary	9	5	4
Primary/Hyphenated	43	25	14

KEY VOTES

1) Change Ed. Funding Formula . . Y
2) State Budget . . . . Y
3) Tougher DUI Level . . . . Y
4) Ban Partial Birth Abortions . . . Y
5) State Employees Pension . . . . . Y
6) Insurance/Domestic Violence . . Y
7) Brownfields . . . . Y
8) Welfare Reform . . . . Y
9) Concealed Guns/Misdemeanor . Y
10) Banks Sell Insurance . . . . Y
11) Pre-Paid College Tuition . . . Y
12) Increase Pull Tab Prizes . . . . Y
13) Utility Deregulation . . . . Y
14) County Obscenity Standards . Y
15) Managed Care Reform . . . . . Y

GROUP RATINGS

	FB	CoC	PrLf	IPPC	ACLU
1997	82	31	1/6	83	70

ELECTION RESULTS

1996 General	Julie A. Curry (D)	22,432	(63.7%)
1996 General	Jerrold H. "Jerry" Stocks (R)	12,759	(36.3%)
1996 Primary	Julie A. Curry (D)	4,720	(100%)
1996 Primary	Jerrold H. "Jerry" Stocks (R)	4,608	(100%)

CAMPAIGN RESOURCES AND EXPENDITURES

1996 Campaign Funds				Top 10 PAC Contributors	
Beg. Balance	$15,350	Individuals	$1,040	1) IHDM . . .$79,538	6) CGranberg .$2,000
Receipts	$158,021	Party	$83,656	2) IPACE . . .$15,959	7) UAW $2,000
Expenditures	$146,816	PACS	$64,433	3) MCIDC . . .$7,000	8) WVWV . . .$2,000
On hand	$26,555	Candidate	$0	4) ITLA $5,000	9) Activator . .$1,523
		Not-itemized	$8,892	5) SEIU $5,000	10) USWA . . .$1,500

NOTE: The General Election Opponent's Campaign Resources and Expenditures are reported in a separate section in the back of the book (pp. 269-284).

GENERAL ELECTION DATA

	Registered Voters	Voter Turnout		Straight Party Voting	
1996	58,231	38,021	65.3%	(R) 4,819 . . .12.7%	(D) 8,019 . . . .21.1%

PRESIDENT

1996	Bill Clinton (D)	19,834	53.5%
	Bob Dole (R)	13,249	35.7%
	Ross Perot (I)	3,786	10.2%
1992	Bill Clinton (D	21,990	53.7%
	George Bush (R)	11,345	27.7%
	Ross Perot (I)	7,599	18.6%

UNITED STATES SENATE

1996	Richard J. Durbin (D)	21,000	57.0%
	Al Salvi (R)	14,893	40.4%

GOVERNOR

1994	Jim Edgar (R)	18,121	62.4%
	Dawn Clark Netsch (D)	10,931	37.6%

Representative N. Duane Noland (R)

District Office: 788 North Sunnyside Rd., Decatur 62522
Phone (217) 428-4068; (217) 428-4089 (fax)
Springfield Office: Room 2112-N Stratton Bldg., Springfield 62706
Phone (217) 782-8176; (217) 782-1275 (fax)

Legislative Assignments: Committees on Agriculture & Conservation (minority spokesperson); Insurance; Registration & Regulation; Appropriations-Public Safety.

Public Service: Representative (1990-present); former board member of the Illinois Farm Bureau and Illinois Corn Growers Association.

Personal: Farmer; born September 12, 1956, Blue Mound; University of Illinois, B. A. in agriculture education/economics; married (Tina), three children.

1997 BILL PASSAGE RATIO	Introduced	Passed House of Origin	Passed GA
Primary	13	7	6
Primary/Hyphenated	32	23	16

KEY VOTES

1) Change Ed. Funding Formula . . N	6) Insurance/Domestic Violence . . Y	11) Pre-Paid College Tuition . . . . Y
2) State Budget . . . . Y	7) Brownfields . . . . Y	12) Increase Pull Tab Prizes . . . . Y
3) Tougher DUI Level . . . . Y	8) Welfare Reform . . . . Y	13) Utility Deregulation . . . . . . Y
4) Ban Partial Birth Abortions . . . Y	9) Concealed Guns/Misdemeanor . Y	14) County Obscenity Standards . Y
5) State Employees Pension . . . . . Y	10) Banks Sell Insurance . . . . Y	15) Managed Care Reform . . . . . N

GROUP RATINGS

	FB	CoC	PrLf	IPPC	ACLU
1997	75	77	6/6	0	30

ELECTION RESULTS

1996 General	N. Duane Noland (R)	30,945	(72.1%)
1996 General	Jim Taylor (D)	11,955	(27.9%)
1996 Primary	N. Duane Noland (R)	8,014	(100%)

CAMPAIGN RESOURCES AND EXPENDITURES

1996 Campaign Funds

Beg. Balance	$69,709	Individuals	$8,977
Receipts	$82,718	Party	$1,650
Expenditures	$96,599	PACS	$34,892
On hand	$55,828	Candidate	$0
		Not-itemized	$37,199

Top 10 PAC Contributors

1) IPACE	$3,000	6) IRLA	$900
2) Activator	$1,227	7) IP	$900
3) MWEDA	$1,200	8) CumbGOP	$800
4) IMPAC	$1,100	9) Monsanto	$750
5) GenFence	$1,100	10) ABDI	$700

NOTE: The General Election Opponent's Campaign Resources and Expenditures are reported in a separate section in the back of the book (pp. 269-284).

GENERAL ELECTION DATA

	Registered Voters	Voter Turnout		Straight Party Voting	
1996	63,031	43,831	69.5%	(R) 6,348 . . . 14.5%	(D) 6,139 . . . 14.0%

PRESIDENT

1996	Bill Clinton (D)	18,340	42.8%
	Bob Dole (R)	19,589	45.7%
	Ross Perot (I)	4,638	10.8%
1992	Bill Clinton (D)	21,404	41.4%
	George Bush (R)	20,576	39.8%
	Ross Perot (I)	9,769	18.8%

UNITED STATES SENATE

1996	Richard J. Durbin (D)	20,510	48.2%
	Al Salvi (R)	21,112	49.6%

GOVERNOR

1994	Jim Edgar (R)	24,596	71.0%
	Dawn Clark Netsch (D)	10,024	29.0%

52nd Senate District

House District 103
House District 104

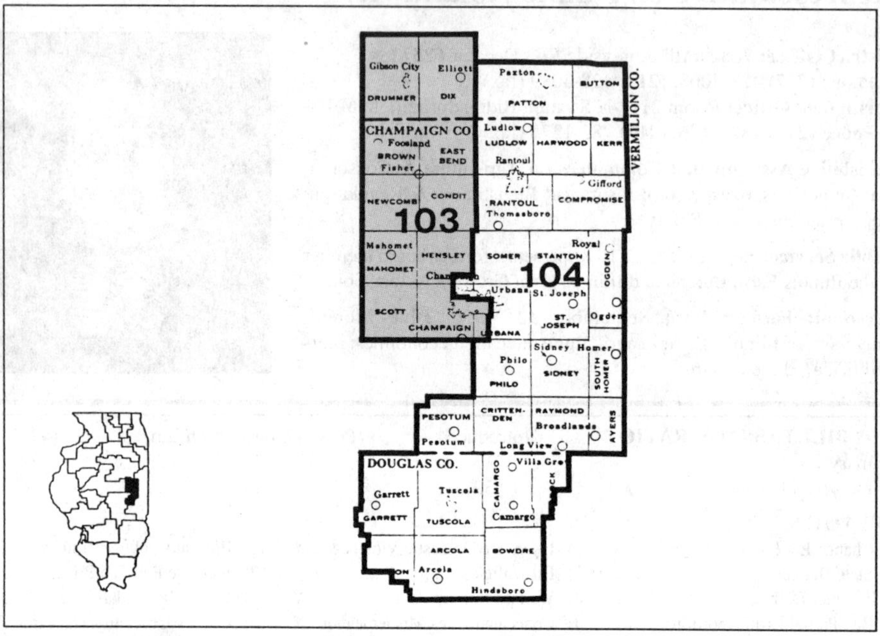

DEMOGRAPHICS (1990)

	S.D. #52	H.D. #103	H.D.#104
VOTING AGE POPULATION	150,306	79,379	70,927
White	86.2%	85.9%	86.5%
Black	7.2%	4.8%	10.0%
Hispanic	2.0%	2.2%	1.8%
Asian	4.4%	6.9%	1.6%
AGE (Total Population)	193,739	96,869	96,870
Under 6	8.2%	6.8%	9.6%
6 to 18	16.8%	15.0%	18.5%
65 and Over	9.7%	7.8%	11.7%
URBAN POPULATION	80.2%	89.0%	71.5%
HOUSING UNITS (Total)	76,778	36,822	39,956
Median Value	$63,714	$76,055	$53,510
Owner Occupied	52.9%	48.5%	57.0%
FAMILY INCOME (Total Families)	44,677	19,024	25,653
Median Income	$35,188	$40,670	$31,541
Below Poverty Level	7.9%	6.2%	9.2%
With Children Under 5	1.8%	1.4%	2.0%
With Children 5 to 17	2.6%	2.3%	2.8%
Headed by Females	4.0%	2.1%	5.5%
INDUSTRY (Total Employed)	96,420	50,733	45,686
Professional/Public Administration	42.9%	49.8%	35.1%
Manufacturing	11.8%	8.7%	15.3%
Retail	17.8%	17.1%	18.7%
Transportation/Communication	5.5%	4.8%	6.3%
Finance/Insurance/Real Estate	4.7%	4.8%	4.5%
Other Service	6.9%	6.4%	7.3%

Senator Stanley B. Weaver (R)

District Office: 1717 Philo Road, Suite 17B, Urbana 61802
Phone (217) 367-0009
Springfield Office: 329 Capitol Bldg., Springfield 62706
Phone (217) 782-6904; (217) 782-7818 (fax)

Legislative Assignments: Senate Majority Leader. Committees on Rules (chair); Executive; Revenue.

Public Service: Senator (1971-present); representative (1969-1971); mayor of Urbana (1957-1969).

Personal: Born May 23, 1925, Harrisburg; graduate of Indiana College of Mortuary Science; served one year in Army/Air Force during World War II; married (Mary E. Smith); two children, two grandchildren.

1997 BILL PASSAGE RATIO

	Introduced	Passed House of Origin	Passed GA
Primary	26	6	5
Primary/Hyphenated	28	7	5

KEY VOTES

1) Senate GOP Ed. $ Plan . . . . . . .Y
2) State Budget . . . . .Y
3) Tougher DUI Level . . . . .Y
4) Ban Partial Birth Abortions . . .Y
5) State Employees Pension . . . . .Y
6) Insurance/Domestic Violence . .Y
7) Brownfields . . . . .Y
8) Welfare Reform . . . . .Y
9) Concealed Guns/Misdemeanor .Y
10) Banks Sell Insurance . . . . . . .Y
11) Pre-Paid College Tuition . . . .Y
12) Increase Pull Tab Prizes . . . .Y
13) Telecommunications Tax . . . .P
14) Delivery Discrimination . . . .P
15) Sell Drivers' Data . . . . .Y

GROUP RATINGS

	FB	CoC	PrLf	IPPC	ACLU
1997	86	100	2/2	0	50

ELECTION RESULTS

1996 General	Stanley B. Weaver (R)	41,032	(58.1%)
1996 General	Jeanne Gerrietts (D)	29,532	(41.9%)
1996 Primary	Stanley B. Weaver (R)	14,116	(100%)

CAMPAIGN RESOURCES AND EXPENDITURES

1996 Campaign Funds

Beg. Balance	$84,397	Individuals	$3,231
Receipts	$60,839	Party	$6,362
Expenditures	$76,359	PACS	$44,800
On hand	$68,877	Candidate	$790
		Not-itemized	$5,656

Top 10 PAC Contributors

1) RSSC	$6,188	6) AT&T	$2,000
2) ISMS	$5,000	7) CPA's	$1,500
3) Allstate	$4,390	8) ABDI	$1,500
4) HI	$2,000	9) CoC	$1,000
5) RPAC	$2,000	10) CUPAC	$1,000

NOTE: The General Election Opponent's Campaign Resources and Expenditures are reported in a separate section in the back of the book (pp. 269-284).

GENERAL ELECTION DATA

	Registered Voters	Voter Turnout		Straight Party Voting	
1996	126,718	75,510	59.6%	(R) 16,838 . . 22.3%	(D) 10,335 . . .13.7%

PRESIDENT

1996	Bill Clinton (D)	35,327	47.9%
	Bob Dole (R)	31,787	43.2%
	Ross Perot (I)	5,524	7.5%
1992	Bill Clinton (D)	38,410	45.5%
	George Bush (R)	30,880	36.6%
	Ross Perot (I)	15,142	17.9%

UNITED STATES SENATE

1996	Richard J. Durbin (D)	36,778	50.5%
	Al Salvi (R)	34,018	46.7%

GOVERNOR

1994	Jim Edgar (R)	35,648	69.8%
	Dawn Clark Netsch (D)	15,457	30.2%

Representative Richard J. "Rick" Winkel, Jr. (R)

District Office: 201 West Springfield, Ste. 1 East A, Champaign 61824
Phone (217) 355-4994; (217) 355-4996 (fax)
Springfield Office: Room 2015-H Stratton Bldg., Springfield 62706
Phone (217) 782-2507

Legislative Assignments: Committees on Appropriations-Education; Higher Education; Judiciary I-Civil Law; State Government Administration & Election Reform; Prison Management Reform; Legislative Audit Commission.

Public Service: Representative (1995-present); board member, Champaign County (1992-1994).

Personal: Attorney; born September 25, 1956, Kankakee; University of Illinois at Urbana-Champaign, B.A. in economics; DePaul University College of Law, J.D.; married (Debra); two children.

1997 BILL PASSAGE RATIO	Introduced	Passed House of Origin	Passed GA
Primary	12	6	3
Primary/Hyphenated	21	12	5

KEY VOTES

1) Change Ed. Funding Formula . . N	6) Insurance/Domestic Violence . . Y	11) Pre-Paid College Tuition . . . . Y
2) State Budget . . . . Y	7) Brownfields . . . . Y	12) Increase Pull Tab Prizes . . . . Y
3) Tougher DUI Level . . . . Y	8) Welfare Reform . . . . Y	13) Utility Deregulation . . . . P
4) Ban Partial Birth Abortions . . . Y	9) Concealed Guns/Misdemeanor . Y	14) County Obscenity Standards . Y
5) State Employees Pension . . . . . Y	10) Banks Sell Insurance . . . . Y	15) Managed Care Reform . . . . . N

GROUP RATINGS

	FB	CoC	PrLf	IPPC	ACLU
1997	57	62	6/6	0	20

ELECTION RESULTS

1996 General	Richard J. "Rick" Winkel, Jr. (R)	20,325	(51.9%)
1996 General	Naomi D. Jakobsson (D)	18,869	(48.1%)
1996 Primary	Richard J. "Rick" Winkel, Jr. (R)	6,576	(100%)
1996 Primary	Naomi D. Jakobsson (D)	3,254	(100%)

CAMPAIGN RESOURCES AND EXPENDITURES

1996 Campaign Funds

Beg. Balance	$16,386	Individuals	$16,364
Receipts	$328,386	Party	$223,782
Expenditures	$341,833	PACS	$68,988
On hand	$2,939	Candidate	$1,650
		Not-itemized	$17,602

Top 10 PAC Contributors

1) HRCC	$142,599	6) CRyder	$5,000
2) FLAD	$54,733	7) MPAC	$5,000
3) IPACE	$10,250	8) CChurchill	$5,000
4) ISMS	$10,000	9) CoC	$2,500
5) CRyan	$10,000	10) C&UPost	$2,300

NOTE: The General Election Opponent's Campaign Resources and Expenditures are reported in a separate section in the back of the book (pp. 269-284).

GENERAL ELECTION DATA

	Registered Voters	Voter Turnout		Straight Party Voting	
1996	71,206	41,258	57.9%	(R) 8,715 . . . 21.1%	(D) 5,977 . . . 14.5%

PRESIDENT

1996	Bill Clinton (D)	19,981	49.5%
	Bob Dole (R)	17,093	42.3%
	Ross Perot (I)	2,614	6.5%
1992	Bill Clinton (D)	21,395	48.0%
	George Bush (R)	15,962	35.6%
	Ross Perot (I)	7,250	16.4%

UNITED STATES SENATE

1996	Richard J. Durbin (D)	20,966	52.6%
	Al Salvi (R)	17,840	44.8%

GOVERNOR

1994	Jim Edgar (R)	17,993	66.6%
	Dawn Clark Netsch (D)	9,016	33.4%

Representative Timothy V. Johnson (R)

District Office: 129 West Main St., Urbana 61801
Phone (217) 384-5336; (217) 367-9025 (fax)
Springfield Office: Room 314 Capitol Bldg., Springfield 62706
Phone (217) 782-8173

Legislative Assignments: Committee on Conflicts of Interest (minority spokesperson).

Public Service: Representative (1977-present); former alderman, Urbana; Republican chairman, Champaign County.

Personal: Attorney; born July 23, 1946, Champaign; University of Illinois, B.A. in liberal arts and sciences and J.D.; eight children.

1997 BILL PASSAGE RATIO	Introduced	Passed House of Origin	Passed GA
Primary	0	0	0
Primary/Hyphenated	0	0	0

KEY VOTES

1) Change Ed. Funding Formula . . Y	6) Insurance/Domestic Violence . . Y	11) Pre-Paid College Tuition . . . . Y
2) State Budget . . . . Y	7) Brownfields . . . . Y	12) Increase Pull Tab Prizes . . . . Y
3) Tougher DUI Level . . . . N	8) Welfare Reform . . . . Y	13) Utility Deregulation . . . . Y
4) Ban Partial Birth Abortions . . . Y	9) Concealed Guns/Misdemeanor . Y	14) County Obscenity Standards . N
5) State Employees Pension . . . . . Y	10) Banks Sell Insurance . . . . Y	15) Managed Care Reform . . . . . Y

GROUP RATINGS

	FB	CoC	PrLf	IPPC	ACLU
1997	86	54	6/6	0	40

ELECTION RESULTS

1996 General	Timothy V. Johnson (R)	20,490	(62.6%)
1996 General	Bob Kirchner (D)	12,255	(37.4%)
1996 Primary	Timothy V. Johnson (R)	8,251	(100%)
1996 Primary	Bob Kirchner (D)	2,664	(100%)

CAMPAIGN RESOURCES AND EXPENDITURES

1996 Campaign Funds		Top 10 PAC Contributors	
Beg. Balance .$30,104	Individuals . . .$8,766	1) ISMS $5,000	6) SPConst . . .$1,000
Receipts $46,121	Party $800	2) LAWPAC . .$1,500	7) Laborers . . .$1,000
Expenditures .$63,187	PACS $24,541	3) MPAC $1,242	8) RPAC $750
On hand $13,038	Candidate $0	4) PIIA $1,000	9) IBA $750
	Not-itemized $12,014	5) ABDI $1,000	10) HOPE $500

NOTE: The General Election Opponent's Campaign Resources and Expenditures are reported in a separate section in the back of the book (pp. 269-284).

GENERAL ELECTION DATA

Registered Voters	Voter Turnout	Straight Party Voting	
1996 55,512	34,252 . . . . .61.7%	(R) 8,123 . . .23.7%	(D) 4,358 . . . .12.7%

PRESIDENT

1996	Bill Clinton (D)	15,346	46.2%
	Bob Dole (R)	14,694	44.2%
	Ross Perot (I)	2,910	8.7%
1992	Bill Clinton (D)	17,015	42.7%
	George Bush (R)	14,918	37.5%
	Ross Perot (I)	7,892	19.8%

UNITED STATES SENATE

1996	Richard J. Durbin (D)	15,812	48.0%
	Al Salvi (R)	16,178	49.1%

GOVERNOR

1994	Jim Edgar (R)	17,655	73.3%
	Dawn Clark Netsch (D)	6,441	26.7%

53rd Senate District

House District 105
House District 106

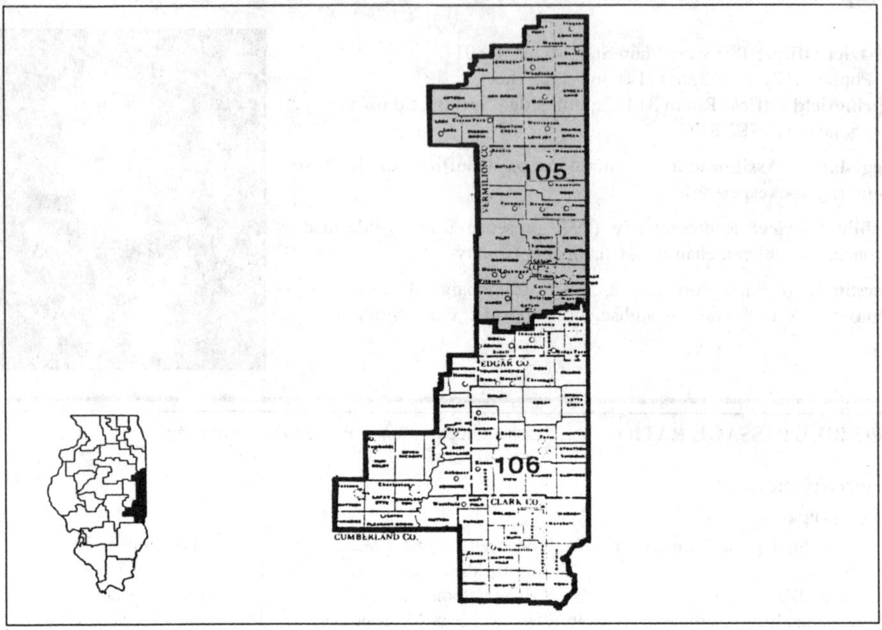

DEMOGRAPHICS (1990)

	S.D. #53	H.D. #105	H.D.#106
VOTING AGE POPULATION	146,660	72,109	74,551
White	94.6%	91.2%	97.8%
Black	4.1%	7.0%	1.2%
Hispanic	0.8%	1.2%	0.5%
Asian	0.4%	0.4%	0.4%
AGE (Total Population)	193,739	96,870	96,869
Under 6	7.7%	8.1%	7.3%
6 to 18	18.4%	18.8%	17.9%
65 and Over	16.2%	16.5%	15.9%
URBAN POPULATION	56.4%	52.9%	59.8%
HOUSING UNITS (Total)	81,101	40,865	40,236
Median Value	$39,130	$39,327	$38,912
Owner Occupied	64.8%	65.2%	64.4%
FAMILY INCOME (Total Families)	51,640	26,702	24,939
Median Income	$30,106	$30,475	$29,657
Below Poverty Level	10.6%	10.9%	10.2%
With Children Under 5	1.9%	1.8%	2.0%
With Children 5 to 17	4.2%	4.3%	4.1%
Headed by Females	5.0%	5.6%	4.3%
INDUSTRY (Total Employed)	84,889	41,433	43,456
Professional/Public Administration	26.4%	24.6%	28.2%
Manufacturing	22.8%	24.9%	20.9%
Retail	18.0%	18.0%	18.0%
Transportation/Communication	6.7%	6.6%	6.9%
Finance/Insurance/Real Estate	4.8%	5.1%	4.4%
Other Service	7.1%	7.4%	6.8%

Senator Judith A. Myers (R)

District Office: 119 1/2 S. Gilbert St., Danville 61832
Phone (217) 443-1997; (217) 443-2725 (fax)
Springfield Office: M-106 Capitol Bldg., Springfield 62706
Phone (217) 782-8899; (217) 782-0650 (fax)

Legislative Assignments: Committees on Agriculture & Conservation; Local Government & Elections; Executive Appointments.

Public Service: Senator (1997); recorder of Vermilion County (1980-1997).

Personal: Born October 29, 1936; B.S. from Purdue University; married (Mel); five children; five grandchildren.

1997 BILL PASSAGE RATIO	Introduced	Passed House of Origin	Passed GA
Primary	1	0	0
Primary/Hyphenated	8	6	4

KEY VOTES

1) Senate GOP Ed. $ Plan . . . . Y	6) Insurance/Domestic Violence . . Y	11) Pre-Paid College Tuition . . . Y
2) State Budget . . . . Y	7) Brownfields . . . . Y	12) Increase Pull Tab Prizes . . . . Y
3) Tougher DUI Level . . . . Y	8) Welfare Reform . . . . Y	13) Telecommunications Tax . . . N
4) Ban Partial Birth Abortions . . . Y	9) Concealed Guns/Misdemeanor . Y	14) Delivery Discrimination . . . . P
5) State Employees Pension . . . . . Y	10) Banks Sell Insurance . . . . Y	15) Sell Drivers' Data . . . . Y

GROUP RATINGS

	FB	CoC	PrLf	IPPC	ACLU
1997	86	100	N/R	0	50

ELECTION RESULTS

1994 General	Harry "Babe" Woodyard (R)	39,810	(69.8%)
1994 General	Charles D. Mattis (D)	17,258	(30.2%)
1994 Primary	Harry "Babe" Woodyard (R)	16,301	(100%)
1994 Primary	Charles D. Mattis (D)	7,595	(100%)

CAMPAIGN RESOURCES AND EXPENDITURES

1996 Campaign Funds				Top 10 PAC Contributors			
Beg. Balance	$ N/A	Individuals	$ N/A	1) N/A	$N/A	6) N/A	$N/A
Receipts	$.N/A	Party	$N/A	2) N/A	$N/A	7) N/A	$N/A
Expenditures	$ N/A	PACS	$N/A	3) N/A	$N/A	8) N/A	$N/A
On hand	$ N/A	Candidate	$N/A	4) N/A	$N/A	9) N/A	$N/A
		Not-itemized	$N/A	5) N/A	$N/A	10) N/A	$N/A

NOTE: The General Election Opponent's Campaign Resources and Expenditures are reported in a separate section in the back of the book (pp. 269-284).

GENERAL ELECTION DATA

	Registered Voter	Voter Turnout		Straight Party Voting			
1996	113,891	76,065	66.8%	(R) 12,827	16.9%	(D)11,064	14.5%

PRESIDENT

1996	Bill Clinton (D)	33,706	45.5%
	Bob Dole (R)	31,502	42.5%
	Ross Perot (I)	8,353	11.3%
1992	Bill Clinton (D)	37,903	43.6%
	George Bush (R)	31,094	35.7%
	Ross Perot (I)	18,031	20.7%

UNITED STATES SENATE

1996	Richard J. Durbin (D)	34,158	46.7%
	Al Salvi (R)	36,413	49.8%

GOVERNOR

1994	Jim Edgar (R)	42,771	76.3%
	Dawn Clark Netsch (D)	13,241	23.7%

Representative William B. "Bill" Black (R)

District Office: 119 1/2 S. Gilbert St., Danville 61832
Phone (217) 431-1986; (217) 431-2088 (fax)
Springfield Office: Room 634 Capitol Bldg., Springfield 62706
Phone (217) 782-4811; (217) 782-1873 (fax)

Legislative Assignments: Assistant Republican Leader; ex officio member of all committees. Committee on Transportation & Motor Vehicles.

Public Service: Representative (1986-present); former board member and chairman, Vermilion County (1976-1985).

Personal: Full-time legislator; born November 11, 1941, Danville; William Jewel College, B.A. in business administration; University of Illinois, M.A. in educational psychology; married (Sharon); two children.

1997 BILL PASSAGE RATIO	Introduced	Passed House of Origin	Passed GA
Primary	19	13	7
Primary/Hyphenated	65	51	27

KEY VOTES

1) Change Ed. Funding Formula . . Y	6) Insurance/Domestic Violence . . Y	11) Pre-Paid College Tuition . . . . Y
2) State Budget . . . . Y	7) Brownfields . . . . Y	12) Increase Pull Tab Prizes . . . . N
3) Tougher DUI Level . . . . N	8) Welfare Reform . . . . Y	13) Utility Deregulation . . . . Y
4) Ban Partial Birth Abortions . . . Y	9) Concealed Guns/Misdemeanor . Y	14) County Obscenity Standards . N
5) State Employees Pension . . . . . Y	10) Banks Sell Insurance . . . . Y	15) Managed Care Reform . . . . . P

GROUP RATINGS

	FB	CoC	PrLf	IPPC	ACLU
1997	82	50	6/6	0	20

ELECTION RESULTS

1996 General	William B. "Bill" Black (R)	27,540	(100%)
1996 Primary	William B. "Bill" Black (R)	9,623	(100%)
1994 General	William B. "Bill" Black (R)	21,023	(77.8%)
1994 General	John T. Thompson, Jr. (D)	5,986	(22.2%)

CAMPAIGN RESOURCES AND EXPENDITURES

1996 Campaign Funds

Beg. Balance	$71,846	Individuals	$1,104
Receipts	$42,149	Party	$250
Expenditures	$44,132	PACS	$25,557
On hand	$69,863	Candidate	$870
		Not-itemized	$14,368

Top 10 PAC Contributors

1) Ameritech . $2,000	6) MACC $1,000
2) ABDI $2,000	7) IPACE $500
3) RPAC $1,050	8) IVendors $500
4) LAWPAC . . $1,000	9) IRoad $500
5) CPA's $1,000	10) IRLA $500

NOTE: The General Election Opponent's Campaign Resources and Expenditures are reported in a separate section in the back of the book (pp. 269-284).

GENERAL ELECTION DATA

	Registered Voters	Voter Turnout		Straight Party Voting	
1996	52,502	36,472	69.5%	(R) 6,511 . . . 17.9%	(D) 5,191 . . . . 14.2%

PRESIDENT

1996	Bill Clinton (D)	16,340	45.9%
	Bob Dole (R)	14,918	41.9%
	Ross Perot (I)	4,064	11.4%
1992	Bill Clinton (D)	18,826	44.1%
	George Bush (R)	14,810	34.7%
	Ross Perot (I)	9,016	21.2%

UNITED STATES SENATE

1996	Richard J. Durbin (D)	16,480	46.8%
	Al Salvi (R)	17,426	49.5%

GOVERNOR

1994	Jim Edgar (R)	20,664	77.2%
	Dawn Clark Netsch (D)	6,109	22.8%

Representative Dale A. Righter (R)

District Office: 105 N. Tenth, Mattoon 61938
Phone (217) 235-6033; (217) 235-6052 (fax)
Springfield Office: Room 2123-O Stratton Bldg., Springfield 62706
Phone (217) 782-6674

Legislative Assignments: Committees on Elementary & Secondary Education; Financial Institutions; Higher Education; Judiciary II-Criminal Law.

Public Service: Representative (Apptd. Sept. 26, 1997-present).

Personal: Born August 23, 1966, Mattoon; Eastern Illinois University, B.A. in accounting; St. Louis University School of Law, J.D.; married (Teresa) two children.

1997 BILL PASSAGE RATIO	Introduced	Passed House of Origin	Passed GA
Primary	N/A	N/A	N/A
Primary/Hyphenated	N/A	N/A	N/A

KEY VOTES

1) Change Ed. Funding Formula . . X	6) Insurance/Domestic Violence . . X	11) Pre-Paid College Tuition X
2) State Budget X	7) Brownfields X	12) Increase Pull Tab Prizes X
3) Tougher DUI Level X	8) Welfare Reform X	13) Utility Deregulation X
4) Ban Partial Birth Abortions . . . X	9) Concealed Guns/Misdemeanor . X	14) County Obscenity Standards . X
5) State Employees Pension X	10) Banks Sell Insurance X	15) Managed Care Reform X

GROUP RATINGS

	FB	CoC	PrLf	IPPC	ACLU
1997	N/R	N/R	N/R	N/R	N/R

ELECTION RESULTS

1996 General	Michael “Mike” Weaver (R)	23,410	(100%)
1996 Primary	Michael “Mike” Weaver (R)	8,058	(100%)
1994 General	Michael “Mike” Weaver (R)	20,768	(69.2%)
1994 General	David Carpenter (D)	9,248	(30.8%)

CAMPAIGN RESOURCES AND EXPENDITURES

1996 Campaign Funds				Top 10 PAC Contributors			
Beg. Balance	N/A	Individuals	N/A	1) N/A	$N/A	6) N/A	$N/A
Receipts	N/A	Party	N/A	2) N/A	$N/A	7) N/A	$N/A
Expenditures	N/A	PACS	N/A	3) N/A	$N/A	8) N/A	$N/A
On hand	N/A	Candidate	N/A	4) N/A	$N/A	9) N/A	$N/A
		Not-itemized	N/A	5) N/A	$N/A	10) N/A	$N/A

NOTE: The General Election Opponent’s Campaign Resources and Expenditures are reported in a separate section in the back of the book (pp. 269-284).

GENERAL ELECTION DATA

	Registered Voters	Voter Turnout		Straight Party Voting	
1996	61,389	39,593	64.5%	(R) 6,316 . . . 16.0%	(D) 5,873 . . . . 14.8%

PRESIDENT

1996	Bill Clinton (D)	17,366	45.0%
	Bob Dole (R)	16,584	43.0%
	Ross Perot (I)	4,289	11.1%
1992	Bill Clinton (D)	19,077	43.0%
	George Bush (R)	16,284	36.7%
	Ross Perot (I)	9,015	20.3%

UNITED STATES SENATE

1996	Richard J. Durbin (D)	17,678	46.6%
	Al Salvi (R)	18,987	50.0%

GOVERNOR

1994	Jim Edgar (R)	22,107	75.6%
	Dawn Clark Netsch (D)	7,132	24.4%

54th Senate District

House District 107
House District 108

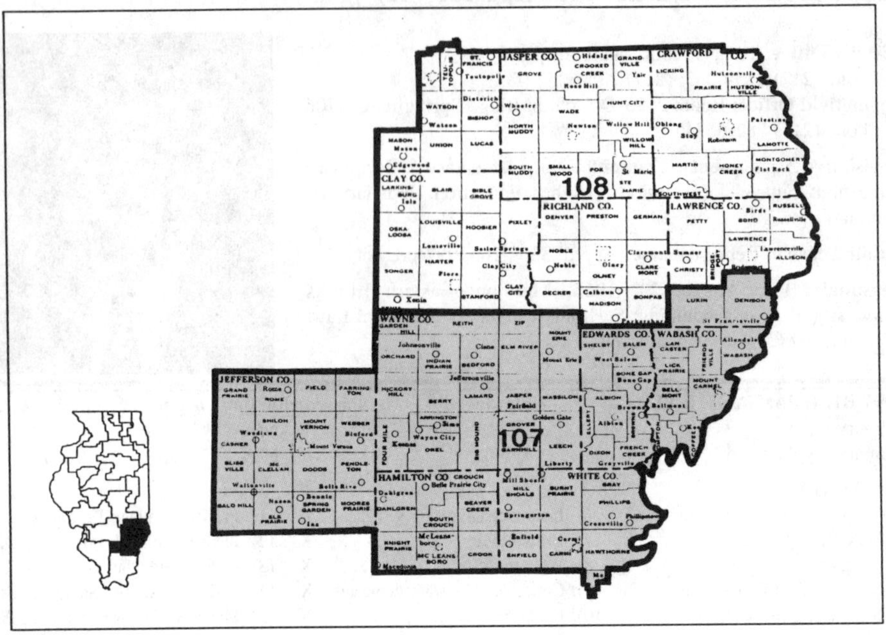

DEMOGRAPHICS (1990)

	S.D. #54	H.D. #107	H.D.#108
VOTING AGE POPULATION	143,492	72,220	71,272
White	98.4%	97.7%	99.2%
Black	0.9%	1.6%	0.2%
Hispanic	0.3%	0.4%	0.3%
Asian	0.2%	0.3%	0.2%
AGE (Total Population)	193,739	96,869	96,870
Under 6	8.4%	8.1%	8.6%
6 to 18	18.9%	18.7%	19.0%
65 and Over	18.1%	18.3%	17.8%
URBAN POPULATION	40.9%	40.2%	41.7%
HOUSING UNITS (Total)	83,550	42,857	40,693
Median Value	$38,513	$37,533	$39,419
Owner Occupied	69.8%	68.5%	71.1%
FAMILY INCOME (Total Families)	55,107	27,756	27,350
Median Income	$27,631	$27,518	$27.758
Below Poverty Level	11.5%	12.6%	10.4%
With Children Under 5	1.9%	2.0%	1.8%
With Children 5 to 17	4.1%	4.4%	3.8%
Headed by Females	4.2%	4.5%	3.9%
INDUSTRY (Total Employed)	81,289	39,604	41,685
Professional/Public Administration	22.7%	23.3%	22.1%
Manufacturing	21.2%	18.3%	23.9%
Retail	17.0%	18.1%	16.0%
Transportation/Communication	6.4%	6.5%	6.3%
Finance/Insurance/Real Estate	4.6%	4.8%	4.5%
Other Service	7.5%	7.9%	7.2%

Senator William L. O'Daniel (D)

District Office: 2929 Broadway, Mt. Vernon 62864
Phone (618) 242-7388; (618) 242-7393 (fax)
Springfield Office: 103-C Capitol Bldg., Springfield 62706
Phone (217) 782-5304; (217) 782-5252 (fax)

Legislative Assignments: Committees on Agriculture & Conservation (minority spokesperson); Transportation; Illinois Commission of Forestry Development; Joint Committee on Administrative Rules.

Public Service: Senator (1985-present); representative (1974-77).

Personal: Farmer/businessman; born December 4, 1923, Union County, KY; married (Norma); five children; eight grandchildren.

1997 BILL PASSAGE RATIO	Introduced	Passed House of Origin	Passed GA
Primary	4	1	1
Primary/Hyphenated	11	7	5

KEY VOTES

1) Senate GOP Ed. $ Plan . . . . N	6) Insurance/Domestic Violence . . Y	11) Pre-Paid College Tuition . . . . Y
2) State Budget . . . . Y	7) Brownfields . . . . Y	12) Increase Pull Tab Prizes . . . . O
3) Tougher DUI Level . . . . Y	8) Welfare Reform . . . . Y	13) Telecommunications Tax . . . Y
4) Ban Partial Birth Abortions . . . Y	9) Concealed Guns/Misdemeanor . Y	14) Delivery Discrimination . . . . Y
5) State Employees Pension . . . . . Y	10) Banks Sell Insurance . . . . Y	15) Sell Drivers' Data . . . . N

GROUP RATINGS

	FB	CoC	PrLf	IPPC	ACLU
1997	91	100	2/2	0	50

ELECTION RESULTS

1996 General	William L. O'Daniel (D)	50,865	(63.0%)
1996 General	Ron Williamson (R)	29,851	(37.0%)
1996 Primary	William L. O'Daniel (D)	9,549	(100%)
1996 Primary	Ron Williamson (R)	10,481	(100%)

CAMPAIGN RESOURCES AND EXPENDITURES

1996 Campaign Funds

Beg. Balance	$65,469	Individuals	$9,750
Receipts	$63,450	Party	$4,900
Expenditures	$52,369	PACS	$40,932
On hand	$76,550	Candidate	$946
		Not-itemized	$6,922

Top 10 PAC Contributors

1) ISMS	$5,023	6) EPAC	$1,000
2) IPACE	$5,000	7) LICID	$1,000
3) MPAC	$5,000	8) CatCEG	$1,000
4) CDS	$4,150	9) CoC	$1,000
5) Sears	$1,150	10) BI	$800

NOTE: The General Election Opponent's Campaign Resources and Expenditures are reported in a separate section in the back of the book (pp. 269-284).

GENERAL ELECTION DATA

	Registered Voters	Voter Turnout		Straight Party Voting			
1996	131,476	86,539	65.8%	(R) 11,391	13.2%	(D) 12,858	14.9%

PRESIDENT

1996	Bill Clinton (D)	35,571	42.3%
	Bob Dole (R)	37,588	44.8%
	Ross Perot (I)	10,223	12.2%
1992	Bill Clinton (D)	40,454	42.9%
	George Bush (R)	35,229	37.3%
	Ross Perot (I)	18,700	19.8%

UNITED STATES SENATE

1996	Richard J. Durbin (D)	36,299	44.4%
	Al Salvi (R)	42,449	52.0%

GOVERNOR

1994	Jim Edgar (R)	46,276	71.0%
	Dawn Clark Netsch (D)	18,868	29.0%

Representative John O. Jones (R)

District Office: P.O. Drawer 1787, 1116 Main St., Mt. Vernon 62864
Phone (618) 242-9511; (618) 242-9516 (fax)
Springfield Office: Room 2111-N Stratton Bldg., Springfield 62706
Phone (217) 782-0471

Legislative Assignments: Committees on Transportation & Motor Vehicles; Agriculture & Conservation; Elementary & Secondary Education; Veterans' Affairs.

Public Service: Representative (1995-present).

Personal: Owner, Jones Tank Truck Service; born October 8, 1940, Broughton; married (Mimi); two children.

1997 BILL PASSAGE RATIO	Introduced	Passed House of Origin	Passed GA
Primary	6	3	3
Primary/Hyphenated	18	15	11

KEY VOTES

1) Change Ed. Funding Formula . . N	6) Insurance/Domestic Violence . . Y	11) Pre-Paid College Tuition . . . . Y
2) State Budget . . . . Y	7) Brownfields . . . . Y	12) Increase Pull Tab Prizes . . . . Y
3) Tougher DUI Level . . . . N	8) Welfare Reform . . . . Y	13) Utility Deregulation . . . . P
4) Ban Partial Birth Abortions . . . Y	9) Concealed Guns/Misdemeanor . Y	14) County Obscenity Standards . Y
5) State Employees Pension . . . . . Y	10) Banks Sell Insurance . . . . Y	15) Managed Care Reform . . . . . N

GROUP RATINGS

	FB	CoC	PrLf	IPPC	ACLU
1997	54	62	6/6	0	30

ELECTION RESULTS

1996 General	John O. Jones (R)	21,785	(53.2%)
1996 General	Joe Bob Pierce (D)	19,155	(46.8%)
1996 Primary	John O. Jones (R)	6,767	(100%)

CAMPAIGN RESOURCES AND EXPENDITURES

1996 Campaign Funds

Beg. Balance	$46,096	Individuals	$11,106
Receipts	$370,601	Party	$262,244
Expenditures	$409,104	PACS	$77,297
On hand	$7,593	Candidate	$0
		Not-itemized	$19,954

Top 10 PAC Contributors

1) HRCC	$136,369	6) MPAC	$6,500
2) FLAD	$92,075	7) CChurchill	$5,000
3) IPACE	$19,500	8) Alliance	$5,000
4) ISMS	$11,000	9) CRyder	$5,000
5) CRyan	$10,000	10) JeffGOP	$3,600

NOTE: The General Election Opponent's Campaign Resources and Expenditures are reported in a separate section in the back of the book (pp. 269-284).

GENERAL ELECTION DATA

	Registered Voters	Voter Turnout		Straight Party Voting	
1996	66,510	42,983	64.6%	(R) 6,031 . . . 14.0%	(D) 7,219 . . . 16.8%

PRESIDENT

1996	Bill Clinton (D)	18,471	44.5%
	Bob Dole (R)	18,025	43.5%
	Ross Perot (I)	4,963	12.0%
1992	Bill Clinton (D)	21,537	44.8%
	George Bush (R)	17,487	36.4%
	Ross Perot (I)	9,036	18.8%

UNITED STATES SENATE

1996	Richard J. Durbin (D)	19,066	47.0%
	Al Salvi (R)	20,056	49.4%

GOVERNOR

1994	Jim Edgar (R)	22,669	69.3%
	Dawn Clark Netsch (D)	10,066	30.7%

Representative Charles A. "Chuck" Hartke (D)

District Office: P.O. Box 1205, 110 East Section, Effingham 62401
Phone (217) 342-2353; (217) 347-3305 (fax)
Springfield Office: Room 2044-J Stratton Bldg., Springfield 62706
Phone (217) 782-2087; (217) 524-0867 (fax)

Legislative Assignments: Majority Conference Chair. Committees on Agriculture & Conservation (vice chair); Transportation & Motor Vehicles; Local Government.

Public Service: Representative (1985-present); U.S. Army Vietnam veteran.

Personal: Farmer; born May 7, 1944, Effingham; married (Kathy); two children.

1997 BILL PASSAGE RATIO	Introduced	Passed House of Origin	Passed GA
Primary	14	6	2
Primary/Hyphenated	31	19	11

KEY VOTES

1) Change Ed. Funding Formula . . Y	6) Insurance/Domestic Violence . . Y	11) Pre-Paid College Tuition . . . . Y
2) State Budget . . . . Y	7) Brownfields . . . . Y	12) Increase Pull Tab Prizes . . . . Y
3) Tougher DUI Level . . . . N	8) Welfare Reform . . . . Y	13) Utility Deregulation . . . . . . Y
4) Ban Partial Birth Abortions . . . Y	9) Concealed Guns/Misdemeanor . Y	14) County Obscenity Standards . Y
5) State Employees Pension . . . . . Y	10) Banks Sell Insurance . . . . Y	15) Managed Care Reform . . . . . Y

GROUP RATINGS

	FB	CoC	PrLf	IPPC	ACLU
1997	86	23	6/6	0	20

ELECTION RESULTS

1996 General	Charles A. "Chuck" Hartke (D)	24,484	(59.1%)
1996 General	Cory M. Jobe (R)	16,918	(40.9%)
1996 Primary	Charles A. "Chuck" Hartke (D)	3,393	(100%)
1996 Primary	Cory M. Jobe (R)	5,249	(100%)

CAMPAIGN RESOURCES AND EXPENDITURES

1996 Campaign Funds

Beg. Balance	$55,702	Individuals	$2,390
Receipts	$74,509	Party	$15,000
Expenditures	$81,867	PACS	$33,630
On hand	$48,344	Candidate	$504
		Not-itemized	$22,985

Top 10 PAC Contributors

1) DSCC	$15,000	6) WMgt	$1,200
2) MCIDC	$2,500	7) P&P	$1,200
3) Activator	$2,360	8) JJM	$1,000
4) ITLA	$2,000	9) Laborers	$700
5) CTCPAC	$1,500	10) JBEsker	$630

NOTE: The General Election Opponent's Campaign Resources and Expenditures are reported in a separate section in the back of the book (pp. 269-284).

GENERAL ELECTION DATA

	Registered Voters	Voter Turnout		Straight Party Voting	
1996	64,966	43,556	67.0%	(R) 5,360 . . . 12.3%	(D) 5,639 . . . 12.9%

PRESIDENT

1996	Bill Clinton (D)	17,100	40.5%
	Bob Dole (R)	19,563	46.3%
	Ross Perot (I)	5,260	12.4%
1992	Bill Clinton (D)	18,917	40.8%
	George Bush (R)	17,742	38.3%
	Ross Perot (I)	9,664	20.9%

UNITED STATES SENATE

1996	Richard J. Durbin (D)	17,233	41.9%
	Al Salvi (R)	22,393	54.5%

GOVERNOR

1994	Jim Edgar (R)	23,607	72.8%
	Dawn Clark Netsch (D)	8,802	27.2%

55th Senate District

House District 109
House District 110

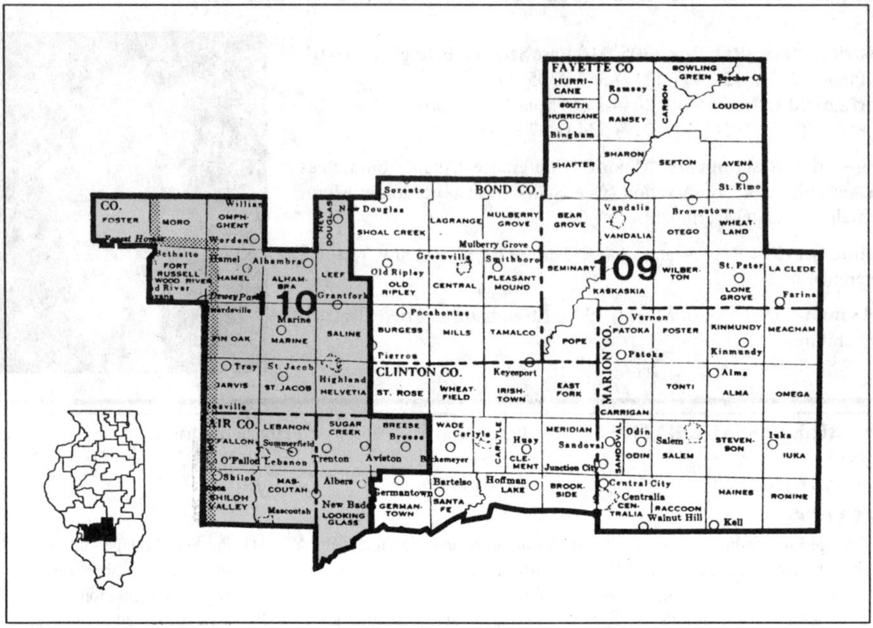

DEMOGRAPHICS (1990)

	S.D. #55	H.D. #109	H.D.#110
VOTING AGE POPULATION	140,831	71,883	68,948
White	94.7%	95.2%	94.2%
Black	3.6%	3.7%	3.6%
Hispanic	0.9%	0.7%	1.0%
Asian	0.6%	0.3%	0.9%
AGE (Total Population)	193,739	96,870	96,869
Under 6	8.9%	8.3%	9.5%
6 to 18	19.8%	18.9%	20.7%
65 and Over	13.8%	16.7%	10.9%
URBAN POPULATION	48.1%	37.3%	59.0%
HOUSING UNITS (Total)	76,010	40,224	35,786
Median Value	$53,599	$38,568	$68,055
Owner Occupied	68.7%	69.7%	67.6%
FAMILY INCOME (Total Families)	52,853	26,137	26,716
Median Income	$33,605	$28.870	$38,824
Below Poverty Level	7.9%	11.4%	4.5%
With Children Under 5	1.4%	1.9%	1.0%
With Children 5 to 17	2.8%	4.0%	1.6%
Headed by Females	3.1%	4.2%	2.0%
INDUSTRY (Total Employed)	84,265	40,545	43,720
Professional/Public Administration	28.1%	26.7%	29.3%
Manufacturing	18.9%	22.3%	15.7%
Retail	17.3%	16.4%	18.2%
Transportation/Communication	7.9%	8.3%	7.6%
Finance/Insurance/Real Estate	5.4%	4.1%	6.6%
Other Service	7.2%	6.3%	8.0%

Senator Frank Watson (R)

District Office: 890 Franklin, Carlyle 62231
Phone (618) 594-4553; (618) 594-4918 (fax)
Springfield Office: 321 Capitol Bldg., Springfield 62706
Phone (217) 782-5755; (217) 782-4079

Legislative Assignments: Assistant Majority Leader. Committees on Agriculture & Conservation; Education; Executive.

Public Service: Senator (1983-present); representative (1978-1983); former trustee and supervisor, Bond County Central Township.

Personal: Pharmacist; born July 26, 1945, St. Louis, Missouri; Purdue University, B.S. in pharmacy; married (Susan Rasler); two children.

1997 BILL PASSAGE RATIO	Introduced	Passed House of Origin	Passed GA
Primary	23	14	12
Primary/Hyphenated	33	20	17

KEY VOTES

1) Senate GOP Ed. $ Plan . . . . . . .Y	6) Insurance/Domestic Violence . .Y	11) Pre-Paid College Tuition . . .Y
2) State Budget . . . . .Y	7) Brownfields . . . . .Y	12) Increase Pull Tab Prizes . . . .Y
3) Tougher DUI Level . . . . .N	8) Welfare Reform . . . . .Y	13) Telecommunications Tax . . .N
4) Ban Partial Birth Abortions . . .Y	9) Concealed Guns/Misdemeanor .Y	14) Delivery Discrimination . . . .P
5) State Employees Pension . . . . .Y	10) Banks Sell Insurance . . . . .Y	15) Sell Drivers' Data . . . . .N

GROUP RATINGS

	FB	CoC	PrLf	IPPC	ACLU
1997	91	100	2/2	0	50

ELECTION RESULTS

1996 General	Frank Watson (R)	52,823	(67.8%)
1996 General	David Ahola (D)	25,041	(32.2%)
1996 Primary	Frank Watson (R)	12,281	(100%)
1996 Primary	David Ahola (D)	7,599	(100%)

CAMPAIGN RESOURCES AND EXPENDITURES

1996 Campaign Funds

Beg. Balance	$119,879	Individuals	$11,560
Receipts	$114,847	Party	$2,834
Expenditures	$168,235	PACS	$67,493
On hand	$66,491	Candidate	$1,311
		Not-itemized	$31,649

Top 10 PAC Contributors

1) MPAC $3,650	6) PIIA $1,500
2) Activator . .$3,423	7) AFFI $1,400
3) IPACE $2,000	8) MidAmAdv $1,180
4) Pharmacy . .$2,000	9) Rehkemper .$1,150
5) Ameritech .$1,750	10) ISMS $1,036

NOTE: The General Election Opponent's Campaign Resources and Expenditures are reported in a separate section in the back of the book (pp. 269-284).

GENERAL ELECTION DATA

Registered Voters	Voter Turnout		Straight Party Voting	
1996 122,112	82,434	67.5%	(R) 12,763 . .15.5%	(D) 14,895 . . .18.1%

PRESIDENT

1996	Bill Clinton (D)	35,633	44.3%
	Bob Dole (R)	35,706	44.4%
	Ross Perot (I)	8,390	10.4%
1992	Bill Clinton (D)	39,042	44.0%
	George Bush (R)	31,733	35.8%
	Ross Perot (I)	17,883	20.2%

UNITED STATES SENATE

1996	Richard J. Durbin (D)	38,961	49.3%
	Al Salvi (R)	37,645	47.6%

GOVERNOR

1994	Jim Edgar (R)	41,349	70.1%
	Dawn Clark Netsch (D)	17,613	29.9%

Representative Kurt M. Granberg (D)

District Office: 230 East Broadway, Centralia 62801
Phone (618) 533-0296; (618) 533-2153 (fax)
Springfield Office: Room 300 Capitol Bldg., Springfield 62706
Phone (217) 782-0066

Legislative Assignments: Assistant Majority Leader; ex officio member of all committees. Committees on Consumer Protection (vice chair); Agriculture & Conservation; Conflicts of Interest.

Public Service: Representative (1983-present).

Personal: Attorney; born June 16, 1953, Carlyle; University of Illinois, B.A. in political science/criminal justice; Chicago-Kent College of Law, J.D.; married (Mary).

1997 BILL PASSAGE RATIO	Introduced	Passed House of Origin	Passed GA
Primary	61	2	1
Primary/Hyphenated	96	23	12

KEY VOTES

1) Change Ed. Funding Formula . . Y	6) Insurance/Domestic Violence . . Y	11) Pre-Paid College Tuition . . . . Y
2) State Budget . . . . Y	7) Brownfields . . . . Y	12) Increase Pull Tab Prizes . . . . Y
3) Tougher DUI Level . . . . Y	8) Welfare Reform . . . . Y	13) Utility Deregulation . . . . Y
4) Ban Partial Birth Abortions . . . Y	9) Concealed Guns/Misdemeanor . Y	14) County Obscenity Standards A
5) State Employees Pension . . . . . Y	10) Banks Sell Insurance . . . . P	15) Managed Care Reform . . . . . Y

GROUP RATINGS

	FB	CoC	PrLf	IPPC	ACLU
1997	86	38	5/6	16	22

ELECTION RESULTS

1996 General	Kurt M. Granberg (D)	25,678	(68.6%)
1996 General	Jackie D. "Butch" Mathus, Jr. (R)	11,767	(31.4%)
1996 Primary	Kurt M. Granberg (D)	4,947	(100%)
1996 Primary	Jackie D. "Butch" Mathus, Jr. (R)	5,104	(100%)

CAMPAIGN RESOURCES AND EXPENDITURES

1996 Campaign Funds				Top 10 PAC Contributors			
Beg. Balance	$103,599	Individuals	$2,795	1) DSCC	$32,500	6) UST	$3,000
Receipts	$125,848	Party	$33,200	2) ISMS	$6,000	7) ILCable	$3,000
Expenditures	$99,522	PACS	$76,027	3) ABDI	$6,000	8) IRLA	$2,500
On hand	$129,925	Candidate	$1,926	4) GGCouncil	$5,000	9) WMgt	$2,400
		Not-itemized	$11,900	5) ITLA	$3,000	10) AFFI	$2,000

NOTE: The General Election Opponent's Campaign Resources and Expenditures are reported in a separate section in the back of the book (pp. 269-284).

GENERAL ELECTION DATA

	Registered Voters	Voter Turnout		Straight Party Voting	
1996	62,840	40,368	64.2%	(R) 5,236 . . . 13.0%	(D) 7,451 . . . 18.5%

PRESIDENT

1996	Bill Clinton (D)	18,314	46.9%
	Bob Dole (R)	16,119	41.3%
	Ross Perot (I)	4,327	11.1%
1992	Bill Clinton (D)	21,901	48.4%
	George Bush (R)	15,062	33.3%
	Ross Perot (I)	8,261	18.3%

UNITED STATES SENATE

1996	Richard J. Durbin (D)	19,953	52.0%
	Al Salvi (R)	17,345	45.2%

GOVERNOR

1994	Jim Edgar (R)	20,822	68.3%
	Dawn Clark Netsch (D)	9,644	31.7%

Representative Ron Stephens (R)

District Office: 535 Edwardsville Rd., Suite 110, Troy 62294
Phone (618) 667-0110; (618) 667-8669 (fax)
Springfield Office: Room 2003-G Stratton Bldg., Springfield 62706
Phone (217) 782-6401; (217) 782-3189 (fax)

Legislative Assignments: Assistant Republican Leader; ex officio member of all committees. Committees on Executive; Registration & Regulation; Appropriations-General Services and Oversight; Electric Utility Deregulation.

Public Service: Representative (1985-91; 1993-present); former trustee, Village of Caseyville; U.S. Vietnam veteran.

Personal: Pharmacist; born February 19, 1948, East St. Louis; St. Louis College of Pharmacy; B.S. in pharmacy; married (Karen); five children.

1997 BILL PASSAGE RATIO	Introduced	Passed House of Origin	Passed GA
Primary	18	4	1
Primary/Hyphenated	36	15	7

KEY VOTES

1) Change Ed. Funding Formula . .N	6) Insurance/Domestic Violence . .Y	11) Pre-Paid College Tuition . . . .Y
2) State Budget . . . . .Y	7) Brownfields . . . . .Y	12) Increase Pull Tab Prizes . . . .Y
3) Tougher DUI Level . . . . .N	8) Welfare Reform . . . . .Y	13) Utility Deregulation . . . . . . .Y
4) Ban Partial Birth Abortions . . .Y	9) Concealed Guns/Misdemeanor .Y	14) County Obscenity Standards Y
5) State Employees Pension . . . . .Y	10) Banks Sell Insurance . . . . .Y	15) Managed Care Reform . . . . .N

GROUP RATINGS

	FB	CoC	PrLf	IPPC	ACLU
1997	64	62	6/6	0	30

ELECTION RESULTS

1996 General	Ron Stephens (R)	26,819	(67.1%)
1996 General	Velda Armes (D)	13,166	(32.9%)
1996 Primary	Ron Stephens (R)	5,761	(100%)
1996 Primary	Velda Armes (D)	3,922	(100%)

CAMPAIGN RESOURCES AND EXPENDITURES

1996 Campaign Funds				Top 10 PAC Contributors			
Beg. Balance	$53,202	Individuals	$3,990	1) IPACE	$5,000	6) MPAC	$2,500
Receipts	$75,446	Party	$5,979	2) FreedomEnt	$5,000	7) RPAC	$2,490
Expenditures	$128,062	PACS	$43,256	3) HomeTeleph	$4,790	8) Activator	$1,967
On hand	$586	Candidate	$5,000	4) HRCC	$3,649	9) ABDI	$1,000
		Not-itemized	$17,221	5) ISMS	$2,517	10) Argosy	$1,000

NOTE: The General Election Opponent's Campaign Resources and Expenditures are reported in a separate section in the back of the book (pp. 269-284).

GENERAL ELECTION DATA

	Registered Voters	Voter Turnout		Straight Party Voting			
1996	59,272	42,066	70.9%	(R) 7,527	17.9%	(D) 7,444	17.7%

PRESIDENT

1996	Bill Clinton (D)	17,319	41.9%
	Bob Dole (R)	19,587	47.4%
	Ross Perot (I)	4,063	9.8%
1992	Bill Clinton (D)	17,141	39.5%
	George Bush (R)	16,671	38.4%
	Ross Perot (I)	9,622	22.1%

UNITED STATES SENATE

1996	Richard J. Durbin (D)	19,008	46.7%
	Al Salvi (R)	20,300	49.9%

GOVERNOR

1994	Jim Edgar (R)	20,527	72.0%
	Dawn Clark Netsch (D)	7,969	28.0%

56th Senate District

House District 111
House District 112

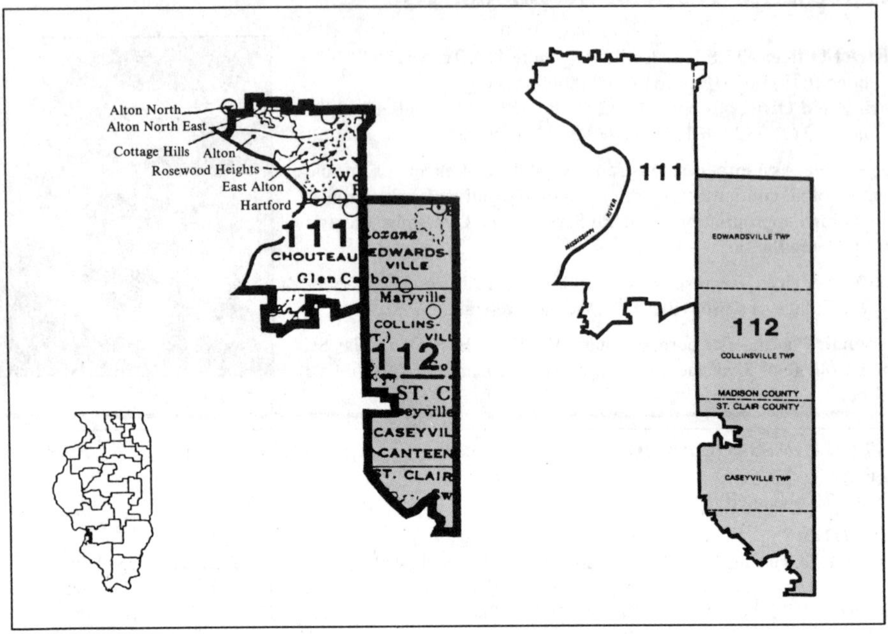

DEMOGRAPHICS (1990)

	S.D. #56	H.D. #111	H.D.#112
VOTING AGE POPULATION	145,588	72,350	73,238
White	92.0%	91.8%	92.2%
Black	5.9%	6.6%	5.2%
Hispanic	1.1%	0.9%	1.3%
Asian	0.7%	0.3%	1.1%
AGE (Total Population)	193,739	96,870	96,869
Under 6	8.4%	8.5%	8.3%
6 to 18	17.9%	18.3%	17.5%
65 and Over	14.1%	15.2%	12.9%
URBAN POPULATION	94.8%	98.5%	91.0%
HOUSING UNITS (Total)	79,249	40,033	39,216
Median Value	$54,580	$43,542	$70,438
Owner Occupied	67.5%	67.8%	67.2%
FAMILY INCOME (Total Families)	53,707	26,923	26,784
Median Income	$36,668	$32,883	$40.755
Below Poverty Level	7.6%	10.1%	5.0%
With Children Under 5	1.6%	2.2%	0.9%
With Children 5 to 17	3.1%	4.2%	2.0%
Headed by Females	4.5%	6.2%	2.8%
INDUSTRY (Total Employed)	89,052	42,129	46,924
Professional/Public Administration	28.2%	26.0%	30.0%
Manufacturing	19.2%	23.1%	15.6%
Retail	18.4%	18.5%	18.4%
Transportation/Communication	7.7%	7.4%	8.0%
Finance/Insurance/Real Estate	7.7%	6.8%	8.6%
Other Service	8.2%	8.0%	8.3%

Senator Evelyn M. Bowles (D)

District Office: 40 Edwardsville Professional Park, Suite 248, Edwardsville 62025
Phone (618) 656-8422; (618) 656-2425 (fax)
Springfield Office: M-103D Capitol Bldg., Springfield 62706
Phone (217) 782-5247

Legislative Assignments: Committees on Local Government & Elections (minority spokesperson); Agriculture & Conservation; Transportation.

Public Service: Senator (1994-present); Madison County Clerk (1974 - 94).

Personal: Full-time legislator; born in Worden; U.S. Coast Guard Women's Reserve Intelligence Division; former school teacher.

1997 BILL PASSAGE RATIO	Introduced	Passed House of Origin	Passed GA
Primary	11	3	2
Primary/Hyphenated	25	12	8

KEY VOTES

1) Senate GOP Ed. $ Plan . . . . . . .N	6) Insurance/Domestic Violence . .Y	11) Pre-Paid College Tuition . . . .Y
2) State Budget . . . . .Y	7) Brownfields . . . . .Y	12) Increase Pull Tab Prizes . . . .O
3) Tougher DUI Level . . . . .Y	8) Welfare Reform . . . . .Y	13) Telecommunications Tax . . .Y
4) Ban Partial Birth Abortions . . .Y	9) Concealed Guns/Misdemeanor .Y	14) Delivery Discrimination . . . .Y
5) State Employees Pension . . . . .Y	10) Bank Sell Insurance . . . . .Y	15) Sell Drivers' Data . . . . .N

GROUP RATINGS

	FB	CoC	PrLf	IPPC	ACLU
1997	82	60	2/2	0	33

ELECTION RESULTS

1994 General	Evelyn M. Bowles (D)	30,463	(57.5%)
1994 General	David R. Tanzyus (R)	22,530	(42.5%)
1994 Primary	Evelyn M. Bowles (D)	15,873	(100%)
1994 Primary	David R. Tanzyus (R)	3,616	(100%)

CAMPAIGN RESOURCES AND EXPENDITURES

1996 Campaign Funds				Top 10 PAC Contributors			
Beg. Balance	$13,980	Individuals	$0	1) IPACE	$1,000	6) AGC	$300
Receipts	$3,900	Party	$0	2) Olin	$500	7) AB	$250
Expenditures	$3,582	PACS	$3,800	3) HOPE	$500	8) Walgreens	$200
On hand	$14,298	Candidate	$0	4) CPA's	$400	9) G&FLC	$200
		Not-itemized	$100	5) BNRR	$300	10) Sears	$150

NOTE: The General Election Opponent's Campaign Resources and Expenditures are reported in a separate section in the back of the book (pp. 269-284).

GENERAL ELECTION DATA

	Registered Voters	Voter Turnout		Straight Party Voting	
1996	116,326	79,381	68.2%	(R) 10,633 . . 13.4%	(D) 25,910 . . . 32.6%

PRESIDENT

1996	Bill Clinton (D)	41,466	53.2%
	Bob Dole (R)	28,269	36.2%
	Ross Perot (I)	7,438	9.5%
1992	Bill Clinton (D)	44,650	50.7%
	George Bush (R)	26,087	29.6%
	Ross Perot (I)	17,402	19.7%

UNITED STATES SENATE

1996	Richard J. Durbin (D)	43,500	56.4%
	Al Salvi (R)	30,360	39.4%

GOVERNOR

1994	Jim Edgar (R)	33,218	64.2%
	Dawn Clark Netsch (D)	18,555	35.8%

Representative Steve Davis (D)

District Office: 29 North Wood River Ave., Wood River 62095
Phone (618) 251-4934; (618) 251-5023 (fax)
Springfield Office: Room 2057-L Stratton Bldg., Springfield 62706
Phone (217) 782-5996

Legislative Assignments: Committees on Veterans' Affairs (chair); Public Utilities; Registration & Regulation; Environment & Energy.

Public Service: Representative (1994-present); former highway commissioner, Wood River Township.

Personal: Full-time legislator; born September 22, 1949; Southern Illinois University-Edwardsville, majoring in engineering; Lewis & Clark Community College; married (Carol); two children.

1997 BILL PASSAGE RATIO	Introduced	Passed House of Origin	Passed GA
Primary	35	8	1
Primary/Hyphenated	69	26	9

KEY VOTES

1) Change Ed. Funding Formula . . Y
2) State Budget . . . . Y
3) Tougher DUI Level . . . . Y
4) Ban Partial Birth Abortions . . . Y
5) State Employees Pension . . . . . Y
6) Insurance/Domestic Violence . . Y
7) Brownfields . . . . Y
8) Welfare Reform . . . . Y
9) Concealed Guns/Misdemeanor . Y
10) Banks Sell Insurance . . . . Y
11) Pre-Paid College Tuition . . . . Y
12) Increase Pull Tab Prizes . . . . Y
13) Utility Deregulation . . . . Y
14) County Obscenity Standards . N
15) Managed Care Reform . . . . . Y

GROUP RATINGS

	FB	CoC	PrLf	IPPC	ACLU
1997	71	31	1/6	83	80

ELECTION RESULTS

1996 General	Steve Davis (D)	22,265	(64.1%)
1996 General	Jim Mihalich (R)	12,470	(35.9%)
1996 Primary	Steve Davis (D)	5,651	(72.5%)
1996 Primary	Charles "Tim" Knott (D)	2,146	(27.5%)

CAMPAIGN RESOURCES AND EXPENDITURES

1996 Campaign Funds

Beg. Balance	$10,263	Individuals	$3,432
Receipts	$164,725	Party	$61, 487
Expenditures	$173,100	PACS	$78,719
On hand	$1,888	Candidate	$0
		Not-itemized	$21,087

Top 10 PAC Contributors

1) IHDM	$58,075	6) JJM	$2,500
2) IPACE	$9,500	7) HG&B	$2,500
3) AFSCME	$9,096	8) DSCC	$2,012
4) ITLA	$5,000	9) USWA	$2,000
5) SEIU	$5,000	10) UAW	$2,000

NOTE: The General Election Opponent's Campaign Resources and Expenditures are reported in a separate section in the back of the book (pp. 269-284).

GENERAL ELECTION DATA

	Registered Voters	Voter Turnout		Straight Party Voting	
1996	55,023	35,988	65.4%	(R) 3,745 . . . 10.4%	(D) 14,312 . . . 39.8%

PRESIDENT

1996	Bill Clinton (D)	20,743	58.8%
	Bob Dole (R)	10,159	28.8%
	Ross Perot (I)	3,924	11.1%
1992	Bill Clinton (D)	23,648	56.7%
	George Bush (R)	9,969	23.9%
	Ross Perot (I)	8,082	19.4%

UNITED STATES SENATE

1996	Richard J. Durbin (D)	21,080	60.4%
	Al Salvi (R)	11,824	33.9%

GOVERNOR

1994	Jim Edgar (R)	14,541	65.4%
	Dawn Clark Netsch (D)	9,702	34.6%

Representative Jay C. Hoffman (D)

District Office: 214 St. Louis St., Edwardsville 62025
Phone (618) 692-9710; (618) 692-9780 (fax)
Springfield Office: Room 2099-M Stratton Bldg., Springfield 62706
Phone (217) 782-8018

Legislative Assignments: Committees on Transportation & Motor Vehicles (chair); Judiciary I-Civil Law; Personnel & Pensions

Public Service: Representative (1991-1997; appointed Oct. 26, 1997-present); assistant state's attorney, St. Clair County.

Personal: Attorney; born November 6, 1961, Highland; Illinois State University, B.S. in finance; St. Louis University Law School; married (Laurie); two children.

1997 BILL PASSAGE RATIO	Introduced	Passed House of Origin	Passed GA
Primary	N/A	N/A	N/A
Primary/Hyphenated	N/A	N/A	N/A

KEY VOTES

1) Change Ed. Funding Formula . . X
2) State Budget X
3) Tougher DUI Level X
4) Ban Partial Birth Abortions . . . X
5) State Employees Pension X
6) Insurance/Domestic Violence . . X
7) Brownfields X
8) Welfare Reform X
9) Concealed Guns/Misdemeanor . X
10) Banks Sell Insurance X
11) Pre-Paid College Tuition X
12) Increase Pull Tab Prizes X
13) Utility Deregulation X
14) County Obscenity Standards . X
15) Managed Care Reform X

GROUP RATINGS

	FB	CoC	PrLf	IPPC	ACLU
1997	N/R	N/R	N/R	N/R	N/R

ELECTION RESULTS

1996 General	Glenn E. Bradford (D)	20,436	(52.0%)
1996 General	Mario Garcia, Jr. (R)	18,857	(48.0%)
1996 Primary	Glenn E. Bradford (D)	4,064	(55.0%)
1996 Primary	Ronald McDonald (D)	3,321	(45.0%)

CAMPAIGN RESOURCES AND EXPENDITURES

1996 Campaign Funds

Beg. Balance	$52,794	Individuals	$0
Receipts	$0	Party	$0
Expenditures	$27,451	PACS	$0
On hand	$25,343	Candidate	$0
		Not-itemized	$0

Top 10 PAC Contributors

1) NA	$N/A	6) N/A	$N/A
2) NA	$N/A	7) N/A	$N/A
3) NA	$N/A	8) N/A	$N/A
4) N/A	$N/A	9) N/A	$N/A
5) N/A	$N/A	10) N/A	$N/A

NOTE: The General Election Opponent's Campaign Resources and Expenditures are reported in a separate section in the back of the book (pp. 269-284).

GENERAL ELECTION DATA

	Registered Voters	Voter Turnout		Straight Party Voting	
1996	61,303	43,393	70.8%	(R) 6,888 . . . 15.9%	(D) 11,598 . . . 26.7%

PRESIDENT

1996	Bill Clinton (D)	20,723	48.5%
	Bob Dole (R)	18,110	42.4%
	Ross Perot (I)	3,514	8.2%
1992	Bill Clinton (D)	21,002	45.2%
	George Bush (R)	16,118	34.7%
	Ross Perot (I)	9,320	20.1%

UNITED STATES SENATE

1996	Richard J. Durbin (D)	22,420	53.1%
	Al Salvi (R)	18,536	43.9%

GOVERNOR

1994	Jim Edgar (R)	18,677	67.8%
	Dawn Clark Netsch (D)	8,853	32.2%

57th Senate District

House District 113
House District 114

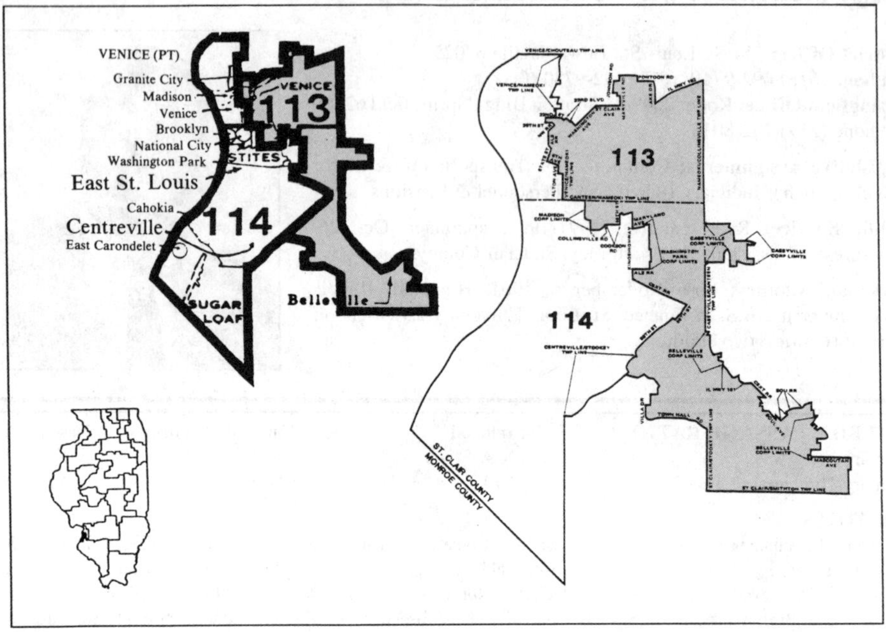

DEMOGRAPHICS (1990)

	S.D. #57	H.D. #113	H.D.#114
VOTING AGE POPULATION	138,054	73,415	64,639
White	66.3%	93.0%	36.1%
Black	31.8%	4.9%	62.3%
Hispanic	1.3%	1.4%	1.2%
Asian	0.4%	0.5%	0.2%
AGE (Total Population)	193,739	96,869	96,870
Under 6	9.9%	8.5%	11.2%
6 to 18	20.5%	16.9%	24.0%
65 and Over	13.6%	16.5%	10.6%
URBAN POPULATION	96.5%	96.2%	96.8%
HOUSING UNITS (Total)	78,697	41,992	36,705
Median Value	$42,355	$54,523	$29,880
Owner Occupied	55.5%	59.8%	50.5%
FAMILY INCOME (Total Families)	49,659	26,022	23,637
Median Income	$27,048	$32,582	$20,933
Below Poverty Level	19.5%	9.2%	30.8%
With Children Under 5	2.7%	1.9%	3.7%
With Children 5 to 17	7.8%	3.8%	12.1%
Headed by Females	13.9%	5.5%	23.1%
INDUSTRY (Total Employed)	73,275	42,915	30,359
Professional/Public Administration	30.1%	29.8%	30.5%
Manufacturing	16.9%	16.1%	18.1%
Retail	18.0%	18.4%	17.3%
Transportation/Communication	8.9%	8.4%	9.5%
Finance/Insurance/Real Estate	6.9%	7.3%	6.4%
Other Service	9.7%	9.0%	10.7%

Senator James F. Clayborne, Jr. II (D)

District Office: 327 Missouri Ave., Suite 422, East St. Louis 62201
Phone (618) 875-1212; (618) 274-3010 (fax)
Springfield Office: 103-B State Capitol, Springfield 62706
Phone (217) 782-5399

Legislative Assignments: Committees on Appropriations; Revenue.

Public Service: Senator (appointed April 17, 1995-present); assistant state's attorney, St. Clair County.

Personal: Attorney; born May 29, 1963, St. Louis, MO; University of Miami Law School; married (Staci); three children.

1997 BILL PASSAGE RATIO	Introduced	Passed House of Origin	Passed GA
Primary	7	0	0
Primary/Hyphenated	18	9	6

KEY VOTES

1) Senate GOP Ed. $ Plan ....N	6) Insurance/Domestic Violence ..Y	11) Pre-Paid College Tuition ....Y
2) State Budget ....Y	7) Brownfields ....Y	12) Increase Pull Tab Prizes ....O
3) Tougher DUI Level ....Y	8) Welfare Reform ....Y	13) Telecommunications Tax ...O
4) Ban Partial Birth Abortions ...Y	9) Concealed Guns/Misdemeanor .Y	14) Delivery Discrimination ....Y
5) State Employees Pension .....Y	10) Banks Sell Insurance ....Y	15) Sell Drivers' Data ....N

GROUP RATINGS

	FB	CoC	PrLf	IPPC	ACLU
1997	64	60	2/2	0	75

ELECTION RESULTS

1996 General	James F. Clayborne, Jr. II (D)	48,193	(100%)
1996 Primary	James F. Clayborne, Jr. II (D)	12,929	(100%)
1992 General	Kenneth Hall (D)	53,604	(75.4%)
1992 General	Wyatt C. Frazier (R)	17,523	(24.6%)

CAMPAIGN RESOURCES AND EXPENDITURES

1996 Campaign Funds				Top 10 PAC Contributors	
Beg. Balance	$58,453	Individuals	$0	1) IPACE $9,000	6) IBA $1,000
Receipts	$36,889	Party	$1,558	2) LAWPAC ..$3,000	7) FDurbin ...$1,000
Expenditures	$33,041	PACS	$34,450	3) ISMS $3,000	8) COBANK .$1,000
On hand	$62,301	Candidate	$0	4) WMgt $2,000	9) KHC $1,000
		Not-itemized	$881	5) ITLA $2,000	10) LICID ...$1,000

NOTE: The General Election Opponent's Campaign Resources and Expenditures are reported in a separate section in the back of the book (pp. 269-284).

GENERAL ELECTION DATA

	Registered Voters	Voter Turnout		Straight Party Voting	
1996	111,667	64,751	58.0%	(R) 5,183 ....8.0%	(D) 20,006 ...30.9%

PRESIDENT

1996	Bill Clinton (D)	42,540	67.6%
	Bob Dole (R)	15,443	24.5%
	Ross Perot (I)	4,255	6.8%
1992	Bill Clinton (D)	48,720	63.9%
	George Bush (R)	16,999	22.3%
	Ross Perot (I)	10,560	13.8%

UNITED STATES SENATE

1996	Richard J. Durbin (D)	44,191	70.0%
	Al Salvi (R)	16,822	26.7%

GOVERNOR

1994	Jim Edgar (R)	23,834	54.4%
	Dawn Clark Netsch (D)	19,949	45.6%

Representative Thomas Holbrook (D)

District Office: 9200 West Main St., Suite 4, Belleville 62223
Phone (618) 394-2211; (618) 394-2210 (fax)
Springfield Office: Room 2062-L Stratton Bldg., Springfield 62706
Phone (217) 782-0104; (217) 782-1333 (fax)

Legislative Assignments: Committees on Local Government (vice-chair); Environment & Energy; Transportation & Motor Vehicles; Veterans' Affairs.

Public Service: Representative (1995-present); board member, St. Clair County.

Personal: Electrical/Instrumentation maintenance; born November 23, 1949, St. Louis, MO.; Southern Illinois University-Edwardsville, B.A. in social science government; married (Molly); one child.

1997 BILL PASSAGE RATIO	Introduced	Passed House of Origin	Passed GA
Primary	24	6	3
Primary/Hyphenated	94	62	33

KEY VOTES

1) Change Ed. Funding Formula . . Y
2) State Budget . . . . Y
3) Tougher DUI Level . . . . N
4) Ban Partial Birth Abortions . . . Y
5) State Employees Pension . . . . . Y
6) Insurance/Domestic Violence . . Y
7) Brownfields . . . . Y
8) Welfare Reform . . . . Y
9) Concealed Guns/Misdemeanor . Y
10) Banks Sell Insurance . . . . Y
11) Pre-Paid College Tuition . . . . Y
12) Increase Pull Tab Prizes . . . . Y
13) Utility Deregulation . . . . Y
14) County Obscenity Standards . Y
15) Managed Care Reform . . . . . Y

GROUP RATINGS

	FB	CoC	PrLf	IPPC	ACLU
1997	82	23	6/6	0	20

ELECTION RESULTS

1996 General	Thomas Holbrook (D)	20,739	(62.2%)
1996 General	Paul A. Whelan (R)	12,578	(37.8%)
1996 Primary	Thomas Holbrook (D)	6,526	(100%)

CAMPAIGN RESOURCES AND EXPENDITURES

1996 Campaign Funds

Beg. Balance	$8,835	Individuals	$3,875
Receipts	$50,911	Party	$1,000
Expenditures	$40,688	PACS	$31,780
On hand	$19,058	Candidate	$0
		Not-itemized	$14,256

Top 10 PAC Contributors

1) IPACE $7,000	6) IFT $800
2) ITLA $2,000	7) IHCA $750
3) USWA $2,000	8) IBA $750
4) UAW $1,000	9) RPAC $700
5) Teamsters . . $1,000	10) CUPAC $650

NOTE: The General Election Opponent's Campaign Resources and Expenditures are reported in a separate section in the back of the book (pp. 269-284).

GENERAL ELECTION DATA

	Registered Voters	Voter Turnout		Straight Party Voting	
1996	54,941	35,639	64.9%	(R) 4,311 . . . 12.1%	(D) 10,743 . . . 30.1%

PRESIDENT

1996	Bill Clinton (D)	18,692	53.4%
	Bob Dole (R)	12,813	36.6%
	Ross Perot (I)	3,121	8.9%
1992	Bill Clinton (D)	20,464	49.1%
	George Bush (R)	13,344	32.0%
	Ross Perot (I)	7,851	18.9%

UNITED STATES SENATE

1996	Richard J. Durbin (D)	19,398	56.3%
	Al Salvi (R)	13,773	40.1%

GOVERNOR

1994	Jim Edgar (R)	16,422	65.2%
	Dawn Clark Netsch (D)	8,751	34.8%

Representative Wyvetter H. Younge (D)

District Office: 1010 Martin Luther King Drive, East St. Louis, 62201
Phone (618) 875-1691; (618) 875-6323 (fax)
Springfield Office: Room L-2 Stratton Bldg., Springfield 62706
Phone (217) 782-5951; (217) 782-8794 (fax)

Legislative Assignments: Appropriations-Education (chairperson).

Public Service: Representative (1975-present).

Personal: Attorney; born August 23, 1930; Hampton Institute, B.S.; St. Louis University School of Law, J.D.; Washington University School of Law, L.L.M.; married (Richard); three children.

1997 BILL PASSAGE RATIO	Introduced	Passed House of Origin	Passed GA
Primary	37	7	1
Primary/Hyphenated	63	12	3

KEY VOTES

1) Change Ed. Funding Formula . . Y	6) Insurance/Domestic Violence . . Y	11) Pre-Paid College Tuition . . . . Y
2) State Budget . . . . Y	7) Brownfields . . . . Y	12) Increase Pull Tab Prizes . . . . Y
3) Tougher DUI Level . . . . Y	8) Welfare Reform . . . . Y	13) Utility Deregulation . . . . Y
4) Ban Partial Birth Abortions . . . N	9) Concealed Guns/Misdemeanor . N	14) County Obscenity Standards . N
5) State Employees Pension . . . . . Y	10) Banks Sell Insurance . . . . Y	15) Managed Care Reform . . . . . Y

GROUP RATINGS

	FB	CoC	PrLf	IPPC	ACLU
1997	86	23	0/6	100	100

ELECTION RESULTS

1996 General	Wyvetter H. Younge (D)	23,219	(88.1%)
1996 General	Alvin E. Piolet (R)	3,143	(11.9%)
1996 Primary	Wyvetter E. Younge (D)	7,450	(100%)
1996 Primary	Alvin E. Piolet (R)	514	(100%)

CAMPAIGN RESOURCES AND EXPENDITURES

1996 Campaign Funds

Beg. Balance	$1,359	Individuals	$1,485
Receipts	$13,387	Party	$1,172
Expenditures	$9,688	PACS	$10,480
On hand	$5,058	Candidate	$250
		Not-itemized	$0

Top 10 PAC Contributors

1) ITLA $1,000	6) ESLFT $500
2) IPACE $1,000	7) CPA's $400
3) MPower . . . $1,000	8) AFSCME . . . $300
4) CTurner . . . $1,000	9) ABDI $300
5) UAW $1,000	10) IFT $300

NOTE: The General Election Opponent's Campaign Resources and Expenditures are reported in a separate section in the back of the book (pp. 269-284).

GENERAL ELECTION DATA

	Registered Voters	Voter Turnout		Straight Party Voting	
1996	56,726	29,112	51.3%	(R) 872 . . . . 3.0%	(D) 9,263 . . . 31.8%

PRESIDENT

1996	Bill Clinton (D)	23,848	85.2%
	Bob Dole (R)	2,630	9.4%
	Ross Perot (I)	1,134	4.0%
1992	Bill Clinton (D)	28,256	81.6%
	George Bush (R)	3,655	10.6%
	Ross Perot (I)	2,709	7.8%

UNITED STATES SENATE

1996	Richard J. Durbin (D)	24,793	86.5%
	Al Salvi (R)	3,049	10.6%

GOVERNOR

1994	Jim Edgar (R)	7,412	39.8%
	Dawn Clark Netsch (D)	11,198	60.2%

58th Senate District

House District 115
House District 116

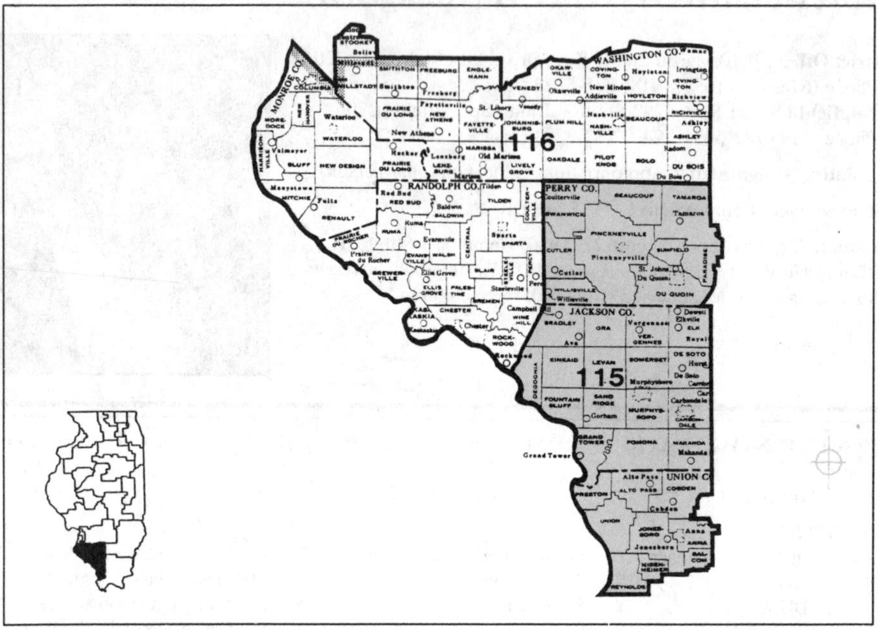

DEMOGRAPHICS (1990)

	S.D. #58	H.D. #115	H.D.#116
VOTING AGE POPULATION	148,178	76,373	71,805
White	92.4%	89.7%	95.2%
Black	5.0%	6.3%	3.7%
Hispanic	1.0%	1.3%	0.8%
Asian	1.4%	2.5%	0.2%
AGE (Total Population)	193,739	96,870	96,869
Under 6	7.6%	7.1%	8.2%
6 to 18	17.8%	16.6%	18.9%
65 and Over	14.2%	13.5%	14.9%
URBAN POPULATION	44.9%	52.7%	37.0%
HOUSING UNITS (Total)	78,603	40,834	37,769
Median Value	$49,948	$43,200	$56,468
Owner Occupied	64.1%	55.9%	73.0%
FAMILY INCOME (Total Families)	49,106	23,017	26,089
Median Income	$31,243	$26,972	$34,934
Below Poverty Level	10.4%	14.5%	6.7%
With Children Under 5	2.0%	3.1%	1.0%
With Children 5 to 17	3.5%	4.7%	2.4%
Headed by Females	4.1%	6.2%	2.3%
INDUSTRY (Total Employed)	83,807	40,916	42,892
Professional/Public Administration	33.0%	41.1%	25.3%
Manufacturing	14.6%	10.4%	18.5%
Retail	16.7%	18.2%	15.3%
Transportation/Communication	6.9%	5.4%	8.4%
Finance/Insurance/Real Estate	5.3%	4.2%	6.3%
Other Service	6.6%	7.0%	6.3%

Senator David Luechtefeld (R)

District Office: 700 N. Front St.; P.O. Box 517; Okawville 62271
Phone (618) 243-9014; (618) 243-5376 (fax)
Springfield Office: M-122 Capitol Bldg., Springfield, 62706
Phone (217) 782-8137

Legislative Assignments: Committees on Government Operations (vice-chair); Agriculture and Conservation (vice-chair); Licensed Activities.

Public Service: Senator (1995-present).

Personal: Former high school teacher/basketball coach; born November 8, 1940, Lively Grove; St. Louis University, Bachelor's degree; Southern Illinois University-Edwardsville, Master's degree; married (Flo); four children.

1997 BILL PASSAGE RATIO	Introduced	Passed House of Origin	Passed GA
Primary	10	5	4
Primary/Hyphenated	22	15	13

KEY VOTES

1) Seante GOP Ed. $ Plan ....Y	6) Insurance/Domestic Violence ..Y	11) Pre-Paid College Tuition ....Y
2) State Budget ....Y	7) Brownfields ....Y	12) Increase Pull Tab Prizes ....N
3) Tougher DUI Level ....Y	8) Welfare Reform ....Y	13) Telecommunications Tax ...N
4) Ban Partial Birth Abortions ...Y	9) Concealed Guns/Misdemeanor .Y	14) Delivery Discrimination ....P
5) State Employees Pension .....Y	10) Banks Sell Insurance ....Y	15) Sell Drivers' Data ....N

GROUP RATINGS

	FB	CoC	PrLf	IPPC	ACLU
1997	91	100	2/2	0	50

ELECTION RESULTS

1996 General	David Luechtefeld (R)	40,689	(50.1%)
1996 General	Barb Brown (D)	40,562	(49.9%)
1996 Primary	David Luechtefeld (R)	11,314	(100%)
1996 Primary	Barb Brown (D)	11,781	(72.6%)

CAMPAIGN RESOURCES AND EXPENDITURES

1996 Campaign Funds				Top 10 PAC Contributors			
Beg. Balance	$25,101	Individuals	$8,743	1) RSSC	$608,774	6) Alliance	$5,134
Receipts	$785,118	Party	$632,220	2) IPACE	$38,148	7) CoC	$5,027
Expenditures	$758,364	PACS	$123,157	3) ISMS	$15,018	8) RMadigan	$4,000
On hand	$51,855	Candidate	$0	4) MPAC	$10,500	9) CRausch	$3,000
		Not-itemized	$20,998	5) CRyan	$6,000	10) Ameritech	$2,500

NOTE: The General Election Opponent's Campaign Resources and Expenditures are reported in a separate section in the back of the book (pp. 269-284).

GENERAL ELECTION DATA

	Registered Voters	Voter Turnout		Straight Party Voting	
1996	132,276	85,416	64.6%	(R) 10,872 . .12.7%	(D) 18,293 . . .21.4%

PRESIDENT

1996	Bill Clinton (D)	40,745	49.3%
	Bob Dole (R)	32,207	39.0%
	Ross Perot (I)	8,961	10.8%
1992	Bill Clinton (D)	44,079	48.8%
	George Bush (R)	29,121	32.3%
	Ross Perot (I)	17,071	18.9%

UNITED STATES SENATE

1996	Richard J. Durbin (D)	42,409	52.1%
	Al Salvi (R)	36,707	45.1%

GOVERNOR

1994	Jim Edgar (R)	41,813	68.3%
	Dawn Clark Netsch (D)	19,377	31.7%

Representative Mike Bost (R)

District Office: 300 East Main St., Carbondale 62901
Phone (618) 457-5787; (618) 457-2990 (fax)
Springfield Office: Room 2020-H Stratton Bldg., Springfield 62706
Phone (217) 782-0387; (217) 782-1275 (fax)

Legislative Assignments: Committees on Elementary & Secondary Education; Higher Education; Local Government; Transportation & Motor Vehicles; Veterans' Affairs.

Public Service: Representative (1995-present).

Personal: Full-time legislator; born December 30, 1960; Murphysboro High School; married (Tracy); three children.

1997 BILL PASSAGE RATIO	Introduced	Passed House of Origin	Passed GA
Primary	13	7	3
Primary/Hyphenated	32	16	10

KEY VOTES

1) Change Ed. Funding Formula . . N	6) Insurance/Domestic Violence . . Y	11) Pre-Paid College Tuition . . . . Y
2) State Budget . . . . Y	7) Brownfields . . . . Y	12) Increase Pull Tab Prizes . . . . Y
3) Tougher DUI Level . . . . Y	8) Welfare Reform . . . . Y	13) Utility Deregulation . . . . P
4) Ban Partial Birth Abortions . . . Y	9) Concealed Guns/Misdemeanor . Y	14) County Obscenity Standards . Y
5) State Employees Pension . . . . . Y	10) Banks Sell Insurance . . . . Y	15) Managed Care Reform . . . . . A

GROUP RATINGS

	FB	CoC	PrLf	IPPC	ACLU
1997	57	50	6/6	0	30

ELECTION RESULTS

1996 General	Mike Bost (R)	19,561	(51.8%)
1996 General	John S. Rendleman (D)	18,188	(48.2%)
1996 Primary	Mike Bost (R)	5,588	(100%)
1996 Primary	John S. Rendleman (D)	5,711	(57.2%)

CAMPAIGN RESOURCES AND EXPENDITURES

1996 Campaign Funds

Beg. Balance	$39,741	Individuals	$13,665
Receipts	$368,800	Party	$259,376
Expenditures	$392,591	PACS	$70,295
On hand	$15,950	Candidate	$0
		Not-itemized	$25,464

Top 10 PAC Contributors

1) HRCC	$161,140	6) MPAC	$6,500
2) FLAD	$66,311	7) Alliance	$5,000
3) CRyan	$10,000	8) CChurchill	$5,000
4) CRyder	$10,000	9) CoC	$4,150
5) ISMS	$10,000	10) SimCon	$2,600

NOTE: The General Election Opponent's Campaign Resources and Expenditures are reported in a separate section in the back of the book (pp. 269-284).

GENERAL ELECTION DATA

	Registered Voters	Voter Turnout		Straight Party Voting (R)		Straight Party Voting (D)	
1996	66,841	39,975	59.8%	4,812	12.0%	9,632	24.1%

PRESIDENT

1996	Bill Clinton (D)	21,023	54.4%
	Bob Dole (R)	13,250	34.3%
	Ross Perot (I)	3,996	10.3%
1992	Bill Clinton (D)	23,178	54.3%
	George Bush (R)	12,491	29.3%
	Ross Perot (I)	6,997	16.4%

UNITED STATES SENATE

1996	Richard J. Durbin (D)	21,911	57.5%
	Al Salvi (R)	15,162	39.8%

GOVERNOR

1994	Jim Edgar (R)	20,060	68.1%
	Dawn Clark Netsch (D)	9,406	31.9%

Representative Dan Reitz (D)

District Office: 128A W. Main, Sparta 62286
Phone (618) 443-5757; (618) 443-3800 (fax)
Springfield Office: Room 2065-L Stratton Bldg., Springfield 62706
Phone (217) 782-1018; (217) 782-0945 (fax)

Legislative Assignments: Committees on Agriculture & Conservation; Environment & Energy; Registration & Regulation; Transportation & Motor Vehicles.

Public Service: Representative (appointed July 16, 1997); chair and member, Randolph County Board (1986-1997).

Personal: Born March 16, 1954, Red Bud; Steeleville High School; former Illinois legislative director for the United Mine Workers; married (Joyce); three children.

1997 BILL PASSAGE RATIO	Introduced	Passed House of Origin	Passed GA
Primary	N/A	N/A	N/A
Primary/Hyphenated	N/A	N/A	N/A

KEY VOTES

1) Change Ed. Funding Formula . .X	6) Insurance/Domestic Violence . .X	11) Pre-Paid College Tuition X
2) State Budget X	7) Brownfields X	12) Increase Pull Tab Prizes X
3) Tougher DUI Level X	8) Welfare Reform X	13) Utility Deregulation X
4) Ban Partial Birth Abortions . . .X	9) Concealed Guns/Misdemeanor .X	14) County Obscenity Standards .X
5) State Employees Pension X	10) Banks Sell Insurance X	15) Managed Care Reform X

GROUP RATINGS

	FB	CoC	PrLf	IPPC	ACLU
1997	N/R	N/R	N/R	N/R	N/R

ELECTION RESULTS

1996 General	Terry W. Deering (D)	29,446	(69.2%)
1996 General	John W. Coats (R)	13,132	(30.8%)
1996 Primary	Terry W. Deering (D)	6,255	(100%)
1996 Primary	John W. Coats (R)	5,415	(100%)

CAMPAIGN RESOURCES AND EXPENDITURES

1996 Campaign Funds				Top 10 PAC Contributors			
Beg. Balance	$N/A	Individuals	$N/A	1) N/A	$N/A	6) N/A	$N/A
Receipts	$N/A	Party	$N/A	2) N/A	$N/A	7) N/A	$N/A
Expenditures	$N/A	PACS	$N/A	3) N/A	$N/A	8) N/A	$N/A
On hand	$N/A	Candidate	$N/A	4) N/A	$N/A	9) N/A	$N/A
		Not-itemized	$N/A	5) N/A	$N/A	10) N/A	$N/A

NOTE: The General Election Opponent's Campaign Resources and Expenditures are reported in a separate section in the back of the book (pp. 269-284).

GENERAL ELECTION DATA

	Registered Voters	Voter Turnout		Straight Party Voting	
1996	65,435	45,441	69.4%	(R) 6,060 . . .13.3%	(D) 8,661 . . . .19.1%

PRESIDENT

1996	Bill Clinton (D)	19,722	44.8%
	Bob Dole (R)	18,957	43.0%
	Ross Perot (I)	4,965	11.3%
1992	Bill Clinton (D)	20,901	43.9%
	George Bush (R)	16,630	34.9%
	Ross Perot (I)	10,074	21.2%

UNITED STATES SENATE

1996	Richard J. Durbin (D)	20,498	47.4%
	Al Salvi (R)	21,545	49.8%

GOVERNOR

1994	Jim Edgar (R)	21,753	68.6%
	Dawn Clark Netsch (D)	9,971	31.4%

59th Senate District

House District 117
House District 118

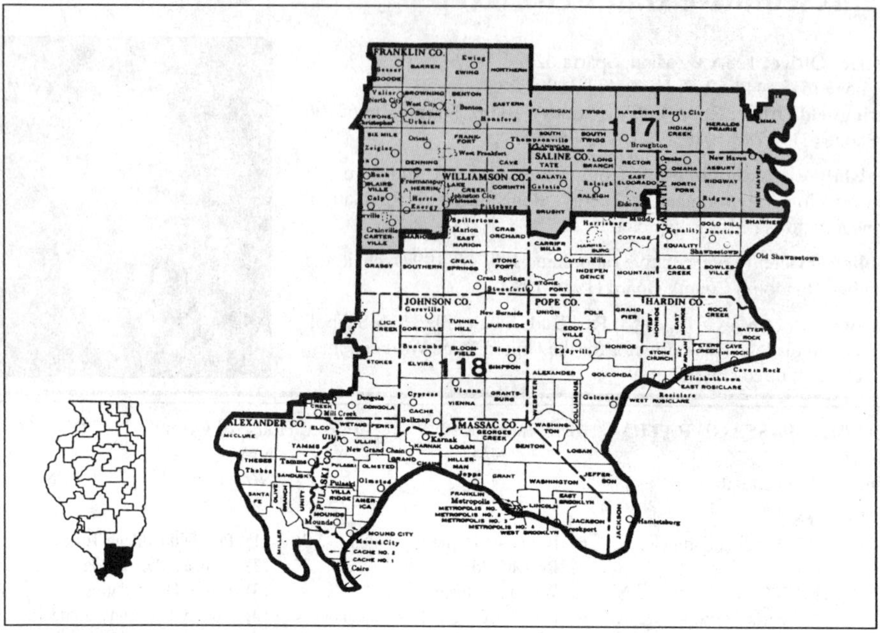

DEMOGRAPHICS (1990)

	S.D. #59	H.D. #117	H.D.#118
VOTING AGE POPULATION	146,801	73,643	73,158
White	94.3%	98.6%	90.0%
Black	4.7%	0.6%	8.9%
Hispanic	0.5%	0.4%	0.7%
Asian	0.2%	0.2%	0.2%
AGE (Total Population)	193,739	96,869	96,870
Under 6	7.5%	7.5%	7.5%
6 to 18	18.2%	17.9%	18.4%
65 and Over	18.5%	19.2%	17.7%
URBAN POPULATION	39.6%	47.8%	31.3%
HOUSING UNITS (Total)	86,915	44,090	42,825
Median Value	$33,899	$33,406	$34,507
Owner Occupied	67.0%	67.4%	66.6%
FAMILY INCOME (Total Families)	54,656	27,588	27,068
Median Income	$25,407	$25,405	$25,408
Below Poverty Level	15.7%	15.1%	16.4%
With Children Under 5	2.7%	2.8%	2.7%
With Children 5 to 17	5.6%	5.4%	5.9%
Headed by Females	6.1%	5.5%	6.7%
INDUSTRY (Total Employed)	71,593	36,192	35,401
Professional/Public Administration	31.2%	30.5%	31.9%
Manufacturing	10.8%	11.4%	10.3%
Retail	17.6%	17.8%	17.4%
Transportation/Communication	8.0%	6.7%	9.2%
Finance/Insurance/Real Estate	4.4%	4.6%	4.1%
Other Service	7.3%	7.6%	6.9%

Senator James F. "Jim" Rea (D)

District Office: 112 East Market St., Christopher 62822
Phone (618) 724-9444; (618) 724-9300 (fax)
Springfield Office: M-103-F Capitol Bldg., Springfield 62706
Phone (217) 782-5509

Legislative Assignments: Committees on Financial Institutions (minority spokesperson); Public Health & Welfare; Joint Committee on Administrative Rules.

Public Service: Senator (1989-present); representative (1979-1989); past president of Christopher Community High School Board of Education; past member of Christopher City Council.

Personal: Full-time legislator; born September 17, 1937, Mulkeytown; Southern Illinois University, B.S. in animal husbandry & biological sciences; M.S. in agriculture industry & community development; National Training Laboratories, special education; married (Josephine); two children; three grandchildren.

1997 BILL PASSAGE RATIO	Introduced	Passed House of Origin	Passed GA
Primary	15	4	2
Primary/Hyphenated	31	14	11

KEY VOTES

1) Senate GOP Ed. $ Plan . . . . . . .N	6) Insurance/Domestic Violence . .Y	11) Pre-Paid College Tuition . . . .Y
2) State Budget . . . . .Y	7) Brownfields . . . . .Y	12) Increase Pull Tab Prizes . . . .Y
3) Tougher DUI Level . . . . .Y	8) Welfare Reform . . . . .Y	13) Telecommunications Tax . . .Y
4) Ban Partial Birth Abortions . . .Y	9) Concealed Guns/Misdemeanor .Y	14) Delivery Discrimination . . . .Y
5) State Employees Pension . . . . .Y	10) Banks Sell Insurance . . . . .Y	15) Sell Drivers' Data . . . . .Y

GROUP RATINGS

	FB	CoC	PrLf	IPPC	ACLU
1997	86	75	2/2	0	50

ELECTION RESULTS

1994 General	James F. "Jim" Rea (D)	49,630	(100%)
1994 Primary	James F. "Jim" Rea (D)	25,204	(100%)
1992 General	James F. "Jim" Rea (D)	74,321	(100%)
1992 Primary	James F. "Jim" Rea (D)	27,518	(100%)

CAMPAIGN RESOURCES AND EXPENDITURES

1996 Campaign Funds				Top 10 PAC Contributors	
Beg. Balance	$139,402	Individuals	$2,150	1) IPACE $4,000	6) PMorris $750
Receipts	$46,921	Party	$375	2) ISMS $3,538	7) ElectEn $750
Expenditures	$44,441	PACS	$28,374	3) Ameritech .$2,400	8) ILCon $500
On hand	$141,882	Candidate	$0	4) UPS $1,000	9) HI $500
		Not-itemized	$16,022	5) WexfordHS . .$850	10) Sears $500

NOTE: The General Election Opponent's Campaign Resources and Expenditures are reported in a separate section in the back of the book (pp. 269-284).

GENERAL ELECTION DATA

	Registered Voters	Voter Turnout		Straight Party Voting	
1996	138,055	87,709	63.5%	(R) 9,018 . . .10.3%	(D) 20,234 . . .23.1%

PRESIDENT

1996	Bill Clinton (D)	44,020	52.1%
	Bob Dole (R)	29,636	35.1%
	Ross Perot (I)	10,394	12.3%
1992	Bill Clinton (D)	52,064	53.4%
	George Bush (R)	30,238	31.0%
	Ross Perot (I)	15,246	15.6%

UNITED STATES SENATE

1996	Richard J. Durbin (D)	46,045	56.0%
	Al Salvi (R)	33,584	40.8%

GOVERNOR

1994	Jim Edgar (R)	46,554	68.5%
	Dawn Clark Netsch (D)	21,363	31.5%

Representative Larry Woolard (D)

District Office: 10400 Terminal Drive, Marion 62959
Phone (618) 997-1171; (618) 997-9148 (fax)
Springfield Office: Room 2060-L Stratton Bldg., Springfield 62706
Phone (217) 782-1051; (217) 782-0882 (fax)

Legislative Assignments: Committees on Agriculture & Conservation (chair); Insurance (vice-chair); Elementary & Secondary Education; Higher Education; Personnel & Pensions.

Public Service: Representative (1989-present); former county commissioner; former Carterville School Board member.

Personal: Businessman, born September 20, 1941, Williamson County; Herrin High School; married (Mary Ann); four children; four grandchildren.

1997 BILL PASSAGE RATIO	Introduced	Passed House of Origin	Passed GA
Primary	33	11	4
Primary/Hyphenated	90	50	30

KEY VOTES

1) Change Ed. Funding Formula . . Y	6) Insurance/Domestic Violence . . Y	11) Pre-Paid College Tuition . . . . Y
2) State Budget . . . . Y	7) Brownfields . . . . Y	12) Increase Pull Tab Prizes . . . . Y
3) Tougher DUI Level . . . . Y	8) Welfare Reform . . . . Y	13) Utility Deregulation . . . . Y
4) Ban Partial Birth Abortions . . . Y	9) Concealed Guns/Misdemeanor . Y	14) County Obscenity Standards . Y
5) State Employees Pension . . . . . Y	10) Banks Sell Insurance . . . . Y	15) Managed Care Reform . . . . . Y

GROUP RATINGS

	FB	CoC	PrLf	IPPC	ACLU
1997	86	38	4/6	33	30

ELECTION RESULTS

1996 General	Larry Woolard (D)	29,688	(72.5%)
1996 General	Philip D. Roberts (R)	11,277	(27.5%)
1996 Primary	Larry Woolard (D)	11,877	(100%)
1996 Primary	Philip D. Roberts (R)	4,481	(100%)

CAMPAIGN RESOURCES AND EXPENDITURES

1996 Campaign Funds		Top 10 PAC Contributors	
Beg. Balance $317	Individuals . . . $5,265	1) ITLA $2,000	6) P&P $1,000
Receipts $70,821	Party $800	2) IBEW $2,000	7) IPACE $1,000
Expenditures . $49,308	PACS $45,439	3) Activator . . . $2,000	8) AFSCME . . . $900
On hand $21,830	Candidate $494	4) IBEWEd $1,600	9) IUOE $800
	Not-itemized $18,823	5) Seasons $1,100	10) ABDI $700

NOTE: The General Election Opponent's Campaign Resources and Expenditures are reported in a separate section in the back of the book (pp. 269-284).

GENERAL ELECTION DATA

	Registered Voters	Voter Turnout		Straight Party Voting	
1996	69,674	43,621	62.6%	(R) 4,209 . . . 9.6%	(D) 12,601 . . . 28.9%

PRESIDENT

1996	Bill Clinton (D)	23,062	54.9%
	Bob Dole (R)	13,495	32.1%
	Ross Perot (I)	5,228	12.4%
1992	Bill Clinton (D)	28,069	56.8%
	George Bush (R)	13,433	27.2%
	Ross Perot (I)	7,877	16.0%

UNITED STATES SENATE

1996	Richard J. Durbin (D)	24,267	59.1%
	Al Salvi (R)	15,496	37.7%

GOVERNOR

1994	Jim Edgar (R)	21,381	64.0%
	Dawn Clark Netsch (D)	12,003	36.0%

Representative David D. Phelps (D)

District Office: 617 East Church St., Suite 8, Harrisburg 62946
Phone (618) 253-8001; (618) 253-8203 (fax)
Springfield Office: Room 2059-L Stratton Bldg., Springfield 62706
Phone (217) 782-5131; (217) 782-0882 (fax)

Legislative Assignments: Committees on Elementary & Secondary Education (chair); Higher Education (vice-chair); Health Care Availabilty & Access; Insurance; Pensions & Personnel; Prison Management Reform.

Public Service: Representative (1985-present); former county clerk, Saline County.

Personal: Teacher; born October 26, 1947, Eldorado; Southern Illinois University, B.S. in social studies and English; married (Leslie); four children.

1997 BILL PASSAGE RATIO	Introduced	Passed House of Origin	Passed GA
Primary	26	8	2
Primary/Hyphenated	49	23	9

KEY VOTES

1) Change Ed. Funding Formula . . Y	6) Insurance/Domestic Violence . . Y	11) Pre-Paid College Tuition . . . . Y
2) State Budget . . . . Y	7) Brownfields . . . . Y	12) Increase Pull Tab Prizes . . . . . P
3) Tougher DUI Level . . . . Y	8) Welfare Reform . . . . Y	13) Utility Deregulation . . . . . . Y
4) Ban Partial Birth Abortions . . . Y	9) Concealed Guns/Misdemeanor . Y	14) County Obscenity Standards . Y
5) State Employees Pension . . . . . Y	10) Banks Sell Insurance . . . . Y	15) Managed Care Reform . . . . . Y

GROUP RATINGS

	FB	CoC	PrLf	IPPC	ACLU
1997	86	33	5/6	16	30

ELECTION RESULTS

1996 General	David D. Phelps (D)	22,893	(55.0%)
1996 General	Jack Hill (R)	18,735	(45.0%)
1996 Primary	David D. Phelps (D)	7,771	(100%)
1996 Primary	Jack Hill (R)	7,477	(100%)

CAMPAIGN RESOURCES AND EXPENDITURES

1996 Campaign Funds				Top 10 PAC Contributors			
Beg. Balance	$16,984	Individuals	$3,880	1) IHDM	$64,158	6) HOPE	$2,400
Receipts	$149,706	Party	$69,158	2) ITLA	$5,000	7) Activator	$2,225
Expenditures	$147,858	PACS	$60,620	3) IPACE	$5,000	8) AFLCIO	$1,600
On hand	$18,832	Candidate	$0	4) CHartke	$5,000	9) USWA	$1,500
		Not-itemized	$16,048	5) AFSCME	$3,125	10) LIPAC	$1,500

NOTE: The General Election Opponent's Campaign Resources and Expenditures are reported in a separate section in the back of the book (pp. 269-284).

GENERAL ELECTION DATA

Registered Voters		Voter Turnout		Straight Party Voting	
1996	68,381	44,088	64.5%	(R) 4,809 . . . 10.9%	(D) 7,633 . . . 17.3%

PRESIDENT

1996	Bill Clinton (D)	20,958	49.3%
	Bob Dole (R)	16,141	37.9%
	Ross Perot (I)	5,166	12.1%
1992	Bill Clinton (D)	23,995	49.8%
	George Bush (R)	16,805	34.9%
	Ross Perot (I)	7,369	15.3%

UNITED STATES SENATE

1996	Richard J. Durbin (D)	21,778	52.9%
	Al Salvi (R)	18,088	43.9%

GOVERNOR

1994	Jim Edgar (R)	25,173	72.9%
	Dawn Clark Netsch (D)	9,360	27.1%

Representative David D. Phelps (D)

[illegible]

General Election Opponents' Campaign Resources and Expenditures

The following pages list campaign finance data for unsuccessful General Assembly candidates in the 1996 general election. Keep in mind that we have compiled information only for those opponents who created a campaign committee with the State Board of Elections. Illinois Election Law requires that candidates for state political offices create a committee and disclose their resources and expenditures when they either raise or spend $1,000 on their campaign efforts. The information found on pages 271-284 was compiled from the semiannual reports required of every political campaign committee registered in Illinois with the State Board of Elections. These reports cover the period from July 1, 1996 to December 31, 1996. Therefore, the information on contributions and expenditures covers primarily the November 1996 general election cycle. The information is not inclusive because candidates do receive contributions for the November election earlier than July 1 and often have expenditures outstanding beyond December of the election year. However, the information does give an indication of the amounts of money raised and spent during a given election cycle.

Information for the beginning balance, receipts, expenditures, and on-hand funds was taken directly from the semiannual reports filed by each candidate's committee. If that information was incomplete or inaccurate, attempts were made to provide the reader with the most accurate data available. All figures have been rounded to the nearest dollar.

The breakdown of contributions by individuals, party sources, PACs (political action committees), candidates, and the "not itemized" section was compiled through a line-item check of the reports filed by the committee. The "candidate" line of this breakdown includes money contributed by the candidate, loans taken out by the candidate, and interest received by the campaign committee.

The top 10 PAC contributors were compiled by a line-item check of the reports filed by the committee. In listing the top 10 PACs, we included partisan committees, such as contributions from the candidate's state and local party funds and transfers from the campaign committees of other candidates. Of course, we also included nonpartisan and special interest PACs as well. The abbreviations of the PACs are listed on the last few pages of this book.

The same campaign resources and expenditures information has been compiled for each member of the General Assembly and is listed on the respective member page.

Listed below are those general election opponents who did not create a committee with the State Board of Elections and apparently did not raise or spend $1,000 for their campaigns.

SENATE:

District 3:	Maggie Kohls (LIB) defeated by Margaret Smith (D) (p. 41)
District 6:	Robert N. Oberg (R) defeated by John J. Cullerton (D) (p. 53)
District 13:	David Whitehead (HWP) defeated by Barack Obama (D) (p. 81)
District 13:	Rosette Caldwell Peyton (R) defeated by Barack Obama (D) (p. 81)
District 15:	Eugene James (R) defeated by William "Bill" Shaw (D) (p. 89)
District 19:	Lance Del Goebel (REF) defeated by William F. Mahar (R) (p. 105)
District 25:	Geraldine Vance Carter (D) defeated by Doris C. Karpiel (R) (p. 129)

HOUSE:

District 2:	Nancy Mercado (R) defeated by Edward Acevedo (D) (p. 35)
District 3:	Augusto Montijo (R) defeated by Miguel A. Santiago (D) (p. 38)
District 4:	John W. Duda (R) defeated by Edgar Lopez (D) (p. 39)
District 6:	Bobby Belk (R) defeated by Shirley M. Jones (D) (p. 43)
District 8:	Les Golden (R) defeated by Calvin L. Giles (D) (p. 47)
District 9:	Marie Ciffone (R) defeated by Arthur L. Turner (D) (p. 50)
District 10:	Earnest L. Thomas (R) defeated by Coy Pugh (D) (p. 51)
District 11:	Rudy Pamintuan (R) defeated by Judy Erwin (D) (p. 54)
District 12:	Beret A. Olson (R) defeated by Sara Feigenholtz (D) (p. 55)
District 17:	Kurt James Eckhardt (R) defeated by Carol Ronen (D) (p. 66)
District 18:	Edward M. Potash (R) defeated by Janice D. "Jan" Schakowsky (D) (p. 67)
District 20:	Joseph Anthony Hornowski (R) defeated by Joseph S. Kotlarz, Jr. (D) (p. 71)
District 21:	Melvin R. Sexton (R) defeated by Mary E. Flowers (D) (p. 74)
District 22:	Terrence F. Goggin (R) defeated by Michael J. Madigan (D) (p. 75)
District 24:	Patricia A. Krasowski (R) defeated by Howard Kenner (D) (p. 79)
District 28:	Derek Banks (HWP) defeated by Thomas J. Dart (D) (p. 87)
District 39:	Keith Murphy (D) defeated by Vincent A. Persico (R) (p. 110)
District 40:	Kevin D. Schuele (D) defeated by Peter Roskam (R) (p. 111)
District 41:	Suzanne Tobin Frankel (D) defeated by Mary Lou Cowlishaw (R) (p. 114)
District 49:	Robert Bob Banks (D) defeated by Carole Pankau (R) (p. 130)
District 50:	Mary Frances Potts (D) defeated by Thomas L. Johnson (R) (p. 131)
District 52:	Robert Boness (D) defeated by Mark H. Beaubien, Jr. (R) (p. 135)
District 62:	Ronald Lee Molinaro III (D) defeated by Robert W. Churchill (R) (p. 155)
District 82:	Tom Wolfe (D) defeated by James H. "Jim" Meyer (R) (p. 195)
District 84:	Alex Arroyo (D) defeated by Tom Cross (R) (p. 199)
District 102:	Jim Taylor (D) defeated by N. Duane Noland (R) (p. 235)
District 114:	Alvin E. Piolet (R) defeated by Wyvetter H. Younge (D) (p. 259)

Senate District 7 **Robert Martwick (D)** opposed Walter W. Dudycz (R) (p. 57)

1996 Campaign Funds				Top 10 PAC Contributors			
Beg. Balance	$26,582	Individuals	$15,410	1) CDS	$228,966	6) CCCTU	$7,000
Receipts	$382,072	Party	$267,818	2) CEJones	$15,000	7) PersPAC	$6,829
Expenditures	$398,474	PACS	$84,423	3) RW	$10,000	8) FCarroll	$5,000
On hand	$10,180	Candidate	$640	4) IPACE	$8,000	9) CNeedham	$4,834
		Not-itemized	$13,780	5) CDeLeo	$7,000	10) IFT	$4,500

Senate District 12 **Glenn B. Wharton (HWP)** opposed Robert S. Molaro (D) (p. 77)

1996 Campaign Funds				Top 10 PAC Contributors			
Beg. Balance	$643	Individuals	$0	1) N/A	$N/A	6) N/A	$N/A
Receipts	$2,593	Party	$0	2) N/A	$N/A	7) N/A	$N/A
Expenditures	$2,672	PACS	$0	3) N/A	$N/A	8) N/A	$N/A
On hand	$564	Candidate	$1,813	4) N/A	$N/A	9) N/A	$N/A
		Not-itemized	$780	5) N/A	$N/A	10) N/A	$N/A

Senate District 18 **Dennis Kibby (D)** opposed Patrick J. O'Malley (R) (p. 101)

1996 Campaign Funds				Top 10 PAC Contributors			
Beg. Balance	$15,750	Individuals	$4,700	1) CDS	$10,931	6) SSFT	$250
Receipts	$32,093	Party	$10,932	2) K&M	$6,161	7) IBEW	$200
Expenditures	$47,843	PACS	$9,145	3) Sprink	$700	8) Plast	$150
On hand	$0	Candidate	$2,040	4) IFT	$684	9) N/A	$N/A
		Not-itemized	$5,276	5) AFLCIO	$350	10) N/A	$N/A

Senate District 19 **Richard R. Della Croce (D)** opposed William F. Mahar (R) (p. 105)

1996 Campaign Funds				Top 10 PAC Contributors			
Beg. Balance	$7,345	Individuals	$1,985	1) CEJones	$19,047	6) CDeLeo	$2,000
Receipts	$68,212	Party	$21,197	2) Innov AD	$6,602	7) MFM	$1,191
Expenditures	$58,787	PACS	$17,916	3) P&S	$4,050	8) IFT	$1,000
On hand	$16,770	Candidate	$23,317	4) IUOE	$2,500	9) ITLA	$1,000
		Not-itemized	$3,797	5) ConsLTD	$2,275	10) Corsair	$700

Senate District 21 **Jennifer Lawson Finlay (D)** opposed Chris Lauzen (R) (p. 113)

1996 Campaign Funds				Top 10 PAC Contributors			
Beg. Balance	$0	Individuals	$1,740	1) WSTU	$500	6) N/A	$N/A
Receipts	$4,244	Party	$1,000	2) CEJones	$500	7) N/A	$N/A
Expenditures	$1,572	PACS	$950	3) CDS	$500	8) N/A	$N/A
On hand	$2,672	Candidate	$0	4) PersPAC	$250	9) N/A	$N/A
		Not-itemized	$554	5) FVBT	$200	10) N/A	$N/A

Senate District 24 **Nancy C. Kenney (D)** opposed Christine Radogno (R) (p 125)

1996 Campaign Funds				Top 10 PAC Contributors			
Beg. Balance	$12,089	Individuals	$5,470	1) CDS	$262,392	6) FCarroll	$8,000
Receipts	$399,772	Party	$300,459	2) IPACE	$19,500	7) CCCTU	$6,300
Expenditures	$404,217	PACS	$83,482	3) CEJones	$18,408	8) CDemuzio	$5,000
On hand	$7,644	Candidate	$0	4) ITLA	$10,000	9) IFT	$4,741
		Not-itemized	$10,361	5) WVWV	$8,000	10) AFSCME	$3,191

Senate District 28 **William M. "Bill" Blaine, Jr. (D)** opposed Martin J. Butler (R) (p. 141)

1996 Campaign Funds		Top 10 PAC Contributors	
Beg. Balance $937	Individuals . . .$1,280	1) BRS $2,900	6) TWU $500
Receipts $15,807	Party $2,450	2) CDS $2,000	7) United $500
Expenditures .$16,604	PACS $7,300	3) ITLA $500	8) UAW $500
On hand $140	Candidate $575	4) IFT $500	9) FJacobs $250
	Not-itemized .$4,202	5) Machinists . . .$500	10) UFCW $250

Senate District 30 **Thomas F. Lachner (R)** opposed Terry Link (D) (p. 149)

1996 Campaign Funds		Top 10 PAC Contributors	
Beg. Balance . .$4,515	Individuals . . .$1,637	1) RSSC . . .$88,664	6) ILCon $3,000
Receipts $171,871	Party $93,164	2) NCS $22,147	7) ISMS $2,748
Expenditures .$164,054	PACS $71,821	3) IHCA $4,000	8) ABDI $2,500
On hand $12,332	Candidate $0	4) HOPE $3,500	9) MPAC $2,000
	Not-itemized .$5,049	5) TrustmarkIns $3,277	10) Baxter $1;500

Senate District 33 **Charles A. Marwig (D)** opposed Steven J. Rauschenberger (R) (p. 161)

1996 Campaign Funds		Top 10 PAC Contributors	
Beg. Balance $0	Individuals $225	1) Painters $4,900	6) Teamsters $250
Receipts $8,475	Party $600	2) Carpenters . .$1,500	7) P&P $150
Expenditures . .$8,321	PACS $7,650	3) FVBT $500	8) N/A . . . .$N/A
On hand $154	Candidate $0	4) CDS $500	9) N/A . . . .$N/A
	Not-itemized $0	5) CFLabor $300	10) N/A . . . .$N/A

Senate District 34 **Carol Jambor-Smith (D)** opposed Dave Syverson (R) (p. 165)

1996 Campaign Funds		Top 10 PAC Contributors	
Beg. Balance . .$6,324	Individuals . . .$1,175	1) CDS $73,356	6) UAW $2,000
Receipts $113,609	Party $74,487	2) IPACE $7,000	7) Teamsters . . .$1,500
Expenditures .$115,397	PACS $26,867	3) PersPAC . . .$3,492	8) LAWPAC . . .$1,500
On hand $4,536	Candidate $0	4) WVWV $2,000	9) Emily $1,000
	Not-itemized .$11,080	5) BPS $2,000	10) IFT $1,000

Senate District 39 **Larry Craig (D)** opposed Dan Cronin (R) (p. 185)

1996 Campaign Funds		Top 10 PAC Contributors	
Beg. Balance $0	Individuals $0	1) CDS $500	6) N/A . . . .$N/A
Receipts $850	Party $500	2) N/A . . . .$N/A	7) N/A . . . .$N/A
Expenditures . .$1,072	PACS $0	3) N/A . . . .$N/A	8) N/A . . . .$N/A
On hand . . . . . .($222)	Candidate $0	4) N/A . . . .$N/A	9) N/A . . . .$N/A
	Not-itemized . . .$350	5) N/A . . . .$N/A	10) N/A . . . .$N/A

Senate District 40 **Aldo A. DeAngelis (R)** opposed Debbie DeFrancesco Halvorson (D) (p.189)

1996 Campaign Funds		Top 10 PAC Contributors	
Beg. Balance $231,719	Individuals . .$27,749	1) RSSC . . .$397,352	6) ChgoCoC . . .$5,000
Receipts $642,760	Party $408,555	2) ISMS $13,400	7) Intercounty . .$5,000
Expenditures .$673,527	PACS $190,615	3) MPAC $9,000	8) HOPE $4,200
On hand $200,952	Candidate $0	4) CRyan $5,000	9) AT&T $3,500
	Not-itemized $15,841	5) PasqCon . . .$5,000	10) RPAC $3,200

Senate District 42 Ed Kelly (D) opposed Edward Petka (R) (p. 197)

1996 Campaign Funds				Top 10 PAC Contributors			
Beg. Balance	$6,173	Individuals	$250	1) CDS	$44,373	6) FCarroll	$3,000
Receipts	$93,148	Party	$48,823	2) IBEW	$9,050	7) IFT	$2,750
Expenditures	$94,709	PACS	$41,050	3) CCL	$5,000	8) IBEW 701	$1,500
On hand	$4,612	Candidate	$0	4) IUOE	$3,500	9) IBEW 197	$1,050
		Not-itemized	$3,025	5) AFSCME	$3,250	10) IPACE	$1,000

Senate District 50 Tom Londrigan (D) opposed Larry K. Bomke (R) (p. 229)

1996 Campaign Funds				Top 10 PAC Contributors			
Beg. Balance	$23,164	Individuals	$3,000	1) CDS	$84,596	6) LAWPAC	$2,500
Receipts	$172,868	Party	$111,745	2) DSCC	$22,000	7) UAW	$2,500
Expenditures	$192,029	PACS	$49,425	3) MCIDC	$6,000	8) Carpenters	$2,000
On hand	$4,003	Candidate	$0	4) ITLA	$5,000	9) FJacobs	$1,500
		Not-itemized	$8,698	5) Teamsters	$2,925	10) CDemuzio	$1,500

Senate District 51 P. Duane Potter (R) opposed Penny Severns (D) (p. 233)

1996 Campaign Funds				Top 10 PAC Contributors			
Beg. Balance	$503	Individuals	$0	1)MaconGOP	$500	6)N/A	$N/A
Receipts	$20,435	Party	$500	2)N/A	$N/A	7)N/A	$N/A
Expenditures	$20,918	PACS	$0	3)N/A	$N/A	8)N/A	$N/A
On hand	$20	Candidate	$9,008	4)N/A	$N/A	9)N/A	$N/A
		Not-itemized	$10,927	5)N/A	$N/A	10)N/A	$N/A

Senate District 52 Jeanne Gerrietts (D) opposed Stanley B. Weaver (R) (p. 237)

1996 Campaign Funds				Top 10 PAC Contributors			
Beg. Balance	$279	Individuals	$7,000	1) CDS	$8,115	6) ChamDem	$300
Receipts	$34,771	Party	$8,665	2) IPACE	$2,500	7) FJacobs	$250
Expenditures	$34,836	PACS	$5,850	3) MCIDC	$1,500	8) SNAPI	$200
On hand	$214	Candidate	$4,000	4) ECILB&C	$750	9) IWPC	$200
		Not-itemized	$9,256	5) P&P	$500	10) SR&R	$150

Senate District 54 Ron Williamson (R) opposed William L. O'Daniel (D) (p. 245)

1996 Campaign Funds				Top 10 PAC Contributors			
Beg. Balance	$505	Individuals	$200	1)CrawPAC	$350	6)N/A	$N/A
Receipts	$3,059	Party	$350	2)N/A	$N/A	7)N/A	$N/A
Expenditures	$3,564	PACS	$0	3)N/A	$N/A	8)N/A	$N/A
On hand	$0	Candidate	$1,800	4)N/A	$N/A	9)N/A	$N/A
		Not-itemized	$709	5)N/A	$N/A	10)N/A	$N/A

Senate District 55 David Ahola (D) opposed Frank Watson (R) (p. 249)

1996 Campaign Funds				Top 10 PAC Contributors			
Beg. Balance	$276	Individuals	$1,108	1) N/A	$N/A	6) N/A	$N/A
Receipts	$4,257	Party	$0	2) N/A	$N/A	7) N/A	$N/A
Expenditures	$4,533	PACS	$0	3) N/A	$N/A	8) N/A	$N/A
On hand	$0	Candidate	$694	4) N/A	$N/A	9) N/A	$N/A
		Not-itemized	$2,455	5) N/A	$N/A	10) N/A	$N/A

Senate District 58 Barb Brown (D) opposed David Luechtefeld (R) (p. 261)

1996 Campaign Funds				Top 10 PAC Contributors	
Beg. Balance	$27,078	Individuals	$20,964	1) CDS $414,151	6) AFLCIO $6,500
Receipts	$602,955	Party	$438,756	2) AFSCME $23,392	7) CClayborne $6,000
Expenditures	$624,745	PACS	$112,187	3) ITLA $10,500	8) CEJones $5,000
On hand	$5,288	Candidate	$450	4) WVWV $8,000	9) IFT $4,500
		Not-itemized	$30,598	5) PersPAC $7,935	10) Laborers $3,500

House District 7 June Edvenson (R) opposed Eugene "Gene" Moore (D) (p. 46)

1996 Campaign Funds				Top 10 PAC Contributors	
Beg. Balance	$0	Individuals	$300	1) N/A $N/A	6) N/A $N/A
Receipts	$1,767	Party	$0	2) N/A $N/A	7) N/A $N/A
Expenditures	$1,767	PACS	$0	3) N/A $N/A	8) N/A $N/A
On hand	$0	Candidate	$1,044	4) N/A $N/A	9) N/A $N/A
		Not-itemized	$423	5) N/A $N/A	10) N/A $N/A

House District 13 Peter Callaghan (R) opposed Ralph C. Capparelli (D) (p. 58)

1996 Campaign Funds				Top 10 PAC Contributors	
Beg. Balance	$978	Individuals	$7,550	1) HRCC $23,120	6) WeepWill $520
Receipts	$92,975	Party	$33,819	2) CDoherty $10,500	7) Hach&Assoc $500
Expenditures	$93,698	PACS	$11,674	3) CMP Inc. $1,000	8) HagDodge $500
On hand	$255	Candidate	$15,900	4) BLA $900	9) Hellas $500
		Not-itemized	$24,032	5) DBA Mag $894	10) ParthRest $500

House District 14 Thomas P. Needham (D) opposed Michael P. McAuliffe (R) (p. 59)

1996 Campaign Funds				Top 10 PAC Contributors	
Beg. Balance	$12,480	Individuals	$16,670	1) IHDM $151,412	6) CLang $3,000
Receipts	$251,272	Party	$182,074	2) DSCC $22,236	7) FMJM $2,729
Expenditures	$256,227	PACS	$38,832	3) ITLA $8,000	8) CTU $2,432
On hand	$7,525	Candidate	$0	4) C&GL $3,000	9) AbbeyPAC $1,500
		Not-itemized	$13,696	5) IFT $3,000	10) CFLabor $1,500

House District 15 Donald M. Hodgkinson (R) opposed Joseph M. Lyons (D) (p. 62)

1996 Campaign Funds				Top 10 PAC Contributors	
Beg. Balance	$6,453	Individuals	$1,123	1) RC Industries $250	6) N/A $N/A
Receipts	$9,723	Party	$0	2) N/A $N/A	7) N/A $N/A
Expenditures	$16,176	PACS	$250	3) N/A $N/A	8) N/A $N/A
On hand	$0	Candidate	$7,300	4) N/A $N/A	9) N/A $N/A
		Not-itemized	$1,050	5) N/A $N/A	10) N/A $N/A

House District 19 James J. Fiduccia (R) opposed Robert J. Bugielski (D) (p. 70)

1996 Campaign Funds				Top 10 PAC Contributors	
Beg. Balance	$0	Individuals	$2,750	1) ParkfieldFord $500	6) N/A $N/A
Receipts	$15,392	Party	$0	2) NSFord $200	7) N/A $N/A
Expenditures	$15,378	PACS	$700	3) N/A $N/A	8) N/A $N/A
On hand	$14	Candidate	$3,325	4) N/A $N/A	9) N/A $N/A
		Not-itemized	$8,617	5) N/A $N/A	10) N/A $N/A

House District 26 **James V. Spring (R)** opposed Charles G. Morrow, III (D) (p. 83)

1996 Campaign Funds		Top 10 PAC Contributors	
Beg. Balance $0	Individuals $0	1) N/A ....$N/A	6) N/A ....$N/A
Receipts $2,090	Party $0	2) N/A ....$N/A	7) N/A ....$N/A
Expenditures ..$1,970	PACS $0	3) N/A ....$N/A	8) N/A ....$N/A
On hand $120	Candidate $1,838	4) N/A ....$N/A	9) N/A ....$N/A
	Not-itemized ...$252	5) N/A ....$N/A	10) N/A ....$N/A

House District 29 **Rich Banske (R)** opposed Arline M. Fantin (D) (p. 90)

1996 Campaign Funds		Top 10 PAC Contributors	
Beg. Balance $957	Individuals $0	1) N/A ....$N/A	6) N/A ....$N/A
Receipts $4,097	Party $0	2) N/A ....$N/A	7) N/A ....$N/A
Expenditures ..$5,054	PACS $0	3) N/A ....$N/A	8) N/A ....$N/A
On hand $0	Candidate $1,270	4) N/A ....$N/A	9) N/A ....$N/A
	Not-itemized .$2,827	5) N/A ....$N/A	10) N/A ....$N/A

House District 31 **John E. Zart (R)** opposed Todd H. Stroger (D) (p. 94)

1996 Campaign Funds		Top 10 PAC Contributors	
Beg. Balance $0	Individuals $260	1) CChurchill ..$1,000	6) N/A ....$N/A
Receipts $6,180	Party $1,000	2) WChevroletInc $520	7) N/A ....$N/A
Expenditures ...$6,195	PACS $1,495	3) CalFed Savings$520	8) N/A ....$N/A
On hand ....($15)	Candidate $0	4) SChicagoDisp .$260	9) N/A ....$N/A
	Not-itemized ..$3,425	5) CenterLounge .$195	10) N/A ....$N/A

House District 34 **Robert F. Lytle (R)** opposed Larry McKeon (D) (p. 99)

1996 Campaign Funds		Top 10 PAC Contributors	
Beg. Balance $214	Individuals ...$1,000	1) FamilyTaxprs$1,000	6) N/A ....$N/A
Receipts $11,253	Party $0	2) Alliance $1,000	7) N/A ....$N/A
Expenditures ..$11,417	PACS $3,750	3) IMPAC $500	8) N/A ....$N/A
On hand $50	Candidate $6,000	4) CAT $500	9) N/A ....$N/A
	Not-itemized ...$503	5) CIPS $250	10) N/A ....$N/A

House District 35 **Jack O'Connor (R)** opposed M. Maggie Crotty (D) (p. 102)

1996 Campaign Funds		Top 10 PAC Contributors	
Beg. Balance ..$32,379	Individuals $5,452	1) HRCC $209,703	6) CoC $2,000
Receipts $341,949	Party $253,494	2) FLAD $40,841	7) FamilyPAC ..$1,770
Expenditures .$335,157	PACS $68,831	3) ISMS $10,000	8) Fremont $1,500
On hand $39,171	Candidate $478	4) MPAC $7,500	9) RPAC $1,300
	Not-itemized .$13,694	5) Evergreen HC $2,000	10) Midwest Auto$1,300

House District 36 **Maureen Murphy (R)** opposed James D. "Jim" Brosnahan (D) (p. 103)

1996 Campaign Funds		Top 10 PAC Contributors	
Beg. Balance .$27,068	Individuals $950	1) HRCC $80,614	6) MPAC $6,000
Receipts $169,677	Party $110,109	2) ISMS $10,000	7) FamilyPAC ..$2,500
Expenditures .$147,482	PACS $50,850	3) CRyan $10,000	8) BaerCmte. ..$2,000
On hand $49,263	Candidate $0	4) FLAD $9,446	9) Fremont $1,500
	Not-itemized .$7,768	5) CChurchill .$8,000	10) ChgoCoC ..$1,500

House District 37 John T. Doody, Jr. (R) opposed Kevin A. McCarthy (D) (p. 106)

1996 Campaign Funds		Top 10 PAC Contributors	
Beg. Balance . .$4,737	Individuals . . .$4,565	1) HRCC . . .$155,070	6) CRyan $10,000
Receipts $306,996	Party $206,991	2) IPACE $28,399	7) MPAC $8,500
Expenditures .$290,365	PACS $83,584	3) FLAD $25,248	8) CMahar $3,123
On hand $21,368	Candidate $0	4) ISMS $11,000	9) ChgoCoC . . .$3,000
	Not-itemized .$11,856	5) CChurchill .$10,000	10) IBA $2,500

House District 38 Lois R. Mayer (D) opposed opposed Renee Kosel (R) (p. 107)

1996 Campaign Funds		Top 10 PAC Contributors	
Beg. Balance .$12,666	Individuals $400	1) IHDM . . .$155,601	6) WVWV $8,000
Receipts $275,876	Party $185,303	2) IPACE $13,819	7) DPI $6,871
Expenditures .$256,935	PACS $81,269	3) DSCC $10,000	8) ITLA $6,000
On hand $31,607	Candidate $0	4) SEIU $10,000	9) IFT $3,000
	Not-itemized .$8,904	5) C&GL $10,000	10) CLang $3,000

House District 42 Barbara Connell Vondrak (D) opposed Suzanne L. Deuchler (R) (p. 115)

1996 Campaign Funds		Top 10 PAC Contributors	
Beg. Balance $0	Individuals $150	1) WSTU $500	6) N/A . . . .$N/A
Receipts $4,841	Party $0	2) Painters $240	7) N/A . . . .$N/A
Expenditures . .$3,839	PACS $890	3) UAW $150	8) N/A . . . .$N/A
On hand $1,002	Candidate $1,100	4) N/A . . . .$N/A	9) N/A . . . .$N/A
	Not-itemized .$2,701	5) N/A . . . .$N/A	10) N/A . . . .$N/A

House District 46 Dennis Hamm (D) opposed Lee A. Daniels (R) (p. 123)

1996 Campaign Funds		Top 10 PAC Contributors	
Beg. Balance $25	Individuals . . .$1,500	1) N/A . . . .$N/A	6) N/A . . . .$N/A
Receipts $2,085	Party $0	2) N/A . . . .$N/A	7) N/A . . . .$N/A
Expenditures . .$1,867	PACS $0	3) N/A . . . .$N/A	8) N/A . . . .$N/A
On hand $243	Candidate $0	4) N/A . . . .$N/A	9) N/A . . . .$N/A
	Not-itemized . . .$585	5) N/A . . . .$N/A	10) N/A . . . .$N/A

House District 47 Mark Pera (D) opposed Eileen Lyons (R) (p. 126)

1996 Campaign Funds		Top 10 PAC Contributors	
Beg. Balance .$24,562	Individuals . . .$2,350	1) IHDM . . .$100,112	6) IFT $7,499
Receipts $223,581	Party $128,769	2) IPACE $26,324	7) PersPAC $4,220
Expenditures .$245,845	PACS $79,544	3) DSCC $23,879	8) DPI $3,040
On hand $2,298	Candidate $293	4) SEIU $10,000	9) CCCTU $2,500
	Not-itemized $12,625	5) ITLA $8,000	10) C&GL $2,000

House District 48 Michael W. Schadt (D) opposed Anne Zickus (R) (p. 127)

1996 Campaign Funds		Top 10 PAC Contributors	
Beg. Balance . .$2,122	Individuals $601	1) P&P $2,000	6) MH&P $350
Receipts $14,255	Party $200	2) WSTU $1,570	7) SMW $350
Expenditures .$16,377	PACS $7,970	3) IPACE $1,000	8) Carpenters $300
On hand $0	Candidate $1,600	4) ILPipeTraders$1,000	9) AFLCIO $250
	Not-itemized .$3,884	5) Sprink $350	10) FMeany $200

House District 51 **Hyman Riebman (D)** opposed Verna L. Clayton (R) (p. 134)

1996 Campaign Funds		Top 10 PAC Contributors	
Beg. Balance .$10,250	Individuals . . .$2,212	1) LAWPAC . .$1,000	6) Robin $250
Receipts $12,095	Party $0	2) D, A&M $1000	7) Field&Sons. . .$250
Expenditures .$15,913	PACS $4,300	3) Maric Wood . .$500	8) Peck&Assoc. . .$150
On hand $6,432	Candidate $0	4) Glink, Martin .$500	9) BlomquistPC . .$150
	Not-itemized .$5,583	5) FisherConst. . .$500	10) N/A . . . .$N/A

House District 54 **Sue A. Walton (D)** opposed Bernard E. Pedersen (R) (p. 139)

1996 Campaign Funds		Top 10 PAC Contributors	
Beg. Balance . .$2,719	Individuals . . .$1,776	1) Clifford Law $5,000	6) SNAPI $200
Receipts $17,666	Party $400	2) COPE 1211 .$2,060	7) CRonen $200
Expenditures .$20,847	PACS $8,798	3) ILNOW $700	8) CStern $200
On hand . . . . . .($462)	Candidate $0	4) Carpenters . . .$500	9) N/A . . . .$N/A
	Not-itemized .$6,692	5) AFLCIO $250	10) N/A . . . .$N/A

House District 55 **Thomas P. Cahill (D)** opposed Rosemary Mulligan (R) (p. 142)

1996 Campaign Funds		Top 10 PAC Contributors	
Beg. Balance . .$1,500	Individuals . . .$2,000	1) Eagle $1,000	6) UAW $250
Receipts $11,759	Party $200	2) FamilyPAC . .$500	7) IBEW $250
Expenditures .$12,995	PACS $3,405	3) Life $330	8) CNP $250
On hand $264	Candidate $0	4) IFT $300	9) NRA $200
	Not-itemized .$6,154	5) Speed $250	10) CCapparelli . .$200

House District 57 **Elaine Nekritz (D)** opposed Elizabeth Coulson (R) (p. 146)

1996 Campaign Funds		Top 10 PAC Contributors	
Beg. Balance .$28,568	Individuals . .$13,804	1) IHDM $51,771	6) UDI $3,000
Receipts $141,899	Party $84,682	2) DSCC $15,960	7) ITLA $2,500
Expenditures .$164,916	PACS $28,010	3) DPI $5,501	8) Statesman . . .$1,500
On hand $5,551	Candidate $0	4) WVWV $4,000	9) IFT $1,250
	Not-itemized $15,403	5) CLang $3,100	10) NFTwpDem $1,250

House District 58 **Kristina "Tina" Escamilla (R)** opposed Jeffrey M. Schoenberg (D) (p. 147)

1996 Campaign Funds		Top 10 PAC Contributors	
Beg. Balance .$22,987	Individuals . .$19,900	1) HRCC $42,806	6) MPAC $2,500
Receipts $119,075	Party $74,756	2) CChurchill .$15,000	7) CatCEG $1,250
Expenditures .$131,603	PACS $19,161	3) NTRegGOP$15,000	8) JUSTPAC $500
On hand $10,459	Candidate $5,258	4) NCS $6,611	9) IROAD $500
	Not-itemized $0	5) URF $2,600	10) ILLumber . . .$500

House District 60 **Joel D. Gingiss (R)** opposed Lauren Beth Gash (D) (p. 151)

1996 Campaign Funds		Top 10 PAC Contributors	
Beg. Balance .$31,252	Individuals . .$19,180	1) HRCC $86,589	6) Duchossois . .$2,000
Receipts $194,673	Party $135,885	2) CChurchill .$20,746	7) NAII $1,150
Expenditures .$225,005	PACS $28,309	3) CRutherford$10,000	8) Ameritech . .$1,130
On hand $920	Candidate $0	4) CPeterson .$10,000	9) CMoore $1,050
	Not-itemized .$11,299	5) CBeaubien .$5,000	10) JUSTPAC . .$1,000

House District 63 **James S. Kappel (D)** opposed Ann Hughes (R) (p. 158)

1996 Campaign Funds		Top 10 PAC Contributors	
Beg. Balance $0	Individuals $200	1) IHDM $2,000	6) N/A . . . .$N/A
Receipts $4,375	Party $2,200	2) CarpetWorld $1,250	7) N/A . . . .$N/A
Expenditures . .$4,375	PACS $1,450	3) SNAPI $200	8) N/A . . . .$N/A
On hand $0	Candidate $0	4) N/A . . . .$N/A	9) N/A . . . .$N/A
	Not-itemized . . .$525	5) N/A . . . .$N/A	10) N/A . . . .$N/A

House District 64 **Joseph H. "Big Joe" Powalowski (D)** opposed Cal Skinner, Jr. (R) (p. 159)

1996 Campaign Funds		Top 10 PAC Contributors	
Beg. Balance $39	Individuals . . .$1,000	1)Highlander . .$1,000	6) N/A . . . .$N/A
Receipts $5,348	Party $0	2) IFT $500	7) N/A . . . .$N/A
Expenditures . .$5,345	PACS $1,900	3) Teamsters . . .$200	8) N/A . . . .$N/A
On hand $42	Candidate $993	4) BSIW $200	9) N/A . . . .$N/A
	Not-itemized .$1,455	5) N/A . . . .$N/A	10) N/A . . . .$N/A

House District 67 **Thomas J. Seymour (R)** opposed Douglas P. Scott (D) (p. 166)

1996 Campaign Funds		Top 10 PAC Contributors	
Beg. Balance . .$1,112	Individuals . . .$6,140	1) FamTaxprs .$11,500	6) SyversonFS .$1,500
Receipts $62,007	Party $17,000	2) HRCC $11,800	7) Park Hills . . .$1,000
Expenditures .$62,386	PACS $26,885	3) OlsonPAC . .$4,000	8) CatCEG $1,000
On hand $733	Candidate $4,750	4) Schlicting . .$2,600	9) CWait $1,000
	Not-itemized .$7,232	5) CWinters . . .$2,000	10) NFIB $995

House District 68 **William A. Vedra (D)** opposed Ronald A. Wait (R) (p. 167)

1996 Campaign Funds		Top 10 PAC Contributors	
Beg. Balance . .$3,708	Individuals $150	1) IHDM $8,938	6) Laborers $500
Receipts $17,289	Party $9,479	2) UAW $2,000	7) AFSCME $400
Expenditures .$19,072	PACS $6,950	3) USWA $1,500	8) IBEW $300
On hand $1,925	Candidate $0	4) BlueSky . . .$1,000	9) ABDI $300
	Not-itemized . . .$710	5) BooneDem . . .$541	10) AFLCIO $250

House District 69 **Victor W. Verni (D)** opposed Dave Winters (R) (p. 170)

1996 Campaign Funds		Top 10 PAC Contributors	
Beg. Balance . .$5,215	Individuals . . .$6,751	1) IHDM . . .$198,495	6) AFSCME . . .$1,640
Receipts $273,454	Party $219,206	2) DSCC $10,045	7) ITLA $1,500
Expenditures .$272,120	PACS $31,126	3) PersPAC . . .$6,116	8) USWA $1,500
On hand $6,549	Candidate $0	4) IPACE $3,000	9) Ameritech . .$1,242
	Not-itemized $16,371	5) UAW $2,000	10) LAWPAC . .$1,000

House District 71 **Phil Banaszek (R)** opposed Michael J. Boland (D) (p. 174)

1996 Campaign Funds		Top 10 PAC Contributors	
Beg. Balance . .$3,765	Individuals $500	1) RIGOP $300	6) N/A . . . .$N/A
Receipts $7,491	Party $400	2) WhitesideGOP $100	7) N/A . . . .$N/A
Expenditures . .$11,010	PACS $0	3) N/A . . . .$N/A	8) N/A . . . .$N/A
On hand $246	Candidate $0	4) N/A . . . .$N/A	9) N/A . . . .$N/A
	Not-itemized .$6,591	5) N/A . . . .$N/A	10) N/A . . . .$N/A

House District 73 **Pennie L. von Bergen Wessels (D)** opposed Gerald L. "Jerry" Mitchell (R) (p. 178)

1996 Campaign Funds		Top 10 PAC Contributors	
Beg. Balance .$16,594	Individuals . . .$3,807	1) IHDM . . .$272,334	6) CGranberg .$7,000
Receipts $368,434	Party $297,914	2) AFSCME .$10,397	7) Laborers $3,000
Expenditures .$348,535	PACS $59,322	3) DSCC $9,804	8) CNovak $3,000
On hand $36,493	Candidate $560	4) SEIU $8,000	9) UAW $2,750
	Not-itemized .$6,831	5) ITLA $7,000	10) IFT $2,500

House District 74 **Mickey R. Martin (D)** opposed I. Ronald Lawfer (R) (p. 179)

1996 Campaign Funds		Top 10 PAC Contributors	
Beg. Balance $363	Individuals $425	1) NWIEIC $1,300	6) NCIL $500
Receipts $12,278	Party $1,012	2) IHDM $1,012	7) IWPC $500
Expenditures . .$12,399	PACS $7,300	3) FCL $1,000	8) P&P $400
On hand $242	Candidate $0	4) NWB&T $900	9) NWICA $300
	Not-itemized . .$3,541	5) Carpenters792 .$700	10) Carpenters . . .$300

House District 75 **Stephen Alan Spangler (R)** opposed Mary K. O'Brien (D) (p. 182)

1996 Campaign Funds		Top 10 PAC Contributors	
Beg. Balance . .$6,543	Individuals . .$11,115	1) HRCC $14,313	6) CardinalTrans $2,000
Receipts $100,386	Party $21,013	2) ISMS $5,000	7) DowUSA . . .$1,500
Expenditures .$103,866	PACS $45,141	3) CRyan $4,000	8) IHCA $1,000
On hand $3,063	Candidate $0	4) MorrisB&T .$3,366	9) MPAC $1,000
	Not-itemized .$23,117	5) GrundyGOP $2,000	10) CatCEG . . .$1,000

House District 76 **Donald Schwanke (R)** opposed Frank J. Mautino (D) (p. 183)

1996 Campaign Funds		Top 10 PAC Contributors	
Beg. Balance $703	Individuals $560	1)LaSal GOP . .$1,000	6)N/A . . . .$N/A
Receipts $9,136	Party $2,250	2)LaSal Cent . .$1,000	7)N/A . . . .$N/A
Expenditures . .$9,697	PACS $0	3)Weller Cong . .$250	8)N/A . . . .$N/A
On hand $142	Candidate $3,700	4)N/A . . . .$N/A	9)N/A . . . .$N/A
	Not-itemized .$2,626	5)N/A . . . .$N/A	10)N/A . . . .$N/A

House District 78 **Tom Berry (D)** opposed Robert A. "Bob" Biggins (R) (p. 187)

1996 Campaign Funds		Top 10 PAC Contributors	
Beg. Balance $722	Individuals $0	1) UTU $1,000	6) N/A . . . .$N/A
Receipts $4,614	Party $0	2) N/A . . . .$N/A	7) N/A . . . .$N/A
Expenditures . .$3,460	PACS $1,000	3) N/A . . . .$N/A	8) N/A . . . .$N/A
On hand $1,876	Candidate $3,460	4) N/A . . . .$N/A	9) N/A . . . .$N/A
	Not-itemized . . .$154	5) N/A . . . .$N/A	10) N/A . . . .$N/A

House District 79 **Marvin Lyzenga (R)** opposed Michael Giglio (D) (p. 190)

1996 Campaign Funds		Top 10 PAC Contributors	
Beg. Balance . .$4,868	Individuals . . .$5,300	1) HRCC . . .$148,127	6) CoC $2,500
Receipts $276,842	Party $215,817	2) FLAD $54,939	7) CatCEG $2,000
Expenditures .$273,281	PACS $42,446	3) ISMS $10,000	8) Fremont $1,500
On hand $8,429	Candidate $0	4) CChurchill .$7,500	9) HomewdDisp $1,250
	Not-itemized $13,279	5) MPAC $2,500	10) JUSTPAC . .$1,000

House District 80 **Flora L. Ciarlo (R)** opposed George F. Scully, Jr. (D) (p. 191)

1996 Campaign Funds		Top 10 PAC Contributors	
Beg. Balance . . $6,337	Individuals . . . $6,242	1) HRCC . . . $153,657	6) StegerPlz . . . $5,250
Receipts $324,245	Party $227,882	2) FLAD $41,560	7) MPAC $5,000
Expenditures . $329,013	PACS $73,701	3) ISMS $10,000	8) GOPWom . . . $3,500
On hand $1,569	Candidate $0	4) CRyan $10,000	9) ChgoCoC . . . $3,177
	Not-itemized $16,420	5) CChurchill . $10,000	10) IBA $3,000

House District 81 **Dave Brockway (D)** opposed Judy Biggert (R) (p. 194)

1996 Campaign Funds		Top 10 PAC Contributors	
Beg. Balance . . $1,675	Individuals . . . . $NA	1) N/A . . . . $N/A	6) N/A . . . . $N/A
Receipts . . . . $N/A	Party . . . . $NA	2) N/A . . . . $N/A	7) N/A . . . . $N/A
Expenditures . . . $N/A	PACS . . . . $NA	3) N/A . . . . $N/A	8) N/A . . . . $N/A
On hand $409	Candidate . . . . . $NA	4) N/A . . . . $N/A	9) N/A . . . . $N/A
	Not-itemized . . . $NA	5) N/A . . . . $N/A	10) N/A . . . . $N/A

House District 89 **Mike Goodman (D)** opposed Jay Ackerman (R) (p. 210)

1996 Campaign Funds		Top 10 PAC Contributors	
Beg. Balance $0	Individuals . . . $4,232	1) IHDM $8,812	6) WoodDem . . $1,500
Receipts $45,153	Party $20,046	2) TazeDem . . . $7,850	7) DSCC $1,389
Expenditures . $45,129	PACS $19,875	3) MCIDC $7,000	8) WCIBCT . . . $1,000
On hand $24	Candidate $1,000	4) Steam $3,000	9) Laborers $700
	Not-itemized $0	5) IUOE $1,500	10) AFLCIO $500

House District 91 **Phil Philipps (R)** opposed Michael K. Smith (D) (p. 214)

1996 Campaign Funds		Top 10 PAC Contributors	
Beg. Balance $755	Individuals . . . $4,780	1) N/A . . . . $N/A	6) N/A . . . . $N/A
Receipts $6,390	Party $0	2) N/A . . . . $N/A	7) N/A . . . . $N/A
Expenditures . . $7,145	PACS $0	3) N/A . . . . $N/A	8) N/A . . . . $N/A
On hand $0	Candidate $1,375	4) N/A . . . . $N/A	9) N/A . . . . $N/A
	Not-itemized . . . $235	5) N/A . . . . $N/A	10) N/A . . . . $N/A

House District 92 **Walter "Wally" Hellstrom, Jr. (R)** opposed Ricca C. Slone (D) (p. 215)

1996 Campaign Funds		Top 10 PAC Contributors	
Beg. Balance . . $2,211	Individuals . . . $1,356	1) CLeitch . . . $18,300	6) PoliceBPAC . . $300
Receipts $26,593	Party $20,902	2) CBlack $1,050	7) PeoGrassroots . $192
Expenditures . $28,804	PACS $2,003	3) CBiggert . . . $1,000	8) PeoGOPWom . $150
On hand $0	Candidate $400	4) Keystone . . . $1,000	9) CAckerman . . . $100
	Not-itemized . $1,932	5) ILCon $500	10) LimestGOP . . $100

House District 94 **Caroline Porter (D)** opposed Donald L. Moffitt (R) (p. 219)

1996 Campaign Funds		Top 10 PAC Contributors	
Beg. Balance . . $4,565	Individuals . . . $2,500	1) Knox Dem . . . $900	6) N/A . . . . $N/A
Receipts $7,234	Party $900	2) USWA $300	7) N/A . . . . $N/A
Expenditures $11,799	PACS $500	3) Laborers $200	8) N/A . . . . $N/A
On hand $0	Candidate $0	4) N/A . . . . $N/A	9) N/A . . . . $N/A
	Not-itemized . $3,334	5) N/A . . . . $N/A	10) N/A . . . . $N/A

House District 95 **Tab Turke (D)** opposed Richard P. Myers (R) (p. 222)

1996 Campaign Funds		Top 10 PAC Contributors	
Beg. Balance . .$6,075	Individuals . . .$5,297	1) IHDM . . .$236,562	6) SEIU $5,000
Receipts $328,660	Party $274,250	2) DSCC $16,193	7) IFT $4,440
Expenditures .$332,232	PACS $46,010	3) CSmith . . .$10,000	8) Life $4,000
On hand $2,503	Candidate $0	4) ITLA $6,000	9) MCIDC $3,500
	Not-itemized .$3,103	5) DPI $5,704	10) CGranberg .$3,000

House District 96 **Paul Lange (D)** opposed Art Tenhouse (R) (p. 223)

1996 Campaign Funds		Top 10 PAC Contributors	
Beg. Balance $89	Individuals . . .$2,250	1) PikeDem $200	6) N/A . . . .$N/A
Receipts $3,915	Party $200	2) N/A . . . .$N/A	7) N/A . . . .$N/A
Expenditures . .$4,004	PACS $0	3) N/A . . . .$N/A	8) N/A . . . .$N/A
On hand $0	Candidate $1,217	4) N/A . . . .$N/A	9) N/A . . . .$N/A
	Not-itemized . . .$248	5) N/A . . . .$N/A	10) N/A . . . .$N/A

House District 98 **Rodney Davis (R)** opposed Gary Hannig (D) (p. 227)

1996 Campaign Funds		Top 10 PAC Contributors	
Beg. Balance .$38,001	Individuals . . .$5,840	1) HRCC $15,549	6) CNoland $800
Receipts $63,541	Party $19,925	2) RodeBrad . .$6,736	7) PetPec $600
Expenditures .$99,494	PACS $17,585	3) MPAC $2,500	8) ILLumber $500
On hand $2,048	Candidate $1,090	4) CatCEG . . .$1,000	9) CStephens $500
	Not-itemized $19,101	5) Alliance $1,000	10) ChristianGOP $500

House District 99 **Leslie J. Graves (D)** opposed Raymond Poe (R) (p. 230)

1996 Campaign Funds		Top 10 PAC Contributors	
Beg. Balance . .$5,202	Individuals . . .$3,034	1) IHDM . . .$113,913	6) IFT $4,060
Receipts $200,763	Party $117,915	2) AFSCME .$13,205	7) UAW $3,500
Expenditures .$195,859	PACS $69,674	3) SEIU $10,000	8) Carpenters . .$3,200
On hand $10,106	Candidate $0	4) MCIDC $7,000	9) ITLA $3,000
	Not-itemized $10,140	5) PersPAC . . .$6,183	10) Teamsters . .$2,500

House District 100 **Marylou Lowder Kent (D)** opposed Gwenn Klingler (R) (p. 231)

1996 Campaign Funds		Top 10 PAC Contributors	
Beg. Balance . .$9,781	Individuals . . .$4,925	1) IHDM . . .$293,269	6) MCIDC $6,500
Receipts $421,541	Party $305,928	2) AFSCME .$17,518	7) KentFoods . .$6,200
Expenditures .$420,013	PACS $94,718	3) SEIU $10,000	8) ITLA $6,000
On hand $11,309	Candidate $0	4) DSCC $7,330	9) CGranberg . .$5,000
	Not-Itemized $15,970	5) WVWV $7,000	10) IFT $4,500

House District 101 **Jerrold H. "Jerry" Stocks (R)** opposed Julie A. Curry (D) (p. 234)

1996 Campaign Funds		Top 10 PAC Contributors	
Beg. Balance . .$8,166	Individuals . .$13,014	1) HRCC $17,456	6) CoC $750
Receipts $58,531	Party $20,454	2) MaconGOP .$2,998	7) Spacemark . . .$600
Expenditures .$65,414	PACS $7,462	3) StocksAg . . .$1,301	8) ILLumber $500
On hand $1,283	Candidate $7,500	4) URF $1,000	9) DecVAClinic . .$400
	Not-itemized $10,101	5) ABC $950	10) FastImpress . .$337

House District 103 Naomi D. Jakobsson (D) opposed Richard J. "Rick" Winkel, Jr. (R) (p. 238)

1996 Campaign Funds		Top 10 PAC Contributors	
Beg. Balance .$12,503	Individuals ...$2,575	1) IHDM ...$241,425	6) ITLA $8,000
Receipts $355,953	Party $262,215	2) WVWV ..$14,000	7) MCIDC $7,000
Expenditures .$360,325	PACS $68,519	3) DSCC $10,000	8) UDI $3,000
On hand $8,131	Candidate $0	4) SEIU $10,000	9) IFT $2,750
	Not-itemized $22,644	5) PersPAC ...$9,803	10) CGranberg .$2,000

House District 104 Bob Kirchner (D) opposed Timothy V. Johnson (R) (p. 239)

1996 Campaign Funds		Top 10 PAC Contributors	
Beg. Balance ..$7,135	Individuals ...$2,172	1) MCIDC $3,000	6) ChamDem $300
Receipts $18,796	Party $300	2) P&P $1,750	7) AFLCIO $250
Expenditures .$25,931	PACS $9,450	3) IBEW $1,000	8) PR&S $250
On hand $0	Candidate $0	4) ECILB&C ...$500	9) SMW $200
	Not-itemized .$6,874	5) ILPipeTraders $500	10) Stonitsch $200

House District 107 Joe Bob Pierce (D) opposed John O. Jones (R) (p. 246)

1996 Campaign Funds		Top 10 PAC Contributors	
Beg. Balance ..$4,242	Individuals ...$2,963	1) IHDM ...$299,408	6) DSCC $10,000
Receipts $434,594	Party $338,714	2) CGranberg .$15,840	7) ITLA $7,000
Expenditures .$431,722	PACS $74,084	3) SEIU $13,000	8) IFT $5,620
On hand $7,114	Candidate $90	4) Laborers ..$12,081	9) CHartke $5,300
	Not-itemized $18,743	5) AFSCME .$10,719	10) PersPAC ...$4,563

House District 108 Cory M. Jobe (R) opposed Charles A. "Chuck" Hartke (D) (p. 247)

1996 Campaign Funds		Top 10 PAC Contributors	
Beg. Balance ..$3,063	Individuals $900	1) Craw PAC ...$450	6) JasperGOP ...$150
Receipts $6,909	Party $1,200	2) CMWeaver ...$250	7) N/A ....$N/A
Expenditures ..$9,972	PACS $200	3) Craw GOP ...$200	8) N/A ....$N/A
On hand $0	Candidate $0	4) Brad Sup $200	9) N/A ....$N/A
	Not-itemized .$4,609	5) CJones $150	10) N/A ....$N/A

House District 109 Jackie D. "Butch" Mathus, Jr. (R) opposed Kurt M. Granberg (D) (p. 250)

1996 Campaign Funds		Top 10 PAC Contributors	
Beg. Balance $279	Individuals $200	1) CWatson $800	6) N/A ....$N/A
Receipts $4,133	Party $1,650	2) IMHA $500	7) N/A ....$N/A
Expenditures ..$4,051	PACS $700	3) FayetteGOP ..$450	8) N/A ....$N/A
On hand $361	Candidate $0	4) SalemGOPWom $400	9) N/A ....$N/A
	Not-itemized .$1,583	5) GC $200	10) N/A ....$N/A

House District 110 Velda Armes (D) opposed Ron Stephens (R) (p. 251)

1996 Campaign Funds		Top 10 PAC Contributors	
Beg. Balance ..$2,814	Individuals ...$1,415	1) IHDM $12,377	6) CPJ $500
Receipts $38,671	Party $13,766	2) CentBank ..$5,000	7) CJHoffman ...$500
Expenditures .$41,467	PACS $9,185	3) ITLA $2,000	8) IUOE143 ....$500
On hand $18	Candidate $6,000	4) LakinLaw ..$1,000	9) WoodysSupply $500
	Not-itemized .$8,305	5) DSCC $639	10) IUOE $500

House District 111 Jim Mihalich (R) opposed Steve Davis (D) (p. 254)

1996 Campaign Funds		Top 10 PAC Contributors	
Beg. Balance .$29,500	Individuals . . .$7,975	1) HRCC $18,697	6) Mad GOP . . .$1,225
Receipts $71,147	Party $28,532	2) AdamsDevlp $4,050	7) CatCEG $1,000
Expenditures .$92,033	PACS $21,005	3) CStephens . .$3,500	8) SIIA $1,000
On hand $8,614	Candidate $0	4) TriadInd . . .$3,000	9) FLAD $1,000
	Not-itemized $13,635	5) CWatson . . .$2,000	10) Alliance . . .$1,000

House District 112 Maria Garcia, Jr. (R) opposed Glenn E. Bradford (D) (p. 255)

1996 Campaign Funds		Top 10 PAC Contributors	
Beg. Balance . .$1,021	Individuals . . .$5,433	1) HRCC . . .$237,137	6) ISMS $2,750
Receipts $331,141	Party $289,510	2) CStephens .$14,910	7) Duchossois . .$2,000
Expenditures .$331,693	PACS $24,122	3) FLAD $10,000	8) CChurchill . .$2,000
On hand $469	Candidate $0	4) CRyder $7,000	9) Fremont $1,750
	Not-itemized $12,076	5) CRutherford $5,200	10) CoC $1500

House District 113 Paul A. Whelan (R) opposed Thomas Holbrook (D) (p. 258)

1996 Campaign Funds		Top 10 PAC Contributors	
Beg. Balance $0	Individuals . . .$6,450	1) HRCC $3,100	6) CStephens $301
Receipts $18,520	Party $4,351	2) KorteConst . . .$500	7) UnionBank . . .$250
Expenditures .$18,520	PACS $1,600	3) StClrCen $500	8) MadGOP $200
On hand $0	Candidate $760	4) ILLumber $500	9) N/A . . . .$N/A
	Not-itemized $5,359	5) TWhelanLaw .$350	10) N/A . . . .$N/A

House District 115 John S. Rendleman (D) opposed Mike Bost (R) (p. 262)

1996 Campaign Funds		Top 10 PAC Contributors	
Beg. Balance $246	Individuals . . .$8,968	1) IHDM . . .$233,170	6) DPI $9,229
Receipts $376,673	Party $289,863	2) FMJM $15,899	7) CGranberg . .$6,632
Expenditures .$374,747	PACS $63,540	3) DSCC $12,994	8) ITLA $6,000
On hand $2,172	Candidate $400	4) IPACE $10,000	9) SEIU $5,000
	Not-itemized $13,929	5) Laborers . . .$9,855	10) AFSCME . .$4,050

House District 116 John W. Coats (R) opposed Terry W. Deering (D) (p. 263)

1996 Campaign Funds		Top 10 PAC Contributors	
Beg. Balance $193	Individuals $900	1) RandGOP $750	6) N/A . . . .$N/A
Receipts $2,457	Party $1,050	2) StClrGOP $300	7) N/A . . . .$N/A
Expenditures . .$2,639	PACS $0	3) N/A . . . .$N/A	8) N/A . . . .$N/A
On hand $11	Candidate $0	4) N/A . . . .$N/A	9) N/A . . . .$N/A
	Not-itemized . . .$507	5) N/A . . . .$N/A	10) N/A . . . .$N/A

House District 117 Philip D. Roberts (R) opposed Larry Woolard (D) (p. 266)

1996 Campaign Funds		Top 10 PAC Contributors	
Beg. Balance $28	Individuals $0	1) N/A . . . .$N/A	6) N/A . . . .$N/A
Receipts $2,975	Party $0	2) N/A . . . .$N/A	7) N/A . . . .$N/A
Expenditures . .$2,837	PACS $0	3) N/A . . . .$N/A	8) N/A . . . .$N/A
On hand $166	Candidate $2,698	4) N/A . . . .$N/A	9) N/A . . . .$N/A
	Not-itemized . . .$277	5) N/A . . . .$N/A	10) N/A . . . .$N/A

House District 118 Jack Hill (R) opposed David D. Phelps (D) (p. 267)

1996 Campaign Funds		Top 10 PAC Contributors	
Beg. Balance . .$5,176	Individuals . . .$3,810	1) HRCC $97,116	6) CatCEG $1,000
Receipts $159,650	Party $107,151	2) CEdgar $5,000	7) IndianapLife .$1,000
Expenditures .$164,591	PACS $10,697	3) PulaskiRB . .$3,320	8) ABC $900
On hand $235	Candidate $5,000	4) CoC $1,700	9) EPAC $750
	Not-itemized $32,992	5) Fremont $1,500	10) CRyan $500

Additional Key Votes

The Senate and House roll call votes described on the following pages (285-341) are included in the *Almanac* to give the reader a more complete picture of member votes than are provided in the key votes portion of each page of the Members and Districts section of this book (pages 32-267) . Some of the roll calls selected as additional key votes are significant due to the partisan or geographic controversy they engendered. Others are significant despite their lack of controversy because of their overall importance in addressing major issues in Illinois.

On pages 287-294 readers will find a list titled Descriptions of Additional Key Votes for the Senate. Likewise on pages 294-303 is a list titled Descriptions of Additional Key Votes for the House. In both cases, the roll calls are listed chronologically for 1997. The type of roll call is described by a sequence of abbreviations that reveal the status of the bill before the chamber. The status abbreviation is followed by the date the roll call vote takes place. The date is followed by a brief description of the bill.

The abbreviations used to denote the status of bills in the Descriptions of Additional Key Votes for the Senate (pages 287-294) and the Descriptions of Additional Key Votes for the House (pages 294-303) are as follows:

- 3RD—third reading
- CONH1—the Senate was voting on whether or not to concur with House amendment #1 to that particular bill
- CONS1—the House was voting on whether or not to concur with Senate amendment #1 to that particular bill
- NCCONH1—the Senate was voting on whether or not to non concur with House amendment #1
- NCONS1—the House was voting on whether or not to non concur with Senate amendment #1
- RECH1—the House was voting whether or not to recede from House amendment #1 to that particular bill
- RECS1—the Senate was voting whether or not to recede from Senate amendment #1 to that particular bill
- CNOTE—the chamber was voting on a motion regarding whether or not a corrections impact note was applicable to the bill
- CC1—the chamber was voting on the adoption of Conference Committee Report #1

As an example, consider the first line in the Descriptions of Additional Key Votes of the Senate list. It reads as follows:

SB	16	3RD	3-6	Provides tax exemptions for aggregate manufacturers.

This means that Senate Bill 16 received a roll call vote on its third reading on March 6, 1997. The bill provides tax exemptions for aggregate manufacturers. We strongly advise the reader to refrain from inferring too much about the substance of the bills (or the motives for the members' votes) based on the description of the bill as provided. The descriptions are for the particular roll call in question and may not reflect the final content or status of that particular piece of legislation (or a member's stand on that issue). For further information about members' positions on legislative issues, the reader should contact that legislator. For further explanation of the bills chosen for this section, contact the Legislative Information System, Room 705 Stratton Office Building, Springfield, Illinois 62706.

For this portion of the *Almanac*, we chose to examine selected 134 roll calls for the senate and 174 for the house. A bill's description in the Descriptions of Additional Key Votes of the Senate may not necessarily correlate to the same numbered bill's description in the Descriptions of Additional Key Votes of the House because many bills were not voted on in both chambers, or some bills may have been changed by amendments in one chamber, giving them more significant language.

Following the Descriptions of Additional Key Votes of the Senate and the Descriptions of Additional Key Votes of the House is a list of Key Votes by Topic Area (pages 304-305) whereon the bills are grouped by topics (abortion, agriculture. etc.). Readers interested in how members voted on a specific topic area may be tempted to use the Key Votes by Topic Area list and the key vote voting records of individual members (pages 32-267) to determine how members vote on specific issues. We would strongly caution, however, that these roll calls cannot give the reader a total picture of a legislator's stand on any given topic. The roll calls we have chosen represent less than five percent of all the bills introduced in the General Assembly. In addition, grouping the bills by topic area is a subjective decision made solely by the researchers. A given bill could be classified under one topic area here, but when viewed in its entirety, it could also be placed in a totally different category.

On pages 306-341 we examine how individual members of the Senate and the House voted on each of these key votes. For these tables, the additional key votes are listed chronologically across the top of several pages with the members names and corresponding votes listed below. The additional key votes for the Senate members are presented first (pages 306-317), followed by the additional key votes for the House members (318-341). For these tables we have used the following abbreviations to designate the members' votes on these bills:

Y— The member voted yes.
N— The member voted no.
P— The member voted present, which has the legal effect of a no vote.
A— The member was absent when that roll call was taken; applies to House

members only and has the legal effect of a no vote.

E— The member received an excused absence for that roll call; applies to House members only and has the legal effect of a no vote.

X— Was not a member of the General Assembly or of that chamber at the time of the roll call.

O— The member was recorded as having not voted; applies to Senate members only and has the legal effect of a no vote.

Descriptions of Additional Key Votes for the Senate

SB	16	3RD	3-6	Provides tax exemptions for aggregate manufacturers.
SB	21	3RD	3-18	Allows townships in Cook County to levy a special tax for improvements to streets.
SB	30	3RD	3-20	Provides that the Secretary of State shall begin replacing multiyear registration (license) plates.
SB	51	3RD	2-6	Omnibus revenue bill, including a provision to allow counties other than Cook to establish a separate deadline for filing a senior citizen tax assessment freeze application.
SB	54	CONH1	6-1	Establishes new rules on developing landfills near a 100-year floodplain.
SB	55	3RD	3-18	Vehicle bill for electric deregulation.
SB	65	3RD	3-19	Creates a minority environmental scholarship program.
SB	69	3RD	3-11	Enables local school districts to levy for technology infrastructure.
SB	76	CONH1	5-22	Establishes new budget proposal procedures.
SB	81	3RD	3-18	Excludes park district recreational programs for the handicapped from the tax caps law.
SB	87	3RD	2-6	Increase authorization in General Obligation Bond Act.
SB	103	CONH1	5-22	Provides procedures for the making and payment of local improvements by special assessment.
SB	107	3RD	3-14	Provides penalties for unlawful use of armor piercing bullets.
SB	110	3RD	3-12	A person may not operate a boat or snowmobile if his or her blood alcohol concentration exceeds the level specified in the Illinois Vehicle Code.
SB	123	3RD	3-19	Creates the Sex Offender Management Board and Fund.
SB	129	3RD	3-20	Prohibits campaign materials from having altered or fraudulent pictures.
SB	140	3RD	3-20	Provides notification requirements for municipalities for proposed pollution control facilities.

SB	160	3RD	3-11	Expands Right of Conscience Act to include health care payers and various health care providers.
SB	166	3RD	3-12	Increases the age for mandatory seat belt use from six to 16.
SB	200	3RD	3-14	Consolidates nonpartisan election dates.
SB	225	3RD	3-20	Allows volunteers to issue citations to handicapped parking violators.
SB	228	3RD	3-18	Creates the Illinois Equal Benefit Opportunity Act of 1997.
SB	230	3RD	3-18	Creates the Partial-birth Abortion Ban Act.
SB	236	3RD	3-11	Experimental procedures on patients in life-threatening situations may be done in accordance with federal rules.
SB	248	CONH1	5-20	Children may bring their own lunch to day care.
SB	317	CC1	5-31	Various changes to Public Aid Code and managed care.
SB	327	3RD	3-19	Authorizes an additional Regional Alzheimer's Disease Assistance Center.
SB	345	CONH2,3	5-22	Further defines an unfit parent; grants grandparents and godparents visitation rights for children in foster care.
SB	366	CONH1	5-21	Expedites the termination of parental rights of unfit parents.
SB	378	3RD	3-20	Implements Uniform State Hazardous Materials Transportation Registration and Permit Program.
SB	381	CC1	5-30	Prisoners responsible for paying costs of frivolous lawsuits.
SB	431	3RD	3-20	Changes the requirements for regional disposable site characterization.
SB	508	3RD	3-17	Provides that a convicted person shall reimburse the Department of Corrections for the costs of incarceration at a rate determined by the department.
SB	557	3RD	3-20	Creates the Alternative Route to Teacher Certification Program.
SB	596	CC1	6-1	Provides that tourism boards and certain convention or civic center boards are "public bodies" under the Open Meetings Act.
SB	600	3RD	3-18	Allows release of certain information to an adopted person, his or her birth parents, and his or her adopted parents after the adopted person turns 18.
SB	680	CC1	6-1	Allows local governments to accept payment by credit card.
SB	700	3RD	3-20	Prohibits the impediment of competition in local telecommunications.

SB	762	3RD	3-20	Eliminates mandatory training requirements for part-time corrections officers.
SB	772	3RD	3-17	Increases penalties for hit and run drivers.
SB	780	3RD	3-17	Provides that DCFS shall give due consideration to a child's heritage when making foster care placement but shall not deny placement of a child on the basis of race.
SB	795	3RD	3-20	Allows Conservation 2000 funds to be used by public and private landowners to protect ecosystems.
SB	796	3RD	3-19	Prohibits prison guards from sexual contact with prisoners.
SB	797	CC1	6-1	Repeals the Meigs Field Act.
SB	806	3RD	3-17	Establishes Illinois Directory of New Hires.
SB	819	3RD	3-18	Provides 30 days to pay for initial annual permit fee to applicants for an air pollution operating permit.
SB	843	3RD	3-17	Provides that neither a local government entity nor employee is liable for an injury caused by a failure to supervise an activity unless guilty of willful and wanton conduct.
SB	856	CONH1,2, 3,4,5	5-22	Omnibus tax bill, includes provisions allowing Department of Revenue to collect child support delinquencies in any manner authorized for all taxes.
SB	858	3RD	3-17	Amends various sections of the Podiatric Medical Practice Act of 1987.
SB	909	CONH1	5-20	Increases the maximum income threshold from \$14,000 annually to \$16,000 for the Circuit Breaker Program.
SB	927	3RD	3-20	Raises the amount of motorcycle registration fee that is used for the Cycle Rider Safety Training Fund and establishes a fee to take the Cycle Rider Training Program.
SB	950	3RD	3-20	Creates a graduated driver's license for drivers under the age of 18.
SB	953	3RD	3-20	Creates the Trademark Registration and Protection Act.
SB	999	CONH1	5-21	Provides that a franchising authority may grant additional cable franchises.
SB	1000	3RD	3-18	Moves the primary election from March to September.
SB	1024	3RD	3-17	Requires employers to report newly hired employees to the Department of Employment Security and requires the department to share that

				information with other governmental agencies for purposes of collecting child support.
SB	1044	3RD	3-20	Requires ATM owners to disclose ATM surcharge fees.
SB	1050	3RD	3-13	Increases student assistance monetary awards for undergraduates.
SB	1084	3RD	3-20	Provides for the creation of one or more Assistive Technology Evaluation and Training Centers.
SB	1101	CC1	6-1	Budget Implementation Act.
SB	1103	3RD	3-18	Bans landscape waste burning in municipalities with a population over 75,000.
SB	1105	3RD	3-20	Provides that a lobbyist shall notify each official on whose behalf an expenditure has been reported within 30 days of filing a report.
HB	8	3RD	5-13	Creates the Genetic Information Privacy Act.
HB	45	3RD	5-13	Increases the maximum Homestead Improvement Exemption to $45,000.
HB	50	3RD	5-15	Creates a pilot project to slow trains traveling through Fox River Grove to a maximum of 50 miles per hour.
HB	56	3RD	5-14	Requires DCFS to provide information on a child's criminal background to the child's foster care providers.
HB	127	CC1	5-31	Revokes or prohibits the issuance of a FOID card to a person who has been convicted of domestic abuse.
HB	154	3RD	5-15	Provides that expressions contained in a high school newspaper are not subject to prior restraint, with certain exceptions.
HB	165	3RD	5-15	Provides language for when expediting termination of parental rights is appropriate.
HB	172	3RD	5-16	Allows for "no knock" search warrants and increases penalties for false emergency 911 calls.
HB	260	3RD	5-16	Limits the use of fees, taxes, or surcharges imposed by local governments on the disposal of solid waste to certain environment-related purposes.
HB	271	3RD	5-13	Requires ATM owners to disclose ATM surcharge fees.
HB	282	3RD	5-16	Creates an income tax credit for corporations that use biodegradable materials made of corn or soybean products.
HB	297	CC1	5-28	Increases dram shop liability.
HB	313	3RD	5-16	Allows state workers to establish credit towards their pensions for prior government experience.

HB	316	3RD	5-13	Requires contractors to use soybean oil-based ink in providing printing services for units of local government.
HB	379	CC1	5-30	Adds certain cases of child abduction to the list of offenses for which an offender must register under the Sex Offender Registration Act.
HB	381	3RD	5-13	Extends the deadline to file for the Senior Citizens Assessment Freeze Homestead Protection by three months if the applicant has a severe medical condition.
HB	424	3RD	5-8	Creates the Illinois River Watershed Restoration Act.
HB	475	3RD	5-16	Requires the Secretary of State to furnish vehicle or driver data at a specified fee.
HB	480	3RD	5-8	Provides rules for petitioning to end township government in a county.
HB	489	3RD	5-13	Creates an off-road vehicle trails program with associated fees.
HB	522	3RD	5-15	Establishes regulation of home medical equipment and services.
HB	524	3RD	5-13	Clarifies that properties located in a TIF district that overlap an enterprise zone are prohibited from receiving a property tax abatement unless certain requirements are met.
HB	540	3RD	5-8	Requires DMH/DD to make at least one site visit a year to its facilities.
HB	581	CC1	6-1	Expands Senior Citizen Real Estate Tax Deferral program to include disabled individuals.
HB	585	3RD	5-8	Changes the method that multistate businesses apportion their income for Illinois tax purposes.
HB	601	3RD	5-13	Changes the auto lease tax structure.
HB	602	3RD	5-15	Implements a graduated fee schedule for certain pesticide registration and licensing fees.
HB	618	3RD	5-8	Increases maximum fines that may be imposed for felonies, misdemeanors and petty offenses.
HB	652	3RD	5-16	Transfers the nonpartisan election of November of odd-numbered years with the nonpartisan election of April of odd-numbered years.
HB	725	3RD	5-15	Expands Right of Conscience Act to include health care payers and various health care providers.
HB	729	3RD	5-14	Provides that all reports filed by political action committees be made available on the World Wide Web.

HB	844	3RD	5-15	Allows for the sale of Collision Damage Waivers for rental cars and creates the Renters Financial Responsibility and Protection Act.
HB	923	3RD	5-8	Provides that the board of trustees from each state university has at least one student member.
HB	951	3RD	5-13	Expands definition of "unfit parent."
HB	968	3RD	5-8	Provides for the replacement of Illinois license plates.
HB	995	3RD	5-16	Grants a Commercial Driver's License waiver to a farmer or member of the family driving a truck-tractor semitrailer.
HB	1004	3RD	5-9	Establishes that the Metropolitan Water Reclamation District cannot construct a reservoir in Lyons Township, except in certain areas.
HB	1029	3RD	5-16	Permits the admissibility of evidence of prior convictions of a defendant for certain domestic violence offenses committed against the same victim.
HB	1080	3RD	5-9	Provides that if a local public aid office has reason to believe that a caretaker's relative is experiencing substance abuse, that caretaker shall be required to submit to testing.
HB	1087	3RD	5-13	Allows a lottery prizewinner to assign all or part of his or her winnings to another person.
HB	1121	CC1	5-29	Changes the auto lease tax structure.
HB	1141	3RD	5-16	Allows the name of a child support obligor who is delinquent on payments to be made available to consumer reporting agencies and newspapers.
HB	1147	3RD	5-16	Creates an infrastructure maintenance fee on telecommunications charges.
HB	1168	3RD	5-13	Makes rewrites to the Illinois Securities Laws.
HB	1169	3RD	5-15	Allows digital imaging to be used for driver's license photos and signatures.
HB	1211	3RD	5-13	Establishes fees for charities and professional fundraisers to be used by the Attorney General's office to disseminate information about charitable organizations.
HB	1219	3RD	5-9	Provides that all sex offenders shall be required to register with local police agencies.
HB	1229	3RD	5-13	Creates the Radon Industry Licensing Act.
HB	1294	3RD	5-13	Establishes in Cook County a pilot program creating an Adolescent Family Life Program for high risk pregnant adolescents who are abusing drugs or alcohol.
HB	1311	3RD	5-13	Creates the Health Care Purchasing Group Act.

HB	1315	3RD	5-9	Allows the death penalty to be imposed on an offender when the victim was over 60 years old and the murder was exceptionally brutal.
HB	1327	3RD	5-13	Makes changes to state and local assessments of students.
HB	1332	3RD	5-13	Provides that insurance companies cannot deny coverage to an individual because that individual has been the victim of abuse.
HB	1337	3RD	5-16	Requires employers to report newly hired employees to the Department of Employment Security and requires the department to share that information with other governmental agencies for purposes of collecting child support.
HB	1347	3RD	5-16	Employers of full-time law enforcement officials or firefighters that are killed or disabled in the line of duty shall continue health benefits for the officer or firefighter or the spouses and children thereof.
HB	1388	3RD	5-13	Establishes a zero tolerance rule for persons who are driving a school bus.
HB	1486	3RD	5-14	Creates the Alzheimer's Special Care Disclosure Act.
HB	1525	3RD	5-14	Requires state universities to offer 50% tuition waivers for undergraduate education to the children of employees of other state universities.
HB	1565	3RD	5-13	Allows HMOs to offer a basic package of health care services to children under the age of 19.
HB	1588	3RD	5-9	Authorizes banks to engage in reverse stock splits.
HB	1618	3RD	5-13	Changes definition of all-terrain vehicle.
HB	1680	3RD	5-13	Creates the Wheat Development Act.
HB	1696	3RD	6-1	Authorizes school districts to impose an income tax on corporations and individuals by referendum.
HB	1707	3RD	5-31	Implements federal requirements on child support.
HB	1881	3RD	5-16	Provides that insurance companies and HMOs must cover certain medical procedures.
HB	2061	3RD	5-14	Creates the Small Business Incubator Fund.
HB	2132	3RD	5-16	Requires school administrators to report certain crimes occurring at or near the school to local police.
HB	2138	3RD	5-9	Allows a defendant to request fingerprint or DNA testing on evidence used to secure a defendant's conviction, if such tests were unavailable at the defendant's trial.
HB	2164	CC1	6-1	Creates a Drycleaner Environmental Response Trust Fund to support remediation of dry cleaning solvent at dry cleaning facilities.

HB	2211	3RD	5-16	Raises the ceiling from $10,0000 to $25,000 on licensed consumer loans and updates the Consumer Installment Loan Act.
HB	2215	CC1	5-31	Provides that pawnbrokers shall be regulated by the Commissioner of Banks and Real Estate.
HB	2262	3RD	5-9	A person may not operate a boat or snowmobile if his or her blood alcohol concentration exceeds the level specified in the Illinois Vehicle Code.

Descriptions of Additional Key Votes for the House

SB	21	3RD	5-13	Allows townships in Cook County to levy a special tax for improvements to streets.
SB	51	3RD	3-21	Omnibus revenue bill, including a provision to allow counties other than Cook to establish a separate deadline for filing a senior citizen tax assessment freeze application.
SB	54	3RD	5-23	Establishes new rules on developing landfills near a 100-year floodplain.
SB	69	3RD	5-8	Enables local school districts to levy for technology infrastructure.
SB	73	3RD	5-16	Provides that the provider of any tangible thing for which an employer is responsible for payment is bound by charges on payments ordered by the Industrial Commission.
SB	76	3RD	5-14	Establishes new budget proposal procedures.
SB	87	3RD	2-19	Increase authorization in General Obligation Bond Act.
SB	103	3RD	5-13	Provides procedures for the making and payment of local improvements by special assessment.
SB	107	3RD	5-9	Provides penalties for unlawful use of armor piercing bullets.
SB	110	3RD	5-13	A person may not operate a boat or snowmobile if his or her blood alcohol concentration exceeds the level specified in the Illinois Vehicle Code.
SB	123	3RD	5-8	Creates the Sex Offender Management Board and Fund.
SB	140	3RD	5-8	Provides notification requirements for municipalities for proposed pollution control facilities.
SB	160	3RD	5 14	Expands Right of Conscience Act to include health care payers and various health care providers.
SB	166	3RD	5-16	Increases the age for mandatory seat belt use from six to 16.

SB	225	3RD	5-12	Allows volunteers to issue citations to handicapped parking violators.
SB	236	3RD	5-9	Experimental procedures on patients in life-threatening situations may be done in accordance with federal rules.
SB	248	3RD	5-9	Children may bring their own lunch to day care.
SB	317	CC1	5-31	Various changes to Public Aid Code and managed care.
SB	327	3RD	5-8	Authorizes an additional Regional Alzheimer's Disease Assistance Center.
SB	345	3RD	5-16	Further defines an unfit parent; grants grandparents and godparents visitation rights for children in foster care.
SB	366	3RD	5-12	Expedites the termination of parental rights of unfit parents.
SB	378	3RD	5-8	Implements Uniform State Hazardous Materials Transportation Registration and Permit Program.
SB	381	CC1	5-31	Prisoners responsible for paying costs of frivolous lawsuits.
SB	431	3RD	5-8	Changes the requirements for regional disposable site characterization.
SB	508	3RD	5-8	Provides that a convicted person shall reimburse the Department of Corrections for the costs of incarceration at a rate determined by the department.
SB	596	CC1	5-31	Provides that tourism boards and certain convention or civic center boards are "public bodies" under the Open Meetings Act.
SB	680	CC1	5-31	Allows local governments to accept payment by credit card.
SB	698	3RD	5-16	Requires the Department of Public Aid to continue to provide assistance to legal aliens.
SB	700	3RD	5-8	Prohibits the impediment of competition in local telecommunications.
SB	762	3RD	5-8	Eliminates mandatory training requirements for part-time corrections officers.
SB	772	3RD	5-13	Increases penalties for hit and run drivers.
SB	777	3RD	5-15	Requires that state contracts of more than $250,000 be signed by a minimum of three executive employees.
SB	795	3RD	5-16	Allows Conservation 2000 funds to be used by public and private landowners to protect ecosystems.
SB	796	3RD	5-8	Prohibits prison guards from sexual contact with prisoners.

SB	797	CC1	6-1	Repeals the Meigs Field Act.
SB	806	CC1	5-31	Establishes Illinois Directory of New Hires.
SB	819	3RD	5-15	Provides 30 days to pay for initial annual permit fee to applicants for an air pollution operating permit.
SB	843	3RD	5-12	Provides that neither a local government entity nor employee is liable for an injury caused by a failure to supervise an activity unless guilty of willful and wanton conduct.
SB	856	3RD	5-16	Omnibus tax bill, includes provisions allowing Department of Revenue to collect child support delinquencies in any manner authorized for all taxes.
SB	858	3RD	5-9	Amends various sections of the Podiatric Medical Practice Act of 1987.
SB	899	3RD	5-16	Provides that contractually representative horsemen's organizations shall have the exclusive authority to represent horsemen.
SB	909	3RD	5-16	Increases the maximum income threshold from $14,000 annually to $16,000 for the Circuit Breaker Program.
SB	927	3RD	5-14	Raises the amount of motorcycle registration fee that is used for the Cycle Rider Safety Training Fund and establishes a fee to take the Cycle Rider Training Program.
SB	950	3RD	5-12	Creates a graduated driver's license for drivers under the age of 18.
SB	953	3RD	5-8	Creates the Trademark Registration and Protection Act.
SB	999	3RD	5-15	Provides that a franchising authority may grant additional cable franchises.
SB	1024	3RD	5-12	Establishes Illinois Directory of New Hires.
SB	1044	3RD	5-12	Requires ATM owners to disclose ATM surcharge fees.
SB	1050	3RD	5-8	Increases student assistance monetary awards for undergraduates.
SB	1084	3RD	5-12	Provides for the creation of one or more Assistive Technology Evaluation and Training Centers.
SB	1101	CC1	6-1	Budget Implementation Act.
SB	1103	3RD	5-16	Bans landscape waste burning in municipalities with a population over 75,000.
SB	1105	3RD	5-23	Provides that a lobbyist shall notify each official on whose behalf an expenditure has been reported within 30 days of filing a report.
HB	8	3RD	4-15	Creates the Genetic Information Privacy Act.

HB	19	3RD	4-25	Amends the Bingo License and Tax Act to increase the aggregate prize limit from $2,250 to $3,250.
HB	38	3RD	4-12	Allows a municipality to demolish a vacant building that is considered hazardous.
HB	45	3RD	4-12	Increases the maximum Homestead Improvement Exemption to $45,000.
HB	46	3RD	4-10	Increases dram shop liability.
HB	50	CONS1	5-19	Creates a pilot project to slow trains traveling through Fox River Grove to a maximum of 50 miles per hour.
HB	56	3RD	3-6	Requires DCFS to provide information on a child's criminal background to the child's foster care providers.
HB	61	3RD	4-24	Regulates electricians and electrical engineers through licensing requirements.
HB	107	3RD	4-19	Requires that health care benefits must provide for a minimum of 96 hours of inpatient care following a mastectomy.
HB	111	3RD	4-10	Requires health care plans to provide coverage for serious mental illness under the same terms as other illnesses.
HB	126	3RD	4-17	Requires Public Aid to continue to provide assistance to legal aliens.
HB	127	CC1	5-31	Revokes or prohibits the issuance of a FOID card to a person who has been convicted of domestic abuse.
HB	154	3RD	4-12	Provides that expressions contained in a high school newspaper are not subject to prior restraint, with certain exceptions.
HB	161	3RD	4-9	Provides that treatment for mental, emotional, or nervous disorders by a licensed clinical professional counselor shall be covered under the Illinois Insurance Code.
HB	165	CONS1	5-22	Provides language for when expediting termination of parental rights is appropriate.
HB	172	CONS1	5-22	Allows for "no knock" search warrants and increases penalties for false emergency 911 calls.
HB	229	CC1	5-31	Raises yearly personal service allowances for members of the General Assembly by $10,000.
HB	253	3RD	4-15	Public Schools Educational Choice Act (title only).
HB	260	3RD	4-18	Technical change to the Illinois Pollution prevention Act.
HB	265	3RD	4-15	Raises to 65 mph the maximum speed limit for trucks, buses, and other large vehicles outside of urban areas.

HB	271	3RD	4-12	Requires ATM owners to disclose ATM surcharge fees.
HB	282	CONS1,2	5-31	Creates an income tax credit for corporations that use biodegradable materials made of corn or soybean products.
HB	297	CC1	5-27	Increases dram shop liability.
HB	313	CONS1,2	5-23	Allows state workers to establish credit towards their pensions for prior government experience.
HB	314	3RD	4-18	Makes senior citizens aged 62 and older (now 65) eligible for the Circuit Breaker Program and increases the household income limit.
HB	316	3RD	4-8	Requires contractors to use soybean oil-based ink in providing printing services for units of local government.
HB	318	3RD	4-15	Allows nonhome-rule municipalities to impose certain taxes to be used for expenditures on capital projects upon approval by referendum.
HB	319	3RD	4-11	Establishes the Freedom of Choice Act, establishing a state policy recognizing a woman's reproductive rights.
HB	347	3RD	4-16	Provides that a person who is a TRS benefit recipient may elect to participate in the State Health Plan.
HB	379	CC1	5-31	Adds certain cases of child abduction to the list of offenses for which an offender must register under the Sex Offender Registration Act.
HB	381	3RD	4-16	Extends the deadline to file for the Senior Citizens Assessment Freeze Homestead Protection by three months if the applicant has a severe medical condition.
HB	383	3RD	4-11	Amends the Public Aid Code, replacing provisions concerning medical assistance and general assistance funding of abortions with identical language prohibiting payment of aid for abortions unless necessary for preserving the woman's life.
HB	391	3RD	4-11	Amends the State Employees Group Insurance Act to remove language prohibiting the coverage of abortions for state employees.
HB	400	3RD	4-10	Creates an income tax credit for taxpayers for amounts spent during the tax year for the tuition and fees of the taxpayer and any dependents.
HB	401	3RD	4-10	Provides the higher education savings accounts are accounts established by qualified taxpayers for the purpose of saving for eligible education-related expenses of the account holder, spouse, or child.

HB	424	3RD	4-16	Creates the Illinois River Watershed Restoration Act.
HB	452	3RD	4-15	Eliminates several special school funds and their levies and provides instead for a general operating fund levy to support these services.
HB	480	3RD	4-19	Provides rules for petitioning to end township government in a county.
HB	489	3RD	4-23	Creates an off-road vehicle trails program with associated fees.
HB	522	3RD	4-15	Establishes regulation of home medical equipment and services.
HB	523	3RD	4-16	Provides that any person who suffers damage (instead of actual damage) may bring an action under the Consumer Fraud and Deceptive Business Practices Act.
HB	524	3RD	4-15	Clarifies that properties located in a TIF district that overlap an enterprise zone are prohibited from receiving a property tax abatement unless certain requirements are met.
HB	540	CONS1,2	5-21	Requires DMH/DD to make at least one site visit a year to its facilities.
HB	571	3RD	4-18	Revises the purposes section of the Truth in Taxation Law in the Property Tax Code.
HB	581	CC1	5-31	Expands Senior Citizen Real Estate Tax Deferral program to include disabled individuals.
HB	585	3RD	4-8	Changes the method that multistate businesses apportion their income for Illinois tax purposes.
HB	586	CONS1	5-22	Allows financial institutions to sell insurance.
HB	591	3RD	4-15	Allows for "no knock" search warrants.
HB	601	3RD	4-24	Changes the auto lease tax structure.
HB	602	3RD	4-24	Implements a graduated fee schedule for certain pesticide registration and licensing fees.
HB	618	CONS1	5-20	Increases the maximum fine that may be imposed for Class 4 felony violations for illegal possession of certain substances.
HB	644	3RD	4-25	Provides for the use of electronic ballot forms.
HB	652	CONS1	5-17	Transfers the nonpartisan election of November of odd-numbered years with the nonpartisan election of April of odd-numbered years.
HB	672	3RD	4-17	Allows statements of economic interest and campaign finance reports to be filed electronically and that they may be made available on the World Wide Web.

HB	725	CONS1	5-22	Expands Right of Conscience Act to include health care payers and various health care providers.
HB	729	CONS2	5-28	Deletes a provision that a person examining a campaign finance statement shall provide personal information and that the political committee may be notified of the examination.
HB	740	3RD	3-21	Increases the length of the minimum school term from 185 to 190 days.
HB	744	3RD	4-23	Allows retired peace officers to carry concealed firearms.
HB	819	3RD	4-15	Creates the Professional Teachers Standards Board and abolishes the State Teacher Certification Board.
HB	844	3RD	3-13	Allows for the sale of Collision Damage Waivers for rental cars and creates the Renters Financial Responsibility and Protection Act.
HB	851	3RD	4-11	Creates the offense of intentional interference with access to health care.
HB	885	3RD	4-23	Prohibits a candidate or public official from accepting contributions from persons licensed under the Horse Racing Act or the Riverboat Gambling Act.
HB	923	3RD	4-11	Provides that the board of trustees from each state university has at least one student member.
HB	951	3RD	4-18	Expands definition of "unfit parent."
HB	968	3RD	4-11	Provides for the replacement of Illinois license plates.
HB	995	3RD	4-8	Grants a Commercial Driver's License waiver to a farmer or member of the family driving a truck-tractor semitrailer.
HB	999	3RD	4-23	Provides an income tax credit to a taxpayer who is the custodian of a qualified pupil for education expenses.
HB	1004	3RD	4-15	Establishes that the Metropolitan Water Reclamation District cannot construct a reservoir in Lyons Township, except in certain areas.
HB	1009	3RD	4-8	Requires that new outdoor swimming pools on private residential property be enclosed by a fence or wall at least 42 inches high.
HB	1025	3RD	4-10	Imposes requirements relating to the selection for the annual Class A and Class AA boys high school basketball site.
HB	1029	3RD	4-19	Permits the admissibility of evidence of prior convictions of a defendant for certain domestic violence offenses committed against the same victim.

HB	1074	3RD	4-17	Provides that no official (now member of the General Assembly) shall accept an honorarium.
HB	1080	3RD	4-17	Provides that if a local public aid office has reason to believe that a caretaker's relative is experiencing substance abuse, that caretaker shall be required to submit to testing.
HB	1090	3RD	4-25	Requires school administrators to report to local law enforcement agencies felony or misdemeanor violations that occur in the schools or at school related activities.
HB	1121	CC1	5-29	Changes the auto lease tax structure.
HB	1141	3RD	4-18	Allows the name of a child support obligor who is delinquent on payments to be made available to consumer reporting agencies and newspapers.
HB	1147	CONS1, 2,3	5-22	Creates an infrastructure maintenance fee on telecommunications charges.
HB	1149	3RD	4-14	Creates a permanent nonprofit organization named the Consumer Insurance Board.
HB	1168	3RD	4-18	Makes rewrites to the Illinois Securities Laws.
HB	1169	3RD	3-21	Allows digital imaging to be used for driver's license photos and signatures.
HB	1207	3RD	4-16	Provides that the Secretary of State shall not issue or renew a driver's license to a person under the age of 21 who has been convicted of a gang-related felony offense.
HB	1211	CONS1	5-22	Establishes fees for charities and professional fundraisers to be used by the Attorney General's office to disseminate information about charitable organizations.
HB	1219	CONS1	5-17	Provides that all sex offenders shall be required to register with local police agencies.
HB	1229	3RD	4-12	Creates the Radon Industry Licensing Act.
HB	1271	3RD	4-25	Creates a Drycleaner Environmental Response Trust Fund to support remediation of dry cleaning solvent at dry cleaning facilities.
HB	1294	3RD	4-11	Establishes in Cook County a pilot program creating an Adolescent Family Life Program for high risk pregnant adolescents who are abusing drugs or alcohol.
HB	1301	3RD	4-14	Creates the Early Childhood Education Collaboration Law to provide education opportunities for children from birth through five years of age.
HB	1302	3RD	4-18	Establishes the Healthy Start Insurance Plan to provide insurance coverage for persons under

				the age of 19 whose family meets certain income criteria.
HB	1303	3RD	4-14	Provides that the Department of Human Services shall administer the Healthy Family Initiative.
HB	1309	3RD	4-17	Provides that solid waste energy facilities must use equipment to separate at least 20% by weight of recyclable materials from the solid waste.
HB	1311	3RD	4-8	Creates the Health Care Purchasing Group Act.
HB	1315	CONS1	5-17	Allows the death penalty to be imposed on an offender when the victim was over 60 years old and the murder was exceptionally brutal.
HB	1332	3RD	4-12	Provides that insurance companies cannot deny coverage to an individual because that individual has been the victim of abuse.
HB	1337	3RD	4-14	Requires employers to report newly hired employees to the Department of Employment Security and requires the department to share that information with other governmental agencies for purposes of collecting child support.
HB	1343	3RD	4-15	Provides that the Department of Public Aid shall maintain a page on the World Wide Web listing individuals delinquent in their child support obligations.
HB	1347	3RD	4-14	Employers of full-time law enforcement officials or firefighters that are killed or disabled in the line of duty shall continue health benefits for the officer or firefighter or the spouses and children thereof.
HB	1388	3RD	4-14	Establishes a zero tolerance rule for persons who are driving a school bus.
HB	1486	3RD	4-10	Creates the Alzheimer's Special Care Disclosure Act.
HB	1504	3RD	4-11	Prohibits the possession and use of tobacco by minors.
HB	1512	3RD	4-11	Prohibits a state officer or employee from receiving payment for vacation, overtime, personal leave, and sick time when leaving service if convicted of a felony relating to his or her state employment.
HB	1525	3RD	4-16	Requires state universities to offer 50% tuition waivers for undergraduate education to the children of employees of other state universities.
HB	1565	3RD	4-18	Allows HMOs to offer a basic package of health care services to children under the age of 19.
HB	1588	3RD	4-14	Authorizes banks to engage in reverse stock splits.
HB	1618	3RD	4-11	Changes definition of all-terrain vehicle.

HB	1627	3RD	4-24	Creates the Business Use Incentives for Large-Scale Development Act.
HB	1680	3RD	4-23	Creates the Wheat Development Act.
HB	1696	3RD	4-25	Creates an income tax credit for taxpayers who sound proof buildings located near O'Hare or Midway airports.
HB	1703	3RD	4-17	Creates the Illinois Family and Medical Leave Act, applicable to employers of 25 or more.
HB	1704	3RD	4-17	Creates the Flex-time Rights Act requiring certain employers to grant leave up to 24 hours.
HB	1707	CONS1	6-1	Implements federal requirements on child support.
HB	1785	3RD	4-14	Creates the Welfare to Work Act which places qualified welfare recipients in state jobs.
HB	1807	3RD	4-11	Amends the Early Intervention Services System Act.
HB	1817	3RD	4-18	Creates the Brownfields Remediation Tax Credit.
HB	1881	CONS1, 2,4	5-22	Provides that insurance companies and HMOs must cover certain medical procedures.
HB	2061	3RD	4-18	Creates the Small Business Incubator Fund.
HB	2132	3RD	4-12	Requires school administrators to report to the police the delivery of cannabis and controlled substances occurring at or near a school.
HB	2138	3RD	4-15	Allows a defendant to request fingerprint or DNA testing on evidence used to secure a defendant's conviction, if such tests were unavailable at the defendant's trial.
HB	2164	CC1	5-31	Creates a Drycleaner Environmental Response Trust Fund to support remediation of dry cleaning solvent at dry cleaning facilities.
HB	2211	CONS1,2	5-21	Amends the Consumer Installment Loan Act.
HB	2215	CC1	5-31	Provides that pawnbrokers shall be regulated by the Commissioner of Banks and Real Estate.
HB	2262	3RD	4-12	A person may not operate a boat or snowmobile if his or her blood alcohol concentration exceeds the level specified in the Illinois Vehicle Code.

Key Votes by Topic Area

Senate Bills

Abortion: SB230
Airports: SB797
Business: SB16, SB806, SB1024, SB1084
Children: SB248, SB345, SB366, SB600, SB780
Consumer Protection: SB953, SB1044
Corrections: SB381, SB508, SB762, SB796
Crime/Drugs/DUI: SB107, SB110, SB123
Education: SB69, SB557, SB1050
Elections/Campaign Finance: SB129, SB200, SB1000
Environment: SB54, SB65, SB140, SB378, SB431, SB795, SB819, SB1103
Gambling: SB899
Health Care: SB160, SB236, SB858
Labor: SB73
Local Government: SB21, SB81, SB103, SB596, SB680, SB843
Salary/Benefit Increases: SB228
Senior Citizens: SB327, SB909
State Budget: SB76, SB87, SB1101
State Government Operations: SB30, SB777, SB1105
Taxes/Fee Increases: SB51, SB856
Transportation/Safety: SB166, SB225, SB772, SB927, SB950
Utilities: SB55, SB700, SB999
Welfare: SB317

House Bills

Abortion: HB319, HB383, HB391
Agriculture: HB282, HB995, HB1680
Airports: HB1696
Banks: HB586, HB1168, HB1588
Business: HB585, HB1337, HB1627, HB2061
Children: HB56, HB165, HB951, HB1141, HB1707, HB1807
Consumer Protection: HB61, HB271, HB522, HB523, HB844, HB1009, HB1211, HB1229
Corrections: HB2138
Crime/Drugs/DUI: HB46, HB172, HB297, HB379, HB591, HB618, HB744, HB1029, HB1207, HB1219, HB1315, HB1388, HB1504
Education: HB154, HB253, HB401, HB452, HB740, HB819, HB923, HB1025, HB1090, HB1301, HB1525, HB2132
Elections/Campaign Finance: HB644, HB652, HB672, HB729, HB885
Environment: HB260,HB424, HB602, HB1271, HB1309, HB1817
Gambling: HB19, HB1087
Gun Control: HB127
Health Care: HB107, HB111, HB540, HB725, HB851
Insurance: HB8, HB161, HB1149, HB1302, HB1311, HB1332, HB1565, HB1881

Local Government: HB38, HB316, HB318, HB480, HB1004
Pensions: HB313, HB347, HB1347
Real Estate: HB45
Salary/Benefit Increases: HB1703, HB1704
Senior Citizens: HB 314, HB381, HB1486
State Government Operations: HB229, HB1074, HB1512
Taxes/Fee Increases: HB400, HB524, HB571, HB581, HB601, HB999, HB1121
Transportation/Safety: HB50, HB265, HB475, HB489, HB968, HB1169, HB1618
Utilities: HB1147
Welfare: HB126, HB1080, HB1294, HB1303, HB1343, HB1785

Senate Member	SB0016	SB0021	SB0030	SB0051	SB0054	SB0055	SB0065	SB0069	SB0076	SB0081	SB0087	SB0103	SB0107	SB0110	SB0123	SB0129	SB0140	SB0160	SB0166	SB0200
Berman	N	Y	Y	Y	Y	N	Y	Y	Y	Y	P	Y	Y	Y	Y	Y	Y	Y	Y	Y
Bomke	Y	N	N	Y	Y	Y	P	Y	Y	N	Y	Y	Y	Y	Y	Y	Y	Y	Y	Y
Bowles	Y	Y	Y	Y	Y	N	Y	Y	Y	Y	Y	Y	Y	Y	Y	Y	Y	Y	Y	Y
Burzynski	Y	N	Y	Y	Y	Y	P	Y	Y	N	Y	Y	Y	Y	Y	Y	Y	Y	Y	Y
Butler	Y	Y	Y	Y	Y	Y	N	Y	Y	Y	Y	Y	Y	Y	Y	Y	Y	Y	Y	Y
Carroll	N	Y	Y	Y	Y	N	Y	Y	Y	P	P	Y	Y	Y	Y	Y	Y	Y	Y	Y
Clayborne	Y	Y	N	Y	Y	N	Y	Y	Y	N	P	Y	Y	Y	Y	Y	Y	Y	Y	Y
Collins	P	Y	Y	Y	Y	N	Y	Y	Y	Y	O	Y	Y	Y	Y	O	Y	Y	Y	Y
Cronin	Y	Y	Y	Y	Y	Y	P	Y	Y	O	Y	Y	Y	Y	Y	Y	Y	Y	Y	Y
Cullerton	P	Y	Y	Y	Y	N	O	Y	Y	Y	N	Y	Y	Y	O	P	Y	Y	Y	Y
DeLeo	Y	Y	Y	Y	Y	N	Y	Y	Y	Y	P	Y	Y	Y	Y	Y	Y	Y	Y	Y
del Valle	Y	Y	Y	Y	Y	N	Y	Y	Y	Y	N	Y	Y	Y	Y	P	Y	Y	Y	Y
Demuzio	Y	Y	N	Y	Y	N	Y	Y	Y	Y	P	Y	Y	Y	Y	Y	Y	Y	Y	Y
Dillard	Y	Y	Y	Y	Y	Y	P	Y	Y	Y	Y	Y	Y	Y	Y	Y	Y	Y	Y	Y
Donahue	Y	Y	N	Y	Y	Y	N	Y	Y	N	Y	Y	Y	Y	Y	Y	Y	Y	Y	Y
Dudycz	Y	Y	Y	Y	Y	Y	N	Y	Y	N	Y	Y	Y	Y	Y	Y	Y	Y	Y	Y
Farley	Y	Y	Y	Y	Y	N	Y	Y	Y	Y	P	Y	Y	Y	Y	Y	Y	Y	Y	Y
Fawell	Y	Y	Y	Y	Y	Y	N	Y	Y	Y	Y	Y	Y	Y	Y	Y	Y	Y	Y	Y
Fitzgerald	Y	N	Y	Y	Y	Y	O	N	Y	N	Y	Y	Y	Y	Y	Y	Y	Y	Y	Y
Garcia	O	Y	N	Y	Y	N	Y	Y	Y	Y	N	Y	Y	Y	Y	P	Y	Y	Y	Y
Geo-Karis	Y	Y	Y	Y	Y	Y	O	Y	Y	Y	Y	Y	Y	Y	Y	Y	Y	Y	Y	Y
Halvorson	Y	Y	P	Y	Y	N	Y	Y	Y	Y	P	Y	Y	Y	Y	Y	Y	Y	Y	Y
Hawkinson	Y	N	N	Y	Y	Y	N	Y	Y	N	Y	Y	Y	Y	Y	Y	Y	Y	Y	Y
Hendon	Y	Y	N	O	Y	N	Y	Y	Y	N	N	Y	Y	Y	Y	N	Y	Y	Y	Y
Jacobs	Y	Y	O	Y	Y	N	Y	Y	Y	Y	Y	Y	Y	Y	Y	Y	Y	Y	Y	Y
Jones, Emil	Y	Y	O	Y	Y	N	Y	Y	Y	Y	N	Y	Y	Y	Y	P	Y	Y	Y	Y
Karpiel	Y	Y	Y	Y	Y	Y	N	Y	Y	Y	Y	Y	Y	Y	Y	Y	Y	Y	Y	Y
Klemm	Y	P	N	Y	Y	Y	N	Y	Y	N	Y	Y	Y	Y	O	Y	Y	Y	O	Y
Lauzen	Y	Y	N	Y	O	Y	P	Y	Y	N	Y	Y	Y	Y	Y	Y	Y	Y	Y	Y
Link	Y	N	Y	Y	Y	N	Y	Y	Y	N	P	Y	Y	Y	Y	Y	Y	Y	Y	Y
Luechtefeld	Y	N	N	Y	Y	Y	P	Y	Y	Y	Y	Y	Y	Y	Y	Y	Y	Y	N	Y
Madigan, Robert	O	Y	Y	Y	Y	Y	O	Y	Y	Y	Y	Y	Y	Y	Y	Y	Y	Y	Y	Y
Mahar	Y	Y	Y	Y	Y	Y	O	Y	Y	N	Y	Y	Y	Y	Y	Y	Y	Y	Y	Y
Maitland	Y	Y	Y	Y	Y	Y	N	Y	Y	N	Y	Y	Y	Y	Y	Y	Y	Y	N	Y
Molaro	Y	Y	Y	Y	O	N	Y	Y	Y	Y	N	Y	Y	Y	O	P	Y	Y	Y	Y
Myers	Y	N	N	X	Y	Y	P	Y	Y	N	X	Y	Y	Y	Y	Y	Y	Y	Y	Y
Obama	Y	Y	Y	Y	Y	N	Y	Y	Y	Y	P	Y	Y	Y	Y	O	Y	Y	Y	Y
O'Daniel	Y	Y	N	Y	Y	N	Y	Y	Y	Y	Y	Y	O	Y	Y	N	Y	Y	Y	Y
O'Malley	P	Y	Y	Y	O	Y	N	Y	Y	Y	Y	Y	Y	Y	Y	Y	Y	Y	Y	Y
Parker	Y	Y	Y	Y	Y	Y	N	Y	Y	Y	Y	Y	Y	Y	Y	Y	Y	Y	Y	Y

SB0225	SB0228	SB0230	SB0236	SB0248	SB0317	SB0327	SB0345	SB0366	SB0378
N	N	N	Y	Y	Y	Y	Y	O	Y
Y	Y	Y	Y	Y	Y	Y	Y	Y	Y
P	Y	Y	Y	Y	Y	Y	Y	Y	Y
Y	Y	Y	Y	Y	Y	Y	Y	Y	Y
Y	Y	Y	Y	O	Y	Y	Y	Y	Y
P	N	N	Y	Y	Y	Y	Y	O	Y
Y	N	Y	Y	Y	Y	Y	Y	Y	Y
Y	O	Y	Y	Y	Y	Y	O	Y	Y
Y	P	Y	Y	O	Y	Y	Y	Y	O
P	Y	N	Y	Y	Y	O	Y	Y	Y
P	Y	Y	Y	Y	Y	Y	Y	Y	Y
Y	N	P	Y	Y	Y	Y	Y	Y	Y
Y	O	Y	Y	Y	Y	Y	Y	Y	Y
Y	Y	Y	Y	Y	Y	Y	Y	Y	Y
Y	Y	Y	Y	Y	Y	Y	Y	Y	Y
Y	Y	Y	Y	Y	Y	Y	Y	Y	Y
Y	Y	N	Y	Y	Y	Y	Y	Y	Y
Y	Y	Y	Y	Y	Y	Y	Y	Y	Y
Y	Y	Y	Y	Y	Y	Y	Y	Y	O
P	N	P	Y	Y	Y	Y	Y	Y	Y
Y	Y	Y	Y	Y	Y	Y	Y	Y	Y
Y	Y	Y	Y	Y	Y	Y	Y	Y	Y
Y	O	Y	Y	Y	Y	Y	Y	Y	Y
Y	P	Y	Y	Y	Y	Y	Y	Y	Y
N	Y	Y	Y	Y	Y	Y	N	Y	Y
Y	O	Y	Y	Y	Y	Y	Y	Y	Y
Y	Y	Y	Y	Y	Y	Y	Y	Y	Y
Y	Y	Y	Y	Y	Y	Y	Y	Y	Y
Y	Y	Y	Y	Y	Y	Y	Y	Y	Y
Y	Y	N	Y	Y	Y	Y	Y	Y	Y
Y	Y	Y	Y	Y	Y	Y	Y	Y	Y
Y	Y	Y	Y	Y	Y	Y	Y	Y	Y
Y	Y	Y	Y	Y	Y	Y	Y	Y	Y
Y	Y	Y	Y	Y	Y	Y	Y	Y	Y
P	N	P	Y	Y	O	Y	Y	Y	Y
Y	Y	Y	Y	Y	Y	Y	Y	Y	Y
Y	N	P	Y	Y	Y	Y	Y	Y	Y
Y	Y	Y	Y	Y	Y	Y	Y	Y	Y
Y	Y	Y	Y	Y	Y	Y	Y	O	Y
Y	Y	N	Y	Y	Y	Y	Y	Y	Y

SB0381	SB0431	SB0508	SB0557	SB0596	SB0660	SB0680	SB0700	SB0762	SB0772
Y	Y	Y	N	Y	Y	Y	Y	Y	P
Y	Y	Y	Y	Y	Y	Y	Y	Y	Y
Y	Y	Y	N	Y	N	Y	Y	Y	Y
Y	Y	Y	Y	Y	N	Y	Y	Y	O
Y	Y	Y	Y	Y	N	Y	Y	Y	Y
Y	Y	Y	N	Y	Y	Y	P	O	P
N	Y	Y	N	Y	P	Y	O	Y	Y
N	O	Y	N	Y	Y	Y	Y	Y	Y
Y	Y	Y	Y	Y	N	Y	Y	Y	Y
Y	Y	Y	N	Y	Y	Y	P	Y	Y
Y	Y	Y	N	Y	Y	Y	Y	Y	Y
N	Y	Y	N	Y	Y	Y	Y	Y	P
O	Y	Y	N	Y	N	Y	Y	Y	Y
Y	Y	Y	Y	Y	Y	Y	Y	Y	Y
Y	Y	Y	Y	Y	Y	Y	Y	Y	P
Y	Y	Y	Y	Y	Y	Y	Y	Y	Y
N	Y	Y	N	O	Y	Y	Y	Y	P
Y	Y	Y	Y	Y	N	Y	Y	Y	P
Y	Y	Y	Y	Y	Y	P	Y	Y	Y
N	Y	Y	N	Y	Y	Y	Y	Y	O
Y	Y	Y	Y	Y	Y	Y	Y	Y	Y
P	Y	Y	N	N	Y	Y	Y	Y	Y
O	Y	Y	Y	Y	N	Y	Y	Y	Y
N	O	Y	N	Y	Y	O	Y	Y	Y
Y	Y	Y	N	N	N	Y	Y	Y	P
N	Y	Y	N	Y	Y	Y	Y	Y	Y
Y	Y	Y	Y	Y	O	Y	Y	Y	O
Y	Y	Y	Y	Y	N	Y	Y	Y	P
Y	Y	Y	Y	N	N	N	Y	Y	Y
N	Y	Y	N	N	Y	Y	Y	Y	Y
Y	Y	Y	Y	N	N	Y	Y	Y	P
Y	Y	Y	P	Y	O	Y	Y	Y	O
Y	Y	O	Y	Y	N	Y	Y	Y	O
Y	Y	Y	Y	Y	Y	Y	Y	Y	N
N	Y	Y	N	O	Y	O	Y	Y	N
Y	Y	Y	Y	Y	Y	Y	Y	Y	Y
N	Y	Y	O	O	Y	Y	P	Y	Y
Y	Y	Y	Y	Y	Y	Y	Y	Y	Y
Y	Y	Y	Y	Y	Y	Y	Y	Y	Y
Y	Y	Y	Y	Y	Y	Y	Y	Y	O

SB0780	SB0795	SB0796	SB0797	SB0806	SB0819	SB0843	SB0856	SB0858
Y	O	Y	Y	Y	Y	Y	Y	O
Y	Y	Y	Y	Y	Y	Y	Y	Y
Y	Y	Y	Y	Y	Y	Y	Y	Y
Y	Y	Y	O	Y	Y	Y	Y	Y
Y	O	Y	Y	Y	Y	Y	Y	Y
Y	Y	Y	Y	Y	Y	Y	Y	O
Y	Y	Y	Y	Y	Y	O	Y	Y
Y	O	Y	Y	Y	Y	Y	Y	Y
Y	Y	Y	Y	Y	Y	O	Y	Y
Y	Y	O	Y	Y	Y	Y	Y	Y
Y	Y	Y	Y	Y	Y	Y	Y	Y
Y	Y	Y	Y	Y	Y	Y	Y	O
Y	O	Y	Y	Y	Y	Y	Y	Y
Y	Y	Y	Y	Y	Y	Y	Y	Y
Y	Y	Y	N	Y	Y	Y	Y	Y
Y	N	Y	Y	Y	Y	Y	Y	Y
Y	Y	Y	Y	Y	Y	Y	Y	Y
Y	Y	Y	Y	Y	Y	Y	Y	Y
Y	O	Y	Y	Y	O	Y	Y	Y
Y	Y	Y	Y	Y	Y	Y	Y	Y
Y	O	Y	Y	Y	Y	Y	Y	Y
Y	Y	Y	Y	Y	Y	Y	Y	Y
Y	Y	Y	Y	Y	Y	Y	Y	Y
P	Y	Y	P	Y	Y	Y	Y	Y
Y	Y	Y	Y	Y	Y	Y	Y	Y
Y	O	O	Y	Y	Y	Y	Y	O
Y	Y	Y	Y	Y	Y	Y	Y	Y
Y	Y	Y	Y	Y	Y	Y	Y	Y
Y	Y	Y	Y	Y	Y	Y	Y	Y
Y	N	Y	Y	Y	Y	Y	Y	Y
Y	Y	Y	P	Y	Y	Y	Y	Y
Y	Y	Y	O	Y	O	Y	Y	Y
O	N	Y	Y	O	Y	O	Y	Y
Y	Y	Y	Y	Y	Y	Y	Y	Y
Y	Y	Y	O	Y	Y	Y	Y	O
Y	Y	Y	Y	Y	Y	Y	Y	Y
Y	Y	Y	Y	Y	Y	Y	Y	Y
Y	Y	Y	O	Y	Y	Y	Y	Y
Y	Y	Y	Y	Y	Y	Y	Y	Y
Y	N	Y	Y	Y	Y	Y	Y	Y

Senate Member	SB0016	SB0021	SB0030	SB0051	SB0054	SB0055	SB0065	SB0069	SB0076	SB0081
Peterson	Y	Y	Y	Y	Y	Y	P	Y	Y	N
Petka	Y	Y	Y	Y	P	Y	N	Y	Y	Y
Philip	Y	Y	Y	Y	Y	Y	N	Y	Y	Y
Radogno	Y	Y	N	Y	Y	Y	N	Y	Y	N
Rauschenberger	N	Y	N	Y	Y	Y	N	N	Y	N
Rea	Y	Y	Y	O	Y	P	Y	Y	Y	Y
Severns	Y	Y	Y	Y	Y	N	Y	Y	Y	Y
Shadid	Y	Y	Y	Y	Y	N	Y	Y	Y	N
Shaw	Y	O	O	Y	Y	O	O	Y	Y	O
Sieben	Y	Y	Y	Y	Y	Y	P	Y	Y	Y
Smith, Margaret	Y	Y	N	Y	Y	N	Y	Y	Y	Y
Syverson	Y	O	N	Y	Y	Y	P	Y	Y	N
Trotter	Y	Y	N	Y	O	N	Y	Y	Y	N
Viverito	Y	Y	Y	Y	Y	N	Y	Y	Y	Y
Walsh, Lawrence	X	X	X	X	Y	X	X	X	Y	X
Walsh, Thomas	Y	Y	Y	Y	Y	Y	N	Y	Y	P
Watson	Y	Y	N	Y	Y	Y	N	Y	Y	Y
Weaver	Y	Y	Y	Y	Y	Y	N	Y	Y	Y
Welch	Y	Y	N	Y	Y	N	Y	Y	Y	Y
Dunn	O	X	X	Y	X	X	X	Y	X	X
Woodyard	X	X	X	O	X	X	X	X	X	X

Senate Member	SB0087	SB0103	SB0107	SB0110	SB0123	SB0129	SB0140	SB0160	SB0166	SB0200
Peterson	Y	Y	Y	Y	Y	Y	Y	Y	Y	Y
Petka	Y	Y	Y	Y	Y	Y	Y	Y	O	Y
Philip	Y	Y	Y	Y	Y	Y	Y	Y	Y	Y
Radogno	Y	Y	Y	Y	Y	Y	Y	Y	Y	Y
Rauschenberger	Y	Y	Y	Y	Y	Y	Y	Y	Y	Y
Rea	O	Y	Y	Y	Y	Y	Y	Y	Y	Y
Severns	Y	Y	Y	Y	Y	Y	Y	Y	Y	Y
Shadid	Y	Y	Y	Y	Y	Y	Y	Y	Y	Y
Shaw	N	Y	O	O	O	O	O	Y	Y	O
Sieben	Y	Y	Y	Y	Y	Y	Y	Y	Y	Y
Smith, Margaret	N	Y	Y	Y	Y	Y	Y	Y	Y	Y
Syverson	Y	Y	Y	Y	Y	Y	Y	Y	Y	Y
Trotter	N	Y	Y	Y	Y	N	O	Y	Y	Y
Viverito	Y	Y	Y	Y	Y	P	Y	Y	O	Y
Walsh, Lawrence	X	N	X	X	X	X	X	X	X	X
Walsh, Thomas	Y	Y	Y	Y	Y	Y	Y	Y	Y	Y
Watson	Y	Y	Y	Y	Y	Y	Y	Y	N	Y
Weaver	Y	Y	Y	Y	Y	Y	Y	Y	Y	Y
Welch	N	Y	Y	Y	Y	Y	Y	Y	Y	Y
Dunn	Y	X	O	Y	X	X	X	Y	Y	O
Woodyard	O	X	X	X	X	X	X	X	X	X

SB02225	SB02228	SB02230	SB02236	SB02248	SB03317	SB03327	SB03345	SB03366	SB03378
Y	Y	Y	Y	Y	Y	Y	Y	Y	Y
Y	Y	Y	Y	Y	Y	Y	O	Y	Y
Y	Y	O	Y	Y	Y	Y	Y	Y	Y
Y	N	Y	Y	Y	Y	Y	Y	Y	Y
Y	Y	Y	Y	Y	Y	N	Y	Y	Y
Y	Y	Y	Y	Y	Y	Y	N	Y	Y
Y	Y	Y	Y	Y	Y	Y	Y	Y	Y
Y	O	Y	Y	Y	O	Y	Y	Y	Y
O	O	O	Y	O	Y	O	Y	Y	O
Y	Y	Y	Y	Y	Y	Y	Y	Y	Y
Y	N	P	Y	Y	Y	Y	Y	Y	Y
Y	Y	Y	Y	Y	Y	Y	Y	Y	Y
Y	N	N	Y	Y	Y	Y	Y	Y	Y
P	Y	Y	Y	Y	Y	Y	Y	Y	Y
X	X	X	X	Y	Y	X	Y	Y	X
Y	Y	Y	Y	Y	Y	Y	Y	Y	Y
Y	Y	Y	Y	Y	Y	Y	Y	Y	Y
Y	Y	Y	Y	Y	Y	Y	Y	Y	Y
Y	Y	Y	Y	Y	Y	Y	Y	Y	Y
X	X	X	Y	X	X	X	X	X	X
X	X	X	X	X	X	X	X	X	X

SB03881	SB04431	SB05038	SB05557	SB05996	SB06000	SB06800	SB07000	SB07762	SB07772
Y	Y	Y	Y	N	Y	Y	Y	Y	P
Y	Y	Y	Y	N	Y	Y	Y	Y	P
Y	O	Y	Y	Y	Y	Y	Y	Y	P
Y	Y	Y	Y	Y	O	Y	Y	Y	Y
Y	Y	Y	Y	Y	Y	O	Y	Y	O
Y	Y	Y	O	Y	Y	Y	Y	Y	O
Y	Y	Y	Y	N	Y	Y	Y	Y	Y
Y	Y	Y	Y	Y	Y	Y	Y	Y	Y
N	O	O	O	Y	O	Y	O	O	O
Y	Y	Y	Y	Y	N	Y	Y	Y	Y
N	Y	Y	N	Y	Y	Y	Y	Y	P
Y	Y	Y	Y	Y	O	Y	Y	Y	Y
N	Y	Y	N	Y	Y	Y	Y	Y	Y
Y	Y	Y	P	Y	Y	Y	Y	Y	Y
Y	X	X	X	N	X	Y	X	X	X
Y	Y	Y	Y	Y	N	Y	P	Y	Y
Y	Y	Y	Y	Y	Y	Y	Y	Y	P
Y	Y	Y	Y	Y	O	Y	Y	Y	P
Y	Y	Y	O	N	N	Y	Y	Y	Y
X	X	X	X	X	X	X	X	X	X
X	X	X	X	X	X	X	X	X	X

SB07880	SB07995	SB07996	SB07997	SB08006	SB08119	SB08433	SB08556	SB08558
Y	Y	Y	Y	Y	Y	Y	Y	Y
Y	Y	Y	Y	Y	Y	Y	Y	Y
Y	Y	Y	Y	Y	Y	Y	Y	Y
Y	N	Y	Y	Y	Y	Y	Y	Y
Y	Y	Y	Y	Y	Y	Y	Y	Y
Y	Y	Y	O	Y	Y	Y	Y	Y
Y	Y	Y	Y	Y	Y	Y	Y	Y
Y	O	Y	Y	Y	Y	Y	Y	Y
O	O	O	Y	O	O	O	Y	O
Y	Y	Y	Y	Y	Y	Y	Y	Y
Y	Y	Y	Y	O	O	Y	Y	Y
Y	O	Y	Y	Y	Y	O	Y	Y
P	Y	O	N	Y	Y	O	Y	Y
Y	Y	Y	Y	Y	Y	Y	Y	O
X	X	X	N	X	X	X	Y	X
Y	Y	Y	Y	Y	Y	Y	Y	Y
Y	Y	Y	Y	Y	Y	Y	Y	Y
Y	Y	Y	Y	Y	Y	Y	Y	Y
Y	Y	Y	N	Y	N	Y	Y	Y
X	X	X	X	X	X	X	X	X
X	X	X	X	X	X	X	X	X

Senate Member	SB0909	SB0927	SB0950	SB0953	SB0999	SB1000	SB1024	SB1044	SB1050	SB1084	SB1101	SB1103	SB1105	HB0008	HB0045	HB0050	HB0056	HB0127	HB0154	HB0165
Berman	Y	O	Y	Y	Y	Y	Y	Y	Y	Y	Y	Y	Y	Y	Y	Y	Y	Y	Y	Y
Bomke	Y	Y	Y	Y	Y	Y	Y	Y	Y	Y	Y	N	Y	Y	Y	Y	Y	Y	Y	Y
Bowles	Y	Y	Y	Y	Y	Y	Y	Y	Y	Y	Y	Y	Y	Y	Y	Y	Y	Y	Y	Y
Burzynski	Y	Y	Y	Y	Y	Y	Y	Y	Y	Y	N	P	Y	Y	Y	Y	Y	Y	Y	Y
Butler	Y	O	Y	Y	Y	Y	Y	Y	Y	Y	Y	Y	Y	Y	Y	Y	Y	Y	Y	Y
Carroll	Y	O	O	Y	Y	N	Y	Y	Y	Y	Y	Y	Y	Y	Y	Y	Y	Y	Y	Y
Clayborne	Y	Y	Y	Y	Y	N	Y	Y	N	Y	Y	Y	O	Y	Y	Y	Y	Y	Y	Y
Collins	Y	Y	Y	Y	O	Y	Y	Y	Y	Y	Y	O	Y	Y	Y	Y	Y	Y	Y	Y
Cronin	Y	Y	Y	Y	Y	Y	Y	Y	Y	Y	Y	P	Y	Y	Y	Y	Y	Y	Y	Y
Cullerton	Y	N	Y	Y	Y	Y	Y	Y	O	Y	Y	Y	Y	Y	Y	Y	O	Y	Y	Y
DeLeo	Y	Y	Y	Y	Y	Y	Y	Y	Y	Y	Y	Y	Y	Y	Y	Y	Y	Y	Y	Y
del Valle	Y	Y	Y	Y	Y	Y	O	Y	Y	Y	Y	Y	Y	Y	Y	Y	Y	Y	Y	Y
Demuzio	Y	Y	Y	Y	Y	Y	Y	Y	Y	Y	Y	Y	Y	Y	Y	Y	Y	Y	Y	Y
Dillard	Y	Y	Y	Y	Y	Y	Y	Y	Y	Y	Y	Y	Y	Y	Y	P	Y	Y	Y	Y
Donahue	Y	N	Y	Y	Y	Y	Y	Y	Y	Y	Y	N	Y	Y	Y	Y	Y	Y	Y	Y
Dudycz	Y	Y	Y	Y	Y	Y	Y	Y	Y	Y	Y	N	Y	Y	Y	Y	Y	Y	Y	Y
Farley	Y	Y	Y	Y	Y	Y	Y	Y	Y	O	Y	Y	Y	Y	Y	Y	Y	Y	Y	Y
Fawell	Y	Y	Y	Y	Y	Y	Y	Y	Y	Y	Y	P	Y	Y	Y	Y	Y	Y	Y	Y
Fitzgerald	Y	Y	Y	Y	Y	Y	Y	P	Y	Y	Y	Y	Y	Y	Y	Y	Y	Y	Y	Y
Garcia	Y	Y	Y	Y	Y	Y	Y	Y	O	Y	Y	Y	Y	Y	O	Y	Y	Y	Y	Y
Geo-Karis	Y	Y	Y	Y	Y	Y	Y	Y	Y	Y	Y	Y	Y	Y	Y	Y	Y	Y	Y	Y
Halvorson	Y	Y	Y	Y	Y	Y	Y	Y	Y	Y	Y	Y	O	Y	Y	Y	Y	Y	Y	Y
Hawkinson	Y	Y	Y	Y	Y	Y	Y	Y	Y	Y	N	N	Y	Y	Y	Y	Y	Y	Y	Y
Hendon	Y	Y	O	O	Y	Y	Y	Y	Y	Y	P	Y	Y	Y	Y	Y	Y	O	Y	Y
Jacobs	Y	Y	N	N	Y	Y	Y	Y	N	Y	Y	Y	Y	Y	Y	Y	Y	Y	Y	Y
Jones, Emil	Y	Y	Y	Y	Y	N	Y	Y	Y	Y	Y	Y	Y	Y	Y	Y	Y	Y	Y	Y
Karpiel	Y	Y	Y	Y	Y	Y	Y	Y	Y	Y	Y	P	Y	Y	Y	Y	Y	Y	Y	Y
Klemm	Y	Y	Y	Y	Y	Y	Y	Y	O	Y	Y	Y	Y	Y	Y	Y	Y	Y	Y	Y
Lauzen	Y	N	Y	Y	P	Y	Y	Y	Y	Y	N	Y	Y	Y	Y	Y	Y	Y	O	Y
Link	Y	Y	Y	Y	Y	Y	Y	Y	Y	Y	Y	Y	Y	Y	Y	Y	Y	Y	Y	Y
Luechtefeld	Y	Y	Y	Y	Y	Y	Y	Y	N	Y	Y	N	Y	Y	Y	Y	Y	Y	Y	Y
Madigan, Robert	Y	Y	Y	Y	Y	Y	Y	Y	Y	Y	O	N	Y	Y	Y	Y	Y	Y	Y	Y
Mahar	Y	Y	Y	O	Y	Y	Y	Y	Y	Y	Y	Y	Y	Y	Y	Y	Y	Y	Y	Y
Maitland	Y	Y	Y	Y	Y	Y	Y	Y	Y	Y	Y	N	Y	Y	Y	Y	Y	Y	Y	Y
Molaro	Y	Y	Y	Y	Y	Y	Y	Y	Y	Y	O	Y	Y	Y	Y	Y	Y	O	Y	Y
Myers	Y	Y	Y	Y	Y	Y	Y	Y	Y	Y	Y	N	Y	Y	Y	Y	Y	Y	Y	Y
Obama	Y	Y	Y	Y	Y	N	Y	Y	Y	Y	N	Y	Y	Y	Y	Y	Y	Y	Y	Y
O'Daniel	Y	Y	Y	Y	Y	Y	Y	Y	Y	Y	Y	Y	Y	O	Y	Y	Y	Y	Y	Y
O'Malley	Y	Y	Y	Y	Y	Y	Y	Y	Y	Y	Y	P	Y	Y	Y	Y	Y	Y	Y	Y
Parker	Y	O	Y	Y	Y	Y	Y	Y	Y	Y	Y	Y	Y	Y	Y	Y	Y	Y	Y	Y

HB0172	HB0260	HB0271	HB0282	HB0297	HB0313	HB0316	HB0379	HB0381	HB0424	HB0475	HB0480	HB0489	HB0522	HB0524	HB0540	HB0581	HB0585	HB0601	HB0602	HB0618	HB0652	HB0725	HB0729	HB0844	HB0923	HB0951	HB0968	HB0995	HB1004
O	Y	Y	Y	Y	Y	Y	Y	Y	Y	Y	Y	Y	Y	Y	Y	Y	Y	Y	Y	Y	Y	Y	Y	Y	Y	Y	Y	N	Y
Y	Y	Y	Y	Y	Y	Y	Y	Y	Y	Y	Y	Y	Y	Y	Y	Y	Y	Y	Y	Y	Y	Y	Y	Y	Y	Y	N	Y	Y
P	N	Y	Y	Y	Y	Y	Y	Y	Y	Y	Y	Y	Y	Y	Y	Y	Y	Y	Y	Y	Y	Y	Y	Y	Y	Y	Y	Y	O
Y	N	Y	Y	Y	Y	Y	Y	Y	Y	N	Y	Y	Y	N	Y	Y	Y	Y	Y	Y	Y	Y	Y	Y	N	Y	Y	Y	Y
Y	Y	Y	Y	Y	Y	Y	Y	Y	Y	Y	Y	Y	Y	Y	Y	Y	Y	Y	Y	Y	Y	Y	Y	Y	Y	Y	Y	Y	Y
Y	Y	Y	Y	Y	Y	Y	Y	Y	Y	Y	Y	Y	Y	Y	Y	Y	Y	Y	Y	Y	Y	Y	Y	Y	Y	Y	Y	O	Y
N	N	Y	Y	Y	Y	Y	Y	Y	Y	Y	Y	Y	Y	O	Y	Y	Y	Y	Y	Y	Y	Y	Y	Y	Y	Y	N	N	Y
O	O	Y	O	Y	O	Y	Y	Y	Y	O	Y	Y	Y	Y	Y	Y	Y	Y	Y	Y	O	Y	Y	Y	Y	Y	N	O	Y
Y	Y	Y	Y	Y	Y	Y	Y	Y	Y	Y	Y	Y	Y	Y	O	Y	Y	Y	Y	Y	Y	Y	Y	Y	Y	Y	Y	O	Y
P	Y	Y	Y	Y	Y	Y	Y	Y	Y	Y	Y	Y	Y	Y	Y	Y	Y	P	Y	Y	Y	Y	Y	Y	Y	Y	O	N	Y
Y	Y	Y	Y	Y	Y	Y	Y	Y	Y	Y	Y	Y	Y	Y	Y	Y	Y	P	Y	Y	Y	Y	Y	Y	Y	Y	N	N	Y
N	Y	Y	Y	Y	Y	Y	Y	Y	Y	N	Y	Y	Y	Y	Y	Y	O	Y	Y	Y	Y	Y	Y	Y	Y	Y	Y	N	O
Y	N	Y	Y	Y	Y	Y	Y	Y	Y	N	Y	Y	Y	Y	Y	Y	Y	Y	O	Y	P	Y	Y	Y	Y	Y	Y	Y	Y
Y	N	Y	Y	Y	Y	Y	Y	Y	Y	Y	Y	Y	Y	Y	Y	Y	Y	Y	Y	Y	Y	Y	O	Y	Y	Y	Y	Y	Y
Y	Y	Y	Y	Y	Y	Y	Y	Y	Y	Y	Y	Y	Y	Y	Y	Y	Y	Y	Y	Y	Y	Y	Y	Y	Y	Y	N	Y	Y
Y	Y	Y	Y	Y	Y	Y	Y	Y	Y	Y	Y	Y	Y	Y	Y	Y	Y	Y	Y	Y	Y	Y	Y	Y	Y	Y	Y	N	Y
Y	Y	Y	Y	Y	Y	Y	Y	Y	Y	N	Y	Y	Y	Y	Y	Y	Y	Y	Y	Y	Y	Y	Y	Y	Y	Y	Y	N	Y
Y	N	Y	Y	Y	Y	Y	Y	Y	Y	N	Y	Y	Y	Y	Y	Y	Y	Y	Y	Y	N	Y	Y	Y	Y	Y	Y	N	Y
Y	N	P	Y	Y	Y	Y	Y	Y	Y	N	Y	P	Y	N	O	Y	Y	Y	Y	Y	Y	Y	Y	Y	Y	Y	Y	Y	Y
O	Y	O	Y	Y	Y	O	O	O	Y	Y	Y	O	Y	O	Y	Y	Y	O	Y	Y	Y	Y	Y	Y	Y	O	Y	N	Y
Y	Y	Y	Y	Y	Y	Y	Y	Y	O	Y	Y	Y	Y	Y	Y	Y	Y	Y	Y	Y	Y	Y	Y	Y	Y	Y	Y	Y	Y
Y	O	Y	Y	Y	Y	Y	Y	Y	Y	Y	Y	Y	Y	Y	Y	Y	Y	Y	O	Y	Y	Y	Y	Y	Y	Y	N	Y	Y
Y	N	Y	Y	Y	Y	Y	O	Y	Y	N	Y	Y	Y	Y	Y	Y	Y	Y	Y	Y	Y	Y	Y	Y	Y	Y	N	Y	Y
N	Y	Y	Y	Y	Y	Y	Y	Y	Y	N	Y	N	Y	Y	Y	Y	Y	Y	Y	Y	Y	Y	Y	P	Y	Y	P	P	Y
Y	N	Y	Y	Y	Y	Y	Y	Y	Y	Y	Y	Y	Y	Y	Y	Y	Y	Y	Y	Y	Y	Y	Y	Y	Y	Y	Y	Y	Y
O	Y	Y	Y	Y	Y	Y	Y	Y	Y	N	Y	Y	Y	Y	Y	Y	Y	P	Y	Y	Y	Y	Y	N	Y	Y	Y	Y	Y
Y	Y	Y	Y	Y	Y	Y	Y	Y	Y	N	Y	Y	Y	Y	Y	Y	Y	Y	Y	Y	P	Y	Y	Y	Y	Y	Y	P	O
Y	Y	Y	Y	Y	Y	Y	Y	Y	Y	Y	Y	Y	Y	N	Y	Y	Y	Y	Y	Y	Y	Y	Y	Y	Y	Y	N	Y	Y
Y	N	Y	Y	Y	N	Y	Y	Y	Y	Y	O	Y	Y	N	P	O	Y	Y	N	Y	Y	Y	Y	Y	Y	Y	N	N	Y
N	Y	Y	Y	Y	Y	Y	Y	Y	Y	N	Y	Y	Y	Y	Y	Y	Y	Y	Y	Y	O	Y	Y	Y	Y	Y	Y	N	Y
Y	N	Y	Y	Y	Y	Y	Y	Y	Y	Y	Y	Y	Y	Y	Y	Y	Y	Y	Y	Y	N	Y	Y	Y	Y	Y	N	Y	Y
Y	Y	Y	Y	Y	Y	Y	Y	Y	Y	Y	Y	Y	Y	Y	P	Y	Y	Y	Y	Y	O	Y	Y	Y	O	Y	Y	Y	Y
Y	N	Y	Y	Y	O	Y	Y	Y	Y	Y	Y	Y	Y	Y	Y	Y	Y	Y	Y	Y	Y	Y	Y	Y	Y	Y	Y	Y	Y
Y	Y	Y	Y	Y	Y	Y	Y	Y	Y	Y	Y	Y	Y	Y	Y	Y	Y	Y	Y	Y	Y	Y	Y	Y	Y	Y	Y	Y	Y
P	O	Y	Y	Y	Y	Y	Y	Y	Y	Y	Y	Y	Y	Y	Y	O	Y	Y	Y	Y	Y	Y	Y	Y	Y	Y	N	N	Y
Y	N	Y	Y	Y	Y	Y	Y	Y	Y	Y	Y	Y	Y	Y	Y	Y	Y	Y	Y	Y	Y	Y	Y	Y	Y	Y	N	Y	Y
N	Y	Y	Y	O	Y	Y	Y	Y	Y	N	Y	Y	Y	Y	Y	Y	Y	Y	Y	Y	Y	Y	Y	O	Y	Y	Y	Y	Y
Y	N	Y	Y	Y	Y	Y	Y	Y	Y	Y	Y	Y	Y	Y	Y	Y	Y	Y	Y	Y	Y	Y	Y	Y	Y	Y	N	Y	Y
N	N	Y	Y	Y	Y	Y	Y	Y	Y	Y	Y	Y	Y	Y	Y	O	Y	Y	Y	Y	Y	Y	O	Y	Y	Y	Y	Y	Y
Y	N	Y	Y	Y	Y	Y	Y	Y	Y	Y	Y	Y	Y	Y	Y	Y	Y	Y	Y	Y	Y	Y	Y	Y	Y	Y	Y	N	Y

Senate Member	SB0909	SB0927	SB0950	SB0953	SB0999	SB1000	SB1024	SB1044	SB1050	SB1084	SB1101	SB1103	SB1105	HB0008	HB0045	HB0050	HB0056	HB0127	HB0154	HB0165
Peterson	Y	Y	Y	Y	Y	N	Y	Y	Y	Y	Y	Y	Y	Y	Y	Y	Y	Y	Y	Y
Petka	Y	Y	Y	Y	Y	Y	Y	Y	Y	Y	Y	N	Y	Y	Y	Y	Y	Y	Y	Y
Philip	Y	Y	Y	Y	Y	Y	Y	Y	Y	Y	Y	N	Y	Y	Y	Y	Y	Y	Y	Y
Radogno	Y	Y	Y	Y	Y	Y	Y	Y	Y	Y	Y	Y	Y	Y	Y	Y	Y	Y	Y	Y
Rauschenberger	O	Y	Y	Y	Y	Y	Y	Y	Y	P	Y	Y	Y	Y	Y	Y	Y	Y	Y	Y
Rea	Y	Y	Y	Y	Y	Y	Y	Y	N	O	Y	Y	Y	Y	Y	Y	Y	Y	Y	Y
Severns	Y	Y	Y	Y	Y	Y	Y	Y	Y	Y	Y	Y	Y	Y	Y	Y	Y	Y	Y	Y
Shadid	Y	Y	Y	Y	Y	Y	Y	Y	Y	Y	N	Y	Y	O	Y	Y	Y	Y	Y	Y
Shaw	Y	O	O	O	Y	O	O	O	O	O	P	O	O	Y	Y	Y	Y	Y	Y	Y
Sieben	Y	Y	Y	Y	Y	Y	Y	Y	N	Y	Y	N	Y	Y	Y	Y	Y	Y	Y	Y
Smith, Margaret	Y	Y	Y	Y	Y	N	Y	Y	O	Y	Y	Y	Y	Y	Y	Y	Y	N	Y	Y
Syverson	Y	Y	Y	Y	Y	Y	Y	Y	Y	Y	Y	P	Y	Y	Y	Y	Y	Y	Y	Y
Trotter	Y	Y	Y	Y	Y	Y	Y	Y	Y	O	Y	Y	Y	Y	Y	Y	O	Y	Y	Y
Viverito	Y	Y	Y	Y	Y	Y	Y	Y	Y	Y	Y	Y	Y	Y	Y	Y	Y	Y	O	Y
Walsh, Lawrence	Y	X	X	X	Y	X	X	X	X	X	Y	X	X	Y	Y	Y	Y	Y	Y	Y
Walsh, Thomas	Y	N	Y	Y	Y	Y	Y	Y	Y	Y	Y	P	Y	Y	Y	Y	Y	Y	Y	Y
Watson	Y	Y	Y	Y	Y	Y	Y	Y	N	Y	Y	N	Y	Y	Y	Y	Y	Y	Y	Y
Weaver	Y	Y	Y	Y	Y	Y	Y	Y	Y	Y	P	N	Y	Y	Y	Y	Y	Y	Y	Y
Welch	Y	Y	Y	N	Y	Y	Y	Y	Y	Y	Y	Y	Y	Y	Y	Y	Y	Y	Y	Y
Dunn	X	X	X	X	X	X	X	X	O	X	X	X	X	X	X	X	X	X	X	X
Woodyard	X	X	X	X	X	X	X	X	X	X	X	X	X	X	X	X	X	X	X	X

HB0172	HB0260	HB0271	HB0282	HB0297	HB0313	HB0316	HB0379	HB0381	HB0424	HB0475	HB0480	HB0489	HB0522	HB0524	HB0540	HB0581	HB0585	HB0601	HB0602	HB0618	HB0652	HB0725	HB0729	HB0824	HB0923	HB0951	HB0968	HB0995	HB1004
Y	Y	Y	Y	Y	Y	Y	Y	Y	Y	Y	Y	Y	Y	Y	Y	Y	Y	Y	Y	Y	N	Y	Y	Y	Y	Y	Y	Y	Y
Y	N	Y	Y	Y	Y	Y	Y	Y	Y	Y	Y	Y	Y	N	O	Y	Y	Y	Y	Y	Y	Y	Y	Y	Y	Y	Y	Y	Y
Y	Y	Y	Y	Y	Y	Y	Y	Y	Y	Y	Y	Y	Y	Y	Y	Y	Y	Y	Y	Y	Y	Y	Y	O	Y	Y	Y	Y	Y
Y	Y	Y	Y	Y	Y	Y	Y	Y	Y	Y	Y	Y	Y	N	Y	Y	Y	Y	Y	Y	Y	Y	Y	Y	Y	Y	Y	Y	Y
Y	N	Y	Y	Y	N	Y	Y	Y	Y	Y	Y	Y	Y	N	P	Y	Y	Y	Y	Y	Y	Y	Y	Y	Y	Y	Y	Y	Y
Y	N	Y	Y	Y	Y	Y	Y	Y	Y	Y	Y	Y	Y	Y	Y	Y	Y	Y	Y	Y	Y	Y	Y	Y	Y	Y	Y	Y	O
Y	Y	Y	Y	Y	Y	Y	Y	O	Y	Y	Y	Y	Y	Y	Y	Y	Y	Y	Y	Y	Y	Y	Y	Y	Y	Y	Y	Y	Y
Y	N	Y	Y	Y	Y	Y	Y	Y	Y	N	Y	Y	Y	Y	Y	Y	Y	Y	O	Y	Y	Y	Y	Y	Y	O	Y	Y	Y
N	N	Y	Y	Y	Y	O	Y	Y	O	N	O	Y	Y	Y	O	Y	O	Y	Y	O	Y	Y	O	P	O	Y	O	N	O
Y	N	Y	Y	Y	Y	O	Y	Y	Y	Y	Y	Y	Y	Y	Y	Y	Y	Y	Y	Y	Y	Y	Y	Y	Y	Y	Y	Y	Y
N	N	Y	Y	Y	Y	Y	Y	Y	Y	Y	Y	Y	Y	Y	Y	Y	Y	Y	Y	Y	Y	Y	Y	Y	Y	Y	P	N	Y
Y	N	Y	Y	Y	Y	Y	Y	Y	O	Y	O	O	Y	N	O	Y	O	Y	Y	O	Y	Y	Y	Y	O	Y	O	Y	Y
N	O	Y	Y	Y	Y	Y	Y	Y	Y	Y	Y	Y	Y	Y	Y	Y	Y	Y	Y	Y	Y	Y	Y	Y	Y	Y	N	N	Y
Y	Y	Y	Y	Y	Y	Y	Y	Y	Y	Y	Y	Y	Y	Y	Y	Y	Y	Y	Y	Y	N	Y	Y	Y	Y	Y	Y	Y	Y
Y	N	Y	Y	Y	Y	Y	Y	Y	Y	Y	Y	Y	Y	Y	Y	Y	Y	Y	N	Y	Y	Y	Y	Y	Y	Y	N	Y	Y
Y	Y	Y	Y	Y	Y	Y	Y	Y	Y	Y	Y	Y	Y	Y	Y	Y	Y	Y	Y	Y	Y	Y	Y	Y	Y	Y	Y	N	Y
Y	Y	Y	Y	Y	Y	Y	Y	Y	Y	Y	Y	Y	Y	Y	Y	Y	Y	Y	Y	Y	N	Y	Y	Y	Y	Y	N	Y	Y
Y	Y	Y	Y	Y	Y	Y	Y	Y	Y	Y	Y	Y	Y	Y	Y	Y	Y	Y	Y	Y	O	Y	Y	Y	Y	Y	Y	Y	Y
Y	N	Y	Y	Y	Y	Y	Y	Y	Y	Y	Y	Y	Y	Y	Y	Y	Y	Y	Y	Y	Y	Y	Y	Y	Y	Y	N	Y	Y
X	X	X	X	X	X	X	X	X	X	X	X	X	X	X	X	X	X	X	X	X	X	X	X	X	X	X	X	X	X
X	X	X	X	X	X	X	X	X	X	X	X	X	X	X	X	X	X	X	X	X	X	X	X	X	X	X	X	X	X

Senate Member	HB 1029	HB 1080	HB 1087	HB 1121	HB 1141	HB 1147	HB 1168	HB 1169	HB 1211	HB 1219	HB 1229	HB 1294	HB 1311	HB 1315	HB 1327	HB 1332	HB 1337	HB 1347	HB 1388	HB 1486
Berman	Y	Y	Y	Y	Y	Y	Y	Y	Y	Y	Y	Y	Y	Y	Y	Y	Y	Y	Y	Y
Bomke	Y	Y	N	Y	Y	Y	Y	Y	Y	Y	Y	Y	Y	Y	Y	Y	Y	Y	Y	Y
Bowles	Y	O	N	Y	Y	Y	Y	Y	Y	O	Y	Y	Y	O	Y	Y	Y	Y	Y	Y
Burzynski	Y	Y	Y	Y	Y	Y	Y	Y	Y	Y	Y	Y	Y	Y	N	Y	Y	Y	Y	Y
Butler	Y	Y	N	Y	Y	Y	Y	Y	Y	Y	Y	Y	Y	Y	O	Y	Y	Y	Y	Y
Carroll	Y	Y	N	Y	Y	P	Y	Y	Y	Y	Y	Y	Y	Y	Y	Y	Y	O	Y	Y
Clayborne	Y	Y	N	Y	Y	Y	Y	O	Y	Y	Y	Y	Y	Y	Y	Y	Y	Y	Y	Y
Collins	O	O	N	Y	O	O	Y	Y	Y	Y	Y	Y	Y	Y	Y	Y	O	O	Y	Y
Cronin	Y	Y	Y	Y	Y	O	Y	O	Y	Y	Y	Y	Y	Y	Y	O	Y	Y	Y	Y
Cullerton	Y	Y	N	Y	Y	Y	Y	Y	Y	Y	Y	Y	Y	Y	Y	Y	Y	O	Y	Y
DeLeo	Y	Y	N	Y	Y	Y	Y	Y	Y	Y	Y	Y	Y	Y	Y	Y	Y	O	Y	Y
del Valle	Y	Y	N	Y	Y	Y	Y	Y	Y	Y	Y	Y	Y	Y	Y	Y	Y	Y	Y	Y
Demuzio	Y	Y	N	Y	Y	Y	Y	Y	Y	Y	Y	Y	Y	Y	Y	Y	Y	Y	Y	Y
Dillard	Y	Y	N	Y	Y	Y	Y	Y	Y	Y	Y	Y	Y	Y	N	Y	Y	Y	Y	Y
Donahue	Y	Y	N	Y	Y	Y	Y	Y	Y	Y	Y	Y	Y	Y	N	Y	Y	Y	Y	Y
Dudycz	Y	Y	Y	Y	Y	Y	Y	Y	Y	Y	Y	Y	Y	Y	Y	Y	Y	Y	Y	Y
Farley	Y	Y	N	Y	Y	Y	Y	Y	Y	Y	Y	Y	Y	Y	Y	Y	Y	Y	Y	Y
Fawell	Y	Y	Y	Y	Y	Y	Y	Y	Y	Y	Y	Y	Y	Y	Y	Y	Y	Y	Y	Y
Fitzgerald	Y	Y	Y	Y	Y	Y	Y	Y	Y	Y	Y	Y	Y	Y	Y	Y	Y	Y	Y	Y
Garcia	Y	Y	O	Y	Y	Y	O	Y	O	Y	O	O	O	Y	O	O	Y	Y	O	Y
Geo-Karis	Y	Y	N	Y	Y	Y	Y	Y	Y	Y	Y	Y	Y	Y	Y	Y	Y	Y	Y	Y
Halvorson	Y	Y	N	Y	Y	Y	Y	Y	Y	Y	Y	Y	Y	Y	Y	Y	Y	Y	Y	Y
Hawkinson	Y	Y	N	Y	Y	Y	Y	Y	Y	Y	Y	Y	Y	Y	N	Y	Y	Y	Y	Y
Hendon	Y	Y	N	O	Y	Y	Y	Y	Y	Y	O	Y	Y	Y	Y	Y	Y	Y	Y	Y
Jacobs	Y	Y	N	Y	Y	Y	Y	Y	Y	Y	Y	Y	Y	Y	N	Y	Y	Y	Y	Y
Jones, Emil	Y	O	N	Y	Y	Y	Y	Y	Y	Y	O	Y	Y	Y	Y	Y	Y	Y	Y	Y
Karpiel	Y	Y	Y	Y	Y	Y	Y	P	Y	Y	Y	Y	Y	Y	Y	Y	Y	P	Y	Y
Klemm	Y	Y	Y	Y	Y	Y	Y	Y	Y	Y	Y	Y	Y	Y	P	Y	Y	Y	Y	Y
Lauzen	Y	Y	Y	Y	Y	N	Y	N	Y	Y	P	Y	O	Y	N	Y	Y	Y	Y	Y
Link	Y	Y	N	Y	Y	Y	Y	Y	Y	Y	Y	Y	Y	Y	Y	Y	Y	Y	Y	Y
Luechtefeld	Y	Y	Y	Y	Y	Y	Y	Y	Y	Y	Y	Y	Y	Y	P	Y	Y	Y	Y	Y
Madigan, Robert	Y	Y	Y	Y	Y	Y	Y	Y	Y	Y	Y	Y	Y	Y	N	Y	Y	Y	Y	Y
Mahar	Y	Y	N	Y	Y	Y	Y	Y	Y	Y	Y	Y	Y	Y	Y	Y	Y	Y	Y	Y
Maitland	Y	Y	N	Y	Y	Y	Y	Y	Y	Y	Y	Y	Y	Y	Y	Y	Y	Y	Y	Y
Molaro	Y	Y	N	Y	Y	Y	Y	Y	Y	Y	Y	Y	Y	Y	Y	Y	Y	Y	Y	Y
Myers	Y	Y	N	Y	Y	Y	Y	Y	Y	Y	Y	Y	Y	Y	Y	Y	Y	Y	Y	Y
Obama	Y	Y	N	Y	Y	Y	Y	Y	Y	Y	Y	Y	Y	Y	Y	Y	Y	Y	Y	Y
O'Daniel	Y	Y	N	Y	Y	Y	Y	Y	Y	Y	Y	Y	Y	Y	Y	Y	Y	Y	Y	Y
O'Malley	Y	Y	P	Y	Y	Y	Y	Y	Y	Y	Y	Y	Y	Y	P	Y	Y	Y	Y	Y
Parker	Y	Y	N	Y	Y	Y	Y	Y	Y	Y	Y	Y	Y	Y	Y	Y	Y	Y	Y	Y

HB 1525	HB 1565	HB 1588	HB 1618	HB 1660	HB 1696	HB 1707	HB 1881	HB 2061	HB 2132	HB 2138	HB 2164	HB 2211	HB 2215	HB 2262
Y	Y	Y	Y	N	Y	Y	Y	Y	Y	Y	Y	Y	Y	Y
Y	Y	Y	Y	Y	Y	Y	Y	Y	Y	Y	Y	Y	Y	Y
Y	Y	O	Y	Y	N	Y	Y	Y	Y	O	Y	Y	Y	O
Y	Y	Y	N	Y	Y	Y	Y	N	Y	Y	Y	Y	Y	Y
Y	Y	Y	Y	Y	Y	Y	Y	Y	Y	Y	Y	Y	Y	Y
N	Y	Y	Y	Y	N	Y	Y	Y	O	Y	Y	Y	O	Y
Y	Y	Y	Y	Y	N	O	Y	N	Y	Y	Y	Y	Y	Y
Y	Y	Y	N	Y	N	Y	O	Y	O	Y	Y	O	Y	Y
Y	Y	Y	Y	Y	Y	Y	Y	Y	Y	Y	Y	Y	Y	Y
Y	Y	Y	Y	Y	N	Y	Y	Y	Y	Y	Y	Y	Y	Y
Y	Y	Y	Y	Y	N	Y	Y	Y	Y	Y	Y	Y	Y	Y
Y	Y	Y	Y	Y	N	Y	Y	Y	Y	Y	Y	Y	Y	O
Y	Y	Y	O	Y	N	Y	Y	Y	Y	Y	Y	Y	Y	Y
Y	Y	Y	Y	Y	Y	Y	Y	Y	Y	Y	Y	Y	Y	Y
Y	Y	Y	Y	Y	N	Y	Y	Y	Y	Y	Y	Y	Y	Y
Y	Y	Y	Y	Y	Y	Y	Y	Y	Y	Y	Y	Y	Y	Y
N	Y	Y	Y	Y	N	Y	Y	Y	Y	Y	Y	Y	Y	Y
Y	Y	Y	Y	Y	Y	Y	Y	Y	Y	Y	Y	Y	Y	Y
Y	Y	P	Y	Y	N	Y	Y	N	Y	Y	Y	P	Y	Y
P	O	Y	O	O	N	Y	Y	Y	Y	Y	Y	Y	Y	Y
Y	Y	P	Y	Y	Y	Y	Y	Y	Y	Y	Y	Y	Y	Y
Y	Y	Y	Y	Y	N	Y	Y	Y	Y	Y	Y	P	Y	Y
Y	Y	O	N	Y	N	Y	Y	Y	Y	Y	Y	Y	Y	Y
Y	Y	Y	Y	Y	N	O	Y	Y	Y	Y	Y	Y	Y	Y
P	Y	Y	Y	Y	N	Y	Y	N	N	Y	Y	Y	Y	Y
Y	Y	Y	Y	Y	N	Y	Y	Y	Y	O	Y	Y	Y	Y
Y	Y	Y	Y	Y	Y	Y	Y	Y	Y	Y	Y	Y	Y	Y
Y	Y	Y	N	Y	Y	Y	Y	Y	Y	Y	Y	Y	Y	Y
N	Y	Y	N	Y	Y	Y	Y	N	Y	Y	Y	Y	Y	Y
Y	Y	Y	Y	Y	N	Y	Y	Y	Y	Y	Y	Y	Y	Y
Y	Y	Y	Y	Y	Y	Y	Y	Y	Y	Y	Y	Y	Y	Y
Y	Y	O	Y	Y	N	Y	Y	O	Y	Y	Y	Y	Y	Y
Y	Y	Y	Y	Y	Y	Y	Y	Y	Y	Y	Y	Y	Y	Y
N	Y	Y	Y	Y	Y	Y	Y	Y	Y	Y	Y	Y	Y	Y
Y	Y	Y	Y	Y	O	O	Y	Y	N	Y	O	Y	O	Y
Y	Y	Y	Y	Y	Y	Y	Y	Y	Y	Y	Y	Y	Y	Y
Y	Y	Y	Y	Y	N	Y	Y	Y	Y	Y	Y	P	Y	Y
Y	Y	Y	Y	Y	N	Y	Y	Y	Y	Y	Y	Y	Y	Y
P	Y	Y	Y	Y	Y	Y	Y	Y	Y	Y	Y	Y	Y	Y
Y	Y	Y	Y	Y	Y	Y	Y	Y	Y	Y	Y	Y	Y	Y

Senate Member	HB1029	HB1080	HB1087	HB1121	HB1141	HB1147	HB1168	HB1169	HB1211	HB1219	HB1229	HB1294	HB1331	HB1335	HB1327	HB1332	HB1337	HB1347	HB1388	HB1486
Peterson	Y	Y	Y	Y	Y	Y	Y	Y	Y	Y	Y	Y	Y	Y	Y	Y	Y	Y	Y	Y
Petka	Y	Y	Y	Y	Y	Y	Y	Y	Y	Y	Y	O	Y	Y	Y	Y	Y	Y	Y	Y
Philip	Y	Y	Y	Y	Y	Y	Y	Y	Y	Y	Y	Y	Y	Y	N	Y	Y	Y	Y	Y
Radogno	Y	Y	Y	Y	Y	Y	Y	O	Y	Y	Y	Y	Y	Y	P	Y	Y	Y	Y	Y
Rauschenberger	Y	Y	N	O	Y	Y	Y	O	Y	Y	Y	Y	Y	Y	N	Y	Y	Y	O	Y
Rea	Y	Y	N	Y	Y	Y	Y	Y	Y	Y	Y	Y	Y	Y	Y	Y	Y	Y	Y	Y
Severns	Y	Y	N	Y	Y	Y	Y	Y	Y	Y	Y	Y	Y	Y	Y	Y	Y	Y	Y	Y
Shadid	Y	Y	N	Y	Y	Y	Y	Y	Y	Y	Y	Y	Y	Y	Y	Y	Y	Y	Y	Y
Shaw	Y	O	N	Y	Y	Y	O	Y	Y	O	Y	Y	Y	O	Y	Y	Y	N	Y	Y
Sieben	Y	Y	N	Y	Y	Y	Y	Y	Y	Y	Y	Y	Y	Y	Y	Y	Y	Y	Y	Y
Smith, Margaret	Y	Y	N	Y	Y	Y	Y	Y	Y	Y	Y	Y	Y	Y	Y	Y	Y	Y	Y	Y
Syverson	Y	Y	Y	Y	Y	Y	Y	Y	Y	Y	Y	Y	Y	Y	N	Y	Y	Y	Y	Y
Trotter	Y	Y	N	Y	Y	Y	Y	Y	Y	Y	Y	Y	Y	Y	Y	Y	Y	Y	Y	Y
Viverito	Y	Y	N	Y	Y	Y	Y	Y	Y	Y	Y	Y	Y	Y	Y	Y	Y	Y	Y	Y
Walsh, Lawrence	Y	Y	Y	Y	Y	Y	Y	Y	Y	Y	Y	Y	Y	Y	Y	Y	Y	Y	Y	Y
Walsh, Thomas	Y	Y	Y	Y	Y	P	Y	Y	Y	Y	Y	Y	Y	Y	Y	Y	Y	Y	Y	Y
Watson	Y	Y	N	Y	Y	Y	Y	Y	Y	Y	Y	Y	Y	Y	N	Y	Y	Y	Y	Y
Weaver	Y	Y	N	Y	Y	Y	Y	Y	Y	Y	Y	Y	Y	Y	N	Y	Y	Y	Y	Y
Welch	Y	Y	Y	Y	Y	Y	Y	Y	Y	Y	Y	Y	Y	Y	Y	Y	Y	Y	Y	Y
Dunn	X	X	X	X	X	X	X	X	X	X	X	X	X	X	X	X	X	X	X	X
Woodyard	X	X	X	X	X	X	X	X	X	X	X	X	X	X	X	X	X	X	X	X

HB 1525	HB 1565	HB 1588	HB 1618	HB 1680	HB 1696	HB 1707	HB 1881	HB 2061	HB 2112	HB 2138	HB 2164	HB 2211	HB 2215	HB 2262
Y	Y	Y	Y	Y	Y	Y	Y	Y	Y	Y	Y	Y	Y	Y
N	Y	Y	Y	Y	Y	Y	Y	N	Y	Y	Y	Y	Y	Y
Y	Y	Y	Y	Y	Y	Y	Y	Y	Y	Y	Y	Y	Y	Y
Y	Y	Y	Y	Y	N	Y	Y	Y	Y	Y	Y	Y	Y	Y
N	Y	Y	Y	Y	Y	Y	Y	N	Y	Y	Y	Y	Y	Y
Y	Y	Y	Y	Y	N	Y	Y	Y	Y	Y	Y	Y	Y	Y
Y	Y	Y	Y	Y	N	Y	Y	Y	Y	Y	Y	Y	Y	Y
Y	Y	Y	Y	Y	N	Y	Y	Y	Y	Y	Y	Y	Y	Y
Y	Y	O	Y	Y	N	Y	Y	O	Y	O	Y	Y	Y	O
Y	Y	Y	Y	Y	Y	Y	Y	Y	Y	Y	Y	Y	Y	Y
P	Y	Y	Y	Y	N	Y	Y	Y	Y	Y	Y	Y	Y	Y
Y	O	Y	Y	Y	Y	Y	Y	Y	Y	Y	Y	Y	Y	Y
P	Y	Y	Y	Y	N	Y	Y	Y	Y	Y	Y	Y	Y	Y
Y	Y	Y	Y	Y	N	Y	Y	Y	Y	Y	Y	Y	Y	Y
Y	Y	Y	Y	Y	N	Y	Y	Y	Y	Y	Y	Y	Y	Y
Y	Y	Y	Y	Y	Y	Y	Y	Y	Y	Y	Y	Y	Y	Y
Y	Y	Y	N	Y	Y	Y	Y	Y	Y	Y	Y	Y	Y	Y
Y	Y	Y	Y	Y	Y	Y	Y	Y	Y	Y	Y	Y	Y	Y
P	Y	Y	Y	Y	N	Y	Y	Y	Y	Y	Y	Y	Y	Y
X	X	X	X	X	X	X	X	X	X	X	X	X	X	X
X	X	X	X	X	X	X	X	X	X	X	X	X	X	X

House Member	SB 0021	SB 0051	SB 0054	SB 0069	SB 0073	SB 0076	SB 0087	SB 0103	SB 0107	SB 0110	SB 0123	SB 0140	SB 0160	SB 0166	SB 0225	SB 0236	SB 0248	SB 0317	SB 0327	SB 0345
Acevedo	Y	Y	Y	Y	Y	Y	Y	Y	Y	Y	Y	Y	Y	Y	Y	Y	Y	Y	Y	Y
Ackerman	N	Y	Y	Y	A	Y	Y	Y	Y	Y	Y	Y	A	N	Y	Y	Y	Y	Y	Y
Beaubien	N	Y	Y	Y	N	Y	Y	Y	Y	Y	Y	Y	Y	Y	Y	Y	Y	Y	Y	Y
Bergman	Y	Y	Y	Y	N	Y	Y	N	Y	Y	A	Y	Y	N	Y	Y	Y	Y	Y	Y
Biggert	N	Y	Y	Y	N	Y	Y	Y	Y	Y	Y	Y	N	N	Y	Y	Y	Y	Y	Y
Biggins	Y	N	Y	Y	N	Y	Y	Y	Y	Y	Y	Y	Y	N	Y	Y	Y	Y	Y	Y
Black	N	Y	Y	Y	Y	Y	Y	N	Y	Y	Y	Y	Y	N	Y	Y	Y	Y	Y	Y
Boland	E	Y	Y	E	Y	Y	Y	E	E	E	E	E	Y	N	E	E	E	Y	E	Y
Bost	N	Y	Y	Y	Y	Y	Y	Y	Y	Y	Y	Y	Y	N	Y	Y	Y	Y	Y	Y
Bradford	Y	N	Y	Y	Y	Y	Y	Y	Y	Y	Y	Y	N	N	Y	Y	Y	Y	Y	Y
Bradley	Y	X	Y	Y	Y	Y	X	Y	Y	Y	Y	Y	Y	Y	Y	Y	Y	Y	Y	Y
Brady	N	N	Y	Y	Y	Y	Y	Y	Y	Y	Y	Y	Y	N	Y	Y	Y	Y	Y	Y
Brosnahan	N	Y	Y	Y	Y	Y	Y	Y	Y	Y	Y	Y	Y	Y	Y	Y	Y	Y	Y	Y
Brown	X	X	X	X	X	X	X	X	X	X	X	X	X	X	X	X	X	X	X	X
Brunsvold	Y	N	Y	Y	Y	Y	Y	Y	Y	Y	Y	Y	Y	P	Y	Y	Y	Y	Y	Y
Bugielski	Y	P	Y	Y	Y	Y	Y	Y	Y	Y	Y	Y	Y	N	Y	Y	Y	Y	Y	Y
Burke	Y	Y	Y	Y	Y	Y	A	Y	Y	Y	Y	Y	Y	P	Y	Y	Y	Y	Y	Y
Capparelli	Y	N	Y	Y	Y	Y	P	Y	Y	Y	Y	Y	Y	N	Y	Y	Y	Y	Y	Y
Churchill	N	Y	Y	Y	N	Y	Y	Y	Y	Y	Y	Y	Y	N	Y	Y	Y	Y	Y	Y
Clayton	N	Y	Y	Y	Y	Y	Y	Y	Y	Y	Y	Y	Y	N	Y	Y	Y	Y	Y	Y
Coulson	Y	Y	Y	Y	P	Y	Y	N	Y	Y	Y	Y	N	Y	Y	Y	Y	Y	Y	Y
Cowlishaw	Y	Y	Y	Y	N	Y	Y	Y	Y	Y	Y	Y	Y	N	Y	Y	Y	Y	Y	Y
Cross	N	N	Y	A	N	Y	Y	N	Y	Y	Y	A	Y	N	Y	Y	Y	Y	Y	Y
Crotty	N	N	Y	Y	Y	Y	Y	Y	Y	Y	Y	Y	N	N	Y	Y	Y	Y	Y	Y
Currie	Y	Y	Y	Y	Y	Y	Y	Y	Y	Y	Y	Y	A	Y	Y	Y	Y	Y	Y	Y
Curry	Y	N	Y	Y	Y	Y	Y	Y	Y	Y	Y	Y	A	Y	Y	Y	Y	Y	Y	Y
Daniels	N	N	Y	Y	N	Y	Y	Y	Y	Y	Y	Y	Y	N	Y	Y	Y	Y	Y	Y
Dart	Y	Y	Y	Y	Y	Y	Y	Y	Y	Y	Y	Y	Y	Y	A	Y	Y	Y	Y	Y
Davis, Monique	Y	Y	Y	Y	Y	Y	P	Y	Y	Y	Y	Y	Y	Y	Y	Y	Y	Y	Y	Y
Davis, Steve	Y	N	Y	Y	Y	Y	Y	Y	Y	Y	Y	Y	Y	N	Y	Y	Y	Y	Y	Y
Deuchler	N	Y	Y	Y	P	Y	Y	Y	Y	Y	Y	Y	N	N	Y	Y	Y	Y	Y	Y
Durkin	Y	N	Y	Y	Y	Y	Y	N	Y	Y	Y	Y	Y	N	Y	Y	Y	Y	Y	Y
Erwin	Y	Y	Y	Y	Y	Y	Y	Y	Y	Y	Y	Y	Y	Y	Y	Y	Y	Y	Y	Y
Fantin	Y	N	Y	Y	Y	Y	Y	Y	Y	Y	Y	Y	N	Y	Y	Y	Y	Y	Y	Y
Feigenholtz	Y	Y	Y	Y	Y	Y	Y	Y	Y	Y	Y	Y	N	Y	Y	Y	Y	Y	Y	Y
Flowers	Y	Y	Y	Y	Y	Y	N	Y	Y	Y	Y	Y	Y	Y	Y	Y	Y	Y	Y	Y
Fritchey	N	Y	Y	Y	Y	Y	Y	Y	Y	Y	Y	Y	Y	Y	Y	Y	Y	Y	Y	Y
Gash	N	Y	Y	Y	Y	Y	Y	Y	Y	Y	Y	Y	Y	Y	Y	Y	Y	Y	Y	Y
Giglio	N	N	Y	Y	Y	Y	N	Y	Y	Y	Y	Y	Y	Y	Y	Y	Y	Y	Y	Y
Giles	Y	Y	Y	Y	Y	Y	Y	Y	Y	Y	Y	Y	Y	Y	Y	Y	Y	Y	Y	Y

SB0366	SB0378	SB0381	SB0431	SB0508	SB0596	SB0680	SB0698	SB0700	SB0762
Y	Y	Y	Y	Y	Y	Y	Y	Y	Y
Y	Y	Y	Y	Y	Y	Y	N	N	Y
Y	Y	Y	Y	Y	Y	Y	Y	Y	Y
Y	Y	Y	Y	Y	Y	Y	N	Y	Y
Y	Y	Y	Y	Y	Y	Y	Y	Y	Y
P	Y	Y	Y	Y	Y	Y	Y	Y	Y
Y	Y	Y	Y	Y	N	Y	N	Y	Y
E	E	Y	E	E	Y	Y	Y	E	E
Y	N	Y	Y	Y	N	Y	N	Y	Y
Y	N	Y	Y	Y	N	Y	Y	Y	Y
Y	Y	Y	Y	Y	Y	Y	Y	Y	Y
Y	Y	Y	Y	Y	Y	Y	Y	Y	Y
Y	N	Y	Y	Y	N	Y	Y	Y	Y
X	X	X	X	X	X	X	X	X	X
Y	Y	Y	Y	Y	Y	Y	Y	Y	Y
Y	Y	Y	Y	Y	Y	Y	Y	Y	Y
Y	Y	Y	Y	N	Y	Y	Y	Y	Y
Y	Y	Y	Y	Y	Y	Y	Y	Y	Y
Y	Y	Y	Y	Y	Y	Y	Y	Y	Y
Y	Y	Y	Y	Y	Y	Y	Y	Y	Y
Y	Y	Y	Y	Y	N	Y	Y	Y	Y
Y	Y	Y	Y	Y	N	Y	Y	Y	Y
Y	Y	Y	Y	Y	Y	Y	Y	Y	Y
Y	N	Y	Y	Y	N	Y	Y	Y	Y
Y	Y	Y	Y	N	Y	Y	Y	Y	Y
Y	Y	Y	Y	Y	N	Y	Y	Y	Y
Y	Y	Y	Y	Y	Y	Y	Y	Y	Y
Y	Y	Y	Y	Y	Y	Y	Y	Y	Y
Y	Y	Y	Y	N	Y	Y	Y	Y	Y
Y	N	Y	Y	Y	N	Y	Y	Y	Y
Y	Y	Y	Y	N	Y	Y	Y	Y	Y
Y	Y	Y	Y	Y	Y	Y	Y	Y	Y
Y	Y	Y	Y	Y	Y	Y	Y	Y	Y
Y	Y	Y	Y	N	Y	Y	Y	Y	A
Y	Y	Y	Y	A	Y	Y	Y	Y	Y
Y	Y	Y	Y	N	Y	Y	Y	Y	Y
Y	N	Y	Y	P	Y	Y	Y	Y	Y
Y	Y	Y	Y	Y	Y	Y	Y	Y	Y
Y	N	Y	Y	Y	N	Y	Y	Y	N
Y	Y	Y	Y	A	Y	Y	Y	Y	Y

SB0772	SB0777	SB0795	SB0796	SB0797	SB0806	SB0819	SB0843	SB0856	SB0858
Y	Y	Y	Y	Y	Y	Y	N	Y	Y
N	Y	Y	Y	Y	Y	Y	Y	Y	Y
N	Y	Y	Y	Y	Y	Y	Y	Y	Y
Y	Y	Y	Y	Y	Y	Y	Y	Y	Y
N	Y	Y	Y	Y	Y	Y	Y	Y	Y
Y	Y	Y	Y	Y	Y	Y	N	Y	Y
N	Y	Y	Y	Y	Y	Y	Y	Y	Y
E	Y	Y	E	Y	Y	N	E	Y	E
N	Y	Y	Y	Y	Y	Y	Y	Y	N
Y	Y	Y	Y	Y	Y	Y	Y	Y	N
Y	Y	Y	Y	Y	Y	Y	Y	Y	Y
N	Y	Y	Y	N	Y	A	Y	Y	Y
Y	Y	Y	Y	Y	Y	Y	Y	Y	N
X	X	X	X	X	X	X	X	X	X
Y	Y	Y	P	Y	Y	Y	Y	Y	Y
Y	Y	Y	Y	Y	Y	Y	Y	Y	Y
N	Y	Y	Y	Y	Y	Y	Y	Y	Y
Y	Y	Y	Y	Y	Y	Y	Y	Y	Y
Y	Y	Y	Y	Y	Y	Y	Y	Y	Y
Y	A	Y	Y	Y	Y	A	N	Y	Y
Y	Y	Y	Y	Y	Y	Y	Y	Y	Y
N	Y	Y	Y	Y	Y	Y	Y	Y	Y
N	Y	Y	Y	Y	Y	N	Y	Y	Y
Y	Y	Y	Y	Y	Y	Y	Y	Y	N
Y	Y	Y	Y	Y	Y	A	Y	Y	Y
Y	Y	Y	Y	Y	Y	Y	Y	Y	N
Y	Y	Y	Y	Y	Y	Y	Y	Y	Y
Y	Y	Y	Y	Y	Y	Y	Y	Y	Y
N	Y	Y	N	Y	Y	Y	Y	Y	Y
Y	Y	Y	Y	Y	Y	Y	Y	Y	N
Y	Y	Y	Y	Y	Y	N	Y	Y	Y
N	Y	Y	Y	Y	Y	Y	Y	Y	N
Y	Y	Y	Y	Y	Y	A	Y	Y	Y
Y	Y	Y	P	Y	Y	A	N	Y	Y
Y	Y	Y	Y	Y	Y	Y	Y	Y	Y
Y	Y	Y	Y	Y	Y	Y	Y	Y	Y
Y	Y	Y	Y	Y	Y	Y	N	Y	Y
Y	Y	Y	Y	Y	Y	Y	Y	Y	Y
Y	Y	Y	Y	Y	Y	Y	Y	Y	N
N	Y	Y	P	Y	Y	Y	N	Y	Y

SB0899	SB0909	SB0927	SB0950	SB0953	SB0999	SB1024	SB1044	SB1050	SB1084
Y	Y	Y	Y	Y	Y	Y	Y	Y	Y
N	Y	Y	Y	Y	Y	Y	Y	Y	Y
N	Y	Y	Y	Y	Y	Y	Y	Y	Y
N	Y	Y	Y	Y	Y	Y	Y	Y	Y
N	Y	Y	Y	Y	Y	Y	Y	Y	Y
N	Y	Y	Y	Y	Y	Y	Y	Y	Y
N	Y	Y	Y	Y	Y	Y	Y	N	Y
Y	Y	Y	E	E	Y	E	E	E	E
N	Y	Y	Y	N	Y	Y	Y	N	Y
Y	Y	Y	N	Y	Y	Y	Y	Y	Y
Y	Y	Y	Y	Y	Y	Y	Y	Y	Y
N	Y	Y	N	Y	Y	Y	Y	Y	Y
N	Y	N	Y	Y	Y	Y	Y	Y	Y
X	X	X	X	X	X	X	X	X	X
Y	Y	Y	N	Y	Y	Y	Y	Y	Y
Y	Y	Y	Y	Y	Y	Y	Y	Y	Y
Y	Y	Y	Y	Y	Y	Y	Y	Y	Y
Y	Y	Y	Y	Y	Y	Y	Y	Y	Y
N	Y	Y	Y	Y	Y	Y	Y	Y	Y
N	Y	Y	Y	Y	Y	Y	Y	Y	Y
N	Y	N	Y	Y	Y	Y	Y	Y	Y
N	Y	Y	Y	Y	Y	Y	Y	Y	Y
N	Y	Y	Y	Y	Y	Y	Y	Y	Y
N	Y	N	Y	Y	Y	Y	Y	Y	A
Y	Y	N	Y	Y	Y	Y	Y	Y	Y
N	Y	N	N	Y	Y	Y	Y	N	Y
N	Y	Y	Y	Y	Y	Y	Y	Y	Y
N	Y	Y	Y	Y	Y	Y	Y	Y	Y
N	Y	Y	N	Y	Y	Y	Y	Y	Y
Y	Y	Y	Y	Y	Y	Y	Y	Y	Y
N	Y	N	Y	Y	Y	Y	Y	Y	Y
N	Y	Y	N	A	Y	Y	Y	Y	Y
N	Y	Y	Y	Y	Y	Y	Y	Y	Y
Y	Y	Y	N	Y	Y	Y	Y	N	Y
N	Y	N	Y	Y	Y	Y	Y	Y	Y
Y	Y	Y	Y	Y	Y	Y	Y	Y	Y
N	Y	N	Y	Y	Y	Y	Y	Y	Y
N	Y	N	Y	Y	Y	Y	Y	Y	Y
N	Y	N	Y	Y	Y	Y	Y	N	Y
P	Y	Y	P	Y	Y	Y	Y	P	Y

House Member	SB0021	SB0051	SB0054	SB0069	SB0073	SB0076	SB0087	SB0103	SB0107	SB0110	SB0123	SB0140	SB0160	SB0166	SB0225	SB0236	SB0248	SB0317	SB0327	SB0345
Granberg	Y	N	Y	A	Y	Y	Y	Y	Y	Y	Y	Y	Y	N	Y	Y	Y	Y	Y	Y
Hannig	Y	Y	Y	Y	Y	Y	Y	Y	Y	Y	Y	Y	Y	N	Y	Y	Y	Y	Y	Y
Hartke	Y	Y	Y	Y	Y	Y	Y	Y	Y	Y	Y	Y	Y	N	Y	Y	Y	Y	Y	Y
Hassert	N	N	Y	Y	N	Y	Y	Y	Y	Y	Y	Y	Y	N	Y	Y	Y	Y	Y	Y
Hoeft	Y	Y	Y	Y	N	Y	Y	Y	Y	Y	Y	Y	Y	Y	Y	Y	Y	Y	Y	Y
Holbrook	Y	N	Y	Y	Y	Y	Y	Y	Y	Y	Y	Y	N	N	Y	Y	Y	Y	Y	Y
Howard	Y	Y	Y	Y	Y	Y	P	Y	Y	A	Y	Y	Y	P	Y	Y	Y	Y	Y	Y
Johnson, Tim	P	Y	Y	Y	N	Y	Y	Y	Y	Y	Y	Y	Y	N	Y	Y	Y	Y	Y	Y
Johnson, Tom	N	Y	Y	Y	Y	Y	Y	Y	Y	Y	Y	Y	Y	N	Y	Y	Y	Y	Y	Y
Jones, John	N	Y	Y	Y	Y	Y	Y	N	Y	Y	Y	Y	Y	N	Y	Y	Y	Y	Y	Y
Jones, Lovana	Y	Y	Y	Y	Y	Y	P	Y	Y	Y	Y	Y	Y	Y	Y	Y	Y	Y	Y	Y
Jones, Shirley	Y	Y	E	Y	Y	Y	Y	Y	Y	Y	Y	Y	Y	Y	Y	Y	Y	Y	Y	Y
Kenner	Y	Y	Y	Y	Y	Y	P	Y	Y	Y	Y	Y	Y	Y	Y	Y	Y	Y	Y	Y
Klingler	N	Y	Y	Y	N	Y	Y	Y	Y	Y	Y	Y	A	A	Y	Y	Y	Y	Y	Y
Kosel	N	Y	Y	Y	N	Y	Y	N	Y	Y	Y	Y	Y	N	Y	Y	Y	Y	Y	Y
Krause	Y	Y	Y	Y	N	Y	Y	Y	Y	Y	Y	Y	N	Y	Y	Y	Y	Y	Y	Y
Kubik	A	E	Y	Y	A	Y	Y	Y	Y	Y	Y	Y	A	N	Y	Y	Y	Y	Y	Y
Lang	Y	Y	Y	Y	Y	Y	Y	Y	Y	Y	Y	Y	Y	Y	Y	Y	Y	Y	Y	Y
Lawfer	N	N	Y	Y	N	Y	Y	N	Y	Y	Y	Y	Y	N	Y	Y	Y	Y	Y	Y
Leitch	N	Y	Y	Y	Y	Y	Y	Y	Y	Y	Y	Y	Y	N	Y	Y	Y	Y	Y	Y
Lindner	Y	Y	Y	Y	N	Y	Y	Y	Y	Y	Y	Y	N	N	Y	Y	Y	Y	Y	Y
Lopez	Y	P	Y	Y	Y	Y	Y	Y	Y	Y	Y	Y	Y	Y	Y	Y	Y	Y	Y	Y
Lyons, Eileen	N	N	Y	Y	Y	Y	Y	N	Y	Y	Y	Y	Y	N	Y	Y	Y	Y	Y	Y
Lyons, Joseph	Y	Y	Y	Y	Y	Y	Y	Y	Y	Y	Y	Y	Y	Y	Y	Y	Y	Y	Y	Y
Madigan, Michael	Y	Y	Y	Y	Y	Y	Y	Y	Y	Y	Y	Y	Y	Y	Y	Y	Y	Y	Y	Y
Mautino	Y	Y	Y	Y	Y	Y	Y	Y	Y	Y	Y	Y	N	N	Y	Y	Y	Y	Y	Y
McAuliffe	N	Y	Y	Y	Y	Y	Y	Y	Y	Y	Y	Y	Y	N	Y	Y	Y	Y	Y	Y
McCarthy	N	N	Y	Y	Y	Y	Y	Y	Y	Y	Y	Y	Y	Y	Y	Y	Y	Y	Y	Y
McGuire	Y	Y	Y	Y	Y	Y	Y	Y	Y	Y	Y	Y	Y	Y	Y	Y	Y	Y	Y	Y
McKeon	Y	Y	Y	Y	Y	Y	Y	Y	Y	Y	Y	Y	Y	Y	Y	Y	Y	Y	Y	Y
Meyer	N	N	Y	Y	P	Y	Y	Y	Y	Y	Y	Y	Y	N	Y	Y	Y	Y	Y	Y
Mitchell	N	Y	Y	Y	Y	Y	Y	N	Y	Y	Y	Y	Y	N	Y	Y	Y	Y	Y	Y
Moffitt	N	Y	Y	Y	Y	Y	Y	Y	Y	Y	Y	Y	Y	N	Y	Y	Y	Y	Y	Y
Moore, Andrea	N	Y	Y	Y	N	Y	Y	Y	Y	Y	Y	Y	Y	N	Y	Y	Y	Y	Y	Y
Moore, Eugene	Y	Y	Y	Y	Y	Y	N	Y	Y	Y	Y	Y	Y	P	Y	Y	Y	Y	Y	Y
Morrow	Y	Y	Y	Y	Y	Y	Y	Y	Y	Y	Y	N	Y	P	Y	Y	Y	Y	Y	Y
Mulligan	N	Y	Y	Y	N	Y	Y	Y	Y	Y	Y	Y	N	N	Y	Y	Y	Y	Y	Y
Murphy	Y	Y	Y	Y	Y	Y	Y	Y	Y	Y	Y	Y	Y	Y	Y	Y	Y	Y	Y	Y
Myers, Richard	N	Y	Y	Y	N	Y	Y	Y	Y	Y	Y	Y	Y	N	Y	Y	Y	Y	Y	Y
Noland	N	N	Y	Y	Y	Y	Y	Y	Y	Y	Y	Y	Y	N	Y	Y	Y	Y	Y	Y

SB0366	SB0378	SB0381	SB0431	SB0508	SB0596	SB0680	SB0698	SB0700	SB0762
Y	Y	Y	Y	Y	Y	Y	Y	Y	Y
Y	Y	Y	Y	Y	Y	Y	Y	Y	Y
Y	Y	Y	Y	Y	A	Y	Y	Y	Y
Y	Y	Y	Y	Y	Y	Y	Y	Y	Y
Y	Y	Y	Y	Y	Y	Y	N	Y	Y
Y	N	Y	Y	Y	Y	Y	Y	Y	Y
A	Y	P	Y	Y	Y	A	Y	Y	Y
P	Y	Y	Y	A	Y	Y	N	Y	Y
Y	A	Y	Y	Y	Y	Y	Y	Y	Y
Y	Y	Y	Y	Y	Y	Y	N	Y	Y
Y	Y	Y	A	P	Y	Y	Y	Y	Y
Y	Y	Y	Y	P	Y	Y	Y	Y	Y
Y	Y	Y	Y	Y	Y	Y	Y	Y	Y
Y	Y	Y	Y	Y	N	Y	Y	Y	Y
Y	N	Y	Y	Y	N	A	N	Y	Y
Y	Y	Y	Y	Y	Y	Y	Y	Y	Y
Y	Y	Y	Y	Y	Y	Y	A	Y	Y
Y	Y	Y	Y	Y	Y	Y	Y	Y	Y
Y	Y	Y	Y	Y	N	Y	N	Y	Y
Y	Y	Y	Y	Y	Y	Y	Y	Y	Y
Y	Y	Y	Y	Y	Y	Y	Y	Y	Y
Y	Y	Y	Y	Y	Y	Y	Y	Y	Y
Y	N	Y	Y	Y	N	Y	Y	Y	Y
Y	N	Y	Y	Y	Y	Y	Y	Y	Y
Y	Y	Y	Y	Y	Y	Y	Y	Y	Y
Y	Y	Y	Y	Y	Y	Y	Y	Y	Y
Y	N	Y	Y	Y	N	Y	Y	Y	Y
Y	N	Y	Y	Y	N	Y	Y	Y	Y
Y	Y	Y	Y	Y	Y	Y	Y	Y	Y
Y	Y	Y	Y	N	Y	Y	Y	Y	Y
Y	Y	Y	Y	Y	Y	Y	Y	Y	Y
Y	Y	Y	Y	Y	Y	Y	Y	Y	Y
Y	Y	Y	Y	Y	Y	Y	Y	Y	Y
Y	Y	Y	Y	Y	Y	Y	Y	Y	Y
Y	Y	Y	Y	N	Y	Y	Y	Y	Y
Y	Y	Y	Y	N	Y	Y	Y	Y	Y
Y	Y	Y	Y	P	Y	Y	Y	Y	Y
Y	Y	Y	Y	P	Y	Y	Y	Y	Y
Y	Y	Y	Y	Y	N	Y	N	N	Y
Y	Y	Y	Y	Y	N	Y	Y	Y	Y

SB0772	SB0777	SB0795	SB0796	SB0797	SB0806	SB0819	SB0843	SB0856	SB0858
Y	Y	Y	Y	Y	Y	A	Y	Y	Y
Y	Y	Y	Y	Y	Y	Y	Y	Y	Y
Y	Y	Y	Y	Y	Y	Y	Y	Y	Y
Y	A	Y	Y	Y	Y	A	Y	Y	Y
Y	Y	Y	Y	Y	Y	Y	N	Y	Y
N	Y	Y	Y	Y	Y	Y	Y	Y	N
P	Y	Y	Y	Y	Y	Y	Y	Y	Y
N	Y	Y	Y	Y	Y	Y	Y	Y	Y
P	Y	Y	Y	Y	Y	Y	Y	Y	Y
Y	Y	Y	Y	Y	Y	Y	N	Y	N
P	Y	Y	Y	Y	Y	A	Y	Y	Y
P	Y	Y	Y	Y	Y	Y	Y	Y	Y
P	Y	Y	N	Y	Y	Y	Y	Y	Y
Y	Y	Y	Y	Y	Y	Y	Y	Y	N
Y	Y	Y	Y	Y	Y	Y	Y	Y	N
Y	A	Y	Y	Y	Y	A	N	Y	Y
A	Y	Y	Y	Y	Y	Y	Y	Y	Y
Y	Y	Y	Y	Y	Y	Y	Y	Y	Y
N	Y	Y	Y	Y	Y	Y	N	Y	N
N	Y	Y	Y	Y	Y	Y	Y	Y	Y
N	Y	Y	Y	Y	Y	Y	Y	Y	Y
Y	Y	Y	Y	Y	Y	N	Y	Y	Y
Y	Y	Y	Y	Y	Y	N	N	Y	Y
Y	Y	Y	Y	Y	Y	Y	N	Y	Y
Y	Y	Y	Y	Y	Y	Y	Y	Y	Y
Y	Y	Y	Y	Y	Y	Y	Y	Y	Y
Y	Y	Y	Y	Y	Y	Y	Y	Y	N
Y	Y	Y	Y	Y	Y	Y	Y	Y	N
Y	Y	Y	Y	Y	Y	Y	Y	Y	Y
Y	Y	Y	Y	Y	Y	N	N	Y	Y
P	Y	Y	Y	Y	Y	Y	Y	Y	Y
Y	Y	Y	Y	Y	Y	Y	Y	Y	N
Y	Y	Y	Y	Y	Y	Y	N	Y	Y
N	Y	Y	Y	Y	Y	N	Y	Y	Y
N	Y	Y	Y	Y	Y	Y	Y	Y	Y
P	Y	Y	Y	Y	Y	Y	Y	Y	Y
N	Y	Y	Y	Y	Y	Y	Y	Y	Y
P	Y	Y	Y	Y	Y	Y	Y	Y	Y
Y	Y	Y	Y	Y	Y	Y	Y	Y	N
N	Y	Y	Y	Y	Y	Y	Y	Y	Y

SB0899	SB0909	SB0927	SB0950	SB0953	SB0999	SB1024	SB1044	SB1050	SB1084
N	Y	Y	Y	Y	Y	Y	Y	Y	Y
Y	Y	Y	N	Y	Y	Y	Y	Y	Y
Y	Y	Y	N	Y	Y	Y	Y	N	Y
N	Y	Y	Y	Y	Y	Y	Y	Y	Y
N	Y	Y	Y	Y	Y	Y	Y	Y	Y
Y	Y	Y	N	Y	Y	Y	Y	Y	Y
Y	Y	Y	N	Y	Y	Y	Y	Y	Y
N	Y	Y	Y	Y	Y	Y	Y	Y	Y
N	Y	Y	N	Y	Y	Y	Y	Y	Y
N	Y	Y	Y	Y	Y	Y	Y	N	Y
Y	Y	Y	P	Y	Y	Y	Y	Y	Y
Y	Y	Y	P	Y	Y	Y	Y	Y	Y
Y	Y	Y	Y	Y	Y	Y	Y	Y	Y
N	Y	Y	Y	N	Y	Y	Y	Y	Y
N	Y	Y	Y	N	Y	Y	Y	Y	Y
N	Y	Y	Y	Y	Y	Y	Y	Y	Y
N	Y	Y	Y	Y	Y	Y	Y	Y	Y
Y	Y	Y	Y	Y	Y	Y	Y	Y	Y
N	Y	Y	Y	Y	Y	Y	P	N	Y
N	Y	Y	N	Y	Y	Y	Y	Y	Y
N	Y	Y	Y	Y	Y	Y	Y	Y	Y
N	Y	Y	Y	Y	Y	Y	Y	Y	Y
N	Y	Y	Y	N	Y	Y	Y	A	Y
Y	Y	A	Y	Y	Y	Y	Y	Y	Y
Y	Y	Y	Y	Y	Y	Y	Y	Y	Y
Y	Y	Y	N	Y	Y	Y	Y	N	Y
N	Y	N	Y	N	Y	Y	Y	Y	Y
N	Y	N	Y	Y	Y	Y	Y	Y	Y
N	Y	Y	Y	Y	Y	Y	Y	Y	Y
Y	Y	Y	Y	Y	Y	Y	Y	Y	Y
N	Y	Y	Y	Y	Y	Y	Y	Y	Y
N	Y	Y	Y	Y	Y	Y	Y	N	Y
N	Y	Y	Y	Y	Y	Y	Y	Y	Y
N	Y	Y	Y	Y	Y	Y	Y	Y	Y
Y	Y	Y	Y	Y	Y	Y	Y	Y	Y
P	Y	Y	N	Y	Y	Y	Y	Y	Y
N	Y	A	P	Y	Y	Y	Y	Y	Y
Y	Y	Y	P	Y	Y	Y	Y	Y	Y
N	Y	Y	Y	Y	Y	Y	Y	Y	Y
N	Y	Y	Y	Y	Y	Y	Y	N	Y

House Member	SB0021	SB0051	SB0054	SB0069	SB0073	SB0076	SB0087	SB0103	SB0107	SB0110	SB0123	SB0140	SB0160	SB0166	SB0225	SB0236	SB0248	SB0317	SB0327	SB0345
Novak	N	N	Y	Y	Y	Y	Y	Y	Y	Y	Y	Y	Y	Y	Y	Y	Y	Y	Y	Y
O'Brien	N	N	Y	Y	Y	Y	Y	Y	Y	Y	Y	Y	Y	N	Y	Y	Y	Y	Y	Y
Pankau	N	Y	Y	Y	N	Y	Y	Y	Y	Y	Y	Y	Y	N	Y	Y	Y	Y	Y	Y
Parke	N	N	Y	Y	Y	Y	Y	Y	Y	Y	Y	Y	Y	N	Y	Y	Y	Y	Y	Y
Persico	Y	Y	Y	Y	N	Y	Y	Y	Y	Y	Y	Y	Y	N	Y	Y	Y	Y	Y	Y
Phelps	Y	N	Y	Y	Y	Y	Y	Y	Y	Y	Y	Y	Y	N	Y	Y	Y	Y	Y	Y
Poe	N	Y	Y	Y	N	Y	Y	N	Y	Y	Y	Y	Y	N	Y	Y	Y	Y	Y	Y
Pugh	Y	Y	Y	Y	Y	Y	Y	Y	Y	Y	Y	Y	Y	P	Y	Y	Y	Y	Y	Y
Reitz	X	X	X	X	X	X	X	X	X	X	X	X	X	X	X	X	X	X	X	X
Ronen	Y	Y	Y	Y	Y	Y	Y	Y	Y	Y	Y	Y	N	Y	Y	Y	Y	Y	Y	Y
Roskam	N	Y	Y	N	N	Y	Y	Y	Y	Y	Y	Y	Y	N	Y	Y	Y	Y	Y	Y
Rutherford	N	N	Y	Y	N	Y	Y	Y	Y	Y	Y	Y	Y	N	Y	Y	Y	Y	Y	Y
Ryder	N	Y	Y	Y	N	Y	Y	Y	Y	Y	Y	Y	Y	N	Y	Y	Y	Y	Y	Y
Santiago	Y	Y	Y	Y	Y	Y	Y	Y	Y	Y	Y	Y	Y	Y	Y	Y	Y	Y	Y	Y
Saviano	Y	Y	Y	Y	N	Y	Y	Y	Y	Y	Y	Y	Y	N	Y	Y	Y	Y	Y	Y
Schakowsky	Y	Y	Y	Y	Y	Y	Y	Y	Y	Y	Y	Y	N	Y	Y	Y	Y	Y	Y	Y
Schoenberg	Y	N	Y	Y	Y	Y	Y	Y	Y	Y	Y	Y	Y	Y	Y	Y	Y	Y	Y	Y
Scott	Y	Y	Y	Y	Y	Y	Y	Y	Y	Y	Y	Y	Y	Y	Y	Y	Y	Y	Y	Y
Scully	N	N	Y	Y	Y	Y	Y	Y	Y	Y	Y	Y	Y	Y	E	Y	Y	Y	Y	Y
Silva	Y	Y	Y	Y	Y	Y	P	Y	Y	Y	Y	Y	N	Y	Y	Y	Y	Y	Y	Y
Skinner	N	Y	Y	Y	Y	Y	N	Y	Y	Y	Y	Y	Y	N	Y	Y	Y	Y	Y	Y
Slone	Y	Y	A	Y	Y	Y	Y	Y	Y	Y	Y	Y	N	Y	Y	Y	Y	Y	Y	Y
Smith, Michael	Y	N	Y	Y	Y	Y	Y	Y	Y	Y	Y	Y	N	A	Y	Y	Y	Y	Y	Y
Stephens	N	Y	Y	Y	P	Y	Y	Y	Y	Y	Y	Y	Y	N	Y	Y	Y	Y	Y	Y
Stroger	Y	Y	Y	Y	Y	Y	P	Y	Y	Y	Y	Y	Y	P	Y	Y	Y	Y	Y	Y
Tenhouse	Y	Y	Y	Y	Y	Y	Y	Y	Y	Y	Y	Y	Y	N	Y	Y	Y	Y	Y	Y
Turner, Arthur	Y	Y	Y	Y	Y	Y	Y	Y	Y	Y	Y	Y	Y	Y	Y	Y	Y	Y	Y	Y
Turner, John	N	N	Y	Y	Y	Y	Y	N	Y	N	Y	A	Y	N	Y	Y	Y	Y	Y	Y
Wait	Y	Y	Y	Y	Y	Y	Y	Y	Y	Y	Y	Y	Y	N	Y	Y	Y	Y	Y	Y
Weaver, Michael	Y	N	Y	Y	Y	Y	Y	Y	Y	Y	Y	Y	A	N	Y	Y	Y	Y	Y	Y
Winkel	N	Y	Y	Y	Y	Y	Y	N	Y	Y	Y	Y	Y	N	Y	Y	Y	Y	Y	Y
Winters	Y	Y	Y	Y	Y	Y	Y	Y	Y	Y	Y	Y	Y	N	Y	Y	Y	Y	Y	Y
Wirsing	N	N	Y	Y	N	Y	Y	Y	Y	Y	Y	Y	Y	N	Y	Y	Y	Y	Y	Y
Wojcik	N	Y	Y	Y	P	Y	Y	Y	Y	Y	Y	Y	Y	N	Y	Y	Y	Y	Y	Y
Wood	N	Y	Y	Y	N	Y	Y	Y	Y	Y	Y	Y	Y	N	Y	Y	Y	Y	Y	Y
Woolard	Y	N	Y	Y	Y	Y	Y	Y	Y	Y	Y	Y	Y	N	Y	Y	Y	Y	Y	Y
Younge	Y	Y	Y	Y	Y	Y	Y	Y	Y	Y	A	Y	Y	Y	A	Y	Y	Y	Y	Y
Zickus	Y	Y	Y	Y	P	Y	Y	N	Y	Y	Y	Y	Y	N	Y	Y	Y	Y	Y	Y
Hughes	N	Y	Y	Y	Y	Y	Y	Y	Y	Y	Y	Y	Y	N	Y	Y	Y	Y	Y	Y
Deering	N	N	Y	Y	Y	Y	Y	Y	Y	Y	Y	A	Y	N	Y	Y	Y	Y	Y	Y
Kotlarz	X	A	X	X	X	X	Y	X	X	X	X	X	X	X	X	X	X	X	X	X

SB0366	SB0378	SB0381	SB0431	SB0508	SB0596	SB0680	SB0698	SB0700	SB0762	SB0772	SB0777	SB0795	SB0796	SB0797	SB0806	SB0819	SB0843	SB0856	SB0858	SB0899	SB0909	SB0927	SB0950	SB0953	SB0999	SB1024	SB1044	SB1050	SB1084
Y	Y	Y	Y	Y	Y	Y	Y	Y	Y	Y	Y	Y	Y	Y	Y	Y	Y	Y	Y	N	Y	Y	N	Y	Y	Y	Y	Y	Y
Y	Y	Y	Y	Y	N	Y	Y	Y	Y	Y	Y	Y	Y	Y	Y	Y	Y	Y	N	N	Y	N	N	Y	Y	Y	Y	Y	Y
Y	Y	Y	Y	Y	Y	Y	Y	Y	Y	N	Y	Y	Y	Y	Y	Y	N	Y	Y	N	Y	Y	Y	Y	Y	Y	Y	Y	Y
Y	Y	Y	Y	Y	Y	Y	Y	Y	Y	A	Y	Y	Y	Y	Y	Y	Y	Y	Y	N	Y	Y	N	Y	Y	Y	Y	Y	Y
Y	Y	Y	Y	Y	Y	Y	Y	Y	Y	N	Y	Y	Y	Y	Y	Y	Y	Y	Y	N	Y	Y	Y	Y	Y	Y	Y	Y	Y
Y	Y	Y	Y	Y	Y	Y	P	Y	Y	Y	Y	Y	Y	Y	Y	Y	Y	Y	P	A	Y	Y	N	Y	Y	Y	Y	N	Y
Y	Y	Y	Y	Y	N	Y	Y	Y	Y	Y	Y	Y	Y	Y	Y	Y	N	Y	N	N	Y	Y	Y	N	Y	Y	Y	Y	Y
Y	Y	Y	Y	N	Y	Y	Y	Y	Y	N	Y	Y	Y	Y	Y	Y	Y	Y	Y	P	Y	Y	N	Y	Y	Y	Y	P	Y
X	X	X	X	X	X	X	X	X	X	X	X	X	X	X	X	X	X	X	X	X	X	X	X	X	X	X	X	X	X
Y	Y	Y	Y	N	Y	Y	Y	Y	Y	Y	Y	Y	Y	Y	Y	Y	Y	Y	Y	Y	Y	N	Y	Y	Y	Y	Y	Y	Y
Y	Y	Y	Y	Y	Y	Y	Y	Y	Y	N	Y	Y	Y	Y	Y	Y	P	Y	Y	N	Y	Y	Y	Y	Y	Y	Y	Y	Y
Y	Y	Y	Y	Y	Y	Y	Y	Y	Y	N	Y	Y	Y	Y	Y	A	Y	Y	Y	N	Y	Y	Y	Y	Y	Y	Y	Y	Y
Y	Y	Y	Y	Y	Y	Y	Y	Y	Y	N	Y	Y	Y	Y	Y	Y	Y	Y	Y	N	Y	Y	Y	Y	Y	Y	Y	Y	Y
Y	Y	Y	Y	Y	Y	Y	Y	Y	Y	Y	Y	Y	Y	Y	Y	N	Y	Y	Y	Y	Y	Y	Y	Y	Y	Y	Y	Y	Y
Y	Y	Y	Y	Y	Y	Y	Y	Y	Y	Y	Y	Y	Y	Y	Y	Y	Y	Y	Y	N	Y	Y	Y	Y	Y	Y	Y	Y	Y
Y	Y	Y	Y	N	Y	Y	Y	Y	Y	Y	Y	Y	Y	Y	Y	N	Y	Y	Y	N	Y	N	Y	Y	Y	Y	Y	Y	Y
Y	Y	Y	Y	Y	Y	Y	Y	Y	Y	Y	Y	Y	Y	Y	Y	N	Y	Y	Y	N	Y	N	Y	Y	Y	Y	Y	Y	Y
Y	Y	Y	Y	N	Y	Y	Y	Y	N	Y	Y	Y	Y	Y	Y	A	Y	Y	Y	Y	Y	Y	Y	Y	Y	Y	Y	Y	Y
Y	N	Y	Y	Y	N	Y	Y	Y	Y	Y	Y	Y	Y	Y	Y	Y	Y	Y	N	N	Y	N	Y	Y	Y	Y	Y	N	Y
Y	Y	Y	Y	N	Y	Y	Y	Y	Y	N	Y	Y	Y	Y	Y	Y	Y	Y	N	N	Y	N	Y	Y	Y	Y	Y	Y	Y
Y	Y	Y	Y	Y	Y	Y	Y	Y	Y	A	Y	Y	Y	Y	Y	Y	Y	Y	Y	N	Y	Y	Y	Y	Y	Y	Y	Y	Y
Y	Y	Y	Y	Y	Y	Y	Y	Y	Y	A	Y	Y	Y	Y	Y	N	Y	Y	Y	Y	Y	Y	Y	Y	Y	Y	Y	Y	Y
Y	Y	Y	Y	Y	Y	Y	A	Y	Y	Y	Y	Y	Y	Y	Y	Y	Y	A	Y	N	Y	Y	Y	Y	Y	Y	Y	Y	Y
Y	Y	Y	Y	Y	Y	Y	N	Y	Y	P	Y	Y	Y	Y	Y	Y	N	Y	Y	N	Y	Y	N	Y	Y	Y	Y	Y	Y
Y	Y	Y	Y	P	Y	Y	Y	Y	Y	N	Y	Y	Y	Y	Y	Y	Y	Y	Y	Y	Y	Y	Y	Y	Y	Y	Y	P	Y
Y	Y	Y	Y	Y	Y	Y	N	Y	Y	N	Y	Y	Y	Y	Y	Y	N	Y	Y	N	Y	Y	N	Y	Y	Y	Y	Y	Y
Y	Y	Y	Y	Y	Y	Y	Y	Y	Y	N	Y	Y	N	Y	Y	Y	Y	Y	Y	N	Y	Y	Y	Y	Y	Y	Y	Y	Y
Y	N	Y	Y	Y	Y	Y	N	Y	Y	N	Y	Y	Y	Y	Y	Y	Y	Y	N	N	Y	Y	N	N	Y	Y	Y	N	Y
Y	Y	Y	Y	Y	Y	Y	Y	Y	Y	Y	Y	Y	Y	Y	Y	Y	N	Y	Y	N	Y	Y	Y	Y	Y	Y	Y	Y	Y
Y	Y	Y	Y	Y	Y	Y	N	Y	Y	N	Y	Y	Y	Y	Y	Y	Y	Y	Y	Y	Y	Y	N	Y	Y	Y	Y	N	Y
Y	Y	Y	Y	Y	N	Y	Y	Y	Y	Y	Y	Y	Y	N	Y	Y	Y	Y	N	N	Y	Y	Y	N	Y	Y	Y	Y	Y
Y	Y	Y	Y	Y	Y	Y	Y	Y	Y	Y	Y	Y	Y	Y	Y	Y	N	Y	Y	N	Y	Y	Y	Y	A	Y	Y	N	Y
Y	Y	Y	Y	Y	N	Y	Y	Y	Y	N	Y	Y	Y	Y	Y	Y	Y	Y	Y	N	Y	Y	Y	N	Y	Y	Y	Y	Y
Y	Y	Y	Y	A	A	Y	Y	Y	Y	N	Y	Y	Y	Y	Y	Y	N	Y	N	N	Y	Y	N	N	Y	Y	Y	Y	Y
Y	N	Y	Y	Y	N	Y	Y	Y	Y	Y	Y	Y	Y	Y	Y	Y	Y	Y	N	N	Y	Y	Y	Y	Y	Y	Y	Y	Y
Y	Y	Y	Y	Y	Y	Y	N	Y	Y	Y	Y	Y	Y	Y	Y	Y	Y	Y	Y	P	Y	Y	N	Y	Y	Y	Y	N	Y
Y	Y	A	Y	N	Y	Y	Y	Y	Y	N	Y	Y	Y	Y	Y	Y	Y	Y	Y	Y	Y	Y	N	Y	Y	Y	Y	Y	Y
Y	N	Y	Y	Y	N	Y	Y	Y	Y	Y	Y	Y	Y	Y	Y	N	N	Y	N	N	Y	Y	Y	Y	Y	Y	Y	N	Y
Y	Y	Y	Y	Y	Y	Y	Y	Y	Y	N	Y	Y	Y	Y	Y	A	Y	Y	Y	N	Y	Y	Y	Y	Y	Y	Y	Y	Y
Y	Y	Y	Y	Y	Y	Y	N	Y	Y	A	Y	Y	Y	Y	Y	Y	Y	Y	N	N	Y	Y	N	N	Y	Y	Y	Y	Y
X	X	X	X	X	X	X	X	X	X	X	X	X	X	X	X	X	X	X	X	X	X	X	X	X	X	X	X	X	X

House Member	SB1101	SB1103	SB1105	HB0008	HB0139	HB0348	HB0445	HB0456	HB0500	HB0556	HB0061	HB0107	HB0111	HB0126	HB0127	HB0154	HB0161	HB0165	HB0172	HB0229
Acevedo	Y	Y	Y	Y	Y	Y	Y	Y	Y	Y	Y	Y	Y	Y	Y	Y	Y	Y	Y	Y
Ackerman	Y	N	Y	Y	N	N	Y	Y	N	Y	N	Y	N	N	N	Y	N	Y	Y	N
Beaubien	Y	Y	Y	N	N	Y	Y	Y	Y	Y	N	A	N	Y	Y	Y	N	Y	Y	N
Bergman	Y	Y	Y	Y	N	Y	Y	Y	Y	Y	N	Y	N	N	Y	Y	N	Y	Y	Y
Biggert	Y	Y	Y	Y	N	N	Y	Y	N	Y	N	Y	Y	Y	N	Y	N	Y	Y	Y
Biggins	Y	Y	Y	Y	N	N	Y	Y	Y	Y	N	N	N	Y	N	Y	N	Y	Y	Y
Black	Y	N	Y	Y	N	N	Y	P	Y	Y	N	Y	Y	N	N	N	N	Y	Y	N
Boland	Y	Y	Y	Y	Y	Y	Y	Y	Y	Y	Y	Y	Y	Y	Y	Y	Y	Y	Y	N
Bost	Y	N	Y	Y	N	N	Y	Y	Y	Y	N	Y	Y	N	Y	Y	N	Y	Y	N
Bradford	Y	Y	Y	Y	N	Y	Y	Y	Y	Y	Y	Y	Y	Y	Y	Y	Y	Y	Y	N
Bradley	Y	Y	Y	Y	Y	X	X	X	Y	X	Y	Y	X	Y	Y	X	X	Y	Y	Y
Brady	Y	N	Y	N	N	N	Y	N	Y	Y	N	N	N	N	N	Y	N	Y	Y	N
Brosnahan	Y	Y	Y	Y	N	Y	Y	Y	Y	Y	Y	Y	Y	N	Y	Y	Y	Y	Y	N
Brown	X	X	X	X	X	X	X	X	X	X	X	X	X	X	X	X	X	X	X	X
Brunsvold	Y	N	Y	Y	Y	Y	Y	N	Y	Y	Y	Y	N	P	N	Y	Y	Y	Y	Y
Bugielski	Y	Y	Y	Y	Y	Y	Y	Y	E	Y	Y	Y	Y	Y	Y	Y	Y	Y	Y	Y
Burke	Y	Y	Y	Y	Y	Y	Y	Y	Y	Y	Y	Y	Y	Y	Y	Y	Y	P	Y	Y
Capparelli	Y	Y	Y	Y	Y	Y	Y	Y	Y	Y	Y	Y	Y	Y	Y	Y	Y	Y	Y	Y
Churchill	Y	N	Y	N	N	N	Y	Y	N	Y	N	N	Y	Y	N	Y	N	Y	Y	N
Clayton	Y	Y	Y	N	N	Y	Y	N	Y	Y	N	Y	N	Y	Y	Y	N	Y	Y	N
Coulson	Y	Y	Y	Y	N	N	Y	Y	Y	Y	N	Y	Y	Y	Y	Y	Y	Y	Y	N
Cowlishaw	Y	Y	Y	Y	N	N	Y	Y	Y	Y	N	Y	Y	Y	Y	Y	N	Y	Y	Y
Cross	Y	Y	Y	N	N	Y	N	Y	N	Y	Y	Y	Y	Y	Y	Y	N	P	Y	N
Crotty	Y	Y	Y	Y	N	Y	Y	Y	N	Y	Y	Y	Y	N	Y	Y	Y	Y	Y	N
Currie	Y	Y	Y	Y	Y	Y	Y	Y	Y	Y	Y	Y	Y	Y	Y	Y	Y	P	Y	Y
Curry	Y	Y	Y	Y	Y	Y	Y	Y	Y	Y	Y	Y	Y	Y	Y	Y	Y	Y	Y	N
Daniels	Y	Y	Y	Y	N	N	Y	Y	N	E	N	Y	Y	Y	Y	Y	N	Y	Y	Y
Dart	Y	Y	Y	Y	E	Y	Y	Y	Y	Y	Y	Y	Y	A	Y	Y	Y	Y	Y	Y
Davis, Monique	Y	Y	Y	Y	Y	P	Y	Y	Y	Y	A	Y	Y	Y	Y	Y	Y	N	Y	Y
Davis, Steve	Y	Y	Y	Y	Y	Y	Y	Y	N	Y	Y	Y	Y	Y	Y	Y	Y	Y	Y	Y
Deuchler	Y	Y	Y	Y	N	N	Y	Y	Y	Y	Y	Y	Y	Y	Y	Y	Y	Y	Y	N
Durkin	Y	Y	Y	N	N	Y	Y	N	Y	Y	Y	Y	N	Y	Y	Y	N	Y	Y	N
Erwin	Y	Y	Y	Y	Y	Y	Y	Y	Y	Y	Y	Y	Y	Y	Y	Y	Y	Y	Y	Y
Fantin	Y	Y	Y	Y	Y	Y	Y	Y	A	Y	Y	Y	Y	Y	Y	N	Y	Y	Y	Y
Feigenholtz	Y	Y	Y	Y	Y	Y	Y	Y	Y	Y	Y	Y	Y	Y	Y	Y	Y	Y	Y	Y
Flowers	Y	Y	Y	Y	N	Y	Y	Y	Y	Y	Y	Y	Y	Y	Y	Y	Y	Y	Y	Y
Fritchey	Y	Y	Y	Y	N	Y	Y	Y	Y	Y	Y	Y	Y	Y	Y	Y	Y	Y	Y	N
Gash	Y	Y	Y	Y	N	Y	Y	Y	Y	Y	Y	E	Y	E	Y	Y	Y	Y	Y	Y
Giglio	Y	Y	Y	Y	Y	Y	Y	Y	Y	Y	Y	Y	Y	N	Y	Y	Y	Y	Y	N
Giles	Y	Y	Y	Y	Y	Y	Y	Y	Y	Y	Y	P	Y	Y	Y	Y	A	P	Y	Y

HB0253	HB0260	HB0265	HB0271	HB0282	HB0297	HB0313	HB0314	HB0316	HB0318
Y	Y	N	Y	Y	Y	Y	Y	Y	N
A	Y	N	Y	Y	Y	Y	N	Y	N
Y	Y	Y	Y	Y	Y	Y	N	Y	N
Y	Y	N	Y	Y	Y	Y	N	Y	N
N	Y	N	Y	Y	Y	Y	N	Y	N
N	Y	Y	Y	Y	Y	Y	N	Y	N
N	N	Y	Y	Y	Y	Y	N	Y	N
N	Y	Y	Y	Y	Y	Y	Y	Y	Y
N	Y	Y	Y	Y	Y	Y	Y	Y	N
N	N	Y	Y	Y	Y	N	Y	Y	N
Y	Y	Y	X	Y	Y	Y	Y	X	N
Y	Y	N	Y	Y	Y	Y	N	Y	N
Y	N	N	Y	Y	Y	N	Y	Y	N
X	X	X	X	X	X	X	X	X	X
N	Y	Y	Y	Y	Y	Y	Y	Y	Y
Y	Y	Y	Y	Y	Y	Y	Y	Y	N
A	Y	Y	Y	Y	Y	Y	Y	Y	N
Y	Y	Y	Y	Y	Y	Y	Y	Y	N
N	Y	Y	Y	Y	Y	Y	N	Y	N
N	Y	Y	Y	Y	Y	Y	Y	Y	Y
N	Y	N	Y	Y	Y	Y	Y	Y	N
Y	Y	Y	Y	Y	Y	Y	Y	Y	N
Y	Y	A	Y	Y	Y	Y	N	Y	N
N	N	N	Y	Y	Y	N	Y	Y	N
N	Y	N	Y	Y	Y	Y	P	Y	Y
N	N	Y	Y	Y	Y	Y	Y	Y	N
N	Y	Y	Y	Y	Y	Y	N	Y	N
Y	Y	N	Y	Y	Y	A	Y	Y	N
N	Y	N	Y	Y	Y	Y	Y	Y	Y
N	Y	Y	Y	Y	Y	Y	Y	Y	N
N	Y	N	Y	Y	Y	Y	N	Y	N
Y	Y	N	Y	Y	Y	Y	A	Y	N
Y	Y	Y	Y	Y	Y	Y	Y	Y	Y
N	Y	Y	Y	Y	Y	Y	Y	Y	Y
N	Y	Y	Y	Y	Y	Y	Y	Y	Y
Y	N	Y	Y	Y	Y	Y	Y	Y	Y
P	Y	N	Y	Y	Y	Y	Y	Y	N
N	E	N	Y	Y	Y	Y	E	Y	N
N	N	Y	Y	Y	Y	N	Y	Y	N
Y	Y	Y	Y	Y	Y	Y	Y	A	Y

HB0319	HB0347	HB0379	HB0381	HB0383	HB0391	HB0400	HB0401	HB0424	HB0452
N	Y	Y	Y	N	Y	Y	Y	Y	Y
N	Y	Y	Y	Y	Y	Y	Y	Y	Y
Y	Y	Y	Y	N	Y	Y	Y	Y	Y
N	N	Y	Y	Y	N	Y	Y	Y	Y
Y	Y	Y	Y	N	Y	Y	Y	Y	Y
N	Y	Y	Y	Y	N	Y	Y	Y	Y
N	Y	Y	Y	Y	N	Y	Y	N	N
Y	Y	Y	Y	N	N	Y	Y	Y	Y
N	Y	Y	Y	Y	N	Y	Y	Y	Y
Y	Y	Y	Y	N	Y	Y	Y	Y	Y
X	Y	Y	Y	X	X	X	X	Y	Y
N	Y	Y	Y	Y	N	Y	Y	Y	Y
N	Y	Y	Y	Y	N	Y	Y	Y	Y
X	X	X	X	X	X	X	X	X	X
N	Y	Y	Y	Y	N	Y	Y	Y	Y
N	Y	Y	Y	Y	N	Y	Y	Y	Y
Y	Y	Y	Y	N	Y	Y	Y	Y	Y
N	Y	Y	Y	Y	N	Y	Y	Y	Y
N	Y	Y	Y	Y	N	Y	Y	Y	Y
Y	Y	Y	Y	N	Y	Y	Y	Y	Y
Y	Y	Y	Y	N	Y	Y	Y	Y	Y
N	A	Y	Y	Y	N	Y	Y	Y	Y
Y	Y	Y	Y	N	Y	Y	Y	Y	Y
Y	Y	Y	Y	Y	N	Y	Y	Y	Y
Y	Y	Y	Y	N	Y	Y	Y	Y	Y
Y	Y	Y	Y	N	Y	Y	Y	Y	Y
N	Y	Y	Y	Y	N	Y	Y	Y	Y
Y	Y	Y	Y	A	Y	Y	Y	Y	Y
Y	Y	Y	Y	N	Y	Y	Y	Y	Y
Y	Y	Y	Y	N	Y	Y	Y	Y	Y
Y	A	Y	Y	N	Y	Y	Y	Y	Y
N	Y	Y	Y	Y	N	Y	Y	Y	Y
Y	Y	Y	Y	N	Y	Y	Y	Y	Y
P	Y	Y	Y	N	Y	Y	Y	Y	Y
Y	Y	Y	Y	N	Y	Y	Y	Y	Y
Y	Y	Y	Y	N	Y	Y	Y	Y	Y
Y	P	Y	Y	N	Y	Y	Y	Y	Y
Y	Y	Y	Y	N	Y	Y	Y	Y	Y
Y	Y	Y	Y	N	Y	Y	Y	Y	Y
A	Y	Y	Y	A	A	Y	Y	Y	P

HB0480	HB0489	HB0522	HB0523	HB0524	HB0540	HB0571	HB0581	HB0585	HB0586
Y	Y	Y	Y	Y	Y	N	Y	N	Y
Y	Y	Y	N	Y	Y	Y	Y	Y	Y
Y	Y	Y	N	Y	Y	Y	Y	Y	Y
Y	Y	Y	N	Y	Y	N	Y	Y	Y
Y	Y	Y	N	Y	Y	N	Y	Y	Y
Y	Y	Y	N	Y	Y	Y	Y	Y	Y
Y	N	N	N	Y	Y	N	Y	Y	Y
Y	Y	N	Y	Y	Y	Y	Y	Y	Y
Y	Y	Y	N	Y	Y	Y	Y	Y	Y
Y	Y	Y	Y	Y	Y	Y	N	N	Y
Y	Y	Y	Y	Y	Y	Y	Y	X	Y
A	N	Y	N	Y	Y	Y	Y	Y	Y
Y	N	Y	Y	Y	Y	Y	N	N	Y
X	X	X	X	X	X	X	X	X	X
Y	Y	Y	Y	Y	Y	Y	Y	Y	Y
Y	Y	Y	Y	Y	Y	Y	Y	Y	Y
Y	A	Y	Y	Y	Y	Y	Y	Y	Y
Y	Y	Y	Y	Y	Y	Y	Y	Y	Y
Y	Y	Y	N	Y	Y	N	Y	Y	Y
Y	Y	Y	N	Y	Y	N	Y	Y	Y
Y	N	Y	N	Y	Y	P	N	Y	Y
Y	Y	Y	N	Y	Y	Y	Y	Y	Y
Y	Y	Y	N	Y	Y	N	Y	Y	Y
Y	N	Y	Y	A	Y	Y	N	N	Y
P	Y	Y	Y	Y	Y	Y	Y	N	Y
Y	Y	Y	Y	Y	Y	Y	N	Y	Y
Y	Y	Y	N	Y	Y	Y	Y	Y	Y
Y	Y	Y	Y	A	Y	Y	Y	P	Y
Y	Y	Y	Y	Y	Y	Y	Y	A	Y
Y	Y	Y	N	Y	Y	Y	N	N	Y
Y	Y	Y	N	Y	Y	N	Y	Y	Y
Y	Y	Y	P	Y	Y	Y	Y	Y	Y
Y	Y	Y	Y	Y	Y	Y	Y	Y	Y
Y	Y	Y	Y	Y	Y	Y	Y	N	Y
Y	E	Y	Y	Y	Y	Y	Y	Y	Y
Y	Y	Y	Y	Y	Y	Y	Y	N	Y
Y	Y	Y	Y	Y	Y	Y	Y	N	Y
E	N	Y	Y	Y	Y	E	Y	Y	Y
Y	Y	Y	Y	Y	Y	Y	N	N	Y
Y	Y	Y	Y	Y	Y	Y	Y	P	Y

House Member	SB1101	SB1103	SB1105	HB0008	HB0019	HB0038	HB0045	HB0046	HB0050	HB0056	HB0061	HB0107	HB0111	HB0126	HB0127	HB0154	HB0161	HB0165	HB0172	HB0229
Granberg	Y	Y	Y	Y	N	Y	Y	N	A	Y	Y	Y	Y	Y	Y	Y	Y	Y	Y	Y
Hannig	Y	N	Y	A	N	Y	Y	Y	Y	Y	Y	Y	N	A	Y	Y	Y	Y	Y	Y
Hartke	Y	N	Y	Y	Y	Y	Y	N	Y	Y	Y	Y	Y	Y	Y	Y	Y	Y	Y	Y
Hassert	Y	Y	Y	Y	N	Y	Y	A	Y	Y	N	Y	N	Y	Y	Y	Y	Y	Y	Y
Hoeft	Y	Y	Y	Y	N	Y	Y	Y	Y	Y	N	Y	N	P	Y	Y	N	Y	Y	N
Holbrook	Y	N	Y	Y	N	Y	Y	N	Y	Y	Y	Y	Y	Y	Y	Y	Y	Y	Y	Y
Howard	Y	Y	Y	Y	Y	Y	Y	Y	Y	Y	A	Y	Y	Y	Y	Y	Y	N	Y	Y
Johnson, Tim	Y	Y	Y	Y	N	N	Y	Y	P	Y	N	Y	N	P	N	Y	N	Y	Y	N
Johnson, Tom	Y	N	Y	Y	N	Y	Y	Y	Y	Y	N	A	N	Y	P	Y	N	N	Y	N
Jones, John	Y	N	Y	Y	N	N	Y	N	Y	Y	N	Y	Y	N	N	Y	N	Y	Y	N
Jones, Lovana	Y	Y	Y	Y	Y	A	A	Y	Y	Y	Y	A	Y	Y	Y	A	Y	N	Y	Y
Jones, Shirley	Y	Y	E	Y	A	Y	Y	Y	Y	E	P	A	Y	Y	Y	Y	Y	N	Y	Y
Kenner	Y	Y	Y	Y	Y	Y	Y	Y	Y	Y	Y	Y	Y	Y	Y	Y	Y	Y	Y	Y
Klingler	Y	Y	Y	Y	N	Y	Y	Y	Y	Y	N	Y	Y	Y	Y	Y	N	Y	Y	N
Kosel	Y	Y	Y	Y	N	N	Y	Y	Y	Y	N	Y	N	N	Y	N	N	Y	Y	N
Krause	Y	Y	Y	Y	N	Y	Y	Y	Y	Y	N	Y	Y	Y	Y	Y	N	Y	Y	Y
Kubik	Y	Y	Y	Y	N	N	Y	Y	Y	Y	N	Y	Y	Y	Y	N	N	Y	Y	Y
Lang	Y	Y	Y	Y	Y	Y	Y	Y	Y	Y	Y	Y	Y	Y	Y	Y	Y	Y	Y	Y
Lawfer	Y	N	Y	Y	N	N	Y	Y	Y	Y	N	N	N	Y	Y	Y	N	Y	Y	N
Leitch	Y	N	Y	Y	N	N	Y	N	Y	Y	N	Y	N	Y	A	Y	A	Y	Y	Y
Lindner	Y	Y	Y	Y	N	Y	Y	Y	Y	Y	N	Y	Y	Y	P	Y	N	Y	Y	N
Lopez	Y	Y	Y	Y	Y	Y	Y	Y	Y	Y	Y	Y	Y	Y	Y	Y	A	Y	Y	Y
Lyons, Eileen	Y	Y	Y	Y	N	Y	Y	Y	Y	Y	N	E	Y	Y	Y	Y	N	Y	Y	N
Lyons, Joseph	Y	Y	Y	Y	Y	Y	Y	Y	Y	Y	Y	Y	Y	Y	Y	Y	Y	Y	Y	Y
Madigan, Michael	Y	Y	Y	Y	Y	Y	Y	Y	Y	Y	Y	Y	Y	Y	Y	Y	Y	Y	Y	Y
Mautino	Y	N	Y	N	N	Y	Y	N	Y	Y	Y	Y	N	Y	N	Y	Y	Y	Y	Y
McAuliffe	Y	Y	Y	Y	N	Y	Y	Y	Y	Y	Y	Y	Y	Y	Y	Y	N	Y	Y	N
McCarthy	Y	Y	Y	Y	Y	Y	Y	Y	Y	Y	Y	Y	Y	Y	Y	Y	Y	Y	Y	N
McGuire	Y	Y	Y	Y	N	Y	Y	Y	Y	Y	Y	Y	Y	Y	Y	Y	Y	Y	Y	N
McKeon	Y	Y	Y	Y	Y	Y	Y	Y	Y	Y	Y	Y	Y	Y	Y	Y	Y	N	Y	Y
Meyer	Y	Y	Y	Y	N	N	Y	Y	Y	Y	N	Y	Y	Y	Y	Y	N	Y	Y	N
Mitchell	Y	Y	Y	Y	N	Y	Y	Y	Y	Y	N	N	N	Y	N	Y	N	Y	Y	N
Moffitt	Y	N	Y	Y	N	Y	Y	Y	Y	Y	Y	Y	N	Y	Y	A	N	Y	Y	N
Moore, Andrea	Y	Y	Y	Y	N	Y	Y	Y	Y	Y	N	Y	Y	Y	Y	Y	N	Y	Y	Y
Moore, Eugene	Y	Y	Y	N	Y	Y	Y	Y	Y	Y	Y	Y	Y	Y	Y	Y	Y	P	Y	Y
Morrow	Y	Y	Y	Y	Y	Y	Y	Y	Y	Y	A	Y	Y	Y	Y	Y	Y	N	Y	Y
Mulligan	Y	Y	Y	Y	N	N	Y	Y	Y	Y	N	Y	Y	Y	Y	Y	N	Y	A	Y
Murphy	Y	Y	Y	P	Y	Y	Y	Y	Y	Y	A	Y	Y	Y	Y	Y	Y	N	Y	Y
Myers, Richard	Y	N	Y	Y	N	Y	Y	Y	Y	Y	N	Y	N	Y	Y	Y	N	Y	Y	N
Noland	Y	N	Y	Y	N	N	Y	Y	Y	Y	N	Y	N	Y	Y	Y	N	Y	Y	N

HB0253	HB0260	HB0265	HB0271	HB0282	HB0297	HB0313	HB0314	HB0316	HB0318	HB0319	HB0347	HB0379	HB0381	HB0383	HB0391	HB0400	HB0401	HB0424	HB0452	HB0480	HB0489	HB0522	HB0523	HB0524	HB0540	HB0571	HB0581	HB0585	HB0586
Y	Y	Y	Y	Y	Y	Y	Y	Y	N	N	Y	Y	Y	N	Y	Y	Y	Y	Y	A	Y	Y	N	Y	Y	Y	Y	Y	P
Y	Y	Y	Y	Y	Y	Y	Y	Y	Y	N	Y	Y	Y	N	Y	Y	Y	Y	Y	Y	Y	Y	Y	Y	Y	Y	Y	Y	Y
Y	Y	Y	Y	Y	Y	Y	Y	Y	Y	N	Y	Y	Y	N	Y	Y	Y	Y	Y	Y	Y	Y	N	Y	Y	Y	Y	N	Y
N	N	Y	Y	Y	Y	Y	N	Y	N	Y	Y	Y	Y	N	Y	Y	Y	Y	Y	Y	Y	Y	N	Y	Y	Y	Y	Y	Y
N	Y	N	Y	Y	Y	Y	N	Y	N	Y	N	Y	Y	N	Y	Y	Y	Y	Y	Y	Y	Y	N	Y	Y	N	N	Y	Y
N	Y	Y	Y	Y	Y	Y	Y	Y	N	N	Y	Y	Y	N	Y	Y	Y	Y	Y	Y	Y	Y	Y	Y	Y	Y	Y	N	Y
P	Y	Y	Y	Y	Y	Y	Y	Y	Y	Y	A	Y	Y	N	Y	Y	Y	A	Y	Y	Y	Y	Y	Y	Y	Y	Y	N	Y
N	Y	Y	Y	Y	Y	Y	Y	Y	N	N	Y	Y	Y	N	Y	Y	Y	Y	Y	Y	Y	Y	N	Y	Y	Y	Y	Y	Y
Y	Y	N	Y	Y	Y	Y	N	Y	N	N	P	Y	Y	N	Y	Y	Y	Y	Y	Y	Y	N	N	Y	Y	Y	Y	Y	Y
Y	N	Y	Y	Y	Y	Y	Y	Y	N	N	Y	Y	Y	N	Y	Y	Y	Y	Y	Y	Y	Y	N	Y	Y	Y	N	Y	Y
N	Y	Y	A	Y	Y	Y	Y	Y	Y	Y	Y	Y	Y	N	Y	Y	Y	Y	Y	A	Y	Y	P	Y	Y	Y	Y	N	Y
Y	Y	Y	Y	Y	Y	E	Y	Y	Y	A	Y	Y	Y	N	Y	Y	Y	Y	Y	Y	Y	Y	P	Y	Y	Y	Y	N	Y
P	Y	Y	Y	Y	Y	Y	Y	Y	Y	Y	Y	Y	Y	N	Y	Y	Y	Y	Y	Y	Y	Y	Y	Y	Y	Y	Y	P	Y
N	Y	Y	Y	Y	Y	Y	Y	Y	N	Y	Y	Y	Y	N	Y	Y	Y	Y	Y	Y	Y	Y	N	Y	Y	Y	Y	Y	Y
N	N	N	Y	Y	Y	N	A	Y	N	Y	Y	Y	Y	Y	N	Y	Y	Y	Y	Y	A	Y	N	Y	Y	Y	N	Y	Y
N	Y	Y	Y	Y	Y	Y	Y	Y	N	Y	Y	Y	Y	N	Y	Y	Y	Y	Y	Y	Y	Y	N	Y	Y	Y	Y	Y	Y
N	Y	Y	Y	Y	Y	Y	N	Y	N	N	Y	Y	Y	Y	A	Y	Y	Y	Y	Y	Y	Y	N	Y	Y	Y	Y	Y	Y
Y	Y	Y	Y	Y	Y	Y	Y	Y	P	Y	Y	Y	Y	N	Y	Y	Y	Y	Y	Y	Y	Y	Y	Y	Y	Y	Y	N	Y
N	Y	N	P	Y	Y	N	N	Y	N	N	Y	Y	Y	Y	N	Y	Y	N	Y	Y	Y	N	N	Y	Y	N	Y	Y	P
Y	Y	Y	Y	Y	Y	Y	N	Y	Y	N	Y	A	Y	Y	N	Y	Y	Y	Y	Y	Y	N	N	Y	Y	N	Y	Y	Y
Y	Y	Y	Y	Y	Y	Y	Y	Y	N	Y	Y	Y	Y	N	Y	Y	Y	Y	Y	Y	Y	Y	P	Y	Y	N	Y	Y	Y
Y	N	Y	Y	Y	Y	Y	Y	E	N	Y	Y	Y	Y	N	Y	Y	Y	Y	Y	Y	N	Y	N	Y	Y	Y	Y	E	Y
N	Y	N	Y	Y	Y	Y	A	Y	N	N	Y	Y	Y	Y	N	Y	Y	Y	Y	E	Y	Y	N	Y	Y	A	Y	Y	Y
Y	Y	Y	Y	Y	Y	Y	Y	Y	N	N	Y	Y	Y	Y	N	Y	Y	Y	Y	Y	Y	Y	Y	Y	Y	Y	Y	N	Y
Y	Y	Y	Y	Y	Y	Y	Y	Y	Y	N	Y	Y	Y	Y	N	Y	Y	Y	Y	Y	Y	Y	Y	Y	Y	Y	Y	N	P
Y	Y	Y	Y	Y	Y	Y	N	A	Y	Y	Y	Y	Y	Y	N	Y	Y	Y	Y	Y	Y	Y	N	Y	Y	Y	Y	Y	Y
Y	N	N	Y	Y	Y	Y	Y	Y	N	N	Y	Y	Y	Y	N	Y	Y	Y	Y	Y	N	Y	N	Y	Y	Y	N	N	Y
A	N	N	Y	Y	Y	N	Y	Y	N	N	Y	Y	Y	Y	N	Y	Y	Y	Y	Y	N	Y	Y	A	Y	Y	N	Y	Y
Y	Y	Y	Y	Y	Y	Y	Y	Y	N	N	Y	Y	Y	Y	N	Y	Y	Y	Y	Y	Y	Y	Y	Y	Y	Y	A	N	Y
N	Y	Y	Y	Y	Y	Y	Y	Y	Y	Y	Y	Y	Y	N	Y	Y	Y	Y	Y	Y	Y	Y	Y	Y	Y	Y	Y	N	Y
N	Y	N	Y	Y	Y	Y	N	Y	N	N	Y	Y	Y	Y	N	Y	Y	Y	Y	Y	Y	Y	N	Y	Y	Y	Y	Y	Y
N	Y	Y	Y	Y	Y	Y	Y	Y	N	N	A	A	Y	N	Y	Y	Y	Y	Y	Y	Y	Y	N	Y	Y	N	N	Y	Y
N	Y	Y	Y	Y	Y	Y	Y	Y	N	N	Y	Y	Y	Y	N	Y	Y	Y	Y	Y	N	Y	N	Y	Y	Y	Y	Y	Y
Y	Y	Y	Y	Y	Y	Y	N	Y	N	Y	A	Y	Y	N	Y	Y	Y	Y	Y	Y	Y	Y	N	Y	Y	N	Y	Y	Y
A	Y	Y	Y	Y	Y	Y	Y	Y	N	Y	Y	Y	Y	N	Y	Y	Y	Y	Y	Y	A	Y	A	Y	Y	Y	Y	Y	Y
Y	Y	N	Y	Y	Y	Y	Y	Y	A	Y	Y	Y	Y	N	Y	Y	Y	Y	Y	Y	Y	Y	Y	Y	Y	Y	Y	P	Y
N	Y	N	Y	Y	Y	Y	A	Y	N	Y	Y	Y	Y	N	Y	Y	Y	Y	Y	Y	Y	Y	N	Y	Y	Y	Y	Y	Y
Y	Y	Y	Y	Y	Y	Y	A	Y	Y	Y	Y	Y	Y	N	Y	Y	Y	Y	Y	Y	Y	Y	P	Y	Y	Y	Y	Y	Y
Y	Y	Y	Y	Y	Y	Y	Y	Y	Y	N	Y	Y	Y	Y	N	Y	Y	Y	Y	Y	Y	Y	N	Y	Y	Y	Y	Y	Y
Y	Y	Y	Y	Y	Y	Y	N	Y	Y	N	Y	Y	Y	Y	N	Y	Y	Y	Y	Y	Y	Y	N	Y	Y	A	Y	Y	Y

House Member	SB 1101	SB 1103	SB 1105	HB 0008	HB 0019	HB 0038	HB 0045	HB 0046	HB 0050	HB 0056	HB 0061	HB 0107	HB 0111	HB 0126	HB 0127	HB 0154	HB 0161	HB 0165	HB 0172	HB 0229
Novak	Y	Y	Y	Y	Y	Y	Y	Y	Y	Y	Y	Y	Y	Y	N	Y	Y	Y	Y	Y
O'Brien	Y	Y	Y	Y	Y	Y	Y	Y	Y	Y	Y	Y	Y	N	Y	Y	Y	Y	Y	N
Pankau	Y	Y	Y	Y	Y	Y	Y	Y	N	Y	N	Y	N	Y	Y	Y	N	Y	Y	N
Parke	Y	P	Y	N	N	N	Y	N	Y	Y	N	N	N	N	Y	Y	N	Y	Y	N
Persico	Y	Y	Y	N	Y	Y	Y	Y	Y	Y	N	Y	Y	Y	Y	Y	Y	Y	Y	Y
Phelps	Y	Y	Y	Y	P	Y	Y	P	Y	Y	Y	Y	Y	Y	N	Y	Y	Y	Y	Y
Poe	Y	N	Y	Y	N	N	Y	Y	Y	Y	N	Y	N	Y	Y	Y	N	Y	Y	N
Pugh	Y	Y	Y	P	Y	Y	Y	Y	Y	Y	Y	Y	Y	Y	Y	P	A	N	Y	Y
Reitz	X	X	X	X	X	X	X	X	X	X	X	Y	X	X	X	X	X	X	X	X
Ronen	Y	Y	Y	Y	Y	Y	Y	Y	Y	Y	Y	Y	Y	Y	Y	Y	Y	P	Y	Y
Roskam	Y	N	Y	N	N	N	Y	P	Y	Y	N	A	N	Y	Y	Y	N	Y	Y	N
Rutherford	Y	N	Y	N	N	N	Y	N	N	Y	N	N	N	N	N	Y	N	Y	Y	N
Ryder	Y	N	Y	Y	N	E	E	Y	N	Y	N	N	Y	Y	N	E	N	Y	Y	N
Santiago	Y	Y	Y	Y	Y	Y	Y	Y	Y	Y	Y	Y	Y	Y	Y	Y	Y	Y	Y	Y
Saviano	Y	Y	Y	Y	N	N	Y	Y	Y	Y	Y	Y	Y	Y	Y	Y	N	Y	Y	Y
Schakowsky	Y	Y	Y	Y	Y	Y	Y	Y	Y	Y	Y	Y	Y	Y	Y	Y	Y	Y	Y	Y
Schoenberg	Y	Y	Y	Y	N	N	Y	Y	Y	Y	Y	Y	Y	Y	Y	Y	Y	Y	Y	Y
Scott	Y	Y	Y	Y	N	Y	Y	Y	Y	Y	Y	Y	Y	Y	Y	Y	Y	Y	Y	Y
Scully	Y	Y	Y	Y	N	Y	Y	Y	Y	Y	Y	Y	Y	Y	Y	Y	Y	Y	Y	N
Silva	Y	Y	Y	Y	Y	Y	Y	Y	Y	Y	Y	Y	A	Y	Y	Y	Y	N	Y	N
Skinner	Y	Y	Y	Y	N	N	P	Y	Y	Y	N	Y	N	N	Y	Y	Y	Y	Y	N
Slone	Y	Y	Y	Y	N	Y	Y	Y	Y	Y	Y	E	Y	Y	Y	Y	Y	Y	Y	Y
Smith, Michael	Y	Y	Y	Y	Y	Y	Y	Y	Y	Y	Y	Y	Y	Y	Y	Y	Y	Y	Y	Y
Stephens	Y	N	Y	Y	N	N	Y	N	Y	Y	N	Y	Y	N	N	Y	A	Y	Y	N
Stroger	Y	Y	Y	Y	Y	Y	Y	Y	Y	Y	Y	Y	Y	Y	Y	Y	Y	P	Y	Y
Tenhouse	Y	N	Y	Y	N	N	Y	Y	Y	Y	N	Y	N	Y	N	Y	N	Y	Y	N
Turner, Arthur	Y	Y	Y	Y	A	Y	Y	Y	Y	Y	Y	Y	Y	Y	P	Y	Y	N	Y	Y
Turner, John	Y	N	Y	N	N	N	Y	N	Y	Y	N	Y	N	Y	N	Y	N	P	Y	N
Wait	Y	N	Y	Y	N	N	Y	Y	Y	Y	P	Y	Y	Y	Y	Y	N	Y	Y	N
Weaver, Michael	Y	N	Y	Y	N	N	Y	N	N	Y	N	Y	Y	Y	N	Y	Y	Y	Y	N
Winkel	Y	A	Y	Y	N	Y	Y	Y	Y	Y	N	Y	Y	Y	Y	Y	Y	Y	Y	N
Winters	Y	N	Y	Y	N	N	Y	Y	Y	Y	P	N	N	Y	Y	Y	N	Y	Y	N
Wirsing	Y	N	Y	Y	N	N	Y	Y	Y	Y	N	N	N	Y	Y	Y	N	Y	Y	N
Wojcik	Y	N	Y	A	N	N	Y	Y	A	Y	N	Y	N	Y	Y	Y	N	Y	Y	A
Wood	Y	A	Y	Y	N	Y	Y	Y	Y	Y	N	Y	Y	Y	Y	Y	N	Y	Y	N
Woolard	Y	Y	Y	Y	Y	Y	Y	N	Y	Y	Y	Y	Y	Y	N	Y	Y	Y	Y	Y
Younge	Y	Y	Y	Y	Y	Y	Y	Y	Y	Y	Y	Y	Y	Y	Y	Y	Y	N	Y	Y
Zickus	Y	N	Y	Y	N	N	Y	Y	Y	Y	N	Y	Y	Y	Y	Y	N	Y	Y	N
Hughes	N	N	Y	N	N	Y	Y	Y	Y	Y	N	N	N	Y	N	Y	N	Y	Y	Y
Deering	Y	Y	Y	Y	Y	Y	Y	N	N	Y	Y	E	N	Y	N	Y	Y	Y	Y	Y
Kotlarz	X	X	X	X	X	X	X	E	X	Y	X	X	E	X	X	X	E	X	X	X

HB0253	HB0260	HB0265	HB0271	HB0282	HB0297	HB0313	HB0314	HB0316	HB0318	HB0319	HB0347	HB0379	HB0381	HB0383	HB0391	HB0400	HB0401	HB0424	HB0452	HB0480	HB0489	HB0522	HB0523	HB0524	HB0540	HB0571	HB0581	HB0585	HB0586
N	Y	Y	Y	Y	Y	Y	Y	Y	P	N	Y	Y	Y	Y	N	Y	Y	Y	N	Y	Y	Y	N	Y	Y	Y	Y	Y	Y
Y	N	Y	Y	Y	Y	N	Y	Y	N	Y	Y	Y	Y	Y	N	Y	Y	Y	Y	Y	N	Y	Y	Y	Y	Y	N	Y	Y
Y	Y	Y	Y	Y	Y	Y	N	A	N	N	P	Y	Y	Y	N	Y	Y	Y	Y	Y	Y	Y	N	Y	Y	N	Y	Y	Y
N	Y	N	Y	Y	Y	Y	N	Y	N	N	Y	Y	Y	Y	N	Y	Y	Y	Y	Y	Y	N	N	Y	Y	A	Y	Y	Y
Y	Y	N	Y	Y	Y	Y	Y	Y	N	Y	Y	Y	Y	Y	N	Y	Y	Y	Y	Y	Y	Y	N	Y	Y	N	Y	Y	Y
N	Y	P	Y	Y	Y	Y	Y	Y	N	N	Y	Y	Y	Y	N	Y	Y	Y	Y	Y	Y	Y	N	Y	Y	Y	Y	Y	Y
N	Y	Y	Y	Y	Y	Y	Y	Y	N	N	Y	Y	Y	Y	N	Y	Y	Y	Y	Y	Y	Y	N	Y	Y	Y	Y	Y	Y
Y	Y	Y	Y	Y	Y	Y	Y	Y	A	Y	Y	Y	Y	N	Y	Y	Y	Y	Y	Y	Y	Y	Y	Y	Y	Y	Y	P	Y
X	X	X	X	X	X	X	X	X	X	X	X	X	X	X	X	X	X	X	X	X	X	X	X	X	X	X	X	X	X
P	Y	N	Y	Y	Y	Y	Y	Y	Y	Y	Y	Y	Y	N	Y	Y	Y	Y	Y	Y	Y	Y	Y	Y	Y	Y	Y	N	Y
Y	Y	N	Y	Y	Y	Y	N	Y	N	N	P	Y	Y	Y	N	Y	Y	Y	Y	Y	N	N	N	Y	Y	Y	Y	Y	Y
Y	Y	Y	Y	Y	Y	Y	N	Y	N	N	Y	Y	N	Y	N	Y	Y	Y	Y	Y	Y	Y	N	Y	Y	Y	Y	Y	Y
Y	Y	Y	E	Y	Y	Y	N	Y	Y	E	Y	Y	Y	E	E	Y	Y	Y	Y	Y	Y	Y	N	Y	Y	N	Y	Y	Y
Y	Y	Y	Y	Y	Y	Y	Y	E	N	N	Y	Y	Y	N	Y	Y	Y	Y	Y	Y	Y	Y	N	Y	Y	Y	Y	E	Y
Y	Y	Y	A	A	Y	Y	N	Y	N	N	Y	Y	Y	Y	N	Y	Y	Y	Y	Y	Y	A	P	Y	Y	N	Y	Y	Y
N	A	N	Y	Y	Y	Y	Y	Y	Y	Y	Y	Y	Y	N	Y	Y	Y	Y	Y	Y	Y	Y	Y	Y	Y	Y	Y	N	N
A	Y	A	Y	Y	Y	Y	Y	Y	A	Y	E	Y	E	N	Y	Y	Y	E	A	Y	E	A	E	A	Y	Y	Y	Y	Y
Y	Y	Y	Y	Y	Y	Y	Y	Y	Y	Y	Y	Y	Y	N	Y	Y	Y	Y	Y	Y	Y	Y	Y	Y	Y	Y	Y	N	Y
Y	N	Y	P	Y	Y	N	Y	Y	N	Y	Y	Y	Y	Y	N	Y	Y	Y	Y	Y	N	Y	Y	Y	Y	Y	N	N	Y
Y	Y	Y	Y	A	Y	Y	Y	Y	N	A	Y	Y	Y	N	Y	Y	Y	Y	Y	Y	Y	Y	Y	Y	Y	Y	Y	N	Y
Y	Y	N	Y	Y	Y	N	Y	Y	N	N	P	Y	Y	Y	N	Y	Y	Y	N	Y	Y	N	N	Y	Y	Y	Y	Y	Y
P	Y	N	Y	Y	Y	Y	N	Y	Y	Y	Y	Y	Y	N	Y	Y	Y	Y	Y	E	Y	Y	Y	Y	Y	N	Y	N	Y
N	Y	Y	Y	Y	Y	Y	Y	Y	Y	Y	Y	Y	Y	Y	N	Y	Y	Y	Y	Y	Y	Y	N	Y	Y	N	Y	N	Y
Y	Y	Y	Y	Y	Y	Y	N	Y	N	N	Y	Y	Y	Y	N	Y	Y	Y	Y	Y	Y	N	N	Y	Y	Y	Y	Y	Y
N	Y	N	Y	Y	Y	Y	Y	Y	Y	Y	Y	Y	Y	N	Y	Y	Y	Y	Y	Y	Y	Y	Y	Y	Y	Y	Y	P	Y
Y	Y	Y	Y	Y	Y	Y	N	Y	N	N	Y	Y	Y	Y	N	Y	Y	Y	Y	Y	Y	Y	N	Y	Y	Y	Y	Y	Y
Y	Y	Y	Y	Y	Y	Y	Y	Y	Y	A	Y	Y	Y	A	Y	Y	Y	Y	Y	Y	Y	Y	P	Y	Y	Y	Y	Y	Y
Y	Y	N	Y	Y	Y	Y	N	Y	N	N	Y	Y	Y	Y	N	Y	Y	Y	Y	Y	Y	Y	N	Y	Y	N	Y	Y	Y
Y	Y	Y	Y	Y	Y	Y	Y	Y	A	N	Y	Y	Y	Y	N	A	Y	Y	Y	Y	A	Y	N	Y	Y	N	N	Y	Y
N	N	Y	Y	Y	Y	Y	Y	Y	N	N	Y	Y	Y	Y	Y	Y	Y	Y	Y	Y	Y	Y	N	Y	Y	N	Y	Y	Y
N	Y	Y	Y	Y	Y	Y	Y	Y	N	N	Y	Y	Y	Y	N	Y	Y	Y	Y	Y	Y	N	N	Y	Y	Y	Y	Y	Y
N	Y	Y	Y	Y	Y	Y	N	Y	N	N	Y	Y	Y	Y	N	Y	Y	Y	Y	Y	Y	N	N	Y	Y	N	Y	Y	Y
N	N	Y	Y	Y	Y	Y	N	Y	N	N	Y	Y	Y	Y	N	Y	Y	Y	Y	Y	Y	N	N	Y	Y	Y	Y	Y	Y
N	Y	N	Y	Y	Y	Y	Y	Y	N	N	Y	Y	Y	Y	N	Y	Y	N	Y	Y	Y	Y	N	Y	Y	Y	Y	Y	Y
N	Y	N	Y	Y	Y	Y	Y	Y	N	Y	Y	Y	Y	N	Y	Y	Y	Y	Y	Y	N	Y	N	Y	Y	Y	Y	Y	Y
N	Y	Y	Y	Y	Y	Y	Y	Y	Y	N	Y	Y	Y	Y	N	Y	Y	Y	Y	Y	Y	Y	N	Y	Y	Y	Y	Y	Y
N	Y	Y	Y	Y	Y	Y	Y	Y	Y	Y	Y	Y	Y	N	Y	Y	Y	Y	Y	P	Y	Y	Y	Y	Y	Y	Y	N	Y
N	Y	N	Y	Y	Y	P	N	Y	N	N	Y	Y	Y	Y	N	Y	Y	Y	Y	Y	Y	Y	N	Y	Y	Y	Y	Y	Y
Y	Y	Y	Y	Y	Y	Y	N	Y	N	Y	Y	Y	Y	N	Y	Y	Y	Y	Y	Y	Y	N	N	Y	Y	N	Y	Y	Y
N	N	Y	Y	Y	Y	Y	Y	Y	Y	N	Y	Y	N	Y	N	Y	Y	N	Y	Y	Y	Y	N	Y	Y	Y	Y	Y	Y
X	X	X	X	X	X	X	X	E	X	X	X	X	X	X	X	E	E	X	X	X	X	X	X	X	X	X	X	E	X

House Member	HB0591	HB0601	HB0602	HB0618	HB0644	HB0652	HB0672	HB0725	HB0729	HB0740	HB0744	HB0819	HB0844	HB0851	HB0885	HB0923	HB0951	HB0968	HB0995	HB0999
Acevedo	Y	Y	Y	Y	Y	Y	Y	Y	Y	Y	Y	Y	Y	N	Y	N	Y	Y	Y	Y
Ackerman	Y	Y	Y	Y	Y	Y	N	Y	Y	Y	P	Y	Y	N	Y	Y	Y	Y	Y	N
Beaubien	Y	Y	N	Y	Y	Y	Y	Y	Y	Y	Y	Y	N	Y	N	Y	Y	Y	Y	N
Bergman	Y	Y	Y	Y	Y	Y	Y	Y	N	Y	Y	Y	Y	N	Y	Y	Y	Y	Y	Y
Biggert	Y	Y	Y	Y	N	N	Y	Y	Y	Y	Y	Y	Y	Y	N	Y	Y	Y	Y	N
Biggins	Y	Y	Y	Y	N	N	Y	Y	Y	Y	N	Y	Y	N	N	Y	Y	Y	Y	Y
Black	Y	Y	N	Y	P	Y	Y	Y	Y	Y	Y	Y	E	N	Y	Y	Y	N	Y	Y
Boland	Y	Y	Y	Y	Y	Y	Y	Y	Y	Y	Y	Y	P	Y	N	Y	Y	P	Y	Y
Bost	Y	Y	N	Y	N	N	Y	Y	Y	Y	Y	Y	Y	N	Y	Y	Y	N	Y	N
Bradford	Y	Y	N	Y	Y	Y	Y	Y	Y	Y	Y	Y	Y	Y	Y	Y	Y	N	Y	N
Bradley	Y	Y	Y	Y	Y	Y	Y	Y	Y	X	Y	Y	X	X	N	X	Y	X	X	Y
Brady	Y	Y	Y	Y	Y	Y	Y	Y	Y	Y	Y	Y	N	N	N	Y	Y	Y	Y	N
Brosnahan	Y	Y	N	Y	Y	N	Y	Y	Y	Y	Y	Y	N	N	Y	Y	Y	N	Y	Y
Brown	X	X	X	X	X	X	X	X	X	X	X	X	X	X	X	X	X	X	X	X
Brunsvold	Y	Y	Y	Y	Y	Y	Y	Y	Y	Y	P	Y	Y	Y	N	N	Y	Y	Y	N
Bugielski	Y	Y	Y	Y	Y	Y	Y	Y	Y	Y	Y	Y	Y	Y	N	Y	Y	N	Y	Y
Burke	P	Y	Y	Y	Y	Y	N	Y	Y	Y	Y	Y	Y	Y	N	Y	Y	N	Y	Y
Capparelli	Y	Y	Y	Y	Y	E	Y	Y	Y	Y	Y	Y	P	Y	Y	Y	Y	Y	Y	Y
Churchill	Y	Y	Y	Y	N	N	Y	Y	Y	Y	Y	Y	Y	N	N	Y	Y	Y	Y	Y
Clayton	Y	Y	Y	Y	Y	Y	Y	Y	Y	Y	Y	Y	N	Y	Y	Y	Y	N	Y	A
Coulson	Y	Y	N	Y	N	Y	Y	Y	Y	Y	N	Y	Y	Y	Y	Y	Y	Y	Y	Y
Cowlishaw	Y	Y	Y	Y	N	Y	A	Y	N	Y	Y	Y	Y	N	Y	Y	Y	Y	Y	Y
Cross	Y	Y	N	Y	Y	Y	Y	Y	Y	Y	Y	Y	Y	Y	P	Y	Y	Y	Y	N
Crotty	Y	Y	N	Y	Y	N	Y	Y	Y	Y	Y	Y	N	Y	Y	Y	Y	N	Y	N
Currie	N	N	Y	Y	Y	Y	Y	Y	Y	Y	N	Y	Y	Y	Y	Y	Y	N	N	N
Curry	Y	Y	Y	Y	Y	Y	Y	Y	Y	Y	P	Y	N	Y	Y	Y	Y	Y	Y	N
Daniels	Y	Y	Y	Y	N	N	Y	Y	Y	Y	Y	Y	Y	N	Y	Y	Y	Y	Y	Y
Dart	P	Y	N	Y	E	Y	Y	Y	Y	Y	Y	Y	N	Y	Y	Y	Y	Y	Y	Y
Davis, Monique	N	Y	Y	Y	N	Y	Y	Y	Y	Y	N	Y	Y	Y	N	Y	Y	Y	Y	N
Davis, Steve	Y	Y	N	Y	Y	Y	Y	Y	Y	Y	Y	Y	N	Y	Y	Y	Y	Y	Y	Y
Deuchler	N	Y	Y	Y	N	Y	Y	Y	Y	Y	Y	Y	E	Y	Y	Y	Y	N	Y	N
Durkin	Y	Y	N	Y	Y	N	Y	Y	Y	Y	Y	Y	Y	Y	N	Y	Y	N	Y	Y
Erwin	Y	Y	Y	Y	Y	Y	Y	Y	Y	Y	A	Y	Y	Y	Y	Y	Y	N	Y	Y
Fantin	N	Y	Y	Y	Y	Y	Y	Y	Y	Y	N	Y	Y	Y	N	N	Y	Y	Y	N
Feigenholtz	N	Y	Y	Y	Y	Y	Y	Y	Y	Y	E	Y	Y	Y	E	Y	Y	Y	Y	N
Flowers	N	Y	Y	Y	Y	Y	Y	Y	Y	Y	N	Y	Y	Y	Y	Y	Y	Y	Y	Y
Fritchey	Y	Y	N	Y	Y	Y	Y	Y	Y	Y	Y	Y	P	Y	P	Y	Y	Y	Y	Y
Gash	Y	Y	Y	Y	Y	Y	Y	Y	Y	Y	N	Y	Y	Y	Y	Y	E	N	Y	N
Giglio	Y	Y	N	Y	Y	Y	Y	Y	Y	Y	Y	Y	Y	Y	Y	Y	Y	Y	N	N
Giles	N	Y	Y	Y	Y	Y	Y	Y	P	Y	N	Y	P	A	N	A	Y	Y	Y	Y

HB 1004	HB 1009	HB 1025	HB 1029	HB 1074	HB 1080	HB 1090	HB 1121	HB 1141	HB 1147	HB 1149	HB 1168	HB 1169	HB 1207	HB 1211	HB 1219	HB 1229	HB 1271	HB 1294	HB 1301	HB 1302	HB 1303	HB 1309	HB 1311
Y	N	Y	Y	Y	Y	Y	Y	Y	Y	N	Y	Y	Y	Y	Y	Y	Y	Y	Y	Y	Y	Y	Y
Y	N	N	Y	Y	Y	N	Y	Y	Y	N	Y	Y	Y	N	Y	Y	N	N	Y	Y	N	Y	Y
Y	N	Y	Y	Y	Y	Y	Y	A	Y	N	Y	Y	Y	Y	Y	Y	N	Y	Y	Y	Y	N	Y
Y	N	Y	Y	Y	Y	N	Y	Y	Y	N	Y	Y	Y	N	Y	Y	N	Y	N	Y	N	Y	Y
Y	N	Y	Y	Y	Y	Y	Y	Y	Y	N	Y	Y	Y	Y	Y	Y	N	Y	Y	Y	Y	N	Y
Y	N	N	Y	Y	Y	N	Y	Y	Y	N	Y	Y	Y	Y	Y	Y	N	N	N	Y	N	N	Y
Y	Y	Y	Y	Y	Y	N	Y	Y	Y	N	Y	Y	Y	N	Y	N	Y	N	Y	Y	Y	Y	Y
Y	Y	Y	Y	Y	Y	Y	Y	Y	Y	Y	Y	Y	Y	Y	Y	Y	Y	Y	Y	Y	Y	N	Y
Y	Y	Y	Y	Y	Y	Y	Y	Y	N	N	Y	Y	Y	N	Y	N	N	N	P	Y	Y	A	Y
Y	Y	Y	Y	Y	Y	Y	Y	Y	N	Y	Y	Y	Y	N	Y	Y	Y	Y	Y	Y	Y	N	Y
N	X	X	Y	Y	Y	Y	Y	A	Y	A	Y	X	Y	Y	Y	X	Y	X	Y	Y	Y	N	X
Y	N	Y	Y	Y	Y	N	Y	Y	Y	N	Y	Y	Y	N	Y	Y	N	N	N	Y	N	N	Y
Y	Y	Y	Y	Y	Y	Y	Y	Y	N	Y	Y	Y	Y	N	Y	Y	Y	Y	Y	Y	Y	N	Y
X	X	X	X	X	X	X	X	X	X	X	X	X	X	X	X	X	X	X	X	X	X	X	X
Y	Y	N	Y	Y	Y	Y	Y	Y	Y	N	Y	Y	Y	Y	Y	Y	N	Y	Y	Y	Y	A	Y
Y	Y	Y	Y	Y	Y	Y	Y	Y	Y	P	Y	Y	Y	Y	Y	Y	Y	Y	Y	Y	Y	Y	Y
Y	Y	N	Y	N	Y	Y	Y	Y	Y	P	Y	Y	Y	N	Y	Y	Y	Y	Y	Y	Y	Y	Y
Y	Y	Y	Y	Y	Y	Y	Y	Y	Y	P	Y	Y	Y	Y	E	Y	Y	Y	Y	Y	Y	Y	Y
Y	Y	N	Y	Y	Y	N	Y	Y	P	N	Y	Y	Y	Y	Y	Y	N	N	Y	Y	N	N	Y
Y	N	Y	Y	Y	Y	Y	Y	Y	Y	N	Y	Y	Y	Y	Y	Y	N	Y	Y	Y	Y	N	Y
Y	N	Y	Y	Y	Y	Y	Y	Y	N	P	Y	Y	Y	N	Y	Y	N	Y	Y	Y	Y	N	Y
Y	Y	N	Y	Y	Y	N	Y	Y	Y	N	Y	Y	Y	N	Y	Y	Y	N	N	Y	N	N	Y
Y	Y	Y	Y	Y	Y	Y	Y	Y	Y	N	Y	Y	Y	Y	Y	Y	N	N	Y	Y	Y	Y	Y
Y	Y	Y	Y	Y	Y	Y	Y	Y	N	Y	Y	Y	Y	N	Y	Y	Y	Y	Y	Y	Y	N	Y
Y	Y	Y	Y	Y	Y	Y	Y	Y	Y	Y	Y	Y	N	Y	Y	Y	Y	Y	Y	Y	Y	N	Y
Y	N	Y	Y	Y	Y	Y	Y	Y	N	N	Y	Y	Y	N	Y	Y	Y	Y	Y	Y	Y	N	Y
Y	Y	N	Y	Y	Y	N	Y	Y	Y	N	Y	Y	Y	Y	Y	Y	N	N	Y	Y	Y	N	Y
Y	Y	Y	Y	Y	Y	E	Y	Y	Y	A	Y	Y	Y	N	Y	Y	E	Y	Y	Y	Y	N	Y
Y	Y	Y	Y	Y	Y	Y	Y	Y	Y	N	Y	Y	N	Y	Y	Y	Y	Y	Y	Y	Y	A	Y
Y	N	Y	Y	Y	Y	Y	Y	Y	Y	N	Y	Y	Y	N	Y	Y	Y	Y	Y	Y	Y	A	Y
Y	N	Y	Y	Y	Y	N	Y	Y	N	N	Y	Y	Y	N	Y	Y	N	Y	Y	Y	A	N	Y
Y	N	Y	Y	Y	Y	Y	Y	Y	Y	N	Y	Y	Y	N	Y	N	N	N	Y	Y	N	N	Y
Y	Y	Y	Y	Y	Y	Y	Y	Y	Y	N	Y	Y	Y	Y	Y	Y	Y	Y	Y	Y	Y	N	Y
N	N	Y	Y	Y	Y	Y	Y	Y	Y	N	Y	Y	P	Y	Y	Y	Y	Y	Y	Y	Y	Y	Y
Y	Y	Y	Y	Y	Y	Y	Y	A	Y	N	Y	Y	P	Y	Y	Y	Y	Y	Y	Y	Y	N	Y
Y	Y	Y	Y	Y	A	Y	Y	Y	Y	Y	Y	Y	P	Y	Y	Y	Y	Y	Y	Y	A	Y	Y
Y	Y	Y	Y	Y	Y	Y	Y	Y	Y	P	Y	Y	P	N	Y	Y	Y	Y	Y	Y	Y	N	Y
Y	Y	Y	E	Y	E	Y	Y	E	Y	N	E	Y	Y	Y	Y	Y	N	Y	Y	E	Y	E	Y
Y	Y	Y	Y	Y	Y	Y	Y	Y	N	Y	Y	Y	Y	N	Y	Y	N	Y	Y	Y	Y	Y	Y
P	Y	Y	Y	P	Y	Y	Y	Y	Y	P	Y	Y	N	A	Y	Y	Y	Y	Y	Y	Y	Y	Y

House Member	HB0591	HB0601	HB0602	HB0618	HB0644	HB0652	HB0672	HB0725	HB0729	HB0740	HB0744	HB0819	HB0844	HB0851	HB0885	HB0923	HB0951	HB0968	HB0995	HB0999
Granberg	Y	Y	Y	Y	Y	Y	Y	Y	Y	Y	A	Y	Y	Y	Y	Y	Y	N	Y	Y
Hannig	Y	Y	Y	Y	Y	Y	Y	Y	Y	Y	Y	Y	Y	Y	Y	N	Y	Y	Y	Y
Hartke	Y	Y	Y	Y	Y	Y	Y	Y	Y	Y	Y	Y	N	N	Y	Y	Y	Y	Y	Y
Hassert	Y	Y	Y	Y	Y	Y	Y	Y	Y	Y	Y	Y	Y	Y	N	Y	Y	Y	Y	Y
Hoeft	Y	Y	Y	Y	N	N	Y	Y	Y	Y	Y	Y	P	Y	Y	Y	Y	N	Y	Y
Holbrook	Y	Y	N	Y	Y	Y	Y	Y	Y	Y	Y	Y	E	N	N	Y	Y	N	Y	Y
Howard	N	Y	Y	Y	Y	Y	Y	Y	Y	Y	P	Y	Y	Y	N	Y	Y	Y	Y	N
Johnson, Tim	Y	Y	Y	Y	Y	N	Y	Y	Y	Y	Y	Y	Y	N	N	Y	Y	Y	Y	N
Johnson, Tom	Y	Y	N	Y	N	Y	Y	Y	Y	Y	Y	Y	Y	N	Y	Y	Y	N	Y	Y
Jones, John	Y	Y	N	Y	N	N	Y	Y	Y	Y	Y	Y	Y	N	Y	Y	Y	N	Y	N
Jones, Lovana	N	Y	Y	Y	Y	Y	P	Y	Y	Y	Y	Y	Y	Y	N	Y	Y	Y	Y	N
Jones, Shirley	N	Y	Y	Y	Y	Y	P	Y	Y	Y	Y	Y	Y	Y	N	Y	Y	Y	Y	N
Kenner	N	Y	Y	Y	Y	Y	N	Y	Y	Y	Y	Y	Y	Y	N	Y	Y	Y	Y	N
Klingler	Y	Y	N	Y	N	N	Y	Y	Y	Y	Y	Y	Y	Y	Y	Y	A	N	Y	N
Kosel	Y	Y	N	A	Y	N	Y	Y	Y	Y	Y	Y	N	N	Y	Y	Y	Y	N	N
Krause	Y	Y	Y	Y	Y	Y	Y	Y	Y	Y	N	Y	Y	Y	Y	Y	Y	N	Y	Y
Kubik	Y	Y	Y	Y	P	Y	Y	Y	Y	E	Y	Y	Y	N	A	Y	Y	Y	Y	N
Lang	Y	Y	Y	Y	Y	Y	Y	Y	Y	Y	P	Y	Y	Y	N	Y	Y	Y	Y	N
Lawfer	Y	Y	Y	Y	N	N	Y	Y	Y	Y	Y	Y	Y	N	Y	Y	Y	N	Y	N
Leitch	Y	Y	Y	Y	A	Y	Y	Y	Y	Y	Y	Y	Y	A	Y	N	Y	N	Y	Y
Lindner	Y	Y	Y	Y	N	N	Y	Y	Y	Y	Y	Y	Y	Y	P	Y	Y	N	Y	Y
Lopez	Y	Y	Y	Y	Y	Y	Y	Y	Y	Y	Y	Y	P	Y	Y	Y	Y	Y	E	Y
Lyons, Eileen	Y	Y	N	Y	N	Y	Y	Y	Y	Y	Y	Y	N	N	Y	Y	Y	N	N	Y
Lyons, Joseph	Y	Y	Y	Y	Y	Y	Y	Y	Y	Y	Y	Y	Y	Y	Y	Y	Y	Y	Y	Y
Madigan, Michael	Y	Y	Y	Y	Y	Y	Y	Y	Y	Y	N	Y	Y	Y	Y	Y	Y	Y	Y	Y
Mautino	Y	Y	Y	Y	Y	Y	Y	Y	Y	Y	N	Y	N	Y	N	N	Y	N	Y	N
McAuliffe	Y	Y	N	Y	Y	Y	Y	Y	Y	Y	Y	Y	Y	N	Y	Y	Y	N	Y	Y
McCarthy	Y	Y	N	Y	Y	Y	Y	Y	Y	Y	Y	Y	N	N	Y	Y	Y	N	N	Y
McGuire	Y	Y	Y	Y	Y	Y	Y	Y	Y	Y	Y	Y	E	Y	Y	Y	Y	A	Y	A
McKeon	Y	Y	Y	Y	Y	Y	Y	Y	Y	Y	Y	Y	Y	Y	Y	Y	Y	P	Y	Y
Meyer	Y	Y	Y	Y	Y	Y	Y	Y	Y	Y	Y	Y	Y	N	Y	Y	Y	Y	Y	N
Mitchell	Y	Y	Y	Y	A	Y	Y	Y	Y	Y	Y	Y	N	Y	Y	Y	Y	N	Y	N
Moffitt	Y	Y	Y	Y	Y	Y	Y	Y	Y	Y	Y	Y	Y	N	Y	A	Y	N	Y	N
Moore, Andrea	Y	Y	Y	Y	Y	Y	Y	Y	Y	Y	Y	Y	Y	Y	Y	Y	Y	Y	Y	Y
Moore, Eugene	N	Y	Y	Y	Y	Y	A	Y	Y	Y	Y	Y	N	Y	N	Y	Y	N	Y	A
Morrow	N	Y	Y	Y	Y	Y	N	Y	E	Y	P	Y	Y	Y	N	Y	Y	P	Y	A
Mulligan	Y	Y	Y	Y	N	Y	Y	N	Y	Y	Y	Y	Y	Y	N	Y	Y	Y	Y	Y
Murphy	N	Y	Y	Y	Y	Y	P	Y	Y	Y	Y	Y	Y	Y	N	Y	Y	Y	Y	N
Myers, Richard	Y	Y	Y	Y	N	N	Y	Y	Y	Y	Y	Y	P	N	Y	Y	Y	N	Y	N
Noland	Y	Y	Y	Y	N	N	Y	Y	Y	Y	Y	Y	Y	N	Y	Y	Y	Y	Y	N

HB 1004	HB 1009	HB 1025	HB 1029	HB 1074	HB 1080	HB 1090	HB 1121	HB 1141	HB 1147	HB 1149	HB 1168	HB 1169	HB 1207	HB 1211	HB 1219	HB 1229	HB 1271	HB 1294	HB 1301	HB 1302	HB 1303	HB 1309	HB 1311
Y	Y	N	Y	Y	Y	Y	Y	Y	Y	N	Y	Y	Y	Y	Y	Y	Y	Y	Y	Y	Y	A	Y
Y	Y	Y	Y	Y	Y	Y	Y	Y	Y	N	Y	Y	Y	Y	Y	Y	Y	Y	Y	Y	Y	A	Y
Y	Y	Y	Y	Y	Y	A	Y	Y	Y	N	Y	Y	Y	Y	Y	Y	Y	Y	Y	N	Y	N	Y
Y	Y	Y	Y	Y	Y	N	Y	Y	Y	N	Y	Y	Y	Y	Y	Y	N	N	Y	Y	Y	N	Y
Y	N	N	Y	Y	Y	Y	Y	Y	Y	N	Y	Y	Y	N	Y	Y	Y	Y	Y	Y	Y	N	Y
Y	Y	Y	Y	Y	Y	Y	Y	Y	Y	N	Y	Y	Y	Y	Y	Y	Y	Y	N	Y	Y	N	Y
Y	Y	Y	Y	Y	Y	Y	Y	Y	Y	P	Y	Y	A	Y	Y	Y	A	Y	Y	Y	Y	Y	Y
Y	N	Y	P	Y	Y	Y	Y	Y	Y	N	Y	Y	Y	Y	Y	Y	N	N	N	Y	N	Y	Y
Y	N	Y	Y	Y	Y	Y	Y	Y	Y	N	Y	Y	Y	Y	Y	Y	N	Y	Y	Y	N	Y	Y
Y	Y	Y	Y	Y	Y	N	Y	Y	N	N	Y	Y	Y	N	Y	N	N	N	Y	Y	Y	N	Y
Y	Y	Y	A	P	Y	Y	Y	Y	Y	P	Y	Y	Y	Y	Y	A	Y	Y	Y	Y	Y	Y	Y
N	Y	Y	Y	A	Y	A	Y	Y	Y	P	Y	Y	Y	Y	Y	Y	Y	Y	Y	Y	Y	Y	Y
P	Y	Y	Y	N	Y	P	Y	Y	Y	P	Y	Y	P	Y	Y	Y	Y	Y	Y	Y	Y	Y	Y
Y	Y	Y	Y	Y	Y	N	Y	Y	N	N	Y	Y	Y	N	Y	N	N	Y	Y	A	Y	N	Y
Y	Y	Y	Y	Y	Y	N	Y	Y	N	N	Y	Y	Y	N	Y	Y	Y	Y	Y	Y	N	N	Y
Y	N	Y	Y	Y	Y	Y	Y	Y	Y	P	Y	Y	Y	Y	Y	Y	N	Y	Y	Y	Y	N	Y
Y	N	N	Y	Y	Y	N	Y	P	Y	N	Y	E	Y	Y	Y	Y	N	N	Y	A	Y	N	Y
Y	Y	Y	Y	Y	Y	Y	Y	Y	Y	Y	Y	Y	Y	Y	Y	Y	Y	Y	Y	Y	Y	A	Y
Y	N	Y	Y	Y	Y	N	Y	Y	N	N	P	Y	Y	N	Y	Y	N	Y	Y	Y	Y	N	Y
Y	N	N	Y	Y	Y	N	Y	Y	Y	N	Y	Y	Y	Y	Y	Y	N	A	Y	Y	Y	N	Y
Y	N	Y	Y	Y	Y	Y	Y	Y	Y	N	Y	Y	Y	Y	Y	Y	N	Y	Y	Y	Y	N	A
Y	E	N	Y	Y	Y	Y	Y	Y	Y	N	Y	Y	Y	Y	Y	Y	Y	Y	Y	Y	Y	N	E
Y	N	N	E	Y	Y	Y	Y	Y	N	A	Y	Y	Y	N	Y	Y	N	Y	Y	A	Y	N	Y
Y	Y	Y	Y	Y	Y	Y	Y	Y	Y	N	Y	Y	Y	Y	Y	Y	Y	Y	Y	Y	Y	N	Y
P	Y	Y	Y	Y	Y	Y	Y	Y	Y	Y	Y	Y	Y	Y	Y	Y	Y	Y	Y	Y	Y	N	Y
Y	N	Y	Y	Y	Y	Y	Y	Y	Y	N	Y	Y	Y	Y	Y	Y	Y	Y	Y	Y	Y	Y	Y
Y	Y	Y	Y	Y	Y	Y	Y	Y	N	N	Y	Y	Y	N	Y	N	N	Y	Y	Y	Y	Y	Y
Y	Y	Y	Y	Y	Y	Y	Y	Y	N	Y	Y	Y	Y	N	Y	Y	Y	Y	Y	Y	Y	N	Y
A	Y	Y	Y	Y	Y	Y	Y	Y	Y	A	Y	Y	Y	Y	Y	Y	Y	Y	Y	Y	Y	N	Y
Y	Y	Y	Y	Y	Y	Y	Y	Y	Y	Y	Y	Y	P	Y	Y	Y	Y	Y	Y	Y	Y	N	Y
Y	N	Y	Y	Y	Y	Y	Y	Y	Y	N	Y	Y	Y	Y	Y	Y	N	N	Y	Y	N	N	Y
Y	N	Y	Y	Y	Y	Y	Y	Y	N	N	Y	Y	Y	N	Y	Y	N	Y	N	N	N	N	Y
Y	Y	N	Y	Y	Y	Y	Y	Y	Y	N	Y	Y	Y	N	Y	N	Y	N	Y	Y	Y	N	Y
Y	N	Y	Y	Y	Y	Y	Y	Y	Y	N	Y	Y	Y	Y	Y	Y	N	Y	Y	N	Y	N	Y
Y	Y	N	Y	N	Y	Y	Y	Y	Y	N	Y	Y	Y	N	Y	Y	Y	Y	Y	Y	Y	Y	Y
P	Y	Y	Y	P	Y	N	Y	Y	Y	N	Y	Y	Y	Y	Y	Y	Y	Y	Y	Y	Y	Y	Y
Y	N	Y	Y	Y	Y	Y	Y	Y	Y	N	Y	Y	Y	A	Y	Y	Y	Y	Y	Y	Y	N	Y
N	Y	Y	Y	P	Y	Y	Y	Y	Y	P	Y	N	Y	Y	Y	Y	Y	Y	Y	Y	Y	Y	Y
Y	N	Y	Y	Y	Y	N	Y	Y	N	N	Y	Y	Y	N	Y	Y	N	N	Y	Y	N	Y	Y
Y	N	Y	Y	Y	Y	N	Y	Y	Y	N	Y	Y	Y	Y	Y	Y	Y	N	Y	Y	N	N	Y

House Member	HB0591	HB0601	HB0602	HB0618	HB0644	HB0652	HB0672	HB0725	HB0729	HB0740	HB0744	HB0819	HB0844	HB0851	HB0885	HB0923	HB0951	HB0968	HB0995	HB0999
Novak	Y	Y	Y	Y	Y	Y	A	Y	Y	Y	N	Y	Y	Y	Y	Y	Y	Y	Y	Y
O'Brien	Y	Y	N	Y	Y	N	A	Y	Y	Y	Y	Y	Y	Y	Y	Y	Y	N	Y	N
Pankau	Y	Y	Y	Y	N	Y	Y	Y	Y	Y	Y	Y	N	N	Y	Y	Y	Y	Y	Y
Parke	Y	Y	Y	Y	Y	Y	Y	Y	Y	Y	Y	Y	Y	N	N	Y	Y	N	Y	Y
Persico	Y	Y	Y	Y	N	Y	Y	Y	Y	Y	N	Y	Y	Y	Y	Y	Y	Y	Y	N
Phelps	Y	Y	Y	Y	Y	Y	Y	Y	Y	Y	P	Y	Y	Y	Y	P	Y	Y	Y	Y
Poe	Y	Y	N	Y	N	Y	Y	Y	Y	Y	Y	Y	Y	N	Y	Y	Y	N	Y	Y
Pugh	A	Y	Y	Y	Y	Y	Y	N	Y	Y	Y	Y	P	Y	N	Y	Y	Y	Y	P
Reitz	X	X	X	X	X	X	X	X	X	X	X	X	X	X	X	X	X	X	X	X
Ronen	N	Y	Y	Y	Y	Y	Y	P	Y	Y	N	Y	Y	Y	Y	Y	Y	N	Y	N
Roskam	Y	Y	Y	Y	N	Y	Y	Y	Y	N	Y	Y	Y	N	Y	Y	Y	Y	Y	Y
Rutherford	Y	Y	Y	Y	N	Y	Y	Y	Y	Y	Y	Y	Y	N	N	N	Y	Y	Y	N
Ryder	Y	Y	Y	Y	N	Y	Y	Y	Y	Y	Y	Y	Y	E	N	E	Y	E	Y	N
Santiago	Y	Y	Y	Y	Y	Y	Y	Y	Y	Y	Y	Y	P	Y	Y	Y	Y	P	E	Y
Saviano	Y	Y	Y	Y	Y	Y	Y	Y	Y	Y	Y	Y	Y	Y	N	Y	Y	N	Y	Y
Schakowsky	N	Y	N	Y	Y	Y	Y	N	Y	Y	N	Y	Y	Y	Y	Y	E	N	P	N
Schoenberg	A	A	Y	Y	Y	Y	Y	Y	Y	Y	E	Y	Y	Y	E	Y	Y	Y	Y	E
Scott	Y	Y	Y	Y	Y	Y	Y	Y	Y	Y	N	Y	Y	Y	N	Y	Y	Y	Y	N
Scully	Y	Y	N	Y	Y	Y	Y	Y	Y	Y	Y	Y	N	Y	Y	Y	Y	N	N	N
Silva	Y	Y	Y	Y	Y	Y	Y	Y	Y	Y	N	Y	Y	Y	Y	Y	Y	N	Y	Y
Skinner	Y	Y	Y	Y	N	Y	Y	Y	Y	Y	Y	Y	Y	N	Y	Y	Y	N	Y	Y
Slone	Y	Y	Y	Y	N	Y	Y	Y	Y	Y	Y	Y	N	Y	Y	Y	Y	Y	Y	N
Smith, Michael	Y	Y	Y	Y	Y	Y	Y	Y	Y	Y	Y	Y	Y	Y	Y	Y	Y	N	Y	N
Stephens	Y	Y	Y	Y	N	N	Y	Y	Y	Y	Y	Y	Y	N	N	Y	Y	N	Y	N
Stroger	N	P	Y	Y	Y	Y	Y	Y	Y	Y	N	Y	Y	Y	N	Y	Y	Y	Y	Y
Tenhouse	Y	Y	N	Y	N	N	Y	Y	Y	Y	Y	Y	Y	N	N	Y	Y	N	Y	N
Turner, Arthur	N	Y	Y	Y	Y	Y	A	Y	Y	Y	Y	Y	Y	Y	N	Y	Y	Y	Y	N
Turner, John	Y	Y	Y	Y	N	Y	Y	Y	Y	Y	Y	Y	Y	N	N	Y	Y	Y	Y	Y
Wait	Y	Y	N	Y	Y	Y	Y	Y	Y	Y	Y	Y	Y	N	Y	Y	Y	N	Y	Y
Weaver, Michael	Y	Y	Y	Y	Y	Y	Y	Y	Y	Y	P	Y	Y	N	Y	Y	Y	N	Y	N
Winkel	Y	Y	N	Y	N	Y	Y	Y	Y	Y	Y	Y	Y	N	Y	Y	Y	N	Y	Y
Winters	Y	Y	Y	Y	N	Y	Y	Y	Y	Y	Y	Y	N	Y	Y	Y	Y	Y	Y	Y
Wirsing	Y	Y	Y	Y	N	Y	Y	Y	Y	Y	Y	Y	Y	N	Y	Y	Y	Y	Y	N
Wojcik	Y	Y	N	Y	Y	N	N	Y	Y	Y	Y	Y	Y	N	N	Y	Y	Y	Y	Y
Wood	Y	Y	N	Y	Y	Y	Y	Y	Y	Y	N	Y	Y	Y	Y	Y	Y	A	Y	Y
Woolard	Y	Y	Y	Y	Y	Y	Y	Y	Y	Y	P	Y	Y	Y	Y	Y	Y	Y	Y	Y
Younge	N	Y	Y	Y	Y	Y	Y	Y	Y	Y	A	Y	Y	Y	N	Y	A	Y	Y	A
Zickus	Y	Y	N	Y	N	Y	Y	Y	Y	Y	Y	Y	N	N	Y	Y	Y	Y	Y	Y
Hughes	Y	Y	Y	Y	Y	Y	Y	Y	Y	Y	N	Y	Y	Y	Y	Y	Y	Y	Y	Y
Deering	Y	Y	Y	Y	Y	Y	A	Y	Y	Y	N	Y	Y	Y	N	Y	Y	Y	Y	Y
Kotlarz	X	X	X	X	X	X	X	X	X	A	X	X	Y	X	X	X	X	X	E	X

HB 1004	HB 1009	HB 1025	HB 1029	HB 1074	HB 1080	HB 1090	HB 1121	HB 1141	HB 1147	HB 1149	HB 1168	HB 1169	HB 1207	HB 1211	HB 1219	HB 1229	HB 1271	HB 1294	HB 1301	HB 1302	HB 1303	HB 1309	HB 1311
N	Y	Y	Y	Y	Y	Y	Y	Y	Y	N	Y	Y	Y	Y	Y	Y	Y	Y	Y	Y	Y	N	Y
N	N	Y	Y	Y	Y	Y	Y	Y	N	N	Y	Y	Y	N	Y	Y	N	Y	Y	Y	Y	N	Y
Y	N	Y	Y	Y	Y	N	Y	Y	Y	N	Y	Y	Y	Y	Y	Y	N	Y	Y	Y	Y	Y	Y
Y	N	Y	Y	N	Y	Y	Y	Y	Y	N	Y	Y	Y	A	Y	N	Y	N	N	Y	N	Y	Y
Y	Y	Y	Y	Y	Y	Y	Y	Y	Y	N	Y	Y	Y	Y	Y	Y	N	N	Y	Y	Y	N	Y
Y	Y	N	Y	Y	Y	Y	Y	Y	P	Y	Y	Y	Y	N	A	Y	N	Y	P	Y	P	Y	Y
Y	N	Y	Y	Y	Y	N	Y	Y	N	N	Y	Y	Y	N	Y	N	Y	N	Y	Y	Y	Y	Y
Y	Y	Y	P	P	Y	P	Y	A	Y	P	Y	Y	N	Y	Y	Y	Y	Y	Y	Y	Y	Y	Y
X	X	X	X	X	X	X	X	X	X	X	X	X	X	X	X	X	X	X	X	X	X	X	X
Y	Y	Y	Y	Y	Y	Y	Y	Y	Y	Y	Y	Y	N	Y	Y	Y	Y	Y	Y	Y	Y	N	Y
Y	N	Y	Y	Y	Y	Y	Y	Y	Y	N	Y	Y	Y	N	Y	N	N	N	N	Y	N	N	Y
Y	N	N	Y	Y	Y	N	Y	Y	Y	N	Y	Y	Y	N	Y	Y	N	N	N	Y	N	Y	Y
Y	N	N	Y	Y	Y	N	Y	Y	Y	N	Y	Y	Y	Y	Y	E	N	E	N	Y	N	Y	Y
A	E	Y	Y	Y	Y	Y	Y	Y	Y	N	Y	Y	Y	Y	Y	Y	Y	Y	Y	Y	Y	Y	E
Y	N	Y	Y	Y	Y	Y	Y	Y	Y	N	Y	Y	Y	N	Y	Y	N	Y	Y	Y	Y	N	Y
Y	Y	Y	Y	Y	Y	Y	Y	Y	Y	Y	E	Y	Y	A	Y	Y	Y	Y	Y	Y	Y	N	Y
A	Y	Y	Y	Y	Y	Y	Y	Y	Y	N	Y	Y	E	Y	Y	Y	N	Y	Y	Y	Y	N	Y
Y	Y	Y	Y	Y	Y	Y	Y	Y	Y	Y	Y	Y	Y	Y	Y	Y	Y	Y	Y	Y	Y	Y	Y
Y	Y	Y	Y	Y	Y	Y	Y	Y	N	Y	Y	Y	Y	N	Y	Y	N	Y	Y	Y	Y	N	Y
Y	Y	A	Y	Y	Y	Y	Y	Y	Y	Y	Y	Y	N	Y	Y	Y	Y	Y	Y	Y	Y	Y	Y
Y	N	Y	Y	Y	Y	Y	Y	Y	Y	N	Y	Y	Y	N	Y	Y	N	Y	N	Y	N	N	Y
N	Y	N	E	Y	Y	Y	Y	Y	Y	N	Y	Y	Y	Y	Y	Y	Y	Y	Y	Y	A	N	Y
Y	Y	N	Y	Y	Y	Y	Y	Y	Y	N	Y	Y	Y	Y	Y	N	Y	Y	Y	Y	Y	N	Y
Y	Y	Y	Y	Y	Y	N	Y	Y	Y	N	Y	Y	Y	N	Y	Y	N	N	N	Y	Y	Y	Y
Y	Y	Y	Y	P	Y	P	Y	Y	Y	N	Y	Y	Y	Y	Y	Y	Y	Y	Y	Y	Y	Y	Y
Y	N	Y	Y	Y	Y	N	Y	Y	Y	N	Y	Y	Y	Y	Y	Y	N	N	Y	Y	Y	Y	Y
N	Y	Y	Y	Y	Y	Y	Y	Y	Y	P	Y	Y	Y	Y	Y	Y	Y	Y	Y	Y	Y	Y	Y
Y	N	Y	Y	Y	Y	Y	Y	Y	Y	N	Y	Y	Y	N	Y	Y	N	N	N	Y	N	N	Y
Y	N	Y	Y	Y	A	N	Y	Y	N	N	Y	Y	Y	N	Y	Y	N	N	N	Y	N	Y	Y
Y	Y	Y	Y	Y	Y	N	Y	Y	Y	N	Y	Y	Y	N	Y	Y	N	Y	Y	Y	Y	Y	Y
Y	N	Y	Y	Y	Y	Y	Y	Y	N	N	Y	Y	Y	N	Y	N	N	N	Y	Y	N	N	Y
Y	Y	Y	Y	Y	Y	N	Y	Y	N	N	Y	Y	Y	N	Y	Y	N	Y	Y	Y	N	N	Y
Y	N	N	Y	Y	Y	N	Y	Y	Y	N	Y	Y	Y	N	Y	Y	N	N	Y	Y	N	N	Y
Y	Y	Y	Y	N	Y	N	Y	Y	Y	N	Y	Y	Y	N	Y	Y	Y	N	Y	Y	Y	Y	Y
Y	N	Y	Y	Y	Y	Y	Y	Y	N	N	Y	Y	Y	N	Y	N	N	N	Y	Y	Y	N	Y
Y	Y	N	Y	Y	Y	Y	Y	Y	N	N	Y	Y	Y	Y	Y	Y	N	Y	Y	Y	Y	Y	Y
Y	Y	Y	Y	Y	Y	Y	Y	Y	Y	Y	Y	Y	N	A	Y	Y	Y	Y	Y	Y	Y	Y	Y
P	N	Y	Y	Y	Y	Y	Y	Y	N	N	Y	Y	Y	N	Y	Y	Y	Y	Y	Y	N	N	Y
Y	N	N	Y	Y	Y	N	Y	Y	Y	N	Y	Y	Y	Y	Y	Y	N	N	Y	N	N	N	Y
N	N	Y	Y	Y	Y	Y	Y	A	Y	N	Y	Y	Y	Y	Y	Y	N	Y	Y	Y	Y	A	Y
X	E	E	X	X	X	X	X	X	X	X	X	A	X	X	X	X	X	X	X	X	X	X	E

House Member	HB 1315	HB 1332	HB 1337	HB 1343	HB 1347	HB 1388	HB 1486	HB 1504	HB 1512	HB 1525	HB 1565	HB 1588	HB 1618	HB 1627	HB 1680	HB 1696	HB 1703	HB 1704	HB 1707	HB 1785
Acevedo	Y	Y	Y	Y	Y	Y	Y	N	Y	Y	Y	Y	Y	N	Y	P	Y	Y	Y	Y
Ackerman	Y	Y	Y	Y	Y	Y	Y	P	Y	Y	Y	Y	N	Y	Y	Y	N	N	Y	Y
Beaubien	Y	Y	Y	Y	Y	Y	Y	Y	Y	N	Y	Y	Y	Y	Y	Y	N	N	Y	N
Bergman	Y	Y	Y	Y	Y	Y	Y	Y	Y	N	Y	Y	Y	N	Y	Y	N	N	Y	N
Biggert	Y	Y	Y	Y	N	Y	Y	Y	Y	Y	Y	Y	Y	Y	Y	Y	N	N	Y	Y
Biggins	Y	Y	Y	Y	Y	Y	Y	Y	Y	N	Y	Y	Y	Y	Y	Y	N	N	Y	N
Black	Y	Y	Y	N	Y	Y	Y	Y	Y	Y	Y	Y	Y	Y	Y	Y	N	Y	Y	Y
Boland	Y	Y	Y	Y	Y	Y	Y	Y	Y	Y	Y	Y	Y	Y	Y	N	Y	Y	Y	Y
Bost	Y	Y	Y	Y	Y	Y	Y	Y	Y	Y	Y	Y	Y	Y	Y	Y	Y	Y	Y	N
Bradford	Y	Y	Y	Y	Y	Y	Y	Y	Y	Y	Y	Y	Y	Y	Y	N	Y	Y	Y	Y
Bradley	Y	X	Y	Y	Y	Y	X	X	X	Y	Y	Y	X	N	Y	P	Y	Y	Y	Y
Brady	Y	Y	Y	Y	Y	Y	Y	Y	Y	Y	Y	Y	Y	Y	Y	Y	N	N	Y	N
Brosnahan	Y	Y	Y	Y	Y	Y	Y	Y	Y	N	Y	Y	N	N	Y	N	Y	Y	Y	N
Brown	X	X	X	X	X	X	X	X	X	X	X	X	X	X	X	X	X	X	X	X
Brunsvold	Y	Y	Y	Y	Y	Y	Y	N	Y	Y	Y	Y	Y	Y	Y	N	Y	Y	Y	Y
Bugielski	Y	Y	Y	Y	Y	Y	Y	Y	Y	Y	Y	Y	Y	N	Y	Y	Y	Y	Y	Y
Burke	Y	Y	Y	Y	Y	Y	Y	Y	Y	Y	Y	Y	Y	N	Y	N	Y	Y	Y	Y
Capparelli	E	Y	Y	Y	Y	Y	Y	Y	Y	Y	Y	Y	Y	N	Y	Y	Y	Y	Y	Y
Churchill	Y	Y	Y	Y	Y	Y	Y	Y	Y	N	Y	Y	Y	Y	Y	Y	N	N	Y	N
Clayton	Y	Y	Y	Y	N	Y	Y	Y	Y	N	Y	Y	Y	N	Y	Y	N	N	Y	N
Coulson	Y	Y	Y	Y	Y	Y	Y	Y	Y	Y	Y	Y	Y	N	Y	Y	N	N	Y	Y
Cowlishaw	Y	Y	Y	Y	Y	Y	Y	Y	Y	N	Y	Y	Y	N	Y	Y	N	N	Y	N
Cross	Y	Y	Y	Y	Y	Y	Y	Y	Y	Y	Y	Y	Y	Y	Y	Y	N	N	Y	Y
Crotty	Y	Y	Y	Y	Y	Y	Y	Y	Y	N	Y	Y	N	N	Y	N	Y	Y	Y	N
Currie	N	A	Y	Y	Y	Y	Y	Y	Y	Y	Y	Y	Y	N	Y	Y	Y	Y	Y	Y
Curry	Y	Y	Y	Y	Y	Y	Y	Y	Y	N	Y	Y	Y	Y	Y	N	Y	Y	Y	Y
Daniels	Y	Y	Y	Y	Y	Y	Y	Y	Y	N	Y	Y	Y	Y	Y	Y	N	N	Y	N
Dart	Y	Y	Y	Y	Y	Y	Y	Y	Y	Y	Y	Y	Y	N	Y	E	Y	Y	Y	Y
Davis, Monique	N	Y	Y	Y	Y	Y	Y	N	Y	Y	Y	Y	Y	N	Y	Y	Y	Y	Y	Y
Davis, Steve	Y	Y	Y	Y	Y	Y	Y	Y	Y	Y	Y	Y	Y	Y	Y	N	Y	Y	Y	Y
Deuchler	Y	Y	Y	Y	Y	Y	Y	Y	Y	Y	Y	Y	Y	P	Y	P	N	N	Y	Y
Durkin	Y	Y	Y	Y	Y	Y	Y	Y	Y	N	Y	Y	Y	Y	Y	Y	N	N	Y	N
Erwin	Y	Y	Y	Y	Y	Y	Y	Y	Y	Y	Y	Y	Y	Y	Y	N	Y	Y	Y	Y
Fantin	P	Y	Y	N	Y	Y	Y	Y	Y	Y	Y	Y	Y	Y	Y	N	Y	Y	Y	Y
Feigenholtz	Y	N	Y	Y	Y	Y	Y	Y	Y	Y	Y	Y	Y	Y	E	N	Y	Y	Y	Y
Flowers	N	P	Y	Y	Y	Y	Y	Y	Y	Y	Y	Y	Y	A	Y	N	Y	Y	Y	Y
Fritchey	Y	Y	Y	P	Y	Y	Y	Y	Y	Y	Y	Y	Y	A	Y	N	Y	Y	Y	Y
Gash	Y	Y	Y	Y	Y	Y	Y	Y	Y	N	E	Y	N	Y	Y	Y	Y	Y	Y	Y
Giglio	Y	Y	Y	Y	Y	Y	Y	Y	Y	N	Y	Y	Y	N	A	N	Y	Y	Y	Y
Giles	N	Y	Y	Y	Y	Y	Y	A	A	Y	Y	Y	A	N	Y	N	Y	Y	P	Y

HB1807	HB1817	HB1881	HB2061	HB2132	HB2138	HB2164	HB2211	HB2215	HB2262
Y	Y	Y	Y	Y	Y	Y	Y	Y	Y
N	Y	Y	N	Y	Y	P	Y	Y	N
Y	Y	Y	Y	Y	Y	Y	Y	Y	Y
N	Y	Y	N	Y	Y	Y	Y	Y	Y
Y	Y	Y	N	Y	Y	N	N	Y	Y
N	Y	Y	N	Y	Y	Y	Y	Y	Y
N	Y	Y	Y	Y	Y	Y	N	N	Y
Y	Y	Y	N	Y	Y	Y	Y	Y	Y
Y	Y	Y	Y	Y	Y	Y	N	Y	Y
N	Y	Y	Y	Y	Y	N	N	Y	A
X	Y	Y	Y	X	Y	Y	Y	Y	X
N	Y	Y	N	Y	Y	N	Y	Y	N
N	N	Y	Y	Y	N	N	Y	Y	Y
X	X	X	X	X	X	X	X	X	X
Y	Y	Y	Y	Y	Y	Y	Y	Y	N
Y	Y	Y	Y	Y	Y	Y	Y	Y	Y
Y	Y	Y	Y	Y	Y	Y	Y	Y	Y
P	Y	Y	Y	Y	Y	Y	Y	Y	Y
Y	Y	Y	N	Y	Y	N	Y	Y	Y
Y	Y	Y	N	Y	Y	N	N	Y	Y
Y	Y	Y	Y	Y	Y	Y	N	Y	Y
N	Y	Y	N	Y	Y	N	Y	Y	Y
N	Y	Y	Y	Y	Y	Y	Y	Y	Y
N	N	Y	Y	Y	N	N	Y	Y	Y
Y	Y	Y	Y	Y	Y	Y	Y	Y	Y
Y	Y	Y	Y	Y	N	A	Y	Y	Y
Y	Y	Y	N	Y	Y	Y	Y	Y	Y
Y	Y	Y	Y	Y	N	Y	Y	Y	Y
Y	Y	Y	Y	Y	Y	Y	Y	A	Y
N	Y	Y	Y	Y	Y	N	Y	Y	Y
N	Y	Y	N	Y	Y	Y	Y	Y	Y
N	Y	Y	N	Y	Y	Y	Y	Y	P
Y	Y	Y	Y	Y	Y	Y	Y	N	Y
Y	Y	Y	Y	Y	Y	Y	Y	Y	Y
Y	Y	Y	Y	Y	Y	Y	Y	Y	Y
Y	Y	Y	Y	Y	Y	Y	Y	Y	Y
Y	Y	Y	Y	Y	N	Y	Y	Y	Y
Y	E	Y	E	Y	Y	N	Y	Y	Y
N	N	Y	Y	Y	N	Y	Y	Y	Y
A	Y	Y	Y	Y	Y	N	Y	Y	Y

House Member	HB 1325	HB 1327	HB 1333	HB 1347	HB 1348	HB 1378	HB 1386	HB 1404	HB 1512	HB 1525	HB 1565	HB 1568	HB 1618	HB 1627	HB 1680	HB 1696	HB 1703	HB 1704	HB 1707	HB 1785
Granberg	Y	Y	Y	Y	Y	Y	Y	Y	Y	Y	Y	Y	N	Y	Y	N	Y	Y	Y	Y
Hannig	Y	Y	Y	Y	Y	Y	Y	Y	Y	Y	Y	Y	N	Y	Y	N	Y	Y	Y	Y
Hartke	Y	Y	Y	Y	Y	Y	Y	Y	Y	Y	Y	Y	Y	Y	Y	N	Y	Y	Y	Y
Hassert	Y	Y	Y	Y	Y	Y	Y	Y	Y	Y	Y	Y	Y	Y	Y	Y	A	N	Y	Y
Hoeft	Y	Y	Y	Y	Y	Y	Y	Y	A	N	Y	Y	Y	N	Y	Y	N	N	Y	Y
Holbrook	Y	Y	Y	Y	Y	Y	Y	Y	Y	Y	Y	Y	Y	Y	Y	N	Y	Y	Y	Y
Howard	Y	Y	Y	Y	A	Y	Y	Y	Y	Y	Y	Y	Y	P	Y	N	Y	Y	Y	Y
Johnson, Tim	Y	Y	Y	Y	Y	Y	Y	Y	Y	N	Y	Y	Y	Y	Y	Y	N	N	Y	N
Johnson, Tom	Y	Y	Y	Y	Y	Y	Y	N	Y	N	Y	Y	Y	N	Y	Y	N	N	Y	Y
Jones, John	Y	Y	Y	Y	Y	Y	Y	Y	Y	Y	Y	Y	Y	A	Y	N	N	Y	Y	N
Jones, Lovana	N	A	Y	Y	Y	Y	Y	P	Y	Y	Y	Y	Y	N	Y	A	P	P	Y	Y
Jones, Shirley	P	Y	Y	Y	Y	Y	Y	P	Y	Y	Y	Y	Y	N	Y	A	P	P	Y	Y
Kenner	Y	A	Y	Y	Y	Y	Y	P	Y	Y	Y	Y	Y	Y	Y	N	Y	Y	Y	Y
Klingler	Y	Y	Y	Y	Y	Y	Y	Y	Y	Y	Y	Y	Y	Y	Y	Y	Y	Y	Y	N
Kosel	Y	Y	Y	Y	Y	Y	Y	Y	Y	Y	Y	Y	Y	Y	Y	Y	Y	Y	Y	N
Krause	Y	Y	Y	Y	Y	Y	Y	Y	Y	Y	Y	Y	Y	N	Y	Y	P	Y	Y	Y
Kubik	Y	Y	Y	Y	Y	Y	Y	P	Y	N	Y	Y	Y	Y	Y	Y	N	N	Y	A
Lang	Y	P	Y	Y	Y	Y	Y	Y	Y	Y	Y	Y	Y	P	Y	N	Y	Y	Y	Y
Lawfer	Y	Y	Y	Y	Y	Y	Y	P	Y	N	Y	P	Y	Y	Y	Y	N	N	Y	N
Leitch	Y	Y	Y	Y	Y	Y	Y	Y	Y	N	Y	Y	N	Y	Y	Y	N	N	Y	Y
Lindner	Y	Y	Y	Y	Y	Y	Y	Y	Y	Y	Y	Y	Y	A	Y	Y	N	N	Y	Y
Lopez	Y	Y	Y	Y	Y	Y	Y	Y	Y	Y	Y	Y	Y	N	Y	N	Y	Y	Y	Y
Lyons, Eileen	Y	Y	Y	Y	Y	Y	Y	Y	Y	N	A	Y	N	N	Y	A	Y	Y	Y	Y
Lyons, Joseph	Y	Y	Y	Y	Y	Y	Y	Y	Y	Y	Y	Y	Y	N	Y	N	Y	Y	Y	Y
Madigan, Michael	Y	Y	Y	Y	Y	Y	Y	Y	Y	Y	Y	Y	Y	Y	Y	P	Y	A	Y	Y
Mautino	Y	Y	Y	Y	Y	Y	Y	Y	Y	Y	Y	Y	Y	Y	Y	N	Y	Y	Y	N
McAuliffe	Y	Y	Y	Y	Y	Y	Y	Y	Y	N	Y	Y	N	N	Y	Y	Y	Y	Y	N
McCarthy	Y	Y	Y	N	Y	Y	Y	Y	Y	N	Y	Y	Y	N	Y	N	Y	Y	Y	N
McGuire	Y	Y	Y	Y	Y	Y	Y	Y	Y	Y	Y	Y	Y	Y	Y	N	Y	Y	Y	Y
McKeon	N	Y	Y	Y	Y	Y	Y	N	Y	Y	Y	Y	Y	N	Y	N	Y	Y	Y	Y
Meyer	Y	Y	Y	Y	Y	Y	Y	Y	Y	Y	Y	Y	Y	Y	Y	Y	N	N	Y	Y
Mitchell	Y	Y	Y	Y	Y	Y	Y	Y	Y	Y	Y	Y	N	Y	Y	Y	Y	N	Y	Y
Moffitt	Y	Y	Y	Y	Y	Y	Y	Y	Y	Y	Y	Y	Y	Y	Y	Y	N	N	Y	Y
Moore, Andrea	Y	Y	Y	Y	Y	Y	Y	Y	Y	Y	A	Y	Y	N	Y	Y	N	N	Y	Y
Moore, Eugene	N	Y	Y	Y	Y	Y	Y	Y	Y	Y	Y	Y	Y	N	Y	N	Y	Y	Y	Y
Morrow	P	Y	Y	Y	Y	Y	A	P	Y	Y	Y	Y	Y	N	Y	N	Y	Y	Y	Y
Mulligan	Y	Y	Y	Y	Y	Y	Y	Y	Y	N	Y	Y	Y	Y	Y	Y	Y	Y	Y	Y
Murphy	N	Y	Y	Y	Y	Y	Y	P	Y	Y	Y	Y	Y	N	Y	A	P	P	Y	Y
Myers, Richard	Y	Y	Y	Y	Y	Y	Y	Y	Y	Y	Y	Y	Y	Y	Y	Y	Y	N	Y	N
Noland	Y	Y	Y	Y	Y	Y	Y	Y	Y	N	Y	Y	N	Y	Y	Y	N	Y	Y	N

HB 1807	HB 1817	HB 1811	HB 2061	HB 2132	HB 2138	HB 2164	HB 2211	HB 2215	HB 2262
Y	Y	Y	Y	Y	N	Y	Y	N	Y
Y	Y	Y	Y	Y	Y	A	Y	Y	Y
Y	Y	Y	Y	Y	Y	Y	Y	Y	Y
Y	Y	Y	Y	Y	Y	Y	Y	Y	Y
Y	Y	Y	Y	Y	Y	Y	Y	Y	Y
N	Y	Y	Y	Y	Y	N	Y	Y	Y
Y	Y	Y	Y	Y	Y	Y	Y	Y	Y
Y	Y	Y	Y	Y	Y	N	Y	Y	A
N	Y	Y	Y	Y	Y	Y	Y	Y	Y
N	Y	Y	Y	Y	Y	N	N	Y	Y
Y	Y	Y	Y	A	Y	Y	Y	N	A
Y	Y	Y	Y	Y	Y	Y	Y	N	Y
Y	Y	Y	Y	Y	Y	Y	Y	P	Y
Y	Y	Y	Y	Y	N	A	N	Y	Y
N	N	Y	Y	Y	Y	Y	N	Y	Y
Y	Y	Y	Y	Y	Y	Y	Y	Y	Y
Y	Y	Y	Y	Y	Y	Y	Y	Y	Y
Y	Y	Y	Y	Y	N	Y	Y	Y	Y
Y	Y	Y	N	Y	Y	N	P	Y	Y
N	Y	Y	N	Y	Y	N	Y	Y	Y
Y	Y	Y	Y	Y	Y	N	Y	Y	Y
Y	Y	Y	Y	Y	Y	Y	Y	Y	Y
Y	Y	Y	A	Y	Y	Y	N	Y	Y
Y	Y	Y	Y	Y	Y	Y	Y	Y	Y
Y	Y	Y	Y	Y	Y	Y	Y	Y	Y
N	Y	Y	Y	Y	Y	N	Y	Y	N
Y	N	Y	N	Y	Y	N	N	Y	Y
N	N	Y	Y	Y	N	N	Y	Y	Y
Y	Y	Y	Y	Y	Y	Y	Y	Y	Y
Y	Y	Y	Y	Y	Y	Y	Y	Y	Y
N	Y	Y	N	Y	Y	Y	Y	Y	Y
N	Y	Y	N	Y	Y	N	N	Y	Y
Y	Y	Y	Y	Y	Y	N	Y	Y	Y
Y	Y	Y	N	Y	Y	Y	Y	Y	Y
Y	Y	Y	Y	Y	Y	Y	Y	Y	Y
Y	A	Y	Y	Y	Y	Y	Y	P	Y
Y	N	Y	A	Y	N	Y	Y	P	Y
Y	Y	Y	Y	Y	Y	Y	Y	N	Y
Y	Y	Y	Y	Y	Y	N	N	Y	Y
N	Y	Y	Y	Y	Y	Y	N	Y	Y

House Member	HB 1315	HB 1332	HB 1337	HB 1343	HB 1347	HB 1388	HB 1486	HB 1504	HB 1512	HB 1525	HB 1565	HB 1588	HB 1618	HB 1627	HB 1680	HB 1696	HB 1703	HB 1704	HB 1707	HB 1785
Novak	Y	Y	Y	Y	Y	Y	Y	Y	Y	Y	Y	Y	Y	Y	Y	N	Y	Y	Y	Y
O'Brien	Y	Y	Y	Y	Y	Y	Y	Y	Y	N	Y	Y	N	Y	Y	N	Y	Y	Y	Y
Pankau	Y	Y	Y	Y	N	Y	Y	Y	Y	N	Y	Y	Y	N	Y	Y	N	Y	Y	Y
Parke	Y	Y	Y	Y	Y	Y	Y	N	Y	N	Y	Y	Y	Y	Y	Y	A	N	Y	N
Persico	Y	Y	Y	Y	Y	Y	Y	Y	Y	Y	Y	Y	Y	N	Y	Y	N	N	Y	Y
Phelps	Y	Y	Y	Y	Y	Y	Y	Y	Y	Y	Y	Y	Y	Y	Y	N	Y	Y	Y	Y
Poe	Y	Y	Y	Y	Y	Y	Y	Y	Y	Y	Y	Y	Y	Y	Y	Y	Y	Y	Y	N
Pugh	N	Y	Y	Y	Y	Y	Y	P	Y	Y	Y	Y	Y	N	Y	N	Y	Y	Y	Y
Reitz	X	X	X	X	X	X	X	X	X	X	X	X	X	X	X	X	X	X	X	X
Ronen	N	N	Y	Y	Y	Y	Y	Y	Y	Y	Y	Y	Y	N	Y	Y	Y	Y	Y	Y
Roskam	Y	Y	Y	Y	Y	Y	Y	N	Y	Y	Y	Y	Y	Y	Y	Y	N	N	Y	Y
Rutherford	Y	Y	Y	Y	Y	Y	Y	Y	Y	N	Y	Y	Y	Y	Y	Y	N	N	Y	N
Ryder	Y	E	Y	Y	Y	Y	Y	E	E	N	Y	Y	E	Y	Y	Y	N	N	Y	N
Santiago	Y	Y	Y	Y	Y	Y	Y	Y	Y	Y	Y	Y	Y	N	Y	N	Y	Y	Y	Y
Saviano	Y	Y	Y	Y	Y	Y	Y	Y	Y	N	Y	Y	Y	N	Y	Y	Y	Y	Y	N
Schakowsky	N	N	Y	Y	Y	Y	Y	Y	Y	Y	Y	Y	N	N	Y	Y	Y	Y	Y	Y
Schoenberg	Y	A	Y	A	Y	Y	Y	Y	Y	N	Y	Y	N	Y	E	Y	Y	Y	Y	Y
Scott	Y	N	Y	Y	Y	Y	Y	Y	Y	N	Y	Y	Y	N	Y	N	Y	Y	Y	Y
Scully	Y	Y	Y	Y	Y	Y	Y	Y	Y	Y	Y	Y	N	N	Y	N	Y	Y	Y	Y
Silva	Y	Y	Y	Y	Y	Y	A	Y	Y	Y	Y	Y	Y	N	Y	N	Y	Y	Y	Y
Skinner	Y	Y	Y	Y	Y	Y	Y	Y	Y	N	Y	Y	Y	N	Y	Y	N	N	Y	Y
Slone	Y	Y	Y	Y	Y	Y	Y	Y	Y	Y	Y	Y	P	N	Y	N	Y	Y	Y	Y
Smith, Michael	Y	Y	Y	Y	Y	Y	Y	Y	Y	Y	Y	Y	Y	Y	Y	N	Y	Y	Y	Y
Stephens	Y	Y	Y	Y	Y	Y	Y	Y	Y	Y	Y	Y	Y	Y	Y	Y	N	Y	Y	N
Stroger	N	Y	Y	Y	Y	Y	Y	P	Y	Y	Y	Y	Y	N	Y	Y	Y	Y	Y	Y
Tenhouse	Y	Y	Y	Y	Y	Y	Y	Y	Y	N	Y	Y	Y	Y	Y	Y	N	Y	Y	Y
Turner, Arthur	Y	Y	Y	Y	Y	Y	Y	P	Y	Y	Y	Y	Y	N	Y	N	Y	Y	Y	Y
Turner, John	Y	Y	Y	Y	Y	Y	Y	Y	Y	N	Y	Y	N	Y	Y	Y	N	N	Y	N
Wait	Y	Y	Y	Y	Y	Y	Y	Y	Y	N	Y	Y	N	N	Y	Y	N	N	Y	N
Weaver, Michael	Y	Y	Y	Y	Y	Y	Y	Y	Y	Y	Y	Y	N	Y	Y	N	Y	Y	Y	Y
Winkel	Y	Y	Y	Y	Y	Y	Y	Y	Y	Y	Y	Y	Y	Y	Y	Y	N	Y	Y	Y
Winters	Y	Y	Y	Y	Y	Y	Y	Y	Y	N	Y	Y	N	Y	Y	Y	N	N	Y	Y
Wirsing	Y	Y	Y	Y	Y	Y	Y	Y	Y	Y	Y	Y	Y	Y	Y	Y	N	N	Y	N
Wojcik	Y	Y	Y	Y	N	Y	Y	N	Y	N	Y	Y	N	Y	Y	Y	N	N	Y	Y
Wood	Y	Y	Y	Y	Y	Y	Y	Y	Y	Y	Y	Y	Y	Y	Y	Y	N	N	Y	Y
Woolard	Y	Y	Y	Y	Y	Y	Y	Y	Y	Y	Y	Y	Y	Y	Y	N	Y	Y	Y	Y
Younge	N	Y	Y	N	Y	Y	Y	Y	Y	Y	Y	Y	Y	P	Y	Y	Y	Y	Y	Y
Zickus	Y	Y	Y	Y	Y	Y	Y	Y	Y	N	Y	Y	Y	Y	Y	Y	N	N	Y	N
Hughes	Y	Y	Y	Y	Y	Y	Y	N	Y	N	Y	Y	N	Y	Y	Y	N	N	Y	A
Deering	Y	Y	Y	Y	Y	Y	Y	Y	Y	Y	Y	Y	Y	Y	Y	N	Y	Y	Y	Y
Kotlarz	X	X	X	X	X	X	E	X	X	X	X	X	X	X	X	X	X	X	X	X

HB1807	HB1817	HB1881	HB2061	HB2113	HB2138	HB2164	HB2211	HB2215	HB2262
Y	Y	Y	Y	Y	Y	Y	Y	Y	Y
Y	Y	Y	Y	Y	Y	N	Y	Y	Y
N	Y	Y	Y	Y	Y	Y	Y	Y	Y
N	Y	Y	Y	Y	Y	N	N	Y	Y
Y	Y	Y	N	Y	Y	Y	Y	Y	Y
P	Y	Y	Y	Y	Y	Y	Y	Y	Y
N	A	Y	Y	Y	Y	N	N	Y	Y
N	Y	Y	Y	P	Y	Y	Y	P	Y
X	X	X	X	X	X	X	X	X	X
Y	Y	Y	Y	Y	Y	Y	Y	Y	Y
N	Y	Y	N	Y	Y	N	N	N	N
N	Y	Y	N	Y	Y	N	Y	Y	N
E	Y	Y	N	E	Y	N	Y	Y	E
Y	Y	Y	Y	Y	Y	Y	Y	Y	Y
Y	Y	Y	N	Y	Y	Y	Y	Y	Y
Y	E	Y	Y	Y	Y	Y	Y	Y	Y
Y	Y	Y	Y	Y	Y	N	Y	Y	Y
Y	Y	Y	Y	Y	Y	Y	Y	Y	Y
N	Y	Y	Y	Y	Y	N	Y	Y	Y
Y	Y	Y	Y	Y	Y	Y	Y	Y	Y
Y	Y	Y	Y	Y	Y	Y	A	Y	Y
Y	Y	Y	Y	Y	Y	Y	Y	Y	Y
Y	Y	Y	Y	Y	Y	Y	Y	Y	Y
N	Y	Y	N	Y	Y	N	Y	Y	A
N	Y	Y	Y	Y	Y	Y	Y	P	Y
Y	Y	Y	Y	Y	Y	N	Y	N	N
Y	Y	Y	Y	Y	Y	Y	Y	P	Y
N	Y	Y	Y	Y	Y	N	Y	Y	N
N	Y	Y	N	Y	Y	N	Y	N	Y
N	Y	Y	Y	Y	Y	N	Y	Y	Y
N	Y	Y	N	Y	Y	Y	N	Y	Y
N	Y	Y	N	Y	Y	N	Y	Y	Y
N	Y	Y	N	Y	Y	Y	Y	Y	A
Y	N	Y	N	Y	Y	Y	N	Y	Y
Y	Y	Y	N	Y	Y	Y	N	Y	Y
Y	Y	Y	Y	Y	Y	Y	Y	Y	Y
Y	Y	Y	Y	Y	Y	A	Y	A	Y
N	Y	Y	Y	Y	Y	Y	N	Y	Y
N	Y	Y	N	Y	Y	P	Y	Y	Y
Y	Y	Y	Y	Y	Y	N	Y	Y	Y
X	X	X	X	X	X	X	X	X	X

Part 3

Appendices

David A. Joens   Kent D. Redfield

Table 1 Illinois at a glance: 10 year comparison*

	1986 - 1987	1996 - 1997
General information		
Population	11,535,000	11,829,940
Resident live births	180,657	185,801
Resident deaths	101,948	108,089
Personal Income ($ millions)	$165,900	$299,054
Per capita income	$14,397	$23,611
Highest point (in feet; Charles Mound, JoDaviess County)	1, 241	1,235
Lowest point (in feet; Cairo on the Ohio River)	269	285
Square miles	55,593	55,593
Education		
Elementary schools:		
public	2,712	2,598
non-public	1,272	1,009
Special education:		
public	N/A	N/A
non-public	133	146
High schools:		
public	714	639
non-public	322	119
Colleges and Universities:		
independent colleges	126	103
public universities	12	12
community colleges	50	49

Table 1 Illinois at a glance: 10 year comparison, continued

	1986 - 1987	1996 - 1997
Services		
Banks:		
State banks[a]	872	745
National banks	400	251
Hospitals	257	242
Mental Health Centers	N/A	21
Public libraries	610	627
Recreational areas:		
State parks	66	63
Fish and wildlife sites	21	30
Historic sites and state memorials	40b	24
State Forests	5	6
Conservation areas	25	26
Churches[b]	9,358	12,376d
Occupations/Professions		
Attorneys	47,400	68,819
Physicians and surgeons	33,799e	34,842
Dentists	9,344	9,598
Registered Nurses	115,610	133,254

[a] State banks include foreign banking for data.

[b] Churches include temples and shrines for data in 1996-1997.

Table 1 Illinois at a glance: 10 year comparison, continued

	1987	1997
Natural and Manufactured Resources		
Coal mines	47	28
Coal resources (billions of tons)	181	49.5 mil.
Grain production		
Corn (billions of bushels)	1.53	1.13
Soybeans (millions of bushels)	382	373.5
Wheat (millions of bushels)	37	68.1
Sorghum (millions of bushels)	36	11.7
Oats (millions of bushels)	12.5	N/A
Manufacturing establishments		
Illinois plants	18,063	18,964
Primary metal industries	502	426
Iron and steel foundries	71	51

Sources: Handbook of Illinois Government, Secretary of State, State of Illinois, 1987-1988, 1997-1998.
* Figures represent the latest data available to the compilers of the *Handbook of Illinois Government*.

Table 2 Illinois constitutional change proposals and state voting since the 1968 proposal to call a Constitutional Convention

Proposed Amendment	Year	For	Against	Passed/Failed
Proposal to Call Constitutional Convention	1968	2,979,977	1,135,440	Passed
Proposed 1970 Constitution	1970	1,122,425	838,168	Passed
Governor's Amendatory Veto	1974	1,302,313	1,329,719	Failed
Personal Property Tax	1978	952,416	733,845	Failed
Veterans' Organizations' Post Homes Exemption	1978	747,907	806,579	Failed
Legislative Article (Cutback Amendment)	1980	2,112,224	962,325	Passed
Revenue Article (Delinquent Tax Sales)	1980	1,857,985	798,422	Passed
Bail & Habeas Corpus	1982	1,389,796	239,380	Passed
Veterans' Property Tax Exemption	1984	1,147,864	1,042,481	Failed
Bail & Habeas Corpus	1986	1,368,242	402,891	Passed
Veterans' Property Tax Exemption	1986	860,609	727,737	Failed
Delinquent Sales Tax	1988	1,497,885	1,035,190	Passed
Voting Qualifications	1988	2,086,744	1,162,258	Passed
Proposed Call for a Constitutional Convention	1988	900,109	2,727,144	Failed
Delinquent Sales Tax	1990	1,004,546	385,772	Passed
Crime Victim's Rights	1992	2,964,592	715,602	Passed
Education	1992	1,882,569	1,417,520	Failed
Effective Dates of Bills	1994	1,476,615	667,585	Passed
Rights After Indictment	1994	1,525,525	906,383	Passed

Note: A proposed amendment becomes effective if approved by either three-fifths of those voting on the question or a majority of those voting in the election.

Sources: *State of Illinois Official Vote, General Election,* November 5, 1968, State Board of Elections, 50-51; *State of Illinois Official Vote, General Election,* November 3, 1970, Secretary of State, 1970, 102-104; *Illinois Blue Book,* Secretary of State, State of Illinois, 1987-88, 541; *State of Illinois Official Vote, General Election,* November 8, 1988, State Board of Elections, 1988, 162-165; *State of Illinois Official Vote, General Election,* November 6, 1990, State Board of Elections, 1990, 180-182; *State of Illinois Official Vote, General Election,* November 3,1992 State Board of Elections, 1992, xvi, xix; *State of Illinois Official Vote, General Election,* November 8, 1994, State board of Elections, vii, x.

Table 3 Constitutional officers: 1997

Attorney General[1] - Jim Ryan
Auditor General[2] - William G. Holland
Comptroller[1] - Loleta A. Didrickson
Superintendent of Education[3] - Joseph A. Spagnolo
Executive Director, State Board of Elections[4] - Ronald D. Michaelson
Governor[1] - Jim Edgar
Lieutenant Governor[1] - Bob Kustra
Secretary of State[1] - George H. Ryan
Treasurer[1] - Judy Baar Topinka

[1] Elected every four years.
[2] Elected by the General Assembly every 10 years.
[3] Appointed by the State Board of Education.
[4] Appointed by the State Board of Elections.

Source: 1997 Roster of State Government Officials, Illinois Issues, 1997, 4-7, 11, 39, 23.

Table 4 Annual salaries of selected legislative, judicial, and executive employees: 1997

Elected Officials

Office/Position	Salary effective 1/10/95
Governor	$126,590
Lt.Governor	$89,357
Secretary of State	$111,697
Comptroller	$96,804
Treasurer	$96,804
Attorney General	$111,697
	Salary effective 7/1/96
General Assembly Member	$47,039
Senator not elected in 1996	$45,669
Senate President and Minority Leader	$19,647
Senate leadership	$14,734
Senate Caucus Chairs	$14,734
Senate Chairs and Spokespersons	$7,369
Speaker and Minority Leader, House of Representatives	$19,647
House Majority Leader	$16,576
Deputy House Leaders	$14,121
House Assistant Leaders	$12,892
House Majority Conference Chairs	$12,892
House Chairs and Spokesperson	$7,369
	Salary effective 7/1/96
Auditor General	$111,697
Deputy Auditor General	$87,887

Table 4 Annual salaries of selected legislative, judicial, and executive employees: 1997, continued

Elected Officials	
Supreme Court justices (7)	$130,250
Appellate Judges (40)	$122,588
Circuit Judges (426)	$112,491
Associate judges (410)	$104,830

Appointed Officials

Office/Position	**Salary effective 7/1/96**
Aging Director	$74,464
Agriculture Director	$89,357
Agriculture Assistant Director	$74,464
Auditor General	$94,535
Deputy Auditor Generals (2)	$87,887
Banks and Real Estate Commissioner	$92,636
Banks and Real Estate First Deputy Commissioner	$85,509
Banks and Real Estate Deputy Commissioners (2)	$78,384
CMS Director	$93,080
CMS Assistant Directors (2)	$78,189
DCFS Director	$94,535
Civil Service Commission Chair	$17,870
Civil Service Commission Members (2)	$12,275 - 13,405*
Commerce Commission Chair	$95,629
Commerce Commission Members (4)	$83,514
DCCA Director	$89,357
DCCA Assistant Director	$74,464
Corrections Director	$104,369
Corrections Assistant Directors (2)	$74,464
Court of Claims Chief Justice	$46,317
Court of Claims Judges (6)	$42,754

Table 4 Annual salaries of selected legislative, judicial, and executive employees: 1997, continued

Appointed Officials

Office/Position	**Salary effective 7/1/96**
Education Labor Relations Board Chair	$68,189 - 74,464 *
Education Labor Relations Board Members (2)	$67,019
State Board of Elections Chair	$41,701
State Board of Elections Vice Chair	$34,254
State Board of Elections Members (6)	$26,808
Emergency Management Agency Director	$72,233
Employment Security Director	$96,804
EPA Director	$89,357
Financial Institutions Director	$74,464
Fire Marshal	$72,223
Human Rights Director	$77,444
Human Rights Commission Chair	$37,232
Human Rights Commission Members (12)	$33,508
Human Services Secretary	$104,369
Human Services Assistant Secretaries (2)	$81,911
Labor Relations Board Chair	$68,189 - 74,464 *
State Labor Board Members (2)	$67,019
Local Labor Board Members (2)	$67,019
Industrial Commission Chair	$89,357
Industrial Commission Members (6)	$85,509
Department of Insurance Director	$81,911
Department of Insurance Assistant Director	$67,019
Department of Labor Director	$81,911
Department of Labor Assistant Director	$67,019
Labor Chief Factory Inspector	$37,232
Labor Superintendent of Safety	$40,955

Table 4 Annual salaries of selected legislative, judicial, and executive employees: 1997, continued

Appointed Officials

Office/Position	Salary effective 7/1/96
Liquor Control Chair	$19,775 - 21,595 *
Liquor Control Secretary	$26,808
Liquor Control Members (4)	$17,871
Lottery Director	$81,911
Military Affairs Adjutant General	$72,233
Military Affairs Assistant Adjutant General (Army)	$64,040
Military Affairs Assistant Adjutant General (Air)	$64,040
Natural Resources Director	$89,357
Natural Resources Assistant Director	$74,464
Natural Resources Examining Officers (4)	$9,210
Natural Resources Mine Officers (6)	$11,168
Nuclear Safety Director	$77,444
Pollution Control Chair	$86,366
Pollution Control Board members (6)	$83,514
Prisoner Review Board Chair	$68,408
Prisoner Review Board Members (11)	$61,283
Department of Professional Regulation Director	$81,911
Property Tax Appeal Board Chair	$46,168
Property Tax Appeal Board Members (4)	$37,232
Public Aid Director	$96,804
Public Aid Assistant Director	$81,911
Public Health Director	$96,804
Public Health Assistant Director	$81,911
Racing Board Members (9 @ $300/day)	$300/day/$8,938/yr
Revenue Director	$96,804
Revenue Assistant Director	$81,911

Table 4 Annual salaries of selected legislative, judicial, and executive employees: 1997, continued

Appointed Officials

Office/Position	Salary effective 7/1/96
State Sanitary District Observer	$22,339
Secretary of State Merit Commission Chair	$10,000 - 12,279 **
Secretary of State Merit Commission Members (4)	$9,210 **
State Police Merit Board Chair	$155-170 *
State Police Merit Board Members (4)	$170
State Police Director	$89,357
State Police Assistant Director	$74,464
Department of Transportation Secretary	$96,804
Department of Transportation Assistant Secretary	$81,911
Veterans' Affairs Director	$72,233
Veterans' Affairs Assistant Director	$64,040

* Effective upon reappointment, will receive the 4/94 CRB of 4.5% (eff 7/94) and 4.5% (eff 7/95).

** Upon reappointment will receive the 7/91 - 7/97 COLAS and the 7/94 CRB 4.5% increase and the 7/95 CRB 4.5 increase.

From telephone interviews with the Comptrollers Office and the Administrative Office of the Illinois Courts on 10/22/97, and from the Legislative Research Unit's *History of Illinois Legislators' Compensation and Expense Allowances,* 1997.

Table 5 Legislative district population characteristics: 1992

Rep. District	Population	Non-Hispanic White	%	Non-Hispanic Black	%	Hispanic	%	Non-Hispanic Asian & Pacific	%
1	96,869	20,379	21.0	4,543	4.7	70,902	73.2	679	0.7
2	96,870	15,597	16.1	2,501	2.6	77,937	80.5	500	0.5
3	96,869	17,363	17.9	9,056	9.3	69,038	71.3	1,046	1.1
4	96,870	20,119	20.8	7,266	7.5	68,275	70.5	675	0.7
5	96,870	21,211	22.0	63,399	65.4	8,413	8.7	3,591	3.7
6	96,869	19,505	20.1	63,087	65.1	4,260	4.4	9,819	10.1
7	96,870	27,996	28.9	63,109	65.1	4,090	4.2	1,447	1.5
8	96,869	25,605	26.4	66,691	68.8	3,244	3.3	1,173	1.2
9	96,869	9,070	9.4	77,421	79.9	9,191	9.5	995	1.0
10	96,870	8,041	8.3	76,344	78.8	11,170	11.5	1,147	1.2
11	96,870	84,430	87.2	5,806	6.0	3,595	3.7	2,855	2.9
12	96,869	71,216	73.5	10,450	10.8	10,287	10.6	4,527	4.7
13	96,869	87,240	90.1	178	0.2	2,571	2.7	6,778	7.0
14	96,870	89,853	92.8	507	0.5	4,150	4.3	2,221	2.3
15	96,870	72,128	74.5	952	1.0	9,861	10.2	13,657	14.1
16	96,869	68,619	70.8	3,370	3.5	8,688	9.0	15,815	16.3
17	96,870	48,939	50.5	18,527	19.1	18,194	18.8	10,503	10.8
18	96,869	57,631	59.5	23,864	24.6	7,953	8.2	7,052	7.3
19	96,870	81,166	83.8	226	0.2	12,817	13.2	2,515	2.6
20	96,869	66,699	68.9	772	.8	21,520	22.2	7,411	7.7
21	96,870	26,537	27.4	63,812	65.9	5,787	6.0	614	0.6
22	96,869	89,952	92.9	103	0.1	5,892	6.1	752	0.8
23	96,870	21,788	22.5	63,233	65.3	11,276	11.6	414	0.4
24	96,869	19,001	19.6	66,248	68.4	11,003	11.4	414	0.4
25	96,870	19,344	20.0	72,259	74.6	1,910	2.0	3,037	3.1
26	96,870	14,852	15.3	70,507	72.8	10,737	11.1	520	0.5
27	96,869	31,916	32.9	63,032	65.1	1,469	1.5	306	0.3
28	96,870	29,129	30.1	63,357	65.4	4,059	4.2	174	0.2

Table 5 Legislative district population characteristics: 1992, continued

Rep. District	Population	Non-Hispanic White	%	Non-Hispanic Black	%	Hispanic	%	Non-Hispanic Asian & Pacific	%
29	96,870	28,915	29.8	63,164	65.2	4,279	4.4	954	0.3
30	96,869	27,500	28.4	63,170	65.2	5,430	5.6	540	0.6
31	96,870	12,439	12.8	63,003	65.0	21,079	21.8	131	0.1
32	96,869	23,630	24.4	63,114	65.2	9,661	10.0	302	0.3
33	96,870	48,450	50.0	3,484	3.6	38,179	39.4	6,149	6.3
34	96,869	49,163	50.7	11,019	11.4	24,476	25.3	11,233	11.6
35	96,869	90,959	93.9	1,861	1.9	2,508	2.6	1,421	1.5
36	96,870	90,576	93.5	1,420	1.5	3,786	4.0	978	1.0
37	96,869	85,900	88.7	6,715	6.9	2,053	2.1	2,108	2.2
38	96,870	85,316	88.1	7,788	8.0	2,428	2.5	1,176	1.2
39	96,869	88,558	91.4	2,003	2.1	2,419	2.5	3,731	3.9
40	96,870	86,979	89.8	2,296	2.4	3,562	3.7	3,877	4.0
41	96,869	88,060	90.9	2,461	2.5	2,034	2.1	4,181	4.3
42	96,870	80,933	83.5	6,935	7.2	7,659	7.9	1,117	1.1
43	96,870	78,476	81.0	116	0.1	16,817	17.4	1,254	1.3
44	96,869	84,752	87.5	2,487	2.6	4,507	4.7	4,967	5.1
45	96,870	83,891	86.6	1,912	2.0	4,205	4.3	6,722	6.9
46	96,869	82,025	84.7	613	0.6	9,923	10.2	4,095	4.2
47	96,869	86,090	88.9	2,390	2.5	7,125	7.4	1,076	1.1
48	96,870	89,243	92.1	2,231	2.3	3,024	3.1	2,231	2.3
49	96,870	80,560	83.2	2,414	2.5	6,531	6.7	7,197	7.4
50	96,869	85,577	88.3	1,296	1.1	6,850	7.1	2,967	3.1
51	96,870	85,742	88.5	1,365	1.4	5,385	5.6	4,258	4.4
52	96,869	89,247	92.1	496	0.5	5,090	6.1	996	1.0
53	96,869	80,621	83.2	2,388	2.5	7,328	7.6	6,328	6.5
54	96,870	89,050	91.9	1,007	1.0	3,507	8.6	3,169	3.3
55	96,870	82,262	84.9	1,096	1.1	6,495	6.7	6,835	7.1
56	96,869	89,157	92.0	603	0.6	9,262	3.4	3,734	3.8

Table 5 Legislative district population characteristics: 1992, continued

Rep. District	Population	Non-Hispanic White	%	Non-Hispanic Black	%	Hispanic	%	Non-Hispanic Asian & Pacific	%
57	96,870	85,721	88.5	789	0.8	4,366	4.5	5,894	6.1
58	96,869	86,359	89.2	2,192	2.3	1,569	1.6	6,632	6.8
59	96,869	57,774	59.6	20,839	21.5	15,456	16.0	2,368	2.4
60	96,870	86,054	88.8	1,571	1.6	5,820	6.0	3,301	3.4
61	96,870	81,983	84.6	4,105	4.3	6,986	7.2	3,440	3.6
62	96,869	84,184	86.9	6,493	6.7	4,650	4.8	1,207	1.2
63	96,870	92,393	95.4	140	0.1	3,568	3.7	572	0.6
64	96,869	92,470	95.5	206	0.2	2,647	2.7	1,388	1.4
65	96,869	87,237	90.1	2,270	2.3	6,069	6.3	1,086	1.1
66	96,870	72,795	75.1	4,932	5.1	15,639	16.1	3,237	3.3
67	96,869	70,444	72.7	19,667	20.3	5,099	5.3	1,282	1.3
68	96,870	91,135	94.1	1,258	1.3	3,298	3.4	957	1.0
69	96,870	91,853	94.8	2,251	2.3	1,708	1.8	810	0.9
70	96,870	89,467	92.4	2,080	2.1	3,321	3.4	1,789	1.8
71	96,870	88,533	91.4	2,825	2.9	4,697	4.8	607	0.6
72	96,869	84,642	87.4	7,560	7.8	3,940	4.1	481	0.5
73	96,870	90,002	92.9	1,566	1.6	4,743	4.9	925	0.3
74	96,869	92,025	95.0	3,214	3.3	1,050	1.1	423	0.4
75	96,870	93,510	96.5	1,038	1.1	1,604	1.7	492	0.5
76	96,869	91,835	94.8	523	0.5	3,837	4.0	510	0.5
77	96,870	79,830	82.4	2,453	2.5	12,535	12.9	1,905	2.0
78	96,869	85,288	88.0	1,008	1.0	7,645	7.9	2,758	2.8
79	96,869	77,401	79.9	15,315	15.8	3,224	3.3	799	0.8
80	96,870	68,269	70.5	19,411	20.0	7,839	8.1	1,089	1.1
81	96,869	86,766	89.6	1,801	1.9	2,683	2.8	5,497	5.7
82	96,869	80,302	82.9	7,618	7.9	3,684	3.8	5,007	5.2
83	96,870	87,711	90.5	3,656	3.8	3,941	4.1	1,389	1.4
84	96,869	69,997	72.3	6,002	6.2	20,007	20.7	624	0.6

Table 5 Legislative district population characteristics: 1992, continued

Rep. District	Population	Non-Hispanic White	%	Non-Hispanic Black	%	Hispanic	%	Non-Hispanic Asian & Pacific	%
85	96,870	74,974	77.4	19,179	19.8	2,098	2.2	418	0.4
86	96,869	63,816	65.8	21,139	21.8	11,062	11.4	574	0.6
87	96,869	91,641	94.6	2,776	2.9	1,718	1.8	542	0.6
88	96,870	89,065	91.9	4,859	5.0	1,422	1.5	1,922	0.4
89	96,869	95,548	98.6	184	0.2	662	0.7	927	0.3
90	96,870	94,469	97.5	1,335	1.4	625	0.6	283	0.3
91	96,869	94,137	97.2	1,536	1.6	671	0.7	310	0.3
92	96,870	72,285	74.6	21,560	22.3	1,705	1.7	999	1.0
93	96,870	91,702	94.7	2,705	2.8	1,068	1.1	1,211	1.3
94	96,869	90,989	93.8	3,434	3.5	1,957	2.0	420	0.4
95	96,870	92,147	95.1	2,926	3.0	741	0.8	859	0.9
96	96,869	94,273	97.3	1,712	1.8	375	0.4	311	0.3
97	96,870	94,781	97.8	1,017	1.1	523	0.5	338	0.3
98	96,869	95,163	98.2	922	1.0	434	0.4	183	0.2
99	96,870	93,538	96.6	1,999	2.1	567	0.6	550	0.6
100	96,869	82,767	85.4	12,309	12.7	754	0.8	825	0.9
101	96,869	83,753	86.5	12,324	12.7	369	0.4	219	0.2
102	96,870	94,161	97.2	1,823	1.9	391	0.4	385	0.4
103	96,869	83,291	86.0	4,929	5.1	2,063	2.1	6,368	6.6
104	96,870	81,755	84.4	11,529	11.9	1,741	1.8	1,574	1.6
105	96,870	85,961	89.8	7,648	7.9	1,533	1.6	519	0.5
106	96,869	94,587	97.6	1,171	1.2	540	0.6	403	0.4
107	96,869	94,000	97.0	2,002	2.1	396	0.4	312	0.3
108	96,870	95,875	99.0	235	0.2	375	0.4	219	0.2
109	96,870	92,237	95.2	3,413	3.5	678	0.7	914	0.3
110	96,869	90,486	93.4	3,979	4.1	1,196	1.2	968	1.0
111	96,870	87,456	90.3	7,729	8.0	964	1.0	935	0.3
112	96,869	88,479	91.3	5,605	5.8	1,405	1.5	1,143	1.2

Table 5 Legislative district population characteristics: 1992, continued

Rep. District	Population	Non-Hispanic White	%	Non-Hispanic Black	%	Hispanic	%	Non-Hispanic Asian & Pacific	%
113	96,869	89,013	91.9	5,419	5.6	1,622	1.7	512	0.5
114	96,870	31,429	32.4	63,823	65.9	1,193	1.2	213	0.2
115	96,870	86,261	89.0	6,767	7.0	1,369	1.4	2,270	2.3
116	96,869	92,621	95.6	3,047	3.1	758	0.8	222	0.2
117	96,869	95,257	98.3	678	0.7	460	0.5	243	0.3
118	96,870	86,014	88.8	9,666	10.0	694	0.7	250	0.3
Total	11,430,602	8,550,208	74.8	1,673,709	14.6	904,446	7.9	275,568	2.4

Source: Data provided by the Illinois Legislative Redistricting Commission as of October 7, 1991.

Table 6 Percentage of partisan votes and General Assembly division: 1920-1996

Election Year*	Division of vote for head of ticket[1]		Illinois House of Representatives[2]		Illinois House of Representatives[2]		Illinois Senate		Illinois Senate	
	D	R	D	R	D	R	D	R	D	R
1920(P)	25.5%	67.8%	58	95	37.9%	62.1%	8	43	15.7%	84.3%
1922(T)	41.2%	54.6%	64	88	41.8%	57.5%	9	42	17.6%	82.4%
1924(P)	23.4%	58.5%	59	94	38.6%	61.4%	14	37	27.5%	72.5%
1926(S)	43.1%	56.9%	60	92	39.2%	60.1%	11	40	21.6%	78.4%
1928(P)	42.3%	56.9%	62	91	40.5%	59.5%	11	40	21.6%	78.4%
1930(S)	64.1%	30.7%	72	81	47.1%	52.9%	18	33	35.3%	64.7%
1932(P)	55.2%	42.1%	80	73	52.3%	47.7%	33	18	64.7%	35.3%
1934(T)	51.2%	42.0%	84	69	54.9%	45.1%	35	16	68.6%	31.4%
1936(P)	57.1%	39.3%	86	67	56.2%	43.8%	33	18	64.7%	35.3%
1938(S)	50.0%	47.1%	74	79	48.4%	51.6%	31	20	60.8%	39.2%
1940(P)	50.3%	48.0%	74	79	48.4%	51.6%	23	28	45.1%	54.9%
1942(S)	45.3%	51.9%	69	84	45.1%	54.9%	23	28	45.1%	54.9%
1944(P)	51.0%	47.5%	74	79	48.4%	51.6%	17	34	33.3%	66.7%
1946(T)	40.9%	54.2%	65	88	42.5%	57.5%	13	38	25.5%	74.5%
1948(P)	48.9%	48.1%	81	72	52.9%	47.1%	18	33	35.3%	64.7%
1950(S)	44.4%	52.3%	69	84	45.1%	54.9%	20	31	39.2%	60.8%
1952(P)	44.1%	53.8%	67	86	43.8%	56.2%	13	38	25.5%	74.5%
1954(S)	52.2%	45.3%	74	79	48.4%	51.6%	19	32	37.3%	62.7%
1956(P)	39.6%	58.5%	83	94	46.9%	53.1%	20	38	34.5%	65.5%
1958(T)	49.3%	45.2%	91	86	51.4%	48.6%	24	34	41.4%	58.6%
1960(P)	49.1%	48.9%	88	89	49.7%	50.3%	27	31	56.6%	53.4%
1962(S)	45.8%	51.4%	87	90	49.2%	50.8%	23	35	39.7%	60.3%
1964(P)	58.2%	39.7%	118	59	66.7%	33.3%	25	33	43.1%	56.9%
1966(S)	42.7%	53.4%	78	99	44.1%	55.9%	20	38	34.5%	65.5%
1968(P)	43.3%	46.1%	83	94	46.3%	53.7%	20	38	34.5%	65.5%

Table 6 Percentage of partisan votes and General Assembly division: 1920-1996, continued

Election Year*	Division of vote for head of ticket[1]		Illinois House of Representatives[2]		Illinois House of Representatives[2]		Illinois Senate		Illinois Senate	
	D	R	D	R	D	R	D	R	D	R
1970(S)	55.3%	40.7%	87	90	49.2%	50.8%	29	29	50.0%	50.0%
1972(P)	39.2%	57.1%	88	89	49.7%	50.3%	29	30	49.2%	50.8%
1974(S)	58.7%	35.2%	101	76	57.1%	42.9%	34	25	57.6%	42.4%
1976(P)	56.9%	49.3%	94	83	53.1%	56.9%	34	25	57.6%	42.4%
1978(S)	43.3%	50.8%	89	88	50.3%	49.7%	32	27	54.2%	45.8%
1980(P)	40.7%	48.4%	86	91	48.6%	51.4%	30	29	50.8%	49.2%
1982(G)	46.9%	47.1%	70	48	59.3%	40.7%	33	26	55.9%	44.1%
1984(P)	42.0%	54.5%	67	51	56.8%	43.2%	31	28	52.5%	47.5%
1986(S)	61.0%	31.6%	67	51	56.8%	53.2%	31	28	52.5%	47.5%
1988(P)	47.2%	49.2%	67	51	56.8%	43.2%	31	28	52.5%	47.5%
1990(S)	61.8%	33.2%	72	46	61.0%	39.0%	31	28	52.5%	47.5%
1992(P)	48.6%	34.3%	67	51	56.7%	43.2%	27	32	45.8%	54.2%
1994(G)	34.4%	63.9%	54	64	45.7%	54.3%	26	33	44.1%	55.9%
1996(P)	54.3%	36.8%	60	58	50.8%	49.2%	28	31	47.5%	52.5%

* The letter in parentheses—P for President, G for Governor, S for U.S. Senator, T for State Treasurer—indicates the highest-ranking office on the ballot at the election.

[1]Total vote exceeds Republican and Democratic vote because it includes third-party votes and the votes of those who did not vote for head of ticket.

[2]Includes incumbents whose seats were not up for election. Where the number of members shown adds to less than the total membership, the difference is due to vacancies or third-party memberships.

Sources: Compiled by the Legislative Research Unit staff from Illinois election statistics published by Secretary of State and State Board of Elections, various years; *Illinois Legislative Handbooks*, various years.

Table 7 Illinois newspaper circulation: 1996

City	Name	County	Population	Circulation	Percent of Pop.
Alton, East Alton	The Telegraph	Madison	51,458	31,325	61
Aurora	The Beacon-News	Kane	99,581	37,964	39
Belleville	Belleville News-Democrat	St. Clair	42,785	50,252	118
Belvidere	Belvidere Daily Republican	Boone	15,958	4,822	31
Benton	Benton Evening News	Franklin	7,216	3,907	55
Bloomington-Normal	The Pantagraph	McLean	91,995	50,670	55
Canton	Daily Ledger	Fulton	13,922	5,851	42
Carbondale-Herrin-Murphysboro	Southern Illinoisan	Jackson & Williamson	47,066	29,626	63
Carmi	Carmi Times	White	5,564	2,612	47
Centralia-Central City-Wamac	Centralia Sentinel	Marion	17,165	15,772	92
Champaign-Urbana	The News Gazette	Champaign	99,846	45,425	46
Charleston	Coles County Daily Times Courier	Coles	20,398	7,472	37
Chicago	Chicago Defender	Cook	2,783,726	19,541	1
	Daily Herald	Cook	2,783,726	128,172	5
	Daily Southtown	Cook	2,783,726	58,034	2
	Chicago Sun-Times	Cook	2,783,726	488,405	18
	Chicago Tribune	Cook	2,783,726	684,366	25
Clinton	Clinton Daily Journal	DeWitt	7,437	3,593	49
Crystal Lake	The Northwest Herald	McHenry	24,512	31,025	127
Danville	Commerical-News	Vermilion	33,828	20,099	60
Decatur	Herald & Review	Macon	83,885	40,830	49
DeKalb	The Daily Chronicle	DeKalb	34,925	10,384	30
Dixon	The Telegraph	Lee	15,144	10,360	69
DuQuion	DuQuion Evening Call	Perry	6,697	4,035	61
Edwardsville	Edwardsville Intelligencer	Madison	14,579	6,894	48
Effingham	Effingham Daily News	Effingham	11,651	12,815	110

Table 7 Illinois newspaper circulation: 1996, continued

City	Name	County	Population	Circulation	Percent of Pop.
Eldorado	Eldorado Daily Journal	Saline	4,536	1,254	28
Elgin	The Courier-News	Cook&Kane	77,010	25,609	34
Flora	The Daily Clay County Advocate-Press	Clay	5,054	3,725	74
Freeport	The Journal-Standard	Stephenson	25,840	16,555	64
Galesburg	The Register-Mail	Knox	33,530	17,518	53
Geneva	Kane County Chronicle	Kane	12,617	13,774	110
Harrisburg	The Daily Register	Saline	9,289	5,643	61
Jacksonville	Jacksonville Journal-Courier	Morgan	19,324	14,457	75
Joliet	Herald-News	Will	76,836	49,390	65
Kankakee	The Daily Journal/The Sunday Journal	Kankakee	27,575	29,162	106
Kewanee	Star-Courier	Henry	12,969	6,547	51
LaSalle-Peru-Oglesby-Spring Valley	News-Tribune	LaSalle & Bureau	27,884	19,416	70
Lawrenceville	Daily Record	Lawrence	4,897	3,947	81
Lincoln	The Courier	Logan	15,418	6,967	46
Litchfield	News-Herald	Montgomery	6,883	5,800	85
Macomb	Macomb Journal	McDonough	19,952	7,450	38
Marion	The Marion Daily Republican	Williamson	14,545	4,545	31
Mattoon	Mattoon Journal-Gazette	Coles	18,441	11,969	65
Moline, East Moline	The Dispatch	Rock Island	63,349	28,247	45
Monmouth	Daily Review Atlas	Warren	9,489	3,416	36
Morris	Daily Herald	Grundy	10,270	7,173	70
Mount Carmel	Daily Republican Register	Wabash	8,287	4,192	51
Mount Vernon	Register-News	Jefferson	16,988	11,904	70
Olney	Olney Daily Mail	Richland	8,664	4,183	49
Ottawa	The Daily Times	LaSalle	17,541	12,580	72

Table 7 Illinois newspaper circulation: 1996, continued

City	Name	County	Population	Circulation	Percent of Pop.
Paris	The Paris Daily Beacon-News	Edgar	8,987	5,542	62
Paxton	Paxton Daily Record	Ford	4,289	1,245	29
Pekin	Pekin Daily Times	Tazewell	32,254	14,565	46
Peoria	Journal Star	Peoria	113,504	76,724	68
Pontiac	The Daily Leader	Livingston	11,428	6,545	58
Quincy	The Quincy Herald-Whig	Adams	39,681	25,074	64
Robinson	Robinson Daily News	Crawford	6,740	6,877	102
Rock Island	The Rock Island Argus	Rock Island	40,552	13,583	34
Rockford	Rockford Register Star	Winnebago	139,426	75,218	54
Shelbyville	Daily Union	Shelby	4,943	4,295	87
Springfield	The State Journal-Register	Sangamon	105,227	66,870	64
Sterling-Rock Falls	The Daily Gazette/Sauk Valley Sunday	Whiteside	24,786	14,423	59
Streator	Streator Times-Press	LaSalle	14,121	8,897	63
Taylorville	The Taylorville Daily Breeze-Courier	Christian	11,133	6,941	62
Watseka	Iroquios County's Times Republic	Iroquios	5,424	3,001	56
Waukegan-North Chicago	The News-Sun	Lake	104,370	34,319	33
West Frankfort	The Daily American	Franklin	8,526	3,375	40

Source: International Year Book, 1996. New York: The Editor and Publisher Company, I-89 – I-104.

Table 8 Illinois television stations: 1996

City	Station	Network	Total TV Households	Net Weekly Circulation	Net Daily Circulation
Bloomington-Normal-Peoria	WYZZ (43)	FOX	594,870	155,477	73,523
Champaign	WCIA (3)	CBS	741,630	285,018	181,913
Champaign	WICD (5)	NBC	464,980	126,820	61,629
Chicago	WBBM (2)	CBS	4,266,170	2,536,404	1,301,296
Chicago	WCFC (38)	Independent	3,418,350	238,421	60,111
Chicago	WCIU (26)	Independent	3,889,460	345,787	121,062
Chicago	WFLD (32)	FOX	25,043,590	2,188,221	930,568
Chicago-Joliet	WGBO (66)	Univision	3,409,770	654,908	240,836
Chicago	WGN (9)	WBN	85,370,590	9,861,905	2,856,776
Chicago	WLS (7)	ABC	4,435,870	2,845,764	1,789,635
Chicago	WMAQ (5)	NBC	4,163,950	2,731,548	1,474,977
Chicago-Gary, In	WPWR (50)	UPN	3,512,660	1,552,877	681,288
Chicago	WSNS (44)	Telemundo	2,914,040	102,804	58,569
Decatur	WAND (17)	ABC	2,549,760	297,145	161,679
Decatur	WFHL (23)	Independent	555,430	32,780	10,992
Harrisburg	WSIL (3)	ABC	580,280	216,096	116,518
LaSalle	WWTO (35)	TBN	758,770	11,738	4,538
Marion	WTCT (27)	Independent	272,490	15,745	6,128
Moline	WQAD (8)	ABC	822,140	282,336	156,509
Mt. Vernon-Salem-Centralia	WCEE (13)	Independent	901,320	75,061	25,653
Peoria	WEEK (25)	NBC	585,890	230,525	132,539
Peoria	WHOI (19)	ABC	581,770	215,342	114,604
Peoria	WMBD (31)	CBS	470,400	220,018	130,441
Quincy-Hannibal,MO	WGEM (10)	NBC	465,570	124,748	76,245
Quincy	WTJR (16)	Independent	124,240	6,450	2,181

Table 8 Illinois television stations: 1996, continued

City	Station	Network	Total TV Households	Net Weekly Circulation	Net Daily Circulation
Rockford	WQRF (39)	FOX	2,287,510	158,243	69,599
Rockford	WREX (13)	NBC	2,831,750	206,543	114,158
Rockford	WTVO (17)	ABC	2,794,020	189,656	98,602
Rockford-Freeport	WIFR (23)	CBS	2,507,430	199,465	110,306
Rock Island	WHBF (4)	CBS	933,280	278,114	144,629
Springfield	WCFN (49)	CBS	260,850	62,550	32,891
Springfield	WICS (20)	NBC	603,110	188,482	113,349
Springfield	WRSP (55)	FOX	646,900	142,287	62,033
Urbana	WCCU (27)	FOX	211,040	81,000	35,006

Source: Adapted from *Cable and Television Factbook 64, TV Stations Volume.* 1997. Washington D.C.: Warren Publishing, Inc. A-360 – A-397.

Table 9 Major Illinois newspaper endorsements of gubernatorial candidates: 1972-1994

Newspaper	1972	1976	1978	1982	1986	1990	1994
Chicago Sun-Times	Ogilvie(R)	Thompson(R)	Thompson(R)	Thompson(R)	Thompson(R)	Edgar(R)	Edgar (R)
Chicago Tribune	Ogilvie(R)	Thompson(R)	Thompson(R)	Thompson(R)	Thompson(R)	Edgar(R)	Edgar (R)
Rockford Register Star	Ogilvie(R)	Thompson(R)	Thompson(R)	Thompson(R)	Thompson(R)	Edgar(R)	Edgar (R)
Moline Daily Dispatch	N/A	Thompson(R)	N/A	Thompson(R)	Thompson(R) and Stevenson(Sol)	Edgar(R)	Edgar (R)
Peoria Journal Star	Ogilvie(R)	Thompson(R)	Thompson(R)	Thompson(R)	Thompson(R)	Edgar(R)	Netsch (D)
Springfield State Journal-Register	Ogilvie(R)	Thompson(R)	Thompson(R)	Thompson(R)	Thompson(R)	Edgar(R)	Edgar (R)
Carbondale Southern Illinoisan	Ogilvie(R)	Thompson(R)	Thompson(R)	Thompson(R)	Thompson(R)	Edgar(R)	Edgar (R)

Sources: "Endorsements," *Chicago Tribune*, Monday, November 6, 1972, Sec. 1, 2; "Endorsements," *Chicago Tribune,* Monday, November 1, 1976, Sec. 4, 2; "Endorsements," *Chicago Tribune,* Tuesday, November 7, 1978, Sec. 3, 2; "Endorsements," *Chicago Tribune,* Tuesday, November 2, 1982, Sec. 1, 18; "Endorsements," *Chicago Tribune,* Tuesday, November 4, 1986, Sec. 1, 18; phone interviews, February 1990; phone interviews, August 1991; phone interviews, July 1995.

Table 10 Illinois governors since 1900

Year	Governor (Political Party)	Born	Died	Age at Inauguration	Total Years in Office	Lt. Governor
1901	Richard Yates (R)	1860	1936	41	4	William A. Northcott (R)
1905	Charles S. Deneen (R)	1863	1940	42	8	Lawrence Y. Sherman (R)
1909	Charles S. Deneen (R)	1863	1940	42	8	John G. Oglesby (R)
1913	Edward F. Dunne (D)	1853	1934	60	4	Barratt O'Hara (D)
1917	Frank O. Lowden (R)	1861	1943	56	4	John G. Oglesby (R)
1921	Len Small (R)	1862	1936	59	8	Fred E. Sterling (R)
1925	Len Small (R)	1862	1936	59	8	Fred E. Sterling (R)
1929	Louis L. Emmerson (R)	1863	1941	66	4	Fred E. Sterling (R)
1933	Henry Horner (D)	1879	1940	54	7	Thomas F. Donovan (D)
1937	Henry Horner (D)	1879	1940	54	7	John H. Stelle (D)
1940	John H. Stelle (D)	1891	1962	49	1	none
1941	Dwight H. Green (R)	1897	1958	44	8	Hugh W. Cross (R)
1945	Dwight H. Green (R)	1897	1958	44	8	Hugh W. Cross (R)
1949	Adlai E. Stevenson (D)	1900	1965	49	4	Sherwood Dixon (D)
1953	William G. Stratton (R)	1914	*	39	8	John Wm. Chapman (R)
1957	William G. Stratton (R)	1914	*	39	8	John Wm. Chapman (R)
1961	Otto Kerner (D)	1908	1975	53	7	Samuel H. Shapiro (D)
1965	Otto Kerner (D)	1908	1975	53	7	Samuel H. Shapiro (D)
1968	Samuel H. Shapiro (D)	1907	1987	61	1	none
1969	Richard B. Ogilvie (R)	1923	1988	46	4	Paul Simon (D)
1973	Daniel Walker (D)	1922	*	51	4	Neil Hartigan (D)
1977	James R. Thompson (R)	1936	*	41	14	Dave O'Neal (R)
1979	James R. Thompson (R)	1936	*	41	14	Dave O'Neal (R)
1983	James R. Thompson (R)	1936	*	41	14	George H. Ryan (R)
1987	James R. Thompson (R)	1936	*	41	14	George H. Ryan (R)
1991	Jim Edgar (R)	1946	*	45	8	Bob Kustra (R)
1995	Jim Edgar (R)	1946	*	45	8	Bob Kustra (R)

Sources: Directory of Illinois State Officials 1995, State of Illinois, 1995, 56; *Illinois Blue Book,* Secretary of State, State of Illinois, 1989, 460; Robert P. Howard, *Mostly Good and Competent Men: Illinois Governors 1818-1988* (Springfield, IL, *Illinois Issues* and Illinois Historical Society, 1989).

Table 11 Illinois gubernatorial political parties since 1900 (1 of 5)

Year	Party	Total Votes	Percent of Vote
1900	Republican	580,199	51.49
	Democrat	518,966	46.06
	Prohibition	15,643	1.39
	People's	1,106	.10
	Socialist Labor	1,319	.12
	Social Democrat	8,611	.76
	United Christian	334	.03
	Union Reform	650	.06
1904	Republican	634,119	59.10
	Democrat	334,880	31.21
	Prohibition	35,389	3.30
	Socialist	59,062	5.50
	Socialist Labor	4,379	.41
	People's	4,364	.41
	Continental	780	.07
1908	Republican	550,076	47.64
	Democrat	526,912	45.64
	Prohibition	33,922	2.94
	Socialist	31,293	2.71
	Socialist Labor	1,526	.13
	Independence	10,883	.94
1912	Republican	318,469	27.39
	Democrat	443,120	38.11
	Prohibition	15,231	1.31
	Socialist Labor	3,980	.34
	Progressive	303,401	26.09

Table 11 Illinois gubernatorial political parties since 1900, continued (2 of 5)

Year	Party	Total Votes	Percent of Vote
1916	Republican	696,535	52.67
	Democrat	556,654	42.09
	Socialist	52,326	3.96
	Prohibition	15,309	1.16
	Socialist Labor	1,739	.13
1920	Republican	1,243,514	58.88
	Democrat	731,643	34.64
	Socialist	58,998	2.79
	Prohibition	9,876	.47
	Farmer-Labor	56,480	2.67
	Single Tax	930	.04
	Socialist Labor	3,020	.14
	Harding-Coolidge Republican	5,985	.28
	Co-operative Party of America	1,260	.06
	Liberal	357	.02
1924	Republican	1,366,436	56.72
	Democrat	1,021,408	42.40
	Socialist	15,191	.63
	Socialist Labor	2,312	.10
	Workers Party of America	2,329	.10
	Commonwealth Land	414	.02
	Independent Republican	1,025	.04
1928	Republican	1,709,818	56.76
	Democrat	1,284,897	42.66
	Socialist	12,974	.43
	Socialist Labor	1,362	.05
	Workers (Communist) Party of America	3,153	.10

Table 11 Illinois gubernatorial political parties since 1900, continued (3 of 5)

Year	Party	Total Votes	Percent of Vote
1932	Republican	1,364,043	40.71
	Democrat	1,930,330	57.62
	Socialist	39,389	1.18
	Socialist Labor	2,896	.09
	Communist	12,466	.37
	Independent	1,182	.04
1936	Republican	1,682,685	43.23
	Democrat	2,067,861	53.13
	Union Progressive	128,962	3.31
	Socialist Labor	2,602	.07
	Prohibition	2,896	.07
	Socialist	6,966	.18
1940	Republican	2,197,778	52.93
	Democrat	1,940,833	46.74
	Socialist	7,523	.18
	Prohibition	6,467	.16
1944	Republican	2,013,270	50.75
	Democrat	1,940,999	48.93
	Socialist Labor	6,906	.17
	Prohibition	5,590	.14
1948	Republican	1,678,007	42.59
	Democrat	2,250,074	57.10
	Prohibition	9,491	.24
	Socialist Labor	2,673	.07

Table 11 Illinois gubernatorial political parties since 1900, continued (4 of 5)

Year	Party	Total Votes	Percent of Vote
1952	Republican	2,317,363	52.48
	Democrat	2,089,721	47.32
	Socialist Labor	8,777	.20
1956	Republican	2,171,786	50.34
	Democrat	2,134,909	49.48
	Socialist Labor	7,874	.18
1960	Republican	2,070,459	44.30
	Democrat	2,594,731	55.51
	Socialist Labor	8,976	.19
1964	Republican	2,239,095	48.08
	Democrat	2,418,394	51.92
1968	Republican	2,307,295	51.21
	Democrat	2,179,501	48.37
	Socialist Labor	19,175	.43
1972	Republican	2,293,809	49.04
	Democrat	2,371,303	50.69
	Socialist Labor	7,966	.17
	Communist	4,592	.10
1976	Republican	3,000,395	64.68
	Democrat	1,610,258	34.71
	Communist	10,091	.22
	Socialist Labor	3,147	.07
	U.S. Labor	2,302	.05
	Socialist Workers	4,926	.11
	Libertarian	7,552	.16

Table 11 Illinois gubernatorial political parties since 1900, continued (5 of 5)

Year	Party	Total Votes	Percent of Vote
1978	Republican	1,859,684	59.04
	Democrat	1,263,134	40.10
	Socialist Workers	11,026	.35
	U.S. Labor	4,737	.15
	Libertarian	11,420	.36
1982	Republican	1,816,101	49.44
	Democrat	1,811,027	49.30
	Libertarian	24,417	.66
	Taxpayers	22,001	.60
1986	Republican	1,655,849	56.42
	Solidarity	1,256,626	42.82
	Libertarian	15,646	.53
	Socialist Workers	6,843	.23
1990	Republican	1,653,126	50.74
	Democrat	1,569,217	48.17
	Solidarity	35,067	1.07
1994	Republican	1,984,318	63.87
	Democrat	1,069,850	34.43
	Libertarian	52,388	1.68

Sources: Samuel K. Gove, ed. *Illinois Votes 1900-1962*, Institute of Government and Public Affairs, University of Illinois, 1963; *Official Vote of the State of Illinois*, General Election, November 3, 1964, Secretary of State, State of Illinois, 1964; *Official Vote of the State of Illinois*, General Election, November 5, 1968, Secretary of State, State of Illinois, 1968; *Official Vote of the State of Illinois,* General Election, November 7, 1972, Secretary of State, State of Illinois, 1972; *State of Illinois Official Vote,* General Election, November 5, 1974, State Board of Elections, State of Illinois, 1974; *State of Illinois Official Vote,* General Election, November 2, 1976, State Board of Elections, State of Illinois, 1976; *State of Illinois Official Vote,* General Election, November 7, 1978, State Board of Elections, State of Illinois, 1978; State of Illinois Official Vote, General Election, November 2, 1982, State Board of Elections, State of Illinois, 1982; *State of Illinois Official Vote*, General Election, November 4, 1986, State Board of Elections, State of Illinois, 1986; *State of Illinois Official Vote*, General Election, November 6, 1990, State Board of Elections, State of Illinois, 1990; *State of Illinois Official Vote*, General Election, November 8, 1994, State Board of Elections, State of Illinois, 1994.

Table 12.1 Gubernatorial election returns statewide summary: 1994

Party	Candidates	Number of Votes	Percent
Republican	Edgar and Kustra	1,984,318	63.9
Democrat	Netsch and Severns	1,069,850	34.4
Libertarian	Kelly and Moldenhauer	52,388	1.7
Total		3,106,556	100.0

Source: *State of Illinois Official Vote,* General Election, November 8, 1994, State Board of Elections, 1994, 1.

Table 12.2 Gubernatorial election returns by county: 1994

County	Republican Number	Percent	Democrat Number	Percent	Libertarian Number	Total Number
Adams	15,656	80	3,573	18	366	19,595
Alexander	2,347	68	1,045	30	41	3,433
Bond	3,628	66	1,731	32	131	5,490
Boone	7,128	75	2,081	22	293	9,502
Brown	1,974	78	527	21	43	2,544
Bureau	9,974	70	3,921	28	271	14,166
Calhoun	1,267	60	802	38	59	2,128
Carroll	4,463	76	1,254	21	119	5,836
Cass	3,205	65	1,632	33	75	4,912
Champaign	30,468	67	14,334	32	662	45,464
Christian	6,880	60	4,411	38	188	11,479
Clark	4,079	72	1,511	27	108	5,698
Clay	3,095	71	1,183	27	71	4,349
Clinton	8,235	70	3,216	28	249	11,695
Cole	11,494	75	3,442	23	309	15,245
Cook	634,353	52	568,737	47	15,854	1,218,944
Crawford	4,978	73	1,733	25	97	6,808
Cumberland	2,909	72	1,027	25	93	4,029
DeKalb	13,354	71	4,942	26	408	18,704
DeWitt	4,218	78	1,294	75	78	5,590
Douglas	4,721	78	1,215	22	85	6,021
DuPage	179,395	79	45,548	20	3,564	228,507
Edgar	4,678	77	1,306	22	60	6,044
Edwards	1,918	70	768	28	44	2,730
Effingham	8,800	75	2,615	22	245	11,660
Fayette	5,112	64	2,128	27	163	7,972
Ford	3,815	81	846	18	63	4,724
Franklin	8,554	60	5,280	37	334	14,168
Fulton	7,490	65	3,737	33	244	11,471

Table 12.2 Gubernatorial election returns by county: 1994, continued

County	Republican Number	Percent	Democrat Number	Percent	Libertarian Number	Total Number
Gallatin	1,534	49	1,537	49	59	3,130
Green	3,457	69	1,462	29	118	5,037
Grundy	8,802	77	2,365	21	210	11,377
Hamilton	2,428	68	1,041	29	78	3,547
Hancock	4,883	75	1,485	23	111	6,479
Hardin	1,839	72	680	27	45	2,564
Henderson	2,336	70	943	28	53	3,332
Henry	11,680	72	4,437	27	205	16,322
Iroquois	9,160	81	1,905	17	184	11,249
Jackson	10,251	65	5,204	33	379	15,834
Jasper	2,357	66	1,162	32	72	3,591
Jefferson	7,840	68	3,414	30	212	11,466
Jersey	4,498	64	2,223	32	278	6,999
JoDaviess	5,293	71	1,985	27	154	7,432
Johnson	3,119	74	977	23	92	4,188
Kane	56,340	75	17,517	23	1,466	75,323
Kankakee	19,282	72	7,148	27	452	26,882
Kendall	9,769	80	2,207	18	270	12,246
Knox	12,935	75	3,964	23	248	17,147
Lake	96,775	73	32,758	25	2,214	131,747
LaSalle	22,685	68	9,725	29	772	33,182
Lawrence	3,561	66	1,707	32	89	5,357
Lee	8,114	75	2,454	23	257	10,825
Livingston	9,782	80	2,267	19	158	12,234
Logan	7,666	77	2,194	22	144	10,004
Macon	22,714	62	13,273	36	530	36,517
Macoupin	9,957	60	6,105	37	403	16,465
Madison	43,806	62	25,008	35	1,794	70,608
Marion	7,734	65	3,918	33	255	11,907

Table 12.2 Gubernatorial election returns by county: 1994, continued

County	Republican Number	Percent	Democrat Number	Percent	Libertarian Number	Total Number
Marshall	3,538	73	1,180	25	100	4,818
Mason	3,546	70	1,463	29	76	5,085
Massac	3,752	78	958	20	73	4,783
McDonough	6,495	71	2,528	28	133	9,156
McHenry	44,414	76	12,596	22	1,292	58,302
McLean	27,216	78	7,144	20	591	34,951
Menard	3,956	73	1,386	26	92	5,434
Mercer	4,550	72	1,695	27	99	6,344
Monroe	5,587	70	2,154	27	228	7,969
Montgomery	6,648	62	3,793	36	236	10,677
Morgan	9,258	74	3,059	24	193	12,510
Moultrie	3,230	68	1,432	30	84	4,746
Ogle	10,285	78	2,444	19	392	13,121
Peoria	36,461	70	14,612	28	945	52,018
Perry	5,856	66	2,820	32	189	8,865
Piatt	4,589	70	1,825	28	107	6,521
Pike	5,199	73	1,737	25	142	7,078
Pope	1,493	75	440	22	54	1,987
Pulaski	2,035	73	712	26	36	2,783
Putnam	1,792	66	850	31	59	2,701
Randolph	7,391	61	4,455	37	272	12,118
Richland	4,216	74	1,419	25	79	5,714
Rock Island	26,901	64	14,238	34	651	41,790
Saline	6,168	65	3,121	33	216	9,505
Sangamon	52,673	68	23,424	30	1,207	77,304
Schuyler	2,346	71	886	27	59	3,291
Scott	1,771	76	525	22	44	2,340
Shelby	5,452	68	2,405	30	159	8,016
Stark	1,730	76	505	22	34	2,269
St. Clair	38,601	61	23,644	37	1,197	63,442

Table 12.2 Gubernatorial election returns by county: 1994, continued

County	Republican Number	Percent	Democrat Number	Percent	Libertarian Number	Total Number
Stephenson	10,372	77	2,773	20	413	13,558
Tazewell	30,478	73	10,432	25	907	41,817
Union	4,810	72	1,729	26	149	6,688
Vermilion	16,813	73	5,855	25	396	23,064
Wabash	2,837	68	1,259	30	73	4,169
Warren	4,400	77	1,203	21	81	5,684
Washington	4,206	72	1,517	26	142	5,865
Wayne	4,667	70	1,829	27	164	6,660
White	3,679	61	2,191	37	120	5,990
Whiteside	12,179	70	4,995	29	303	17,477
Will	71,871	73	24,635	25	1,799	98,305
Williamson	13,737	69	5,603	28	443	19,783
Winnebago	49,053	71	17,087	25	2,557	68,697
Woodford	9,282	78	2,388	20	183	11,853

Source: State of Illinois Official Vote, General Election, November 8, 1994, State Board of Elections, 1994, 1-4.

Table 13.1 Cook County gubernatorial election returns by wards of Chicago: 1994

Ward	Republican Number	Percent	Democrat Number	Percent	Libertarian Number	Percent	Total
1	2,071	36	3,669	63	78	1	5,818
2	2,081	20	8,381	79	120	1	10,582
3	1,056	13	6,943	86	107	1	8,106
4	1,988	15	10,884	84	138	1	13,010
5	2,097	15	11,350	83	149	1	13,596
6	2,382	15	13,845	85	142	1	16,369
7	1,867	16	9,906	88	129	1	11,902
8	2,382	13	15,949	86	173	1	18,504
9	1,764	14	10,552	85	126	1	12,442
10	6,065	56	4,696	43	150	1	10,911
11	5,855	39	8,987	60	161	1	15,003
12	1,614	46	1,869	53	61	2	3,544
13	9,773	47	10,705	52	188	1	20,666
14	5,678	52	5,095	47	170	2	10,943
15	2,005	22	6,877	76	120	1	9,002
16	1,271	18	5,557	80	91	1	6,919
17	1,518	14	9,510	85	143	1	11,171
18	6,982	38	11,156	61	213	1	18,351
19	10,680	47	11,628	51	310	1	22,618
20	1,219	12	8,661	87	128	1	10,008
21	2,444	14	14,251	84	184	1	16,879
22	1,228	26	3,398	73	57	1	4,683
23	12,949	61	8,081	38	269	1	21,299
24	1,184	13	7,623	85	125	1	8,932
25	1,980	41	2,744	57	57	1	4,781
26	2,127	36	3,743	63	84	1	5,954
27	2,201	24	7,003	75	123	1	9,327
28	1,202	13	7,739	86	92	1	9,033
29	2,053	20	7,900	78	147	1	10,100
30	5,663	58	4,013	41	163	2	9,839

Table 13.1 Cook County gubernatorial election returns by wards of Chicago: 1994, continued

Ward	Republican Number	Percent	Democrat Number	Percent	Libertarian Number	Percent	Total
31	2,794	46	3,186	52	89	1	6,069
32	5,042	42	6,719	56	200	2	11,961
33	4,225	46	4,884	53	162	2	9,271
34	1,988	13	13,026	86	155	1	15,169
35	2,438	42	3,329	57	95	2	5,862
36	11,000	62	6,374	36	224	1	17,598
37	1,359	15	7,826	84	102	1	9,287
38	9,623	64	5,281	35	219	1	15,123
39	6,074	54	4,912	44	164	1	11,150
40	4,461	45	5,353	54	128	1	9,942
41	13,820	68	6,069	30	289	1	20, 178
42	9,035	51	8,365	48	177	1	17,577
43	7,256	48	7,817	51	175	1	15,248
44	5,642	39	8,714	60	188	1	14,544
45	11,051	61	6,698	37	249	1	17,998
46	3,507	34	6,789	65	152	1	10,448
47	5,376	46	6,864	55	199	2	12,439
48	3,925	35	6,976	63	162	1	11,063
49	2,351	30	5,426	69	152	2	7,917
50	4,713	39	7,289	60	140	1	12,142
Absentee	379	45	450	54	8	1	837
Total	219,438	33	375,062	66	7,627	2	602,127

Source: *State of Illinois Official Vote*, General Election, November 8, 1994, State Board of Elections, 1994, 208-209.

Table 13.2 Cook County gubernatorial election returns by township: 1994

Township	Republican Number	Percent	Democrat Number	Percent	Libertarian Number	Percent	Total
Barrington	3,232	84	565	15	52	1	3,849
Berwyn	8,289	69	3,566	30	209	2	12,064
Bloom	15,706	63	8,710	35	321	1	24,737
Bremen	15,555	60	9,764	40	410	2	25,729
Calumet	1,449	40	2,104	58	60	2	3,613
Cicero	9,754	80	2,284	19	160	1	12,198
Elk Grove	16,108	79	3,991	20	247	1	20,346
Evanston	7,936	39	12,363	60	214	1	20,513
Hanover	8,488	75	2,600	23	238	2	11,326
Lemont	3,469	75	1,047	23	81	2	4,597
Leyden	18,158	76	5,361	22	338	1	23,857
Lyons	21,935	72	8,086	27	414	1	30,435
Maine	26,693	65	9,359	40	487	2	36,539
New Trier	15,429	56	8,037	27	189	1	23,655
Niles	17,025	56	12,895	49	276	1	30,196
Northfield	18,917	72	7,311	28	204	1	26,432
Norwood Park	5,469	74	1,855	25	91	1	7,415
Oak Park	6,727	43	8,760	56	192	1	15,679
Orland	15,658	75	4,898	25	257	1	20,813
Palatine	18,731	79	4,578	19	416	2	23,725
Palos	11,548	73	4,036	26	205	1	15,789
Proviso	23,134	60	14,925	39	500	1	38,559
Rich	9,942	56	7,678	43	230	1	17,850
River Forest	2,654	67	1,244	32	45	1	3,943
Riverside	4,224	74	1,418	25	84	1	5,726
Schaumburg	19,071	77	5,331	21	354	1	24,756

Table 13.2 Cook County gubernatorial election returns by township: 1994, continued

Township	Republican Number	Percent	Democrat Number	Percent	Libertarian Number	Percent	Total
Stickney	6,267	66	3,090	32	182	2	9,539
Thornton	23,073	56	17,266	44	565	1	40,904
Wheeling	30,002	76	8,816	22	522	1	39,340
Worth	30,278	71	11,737	27	644	1	42,659
Total	414,939	58	193,675	41	8,187	1	616,801

Source: State of Illinois Official Vote, General Election, November 8, 1994, State Board of Elections, 1994, 198-199.

Table 14.1 Popular votes for president in the United States: 1900-1996

Year	Republican	Percent	Democrat	Percent	Other	Percent
1900	7,218,039	51.7	6,358,345	45.5	394,086	2.8
1904	7,626,593	56.4	5,082,898	37.6	809,473	6.0
1908	7,676,258	51.6	6,406,801	43.0	799,675	5.4
1912	3,486,333	23.2	6,293,152	41.8	5,261,478	35.0
1916	8,546,789	46.1	9,126,300	49.2	861,933	4.7
1920	16,133,314	60.3	9,140,884	34.2	1,479,588	5.5
1924	15,717,553	54.1	8,386,169	28.8	4,972,237	17.1
1928	21,411,991	58.2	15,000,185	40.8	378,188	1.0
1932	15,758,397	39.6	22,825,016	57.4	1,165,969	2.9
1936	16,679,543	36.5	27,747,636	60.8	1,215,124	2.7
1940	22,336,260	44.8	27,263,448	54.7	240,735	.5
1944	22,013,372	45.9	25,611,936	53.4	349,511	.7
1948	21,970,017	45.1	24,105,587	49.5	2,616,838	5.4
1952	33,936,137	55.1	27,314,649	44.4	300,332	.5
1956	35,585,245	57.4	26,030,172	42.0	409,955	.7
1960	34,106,671	49.6	34,221,344	49.7	500,945	.7
1964	27,177,838	38.5	43,126,584	61.0	336,682	.5
1968	31,785,148	43.4	31,274,503	42.7	10,143,719	13.9
1972	47,170,179	60.7	29,171,791	37.5	1,385,622	1.8
1976	39,147,793	48.0	40,830,763	50.1	1,577,333	1.9
1980	43,904,153	50.7	35,483,883	41.0	7,127,185	8.2
1984	54,455,074	58.8	37,577,137	40.6	548,382	.6
1988	48,642,640	53.1	41,716,679	45.5	1,227,406	1.3
1992	38,167,416	37.7	43,728,275	43.2	19,237,247	19.0
1996	39,197,755	40.7	47,402,357	49.2	9,674,858	10.0

Sources: Congressional Quarterly's Guide to U.S. Elections, 2nd ed. (Washington, D.C.: Congressional Quarterly, Inc., 1985), 345-366; *Statistics of the Presidential and Congressional Election of November 8, 1988* (Washington, D.C.: U.S. Government Printing Office, 1989), 13-14; *Statistics of the Presidential and Congressional Election of November 7, 1992* (Washington, D.C.: U.S. Government Printing Office, 1993), 3552. *Congressional Quarterly Almanac, Vol. LII* (Washington D.C.: Congressional Quarterly Inc., 1996), 11-16.

Table 14.2 Popular votes for president in Illinois: 1900-1996

Year	Republican	Percent	Democrat	Percent	Other	Percent
1900	597,985	52.8	503,061	44.4	30,852	2.8
1904	632,645	58.8	327,606	30.4	116,244	10.7
1908	629,932	54.5	450,810	39.0	74,512	6.4
1912	253,593	22.1	405,048	35.3	487,532	42.5
1916	1,152,549	52.6	950,229	43.3	89,929	4.1
1920	1,420,480	67.8	534,395	25.5	139,840	6.8
1924	1,453,321	58.8	576,975	23.4	439,771	17.8
1928	1,770,723	57.0	1,312,235	42.2	24,531	.8
1932	1,432,756	42.0	1,882,304	55.2	92,866	2.8
1936	1,570,393	39.7	2,282,999	57.7	102,322	2.6
1940	2,047,240	48.5	2,149,934	51.0	20,104	.5
1944	1,939,314	48.1	2,079,479	51.5	17,268	.4
1948	1,961,103	49.2	1,994,715	50.1	28,228	.7
1952	2,457,327	54.8	2,013,920	44.9	9,811	.2
1956	2,623,327	59.5	1,775,682	40.3	8,398	.2
1960	2,368,988	49.8	2,377,846	50.0	10,575	.2
1964	1,905,946	40.5	2,796,833	59.5	62	0
1968	2,174,774	47.1	2,039,814	44.2	405,161	8.8
1972	2,788,179	59.0	1,913,472	40.5	21,585	.5
1976	2,364,269	50.1	2,271,295	48.1	83,350	1.8
1980	2,358,049	49.6	1,981,413	41.7	410,259	8.6
1984	2,707,103	56.2	2,086,499	43.3	25,486	.5
1988	2,310,939	50.7	2,215,940	48.6	32,241	.7
1992	1,718,190	34.9	2,379,510	48.3	832,044	16.9
1996	1,587,021	36.8	2,341,744	54.3	382,626	8.9

Sources: Congressional Quarterly's Guide to U.S. Elections, 2nd ed. (Washington, D.C.: Congressional Quarterly, Inc., 1985), 345-366; *Statistics of the Presidential and Congressional Election of November 8, 1988* (Washington, D.C.: U.S. Government Printing Office, 1989) 13-14; *Statistics of the Presidential and Congressional Election of November 7, 1992* (Washington, D.C.: U.S. Government Printing Office, 1993) 3552. *State of Illinois Official Vote, General Election, November 3, 1996,* State Board of Elections, State of Illinois, 1996.

Table 15.1 U.S. Senate results for Illinois' congressional delegation since 1918

Year	Number of Senators		Gains/Losses	
	Democrat	Republican	Democrat	Republican
1918	0	2		
1920	0	2	0	0
1924	0	2	0	0
1926	0	2	0	0
1928*	0	2	0	0
1930	1	1	+1	-1
1932	2	0	+1	-1
1936	2	0	0	0
1938	2	0	0	0
1940*	1	1	-1	+1
1942	0	2	-1	+1
1944	1	1	+1	-1
1948	2	0	+1	-1
1950	1	1	-1	+1
1954	1	1	0	0
1956	1	1	0	0
1960	1	1	0	0
1962	1	1	0	0
1966	0	2	-1	+1
1968	0	2	0	0
1970	1	1	+1	-1
1972	1	1	0	0
1974	1	1	0	0
1978	1	1	0	0
1980	1	1	0	0

Table 15.1 U.S. Senate results for Illinois' congressional delegation since 1918, continued

Year	Number of Senators: Democrat	Number of Senators: Republican	Gains/Losses: Democrat	Gains/Losses: Republican
1982	1	1	0	0
1984	2	0	+1	-1
1986	2	0	0	0
1988	2	0	0	0
1990	2	0	0	0
1992	2	0	0	0
1994	2	0	0	0
1996	2	0	0	0

* Special election.

Sources: Congressional Quarterly's Guide to U.S. Elections, 2nd ed. (Washington, D.C.: Congressional Quarterly, Inc., 1985), 615; *State of Illinois Official Vote*, General Election, November 4, 1986, State Board of Elections, State of Illinois, 1986, 10-11; *State of Illinois Official Vote,* General Election, November 6, 1990, State Board of Elections, State of Illinois, 1990, 1; *State of Illinois Official Vote,* General Election, November 3, 1992, State Board of Elections, State of Illinois, 1992, 11; *State of Illinois Official Vote,* General Election, November 8, 1994, State Board of Elections, 1994. *State of Illinois Official Vote*, General Election, November 5, 1996, State Board of Elections, State of Illinois, 1996, 12-96.

Table 15.2 U.S. House results for Illinois' congressional delegation since 1900

	Number of Representatives			Gains/Losses		
Year	**Democrat**	**Republican**	**Other**	**Democrat**	**Republican**	**Other**
1900	11	11	0			
1902[a]	8	17	0	-3	+6	
1904	1	24	0	-7	+7	
1906	5	20	0	+4	-4	
1908	6	19	0	+1	-1	
1910	11	14	0	+5	-5	
1912[b]	20	5	2	+9	-9	+2
1914	10	16	1	-10	+11	-1
1916	6	21	0	-4	+5	-1
1918	5	22	0	-1	+1	
1920	3	24	0	-2	+2	
1922	7	20	0	+4	-4	
1924	5	22	0	-2	+2	
1926	7	20	0	+2	-2	
1928	6	21	0	-1	+1	
1930	12	15	0	+6	-6	
1932	19	8	0	+7	-7	
1934	21	6	0	+2	-2	
1936	21	6	0	0	0	
1938	17	10	0	-4	+4	
1940	11	16	0	-6	+6	
1942[c]	7	19	0	-4	+3	
1944	11	15	0	+4	-4	
1946	6	20	0	-5	+5	
1948[d]	12	14	0	+6	-6	
1950	8	18	0	-4	+4	
1952[e]	9	16	0	+1	-2	
1954	12	13	0	+3	-3	
1956	11	14	0	-1	+1	
1958	14	11	0	+3	-3	
1960	14	11	0	0	0	

Table 15.2 U.S. House results for Illinois' congressional delegation since 1900, continued

	Number of Representatives			Gains/Losses		
Year	**Democrat**	**Republican**	**Other**	**Democrat**	**Republican**	**Other**
1962[f]	12	12	0	-2	+1	
1964	13	11	0	+1	-1	
1966	12	12	0	-1	+1	
1968	12	12	0	0	0	
1970	12	12	0	0	0	
1972	10	14	0	-2	+2	
1974	13	11	0	+3	-3	
1976	12	12	0	-1	+1	
1978	10	14	0	-2	+2	
1980	10	14	0	0	0	
1982[g]	12	10	0	+2	-4	
1984	13	9	0	+1	-1	
1986	13	9	0	0	0	
1988	14	8	0	+1	-1	
1990	15	7	0	+1	-1	
1992[h]	12	8	0	-3	+1	
1994	10	10	0	-2	+2	
1996	10	10	0	0	0	

[a]1902 - added three representative positions; [b]1912 – added two at-large representative positions; [c]1942 – eliminated one at-large representative position; [d]1948 - added one representative position; [e]1952 - eliminated one representative position; [f]1962 - eliminated one representative position; [g]1982 - eliminated two representative positions; [h]1992 - eliminated two representative positions

Sources: Congressional Quarterly's Guide to U.S. Elections, 3rd ed. (Washington, D.C.: Congressional Quarterly, Inc., 1994) 1085-1322; *State of Illinois Official Vote*, General Election, November 8, 1994, State Board of Elections, 1994, 23-35. *State of Illinois Official Vote*, General Election, November 5, 1996, 17-29.

Table 16 Size of Illinois delegations to national party conventions: 1932-1996

Year	Illinois Democratic Votes	Democratic Convention Total Votes	Percent of Total Convention Votes	Illinois Republican Votes	Republican Convention Total Votes	Percent of Total Convention Votes
1996	193	4,289	5	69	1,990	4
1992	195	4,288	5	85	2,210	4
1988	200	4,055	5	92	2,241	4
1984	194	3,933	5	93	2,235	4
1980	179	3,331	5	102	1,994	5
1976	169	3,008	6	101	2,259	4
1972	170	3,016	6	58	1,348	4
1968	118	2,622	5	58	1,333	4
1964	114	2,316	5	58	1,308	4
1960	69	1,521	5	60	1,331	5
1956	64	1,372	5	60	1,323	5
1952	60	1,230	5	60	1,206	5
1948	60	1,234	5	56	1,094	5
1944	58	1,176	5	59	1,059	6
1940	58	1,100	5	58	1,000	6
1936	58	1,100	5	57	1,003	6
1932	58	1,154	5	61	1,154	5

Sources: *Congressional Quarterly Weekly Report* (Supplement), August 17, 1996 (Washington, D.C.: Congressional Quarterly, Inc., 1996), 60-61; *Congressional Quarterly Weekly Report* (Supplement), August 3, 1996 (Washington, D.C.: Congressional Quarterly, Inc., 1996), 45; *Congressional Quarterly Weekly Report*, August 8, 1992 (Washington, D.C.: Congressional Quarterly, Inc., 1992), 78; *Congressional Quarterly Weekly Report,* July 25, 1992 (Washington, D.C.: Congressional Quarterly, Inc., 1992), 2220; *Congressional Quarterly Weekly Report,* July 9, 1988 (Washington, D.C.: Congressional Quarterly, Inc., 1988), 1872-1892; *Congressional Quarterly Weekly Report,* August 6, 1988 (Washington, D.C.: Congressional Quarterly, Inc., 1988), 2155-2174; *Congressional Quarterly's Guide to U.S. Elections,* 2nd ed. (Washington, D.C.: Congressional Quarterly, Inc., 1985), 198-221; Richard C. Bain & Judith H. Parris, *Convention Decisions and Voting Records,* 2nd ed. (Washington, D.C.: Brookings Institute, 1973) Appendix C; Clarence Cannon, *The Official Manual for the Democratic National Convention of 1964*, 1964, 16-17.

Table 17.1 Citizens' perceptions of the most important problem facing Illinois: 1996

Statewide	**Crime 21%**	**Education 22%**	**Taxes 13%**	**Unemployment 9%**
Region				
Chicago	24	20	8	8
Suburban Cook	17	28	7	8
Collar Counties	22	23	24	4
Northern Illinois	22	28	12	9
Central Illinois	18	19	14	14
Southern Illinois	23	14	12	10
Age				
18-34	22	19	12	8
35-60	20	24	13	11
Over 60	22	24	12	5
Race				
White	19	25	14	7
Black	31	11	4	14
Gender				
Male	24	20	16	9
Female	18	24	10	9

Source: Illinois Policy Survey 1996 (DeKalb: Center for Governmental Studies, Northern Illinois University, 1996).

Table 17.2 Citizens' perceptions of the most important problem facing Illinois: 1994

Statewide	Crime 39%	Education 18%	Taxes 10%	Unemployment 6%
Region				
Chicago	48	14	3	7
Suburban Cook	46	18	8	6
Collar Counties	38	37	12	3
Northern Illinois	36	17	14	6
Central Illinois	35	15	15	5
Southern Illinois	22	17	15	9
Age				
18-34	39	19	8	3
35-60	35	20	12	9
Over 60	49	11	10	3
Race				
White	38	19	12	5
Black	42	8	4	11
Gender				
Male	43	14	12	8
Female	36	22	8	4

Source: Illinois Policy Survey 1994 (DeKalb: Center for Governmental Studies, Northern Illinois University, 1994), 4.

Table 17.3 Citizens' perceptions of the most important problem facing Illinois: 1992

Problem	**State**	**Balance Chicago**	**Collar Cook**	**Northern Counties**[1]	**Central Illinois**[2]	**Southern Illinois**[3]	**Illinois**[4]
Education	17.3%	12.4%	17.3%	16.4%	26.7%	19.0%	19.6%
Taxes & Spending	14.6%	7.8%	17.5%	19.1%	15.1%	13.7%	17.4%
Drugs	2.9%	6.0%	1.1%	2.4%	1.5%	1.8%	2.7%
Unemployment	25.0%	22.9%	32.5%	20.8%	21.7%	23.8%	27.3%
Other Economic	12.4%	14.1%	7.8%	11.0%	12.0%	19.0%	10.3%
Environment	.5%	N/A	N/A	N/A	3.9%	N/A	1.1%
Social	11.8%	20.8%	14.4%	11.3%	6.9%	2.4%	5.5%
Other	10.6%	13.1%	4.6%	11.5%	10.2%	13.5%	10.8%
No problem/don't know	5.0%	2.9%	4.9%	7.4%	2.0%	6.8%	5.5%

[1] Lake, McHenry, Kane, Will, DuPage.
[2] Boone, Winnebago, Stephenson, JoDaviess, Carroll, Whiteside, Lee, Ogle, DeKalb, LaSalle, Grundy, Bureau, Henry, Rock Island, Mercer, Putnam, Kendall.
[3] Henderson, Warren, Knox, Stark, Marshall, Livingston, Kankakee, Piatt, Champaign, Iroquois, Ford, McLean, Woodford, Peoria, Fulton, McDonough, Moultrie, Logan, Hancock, Adams, Schuyler, Brown, Pike, Mason, Cass, Coles, Vermilion, Morgan, Menard, Sangamon, Tazewell, DeWitt, Macon, Christian, Douglas, Edgar, Scott.
[4] Calhoun, Greene, Macoupin, Montgomery, Shelby, Cumberland, Clark, Franklin, Saline, Johnson, Pulaski, Crawford, Jasper, Effingham, Fayette, Bond, Madison, Jersey, Hamilton, Williamson, Pope, Alexander, St. Clair, Clinton, Marion, Clay, Richland, Lawrence, Wabash, White, Jackson, Hardin, Edwards, Wayne, Jefferson, Washington, Monroe, Randolph, Perry, Gallatin, Union, Massac.

Source: Illinois Policy Survey 1992 (DeKalb, Illinois: Center for Governmental Studies, Northern Illinois University, 1992), 4.

Table 17.4 Citizens' perceptions of the Illinois General Assembly: 1984-1996

Year	Excellent/Good	Fair	Poor/Very Poor	Don't Know
1984	26%	43%	10%	21%
1985	31%	39%	10%	20%
1986	27%	40%	10%	23%
1987	22%	46%	14%	18%
1988	28%	39%	14%	19%
1989	22%	40%	16%	22%
1990	20%	45%	15%	20%
1991	16/26%*	47/45%*	20/12%*	17/16%*
1992	14%	N/A	21%	N/A
1993	15%	N/A	24%	N/A
1994	14%	N/A	14%	N/A
1996	22%	N/A	12%	N/A

* Number represents citizens' perceptions of their own state legislators.

Sources: Illinois Policy Survey 1991-1996 (DeKalb, Illinois: Center for Governmental Studies, Northern Illinois University, 1991-1996).

Table 18.1 Total number of registered lobbyists in Illinois: 1984-1997

1984	1985	1986	1987	1988	1989	1990	1991	1992	1993	1994*	1995	1996	1997
592	699	639	595	658	776	806	863	884	1,003	1,422	1,653	1,645	1,692

Source: Index Division, Secretary of State's Office, State of Illinois.
* New lobbyist registration law went into effect.

Table 18.2 Lobbyist registration and reporting totals: 1994-1996

Expenditure	1994	1995	1996
Travel & Lodging	$18,964	$50,218	$33,153
Meals, Beverages & Entertainment	$774,239	$937,568	$1,071,364
Gifts	$186,921	$209,591	$203,553
Honoraria	$8,261	$9,870	$1,975
Grass Roots	$1,791	$1,572	$3,276
Totals	$990,176	$1,208,819	$1,313,303

Source: Index Division, Secretary of State's Office, State of Illinois.

Table 19.1 Top 10 interest groups in contributions to legislative elections 1994 (January 1, 1993 through December 31, 1994) and 1996 (January 1, 1995 through December 31, 1996) election cycles (amounts in units of $1,000)

Name	Legis. Elect. Expend.	$ to Democr. Leader/ Chamber	$ to Repub. Leader/ Chamber	$ to Incumb. Democr. Legis.	$ to Incumb. Repub. Legis.	$ to Democr. Non-incumb.	% to Repub. Non-incumb.
1994							
Medical Society	1,372	52	335	153	516	63	252
Illinois Education Association (IPACE)	1,045	89	3	635	222	76	20
Manufacturers' Association PAC (MPAC)	448	9	141	24	142	1	131
Beer Distributors PAC (ABDI)	414	70	62	144	112	9	17
Trial Lawyers Association PAC	395	56	11	199	17	84	28
Bankers Association PAC	372	62	77	107	115	3	8
Realtors Association PAC	300	50	59	80	95	3	13
Hospital Association PAC (HOPE)	261	68	56	65	61	3	8
CPA Association PAC	230	29	25	81	84	4	7
AFSCME-Illinois PAC	214	86	10	75	17	24	2
1995-1996							
Medical Society PAC	1,420	33	546	151	514	63	113
Illinois Education Association (IPACE)	1,257	40	44	446	401	196	130
Manufacturers' Association PAC (MPAC)	781	15	318	56	324	5	63
Hospital Association PAC (HOPE)	516	127	211	54	110	6	8
Bankers Association PAC	475	69	4	190	5	200	7
Trial Lawyers Association PAC	449	58	78	120	171	13	9
Beer Distributors PAC (ABDI)	476	71	107	122	159	7	10
Ameritech	353	39	96	62	132	7	17
Realtors Association PAC	348	43	91	55	149	3	7
Philip Morris	313	60	178	25	48	1	1

Source: Data compiled from the "Campaign Finance Project" of *Illinois Issues*, University of Illinois at Springfield.

Table 19.2 Total campaign spending and increases in spending

1990, 1992, 1994, 1996 comparison of general election spending for governor, statewide, and legislative candidates (in million $)

	1990	**1992**	**1994**	**1996**
Governor	15.6	—	12.4	—
Statewide	7.8	—	10.3	—
Legislative	9.5	18.2	18.5	26.3
Total	32.9	18.2	41.2	26.3

Total spending by legislative candidates

	Primary	**General**	**Total**
94 Legislative Candidates	6.4	18.5	24.9
96 Legislative Candidates	7.8	26.3	34.1

10 most expensive house races and 5 most expensive senate races per year - general election

	1990	**1992**	**1994**	**1996**
House	2.40	3.17	5.33	7.19
Senate	1.62	3.02	3.16	5.29

Most expensive individual legislative races - general election (both candidates)

House	**Senate**
1990 = $322,000	1990 = $ 808,000
1992 = $361,000	1992 = $ 763,000
1994 = $701,000	1994 = $1,345,000
1996 = $841,000	1996 = $1,388,000

Number of legislative races where combined spending exceeded $300,000 - general election

1990 = 4	1992 = 16	1994 = 25	1996 = 28

Number of legislative races where combined spending exceeded $1,000,000 - general election

1990 = 0	1992 = 0	1994 = 1	1996 = 4

Source: Data for 1996 were compiled from tables provided by Kent D. Redfield, 1997 (Springfield, Ill.: Institute for Public Affairs, University of Illinois at Springfield). Data for 1990 were compiled from Kent D. Redfield, 1995 *Cash Clout* (Springfield, Ill: Institute for Public Affairs, University of Illinois at Springfield). Data for 1994 were compiled from reports by the Illinois Campaign Finance Project, a project of *Illinois Issues* magazine and the Institute for Public Affairs, University of Illinois at Springfield.

Table 19.3 Competition in the funding of legislative races

Total number of "no contest" legislative races - general election (Winner had no opponent or opponent spent less than $50,000 and received less than 40% of the vote.)

1990	16 senate (of 20)	1994	15 senate (of 21)
	97 house (of 118)		85 house (of 118)
	113 of 138 races (82 percent)		**100 of 139 races (72 percent)**
1992	47 senate (of 59)	1996	32 senate (of 39)
	95 house (of 118)		91 house (of 118)
	142 of 177 races (80%)		**123 of 157 races (80%)**

Least spent by a winning candidate who had an opponent

1994	$11,857 house	$21,024 senate
1996	$ 9,512 house	$22,104 senate

Source: Data were compiled from tables provided by Kent D. Redfield, 1997 (Springfield, Ill.: Institute for Public Affairs, University of Illinois at Springfield).

Table 19.4 Legislative leaders - receipts and expenditures

Campaign contribution receipts by legislative leaders and chamber committees (in million $)

	1990	**1992**	**1994**	**1996**
Senate Republicans	1.534	2.498	3.085	4.731
Senate Democrats	1.468	1.868	1.964	1.885
House Republicans	1.670	3.005	4.252	8.799
House Democrats	2.453	4.153	6.123	5.557
Total	7.125	11.524	15.424	20.972

Source: Data for were compiled from tables provided by Kent D. Redfield, 1997 (Springfield, Ill.: Institute for Public Affairs, University of Illinois at Springfield).

Table 19.5 Targeted races - spending totals and sources of funds

Candidates in targeted races - 1996 general election receipts (in million $)

House Republican (27 candidates)			**House Democratic (27 candidates)**		
Legislative leader	3.832	58%	Legislative leader	3.752	56%
Other political	.487	8%	Other political	.643	9%
Individual/Not-item	.731	11%	Individual/Not item	.645	9%
Interest groups	1.542	23%	Interest groups	1.781	26%
Total	6.592	100%	Total	$6.821	100%

Average receipts for house Republican candidate	= $244,000 ($142,000 from leader)
Average receipts for house Democratic candidate	= $253,000 ($139,000 from leader)
Average total receipts for targeted house race	= $497,000

Senate Republican (7 candidates)			**Senate Democratic (7 candidates)**		
Legislative leader	2.596	69%	Legislative leader	1.484	63%
Other political	.095	2%	Other political	.042	2%
Individual/Not-item	.291	8%	Individual/Not-item	.252	11%
Interest groups	.779	21%	Interest groups	.555	24%
Total	3.761	100%	Total	$2.333	100%

Average receipts for senate Republican candidate	= $537,000 ($371,000 from leader)
Average receipts for senate Democratic candidate	= $333,000 ($212,000 from leader)
Average total receipts for targeted senate race	= $870,000

Sources for Tables 19.1, 19.2,19.3, 19.4 and 19.5: Data were compiled from tables provided by Kent D. Redfield, 1997 (Springfield, IL.: Institute for Public Affairs, University of Illinois at Springfield).

Table 20 Blacks, Hispanics, and women as a percentage of state legislators and voting-age population (VAP) for Illinois and neighboring states: 1996

		Black*			Hispanic			Women		
State	Number of Legislators	Number of Legislators	Percent	Percent VAP	Number of Legislators	Percent	Percent VAP	Number of Legislators	Percent	Percent VAP
Illinois	177	22	12.4	14.0	6	3.4	7.7	46	26.0	52.2
Indiana	150	12	8.0	7.4	1	0.7	1.8	31	21.0	52.3
Iowa	150	1	0.7	1.8	0	0.0	1.2	31	21.0	52.3
Kentucky	138	5	3.6	6.8	0	0.0	0.6	13	9.0	52.4
Missouri	197	16	8.1	9.8	0	0.0	1.7	43	22.0	52.8
Wisconsin	132	8	6.1	4.3	0	0.0	1.2	31	23.0	51.8
U.S.	7,424	557	7.5	11.4	174	2.3	7.9	1,594	21.0	52.0

*Figures are for 1994, the most recently reported year.

Note: Hispanic refers to ethnicity not race.

Sources: *Projections of Voting Age Population for States: November, 1994,* U.S. Department of Commerce, Bureau of the Census, 10-12; National Conference of State Legislatures, August, 1995, National Conference of State Legislatures, 1997.

Table 21.1 Age of Illinois legislators: 1997

		Democrats (60)		Republicans (58)		Total (118)	
House	**Age**	**#'s**	**%**	**#'s**	**%**	**#'s**	**%**
	21-39	15	25	7	12	22	19
	40-49	19	32	15	26	34	29
	50+	23	38	33	57	56	47
	Not available	3	5	3	5	6	5

		Democrats (28)		Republicans (31)		Total (59)	
Senate	**Age**	**#'s**	**%**	**#'s**	**%**	**#'s**	**%**
	21-39	3	11	3	10	6	10
	40-49	10	36	10	32	20	34
	50+	15	53	18	58	33	56
	Not available	0	0	0	0	0	0

Sources: Compiled from Part II, General Assembly Members of the *Almanac of Illinois Politics 1994,* Institute for Public Affairs, Sangamon State University, Springfield, IL, and Part II, General Assembly Members of the *Almanac of Illinois Politics 1996,* Institute for Public Affairs, University of Illinois at Springfield, Springfield, IL.

Table 21.2 Gender of Illinois legislators: 1997

House	Democrats (60)		Republicans (58)		Total (118)	
	Number	Percent	Number	Percent	Number	Percent
Male	42	70	42	72	84	71
Female	18	30	16	28	34	29

Senate	Democrats (28)		Republicans (31)		Total (59)	
	Number	Percent	Number	Percent	Number	Percent
Male	23	82	24	77	47	80
Female	5	18	7	23	12	20

Total House & Senate Membership	Democrats (88)		Republicans (89)		Total (177)	
	Number	Percent	Number	Percent	Number	Percent
Male	65	74	66	74	131	74
Female	23	26	23	26	46	26

Sources: Compiled from Part II, General Assembly Members of the *Almanac of Illinois Politics—1998*, Institute for Public Affairs, University of Illinois at Springfield, Springfield, IL. and from responses to questionnaires sent to legislators.

Table 21.3 Race of Illinois legislators: 1997

House	Race	Number	Percent
	White	100	85
	Black	14	12
	Hispanic	4	3
	Total	118	100

Senate	Race	Number	Percent
	White	49	83
	Black	8	14
	Hispanic	2	3
	Total	59	100

Total House & Senate Membership	Race	Number	Percent
	White	149	84
	Black	22	12
	Hispanic	6	4
	Total	177	100

Sources: Compiled from Part II, General Assembly Members of the *Almanac of Illinois Politics—1998*, Institute for Public Affairs, University of Illinois at Springfield, Springfield, IL. and from responses to questionnaires sent to legislators.

Table 21.4 Education of Illinois legislators: 1997

House	**Democrats (60)**		**Republicans (58)**		**Total (118)**	
	Number	**Percent**	**Number**	**Percent**	**Number**	**Percent**
H.S. Diploma	9	15	6	10	15	13
College Degree	26	43	26	45	52	44
Graduate Degree	25	42	26	45	51	43

Senate	**Democrats (28)**		**Republicans (31)**		**Total (59)**	
	Number	**Percent**	**Number**	**Percent**	**Number**	**Percent**
H.S. Diploma	5	18	1	3	6	10
College Degree	12	43	17	55	29	49
Graduate Degree	11	39	13	42	24	41

Total House & Senate Membership	**Democrats (88)**		**Republicans (89)**		**Total (177)**	
	Number	**Percent**	**Number**	**Percent**	**Number**	**Percent**
H.S. Diploma	14	16	7	8	21	12
College Degree	38	43	43	48	81	46
Graduate Degree	36	41	39	44	75	42

Sources: Compiled from Part II, General Assembly Members of the *Almanac of Illinois Politics—1998*, Institute for Public Affairs, University of Illinois at Springfield, Springfield, IL.

Table 21.5 Principal occupation listing of Illinois legislators: 1997

House	**Democrats (60)**		**Republicans (58)**		**Total (118)**	
	Number	**Percent**	**Number**	**Percent**	**Number**	**Percent**
Full-time legislator	26	44	14	25	40	34
Lawyer	11	19	16	28	27	23
Business/Finance	6	10	6	11	12	11
Real Estate/Insurance	2	4	5	9	7	6
Local Government	4	7	1	2	5	5
Educator	4	7	4	7	8	7
Health/Social Service	0	0	1	2	1	1
Farmer	1	2	6	11	7	6
Other	6	10	5	9	11	10

Senate	**Democrats (28)**		**Republicans (31)**		**Total (59)**	
	Number	**Percent**	**Number**	**Percent**	**Number**	**Percent**
Full-time legislator	14	50	11	35	25	42
Lawyer	8	29	6	19	14	25
Business/Finance	2	7	6	19	8	14
Real Estate/Insurance	0	0	0	0	0	0
Local Government	0	0	0	0	0	0
Educator	1	4	1	3	2	3
Health/Social Service	1	4	1	3	2	3
Farmer	1	4	1	3	2	3
Other	1	4	5	16	6	10

Table 21.5 Principal occupation listing of Illinois legislators: 1997, continued

Total House & Senate Membership	Democrats (88)		Republicans (89)		Total (177)	
	Number	Percent	Number	Percent	Number	Percent
Full-time legislator	40	45	25	28	65	37
Lawyer	19	22	22	25	41	23
Business/Finance	8	9	12	13	20	11
Real Estate/Insurance	2	2	5	6	7	4
Local Government	4	5	1	1	5	3
Educator	5	6	5	6	10	6
Health/Social Service	1	1	2	2	3	2
Farmer	2	2	7	8	9	5
Other	7	8	10	11	17	9

Sources: Compiled from Part II, General Assembly Members of the *Almanac of Illinois Politics—1998*, Institute for Public Affairs, University of Illinois at Springfield, Springfield, IL. and from responses to questionnaires sent to legislators.

Table 21.6 Tenure of Illinois legislators: 1997

House	**Democrats (60)**		**Republicans (58)**		**Total (118)**	
	Number	**Percent**	**Number**	**Percent**	**Number**	**Percent**
Freshman	14	23	7	12	21	18
1-2 terms	10	17	11	19	21	18
3 + terms	36	60	40	69	76	64

Senate	**Democrats (28)**		**Republicans (31)**		**Total (59)**	
	Number	**Percent**	**Number**	**Percent**	**Number**	**Percent**
Freshman	3	11	2	6	5	8
1-2 terms	4	14	3	10	7	12
3 + terms	21	75	26	84	47	80

Sources: Compiled from Part II, General Assembly Members of the *Almanac of Illinois Politics—1998*, Institute for Public Affairs, University of Illinois at Springfield, Springfield, IL. and from responses to questionnaires sent to legislators.

Table 22 Leadership of the Illinois General Assembly: 1997

Senate	House
Senate Majority (Republicans)	**House Majority (Democrats)**
Senate President - James "Pate" Philip	Speaker - Michael J. Madigan
Senate Majority Leader - Stanley B. Weaver	Majority Leader - Barbara Flynn Currie
Assistant Majority Leaders:	Deputy Majority Leader - Ralph Capparelli
Walter W. Dudycz	Assistant Majority Leaders:
Adeline Jay Geo-Karis	Kurt Granberg
Laura Kent Donahue	Gary Hannig
John W. Maitland	Lou Jones
Frank C. Watson	Miguel Santiago
Republican Caucus Chair - Doris C. Karpiel	Lou Lang
Majority Caucus Secretary - Edward F. Petka	Joel Brunsvold
	Majority Conference Chair - Charles Hartke
Senate Minority (Democrats)	**House Minority (Republicans)**
Minority Leader - Emil Jones Jr.	Minority Leader - Lee A. Daniels
Assistant Minority Leaders:	Deputy Minority Leaders:
Howard W. Carroll	Robert Churchill
Vince Demuzio	Tom Ryder
Miguel A. del Valle	Assistant Deputy Minority Leaders:
Patrick Welch	Judy Biggert
William Shaw	Bill Black
Democrat Caucus Chair - James DeLeo	Jack Kubik
Deputy Minority Caucus Chair - Margaret Smith	David Leitch
	Ron Stephens
	Kathleen Wojcik
	Republican Conference Chair - Art Tenhouse

Source: 1997 Roster of State Government Officials, Illinois Issues, 1997, 18, 24.

Table 23.1 Membership of Illinois General Assembly Senate committees: 1997

Senate Committees	Democrats	Republicans
Agriculture & Conservation Chair: Sieben, Todd Vice Chair: Luechtefeld, David Min. Spokesperson: O'Daniel, William	Bowles, Link, L. Walsh	Hawkinson, R. A. Madigan, Myers, Watson
Appropriations Chair: Rauschenberger, Steven Vice Chair: Donahue, Laura Kent Min. Spokesperson: Trotter, Donne	Carroll, Clayborne, Smith, Welch	Bomke, Fawell, Lauzen, Maitland, Syverson, T. Walsh
Commerce & Industry Chair: Lauzen, Chris Vice Chair: Radogno, Christine Min. Spokesperson: Garcia, Jesus	Farley, Hendon, Smith	Dillard, Geo-Karis, Klemm
Education Chair: Cronin, Dan Vice Chair: O'Malley, Patrick Min. Spokesperson: Berman, Arthur	Collins, Demuzio, Halvorson	Butler, Karpiel, Sieben, Watson
Environment & Energy Chair: Mahar, William Vice Chair: Maitland, John Min. Spokesperson: Farley, Bruce	Jacobs, Shaw, Trotter	Dillard, Donahue, Karpiel, Rauschenberger
Executive Chair: Klemm, Dick Vice Chair: Petka, Ed Min. Spokesperson: Collins, Earlean	del Valle, Demuzio, E. Jones, Severns	Dudycz, Karpiel, Maitland, Philip, Watson, W. B. Weaver

Table 23.1 Membership of Illinois General Assembly Senate committees: 1997, continued

Executive Appointments		
Chair: Petka, Ed Vice Chair: Bomke, Larry Min. Spokesperson: Hendon, Rickey	Carroll, DeLeo, Shadid	Burzynski, Myers, T. Walsh
Financial Institutions		
Chair: O'Malley, Patrick Vice Chair: Walsh, Tom Min. Spokesperson: Rea, Jim	Carroll, Halvorson, Hendon	Butler, Geo-Karis, Parker
Insurance, Pensions & Licensed Activities		
Chair: Madigan, Robert Vice Chair: Walsh, Tom Min. Spokesperson: Jacobs, Denny	Berman, Cullerton, Molaro	Fitzgerald, O'Malley, Peterson, Petka
Judiciary		
Chair: Hawkinson, Carl Vice Chair: Dillard, Kirk Min. Spokesperson: Cullerton, John	Obama, Shadid, Shaw	Cronin, Geo-Karis, O'Malley, Petka
Licensed Activities		
Chair: Burzynski, J. Bradley Vice Chair: Karpiel, Doris Min. Spokesperson: Molaro, Robert	del Valle, DeLeo, Viverito	Luechtefeld, R. A. Madigan, Peterson
Local Government & Elections		
Chair: Butler, Marty Vice Chair: Bomke, Larry Min. Spokesperson: Bowles, Evelyn	Link, Shaw, Trotter	Dudycz, Klemm, Myers, Rauschenberger

Table 23.1 Membership of Illinois General Assembly Senate committees: 1997, continued

Public Health & Welfare Chair: Syverson, Dave Vice Chair: Parker, Kathleen Min. Spokesperson: Smith, Margaret	Garcia, Obama, Rea	Cronin, Donahue, Mahar, Radogno
Revenue Chair: Peterson, William Vice Chair: Lauzen, Chris Min. Spokesperson: Severns, Penny	Berman, Clayborne, Welch	Fawell, Fitzgerald, Radogno, Weaver
Rules Chair: Weaver, Stanley Vice Chair: Dillard, Kirk Min. Spokesperson: Demuzio, Vince	Cullerton	Dudycz
State Government Operations Chair: Fitzgerald, Peter Vice Chair: Luechtefeld, David Min. Spokesperson: Viverito, Louis	Link, Obama, L. Walsh	Burzynski, Donahue, Sieben
Transportation Chair: Fawell, Beverly Vice Chair: Parker, Kathleen Min. Spokesperson: Shadid, George	Bowles, O'Daniel, Molaro	Dudycz, Hawkinson, Mahar, Syverson

Table 23.2 Membership of Illinois General Assembly House committees: 1997

Aging		
Chair: McGuire, Jack Vice Chair: Lyons, Joseph Min. Spokesperson: Lawfer, Ronald	Brosnahan, Crotty, Fantin, Feigenholtz, Giles, McKeon, Scott, Scully, Silva	Coulson, Cowlishaw, Klingler, Kosel, Krause, E. Lyons, Mitchell, Saviano, Wood
Agriculture & Conservation		
Chair: Woolard, Larry Vice Chair: Hartke, Chuck Min. Spokesperson: Noland, Duane	Brunsvold, Granberg, Hannig, O'Brien, Reitz, Smith	Ackerman, Jones, Lawfer, Myers, Poe, Turner
Appropriations Education		
Chair: Younge, Wyvetter Vice Chair: Lopez, Edgar Min. Spokesperson: Durkin, Jim	Bradford, Crotty, Howard, Jones, Santiago, Scully, Silva, Slone	Cowlishaw, Mitchell, Myers, Poe, Skinner, Winkel, Wirsing, Wood
Appropriations General Services		
Chair: Schoenberg, Jeff Vice Chair: Gash, Lauren Beth Min. Spokesperson: Biggins, Bob	Brosnahan, Curry, Feigenholtz, Fritchey, Kenner, Scully, Silva	Bergman, Coulson, Deuchler, Lindner, Roskam, Stephens, Winters
Appropriations Human Services		
Chair: Davis, Monique Vice Chair: Pugh, Coy Min. Spokesperson: Mulligan, Rosemary	Flowers, Kenner, Ronen, Schakowsky	Beaubien, Biggert, Leitch, Saviano
Appropriations Public Safety		
Chair: Morrow, Charles Vice Chair: Mautino, Frank Min. Spokesperson: Skinner, Cal	Acevedo, L. Jones, J. Lyons, McGuire, Santiago	McAuliffe, Moffitt, Noland, Pankau, Wait

Table 23.2 Membership of Illinois General Assembly House committees: 1997, continued

Children & Youth Chair: Ronen, Carol Vice Chair: Howard, Connie Min. Spokesperson: Lindner, Patricia	Crotty, Erwin, Feigenholtz, Gash	Cross, Klingler, Mulligan, Roskam
Conflicts of Interest Chair: Lang, Lou Min. Spokesperson: Johnson, Tim	Granberg, Scott, Turner	Biggert, Churchill, Kubik
Consumer Protection Chair: Lopez, Edgar Vice Chair: Granberg, Kurt Min. Spokesperson: Moffitt, Donald	Acevedo, Curry, Fritchey, McCarthy	Bergman, Parke, Wojcik, Zickus
Elementary & Secondary Education Chair: Phelps, David Vice Chair: Davis, Monique Min. Spokesperson: Cowlishaw, Mary Lou	Boland, Crotty, Curry, Gash, Giles, Mautino, Murphy, Smith, Woolard	Bost, Hoeft, Jones, Johnson, Kosel, Mitchell, Persico, Poe, Righter
Environment & Energy Chair: Novak, Phil Min. Spokesperson: Hassert, Brent	Bradley, Davis, Holbrook, Howard, S. Jones, Murphy, O'Brien, Reitz, Scott, Slone,	Beaubien, Brady, Brown, Durkin, Hoeft, Lawfer, Meyer, Moore, Parke, Persico Smith
Executive Chair: Burke, Daniel Vice Chair: Fritchey, John Min. Spokesperson: Rutherford, Dan	Bugielski, Capparelli, Lopez, J. Lyons, McGuire, Santiago	Ackerman, Biggins, Clayton, Hassert, Kubik, Stephens
Financial Institutions Chair: Bugielski, Robert Min. Spokesperson: Deuchler, Suzanne	Burke, Capparelli, Davis, Giles, S. Jones, Lang, Lopez, Mautino, Morrow, Novak, Pugh, Santiago, Schoenberg	Biggins, Brady, Durkin, Hassert, Lindner, McAuliffe, Meyer, Persico, Righter, Rutherford, Saviano, Wojcik, Wood

Table 23.2 Membership of Illinois General Assembly House committees: 1997, continued

Health Care Availability & Access		
Chair: Flowers, Mary Vice Chair: Feigenholtz, Sara Min. Spokesperson: Krause, Carolyn	Brosnahan, Dart, Kenner, McCarthy, McKeon, E. Moore, Murphy, Phelps, Ronen, Schakowsky, Silva, Slone, Stroger	Brown, Clayton, Coulson, Cross, Klingler, Lyons, A. Moore, Mulligan, Pankau, Ryder, Skinner, Tenhouse, Zickus
Higher Education		
Chair: Erwin, Judy Vice Chair: Phelps, David Min. Spokesperson: Wirsing, David	Bradford, Fantin, Giles, McCarthy, McKeon, Woolard	Bost, Klingler, Myers, Poe, Righter, Winkel
Human Services		
Chair: Pugh, Coy Vice Chair: Schoenberg, Jeff Min. Spokesperson: Zickus, Anne	Flowers, Howard, McKeon, Stroger	Bergman, Deuchler, Mulligan, Winters
Insurance		
Chair: Mautino, Frank Vice Chair: Woolard, Larry Min. Spokesperson: Brady, Bill	Boland, Bradley, Bugielski, Giles, Kenner, Lopez, E. Moore, Phelps, Silva, Stroger	Brown, Hassert, Hoeft, Meyer, Noland, Parke, Persico, Rutherford, Ryder, Winters
Judiciary Civil Law		
Chair: Dart, Tom Vice Chair: Scott, Douglas Min. Spokesperson: Cross, Tom	Brosnahan, Hoffman, Lang, Scully	Biggert, Turner, Wait, Winkel
Judiciary Criminal Law		
Chair: Gash, Lauren Beth Vice Chair: Smith, Michael Min. Spokesperson: Roskam, Peter	Acevedo, Bradley, Erwin, Jones, McKeon, O'Brien	Cross, Johnson, Lindner, Lyons, Righter, Turner

Table 23.2 Membership of Illinois General Assembly House committees: 1997, continued

Labor & Commerce Chair: Schakowsky, Janice Vice Chair: Kenner, Howard Min. Spokesperson: Parke, Terry	Brosnahan, Davis, Giglio, Howard, S. Jones, McGuire, McKeon, Murphy, Slone	Ackerman, Biggert, Johnson, E. Lyons, A. Moore, Roskam, Skinner, Winters, Wood
Local Government Chair: Stroger, Todd Vice Chair: Holbrook, Tom Min. Spokesperson: Turner, John	Acevedo, Fritchey, Hartke, Mautino, Scott, Scully, Smith	Bergman, Bost, Kosel, Lawfer, Mitchell, Moffitt, Wait
Personnel & Pensions Chair: Murphy, Harold Min. Spokesperson: Hoeft, Douglas	Hoffman, Mautino, E. Moore, Phelps, Stroger, Woolard	Beaubien, Deuchler, Durkin, McAuliffe, Poe
Prison Management Reform Chair: Dart, Tom Min. Spokesperson: Johnson, Tom	Erwin, Gash, L. Jones, Phelps	Durkin, Roskam, Skinner, Winkel
Public Utilities Chair: Jones, Shirley Vice Chair: Morrow, Charles Min. Spokesperson: Ackerman, Jay	M. Davis, S. Davis, L. Jones, McCarthy	Cowlishaw, Leitch, A. Moore, Wirsing
Registration & Regulation Chair: Saviano, Skip Vice Chair: Pankau Min. Spokesperson: L. Jone	Burke, Boland, Bugielski, Capparelli, Crotty, Feigenholtz, L. Jones, Lopez, Reitz, Santiago	Beaubien, Coulson, Krause, Lindner, Meyer, Mulligan, Noland, Stephens, Turner, Wojcik, Zickus

Table 23.2 Membership of Illinois General Assembly House committees: 1997, continued

Revenue		
Chair: Moore, Eugene Vice Chair: Fantin, Arline Min. Spokesperson: Moore, Andrea	Brunsvold, Currie, Dart, Turner	Biggins, Krause, Kubik, Pankau
Rules		
Chair: Currie, Barbara Flynn	Hannig, Turner	Churchill, Ryder
State Gov Admin & Election Reform		
Chair: Giles, Calvin Vice Chair: Curry, Julie Min. Spokesperson: Clayton, Verna	Bradley, Dart, Lang, Lyons, McCarthy	Brady, Cross, Rutherford, Winkel, Wirsing
Transportation & Motor Vehicles		
Chair: Hoffman, Jay Vice Chair: Murphy, Harold Min. Spokesperson: Wait, Ron	Fantin, Giglio, Hartke, Holbrook, J. Lyons, McGuire, Novak, O'Brien, Reitz	Black, Bost, Clayton, Jones, Kosel, McAuliffe, Moffitt, Myers, Zickus
Veterans' Affairs		
Chair: Davis, Steve Vice Chair: Boland, Mike Min. Spokesperson: Meyer, Jim	Bradford, Giglio, Holbrook, Novak	Bost, Johnson, J. Jones, Tenhouse

Source: House of Representative's Clerk's Office, 1997. Secretary of the Senate's Office, 1997.

Table 24 Incumbent advantage in the Illinois General Assembly: 1976-1996

	1996	1994	1992	1990	1988	1986	1984	1982	1980	1978	1976
House of Representatives											
Incumbent Democrats											
Running	46	56	52	61	64	63	62	61	81	74	78
Winning	46	43	47	61	63	63[a]	58	53	75	69	75
Incumbent Republicans											
Running	56	47	28	47	48	45	39	49	70	75	63
Winning	52	47	24	43	47	44	39	34	68	72	61
Percent Reelected	96	87	89	96	98	99	96	79[b]	95	95	96
Senate											
Incumbent Democrats											
Running	16	9	20	10	21	19	10	24	9	15	17
Winning	16	8	19	10	21	18	9	23	8	13	15
Incumbent Republicans											
Running	19	9	29	10	18	15	7	22	5	14	11
Winning	18	9	27	10	18	14	7	19	5	14	11
Percent Reelected	98	94	94	100	100	94	94	91	93	93	93

[a] Ray A. Christensen (D-85) declared winner after original outcome was challenged.
[b] Prior to the 1982 reapportionment, three House members were elected from each of the 59 legislative districts for a total of 177 House members. In 1982 the size of the House was reduced to 118 members who were elected from single-member districts.

Sources: Campaign finance database, Illinois Legislative Studies Center, University of Illinois at Springfield, 1995; *1993 Illinois Roster-88th General Assembly,* Electric Cooperatives of Illinois, 41-70; *1991 Illinois Roster-87th General Assembly*, Electric Cooperatives of Illinois, 34-72; *State of Illinois Official Vote,* General Election, November 6, 1990, State Board of Elections, 1990, 47-92; *Illinois Blue Book,* Secretary of State, State of Illinois, 1988, 62-63; *State of Illinois Official Vote,* General Election, November 8, 1988, State Board of Elections, 1988, 32-87; Michael D. Klemens, "1988 Legislative Elections Give New Meaning to `Power of Incumbency,'" *Illinois Issues,* December 1988, 15-16; Michael D. Klemens, "Lawmakers' Class of '88: One Bona Fide Surprise," *Illinois Issues,* January 1989, 19-21; Michael D. Klemens, "Expectations of the Rookie Legislators," *Illinois Issues,* January 1987, 15-17; Michael D. Klemens, "Don't Vote for Nobody Nobody Knows," *Illinois Issues*, December 1986, 4-7; *Illinois Blue Book*, Secretary of State, State of Illinois, 1984, 58-59; *State of Illinois Official Vote,* General Election, November 6, 1984, State Board of Elections, 1984, 34-62; *Illinois Blue Book*, Secretary of State, State of Illinois, 1982, 58-59; *State of Illinois Official Vote,* General Election, November 2, 1982, State Board of Elections, 1982, 40-85; Paul M. Green et al., Illinois Elections, 3rd ed. (Springfield, Illinois: *Illinois Issues,* 1986) 93-96; *Illinois Blue Book,* Secretary of State, State of Illinois, 1980, 58-59; *State of Illinois Official Vote,* General Election, November 4, 1980, State Board of Elections, 1980, 33-52; David H. Everson, "The Bullet Bites the Dust: Will the Cutback Amendment Bring Competition and Accountability?" *Illinois Issues,* March 6, 1981, 10-15; *Illinois Blue Book,* Secretary of State, State of Illinois, 1978, 60-61; *State of Illinois Official Vote,* General Election, November 7, 1978, State Board of Elections, 1978, 56-78; Gary Adkins, "The Election Message," *Illinois Issues,* December 1978, 2; "Elections: Democrats Win Clear Majority in General Assembly," *Illinois Issues,* January 1977, 25-26; *State of Illinois Official Vote* 1996; *State of Illinois Official Vote* 1994; Illinois Handbook of Government 1997-1998.

Table 25 Party advantage in the Illinois General Assembly: 1976-1996

	1996	1994	1992	1990	1988	1986	1984	1982	1980	1978	1976
House											
Democrats	60	55	67	72	67	68	67	70	85	88	93
Republicans	58	63	51	46	51	50	51	48	91	88	83
Independents	0	0	0	0	0	0	0	0	1*	1*	1*
Senate											
Democrats	28	27	27	31	31	31	31	33	30	32	34
Republicans	31	32	32	28	28	28	28	26	29	27	25
Independents	0	0	0	0	0	0	0	0	0	0	0

*Although Taylor Pouncey ran as an independent, he voted with the Democratic Party for speaker of the House.

Sources: 1997-1998 Handbook of Illinois Government, State of Illinois, 1997, 18-19; *1995-1996 Handbook of Illinois Government,* State of Illinois, 1995, 23-52; *1993 Roster of State Government Officials, Illinois Issues,* April 1993, 17,25; *1991 Roster of State Government Officials, Illinois Issues,* April 1991, 23,33; Michael D. Klemens, "Lawmakers' Class of '88: One Bona Fide Surprise," *Illinois Issues* January 1989, 19-21: *Illinois Blue Book,* Secretary of State, State of Illinois, 1988, 62-63; *State of Illinois Official Vote,* General Election, November 8, 1988, State Board of Elections, 1988, 32-87; Michael D. Klemens, "1988 Legislative Elections Give New Meaning to `Power of Incumbency,'" *Illinois Issues,* December 1988, 15-16; Michael D. Klemens, "Expectations of the Rookie Legislators," *Illinois Issues,* January 1987, 15-17; Michael D. Klemens, "Don't Vote for Nobody Nobody Knows," *Illinois Issues*, December 1986, 4-7; *Illinois Blue Book,* Secretary of State, State of Illinois, 1984, 58-59; *State of Illinois Official Vote,* General Elections, November 6, 1984, State Board of Elections, 1984, 34-62; *Illinois Blue Book,* Secretary of State, State of Illinois, 1982, 58-59; *State of Illinois Official Vote,* General Election, November 2, 1982, State Board of Elections, 1982, 40-85; Paul M. Green et al., *Illinois Elections*, 3rd ed. (Springfield, Illinois; *Illinois Issues,* 1986) 93-96; *Illinois Blue Book*, Secretary of State, State of Illinois, 1980, 58-59; *State of Illinois Official Vote*, General Election, November 4, 1980, State Board of Elections, 1980, 33-52; David H. Everson, "The Bullet Bites the Dust: Will the Cutback Amendment Bring Competition and Accountability?" *Illinois Issues,* March 1981, 10-15; *Illinois Blue Book,* Secretary of State, State of Illinois, 1978, 60-61; *State of Illinois Official Vote,* General Election, November 7, 1978, State Board of Elections, 1978, 56-78; Gary Adkins, "The Election Message," *Illinois Issues,* December 1978, 2; "Elections: Democrats Win Clear Majority in General Assembly," *Illinois Issues,* January 1977, 25-26.

Table 26 Illinois General Assembly workload: 1977-1996

	1977-78	1979-80	1981-82	1983-84	1985-86	1987-88	1989-90	1991-92	1993-94	1995-96*
Bills introduced	5,345	5,689	4,383	5,251	5,990	6,591	6,569	6,505	6,128	5,686
Senate	1,893	2,045	1,693	1,960	2,317	2,280	2,321	2,247	1,854	1,948
House	3,452	3,644	2,690	3,291	3,673	4,311	4,248	4,258	4,274	3,738
Sent to governor	1,736	1,711	1,159	1,722	1,606	1,659	1,687	1,528	775	722
Senate	695	672	568	713	734	686	655	623	325	341
House	1,041	1,039	591	1,009	872	973	1,032	905	450	381
Percent	32.4	30.0	26.4	32.7	26.8	25.2	25.7	23.5	12.6	12.7
Bill signed**	1,401	1,434	958	1,335	1,365	1,331	1,393	1,264	671	654
Senate	546	555	473	537	635	568	527	527	286	312
House	855	879	485	798	730	763	866	737	385	342
Percent	80.7	83.8	82.6	77.5	84.9	80.2	82.6	82.7	86.6	90.6
Appropriation reduced or item vetoed	39	49	131	68	135	107	40	26	0	0
Senate	21	28	80	37	78	56	22	14	0	0
House	18	21	51	31	57	51	18	12	0	0
Percent	2.4	2.8	11.3	3.9	8.4	6.4	2.4	1.7	0.0	0.0
Vetoed in full	219	154	99	200	126	195	154	174	54	21
Senate	91	72	48	90	61	62	79	64	18	12
House	128	82	51	110	65	133	75	110	36	9
Percent	12.6	9.0	8.5	11.6	7.8	11.8	9.1	11.4	7.0	2.9
Overridden	17	28	6	30	19	19	19	14	4	3
Senate	5	15	3	13	9	7	8	8	3	2
House	12	13	3	17	10	12	11	6	1	1
Percent	7.7	18.1	6.0	15.0	15.0	9.7	12.3	8.0	7.4	14.3

Table 26 Illinois General Assembly workload: 1977-1996, continued

	1977-78	1979-80	1981-82	1983-84	1985-86	1987-88	1989-90	1991-92	1993-94	1995-96*
Amendatory vetoes	116	123	102	187	115	133	140	90	50	47
Senate	58	45	47	86	38	58	49	32	21	17
House	58	78	55	101	77	75	91	58	29	30
Percent	6.6	7.1	8.8	10.8	7.1	8.0	8.3	5.9	6.5	6.5
Adopted	95	107	89	151	92	87	70	64	16	22
Senate	50	41	41	70	35	39	24	23	9	7
House	45	66	48	81	57	48	46	41	7	5
Percent	81.8	86.9	87.2	80.7	80.0	65.4	50.0	71.1	32.0	46.8
Overridden	3	6	6	20	6	14	8	2	1	0
Senate	2	1	4	8	0	4	1	0	0	0
House	1	5	2	12	6	10	7	2	1	0
Percent	2.5	4.8	5.8	10.6	5.2	10.5	5.7	2.2	2.0	0.0
No action	18	10	7	16	17	32	62	21	33	4
Senate	6	3	2	8	3	14	24	8	12	3
House	12	7	5	8	14	18	38	13	21	1
Percent	15.5	8.1	6.8	8.5	14.7	24.1	44.3	26.7	66.0	8.5
Bills enacted	1,516	1,575	1,059	1,536	1,482	1,451	1,490	1,280	692	679
as a % of bills										
introduced	28.3	27.6	24.1	29.2	24.7	22.0	22.7	19.7	11.3	11.9
sent to governor	97.3	92.0	91.3	89.1	92.2	87.5	88.3	83.8	89.3	94.0

*Through September 23, 1996
**Includes appropriation bills reduced or item vetoed, and bills filed without governor's signature

Source: Compiled by Legislative Research Unit from *Illinois Revised Statutes; Legislative Synopsis and Digest;* and Legislative Information System reports.

Table 27 Illinois General Assembly staff: 1975-1997 (selected years)

Year	Staff	Committee	Chicago	Leadership	Total
1975	Senate Majority (D)	17	*	10	27
	Senate Minority (R)	23	*	10	33
	House Majority (D)	29	*	14	43
	House Minority (R)	24	*	9	33
1980	Senate Majority (D)	22	4	20	46
	Senate Minority (R)	21	2	16	39
	House Majority (R)	26	1	21	48
	House Minority (D)	24	2	16	42
1985	Senate Majority (D)	24	9	38	71
	Senate Minority (R)	25	4	26	55
	House Majority (D)	21	15	64	100
	House Minority (R)	24	13	34	71
1988	Senate Majority (D)	23	12	37	72
	Senate Minority (R)	25	5	28	58
	House Majority (D)	20	19	70	109
	House Minority (R)	23	14	45	82
1989	Senate Majority (D)	28	12	36	76
	Senate Minority (R)	26	8	26	60
	House Majority (D)	23	29	78	130
	House Minority (R)	28	11	50	89
1990	Senate Majority (D)	37	16	27	80
	Senate Minority (R)	35	7	25	67
	House Majority (D)	66	23	26	115
	House Minority (R)	45	8	33	86

Table 27 Illinois General Assembly staff: 1975-1997 (selected years), continued

Year	Staff	Committee	Chicago	Leadership	Total
1993	Senate Majority (R)	27	5	22	54
	Senate Minority (D)	21	7	27	55
	House Majority (D)	23	15	46	84
	House Minority (R)	43	11	13	67
1995	Senate Majority (R)	24	3	20	47
	Senate Minority (D)	26	3	25	54
	House Majority (R)	34	8	16	58
	House Minority (D)	25	11	33	69
1997	Senate Majority (R)	25	4	19	46
	Senate Minority (D)	22	1	29	52
	House Majority (D)	44	10	30	84
	House Minority (R)	26	15	29	70

* Number of Chicago staff included in Leadership staff.

Sources: *1970 Illinois Legislative Directory,* Illinois Legislative Council, 1970, 1-5; *Illinois General Assembly Directory,* Illinois Legislative Council, April 1975, 1-14; *Directory of State Officials,* Illinois Legislative Council, March 1980, 7-23; *Directory of State Officials,* Legislative Research Unit, April 1985, 5-29; *Directory of Illinois State Officials,* Legislative Research Unit, March 1988, 5-35; *Directory of Illinois State Officials,* Legislative Research Unit, March 1989, 5-36; *Roster of the 87th General Assembly & Staff: Revised October 1991,* Legislative Research Unit, 1991; *Directory of Illinois State Officials,* Legislative Research Unit, April 1993, 5-38.

Table 28 Directors and number of paid employees for Illinois code departments: 1997

Department	Director	Number of Employees
Department on Aging	Maralee I. Lindley	105
Department of Agriculture	Rebecca C. Doyle	653
Department of Central Management Services	Michael S. Schwartz	1,322
Department of Children and Family Services	Jess McDonald	4,289
Department of Commerce and Community Affairs	Dennis Whetstone	542
Department of Corrections	Odie Washington	14,651
Department of Employment Security	Lynn Quigley Doherty	2,132
Department of Financial Institutions	Frank C. Casillas	168
Department of Human Rights	Rose Mary Bombela	202
Department of Human Services	Howard Peters	20,283
Department of Insurance		372
Department of Labor	Shinae Chun	91
Department of Lottery	Lori Spear Montana	295
Department of Military Affairs	Richard G. Austin	300
Department of Natural Resources	Brent Manning	2,216
Department of Nuclear Safety	Thomas W. Ortciger	233
Department of Professional Regulation	Nikki Zollar	317
Department of Public Aid	Robert W. Wright	2,474
Department of Public Health	John R. Lumpkin M.D.	1,315
Department of Revenue	Kenneth E. Zehnder	2,495
Department of State Police	Terrance W. Gainer	3,679
Department of Transportation	Kirk Brown	6,717
Department of Veterans' Affairs	Robert Foster	1,059

Sources: 1997 Roster of State Government Officials, Illinois Issues, 1997, 8-17; *Directory of Illinois State Officials,* Legislative Research Unit, 1997.

Table 29.1: Staff directors—office of the governor: 1997

Chief of Staff	Mark Boozell	Transportation	Tom Livingston
Deputy Chief of Staff	Andrew Foster	Education	Allen Grosboll
Deputy Chief of Staff	Allen Grosboll	Ethnic Affairs	Patricia Michalski
Senior Assistant to the Governor	Valerie Brooks	Higher Education	Tom Livingston
Chief Legal Counsel	Elena Kezelis	Personnel/Labor/Boards and Commission	Janis Cellini
Senior Personal Assistant to the Governor	Michael McCormick	Press Secretary	Thomas Hardy
Director of Scheduling	Joe Khayyat	Legislative Affairs	Deno Peridou
Washington D.C. Director	Terri Moreland	Deputy Director	Scott Kaiser
Environmental/Agriculture	Allen Grosboll	Human Services	Kimberly Cox/Phallisha Horton-Newsome
Human Services	Valerie Brooks	Business and Economic Development/ Financial Regulation	Terry Harvill
Government Operations	Allen Grosboll	Environment/Natural Resources/Cultural Affairs	Erica Mair
State-Bonding Authorities	Elena Kezelis	Elementary/Secondary Education	Bob Hansen
Law Enforcement/Public Safety	Elena Kezelis	Job Training	Tim Probst
Bureau of the Budget	Stephen Schnorf	Bonding Authorities	Scott Rice
Internship Program	Edna Walden		
Governor's Office	Donna Fitts		
Business and Economic Development	Andrew Foster		
Retirement Systems	Elena Kezelis		

Table 29.2: Departments and agencies administered through the office of the governor: 1998

Governor

- Education
  - State Board of Education
  - Student Assistance Commission
  - Board of Higher Education
    - Board of Trustees of University of Illinois
    - Board of Trustees of Southern Illinois University
    - Board of Trustees of Chicago State University
    - Board of Trustees of Eastern Illinois University
    - Board of Trustees of Governors State University
    - Board of Trustees of Northeastern Illinois University
    - Board of Trustees of Western Illinois University
    - Board of Trustees of Illinois State University
    - Board of Trustees of Northern Illinois University
    - Community College Board
- State Board of Elections
- Major State Departments and Agencies
  - Aging
  - Agriculture
  - Central Management Services
  - Children and Family Services
  - Commerce and Community Affairs
  - Corrections
  - Emergency Management Agency
  - Employment Security
  - Environmental Protection Agency
  - Financial Institutions
  - Historic Preservation Agency
  - Human Rights
  - Human Services
  - Insurance
  - Labor
  - Lottery
  - Natural Resources
  - Nuclear Safety
  - Professional Regulation
  - Public Aid
  - Public Health
  - Revenue
  - State Police
  - Transportation
  - Veterans' Affairs
- Bureau of the Budget
- Department of Military Affairs
- Other Agencies, Boards, and Authorities
  - Regulatory Boards
  - Boards and Commissions
  - Public Safety Agencies
  - Financing Authorities
  - Environmental Agencies
  - Miscellaneous Agencies

Source: Adapted from *Illinois Handbook of Government 1997-1998.* Secretary of State, 1997. P 56.

Table 30: Organization of the Illinois court system (number of justices)

The Supreme Court of Illinois (7 justices)

1st Appellate District (24 justices)	2nd Appellate District (9 justices)	3rd Appellate District (6 justices)	4th Appellate District (6 justices)	5th Appellate District (7 justices)
Cook County Circuit	15th Circuit 16th Circuit 17th Circuit 18th Circuit 19th Circuit	9th Circuit 10th Circuit 12th Circuit 13th Circuit 14th Circuit 21st Circuit	5th Circuit 6th Circuit 7th Circuit 8th Circuit 11th Circuit	1st Circuit 2nd Circuit 3rd Circuit 4th Circuit 20th Circuit

Note: The number of appellate justices as of December 20, 1995.
Source: Administrative Office of the Illinois Courts, State of Illinois, 1995.

Table 31.1 Election results for Illinois Supreme Court justices since new constitution (first election)

Year	Justice	Judicial District	Party	Percentage of Vote
1976	William G. Clark	1st	Democrat	58
1976	James A. Dooley	1st	Democrat	64
1976	Thomas J. Moran	2nd	Republican	6
1980	Seymour Simon	1st	Democrat	61
1984	Ben Miller	4th	Republican	6
1988	Horace L. Calvo	5th	Democrat	53
1990	Charles E. Freeman	1st	Democrat	62
1990	Michael A. Bilandic	1st	Democrat	69
1990	James D. Heiple	3rd	Republican	50
1992	Mary Ann Grohwin McMorrow	1st	Democrat	69
1992	John L. Nickels	2nd	Republican	100

Source: State of Illinois Official Vote, cast at the 1974-1992 General Elections, State Board of Elections, State of Illinois, 1976, 1980, 1984, 1988, 1990, 1992.

Table 31.2 Reelection results for Illinois Supreme Court justices since new constitution (retention election)

Year	Justice	Judicial District	Percentage of Vote
1974	Daniel P. Ward	1st	82
1974	Joseph Burke	1st	72
1974	John T. Dempsey	1st	80
1974	Thaddeus V. Adesko	1st	62
1974	Thomas J. Moran	2nd	74
1976	Howard C. Ryan	3rd	80
1986	William G. Clark	1st	81
1986	Thomas J. Moran	2nd	79
1986	Howard C. Ryan	3rd	78
1994	Benjamin K. Miller	4th	79

Source: State of Illinois Official Vote, cast at the 1974-1994 General Elections, State Board of Elections, State of Illinois, 1974, 1976, 1986, 1994.

Table 32.1 Caseload of the Illinois Supreme Court: 1970-1996

Year	Number of Petitions for Leave to Appeal	Number of Petitions for Rehearing	Number of Cases Decided with Full Opinions
1970	344	87	345
1971	335	77	208
1972	447	70	246
1973	555	46	207
1974	644	64	228
1975	655	60	183
1976	761	76	236
1977	918	68	219
1978	989	64	195
1979	1,026	61	219
1980	1,160	65	231
1981	1,380	66	208
1982	1,468	61	199
1983	1,362	77	257
1984	1,468	59	200
1985	*	*	*
1986	1,617	71	156
1987	1,547	43	139
1988	1,361	57	181
1989	1,321	64	162
1990	1,444	54	125
1991	1,526	51	124
1992	1,561	68	104
1993	1,568	52	116
1994	1,586	55	121
1995	1,767	54	102
1996	1,966	58	89

* Not reported.

Sources: Administrative Office of the Illinois Courts, correspondence, August 1995; *Annual Reports of the Supreme Court of Illinois*, Administrative Office of the Illinois Courts, State of Illinois, 1970-1996.

Table 32.2 Caseload of the Illinois Appellate Courts: 1970-1996

Year	Number of Cases Pending *	Number of Cases Filed	Number of Cases Disposed of	Number of Cases Disposed with Full Opinions
1970	1,901	1,856	1,496	1,079
1971	2,261	2,499	1,944	1,410
1972	2,816	3,020	2,526	1,763
1973	3,310	3,044	2,958	2,037
1974	3,396	3,259	3,071	2,214
1975	3,584	4,135	3,645	2,394
1976	4,073	3,973	3,935	1,952
1977	4,111	4,381	4,579	2,198
1978	3,913	4,337	4,472	2,087
1979	3,852	5,651	4,660	2,092
1980	4,924	6,479	6,153	2,523
1981	8,341	9,587	9,306	2,943
1982	5,635	6,687	6,500	1,446
1983	5,938	6,815	7,396	1,523
1984	5,501	6,916	6,891	1,503
1985	**	**	**	**
1986	6,325	7,334	7,007	1,761
1987	6,868	7,651	7,451	2,024
1988	7,371	7,635	7,495	1,880
1989	7,908	7,507	7,625	2,042
1990	8,320	7,715	7,830	2,035
1991	8,570	8,297	8,458	2,249
1992	8,695	8,756	8,242	2,177
1993	9,375	8,915	8,528	2,144
1994	9,935	8,732	9,295	1,630
1995	9,525	8,849	9,646	1,051
1996	8,898	8,834	9,243	1,071

* Cases pending at the beginning of the callendar year. ** Not reported.

Sources: Administrative Office of the Illinois Courts, correspondence, August 1995; *Annual Reports of the Supreme Court of Illinois,* Administrative Office of the Illinois Courts, State of Illinois, 1970-1996.

Table 32.3 Caseload of the Illinois circuit courts: 1971-1996

Year	Number of Cases Filed/Begun	Number of Cases Reinstated	Net Added	Number of Cases Disposed of
1971	3,025,995	11,816	3,037,811	2,960,489
1972	2,898,226	14,732	2,912,958	2,868,718
1973	3,052,145	14,015	3,066,160	2,895,348
1974	3,114,194	24,777	3,138,971	2,989,263
1975	3,398,709	19,968	3,418,677	3,263,365
1976	3,464,746	19,826	3,484,572	3,268,838
1977	3,504,680	19,776	3,524,456	3,369,022
1978	7,583,557	50,392	7,633,949	5,209,264
1979	8,021,778	25,203	8,046,981	5,067,905
1980	7,831,646	25,111	7,856,757	5,342,324
1981	7,974,160	35,269	8,009,429	5,660,191
1982	7,426,028	43,963	7,469,991	5,443,478
1983	7,910,216	56,032	7,996,248	5,888,994
1984	7,644,544	115,861	7,760,405	5,773,661
1985	*	*	*	*
1986	7,421,747	75,779	7,497,573	4,890,414
1987	7,136,409	76,867	7,213,267	5,352,130
1988	8,715,839	136,173	8,852,031	5,229,493
1989	9,033,393	68,679	10,102,072	6,954,842
1990	7,582,311	72,350	7,654,661	6,524,294
1991	4,144,391[a]	87,209	4,231,600[a]	4,616,583[a]
1992	4,203,326[a]	108,856	4,312,182[a]	5,045,433[a]
1993	4,069,484[a]	**	N/A	4,163,774[a]
1994	4,126,740[a]	**	N/A	3,905,539[a]
1995	4,249,833	15,232	N/A	4,181,238
1996	4,390,047	48,786	N/A	4,117,153

* Not reported. ** Included in "Filed/Begun" figures. [a] Does not include Cook County parking tickets.

Sources: Annual Reports of the Supreme Court of Illinois, Administrative Office of the Illinois Courts, State of Illinois, 1970-1996.

Table 33 Twenty-year history of general funds revenues and expenditures: 1974-1995 ($ millions)

Fiscal Year	Total Revenues	Change Amount	Percent	Total Expenditures	Change Amount	Percent	June 30 Available Balance	Surplus or Deficit
1974	4,501	329	7.9	4,435	351	8.6	453	66
1975	4,910	409	9.1	5,048	613	13.8	315	-138
1976	5,462	552	11.2	5,651	603	11.9	126	-189
1977	5,930	468	8.6	6,004	353	6.2	52	-74
1978	6,343	413	7.0	6,309	305	5.1	86	34
1979	7,055	712	11.2	6,751	442	7.0	390	304
1980	7,442	387	5.5	7,442	691	10.2	390	0
1981	8,100	658	8.8	8,293	851	11.4	197	-193
1982	8,265	165	2.0	8,275	-18	-0.2	187	-10
1983	8,437	172	2.1	8,514	239	2.9	110	-77
1984	9,707	1,270	15.1	9,600	1,086	12.8	217	107
1985	10,317	610	6.3	10,055	455	4.7	479	262
1986	10,583	266	2.6	10,774	719	7.2	288	-191
1987	11,057	474	4.5	11,191	417	3.9	154	-134
1988	11,620	563	5.1	11,528	337	3.0	246	92
1989	12,133	513	4.4	11,838	310	2.7	541	295
1990	12,841	708	5.8	12,987	1,149	9.7	395	-146
1991	13,261	420	3.3	13,556	569	4.4	100	-295
1992	14,217	956	7.2	14,186	630	4.6	131	31
1993	15,050	833	5.9	15,009	823	5.8	172	41
1994	16,186	1,136	7.5	16,128	1,119	7.5	230	58
1995	17,302	1,116	6.9	17,201	1,073	6.7	331	101

Sources: *Comptroller's Monthly Fiscal Report,* Comptroller's Office, State of Illinois, July 1981, 2; Comptroller's Office, State of Illinois, July, 1993; Comptroller's Office, State of Illinois, July 1995.

Table 34 State expenditures for education and public aid; number of state employees and payroll

	Public Aid FY 1996			Education 95-96			State Employees CY1996			State Payroll CY1996		
County	Amount (million)	Percent of total	Rank	Amount (million)	Percent of total	Rank	Number	Percent of total	Rank	Amount (million)	Percent of total	Rank
Adams	30.5	0.43	25	26.3	0.78	21	941	0.63	32	25.3	0.63	32
Alexander	12.7	0.18	47	7.7	0.23	69	186	0.12	76	5.2	0.13	72
Bond	8.5	0.12	64	7.1	0.21	72	293	0.19	60	8.4	0.21	59
Boone	10.2	0.15	55	9.3	0.28	59	200	0.13	73	5.2	0.13	71
Brown	1.9	0.03	98	2.1	0.06	101	255	0.17	65	7.3	0.18	62
Bureau	11.8	0.17	49	16.4	0.49	37	345	0.23	56	7.9	0.20	60
Calhoun	1.5	0.02	101	2.4	0.07	100	110	0.07	90	2.9	0.07	87
Carroll	6.5	0.09	78	7.7	0.23	68	136	0.09	84	4.0	0.10	82
Cass	9.2	0.13	62	6.6	0.19	76	441	0.29	49	12.0	0.30	50
Champaign	56.8	0.81	14	41.4	1.23	16	11,348	7.55	3	265.7	6.58	3
Christian	20.1	0.29	33	14.9	0.44	39	1,030	0.69	26	29.4	0.73	27
Clark	6.2	0.09	80	8.7	0.26	62	221	0.15	68	4.8	0.12	76
Clay	10.7	0.15	53	8.4	0.25	66	76	0.05	96	2.1	0.05	96
Clinton	18.1	0.26	37	14.0	0.42	41	643	0.43	41	18.3	0.45	40
Coles	29.6	0.42	26	18.0	0.54	33	1,650	1.10	18	40.7	1.01	20
Cook	4,295.5	61.05	1	1,238.4	36.78	1	38,562	25.66	1	997.3	24.69	1
Crawford	7.3	0.10	74	7.9	0.23	67	306	0.20	59	8.7	0.21	57
Cumberland	4.3	0.06	87	5.7	0.17	82	150	0.10	81	3.4	0.09	85
DeKalb	28.6	0.41	29	20.2	0.60	30	3,479	2.32	8	79.6	1.97	8
DeWitt	7.7	0.11	70	3.7	0.11	90	241	0.16	67	5.4	0.13	70
Douglas	8.2	0.12	66	6.3	0.19	79	286	0.19	61	6.4	0.16	65
DuPage	171.0	2.43	3	98.6	2.93	6	4,531	3.02	5	127.6	3.16	4
Edgar	9.5	0.14	59	9.8	0.29	52	394	0.26	51	11.5	0.28	51
Edwards	1.9	0.03	99	3.1	0.09	97	48	0.03	102	1.3	0.03	102
Effingham	11.5	0.16	50	15.1	0.45	38	462	0.31	48	14.3	0.35	45
Fayette	12.1	0.17	48	9.5	0.28	56	530	0.35	44	16.1	0.40	42
Ford	6.6	0.09	77	5.6	0.17	83	167	0.11	79	3.8	0.09	83
Franklin	28.6	0.41	28	23.5	0.70	26	653	0.43	39	16.2	0.40	41

Table 34 State expenditures for education and public aid; number of state employees and payroll, continued

	Public Aid FY 1996			Education 95-96			State Employees CY1996			State Payroll CY1996		
County	Amount (million)	Percent of total	Rank	Amount (million)	Percent of total	Rank	Number	Percent of total	Rank	Amount (million)	Percent of total	Rank
Fulton	28.8	0.41	27	20.9	0.62	28	647	0.43	40	18.5	0.46	38
Gallatin	6.4	0.09	79	3.1	0.09	96	68	0.05	98	1.9	0.05	97
Green	7.5	0.11	73	7.4	0.22	71	321	0.21	58	8.5	0.21	58
Grundy	8.3	0.12	65	5.8	0.17	80	372	0.25	52	9.1	0.23	54
Hamilton	6.0	0.09	82	4.9	0.15	85	113	0.08	89	2.9	0.07	88
Hancock	7.5	0.11	71	11.7	0.35	48	218	0.15	69	4.3	0.11	79
Hardin	3.9	0.05	90	3.4	0.10	93	134	0.09	85	4.2	0.10	81
Henderson	2.2	0.03	97	3.4	0.10	94	65	0.04	100	1.4	0.03	101
Henry	17.1	0.24	40	25.4	0.76	22	357	0.24	54	9.4	0.23	52
Iroquois	16.0	0.23	42	12.9	0.38	43	364	0.24	53	8.9	0.22	56
Jackson	34.3	0.49	22	25.1	0.75	24	5,072	3.38	4	110.8	2.74	5
Jasper	2.9	0.04	94	3.5	0.10	92	115	0.08	88	2.9	0.07	89
Jefferson	24.4	0.35	31	19.8	0.59	31	436	0.29	50	13.0	0.32	47
Jersey	9.9	0.14	57	8.6	0.26	63	243	0.16	66	6.2	0.15	66
JoDaviess	3.1	0.04	92	6.7	0.20	75	104	0.07	95	2.3	0.06	95
Johnson	4.5	0.06	86	5.4	0.16	84	687	0.46	37	21.8	0.54	37
Kane	129.6	1.84	7	109.2	3.24	4	3,164	2.11	10	91.0	2.25	7
Kankakee	69.6	0.99	11	45.7	1.36	13	2,462	1.64	12	68.6	1.70	12
Kendall	4.3	0.06	89	11.8	0.35	47	264	0.18	64	6.5	0.16	64
Knox	41.7	0.59	18	20.9	0.62	29	643	0.43	41	18.3	0.45	39
LaSalle	41.7	0.59	17	33.1	0.98	19	1,544	1.03	19	44.3	1.10	18
Lake	151.6	2.15	4	116.1	3.45	3	2,579	1.72	11	68.6	1.70	11
Lawrence	14.1	0.20	44	9.2	0.27	60	105	0.07	94	2.8	0.07	93
Lee	16.3	0.23	41	12.0	0.36	46	1,024	0.68	27	32.4	0.80	25
Livingston	13.7	0.19	46	17.7	0.52	35	1,166	0.78	16	34.5	0.85	23
Logan	17.2	0.24	39	7.6	0.23	70	1,727	1.15	14	51.1	1.26	14
Macon	64.1	0.91	13	47.5	1.41	12	982	0.65	30	25.7	0.64	31
Macoupin	23.9	0.34	32	29.3	0.87	20	1,070	0.71	25	29.7	0.74	26

Table 34 State expenditures for education and public aid; number of state employees and payroll, continued

	Public Aid FY 1996			Education 95-96			State Employees CY1996			State Payroll CY1996		
County	Amount (million)	Percent of total	Rank	Amount (million)	Percent of total	Rank	Number	Percent of total	Rank	Amount (million)	Percent of total	Rank
Madison	147.4	2.10	5	95.1	2.82	7	3,329	2.22	9	75.3	1.86	10
Marion	31.1	0.44	24	25.2	0.75	23	985	0.66	28	27.0	0.67	30
Marshall	4.8	0.07	85	4.0	0.12	88	120	0.08	87	2.8	0.07	91
Mason	7.8	0.11	69	9.6	0.28	55	487	0.32	46	12.3	0.30	48
Massac	10.9	0.15	52	6.7	0.20	74	154	0.10	80	4.3	0.11	80
McDonough	10.2	0.14	56	10.5	0.31	51	1,971	1.31	14	47.5	1.18	16
McHenry	35.9	0.51	19	35.9	1.07	17	889	.59	35	23.1	0.57	36
McLean	34.9	0.50	20	33.9	1.01	18	3,833	2.55	6	78.2	1.94	9
Menard	3.7	0.05	91	6.3	0.19	78	1,183	0.79	23	35.9	0.89	22
Mercer	5.9	0.08	83	4.7	0.14	86	128	0.09	86	3.3	0.08	86
Monroe	7.5	0.11	72	8.5	0.25	64	171	0.11	78	4.9	0.12	75
Montgomery	17.9	0.26	38	14.0	0.42	42	984	0.65	29	29.2	0.72	28
Morgan	19.4	0.28	35	11.2	0.33	49	1,733	1.15	15	52.4	1.30	13
Moultrie	6.2	0.09	81	4.4	0.13	87	146	0.10	82	3.6	0.09	84
Ogle	14.0	0.20	45	17.8	0.53	34	524	0.35	45	13.1	0.32	46
Peoria	108.8	1.55	9	66.9	1.99	9	1,536	1.02	20	42.7	1.06	19
Perry	9.8	0.14	58	9.5	0.28	57	677	0.45	38	12.0	0.30	49
Piatt	4.9	0.07	84	3.8	0.11	89	338	0.22	57	9.0	0.22	55
Pike	8.9	0.13	63	9.3	0.28	58	348	0.23	55	9.0	0.23	53
Pope	2.3	0.03	96	2.5	0.07	99	142	0.09	83	4.5	0.11	78
Pulaski	4.3	0.06	88	6.7	0.20	73	193	0.13	75	5.6	0.14	69
Putnam	0.6	0.01	102	0.9	0.03	102	67	0.04	99	1.7	0.04	99
Randolph	15.1	0.21	43	12.7	0.38	44	1,266	0.84	22	39.5	0.98	21
Richland	9.3	0.13	61	8.4	0.25	65	106	0.07	92	2.9	0.07	90
Rock Island	67.8	0.96	12	58.7	1.74	10	844	0.56	36	23.6	0.59	35
Saline	27.2	0.39	30	14.8	0.44	40	479	0.32	47	14.6	0.36	44
Sangamon	76.6	1.09	10	55.4	1.65	11	20,119	13.39	2	656.4	16.25	2
Schuyler	2.4	0.03	95	3.6	0.11	91	278	0.12	77	5.2	0.13	73

Table 34 State expenditures for education and public aid; number of state employees and payroll, continued

	Public Aid FY 1996			Education 95-96			State Employees CY1996			State Payroll CY1996		
County	Amount (million)	Percent of total	Rank	Amount (million)	Percent of total	Rank	Number	Percent of total	Rank	Amount (million)	Percent of total	Rank
Scott	1.9	0.03	100	3.2	0.09	95	199	0.13	74	5.1	0.13	74
Shelby	7.9	0.11	68	12.2	0.36	45	202	0.13	72	4.6	0.11	77
St.Clair	210.1	2.99	2	137.9	4.09	2	2,110	1.40	13	50.2	1.24	15
Stark	2.9	0.04	93	3.1	0.09	98	71	0.05	97	1.7	0.04	98
Stephenson	19.4	0.28	34	18.2	0.54	32	217	0.14	70	5.7	0.14	68
Tazewell	49.5	0.70	16	43.7	1.30	14	937	0.62	33	23.7	0.59	34
Union	18.8	0.27	36	10.9	0.32	50	954	0.63	31	27.8	0.69	29
Vermilion	51.9	0.74	15	43.3	1.29	15	893	0.59	34	24.8	0.61	33
Wabash	6.9	0.10	76	6.5	0.19	77	52	0.03	101	1.40	0.04	100
Warren	7.9	0.11	67	8.7	0.26	61	273	0.18	63	7.8	0.19	61
Washington	9.4	0.13	60	5.8	0.17	81	208	0.14	71	5.7	0.14	67
Wayne	7.1	0.10	75	9.8	0.29	53	109	0.07	91	2.6	0.06	94
White	10.5	0.15	54	9.7	0.29	54	106	0.07	92	2.8	0.07	92
Whiteside	34.2	0.49	23	24.0	0.71	25	562	0.37	43	15.3	0.38	43
Will	121.9	1.73	8	100.3	2.98	5	3,480	2.32	7	103.6	2.56	6
Williamson	34.5	0.49	21	23.3	0.69	27	1,278	0.85	21	33.8	0.84	24
Winnebago	136.5	1.94	6	81.4	2.42	8	1,693	1.13	17	45.7	1.13	17
Woodford	10.9	0.16	51	17.4	0.52	36	274	0.18	62	6.8	0.17	63

Source: Comptroller's Office, State of Illinois, 1997; Illinois Department of Human Services, Bureau of Research and Analysis, Fiscal Year 1996; ISBE 95-96 Audited Annual Financial Reports.

Table 35 County, municipal, and township governmental units in Illinois: census years 1952-1995

Year	County	Municipal	School Districts	Special Districts*	Township
1952	102	1,157	3,484	1,546	1,433
1962	102	1,251	1,540	2,126	1,433
1972	102	1,267	1,177	2,407	1,432
1982	102	1,280	1,049	2,602	1,434
1992	102	1,280	976	2,166	1,434
1995	102	1,287	947	2,190	1,432

* With power to tax.

Sources: Department of Revenue, written correspondence, October 1997; 1987 Census of Governments: Government Organization, vol. 1, no. 1, U.S. Department of Commerce, Bureau of the Census, 1987.

Table 36 Fiscal year 1998 total funds by agency (dollars in thousands)

	FY97 Approp. with Supplement	FY98 Governor	FY98$ Final Action	Change% FY97-98 Final	Change FY97-98 Final
Fiscal year 1998 total funds	34,609,543.5	34,628,719.1	35,549,105.5	+939,562.0	+2.7%
Legislative agencies	63,639.2	64,258.9	66,896.5	+3,257.3	+5.1
General Assembly Operations	33,733.3	33,826.3	34,850.4	+1,117.1	+3.3
General Assembly Retirement Systems	2,400.0	3,113.0	3,113.0	+713.0	+29.7
Legislative Support Agencies	12,299.4	12,449.5	13,869.4	+1,570.0	+12.8
Auditor General	15,206.5	14,870.1	15,063.7	-142.8	-0.9
Judicial agencies	250,159.1	274,116.3	263,534.2	+13,375.1	+5.3
Supreme Court	218,884.6	239,818.5	228,515.4	+9,630.8	+4.4
Judges Retirement System	13,747.0	15,664.0	15,664.0	+1,917.0	+13.9
Judicial Inquiry Board	344.7	510.9	548.3	+203.6	+59.1
Appellate Defender	9,679.3	9,972.7	9,243.5	-435.8	-4.5
Appellate Prosecutor	7,503.5	8,150.2	9,563.0	+2,059.5	+27.4
Constitutional officers	1,179,803.9	1,135,454.2	1,146,139.7	-33,664.2	-2.9
Governor	7,817.8	8,203.7	8,165.1	+347.3	+4.4
Lieutenant Governor	3,024.3	2,914.3	2,914.3	-110.0	-3.6
Attorney General	37,950.8	42,660.7	44,160.8	+6,210.0	+16.4
Secretary of State	289,847.8	289,534.6	299,064.6	+9,216.8	+3.2
Comptroller	48,322.7	50,508.6	50,264.1	+1,941.4	+4.0
Treasurer	792,840.5	741,632.3	741,570.8	-51,269.7	-6.5
Code departments	22,499,632.0	22,330,308.4	23,222,424.7	+722,792.7	+3.2
Aging	201,313.3	205,017.5	211,788.1	+10,474.8	+5.2
Agriculture	80,516.5	94,314.7	94,636.7	+14,120.2	+17.5
Central Management Services	1,770,869.9	1,756,304.6	1,745,656.8	-25,213.1	-1.4
Children & Family Services	1,334,633.4	1,343,470.0	1,341,958.1	+7,324.7	+0.5
Commerce & Community Affairs	784,650.0	791,144.1	813,238.6	+28,588.6	+3.6

Table 36 Fiscal year 1998 total funds by agency (dollars in thousands), continued

	FY97 Approp. with Supplement	FY98 Governor	FY98$ Final Action	Change% FY97-98 Final	Change FY97-98 Final
Corrections	915,022.9	992,663.2	1,030,570.5	+115,547.6	+12.6
Employment Security	210,734.0	222,160.3	222,160.3	+11,426.3	+5.4
Financial Institutions	13,774.6	14,474.1	14,363.0	+588.4	+4.3
Human Rights	8,830.0	9,204.2	9,107.2	+277.2	+3.1
Department of Human Services	4,222,541.5	4,297,189.0	4,341,010.9	+118,469.4	+2.8
Insurance	22,780.0	24,353.6	24,349.9	+1,569.9	+6.9
Labor	5,228.6	5,503.1	5,502.0	+273.4	+5.2
Lottery	383,317.8	364,767.4	364,092.2	-19,225.6	-5.0
Military Affairs	26,648.8	27,534.4	27,909.1	+1,260.3	+4.7
Natural Resources	356,891.9	352,293.1	418,393.7	+61,501.8	+17.2
Nuclear Safety	32,758.8	32,899.7	29,410.4	+3,348.4	-10.2
Professional Regulation	20,544.6	21,580.9	21,572.9	+1,028.3	+5.0
Public Aid	5,865,441.7	5,752,295.1	5,745,355.0	-120,086.7	-2.0
Public Health	178,752.6	190,058.1	193,198.5	+14,445.9	+8.1
Revenue	560,066.5	586,427.8	681,681.5	+121,615.0	+21.7
State Police	264,769.8	280,013.0	283,756.5	+18,986.7	+7.2
Transportation New Appropriations	2,820,509.2	2,666,877.5	2,690,269.1	-130,240.1	-4.6
Transportation Reappropriations	2,364,458.6	2,240,958.6	2,853,439.3	+488,980.7	+20.7
Veterans' Affairs	54,577.0	58,804.4	59,004.4	+4,472.4	+8.1
Other agencies	2,721,469.9	2,742,814.8	2,636,684.7	-84,785.2	-3.1
Arts Council	8,007.0	13,105.8	14,135.8	+6,128.8	+76.5
Banks & Real Estate	23,135.5	24,339.8	24,328.7	+1,193.2	+5.2
Build Illinois Reappropriations	262,426.1	178,860.9	179,861.1	-82,565.0	-31.5
Bureau of the Budget	206,053.5	211,025.6	211,022.0	+4,968.5	+2.4
Capital Development Board Operations	9,572.4	10,270.0	10,186.0	+613.6	+6.4
Capital Development Board New Appropriations	515,876.2	338,613.9	108,478.0	-407,398.2	-79.0
Capital Development Board Reappropriations	528,753.8	773,743.9	863,383.2	+334,629.4	+63.3
Civil Service Commission	380.7	401.0	378.0	-2.7	-0.7

Table 36 Fiscal year 1998 total funds by agency (dollars in thousands), continued

	FY97 Approp. with Supplement	FY98 Governor	FY98$ Final Action	Change% FY97-98 Final	Change FY97-98 Final
Commerce Commission	32,968.2	31,369.1	32,286.7	-681.5	-2.1
Comprehensive Health Insurance Plan	17,324.3	17,324.3	17,324.3	0.0	0.0
Court of Claims—Awards	21,317.8	0.0	2,978.7	+18,339.1	-86.0
Court of Claims—Operations	13,357.9	18,505.4	18,385.4	+5,027.5	+37.6
Criminal Justice Information Authority	74,807.8	91,747.7	91,248.5	-16,936.6	+22.6
Deaf and Hard of Hearing Commission	0.0	300.0	300.0	+300.0	+100.0
East St. Louis Financial Advisory Authority	280.0	280.0	280.0	0.0	0.0
Environmental Protection Agency	618,378.2	697,469.9	720,228.0	+101,849.8	+16.5
Environmental Protection Trust Fund Commission	3,225.0	3,481.0	3,481.0	+256.0	+7.9
Emergency Management Agency	153,771.6	90,248.5	91,248.5	-62,523.1	-40.7
Farm Development Authority	4,079.4	4,079.4	4,079.4	0.0	0.0
Guardianship & Advocacy Commission	6,041.4	6,486.2	6,511.2	+469.8	+7.8
Health Care Cost Containment Council	1,334.0	1,373.1	1,373.1	+39.1	+2.9
Historic Preservation Agency	15,690.1	15,140.8	16,815.8	+1,125.7	+7.2
Human Rights Commission	1,786.7	1,988.1	1,983.8	+197.1	+11.0
Industrial Commission	9,198.8	9.696.1	9,677.2	+478.4	+5.2
Liquor Control Commission	3,610.6	3,654.1	4,022.2	+411.6	+11.4
Local Law Enforcement Officers Training Board	10,749.5	11,001.6	11,001.6	+252.1	+2.3
Medical District Commission	5,648.7	6,592.3	8,980.0	+3,331.3	+59.0
Metropolitan Pier & Exposition Authority	98,950.0	103,500.0	103,500.0	+4,550.0	+4.6
Planning Council on Developmental Disabilities	3,560.6	4,561.5	4,561.5	+1,000.9	+28.1
Pollution Control Board	1,918.8	1,918.8	1,918.8	0.0	0.0
Prairie State 2000 Authority	7,557.8	7,472.4	7,471.0	-86.8	-1.1
Prisoner Review Board	1,068.1	1,148.5	1,148.5	+80.4	+7.5
Property Tax Appeal Board	2,736.0	3,547.6	3,544.3	+808.3	+29.5
Racing Board	11,259.6	11,348.2	11,353.2	+93.6	+0.8
Savings & Residential Finance	0.0	0.0	0.0	0.0	0.0

Table 36 Fiscal year 1998 total funds by agency (dollars in thousands), continued

	FY97 Approp. with Supplement	FY98 Governor	FY98$ Final Action	Change% FY97-98 Final	Change FY97-98 Final
Sports Facilities Authority	18,000.0	18,000.0	18,000.0	0.0	0.0
State Board of Elections	5,442.1	5,657.1	5,657.1	+215.0	+4.0
State Employees' Retirement System	8,579.0	9,317.4	9,317.4	+738.4	+8.6
State Fire Marshal	12,341.5	12,809.5	13,309.5	+968.0	+7.8
State & Local Labor Relations Board	1,674.8	1,758.6	1,752.6	+77.8	+4.6
State Police Merit Board	606.4	676.7	676.7	+70.3	+11.6
K-12 Education	5,343,984.9	5,692,012.0	5,806,077.0	+462,092.1	+8.6
State Board of Education	5,342,742.8	5,690,644.1	5,804,712.1	+461,969.3	+8.6
Illinois Educational Labor Relations Board	1,242.1	1,317.9	1,314.9	+72.8	+5.9
Teachers Retirement & Chicago Pensions	0.0	50.0	50.0	+50.0	+100.0
Higher Education	2,550,854.5	2,389,754.5	2,407,348.7	-143,505.8	-5.6
Board of Higher Education	81,248.0	138,822.3	138,147.3	+56,899.3	+70.0
Chicago State University	43,886.2	31,910.8	34,110.8	-9,775.4	-22.3
Eastern Illinois University	64,939.2	42,402.0	41,870.4	-23,068.8	-35.5
Governor's State University	29,931.7	21,990.1	23,182.8	-6,758.9	-22.5
Illinois Community College Board	274,598.6	285,530.4	285,649.4	+11,050.8	+4.0
Illinois State University	116,093.2	75,695.4	75,540.1	-40,553.1	-34.9
Illinois Student Assistance Commission	516,826.7	535,953.0	536,116.7	+19,290.0	+3.7
Math & Science Academy	13,367.8	14,022.5	13,650.1	+282.3	+2.1
Northeastern Illinois University	50,088.5	36,024.1	36,024.1	-14,064.4	-28.1
Northern Illinois University	94,466.7	97,409.6	96,971.1	+2,504.4	+2.7
Southern Illinois University	194,075.9	200,170.5	199,503.4	+5,427.5	+2.8
Universities Civil Service Merit Board	1,144.9	1.192.0	1,176.1	+31.2	+2.7
Universities Retirement Systems	159,547.0	201,624.0	201,624.0	+42,077.0	+26.4
University of Illinois	839,392.9	654,796.8	671,339.7	-168,053.2	-20.0
Western Illinois University	71,247.2	52,211.0	52,442.7	-18,804.5	-26.4

Source: Senate Democrat FY98 Budget Wrapup, State of Illinois, 1997.

Table 37 General funds expenditures by major function: fiscal years 1977-1997 ($ millions)

Year	Education	Health & Social Services	Income Support
FY77	2,438	1,499	1,044
FY78	2,557	1,597	1,011
FY79	2,769	1,753	1,003
FY80	2,970	2,006	1,021
FY81	3,195	2,197	1,141
FY82	3,156	2,383	1,249
FY83	2,974	2,364	1,285
FY84	3,212	2,438	1,330
FY85	3,441	2,657	1,348
FY86	3,870	2,790	1,415
FY87	4,144	2,868	1,417
FY88	3,965	3,092	1,346
FY89	4,165	3,476	1,351
FY90	4,915	3,875	1,400
FY91	4,995	4,196	1,496
FY92	4,902	4,708	1,502
FY93	4,922	5,022	1,352
FY94	5,114	5,410	1,421
FY95	5,404	6,339	1,524
FY96	5,695	6,805	1.472
FY97	6,102	6,723	1,423

Source: Illinois Annual Report, Office of the Comptroller, State of Illinois, 1974-1997.

Table 38 Monthly average of persons receiving AFDC/TANF* and grant amounts: 1977-1996

Year	**Monthly Average of Persons Receiving AFDC/TANF**	**Total CY Payments**
1977	757,832	723,142,000
1978	705,904	696,024,031
1979	668,512	700,313,964
1980	673,993	747,298,283
1981	711,036	840,428,317
1982	714,710	834,011,861
1983	739,622	851,453,717
1984	746,040	862,886,450
1985	739,596	904,385,524
1986	740,837	903,261,710
1987	716,338	876,043,975
1988	669,744	818,395,624
1989	637,194	781,578,499
1990	651,405	868,644,544
1991	689,293	922,085,990
1992	693,617	920,954,957
1993	703,276	950,565,394
1994	726,789	1,010,086,898
1995	702,918	1,000,959,568
1996	663,724	969,321,735

* TANF, (Temporary Assistance to Needy Families), replaced AFDC effective July1, 1997.

Sources: Bureau of Research and Analysis, Department of Public Health, Springfield, November, 1997.

Table 39.1 County population totals: 1980 and 1990

County	1980	1990	Difference in Pop. 1980-1990	% Difference in Pop. 1980-1990
Adams	71,622	66,090	-5,532	-7.72
Alexander	12,264	10,626	-1,638	-13.36
Bond	16,224	14,991	-1,233	-7.60
Boone	28,630	30,806	2,176	7.60
Brown	5,411	5,836	425	7.85
Bureau	39,114	35,688	-3,426	-8.76
Calhoun	5,867	5,322	-545	-9.29
Carroll	18,779	16,805	-1,974	-10.51
Cass	15,084	13,437	-1.647	-10.92
Champaign	168,392	173,025	4,633	2.75
Christian	36,466	34,418	-2,028	-5.56
Clark	16,913	15,921	-992	-5.87
Clay	15,283	14,460	-823	-5.39
Clinton	32,617	33,944	1,327	4.07
Coles	52,992	51,644	-1,348	-2.54
Cook	5,253,190	5,105,067	-148,123	-2.82
Crawford	20,818	19,464	-1,354	-6.50
Cumberland	11,062	10,670	-392	-3.54
DeKalb	74,624	77,932	3,308	4.43
DeWitt	18,108	16,516	-1,592	-8.79
Douglas	19,774	19,464	-310	-1.57
DuPage	658,177	781,666	123,489	18.76
Edgar	21,725	19,595	-2,130	-9.80
Edwards	7,961	7,440	-521	-6.54
Effingham	30,944	31,704	760	2.46
Fayette	22,167	20,893	-1,274	-5.75
Ford	15,265	14,275	-990	-6.49

Table 39.1 County population totals: 1980 and 1990, continued

County	1980	1990	Difference in Pop. 1980-1990	% Difference in Pop. 1980-1990
Franklin	43,201	40,319	-2,882	-6.67
Fulton	43,687	38,080	-5,607	-12.83
Gallatin	7,590	6,909	-681	-8.97
Greene	16,661	15,317	-1,344	-8.07
Grundy	30,582	32,337	1,755	5.74
Hamilton	9,172	8,499	-673	-7.34
Hancock	23,877	21,373	-2,504	-10.49
Hardin	5,383	5,189	-194	-3.60
Henderson	9,114	8,096	-1,018	-11.17
Henry	57,968	51,159	-6,809	-11.75
Iroquois	32,976	30,787	-2,189	-6.64
Jackson	61,522	61,067	-455	0.74
Jasper	11,318	10,609	-709	-6.26
Jefferson	36,354	37,020	666	1.83
Jersey	20,538	20,539	1	0.00
JoDaviess	23,520	21,821	-1,699	-7.22
Johnson	9,624	11,347	1,723	17.90
Kane	278,405	317,471	39,066	14.03
Kankakee	102,926	96,255	-6,671	-6.48
Kendall	37,202	39,413	2,211	5.94
Knox	61,607	56,393	-5,214	-8.46
Lake	440,372	516,418	76,046	17.27
LaSalle	109,139	106,913	-2,226	-2.04
Lawrence	17,807	15,972	-1,835	-10.30
Lee	36,328	34,392	-1,936	-5.33
Livingston	41,381	39,301	-2,080	-5.03
Logan	31,802	30,798	-1,004	-3.16
Macon	131,375	117,206	-14,169	-10.79

Table 39.1 County population totals: 1980 and 1990, continued

County	1980	1990	Difference in Pop. 1980-1990	% Difference in Pop. 1980-1990
Macoupin	49,384	47,679	-1,705	-3.45
Madison	247,671	249,238	1,567	0.63
Marion	43,523	41,561	-1,962	-4.51
Marshall	14,479	12,846	-1,633	-11.28
Mason	19,492	16,269	-3,223	-16.53
Massac	14,990	14,752	-238	-1.59
McDonough	37,236	35,244	-1,992	-5.35
McHenry	147,724	183,241	35,517	24.04
McLean	119,149	129,180	10,031	8.42
Menard	11,700	11,164	-536	-4.58
Mercer	19,286	17,290	-1,996	-10.35
Monroe	20,117	22,422	2,305	11.46
Montgomery	31,686	30,728	-958	-3.02
Morgan	37,502	36,397	-1,105	-2.95
Moultrie	14,546	13,930	-616	-4.23
Ogle	46,338	45,957	-381	-0.82
Peoria	200,466	182,827	-17,639	-8.80
Perry	21,714	21,412	-302	-1.39
Piatt	16,581	15,548	-1,033	-6.23
Pike	18,896	17,577	-1,319	-6.98
Pope	4,404	4,373	-31	-0.70
Pulaski	8,840	7,523	-1,317	-14.90
Putnam	6,085	5,730	-355	-5.83
Randolph	35,566	34,583	-983	-2.76
Richland	17,587	16,545	-1,042	-5.92
Rock Island	165,968	148,723	-17,245	-10.39
Saline	27,360	26,551	-809	-2.96
Sangamon	176,089	178,386	2,297	1.30

Table 39.1 County population totals: 1980 and 1990, continued

County	1980	1990	Difference in Pop. 1980-1990	% Difference in Pop. 1980-1990
Schuyler	8,365	7,498	-867	-10.36
Scott	6,142	5,644	-498	-8.11
Shelby	23,923	22,261	-1,662	-6.95
St. Clair	265,469	262,852	-2,617	-0.99
Stark	7,389	6,534	-855	-11.57
Stephenson	49,536	48,052	-1,484	-3.00
Tazewell	132,078	123,692	-8,386	-6.35
Union	16,851	17,619	768	4.56
Vermilion	95,222	88,257	-6,965	-7.31
Wabash	13,713	13,111	-602	-4.39
Warren	21,943	19,181	-2,762	-12.59
Washington	15,472	14,965	-507	-3.28
Wayne	18,059	17,241	-818	-4.53
White	17,864	16,522	-1,342	-7.51
Whiteside	65,970	60,186	-5,784	-8.77
Will	324,460	357,313	32,853	10.13
Williamson	56,538	57,733	1,195	2.11
Winnebago	250,884	252,913	2,029	0.81
Woodford	33,320	32,653	-667	-2.00
Total State Population	11,422,421	11,434,582	12,161	0.11

Source: Illinois State Data Center Cooperative, Illinois Bureau of the Budget, Office of the Governor, State of Illinois, 1991.

Table 39.2 Population and rank of Illinois counties: 1994

	Population		Rank	Change	
	1990 Census	July 1, 1994		Number	Percent
Adams	66,090	67,714	21	1,624	2.5
Alexander	10,626	10,309	89	-317	-3.0
Bond	14,991	15,250	76	259	1.7
Boone	30,806	34,785	41	3,979	12.9
Brown	5,836	6,019	97	183	3.1
Bureau	35,688	36,074	38	386	1.1
Calhoun	5,322	5,016	101	-306	-5.7
Carroll	16,805	16,787	70	-18	-0.1
Cass	13,437	13,358	82	-79	-0.6
Champaign	173,025	167,485	12	-5,540	-3.2
Christian	34,418	34,736	43	318	0.9
Clark	15,921	16,244	71	323	2.0
Clay	14,460	14,408	79	-52	-0.4
Clinton	33,944	34,776	42	832	2.5
Coles	51,644	52,129	26	485	0.9
Cook	5,105,044	5,141,375	1	36,331	0.7
Crawford	19,464	19,969	59	505	2.6
Cumberland	10,670	11,030	87	360	3.4
DeKalb	77,932	82,058	20	4,126	5.3
DeWitt	16,516	16,906	67	390	2.4
Douglas	19,464	19,646	60	182	0.9
DuPage	781,689	843,067	2	61,378	7.9
Edgar	19,595	19,616	61	21	0.1
Edwards	7,440	7,287	94	-153	-2.1
Effingham	31,704	32,675	47	971	3.1
Fayette	20,893	20,960	58	67	0.3
Ford	14,275	13,920	81	-355	-2.5

Table 39.2 Population and rank of Illinois counties: 1994, continued

	Population		Rank	Change	
	1990 Census	July 1, 1994		Number	Percent
Franklin	40,319	40,623	33	304	0.8
Fulton	38,080	38,121	35	41	0.1
Gallatin	6,909	6,801	95	-108	-1.6
Greene	15,317	15,357	75	40	0.3
Grundy	32,337	34,735	44	2,398	7.4
Hamilton	8,499	8,453	90	-46	-0.5
Hancock	21,373	21,447	55	74	0.3
Hardin	5,189	5,162	100	-27	-0.5
Henderson	8,096	8,244	91	148	1.8
Henry	51,159	51,520	27	361	0.7
Iroquois	30,787	31,428	48	641	2.1
Jackson	61,067	61,741	22	674	1.1
Jasper	10,609	10,638	88	29	0.3
Jefferson	37,020	37,261	36	241	0.7
Jersey	20,539	20,975	57	436	2.1
JoDaviess	21,821	22,108	54	287	1.3
Johnson	11,347	11,992	85	645	5.7
Kane	317,471	348,590	5	31,119	9.8
Kankakee	96,255	101,290	18	5,035	5.2
Kendall	39,416	44,091	31	4,675	11.9
Knox	56,393	55,855	25	-538	-1.0
Lake	516,418	559,392	3	42,974	8.3
LaSalle	106,913	109,408	17	2,495	2.3
Lawrence	15,972	15,941	73	-31	-0.2
Lee	34,392	35,489	40	1,097	3.2
Livingston	39,301	40,185	34	884	2.2

Table 39.2 Population and rank of Illinois counties: 1994, continued

	Population		Rank	Change	
	1990 Census	July 1, 1994		Number	Percent
Logan	30,798	30,767	49	-31	-0.1
Macon	117,206	116,588	16	-618	-0.5
Macoupin	47,679	48,594	30	915	1.9
Madison	249,238	255,105	8	5,867	2.4
Marion	41,561	41,783	32	222	0.5
Marshall	12,846	12,761	84	-85	-0.7
Mason	16,269	16,790	69	521	3.2
Massac	14,752	15,189	77	437	3.0
McDonough	35,244	35,581	39	337	1.0
McHenry	183,241	215,945	9	32,704	17.8
McLean	129,180	137,577	14	8,397	6.5
Menard	11,164	11,925	86	761	6.8
Mercer	17,290	17,452	64	162	0.9
Monroe	22,422	24,165	52	1,743	7.8
Montgomery	30,728	30,721	50	-7	0.0
Morgan	36,397	36,199	37	-198	-0.5
Moultrie	13,930	14,083	80	153	1.1
Ogle	45,957	48,802	29	2,845	6.2
Peoria	182,827	183,159	11	332	0.2
Perry	21,412	21,268	56	-144	-0.7
Piatt	15,548	15,967	72	419	2.7
Pike	17,577	17,162	66	-415	-2.4
Pope	4,373	4,576	102	203	4.6
Pulaski	7,523	7,404	93	-119	-1.6
Putnam	5,730	5,783	98	53	0.9
Randolph	34,583	34,443	45	-140	-0.4

Table 39.2 Population and rank of Illinois counties: 1994, continued

	Population		Rank	Change	
	1990 Census	July 1, 1994		Number	Percent
Richland	16,545	16,846	68	301	1.8
Rock Island	148,723	150,305	13	1,582	1.1
Saline	26,551	26,698	51	147	0.6
Sangamon	178,386	183,908	10	5,522	3.1
Schuyler	7,498	7,630	92	132	1.8
Scott	5,644	5,643	99	-1	0.0
Shelby	22,261	22,478	53	217	1.0
St. Clair	262,852	265,440	6	2,588	1.0
Stark	6,534	6,305	96	-229	-3.5
Stephenson	48,052	49,095	28	1,043	2.2
Tazewell	123,692	126,417	15	2,725	2.2
Union	17,619	17,990	63	371	2.1
Vermilion	88,257	87,327	19	-930	-1.1
Wabash	13,111	12,898	83	-213	-1.6
Warren	19,181	18,934	62	-247	-1.3
Washington	14,965	15,055	78	90	0.6
Wayne	17,241	17,168	65	-73	-0.4
White	16,522	15,914	74	-608	-3.7
Whiteside	60,186	60,298	23	112	0.2
Will	357,313	398,706	4	41,393	11.6
Williamson	57,733	59,407	24	1,674	2.9
Winnebago	252,913	263,122	7	10,209	4.0
Woodford	32,653	33,955	46	1,302	4.0

Source: Compiled by the Legislative Research Unit, 1995, from U.S. Department of Commerce, Bureau of the Census, "Estimates of Resident Population of State and Counties and Percent Change, April 1, 1990 to July 1, 1994," CENDATA (Dialog® online system).

Abbreviations

AB	Anheuser Busch
AbbeyBlders	Abbey Builders
AbbeyPAC	Abbey PAC
ABC	ABC PAC
ABCI	American Bare Conductor, Inc.
ABDI	Associated Beer Distributors of Illinois
Activator	Illinois Farm Bureau
ACPA	American Crop Protection Association
AdamsDevlp	Adams Development
ADM	Archer Daniels Midland Company
ADS	American Disposal Services, Inc.
AFFI	Associated Fire Fighters of Illinois
AFLCIO	American Federation of Labor and Congress of Industrial Organizations
AFSCME	Association of Federal, State, County & Municipal Employees
AGC	Association of General Contractors of Illinois PAC
AIA	American Insurance Association
AlarmDet	Alarm Detection Systems
ALEX	American Legislative Exchange Co.
AlivioMC	Alivio Medical Center
Alliance	Alliance for Illinois School Boards
Allstate	Allstate Insurance PAC
Alt&Gray	Altheimer & Gray
Ameritech	Ameritech Corporation PA C
Amoco	Amoco Oil PAC
ANA	American Naprapathic Association PAC
AntiochMB	Antioch Missionary Baptist Church
AO&R	Anesi, Ozmon & Rodin Ltd.
AQC	Ashley's Quality Care
ARC	Arlington International Racecourse, Ltd.
Argosy	Argosy Gaming Company
ASBA	American Small Business Advisors
AT&T	American Telephone and Telegraph PAC
AULife	American Union Life Insurance Company
Auto	Chicago Auto Trade Association PAC
AVentures	ArcVentures LLC
B&HCPA	Bolling & Hill, CPAs
BaerCmte	Baer Committee

BAGChgo	Builders Association of Greater Chicago
BankersL&C	Bankers Life and Casualty
Baxter	Baxter Healthcare Corp.
BCongress	Blagojevich for Congress
Benchmark	Benchmark Real Estate Services Inc.
BFerris	Browning Ferris Corporate PAC
BI	Bank of Illinois
BlomquistPC	Ernest Blomquist III, PC
BLA	Bollinger, Loch & Associates
BlueSky	Blue Sky Banners
BNRR	Burlington Northern Railroad
BooneDem	Boone County Democrats
BPS	BPS Inc.
BradSup	Bradford Supply
BRS	Brotherhood of Railroad Signalmen
BSDCorp	BSD Corp.
BSIW	Bridge Structural Iron Workers (IPAL)
CAckerman	Citizens for Ackerman
CalFed Savings	Calumet Federal Savings
C&GL	Construction & General Laborers
C&L	Coopers & Lybrand
C&UPost	C&U Poster Advertising Co.
CAE	Concerned Assoc. Employees
CAR	Illinois Automotive Dealers Association
CardinalTrans	Cardinal Transportation, Inc.
Carmichael	Carmichael Leasing Co.
Carpenters	Carpenters Union PAC
CarpetWorld	CarpetWorld, Inc.
CAT	Caterpillar
CatCEG	Caterpillar Committee for Effective Government
CBA	Community Bankers Association
CBeaubien	Committee to Elect Mark Beaubien
CBiggert	Citizens for Judy Biggert
CBlack	Citizens for Bill Black
CB&T	Capitol Bank and Trust
CBOT	Chicago Board of Trade
CCapparelli	Citizens for Capparelli
CCCTU	Cook County College Teachers Union
CCEx	Community Currency Exchanges of Illinois
CChurchill	Citizens for Bob Churchill
CCL	Construction and Common Laborers
CClayborne	Committee to Elect James Clayborne
CDart	Citizens for Thomas Dart
CDavis	Davis for Congress
CDeLeo	Committee to Elect James A. DeLeo
CDemuzio	Committee for Senator Vince Demuzio
CDoherty	Citizens for Doherty

CDonahue	Laura Kent Donahue Campaign Committee
CDStephens	Citizens for Don Stephens
CDS	Citizens for Democratic Senate
CEdgar	Citizens for Edgar
CEJones	Citizens for Emil Jones
CentBank	Central Bank
CenterLounge	Center Lounge
CentTel	Central Telephone Company of Illinois
Cent21	Century 21 ABC Schiro Group
CFeigenholtz	Citizens for Feigenholtz
CFFU	Chicago Firefighters Union PAC
CFLabor	Chicago Federation of Labor
CGarcia	Citzens for Jesus Garcia
CGranberg	Citizens for Kurt Granberg
ChamDem	Champaign County Democratic Party
Chamelin	Chamelin & Associates
CHartke	Citizens for Hartke
ChaufCars	Chauffered Cars Inc.
CHB	Community Home Builders
ChgoCoC	Chicagoland Chamber of Commerce
Christian GOP	Christian County Republican Party
CIEquip	Central Illinois Equipment Company
CILCO	Central Illinois Light Company
CIPS	Central Illinois Public Service Co. PAC
CJHoffman	Committee to Elect Jay Hoffman
CJones	Citizens for John Jones
CKrause	Citizens for Carolyn Krause
CLang	Citizens for Lou Lang
ClarkR&M	Clark Refining & Marketing Inc.
Classic Chev	Classic Chevrolet
CLeitch	Citizens for David Leitch
CliffordLaw	Clifford Law Offices
CLM	Committee for Betty Loren-Maltese
CMahar	Citizens for Bill Mahar, Jr.
CMC	Charter Medical Corp.
CMEx	Chicago Mercantile Exchange
CMoore	Citizens for Andrea Moore
CMP Inc.	CMP Inc.
CMSmith	Citizens for Mary Ann Smith
CMWeaver	Citizens to Elect Mike Weaver
CNA	CNA Insurance Corporate PAC
CNeedham	Citizens for Needham
CNoland	Citizens for Duane Noland
CNovak	Citizens for Phil Novak
CNP	Computer Network Performance
COBANK	Community Banks of Illinois PAC
CoC	Illinois Chamber of Commerce

ConElectric	Continental Electric
ConsLTD	Consultants Ltd.
COPE1211	COPE1211
Corey-Steel	Corey-Steel Company
Corsair	Corsair Systems
CPA's	Certified Public Accountants Illinois PAC
CParker	Citizens for Kathy Parker
CPeterson	Citzens for Peterson
CPhilip	James Pate Philip Campaign Fund
CPJ	Callis, Papa, Jentsen
CrawGOP	Crawford County GOP
CrawPAC	Craw-PAC
CRausch	Citizens for Rauschenberger
CRock	Citizens for Phil Rock
CRonen	Citizens for Carol Ronen
CRutherford	Dan Rutherford Campaign Committee
CRyan	Citizens for George Ryan
CRyder	Citizens for Tom Ryder
CSchulter	Citizens for Gene Schulter
CSheahan	Citizens for Michael Sheahan
CSieben	Citizens for Todd Sieben
CSJBOP	Central States Joint Board PAC
CSmith	Citziens for Mike Smith
CStephens	Citizens for Ron Stephens
CStern	Stern for Illinois Committee
CSX	CSX Transportation
CTaddeo	Citizens for August Taddeo
CTCPAC	Construction Trades Craft Committee
CTurner	Citizens for Arthur Turner
CTU	Chicago Teachers Union
CubaGOP	Cuba Township Republicans
CumbGOP	Cumberland County Republican Central Committee
CUPAC	Credit Unions of Illinois PAC
CWadas	Cmte to Elect Kenneth J. Wadas
CWait	Citizens for Ron Wait
CWalsh	Citizens to Reelect Thomas Walsh
CWatson	Citizens for Frank Watson
CWennlund	Citizens for Larry Wennlund
CWinters	David F. Winters Campaign Fund
CyborFire	Cybor Fire Protection Co.
D, A&M	Denkewalter, Angelo & Minkow
DBA Mag	DBA Magnums
DecVAClinic	VA Clinic of Decatur
DelCar	Delaware Car Rental
Do-All	Do-All Fence
Dominick's	Dominick's Finer Foods Inc.
DowUSA	Dow USA

DPI	Democrat Party of Illinois
DSCC	Democratic Senatorial Campaign Committee
Duchossois	Duchossois Industries
DystelInc	Jane D. Dystel, Inc.
Eagle	Eagle Forum
ECILB&C	East Central Illinois Building and Construction Trades
Egbert	Egbert Family Ltd. Partnership
Elect	Elect, Markham, Illinois
ElectEn	Electric Energy Inc.
ElPasoAuto	El Paso Auto
EmergMed	Emergency Med Pac
Emerson	Illinois Emerson Corporate PAC
Emily	Emily's List
Empress	Empress Riverboat Casino
EMS	Express Mailing Service
EPAC	Employers Political Action Committee
ESLFT	East St. Louis Federation of Teachers
EvergreenHC	Evergreen Health Care SC
Excalibur	Excalibur
FamilyPAC	Family PAC
FamTaxprs	Family Taxpayer's Network
FastImpress	Fast Impressions
FayetteGOP	Fayette County Republican Party
FBSchaum	First Bank of Schaumburg
FCB	1st Chicago Builders
FCCSPAC	First Chicago Corp. State PAC
FCNBD	First of Chicago NBD Corp. PAC
FCarroll	Friends of Howard Carroll
FCL	Freeport Central Labor
FDurbin	Friends of Dick Durbin
FHalvorson	Friends of Debbie Halvorson
Fidelity	Fidelity Group Ltd.
Field&Sons	H. Field & Sons, Inc.
FirstComm	The First Commercial Bank
FisherConst.	Fisher Construction Co.
FJacobs	Friends of Denny Jacobs
FKubik	Friends of Jack Kubik
FLAD	Friends of Lee A. Daniels
FLEvans	Friends of Lane Evans
FloodBros	Flood Brothers Disposal & Recycling System
FMeany	Friends of Kathleen Meany
FMJM	Friends of Michael J. Madigan
FOP	Fraternal Order of Police
FoxCollision	Fox Collision Experts
FreedomEnt	Freedom Enterprises
Fremont	Fremont Comp Insurance Group
FRobShaw	Friends 9th Ward Alderman Robert Shaw

FSaviano	Friends for Saviano
FVBT	Fox Valley Building Trades
FZuccarelli	Friends of Frank Zuccarelli
G&E Sales	G&E Sales Corp.
G&FLC	Grain & Feed Legislative Council
G&S	Grover and Sullivan
GC	General Contractors
GDC	Gardner Denver Cooper Ind.
Gen Fence	General Fence Company
Geske	Geske & Sons, Inc.
GGCouncil	Good Government Council
Glencrest	Glencrest Nursing & Rehab Centre Ltd.
Glink,Martin	Glink, Martin Law Offices
GOA	Greater O'Hare Association
GOInc.	Gorski Osterholdt Inc.
GOPAC	GOP Political Action Committee (Federal Account)
GOPWom	Republican Women's PAC of IL
Gottlieb	Gottlieb Memorial Hospital
GrundyGOP	Grundy County Republican Party
Guerine	Guerine & Company Inc.
GTE	General Telephone Corporate PAC
GTENorth	GTE North
Hach&Assoc	William Hach & Associates
HagDodge	Haggerty Dodge Inc.
Harrah's	Harrah's Operation Company Inc.
Haste	Haste Real Estate
Haymrkt	Haymarket House
HBPAC	Home Builders Association of Illinois PAC
Hellas	Hellas Cafe
Heritage	Heritage Enterprises Inc.
HeritBank	Heritage Bank
HG&B	Hopkins, Goldenberg & Bilbrey, PC
HI	Household International
Highlander	Highlander Magazine
HMLTD	Hoffman-McPike Ltd.
Hollywood	Hollywood Casinos
HomeTeleph	Home Telephone Co.
HomewdDisp	Homewood Disposal Service Inc.
HOPE	Hospitals Organized for Political Education
HRCC	Illinois House Republican Campaign Committee
Humana	Humana
HuntInc.	J Alexander Hunt Inc.
IAC	Inter American Communications
IAHMO	Illinois Association of HMO's
IAMB	Illinois Association of Mortgage Brokers
IBA	Illinois Bankers Association PAC
IBEW	International Brotherhood of Electrical Workers

IBEWEd	International Brotherhood of Electrical Workers Education Committee
ICAPAC	Illinois Collection Association PAC
IFDA	Illinois Funeral Directors Association PAC
IFHR	Illinois Federation for Human Rights
IFT	Illinois Federation of Teachers
IHCA	Illinois Health Care Association
IHDM	Illinois House Democrat Majority
IHHA	Illinois Horsemen's & Harnessmen's Association
IHHSA	Illinois Hospital & Health Care Systems Assn.
IHIPAC	Illinois Housing Institute PAC
ILBC	Illinois Legislative Black Caucus
ILCable	Illinois Cable TV Association
ILCasualty	Illinois Casualty
ILCentral	Illinois Central Railroad
ILCon	Illinois Construction Industry PAC
ILFI	Illinois League of Financial Institutions PAC
ILLumber	Illinois Lumbermens Association PAC
ILNOW	Illinois National Organization for Women
ILPipeTraders	Illinois Pipe Traders PEC
ILRest	Illinois Restaurant Association PAC
IMAPAC	Illinois Medical Anesthesiologists PAC
IMHA	Illinois Manufactured Housing Association
IMPAC	Illinois Merchants PAC
IMPACT	IMPACT-AIDS Project Fund
IndFinance	Independent Finance
IndianapLife	Indianapolis Life
Inland	Inland Group Inc., PAC
Innov-AD	Innov-AD
Intercounty	Intercounty Title Company
INTIC	INTIC
IP	Illinois Power PAC
IPACE	Illinois Education Association PAC
IPMA	IL Petroleum Marketers Association
IPTPAC	Illinois Physical Therapy PAC
IRLA	Illinois Retail Liquor Association
IRMA	Illinois Retail Merchants Association
IRoad	Illinois Roadbuilders Association
ISMS	Illinois State Medical Society
ISPP	Illinois School Pyschologist PAC
ITLA	Illinois Trial Lawyers Association PAC
IUOE	International Union of Operating Engineers
IVendors	Illinois Vendors' Association PAC
IWPC	Illinois Womens Political Caucus
J&BElectric	Jamerson & Bauwens Electrical Contr.
JACPAC	Jacksonville Chamber of Commerce PAC
JasperGOP	Jasper County Republican Party

JBEsker	JB Esker and Sons
JeffGOP	Jefferson Couny GOP
Jimenez	Jimenez Interprice Inc.
JJM	JJM PAC
JUSTPAC	Illinois Civil Justice League PAC
K&Ellis	Kirkland & Ellis PAC
K&M	Knepper & Moga
KentFoods	Kent Foods, Inc.
KenwoodLiq	Kenwood Liquors
Keystone	Keystone Consolidated Industries PAC
KHC	Kenwood Healthcare Center
Knapheide	Kanpheide Manufactunog Co.
KnoxDem	Knox County Democratic Party
KorteConst	Korte Construction Company
KP&A	Keith Parker and Associates
Kraft	Kraft General Foods
Laborers	Laborers Union
Laidlaw	Laidlaw Waste Systems
LakinLaw	Lakin Law Firm
LamonicaBev	Lamonica Beverages, Inc.
Landmark	Landmark Financial
LaSalCent	LaSalle County Republican Century Club
LaSalGOP	LaSalle County GOP
LavinPC	Terrence Lavin, PC
LAWPAC	Illinois State Bar Associadon
LCR	Lake County Riverboat Project
LCI	Legislative Consultants of IL
LCRE	Lincoln Central Real Estate
LCTU	Lake County Teachers Union PEC
LibertyLM	Libertyville Lincoln Mercury
LICID	Legislative Interest Committee of Illinois Dentists
Life	Illinois Citizens for Life
LimestGOP	Limestone Township Republican Club
LIPAC	IL Life Insurance PAC
LLDC	Lincoln Land Development Company
Local 1001	Local 1001
LUPAC	Illinois Life Underwriters PAC
LynnMarketing	Lynn Marketing
MACC	MACC of Illinois, Inc.
Machinists	Machinists' Union PAC
Macom	Macom Corp
MaconGOP	Macon County Republican Party
MadGOP	Madison County Republican Club
MAMP	Mt. Auburn Memorial Park Inc.
M&B	Moss & Bloomberg
Maric Wood	Maric Woodworking
MASILA	MASILA

MaxManor	Maxwell Manor Nursing Home
MBPlatt	Mayer, Brown and Platt Law Firm
MCI	MCI Telecommunications Corp.
MCIDC	Mid-Central Illinois District Carpenters
McLFB	McLean County Farm Bureau
MCMgt	M C Management Co.
Medco	Medco Physicans Unlimited
MedMan	Medina Manor Retirement & Nursing Center
Mentzer	Mentzer Media
Merck	Merck & Company
MetroPrim	Metro Primary Care Network Corp.
MFM	Miller, Fanucchi, McGing
MH&P	Marble Helpers & Polishers
MidAmAdv	Mid-America Advertising Inc.
MidAmFed	Mid-America Federal PAC
Midas	Midas International Corp.
Midwest Auto	Midwest Auto Security Inc.
Miller	Miller Brewing Co.
Monroe	Monroe Truck Equipment
Monsanto	Monsanto Corporate PAC
MorrisB&T	Morris Business and Technology Center
MPAC	Illinios Manufacturer's Association PAC
MPower	Illinois Association of Rehabilitation Facilities PAC
MR&C	Roger C. Marquardt & Co.
MWEDA	Mid West Equipment Dealers Association
NAII	National Association of Independent Insurance IL State PAC
N&STruck	Nagel & Siebert Trucking
NASW	National Association of Social Workers
NCBank	North Community Bank
NCIL	North Central Illinois Laborers
NCS	National Communications Specialists
NDC	Northwest Display Corp.
NeidlesEnt	Neidles Enterprises, Inc.
NFBC	National Family Business Council
NFIB	National Federation of Independent Businesses
NFTwpDem	NorthField Township Democrats
NIBC	Northern Illinois Building Contractors
NICA	Northern Illinois Contractors Association
NIGAS	Northern Illinois Gas Company
NJC	National Jockey Club
Norfolk	Norfolk Southern
NRA	National Rifle Association
NRCC	National Republican Congressional Committee
NSBSI	National School Bus Service Inc.
NSFord	North Side Ford
NTGOP	New Trier Township GOP
NTRegGOP	New Trier Regular GOP

NWB&T	North Western Illinois Building and Trades
NWICA	North Westem Illinois Contractors Association
NWIEIC	NorthWest Illinois Eastern Iowa Council of Carpenters
Oak	The Oak Agency
OBriens	O'Briens Restaurant
OGroup	The Owens Group, Inc.
OGServices	O G Services Corp.
Olin	Olin Corporate PAC
OlsonPAC	Olson PAC
OxfordFin	Oxford Financial Corp.
Pacini	Pacini Realty
Painters	Painters
P&P	Plumbers & Pipefitters
P&S	Penn & Schoen
Park Hills	Park Hills Subdivision
ParkfieldFord	Parkfield Ford
ParthRest	Parthenon Restaurant
PasqCons	Pasquinelli Construction
PCPLTD	Prudential Cullinan Properties, Ltd.
Peck&Assoc.	Peck, Kerry & Associates
PeoGOPWom	Peoria County Republican Women
PeoGrassroots	Peoria County Grassroots Committee
PersPAC	Personal PAC
PetPec	Petroleum PEC of IL
Pharmacy	Illinois Pharmacy Association PAC
PIIA	Professional Independent Insurance Agents PAC
PikeDem	Pike Couny Democrats
Pioneer	Pioneer Financial Services Inc.
PKMall	PK Mall Inc
Plast	Plasterer's
Players	Players Riverboat Casino
Plumb93	Plumbers Local Union #93Pol Fund
PMC	Property Management Corp.
PMorris	Philip Morris
PNovak	Philip Novak Campaign Fund
PoliceBPAC	Policemen's Benevolent PAC
Portillo's	Portillo's Hot Dogs Inc.
PR&S	Power, Rogers & Smith, PC
Prohealth	Prohealth Inc.
ProSelect	Pro Select
PSalvi	Law Offices of Patrick A. Salvi
PulaskiRB	Pulaski County Republican Boosters
QCFL	Quad Cities Federation of Labor
QMS	Quicksilver Messenger Service
Quantum	Quantum Foods Great Steaks
Quidlibet	Quidlibet Research Inc.
RAI	Racing Association of Illinois

Railroad	Illinois Railroad Association PAC
RandGOP	Randolph County Republican Century Club
RC Industries	RC Industries
Rehkemper	Rehkemper & Sons Inc.
RepubTob	Republic Tobacco
RezCon	Rezko Concession Inc
Ribs&Bibs	Ribs&Bibs
RIGOP	Rock Island County Republican Party
RJR	R.J. Reynolds
RMadigan	Robert Madigan for State Senate
Robin	Neil A. Robin, Ltd.
RodeBrad	RodeBrad of Taylorville
RosemontExpo	Rosemont Exposition Services, Inc.
RPAC	Illinois Realtors Association PAC
RPLMgt.	RPL Management
RRDonnelly	RR Donnelly & Sons, Co.
RSSC	Republican State Senate Campaign Committee
RubloffDevlp	Rubloff Development
RW	Rudnick & Wolfe
SachsErn	Sachs, Earnest & Associates Ltd.
SalemGOPWom	Salem Republican Womens Club
S&Austin	Sidley & Austin
SASPAC	SASPAC
SChicagoDisp	South Chicago Disposal
Schlicting	Schlicting & Sons
Sears	Sears Roebuck & Co.
Seasons	Seasons at Rend Lake
Sec-Master	Security-Master
SEIU	Service Employees Council
SEIU/GSEU73	Service Employees Council/GSEU73
ShyWays	ShyWays
Signature	Signature Housing Solutions, Inc.
SIIA	SIIA
SimCon	E.T. Simonds Construction
SJP	Summer Jam Productions
SMCorp	Sheck Mechanical Corp.
SMS	Smith Barney Shearson
SMW	Sheet Metal Workers
SNAPI	Illinois Nurses' Association
Spacemark	Spacemark Inc.
Speed	Speed System International
SPConst	Scheitlein Peters Construction
Sprink	Sprinkler Fitters
Sprint	Sprint Corporate PAC
SR&D	Storino, Ramello & Durkin
SR&R	Sahner, Robin & Roznick
SSFT	Southwest Suburban Federation of Teachers

Starrett	Starrett Medical Associates
Statesman	Statesman of the Year State & Local PAC
StClrCen	St. Clair County Republican Century Club
StClrGOP	St. Clair County Republicans
Steam	Steamfitters
StegerPlz	Steger Plaza, Ltd.
StocksAg	Stocks Ag-Lines Inc.
Stonitsch	Stonitsch Financial
Sundstrand	Sundstrand Good Government Program
SyversonFS	Syverson for Senate
TAC	Treasurer's Action Committee
TazeDem	Tazewell County Democratic Party
TCI	TCI Communications Inc.
TDems	Thornton Township Democratic Org.
Teamsters	Teamsters Union
TIP	Hotel & Restaurant Employees' Union
TMRS	TMRS Ent Inc.
Tombstone	Tombstone Inn
TORVAC	TORVAC
TriadInd	Triad Industries
TriPClub	Triple "P" Club
Truck	Trucking Industry PAC
TrustmarkIns	Trustmark Insurance Company
TuthillCorp.	Tuthill Corporation
TWhelanLaw	Law Offices of Timothy Whelan, PC
TWU	Transportation Workers Union
UAW	United Auto Workers
UDI	United Democrats of Illinois
UFCW	United Food & Commercial Workers
UltraInk	Ultra Ink Inc.
Union Pacific	Union Pacific RR
UnionBank	Union Bank of Illinois
UNIPAC	Unicom PAC
UNISTAT	UNISTAT
United	United Airlines
Unity HMO	Unity HMO of IL Inc.
Uno-Ven	Uno-Ven Co.
UPI	University Professionals of Illinois
UPS	United Parcel Services PAC
UrbReal Estate	Urban Real Estate, Res., Inc.
URF	United Republican Fund
UST	UST Public Affairs Inc.
USWA	United Steel Worker of America
UTU	Union Transportation Union TPEL
ValleyAm	Valley Ambulatory Surgery Center
Victory Fund	Victory Fund PAC
VIPNR	Voter's Improvement Party of North Riverside

VSGrinding	VS Grinding Company Inc.
Walgreens	Walgreens Drug Stores PAC
WauDems	Waukegan Township Democrats
WChevroletInc	William Chevrolet Inc.
WCIBCT	West Central Illinois Building and Construction Trades
WCLA	Workers Compensation Lawyers Association
WeepWill	Weeping Willow construction
WellerCong	Weller for Congress
WexfordHS	Wexford Health Services Insurance
WhitesideGOP	Whiteside County Republican Party
WilliamsBros	Williams Brothers Construction Inc.
WilsonCon	Wilson Cons. Mgmt. Corp.
WiltonInd	Wilton Industries, Inc.
WMgt	Waste Management PAC
WomensCamp	Women's Campaign Fund
WoodDem	Woodford County Democratic Party
WoodysSupply	Woody's Supply Company
WSTU	West Suburban Teachers Union
WVWV	Women's Voices Women's Votes
Zeman	Zeman Realty
Zurich-Amer	Zurich-American State & Local PAC

About the Authors

David A. Joens is assistant to the director of the Illinois Legislative Studies Center, University of Illinois at Springfield. Prior to coming to the university, he served as a staff member for the Illinois Senate for seven years.

Paul Kleppner, Ph.D., is distinguished research professor of history and political science and director of the Office for Social Policy Research at Northern Illinois University in DeKalb.

Samuel J. Pernacciaro, Ph.D., is associate professor of political science at the University of Wisconsin—Parkside and research associate at the LaFollette Institute, University of Wisconsin—Madison. He coauthored *Roll Call: Patterns of Voting in the Sixth Illinois Constitutional Convention* in 1975.

Kent D. Redfield, Ph.D., is associate director of the Illinois Legislative Studies Center and professor of political studies at the University of Illinois at Springfield. He is director of the Illinois Legislative Staff Internship Program. With Jack R. Van Der Slik, he is the coauthor of *Lawmaking in Illinois.* He has served as the primary investigator for the Illinois Campaign Finance project and is the author of *Cash Clout: Political Money in Illinois Legislative Elections.*

Jack R. Van Der Slik, editor, is director of the Illinois Legislative Studies Center and professor of political studies at the University of Illinois at Springfield. He is author of *American Legislative Processes* and coauthor, with Kent D. Redfield, of *Lawmaking in Illinois.* His most recent book is *One for All and All for Illinois: Representing the Land of Lincoln in Congress.*